CAMBRIDGE STUDIES IN LAW AND SOCIETY

Founded in 1997, Cambridge Studies in Law and Society is a hub for leading scholarship in socio-legal studies. Located at the intersection of law, the humanities, and the social sciences, it publishes empirically innovative and theoretically sophisticated work on law's manifestations in everyday life: from discourses to practices, and from institutions to cultures. The series editors have longstanding expertise in the interdisciplinary study of law, and welcome contributions that place legal phenomena in national, comparative, or international perspective. Series authors come from a range of disciplines, including anthropology, history, law, literature, political science, and sociology.

CAMBRIDGE
STUDIES IN
LAW AND SOCIETY

A list of books in the series can be found at the back of this book.

A SOCIOLOGY OF POST-IMPERIAL CONSTITUTIONS

Covering the period from the eighteenth century to the present, *A Sociology of Post-Imperial Constitutions* combines global history and historical legal sociology to explain how democratic constitutions were created by imperialism and military policies related to imperialism. It challenges common views about the relation between democracy and peace, examining how, in different locations and different periods, the constitutional ordering of citizenship both reflected and perpetuated warfare. It also isolates the features of constitutional systems that have been successful in obviating military violence, separating democracy from its military origins. It discusses how the emergence of democratic government after 1945 depended on a dialectical transformation of the war/law nexus in constitutional rule. It then assesses ways in which, and the reasons why, some contemporary constitutions have begun to remilitarize their societies and to rearticulate military constructs of legitimacy.

CHRIS THORNHILL is Professor of Law at the University of Birmingham. He has held professorships in politics, sociology and law in Glasgow, Manchester and Bielefeld. He has received prizes for research in law and society from the Humboldt Foundation, Deutsche Gesellschaft für Soziologie and the World Complexity Science Academy. This is his third book in Cambridge Studies in Law and Society, following *A Sociology of Constitutions* (2011) and *A Sociology of Transnational Constitutions* (2016).

A SOCIOLOGY OF POST-IMPERIAL CONSTITUTIONS

Suppressed Civil War and Colonized Citizens

Chris Thornhill
University of Birmingham

CAMBRIDGE
UNIVERSITY PRESS

CAMBRIDGE
UNIVERSITY PRESS

Shaftesbury Road, Cambridge CB2 8EA, United Kingdom

One Liberty Plaza, 20th Floor, New York, NY 10006, USA

477 Williamstown Road, Port Melbourne, VIC 3207, Australia

314–321, 3rd Floor, Plot 3, Splendor Forum, Jasola District Centre, New Delhi – 110025, India

103 Penang Road, #05–06/07, Visioncrest Commercial, Singapore 238467

Cambridge University Press is part of Cambridge University Press & Assessment, a department of the University of Cambridge.

We share the University's mission to contribute to society through the pursuit of education, learning and research at the highest international levels of excellence.

www.cambridge.org
Information on this title: www.cambridge.org/9781316513941

DOI: 10.1017/9781009076388

When citing this work, please include a reference to the DOI 10.1017/9781009076388

First published 2025

A catalogue record for this publication is available from the British Library

A Cataloging-in-Publication data record for this book is available from the Library of Congres

ISBN 978-1-316-51394-1 Hardback

For Atina, Grace and John

CONTENTS

ACKNOWLEDGEMENTS

This book has been largely elaborated through discussions with three good friends: Hauke Brunkhorst, Atina Krajewska, and Ben Morris, who have listened to and disputed numerous claims in this book with me over recent years. My gratitude goes to each of them, and my debt to them for our conversations, at times straining the bonds of friendship, is immense. In addition, I wish to thank the following colleagues for stimulating conversations during the writing of this book: Guilherme de Azevedo, Juan Barrero Berardinelli, Gilberto Bercovici, Marta Bucholc, Carina Calabria, Emilios Christodoulidis, Lucas Delgado, Damla Erkan, Gorm Harste, Ingunn Ikdahl, Andreas Krampe, Julieta Lemaitre, Gilmar Mendes, Drew Milne, Tolibjon Mustafoev, Finola O'Sullivan, William Outhwaite, Rachel Pougnet, Darrow Schecter, Ulisses Schwarz, Maria Smirnova, Stephan Stetter, Rustamjon Urinbojev, Rafael Valim, Gert Verschraegen, Guoshu Yang, Chuxi Zhang.

Some research for this book was funded by the Norwegian Research Council and some of it was funded by the Swedish Research Council. Some research was undertaken during visiting professorships at the University of Flensburg, funded by the Alexander von Humboldt Foundation; at the Instituto de Direito Publico (Brasilia); at Unisinos (Porto Alegre); at Mackenzie University (São Paulo); and at the Institut für Militärgeschichte und Sozialwissenschaften der Bundeswehr (Potsdam). I warmly thank all funding bodies and hosts that made the research possible.

INTRODUCTION

EMPIRES AND CONSTITUTIONS: SOME DEFINITIONS

The first claim in this book is that the development of constitutional law has a dialectical relation to imperialism, and to military forces that accompany imperialism. From their first emergence, modern constitutions formed components in lines of state-building connected to inter-imperial rivalry, and they reflected the interlinking of states in a transnational military system. In this process, imperialism shaped the creation of constitutions in different ways. Many states acquired constitutions as they were separated from existing empires, so that national self-determination became the wellspring of constitutional law.[1] With some qualified exceptions after 1848, constitutions, as a rule, established normative foundations for governments, based in ideals of national citizenship, which were distinct from the institutional substructures imposed by imperialism. In many contexts, however, constitutions were built on norms of citizenship established in empires to serve imperialist ends. Many states acquired constitutions as they reconfigured their foundations while remaining empires, and many states became empires as soon as they acquired constitutions. Well into the twentieth century, a crisis of imperialism lay in the background to the formation of much constitutional law, and most constitutions were written so that states could adapt to or recover from such a crisis.

[1] One historian states simply that the constitutional moments that occurred in the American and French Revolutions started the longer process 'later described as "decolonization"' (Ahmed 2014: 1). In a similar context, one historian argues that the momentum towards 'self-determination and national sovereignty' was initiated in the American and French Revolutions (Üngör 2011: 2).

This meant that many constitutions replicated imperatives and conflicts inherent in imperialism, and many states constructed on a constitutional basis soon perpetrated actions typical of empires. Even in constitutions that detached the space occupied by nation states from empires, constitutional law rarely merely supplanted imperial rule, and constitutionalism usually evolved as a legal order for managing state actions in a form close to imperialism. As outlined in Chapter 1, the original forces that created constitutional law resulted from a reorganization of national societies in the face of imperial violence, and this origin frequently shaped societies in distinctive imperial fashion.

This background explains the title of this book, which defines its primary object as *post-imperial* constitutions. Many books have examined the development of *postcolonial law* in contemporary society. However, this book claims that the concept of *post-imperial law* most adequately captures the construction of modern constitutional order at the global level. It uses this term to describe how imperialism formed an overarching structure that diversely shaped the global development of constitutional law both in colonizing and in colonized zones. In so doing, it uses the prefix 'post' in 'post-imperial constitutionalism' carefully. This prefix is employed to indicate that constitutions typically emerged in different parts of imperial systems. In such contexts, constitutions were established to place government on discernibly national and symbolically consensual foundations, specifically opposed to imperial patterns of legitimacy. Yet, in so doing, they frequently perpetuated imperialism at the interstate level and reproduced or even intensified features of imperialism in domestic societies, so that imperialist impulses remained palpable in the constitutional polities that replaced, or grew within, empires. In many contexts, constitutions constructed national societies in a form that extended imperial modes of social formation, and, over long historical sequences, they often served the constant reconfiguration of imperialism. At least until 1945, many constitutions were post-imperial and imperialist at the same time, as they articulated patterns of legitimacy separate from empires but also reproduced imperialism as a global system. The concept of the *post-imperial constitution* is selected here as a dialectical term to interpret these realities. Strictly, only the British constitution can be classified, simply, as an *imperial* constitution.

The second claim in this book is rather more straightforward. This claim is that the link between imperialism and constitutionalism meant that constitutions promoted military violence in various ways. It is often noted that the transition from empire to nation is a primary cause of military conflict, a fact explained by such factors as border disputes and ethnic irredentism.[2] On the account offered here, however, a deeper structural nexus exists between constitutions, imperialism and violence. Typically, constitutions were formed in environments marked by increased militarization of inter-imperial relations. In such contexts, they were designed to establish a sovereign order for the control of military force in society. A primary function of most constitutions was to separate citizens of one state from citizens of other states, defining national membership as a source of military duties in a system of military antagonism.[3] Moreover, the birth of constitutionalism coincided with the arming of national citizens, most of whom were not professionally trained as soldiers, a prospect that had alarmed earlier regents who feared an armed populace would turn against them. In such contexts, most constitutions created an enduring source of militarism in societies defined by constitutional rule. Since the advent of constitutions, self-evidently, many states without constitutions have declared war, and many have experienced civil war. No claim is made here that constitutional organization is an exclusive cause of military conflict, internal or external. However, constitutions usually brought substantial changes in warfare. Most states situated on a trajectory of constitutional organization experienced devastating war.[4] War between such states was qualitatively different from earlier wars, as warfare defined the conditions of citizenship in belligerent societies, and it entailed conflicts between constitutionally implicated citizens, in which one society, as a whole, fought against a different society, as a whole. In such wars, states frequently mobilized larger armies, and they sacrificed a larger number of soldiers than had earlier states.[5] Moreover, as

[2] See Wimmer 2013: 23–24, 110. On my account, the division sometimes posited between 'revolutionary wars' and 'wars driven by the politics of nation building' is not fully tenable (Wimmer and Min 2006: 876). Major revolutionary wars were caused by imperial fragmentation and nation-building was conducted in revolutionary fashion (France 1792; Russia 1918). Most importantly, revolutionary wars often transformed empires in ways analogous to secessionist wars, as they nationalized core states within empires.

[3] See pp. 134–5, 137, 197–8.

[4] Following one classic account of the correlates of war, nine of the ten states that lost most citizens in battle from 1815 to the 1980s were on a trajectory of constitutional organization and experienced intense conflicts as a result (Small and Singer 1982: 179). These states are Austria, France, Germany, Italy, Japan, Russia, Spain, Turkey and the UK; China is the exception. In each case, warfare tended to occur after or in the longer wake of intensified constitutional experiments, and constitutions were substantially forged in war, of different kinds, usually linked to imperialism.

[5] See pp. 68–70.

constitutions made all members of society present in warfare, they militarized domestic societies, and conflicts between domestic groups were inflamed by the fact that these groups encountered each other, as members of the same nation, in military environments.

The term *militarism* is used here in encompassing sociological fashion, and it extends further than most definitions, which tend to focus on civil–military relations, foreign policy and governmental use of military force. Militarism here describes a condition with some or all of the following features: (1) military prerogatives shape political institutions and military actors establish primary obligations for subjects in society; (2) military groups may have privileged social positions and define conditions of access to political power; (3) military demands and duties pervasively shape social and political behaviour beyond the strict military domain; (4) internal social conflicts are likely to engender and be resolved by military violence.[6] Militarism, further, often results in war – at least it intensifies conflict potentials in society likely to lead to war. The distinctive aspect of this definition is that it identifies militarization both in vertical and in lateral interactions in society, and it examines how factors in both dimensions create military violence. As explained in different chapters of this book, many major modern wars have been linked to contests over citizenship in the lateral dimension of society, resulting from constitutional organization. In most polities on a constitutional pathway, constitutions have created a deep causal convergence between intra-societal and international conflict, such that internal conflicts originated in, and in turn intensified, external military pressures.

On this dual premise, this book charts the long-term evolution of constitutional law since the last decades of the eighteenth century, when constitutions first became central institutions in governmental order. It shows how constitutions were initially defined by military imperatives arising from imperialism, which imprinted a military form on nation states. This form was globalized over time, with variations. This book then shows how, until relatively recently, constitutions produced ideas of governmental legitimacy that tended to induce

[6] This approach differs from accounts of militarism focused solely on civil–political relations. It is close to analysis of militarism as a cultural condition (Vagts 1981: 13) and it follows descriptions of militarism as a diffuse set of orientations that shape identity and nationhood (see Ben-Eliezer 2019: 26). However, it implies that, in most militarized contexts, external and internal militarism overlapped.

military violence, so that constitutionally ordered states frequently engendered militarism, both in their own societies and beyond.

Imperialism resists easy definition, and the ambiguities inherent in this concept are often mentioned in this book. For the sake of clarity, the following definition of imperialism is adopted. Imperialism is construed here as a form of sociopolitical administration that involves the extraction of land, labour and resources from prior inhabitants of a territory by colonizing agents. This administration is organized in a system that the parties from whom land, labour and resources are extracted cannot unilaterally terminate or even modify. Different groups are governed by different means under varying legal norms, enforced with different degrees of consensus and coercion. Military force is fundamental to imperialism, and relations between metropolitan and colonized subjects are sustained, whether directly or remotely, by military means. The military usually retains a key role in supporting governmental coercion in colonial territories; in fact, colonial societies retain features of military occupation.[7] Naturally, the daily government of colonized societies inside empires may rest on conventional agreements between implicated groups. By the twentieth century, imperialism had lost some characteristics of simple military occupation.[8] For instance, the British Empire was structured around a system of indirect rule that involved the co-opting of elites into colonial service and the avoidance of manifest military repression. Long before the twentieth century, the Ottoman Empire had established a complex semi-consensual patchwork to support imperial authority. Yet an empire is a type of polity in which power has violent purposes, so that – with internal and external variations – social roles are deeply defined by the extraction and enforcement of violence. As examined repeatedly below, one vital feature of empires is that they create diffuse polities in which the legal limits of the polity are hard to determine. Centrally, subjects of empires are often also military adversaries of empires, such that external war and civil war converge.

The third claim in this book is of a broader nature. This claim is that constitutions reflect an uncertain distinction between nations and

[7] See pp. 149–51. One recent account of British colonization in India states that, in the early colonial period, the military was the 'marrow' of the imperial regime. Then, the later colonial period still showed the 'preponderance of the military over all other competing demands' (Sehgal 2021: 235–237).

[8] See p. 169.

empires, and they create a system of administration and legitimation in which the internal and external acts of states are not fully separate.

It is a sociological commonplace that the period since the eighteenth century witnessed the rise of modern sovereign states exercising control of the means of violence inside national society (Weber 1921/2: 30). Moreover, it is often argued that nation states are ruled by governments based in a clear distinction between internal and external functions. Such analysis implies that, through their development, modern states became less disposed to violence in their internal actions than in their external behaviour; this view is supported by renowned sociologists and observers of international politics (Elias 1976: 354; Linklater 2017: 422).[9] However, this book challenges this view, claiming that such views are selectively focused. In modern history, the dominant political form has been, not the sovereign *nation state*, but the diffuse *empire*. It was only after 1945 that nation states replaced empires as primary systems of social organization. In most contexts, national political institutions have been profoundly shaped by the intersection between empire and nation, in which traditional concepts of sovereignty cannot be applied without qualification.

For example, aspects of the above definition of imperialism can be applied to many modern nations, and, beneath the surface of many national societies, we can observe unilateral acts of territorial annexation. Most modern European states have their origins in diffuse composite territories, which were unified by incremental processes of centralization in which military actors performed primary roles.[10] Broadly, many European states developed through a two-stage pattern of imperialism. First, in their original emergence, European states developed through personal imperialism in which regents allotted privileges to local landholding elites to secure their frontiers, so that governments acquired national form by establishing lateral attachments with politically relevant actors. Second, in their modern form, most states developed by transforming such lateral agreements into vertical agreements, which reduced the power of landholders as a precondition for territorial order. This process was usually realized as states imposed direct military duties on individual citizens, so that

[9] Interestingly, Michael Mann (2012: 361) is an expert in interpreting state formation and imperialism, but he does not link his formative analysis of the states to his discussion of empires.

[10] One historian has claimed that Great Britain was the only non-unitary state in eighteenth-century Europe (Higginbotham 2005: 70). However, Poland, Prussia, Austria (if it existed) and (more arguably) Spain were composite states.

they integrated their citizens through military organizations. In different ways, the spatial processes that created national societies were not categorically distinct from imperialism. In fact, common nation-building trajectories often formed a template for modern empires.[11]

In addition, most European states were formed as they extended their institutional capacities outwards, so that the internal construction of state institutions coincided with the external imposition of imperial rule. Of course, Charles Tilly diagnosed the deep link between state formation and military mobilization and the equally deep link between military pressures and democratic integration.[12] Yet he was less attentive to the fact that, in most historical settings, state formation depended on military circumstances related to imperialism.[13] Before the rise of modern overseas empires, states were scarcely formed on a national design; at this time, most nations evolved in composite form and national governments had limited reach in domestic societies. Most notably, before the rise of modern empires, states rarely fought wars as nations, and the military capacities of states were limited. Before the eighteenth century, most large armies were recruited on a transactional basis from military entrepreneurs and they were deployed in wars for private interests – usually because of dynastic rivalries, often caused by succession crises. Through the eighteenth century, armies increased in size and were more strictly subject to national control, but they were not primarily recruited from national populations. In fact, the disarming of national populations, ensuring some distinction between civil and military functions, was a vital premise for early modern government, and it persisted until the later eighteenth century.[14] It was only after the constitutional revolutions in the late eighteenth and nineteenth centuries that armies were mainly recruited amongst national citizens, defined by national affiliations, such that states obtained direct purchase on their citizens. This state-building moment was closely connected to imperialism, and it reflected a deep intensification of inter-imperial conflict. In most settings, this development profoundly shaped the societies that provided soldiers. Societies acquired more integrated national form as states promoted the general extraction of military force, which supported the building of centralized institutions, linking all persons directly to the

[11] See discussions in Chapter 1.

[12] Tilly (2004: 89–90). See for similar analysis Levi (1996: 109).

[13] The common impact of imperialism on citizenship formation is not noted in Mann's (1987) typology of paths to citizenship.

[14] On this point, see excellent discussion in Rink (1999: 37).

state. It was at this time that wars presented legitimational challenges for all society, as military initiatives required governments to account for their actions amongst the citizens affected by them. In many cases, this defined the basic patterns of citizenship that typify modern nationhood, and citizenship evolved as an internal attachment between states and citizens as states widened their reach externally. These processes normally occurred because military force was required to govern external territories and citizenship rights were promoted as social agents were linked to the state as providers of military force.

Typically, in sum, nation states hardly existed before they were empires, and empires were rarely constructed by fully formed nation states. Some historians argue that Russia was unusual amongst modern polities as it was an empire before it became a nation state.[15] However, nothing is peculiar in this feature. Great Britain approached territorial integration as it became an empire in the eighteenth century. It then established a shared legal-political regime for its citizens through the late nineteenth century, closely mirroring stages of external expansion. The USA approached consolidation as a nation state as it annexed territories previously held by other peoples and empires; in essence, it became a nation state as it became an empire.[16] In the case of Germany, national integration and imperialism interacted inseparably in creating the first modern German nation state (termed an empire – a *Reich*) in the 1870s. Similar processes can be observed in Italy, Spain, Japan and, later, in Poland. In Austria and Turkey, the later nineteenth century was dominated by the endeavour to transform empires into polities supported by national or semi-national affiliations.

In each point, many governments reinforced their sovereign status through acts of control in which a strict, positive distinction between the inside and the outside of national society was not manifest. Generally, the rise of imperialism was not a phenomenon that was simply external to colonizing societies. Rather, it was a process that created and transfigured colonizing societies such that, in many cases, metropolitan and colonized regions evolved as two parts of the same imperial society or *imperial system*.[17]

Against this background, this book examines constitutions from a distinct perspective. Nation states and empires are usually seen as

[15] Blauvelt (2003: 42).
[16] Saler (2015: 19).
[17] Here, the book builds on recent historical research. See the critical assessment of the 'notion of a clear-cut break between empire and nation' in Esherick, Kayali and Young (2006: 13). Other

strictly differentiated systems of rule.[18] Moreover, many constitutions were originally legitimated by the claim that they established national governments on foundations that were opposed to imperialism. This was expressed in the first constitutions in revolutionary America and Europe, where constitutional citizenship was defined as membership in a political community decisively distinct from an empire.[19] Still today, constitutions are presented as expressions of nation-building commitments. However, this book shows how constitutions effected complex patterns of transformation in society, and they were mainly used to manage the effects of international pressures. As a result, they often organized societies in a hybrid form between nations and empires, extending imperial logics into national society. Of course, it is essential to differentiate between polities formed at different locations in imperial systems, as metropolitan states and colonial states usually developed on very different constitutional pathways. However, from the eighteenth century, imperialism formed an encompassing world system, and it shaped affected states in partly overlapping manner, regardless of whether states emerged at the metropolitan side or at the colonial side of imperial systems. Quite generally, the book argues that constitutions have typically been imprinted on national societies as the *form of sovereignty* adapted to a world created by imperialism. Owing to this form of sovereignty, constitutions shaped social order around imperatives in which the inside and the outside of national society overlapped, and the distinction between empire and nation was not clear. As discussed in Chapters 1–5, constitutions often distilled constructs of citizenship on premises first used to support empires. In some

historians observe the 'entanglement of nation and empire' in European history, explaining how empires were often sites of 'advanced nation-building projects' (Berger and Miller 2015: 4–5). The convergence of nation-building and empire-building is central to the observations of Osterhammel (2009: 603), who analyses the period of nationalism as congruent with a 'world of empires'. Speaking of the Ottoman Empire, one historian focuses on the 'fraught notion of a break between empire and nation' (Kayali 2021: 16). One historian proposes the concept of 'the "nation-state/empire" . . ... as a basic unit in an analysis of international politics for the period between the late nineteenth century and 1945' (Akami 2012: 178). See for overlapping conceptions Khalid (2006: 251); Kamissek (2018: 271); Malešević (2019: 70).

18 The claim is common that empires are based 'asymmetrical' constructions of power and 'hierarchical relations of law and membership', while nations are formed through 'social integration' in Jureit (2019: 109). For related statements, see Kivelson and Suny (2017: 12). The claim is also frequent that 'the nation-state tends to homogenize those inside its borders and exclude those who do not belong, while the empire reaches outward and draws, usually coercively, peoples whose difference is made explicit under its rule' (Burbank and Cooper (2011: 8)). See congruent classical analysis in Eisenstadt (1993: 20).

19 See pp. 57, 73.

instances, the ideal of national sovereignty condensed in constitutional law had an intrinsically imperial focus. Many states legitimated by ideals of national citizenship were propelled onto an expansionist trajectory, so that they were not obviously separate from empires. At different points in the book, the concept of the *imperial nation* is used to explain the formation of constitutionally ordered states. This view of constitutions is advanced as an interpretive framework through the book. Using this perspective, the book analyses constitutions in different global regions, including Eastern and Western Europe, the Middle East, North and South America, Asia and Africa, as texts that translated imperial impulses into legal-political form.

To examine these matters, this book defines a constitution in the following terms. A constitution is observed here, first, as a legal order that allocates powers in the state and constructs the legitimacy of the state on public premises rooted in consensual attachments between citizens and government. As such, a constitution need not be democratic. Very few constitutions became truly democratic until after 1945. Yet a constitution must contain some commitment to popular electoral representation, and it generates legitimacy by establishing *a norm of inclusion oriented towards full democracy*. On this definition, modern constitutions appeared in North America and Europe between 1776 and 1795. Characteristic of modern constitutions is that they define a legitimate state as one whose authority is based in the *construction of all citizens as politically implicated actors* whose will is manifested through elections, with varying degrees of popular participation. Second, a constitution is observed here as a legal order that presents the state as a public order because it creates rules for the definition and protection of citizens. That is, constitutions present governmental legitimacy as the result of a legal regime to guarantee rights of citizenship, usually granting all citizens certain personal and procedural rights, and assigning rights of political participation to some social groups. This book restricts its focus to states that have entered enduring trajectories of constitutional formation based in this model. For this reason, although China comes into focus at different points in the book, China is not examined in depth.

CONSTITUTIONS AND EARLY IMPERIALISM

The connection between imperialism and constitutionalism was evident in the origins of constitutional formation. In medieval Europe, many polities developed semi-constitutional procedures for collective deliberation. Such procedures were usually focused on the conduct of war, and their purpose was both to organize military supply and to ensure the military loyalty of regional elites at the margins of the polity. Subsequently, late medieval Europe witnessed the formation of estate-based constitutions. In such arrangements, the power of estates to influence governmental policy was strongest in times of military activity, in which fiscal demands placed on government were high. In early modern Europe, some states with estate-based constitutions underwent extensive territorial expansion and representative bodies played important roles in subjecting colonized regions to central government. In post-medieval Poland, for example, institutions facilitating political representation were used to connect different parts of the polity as it expanded across large regional spaces.[20] Later, the reinforcement of parliamentary rule in post-1688 England supported the early growth of empire and sustained the fiscal institutions that made imperialism possible. Despite these connections, however, early constitutional systems were largely intended to secure privately financed supplies of troops; such force was usually provided by corporate bodies such as companies, foreign financiers or noble administrative districts. This meant that, to obtain soldiers, governments entered private contracts with military corporations, and constitutions were not required to facilitate the immediate extraction of military capacity from society.[21] By consequence, most constitutions restricted full rights of citizenship to select social groups.

The causal thread connecting constitutionalism and imperialism became most palpable in the eighteenth century. Each major constitutional system formed at this time evolved in a context in which imperialism pervasively shaped processes of polity-building. Each system constructed a legal order designed to promote direct communication between government and citizens, especially in matters relating to military recruitment. At this time, the first written constitutions were implemented in the regions that became the USA, Poland and France, and they established a formally agreed order to legitimate governmental power. These constitutions were created in diverse environments and for different purposes. The federal constitution of the USA was the only national constitution that remained in force for any length of time. However, all these constitutions ordered state institutions in response

[20] This is documented at different points in Polish state formation. See discussion in Mazur (2006: 134) and Kupisz (2008: 25).

[21] See discussion of the end of this system at pp. 47–8, 70.

to imperialism, and all based the legitimacy of government in ideas of general citizenship able to sustain imperialism.

Each early constitution-making situation was caused by the Seven Years' War. This multifocal war involved conflict over maritime domination between France, Britain and Spain, especially in North America and the Caribbean. It also involved conflict for domination in parts of Central and Eastern Europe between Russia, Prussia and the Habsburg dynasty. As examined below, this war created great global demand for military force, and it was conducted in scenarios separated by large geographical distances. Through this war, crucially, European imperialism underwent a deep transformation. Before the eighteenth century, European empires were mainly personal empires or trading empires organized around relatively loose affiliations between metropolitan and colonial regions.[22] By circa 1750, however, empires began to operate as more robustly constructed administrative entities, imposing concentrated military and fiscal domination on their populations. As discussed in Chapters 1–5, the intensification of empire in the eighteenth century was expressed, diversely, in the fact that different empires promoted new concepts of imperial membership, in which the distinction between metropolitan subjects and colonial subjects was reduced. In fact, owing to military pressures, empires began to acquire functions now usually associated with nations, and they promoted increasingly uniform ideas of legal obligation, close to imperial citizenship. Importantly, this transformation of empires was one aspect of a wider process of transformation that occurred in the eighteenth century. At this time, many national societies moved away from patterns of social integration predominantly based in lateral attachments between particular groups and agents towards a model of social integration based in vertical attachments, linking individual agents more directly to state in institutions. The transformation of nations and the transformation of empires at this point were closely linked phenomena.

The transformation of imperialism shaped the rise of constitutionalism in diverse ways. Generally, the rise of imperialism meant that military pressures assumed increased force in connecting state and societal actors. Early constitutions then formed a structural reaction to this change as they enabled governments to produce legitimacy for their actions in societies defined by vertical affiliation and membership. This occurred in variations, some more specific to Europe, some more

[22] See pp. 40, 220–1.

general. Yet, broadly, constitutions responded to these transformations in three fundamental ways.

First, the relation between imperialism and early constitutionalism is seen in the fact that early constitutions established governmental orders that enacted a *legal transformation of geographical space*. This process was already advanced before written constitutions became common. Before the 1780s, most European societies had seen extensive legal codification, establishing shared legal obligations for social actors, which went some way towards placing national societies under a unified legal apparatus.[23] However, early constitutions were written as texts that authorized general legal norms across society, which meant that all persons were connected to governments through formally defined obligations. This transformation marked the beginning of modern citizenship as it created a legal regime bearing equally on all territorial residents, albeit usually with status variations. This was shaped by the principle that mere occupancy of land could not produce binding rights or duties, and that inhabitants of a given territory only entered binding obligations if occupancy of territory was subject to unifying legal duties.

Such legal reorganization was directed against modes of government based in informal authority. In European contexts, it was directed against aristocratic independence. In the Americas, it was directed against colonial rule. In both settings, the legal ordering of social space clearly articulated patterns of imperialism. At one level, legal codification was an act of colonization, as it led to the displacement of local elites from inherited social positions and transposed societal control onto a vertical axis.[24] It tended also to reduce the autonomy of religious organizations and to ensure that the legitimation of authority was concentrated in the state. However, legal codification was usually accelerated in societies in which governments were involved in external military expansion. As discussed below, the supreme acts of legal codification – the creation of constitutions – almost invariably coincided with inter-imperial conflict.

Second, the force of imperialism in shaping modern constitutionalism can be observed in the fact that early constitutions organized political institutions in the face of war. In each instance, constitutions transformed the military orders of early modern society into public organizations in which military obligations of national populations were more

[23] See pp. 72–3, 96, 101.

[24] See p. 96. My account overlaps with Osterhammel's (2009: 168) idea of the 'ordering of space'.

fully controlled by the state. At a fundamental level, the essential legal norms that support constitutions originated in military law. This can be seen through legal-historical analysis. Before the eighteenth century, as mentioned, armies had usually been assembled by groups of nobles, entrepreneurs, and commissioned recruiters, who were bound to their soldiers through private-legal monetary agreements. This contractual relation formed the most sensitive point in early modern statehood, as the private-legal premise of military recruitment meant that armies were costly, unruly and often unreliable. During the emergence of early public law, increasing emphasis was placed on the insistence that regents should possess the sole power to approve military contracts, so that private actors could not raise troops except in the royal name. In the middle part of the eighteenth century, before modern constitutional law was consolidated, military law clearly subordinated military organizations to central authority, and the control of military contracts was an essential feature of the emerging sovereign state.[25] Subsequently, early constitutions built on and enlarged this foundation and reinforced the strictly public-law dimensions of military law. Manifestly, constitutions created representative procedures in which citizens could elect governments, so that states could negotiate directly with citizens about military finance. In this regard, constitutions established agreements between public bodies and citizens to secure military capacity, and they made it possible for governments to rebuild military institutions in rapid time.[26] In most contexts, further, early constitutions tied citizenship to military service and a deep military emphasis was inherent in the legitimational diction of early constitutional law.

Of course, from the 1770s on, most constitutions prescribed procedures to functionally separate government from militaries. This is visible, emblematically, in the 1791 constitution of France, which dictated that the army should be 'essentially obedient' and could never assume a deliberative role in politics (Title IV/12). This is also reflected in *Federalist* 41, where James Madison argued that armies pose a constitutional threat, to be checked by provisions that limit the term of revenues granted to them.[27] Such caution remained

[25] See this formulation in France in Briquet (1728: 1–2). For one construction of military law as a fundamental part of public law, see the discussion of Prussia in Müller (1760: 13).

[26] Some observers have noted that constitutional transitions after 1945 brought militaries to central political roles, as armies formed the 'most organized, national-oriented social force' (Hinnebusch 1990: 11). However, this can be generalized across most constitution-making scenarios.

[27] References are to the 1987 edition of the *Federalist*, based on the 1787/8 publication (Madison, Hamilton and Jay 1987 [1787–8]: 269).

a common part of constitutional law.[28] Nonetheless, such rules only had superficial effects, and a deep attachment to the military defined the core of early constitutional law. As discussed below, constitutions were formed in imperial states, in colonies and in states acting as both colonies and as empires, and, in each setting, they were used for military ends, to solidify military force in the state. Central to each early constitution was a concept of the citizen, presented as a member of a publicly defined nation, who obtained certain legal-political rights through constitutional law, and who was required, by way of payment for these rights, to perform military service (conscription) for the government. Early constitutions evolved, in essence, as *military contracts* in which the brokering of military supply, which, in private-legal form, lay at the heart of earlier estate-based constitutions, was translated into a system of near-universal public obligations. The basic legitimational unit of the modern political order – the citizen – was constructed as a means of generating military violence for the state. Of course, this unit initially comprised all members of society, whose utility was immediately determined by warfare. However, by the age of total war, women also became citizens through and after war, as warfare integrated women in constitutional bargaining structures because it transformed labour markets and made women indispensable to the government.

In different ways, the military transactions underlying constitutional law resulted from imperialism. In the longer wake of 1648, many European states had – with variations – promoted policies to ensure that armies were centralized and military positions were staffed by accountable officeholders. By 1750, many states possessed substantial standing armies, comprising soldiers paid either directly or indirectly from the public purse. These armies were partly filled by mercenaries and foreign recruits, but they were subject directly to national authority. Over time, however, the pressures of inter-imperial warfare, especially in the Seven Years' War, meant that the maintenance of permanent standing armies became expensive. Accordingly, each early constitution was drafted at a time when states were overstretched by military financing, and they were conceived as instruments to establish new lines of military supply. Further, early constitutions took shape in environments in which governments already promoted in rudimentary form the recruitment of national conscript armies, in

[28] See pp. 68, 77, 213, 245, 256.

which subjects were mobilized as soldiers because of their residence in a particular region. By the later eighteenth century, the reliance of governments on large armies led to the increasing enlistment of conscripts and militias, and the widening of international empires was reflected in the expansion of military service. Militia service began in France in the 1680s, but it was formalized between 1719 and 1726. In Spain, it was imposed stepwise in the 1730s, the 1760s and the 1770s. Prussia was an important pioneer in this regard. By the 1730s, the Prussian monarchy introduced a cantonal system of recruitment that enforced selective involuntary conscription. Militia service was expanded in Britain in 1757, and it was common in British colonies in the North Atlantic at this time. The writing of constitutions after 1775 was closely tied to such recruitment patterns. Early constitutions were usually written in regions where the role of militias had been widened, and they served to transform militia service into national service. In this respect, early constitutions often built upon military affiliations already constructed by empires, and, throughout history, constitutions have frequently evolved as documents that translated military attachments formed by empires into national legal obligations.

Third, the influence of imperialism on early constitutionalism is tangible in the fact that the first constitutions reacted to transformations in labour markets, reflecting the long emergence of early capitalist economies. By the later decades of the eighteenth century, most European societies were in the middle of a process in which workers in rural communities were being liberated from coerced labour, so that the obligations attached to serfdom were progressively weakened. This was clearly expressed in acts of legal codification in the eighteenth century, which tended to support the recognition of legal rights for peasants.[29] As a result, for the first time in modern history, governments were consolidated on a material foundation in which economic production was (formally) based in increasingly free individual labour, so that public support for government was not purchased through legislation to reinforce serfdom or other unfree economic practices. Most constitutions brought these developments towards completion, and they constructed governmental legitimacy around an idea of the citizen as an autonomous economic agent. All early constitutions contained provisions to abolish or at least to reduce the force of coercive labour systems, and they began to assign some political rights to persons

29 See p. 96.

extricated from the bonds of serfdom. In this context, the transformation of subjects into citizens at the core of modern constitutionalism reflected in legally abstracted form the end of a longer process of social formation in which the local obligations of feudalism had been qualified, and single persons in society had been placed in a more vertical relation to central governments.

In vital respects, the liberation of agricultural labour that began to prevail in eighteenth-century Europe was the outcome of imperialism, and it was determined by military forces. By the Seven Years' War, the consumption of soldiers by national governments had increased markedly and governments were forced to reach deeper into their populations to extract military personnel and monetary resources. On one hand, such military expansion imposed fiscal burdens on national states that necessitated agricultural reform and proto-capitalist innovation, to augment agrarian production and to increase taxes levied on agricultural products. One outcome of such policies was that serfs were released from traditional obligations, so that economic modernization for military purposes increased social liberty. One motivation for the weakening of serfdom in Europe was that it increased the capacity of national governments to tax agrarian products and to use tax to finance armies. However, such reforms had a more immediate military purpose. Serfdom conflicted with national initiatives for military conscription, and it obstructed the direct recruitment of soldiers for national armies. The abolition of serfdom allowed governments to obtain immediate access to potential soldiers; early national armies placed serfs in direct relation to their regents, which then altered their relation to their territorial lords, forming a tight individual line of obligation between subjects and state.[30] Both the liberation of labour and the transformation of the serf into the soldier that early constitutionalism promoted can be ascribed, in part at least, to military pressures resulting from imperialism. The rise of early capitalism and demands for military reform were closely interlocked, and both were causally attached to imperialism. Together, these forces promoted a *military-economic logic of individualization* in early national societies. In this process, persons

[30] In eighteenth-century Spain, for example, militia service conferred privileged legal status on soldiers, as it designated them as royal soldiers and separated them from some customary legal obligations (see Andújar Castillo 1991: 12). In Russia, military service provided an important pathway out of servitude. In other territories, military service was introduced as serfdom was abolished.

were extracted from rural economies, religious corporations and local administrations and placed in life horizons defined by individual economic contracts towards other people and individual military contracts towards the state. This process of military-economic individualization usually reinforced secular constructions of legitimacy for the state as it transferred the source of societal duties from religious to governmental institutions.[31]

As discussed throughout this book, the impact of these processes on constitutional organization remained pervasive long after the first wave of constitution making. It took approximately a century from the 1770s until constitutional rule became a common system of political organization. By this time, the original functions of constitutionalism – the legal construction of space, the formation of citizenship through military obligations, and the solidification of individualized labour markets – had acquired a strategic emphasis. In their initial development, however, constitutions built on processes that, owing to imperialism, were already structural to society. In this setting, constitutions established a legal order in which states could manage the internal preconditions of their sovereignty and stabilize their position in relation to changing external security challenges. This created a global path dependency in which the integration of citizens as constitutional subjects was directly determined by military pressures resulting from imperialism.

LEGITIMACY AND THE PATHOLOGIES OF CONSTITUTIONALISM

In these respects, modern constitutional law developed in the eighteenth century as a reaction to imperial pressures. At the same time, it developed as a mechanism for managing the social and military crises that imperialism engendered. The aggregate of interlinked dynamics outlined above was caused by deep social contradictions in imperial societies in which traditional structures for the administration of military force lost efficacy so that governments were compelled to alter the instruments used for organizing violence. By the later eighteenth century, governments were able to conduct external military conflict only

[31] In classical sociology, war is seen as countervailing individualism (Durkheim 1950: 92). However, to support my claims, one specialist in French military history explains how, with conscription laws introduced in 1793, the individual replaced the *collectivité* as the basic unit of political obligation (Vallée 1937: 9). One analysis of Japan supports my argument by explaining how rural populations in nineteenth-century Japan first experienced individual integration through military organizations (Smethurst 1974: 87–88).

if they deepened their legitimational support in national society, especially in matters concerning military supply. To obtain such support, governments were forced to interact more directly with their populations and to create instruments that incentivized popular military engagement so that imperial environments forced states to acquire more fully national form. In projecting uniform ideas of citizenship and establishing representative organs, constitutions played a central role in structuring this process, and they were designed to create a legal-political (legitimational) order in which states could articulate bargains over military supply and military capacities could be reconsolidated.

Crucial in this respect, however, is the fact that constitutions did little to assuage social contradictions in imperial societies. Distinctively, modern constitutions usually reacted to structural challenges caused by imperialism by defining the state as an organization with immediate responsibility for all society, legitimated by the idea that it expressed a concept of sovereignty in which all citizens were implicated. On this basis, modern constitutional law brought contradictions between social groups to increased political prominence, so that civil conflicts tended, under certain circumstances, to encompass the whole of society and to incite violence that embraced large social factions.[32] As a result, most constitutions created governments that acted towards their own populations as they acted towards external populations. Moreover, as members of society were linked to state institutions by military procedures, these conflicts were frequently articulated through military organizations, and armies were often brought into central political roles.

These outcomes are visible in the primary social functions of constitutions, each of which stimulated heightened social conflict.

First, the fact that constitutions induced the legal transformation of geographical space stimulated lateral violence in society, and, once subject to constitutional organization, most societies experienced deeply polarized attitudes towards legal integration. In most emerging nations, the construction of legal categories of citizenship was experienced by some groups as a process that resembled imperialism, and it instilled a deeply conflictual grammar, frequently close to civil war, at the heart of national society.[33] By the nineteenth century, the formation of constitutionally ordered nation states often depended on the

[32] For a similar claim, see Rougier (1903: 556).
[33] See discussion of early cases in Chapter 1.

forcible imposition of a unified legal order on society. In European polities such as Germany, Italy, Spain and Poland, strategies of military centralization were eventually required to impose constitutional law on society, and the military served as a primary organ of integration. In Latin America, constitutional law was frequently employed as an instrument of internal colonization, as elites utilized it both to harden their domestic positions and to incorporate regional groups in emerging states. In such processes, early constitutional systems emulated techniques of political centralization previously used in empires.

Second, the fact that constitutional law served the recruitment of soldiers had clear implications for social violence.

On one hand, early constitutions were designed to mobilize armed citizens, *soldats-citoyens*, to fight for constitutionally defined states. As examined in Chapters 1–5, the military idea of the citizen at the centre of modern constitutionalism typically meant that most early experiences of constitutional government had some military dimensions. However, the *soldat-citoyen* was rarely based in uniform social support for constitutional rule, and the mobilization of citizens in support of constitutional government usually triggered counter-mobilization. This aspect of constitutionalism meant that, for many, national citizenship was an intensely undesired condition as the assumption of rights of legal membership entailed exposure both to violence and to military ideology: the constitutional personality of the citizen was inextricably attached to the potential experience of violent death. Unsurprisingly, in most early constitutional states, some newly enfranchised citizens went to great lengths to avoid citizenship and the military duties that went with it. Exemplified by the Vendée, early constitutional regimes repeatedly provoked conscription rebellions, close to civil war.[34] More profoundly, the military substance of constitutionalism meant that the citizen was placed at the legitimational centre of government in a form that lacked universal social appeal. Most constitutional states constructed their legitimacy around subjects mobilized for military purposes, but they were forced to manufacture consent for their actions amongst the military subjects on whom they relied.

These factors had several consequences. Generally, as constitutional rule was designed to secure military force for government, constitutions placed military actors in prominent positions, allowing them to determine the form of the state. Often, further, constitution making

[34] See examples at pp. 47, 85, 153, 285.

converged with civil war and rival political factions were linked to opposing groups in the army. In many such contexts, the army acquired central administrative functions in society, such that the preservation of public order became a designated role of the military.[35] Before the 1780s, the maintenance of social peace was mainly entrusted to local and religious bodies. However, as modern constitutions set out norms of national representation to support the legitimation of law, they also established provisions for enforcing emergency laws. In such provisions, they defined the conditions in which laws could be enforced without compliance with regular procedures – typically against internal actors and insurgents.[36] This meant that political exceptionalism became a common feature of constitutional rule, and constitutionalism was intertwined with the use of military units to enforce the law without social support. More structurally, the undesirability of the roles conferred on citizens in early constitutional law created a set of constitutional-legitimational problems that shaped the entire history of modern statehood. Throughout the nineteenth century, states consolidated their social positions by managing conflicts between the citizens to which they attached their legitimacy, and the organization of military force for external war was flanked by policies for the pacification of national society and the avoidance of civil conflict. This was partly reflected in constitutional measures to soften material antagonisms; for example, in early social-welfare policies.[37] As discussed below, after circa 1870, welfare systems developed, in part, as integration mechanisms designed to manage social conflicts caused by militarism.[38] Yet, in many cases, national states controlled the social conflicts that they internalized by forcibly regulating those groups – usually distinct religious, ethnic or sociopolitical sectors – who were not easily harnessed to the military form of the citizen. Moreover, states often used war itself to extract legitimation from their citizens. Many wars, especially the Franco-Prussian War and World War I, were partly initiated by belligerent states to manifest popular acclamation for governments.[39] Such

[35] See pp. 68, 110.

[36] The 1791 constitution of France provided for a 'public force' to ensure the maintenance of order (IV/1). Articles 365 and 366 of the 1795 constitution of France allowed the use of the military against domestic groups. In the 1848 constitution of France, Art. 106 contained state-of-siege provisions. Other early constitutions followed suit. The Prussian constitution of 1850 contained provisions for the exceptional suspension of basic protections (Art. 111).

[37] See pp. 140–1.

[38] See p. 134.

[39] This theory is often rejected in political science, although it is partly supported in Blainey (1988: 78–82) and Gelpi (1997: 277). This approach is more widespread amongst historians.

conscious promotion of military citizenship was always perilous for national governments, and it tied their legitimacy to contingent events. When military initiatives failed, belligerent states normally experienced acute legitimational crisis and, frequently, soldiers led revolts against their governments. The Napoleonic Wars, the Crimean War, the Austro-Sardinian War, the Austro-Prussian war, the Franco-Prussian War, the Russo-Ottoman War (1877–8), the Russo-Japanese War and World War I all caused deep constitutional transformation in the states that fared poorly in conflict. In most such cases, military defeat created extreme political instability, usually expressed both in constitutional reform and in intensified militarism, in the polities in question.

Third, the fact that constitutional law was related to agrarian reform and the reconstruction of labour markets created a volatile focus of violence in society. Through the rise of constitutional law, most states – in essence – entered a bargain with their citizens in which some basic rights were given to involuntary labourers, who were extracted from coercive labour regimes in return for military force. This was visible in the constitutional position of serfs in revolutionary Europe, but it was partly mirrored, simultaneously, in the constitutional position of slaves in the Americas. One result of this was that responsibility for peasant economies was removed from regional authorities and national governments assumed increasing duties in regulating labour markets and labour-related disputes between different groups of citizens. In Europe, different governments approached these contradictions in different ways. Through the earlier nineteenth century, most states simply retracted from peasants the rights originally promised to them in constitutional law. Across Europe, the legal abolition of serfdom was frequently not concluded until the decades after 1848. During the nineteenth century, nonetheless, national governments were confronted with an abiding structural predicament which could not be papered over by simple exclusion or repression. As states were formed in the context of imperialism and related interstate conflict, they remained enduringly dependent on national military resources and personnel, and they were forced to establish some general construction of citizenship in order to mobilize soldiers. This had the consequence that, by the latter part of the nineteenth century, problems of social

For one of its exponents, see Wehler (1972: 455). I agree with the claim that external mobilization by military leaders is often similar to a domestic coup, as it effects violent repression and regime change in the belligerent polity (Dassel 1998: 122).

management resulting from the abolition of serfdom could not be deflected from the political arena. By 1900, most European states were engaged in the political and economic integration of social groups with histories of unfree labour, and some political rights for classes comprising former forced workers were granted in most polities. In many states, however, this led to the militarization of conflicts between groups with different economic prerogatives and different positions in national economic systems. Indeed, the militarization of intra-societal conflicts can be viewed as the price states paid for their original promotion of citizenship as a military contract.

In each point, constitutional rule evolved as a legal-political order with a dialectical relation to social violence. Constitutions acquired prominence as the form of sovereignty pressed into society by pressures for vertical integration released by imperialism, forming a bargaining system to stabilize legitimacy for national governments in face of changing military constellations. Yet this form usually affected society in unpredictable fashion. Although vertical integration was strongly linked to the separation of individual subjects from traditional (local or religious) milieux, it induced multiple experiences of collective violence, and few bargaining systems used to absorb such integration held up in face of the antagonisms that they released. From the eighteenth century, governments constructed their legitimacy as they elaborated sets of rights for their subjects.[40] Under most constitutions, the formation of such rights brought collective violence to the surface of society, and many constitutions created polities in which civil war and inter-state war overlapped. Typically, constitutions brought national armies into central governmental roles and they imprinted a military form on national political systems: *they promoted vertical militarization*. Once created, constitutional states were frequently forced to operate in an external landscape defined by imperial rivalry, which necessarily cemented the position of military forces. Moreover, the vertical impact of constitutions transmitted violent social conflict through society at large, so that horizontal attachments that connected society were also defined by military volatility: *they promoted lateral militarization*. This was evident in the first constitutions created in the eighteenth century. However, this dimension of constitutional violence did not recede and it afflicted constitutional rule, at different points in imperial systems, well into the twentieth century. In most cases, the vertical integration

[40] See pp. 139–43.

of citizens gave rise to deep militarism in the lateral dimensions of society. In this regard, many constitutional states immediately acquired primary characteristics of empires: (1) their internal and external military actions converged, and they created integration regimes for citizens to meet external military needs; (2) they legitimated themselves in coercive categories that produced lateral violence inside domestic societies; (3) this production of internal violence often led to the intensification of external violence.

On this basis, constitutional law expresses a deep paradox for modern society. Constitutions developed as legal documents that stabilized the essential political rights that typify modern life, extracting legitimacy from politically implicated citizens and creating sovereign states with powerful integration functions. Yet constitutions extracted legitimacy from citizens in unreliable, violent form and they usually engendered *more violence*, unsettling the states whose sovereignty they were intended to uphold. As a result, although conceived to organize nations, most post-imperial constitutions rapidly reproduced elements of imperialism.

IMPERIALISM, CONSTITUTIONS AND INTERNATIONAL LAW

The relation of constitutional law to violence is further reflected in the historical links between constitutional law and international law. In the early development of constitutionalism, it was often claimed that constitutional states were unlikely to violate provisions for international peace.[41] Today, this assumption is reflected in claims that national constitutional law and international law contain convergent moral claims.[42] However, constitutional law and international law frequently evolved as alternative ways of managing the violence sovereign states produced, and of absorbing the effects of imperialism. Accordingly, throughout history, constitutions typically presented models of legitimacy that contradict norms established at the international level, often generating expressions of violence that international law was intended to avert.

Before the rise of modern constitutions, some principles of international order for European society had resulted from the Peace

[41] See p. 73.
[42] See for prominent examples Brunkhorst (2002: 110) and Habermas (2012).

Treaties of Westphalia of 1648, bringing an end to the Thirty Years' War. Both the actual force and the novelty of these treaties are questionable, and the importance ascribed to them is often more symbolic than real. Yet these treaties established a normative climate that framed the emerging European state system, and they had important consequences for the management of violence.

These treaties began to endorse norms of state action and responsibility that identified core political domains, especially in questions of security, that were formally subject to the authority of heads of state. In the Holy Roman Empire, the main scenario of the Thirty Years' War, the treaties established a multilateral security community, comprising separate princely states, in which treaties agreed between these states assumed contractual status.[43] First, this meant that princes had acquired sovereign responsibility for their territories. However, it also meant that the emperor could not declare war without approval of the territorial princes whose domains formed the empire. This was set out in the Art. VIII, §2 of the Treaty of Osnabrück (1648). In addition, these treaties stipulated that princes could not form alliances against the empire or against the terms of peace. These treaties also led to the establishment of a permanent Diet in Regensburg, operative from 1663, which discharged policies of *securitas publica*.[44] In this context, interstate war became a matter subject to international law, and, in parts of Europe, war was determined by norms established between sovereign states.[45] This was reflected in the institutionalization of peace congresses to manage interstate conflict – for example, in Cambrai in the 1720s. This period also saw the expansion of diplomatic bodies as permanent institutions in which heads of state devolved representative functions to formal emissaries, thereby institutionalizing interstate interaction as a strict attribute of regents.

In these respects, these treaties were intended to obviate the experience of warfare that typified the Thirty Years' War (1618–48), and they promoted a concept of statehood to restrict the effects of war. Between 1618 and 1648, armies had largely been raised by private agents, possessing limited loyalty to regents and governments, and they were rarely supported by adequate fiscal resources. Consequently, the violent quest for booty by private soldiers was a constant feature of war, and it

[43] Böckenförde (1969: 452).

[44] On the role of the Diet in serving to guarantee interstate peace, see Schindling (1991: 177–185).

[45] See Berber (1964: 191).

frequently destroyed elemental structures of public order. As a result, the Thirty Years' War had an indistinct military form. It had many hallmarks of an intra-imperial war. Battles were fought between armies (notionally) attached to the Holy Roman Empire and armies mobilized – in part – by emerging states within the empire, seeking some degree of autonomy from it. However, it had hallmarks of a civil war; it was fought between armies of different states in the Holy Roman Empire, and it entailed extreme hostility between armies and catastrophic penetration of warfare into the civil sphere. Against this background, the treaties of 1648 were intended to manage military conflict in a context marked by imperial collapse. They constructed state responsibilities, in part, to avert, or at least to confine, war, and they sought to ensure that war could be ordered in a form that was legally distinct from civil war. Importantly, such ideas were reflected in the development of military law in emerging national societies, which, as discussed, was used to concentrate military power in the state. The decades after 1648 saw frequent and lengthy wars in which the efficacy of such norms was always limited. Yet in the eighteenth century, sovereign states asserted control of military supply and armies were increasingly sustained by national fiscal systems: this was one precondition for the rise of standing armies. Accordingly, the use of military force was circumscribed and societies in some parts of Europe were partly demilitarized, so that the avoidance of uncontrolled war became a shared commitment.[46] Importantly, standing armies were rarely used for public-order functions against citizens. Whether accurately or not, one leading observer commented in the 1770s that, through the eighteenth century, 'wars became less cruel'; this was partly because 'vanquished peoples' were not subject to harsh acts of requisitioning and extraction.[47]

The period of constitution making in the later eighteenth century was a period in which the principles of the post-1648 world reached the end of their sustainability, and this was largely the consequence of imperialism. This can be seen in the historical contexts in which constitutions evolved. At a specific level, as mentioned, the wave of

[46] See my earlier claim in Thornhill (2021: 56–57). See the observation that 'the militarization of society in the *Ancien Régime*' was limited by the fact that regents separated armies from society (Carl 1993: 11).

[47] Guibert (1803: 263). This is echoed in sociological analysis in Luard (1986: 126). One commentary explains how, after around 1700, there evolved a 'clearly marked separation between the space of combat and the spaces where civil peace was preserved', so that 'wars were more effectively circumscribed' (Cornette 1993: 33).

constitution making in the late eighteenth century was caused by the Seven Years' War. The Seven Years' War itself had its origins in Europe in the Prussian annexation of Silesia from the Habsburgs beginning in 1740, which initiated the dissolution of the interstate structure created in 1648.[48] This conflict involved deep societal annexation and the military imposition of civil government by one German state on subjects of a rival German state, both of which were positioned within the Holy Roman Empire. As such, 1740 initiated a period of interstate antagonism in which competition for supremacy in Central Europe was intensified and the distinction between interstate war and civil war lost clarity. At a more general level, the first wave of constitution making originated in conditions in which laws of war lost efficacy. Outside Europe, the Seven Years' War was caused by minor territorial disputes between Britain and France in Pennsylvania. In this environment, central state institutions had only limited control of their armies and warfare was not easily subject to laws of sovereignty. For example, the British military effort required large-scale conscription of colonial subjects whose loyalty to the British government was at times uncertain. This war entailed the mobilization of military units in informal conflicts or remote settings, so that laws of war intended to tame military conflict could scarcely be enforced. Essentially, the principles of sovereignty and state responsibility set out in 1648 encountered their limits in colonial wars, which became widespread through the eighteenth century. In promoting colonization, sovereign states engaged in conflicts with multiple populations, often only informally attached to flags of state, and they were required to mobilize armies in rough terrains outside regular command structures. By the revolutionary period, the rising frequency of imperial conflicts meant that the constraints on warfare notionally established after 1648 had been eroded. It was in such conditions that the early impetus to constitutional order took place. States turned to their citizens as providers of violence in environments where sovereign administration of warfare was limited, and citizens acquired constitutional roles as interstate war and civil war converged.

Over a longer period, the constitutional construction of government recurrently reflected and induced modes of violence that

[48] In discussions of Prussian history, this war served to 'transform the situation in Europe' as it involved widespread use of 'irregular forces' (Grünhagen 1890: 3, 307–308). Early military theorists viewed this war as an 'epochal event' 'in military history' and even in 'world history' (Berenhorst 1872: 52–53). More recently, this war is described as 'the beginning of a new epoque' both in terms of its distinct nature and its impact on the European balance of power (Bein 1994: 56).

fractured international security structures. Generally, constitutions were formed in five major waves, each with different emphases. These waves were essentially as follows: (1) the period from 1776 to 1824; (2) the period from 1848 to 1891; (3) the period from 1916 to 1920; (4) the period from 1945 to the 1960s; (5) the period starting in the 1980s. A smaller sub-cluster of constitutions can be found after 1905 in Iran, Russia, China, Mexico and Turkey, which were arguably less effective in creating representative systems. In each wave, constitutions formed reactions to an international order, put in place to organize sovereign states and to structure military relations in settings that resulted from imperial conflicts. As discussed, the first wave of constitution making occurred against the background of the Treaties of Westphalia. Later, the second constitutional wave occurred through the long dissolution of the European order of public law created by the Congress of Vienna in 1815. The Congress of Vienna established a system of inter-monarchical peace designed to limit warfare by re-stabilizing existing imperial blocs after the Napoleonic interlude. Initially, this system was intended to restrict nationalist movements in European societies, limiting sovereign titles to formal heads of state. Ultimately, this system created the basis for the inter-imperial order that evolved in the later nineteenth century. Then, the third constitutional wave coincided with the formation of the League of Nations in 1919–20. The approach of the League of Nations to imperialism was equivocating. It was partly intended to oversee the dismantling of major empires in Europe, reflecting Woodrow Wilson's ideals of national self-determination and the primacy of the nation state. However, like the Congress of Vienna, it stabilized some empires, notably those centred in London and Paris, at the expense of others.[49] This was partly because the USA did not ratify the covenant of the League of Nations. It meant that Germany, Austria and Turkey emerged after 1919 as post-imperial polities bordered by strengthened empires. The fourth constitutional wave converged with the creation of the United Nations, one of whose primary functions was to manage the dissolution of European empires in Asia and Africa and to stabilize nation states in this context. The fifth wave of constitution making was shaped by the rise of an international human rights consensus in the 1980s.

[49] One excellent account describes its results as 'a shameless betrayal of the promises of self-determination' (Pedersen 2015: 77).

In each period, constitutions developed in complex relation to international law, which was in turn positioned in a complex relation to imperial power. In essence, in each step, the corpus of international law developed as a set of instruments for ordering sovereign statehood in contexts defined by imperialism, and the major international moments of legal foundation coincided with the crisis of an imperial or an inter-imperial structure. This can be seen in 1648, 1815, 1919–20 and 1945. Of course, such normative structures clearly perpetuated extreme violence in some regions, as they were usually designed to legitimate violent state action in regions not protected by the title of sovereignty.[50] Despite this, at different junctures, law-based security systems were established, whose purpose was to manage violence and to prevent the diffuse societalization of war. This phenomenon is addressed in different historical locations throughout this book. In such settings, however, international law usually collapsed because it could not contain imperialism and imperialism strained the models of sovereignty around which international order was designed. Against this background, constitutions were initially written at moments when international arrangements to manage violence began to fracture. This can be seen from the 1770s, as the Westphalian order was fragmenting; after 1848, as the Viennese system was beginning to dissolve; after 1918, as the international order around the League of Nations was critically weakened at the moment of its inception. In each setting, constitutions were established in a dialectical relation with international law. On one hand, constitutions replicated the focus of international law as they solidified the sovereign authority of states, allowing states to stand as independent entities in the international system. On the other hand, as they constructed vertical foundations for nation states, constitutions had intra-societal consequences that weakened the states that they supported, and they often organized national populations in forms that could not be contained in the international order of sovereign states. Each constitutional moment in the earlier waves of constitutionalism – around 1789, after 1848, after 1920 – gave rise to states that mobilized their populations for the sake of sovereignty yet which, in so doing, triggered acute violence, both internally and externally. As discussed at different points below, constitutions were often

[50] See the claim that the 'universalization of international law', based in positivist accounts of sovereign statehood, served the imperialist expansion of European states in the nineteenth century in Anghie (2005: 32–33). See further discussion at p. 150.

constructed amidst irregular warfare and their results sat uneasily with the ideals of international law, focused on the containment of violence.

These processes occurred in many variations, and, at different times, constitutionally ordered societies were marked by predominantly lateral or predominantly vertical models of military violence. However, up to circa 1945, societies usually became more constitutionalized as they were more militarized, and they became more militarized as they were more thoroughly constitutionalized. Few polities created constitutional rights without exposing citizens to war, and the patterns of integration typical of constitutional law rarely developed independently of military pressures. However, few states controlled the military outcomes of this process. It was only after 1945 that constitutions began to frame legitimacy in categories that were more convergent with international law.

RESEARCH LANDSCAPE

In presenting this analysis, this book challenges three common outlooks in research on constitutional law and the legal foundations of statehood.

First, this book builds on the common sociological interpretation of a constitution as a textually ordered agreement that supports the integration processes that underlie national societies. Most constitutional theorists with a sociological disposition argue that constitutions allow the enactment of citizenship in relatively peaceful fashion, sustaining the long-term integration of different social groups and creating a premise for democracy in civil society.[51] By contrast, this book claims that constitutions have usually promoted social integration by establishing legal structures conditioned by external military dynamics, in which armies acquire a primary role.[52] Of course, constitutions do more than manage military capacity, and they reflect bargains between different groups in society. However, in most contexts, acts of constitution making served to restructure society's military basis, and they formed, essentially, a *security constitution* for national society: they resulted, not from *civil society*, but from *military society*.[53] In this respect,

[51] See classic statements of this view in Durkheim (1950: 99), Parsons (1965), and Habermas (1973: 148).

[52] Amongst early sociologists, Franklin Henry Giddings (1901: 3) identified the close relation between democracy and empire.

[53] The parallel concept of 'war society' is used in related, slightly narrower fashion in Kruse (2015: 12).

the book advances some arguments that converge with claims often viewed as Foucauldian, as it indicates that constitutional democracy first developed as an apparatus for physical administration. However, its conclusions are anything but Foucauldian. It is supported by a long-term constitutional theory of social integration, which outlines the conditions under which states may exercise sovereignty in effective, relatively legitimated fashion.

Second, this book opposes a central presumption amongst constitutionalists, who analyse constitutional law as part of the doctrine of limited government. On this common account, constitutions are perceived as consensual devices for framing domestic government, taming the excesses of political arbitrariness, and establishing a procedural order for the use of public authority. This book argues that the rights secured under classical constitutional law usually resulted, not from moments of deliberation between citizens, but from wars. Few enduring constitutional systems were created by peaceful change, and the hard apparatus of constitutional law was usually driven into society by war. To be sure, most states weakened constitutional rights *during actual warfare*, as exceptional powers were transferred to executive branches of government, especially in the surveillance of internal dissidents.[54] Many states also preserved intensified executive powers directly after wars.[55] Yet most states that assumed constitutional form were created through *military bargaining* between government and citizens: that is, they were normally formed in periods leading up to war, when governments were forced to motivate soldiers, and in the longer wake of war, when governments rewarded, pacified and reintegrated soldiers. This meant that constitutions formed political designs for creating legitimacy for government in military environments. As a result, most wars created a complex and intricate constitutional balance in which some coercive powers of executive bodies were augmented, but the rights of citizens to shape the legislation defining such powers increased sharply.[56] Self-evidently, not all wars led to the reinforcement of constitutional rule. Yet until the late twentieth century, few constitutions were not established as wars forced populations into proximity to government. As discussed below, the primary problem of constitutionalism arose from the fact that states

[54] See examples at pp. 176, 196.

[55] Amongst the most famous twentieth-century examples are, in the UK, the Emergency Powers Act (1920), and, in the USA, the Internal Security Act (1950).

[56] I agree that there is no simple *ratchet effect* in the relation between war and rights (Posner and Vermeule 2003: 610). The claim that war leads to executive reinforcement and weakens constitutional rights reflects a simplified dichotomy.

usually became more democratic when exposed to war, which often meant that democratic interactions had a strong military character, and wars affected constitutional formation by generating liberty and repression together, both in exponentially heightened fashion.

In analysing these factors, this book builds on research that assesses the relation between the construction of constitutional rights and warfare, explaining how militarism often creates implied political and social bargains that expand constitutional provisions.[57] It also elaborates on research that has illuminated the origins of constitutionalism in imperial constellations.[58] However, its focus differs from existing research. It attempts to illustrate how constitutional bargains created through military demands were often liable to fracture, and it outlines a theory of constitutional democracy that shows how constitutions experienced crisis when the military bargains that supported them proved unsustainable. That is, constitutions were created to broker military capacity, and they integrated national citizens to that end. However, these bargains were susceptible to engender renewed military violence – in different social dimensions. Finally, it seeks to explain how crises inherent in such functions can be managed. On this basis, the book claims that a new vocabulary is required to interpret constitutions which assesses how the formation of constitutional rights is both determined by and likely to induce military conflict.

Third, as mentioned, this book expounds the view that constitutional regimes are causally related to war. Constitutional regimes are – typically – the results of war, so that war and constitutional government are linked in a complex legitimational nexus. Moreover, constitutions organize society around violent bargains and vertically constructed obligations, which often promote intra-societal conflicts that induce warfare. In this component, the book uses a method based in the historical sociology of law to elucidate the causes of war. That is, it reconstructs the broad social constellations in which constitutions were created and, in so doing, it describes how, through constitutions, governments internalized deep structural emphases towards violence, and how this affected democratization and its outcomes. It utilizes this

[57] This aspect of the book builds on research that examines war as the basis for social bargains that created basic rights. This is exemplified by Tilly (1990: 83), Krebs (2006: 29; 2009), different chapters in Kier and Krebs (2012), Rousseau (2021: 23) and Obinger (2020: 9).

[58] See my earlier account in Thornhill (2021). This has also been addressed in Colley (2021), who does not focus on democratic problems arising from this connection.

method to question the claim, common amongst theorists of international relations, that democratic states show limited willingness to declare war, *at least against each other*.[59]

This book questions assumptions about *inter-democratic peace*, first, by arguing that war is not a simple interstate practice involving the declaration of hostility by one state against a different state, in which the inside and the outside of society are strictly separate. Instead, war needs to be understood more broadly in terms that incorporate multiple patterns of conflict. As the book argues against conceptual purism in defining nations, it also argues against purism in defining wars. During their constitutional evolution, most societies experienced acute intergroup hostilities, many of which fell between strictly distinct categories of interstate war, civil war and civil disorder. Indeed, most societies entered periods of violence in which wars had convergent internal and external dimensions, both of which were linked to conflicts over citizenship. Moreover, imperialism held many democratizing societies in states of violence, not simply classifiable as war, in which political order depended on military force. In analysing these phenomena, the book shows how internal and external violence are not always fully separate, and different forms of violence contain aspects of war.

This book questions the inter-democratic peace theory, second, by claiming that exponents of such theory usually show an unnuanced understanding of democracy, which does not fully address the restrictions imposed on popular representation in most purportedly 'democratic' states.[60] The relation between war and democracy is a hard case for testing whether a state is democratic, as war is a situation in which the decisions of some people have mortal outcomes for many others. Therefore, it is reasonable to claim that a state warranting classification as a democracy is one whose government allots to people expected to fight and die for it (potential soldiers) the right to vote for it. This definition was implicitly proposed by Max Weber around 1918

[59] This idea was popularized by Kant (1976: 197). See the later claim that 'constitutional constraints eliminate autocratic caprice in waging war' in Oneal and Russett (1997: 268). The assertion that democracies do not wage war on each other is clearly stated in Maoz and Russett (1993: 636) and Rummel (1995: 458). For more emphatic support for this theory, see Levy (1988: 662) and Weart (1998: 13). For a sceptical approach, see Gleditsch (1992: 37). My analysis is close to the claim that 'semidemocracy is associated with an increased likelihood of civil war' in Henderson (2002: 119).

[60] On one account, electoral enfranchisement of ten per cent of the adult population qualifies a state as democratic (Levy 1988: 662). However, states permitting fractional enfranchisement usually did so for deliberately non-democratic reasons: to discriminate strategically against non-enfranchised social groups.

(1921: 308) and it is taken here as a threshold for the categorization of a polity as democratic. Moreover, it is reasonable to claim that a state warranting recognition as a democracy will enable other adults immediately affected by conflict, including female citizens, to take part in national elections for governments that conduct war. In other words, a democracy needs to be defined as a state that allows full male and female suffrage. If the first part of this definition is accepted, very few states were democratic for any length of time before 1918. If the second part is accepted, there were very few enduring democracies before 1945. Most 'democracies' that existed before 1945 were only partial or intermittent democracies, in which large sectors of the population were normally excluded from electoral participation because of their class, ethnicity or gender. When such 'democracies' declared war, they only legitimated this declaration to select domestic groups, often not including persons mobilized as combatants: simply, *such decisions were not democratic*.

If this definition of democracy is applied, inter-democratic peace theory is on shaky ground. Importantly, evidence to support such theory is often extracted from analysis of World War I, assuming that this war was fought between democracies (France, UK, USA) and autocracies (Germany, Turkey, Austria–Hungary) (Weart 1998: 144). However, no belligerent state in 1914 was genuinely democratic. New Zealand was democratic, but it entered the war as part of the British Empire. France was the most democratic major European state at this point, although French women could not vote until 1944–5. Measured by the proportion of the population that could vote, Germany was far more democratic in 1914 than the UK. The UK only had circa 60 per cent male enfranchisement in 1914; many working-class men were excluded from voting, so that many persons called up for military service from 1916 were not enfranchised until 1918 (if they were still alive). Potential military recruits had far stronger political representation in Germany than in the UK. The conflict began with the declaration of war by Austria on Serbia, neither of which states were fully democratic, but both of which had deeper enfranchisement than the UK.[61] Belgium, the country invaded by Germany in 1914, was hardly

[61] On one calculation Serbia, whose electoral system had a property threshold and prevented soldiers from voting, had circa 70 per cent male enfranchisement before 1918 (Popović-Obradović 2013: 233–234). This was roughly 10 per cent higher than the basic franchise in Britain, and Britain had substantial plural voting. The Austrian part of Austria-Hungary had full male suffrage from 1907.

a democracy – it had a system of plural voting whose purpose was to prevent equal male suffrage.[62] In this context, it is difficult to see relative democratization as a factor that impacted on the *war proneness* of European states at this time. The same logic applies to the Balkan Wars (1912–13), in which the protagonists were undergoing sporadic democratic reinforcement. Moreover, one reason why, before 1945, predominantly democratic states were reluctant to declare war is that many polities with the extensive enfranchisement had small populations (for example, Sweden, Denmark, Norway, New Zealand). Their motives for not declaring war on other states were probably based, not on constitutional accountability, but on a survival calculus. After 1945, then, many democracies were allied to a global superpower, the USA. The USA frequently initiated war against other states and tolerated war by its allies against non-allied states. It also overthrew several democratizing governments through *actions (formally) short of war*.[63] Yet, the USA reduced the probability that democracies allied to it would declare war on each other. Here too, the extent to which relative belligerence was conditioned by democracy is at least disputable.

Against this background, this book claims that a dynamic reciprocal link needs to be posited between war and democracy, in which internal democratization often depended on war. To capture this link, *partial democratization* is advanced here as a framework for examining propensities for war amongst states. Large-scale interstate wars before 1939 were typically conflicts between states that had obtained only partial democratic features, and, in this process, war had usually accelerated their elaboration of inclusive constitutional norms. Before 1945, in fact, most military conflicts were conducted by *partly democratized states* against *peoples that did not live under sovereign states*: they were imperial wars. Generally, the tortuous path *towards* constitutional democracy is the condition in which war has commonly arisen, and, in such settings, war, constitutional democracy and imperialism have been intrinsically intertwined.[64] Up to 1945, constitutional inclusion was usually driven by the global imperial system, and, as examined below, it tended to create partial democracies, democratic enough to support national

[62] Electoral rights became universal, but not equal, for Belgian men through the amended constitution of 1893. However, the revised Art. 47 of the constitution allowed some men – namely, those who met a certain property threshold or had attained a certain educational level – to cast more votes than others. This meant that there was a relative concentration of power in a small, privileged group of men. At the same time, all German men could vote.

[63] See discussion in Chapter 6.

[64] Here my claims converge with Mansfield and Snyder (1995: 7–8; 2002: 299).

armies but not democratic enough to transform the state.[65] Partial democracies, in turn, induced many wars – civil wars, interstate wars or wars containing both elements. Some of the most aggressive states in world history, such as Germany, Japan and Italy in the 1930s, were tangibly the products of democratization. Their external military actions reflected internal conflicts that had arisen due to imperial pressures and because of social and political bargains established during (partly) democratic interludes, preceding transitions to extreme authoritarianism. In such cases, external and internal wars were not easily separable, and constitutional systems reflected inter-group interactions of a hostile nature that spilled over into external violence. Moreover, wars usually had convergent outcomes in participant states. As discussed, wars intensified democratization in belligerent states, at least in those that remained sovereign after conflict. But they also shaped constitutions in a form that remained sensitive to militarization. It was only after 1945 that constitutions were able to stabilize peace, internally and externally.

In this light, this book contributes distinctively to debate about war and democracy as it explains how the links between democratization and war have fluctuated over time, and it identifies the constitutional and legitimational forms that have proved most likely to secure peaceful democratic rule. In this regard, it seeks to draw insights from periods marked by the reduction of *democratic militarization*, and it isolates the models of constitutional law that create legitimacy for government in a form able to pacify society. This analysis may contribute to explaining the preconditions of interstate war. One implication in the book is that deep-rooted propensities in democracy are always likely to induce a remilitarization of citizenship. Democracy thus presupposes constitutional designs that avert this.

The first chapters of this book explain how constitutional systems were created by war, usually of an inter-imperial nature. These sections show how military pressures on constitutions fractured constitutional order, often elevating military actors to prominent positions and inducing internal and external conflict. A theory of the *occupation constitution* is proposed to capture this; this theory argues that, in different dimensions, constitutions evolved as elements in complex processes of military occupancy. The later chapters explain how constitutions learned to limit the structural paradoxes on which they were based. These chapters assess

65 See discussion in Chapter 2.

how, after 1945, democracy developed through the management of the violence from which it originated. Here, the book advances a theory of *world law* to argue that constitutional models eventually secured democracy as they preserved aspects of constitutional law created by violence, but they also separated governments from their military origins. The book concludes by underlining the intense precariousness of constitutional democracy, outlining how the original attachments between constitutional law and violence are currently being rearticulated. In this last respect, the book adds to literature on world systems. Its claim is that imperialism constituted a world system of violence, which was reflected through the early development of constitutionalism, as constitutions allowed states to position themselves in this world system. Then, after 1945, the world system changed and constitutions reflected this change. The final chapter of the book, Chapter 10, outlines ways in which the world system is changing once more, expressed in new constitutional techniques for legitimacy production.

CHAPTER ONE

IMPERIALISM AND THE ORIGINS OF CONSTITUTIONS

INTRODUCTION

The late eighteenth century, between 1776 and 1795, is the period in which modern constitutionalism emerged. As mentioned in the Introduction, arrangements for political representation had existed before this period. However, it was in this period when constitutional texts matching the definition given in the Introduction were first written. Despite their great variations, constitutions of this time established the principle that citizens exercising political rights form the primary source of legitimate authority, so that laws require the collective recognition of citizens to manifest legitimacy. At this time, constitutions also began to identify citizens as bearers of protected rights. The core constitutional lineages of this time took shape in the USA, Poland and France.

The emergence of the first modern constitutions occurred in a broad context in which European imperialism was undergoing rapid transformation. The middle decades of the eighteenth century were an era, generally, in which imperial polities reorganized their relations with their colonies and overseas territories. This coincided with increases in the mobility of goods and labour between metropolitan and colonial regions, such that the fabrics of trade connecting different imperial regions became thicker.[1] At this time, in consequence, imperialism formed a broad constellation in which state-building and empire-building processes became less distinct. Institutions increasingly reached across the partitions

[1] See accounts of this in Steele (1986: 229) and Hancock (1995: 383–388).

between colonizing and colonized territories, tying subjects more directly to imperial centres and producing loyalties and conflicts that were uncertainly positioned between the external and the internal dimensions of different states. Through this intensification of imperialism, military units acquired new salience, often forming the main links between metropolitan and colonial regions. In some settings, military bodies dictated terms of membership and affiliation for inhabitants of all imperial domains.

Early constitutions were created in this changing imperial context. Constitutional law normally evolved in situations where empires had experienced protracted military concentration, and constitutions served to sustain political systems in settings marked by social and legal forms resulting from this. In such contexts, constitutions were formed on both sides of imperial systems, as colonizing and colonized regions reacted in parallel ways to the logic of imperial transformation. However, even where they supported new states, constitutions were formed *within empires*, and they were born from over-layered conflicts traversing different points in imperial systems and involving multiple actors with motivations shaped by empires. Moreover, early national constitutions reproduced and extended patterns of organization already devised in empires to stabilize imperial transformation. In particular, early constitutions promoted new ideas of citizenship to unify national societies, especially in the military dimension. Yet such principles were typically grafted onto normative structures already established in empires in order to unify imperial domains. In each respect, states utilized constitutions to adapt to realities configured by imperialism and, once organized in constitutional form, states were typically integrated into a system of inter-imperial relations. In primary cases, constitutionally ordered states retained core features of empires, and they used their constitutional support as a basis for outward expansion. In addition, early constitutions often emanated from armies and they created regimes in which military attachments shaped political order, often leading to intense social conflict. In each point, the uncertain distinction between the inside and the outside of society became a characteristic of constitutional states.

THREE LINES OF MODERN CONSTITUTIONALISM

1 USA

The first line of modern constitution making began in the British colonies in North America, which obtained independence and eventually created a unified state in the revolutionary period of 1775–91. In this environment, the origins of constitutional law were defined by changes in imperial society.

The emergence of revolutionary constitutionalism in the British colonies was originally shaped by transformation in the British Empire. During its foundation, the British Empire in the North Atlantic was a loose agglomerate of territories possessing diverse legal relations to the English (later British) crown. Some colonies were founded through royal charters (Virginia, New Hampshire, Massachusetts); some were based in proprietary grants, close to personal fiefs (Pennsylvania, New Jersey, New York, the Carolinas, Maryland); others, such as Rhode Island and Connecticut, had corporate charters guaranteeing almost unlimited self-government. Generally, however, the relation between the colonies and the metropolitan power was determined by the fact that many colonies were established by individual ventures. Before the founding of Georgia in 1732, which was initially governed by trustees in London and became a royal colony in 1752, Jamaica was the only English colony created by direct royal intervention as it was transferred to the English crown by treaty.[2] Consequently, colonial relations to Britain were mainly mediated through attachments of a commercial nature. The military basis for imperial rule in the northern Atlantic was initially relatively weak, although surely not non-existent. Even in colonies administered by royal governors, British military presence was low.[3] This was not unique to the North Atlantic. British expansion in the region now belonging to India was only loosely shaped by public institutions. The role of the British East India Company in consolidating British control in India was often compared to the acts of commercial organizations in creating colonies in America.[4]

By the middle of the eighteenth century, the British Atlantic colonies had begun to witness a solidification of imperialism. This

[2] Greene (1994: 15).

[3] This view is expressed in Shy (1965: 39), Olson (1992: 108) and Shannon (2000: 13). This view has been challenged by Webb (1979: xviii), who argues that, by the 1670s, the British Empire rested on military force condensed in the authority of the governors-general. Webb's 1997: 2) view is that 'English colonial policy was as much military as it was commercial'. This view supports basic claims in this book. Yet, until the 1750s, empires were generally held together by small armies, and the British Empire was no exception. On one calculation, British forces in American colonies in the earlier years of the wars of independence amounted to about 50,000 (Collins 2010: 32).

[4] See Pownall (1781: 8–9). See also the account of the 'company model of empire' (Burbank and Cooper 2011: 173).

solidification was shaped by intensifying conflicts between the British government and other states with colonial pretensions in the Atlantic region. Such conflicts culminated in the Seven Years' War, which was subdivided globally into numerous theatres of war. As mentioned, the primary hostility in this war, between Britain and France, resulted mainly from territorial disputes in backcountry Pennsylvania. Such disputes would have assumed limited importance before the thickening of imperial government. However, these disputes gave rise to substantial mobilization of troops at the imperial centre, eventually involving multiple military clashes between Britain and France across northern America. This solidification was also reflected in a series of institutional changes. Through the eighteenth century, the British colonies in the Atlantic were more closely assimilated to the imperial polity, whose legislative centre was in London. Military bodies played a central role in this transformation and military pressures drew the imperial polity together. This was partly a process of subordination, as British military bodies stationed in the colonies bound colonies and metropole together in military hierarchies. However, this process linked the empire and the colonies at a lateral level, and it conferred specific constitutional distinction on colonial citizens and on colonial institutions, which began to operate as organic parts of the empire. Intensified imperialism was not clearly distinct from extended state formation. It created the basis for a large, decentralized North Atlantic polity. Together, these factors created the constitutional conjuncture for the American Revolution.

First, during the Seven Years' War, the British army acquired greater prominence in the North Atlantic, frequently forming the most immediate contact between inhabitants of British colonies and the metropolitan government. Initially, the British army appeared in colonial America as an organization whose purpose was to defend British territory inhabited by British–American subjects against French troops. In many respects, such territorial defence was a joint endeavour. It involved common military mobilization in Britain and in the colonies in which colonial troops were often subject to British military articles, forming parts of the British army. With regional variations, the Seven Years' War saw extensive conscription in the American colonies, both in state militias and in quotas dispatched to the British army. In some areas, British colonial warfare induced unprecedented militarization in American society. Many colonies introduced draft and anti-desertion laws in the Seven Years' War, and members of colonial populations, often residing in remote rural localities, were connected through military organizations.[5] This process necessarily strengthened ideas of imperial citizenship; the shared discharge of military duties meant that colonists entered unprecedented immediacy to each other and to the imperial polity. Ultimately, the imperialist objectives of the British crown were successfully achieved and France was defeated in 1763. Through the latter stages of the war, the British Empire underwent great enlargement and British–American subjects jointly engaged in an expansionist war. The Treaty of Paris in 1763 then transformed the legal nature of lands Britain held in America. As mentioned, most American lands had initially been occupied by private enterprise or charter. From this point on, military conquest, coordinated by public institutions tied to the British crown and sanctioned by international treaty, formed the legal basis for British control in large parts of the empire.

At one level, the Seven Years' War connected Britain and its colonies in an increasingly dense system of institutional integration and shared citizenship. However, for many inhabitants of the American colonies, integration in the British polity had ambiguous implications and their position in the polity after 1763 was uncertain. Through the war, imperial subjects from Britain became visible in the colonies as a governing group that conducted rapid military expansion in former French parts of North America. Clearly, American residents participated fully in this process; as soldiers and settlers, they were centrally involved in territorial acquisition. However, this military enlargement altered the position of British government in American colonies, where, previously, most regions had experienced only light imperial rule. Indeed, the increased British military presence raised sensitive constitutional questions about the relation of the British army to American colonies and about the powers the British army could exercise. Above all, this placed inhabitants of the American colonies in a strained constitutional position as many of them had been deployed by an army for shared imperial protection, but this army then asserted external military authority in their domains, acting – in effect – as an occupation force in their society. Through this, British expansion in North America meant that inhabitants of British colonies were

[5] Such laws were passed in Massachusetts (1754), Virginia (1755) and Pennsylvania (1756). On one account, during the Seven Years' War, Massachusetts drafted more than 30 per cent of eligible males (Higginbotham 1988: 28). One historian estimates that 51,000 provincial troops were mustered in the war (Ruddiman 2014: 19).

expected to act as colonizers and objects of colonization at the same time. The problems inherent in such experiences were reinforced by the fact that colonial inhabitants were not well treated by agents of the British army. Relations between military and civilian authorities in the Seven Years' War were often poor and protest about British requisitioning, impressment and quartering of troops was frequent.[6] American soldiers were not highly regarded in the British army and colonial troops and state militias were often ridiculed. This was not improved by the fact that, at least in earlier initiatives, the British military leadership lacked competence.[7]

Ambiguities in this situation were greatly exacerbated by the fact that, after the end of the Seven Years' War, the British military presence was not withdrawn and a British standing army became a feature of colonial administration. Moreover, as the British army had been stationed to defend the boundaries of the British Empire in North America, the government in Westminster demanded that fiscal resources to support the army should be levied in the colonies. This created a situation in which the British empire became institutionally present both as an external military force and as a fiscal state. These processes were reflected initially in policies introduced by Grenville in 1763–5, in which the British government passed new laws to generate more tax and strengthen British control over the colonies.[8] This culminated in the Stamp Act (1765) and the Townshend Acts (1767), which imposed new taxes on American colonial assemblies.

Second, during the Seven Years' War, powers exercised by colonial assemblies in North America were extended, as such legislatures assumed central roles in the war effort.[9] Throughout the war, the lower houses of many state assemblies obtained increased responsibility for raising and provisioning troops, and the Westminster government widened the functions of such legislatures because it relied on them for resources and revenue.[10] Through this process, elected members of colonial assemblies acquired new authority. In states subject directly to British government, such officials were able to assert powers originally exercised by royal governors, including some control of public spending, the framing of financial legislation and the regulation of

[6] This is described in Rogers (1974: 79), Ward (2003: 82–86) and Ward (2006: 3).
[7] On hostile perceptions of redcoats amongst American residents, see Anderson (1984: 111, 141).
[8] See related analysis in Tucker and Hendrickson (1982: 3, 75).
[9] For discussion of this process in Pennsylvania, see Pearl (2020: 83).
[10] Different cases are discussed in Greene (1994: 168–179), Anderson (2000: 241), Ward (2003: 3) and Pearl (2020: 83).

militias.[11] By consequence, members of colonial legislatures consolidated their position as actors in a colonial constitution, claiming a distinct set of rights and obligations. One outcome of this was, naturally, that such legislatures, reinforced by colonial war, were reluctant to surrender their constitutional powers after 1763. After 1763, spokespersons for American liberties used this position to declare that 'rights granted to the British colonies' necessarily included 'equal freedom with the mother state'. This theory resulted in the claim that the British Empire 'consists of many separate governments' in which 'no single part' could impose its power on other parts.[12] Leading advocates of increased autonomy in the American colonies justified their opposition to Britain, not simply by denouncing the presence of British armies, but by condemning the methods used to finance imperial armies as violations of a transatlantic constitution. Critics of the empire advocated 'harmony between Great Britain and these colonies, ON A CONSTITUTIONAL FOUNDATION'.[13]

Together, these factors set in motion the tax revolt that eventually led to the wars of American independence.[14] Through its military consolidation in the eighteenth century, the British Empire embarked on a paradoxical pattern of formation. The empire asserted greater control of its constituent parts, and, owing to warfare, imperial subjects were integrated in a shared set of loyalties and duties as imperial citizens. At the same time, citizenship remained asymmetrical and rights granted in warfare lost force outside military environments. This stimulated a deep constitutional conflict. In this conflict, British colonies, perceived by many of their inhabitants as parts of an extended imperial polity, were expected to finance an army, which some of their inhabitants perceived as part of an external occupation regime. This conflict occurred against a background in which, within the colonial states, legislative bodies had assumed augmented constitutional powers, amongst which the power to approve or reject fiscal extraction was jealously guarded. This conflict culminated in British military occupation of regions that were recalcitrant in complying with imperial levies, notably the port of Boston in 1768. In this event, the arrival of British troops to defend metropolitan claims against Bostonians visibly stirred

11 See Greene (1963: 70–1).

12 Hopkins (1765: 5, 19).

13 Dickinson (1774: 24).

14 See the contemporary response to the Stamp Act: 'It is an essential principle of the English Constitution, that the subject shall not be taxed without his Consent, which hath not been introduced by any particular Law' (Dulany 1766: 7).

memories of the arrival of British redcoats to defend imperial rights against the French only ten years previously. Hatred for the invasion was increased by the fact that, as heirs to the British Whig tradition, members of colonial elites despised standing armies, depicting the British military presence in North America as a tyrannical regime.[15] In each respect, conflict was concentrated on the implementation of a constitutional order to support military occupation.

1(a): Imperial Civil War 1

By 1776, members of the colonial elites in British North America asserted independence from the British Empire, in which their constitutional self-understanding had originated. At one level, the constitutional situation that appeared around 1776 formed the template for modern nationalism, as it resulted, simply, in revolution by a colonial population against an empire. This was expressed in the constitutional diction of the revolutionary period, as citizens justified new laws by proclaiming that voluntary personal attachments were the only source of political duty. For example, the authors of the constitution of New York (1777) declared that their authority to write the constitution arose from the fact that all power had 'reverted to the people' because of the transgressions of the British king. Yet the American Revolution was not simply an expression of external, anti-colonial sentiment. The move towards independence in the British–American colonies was initially an intra-polity conflict concerning the authority of British political institutions and the obligations of colonial subjects towards them. As such, this event displayed the denser, interlocked implications of imperialism for societies of the eighteenth century. The American Revolution articulated the intricate linkage between nation-building and imperialism, and it contained antagonisms that fused elements of anti-imperial war, of civil war, of wars of national unification – and, ultimately, of imperial conquest.

By 1763, as discussed, the British imperial polity had been transformed by protracted warfare and its fiscal and military demands on its subjects had increased consonantly, both in metropolitan Britain and in its North American colonies. In this respect, Britain did not differ greatly from other European polities of the eighteenth century. On the contrary, the fact that the British imperial government became

[15] The main protest in the Boston press referred to the fact that 'quartering troops upon British Americans' violated the Bill of Rights (Dickerson 1970: 74).

manifest in America as an organization that implanted new military bases in society and extracted revenue from traditionally privileged elites was a geographically enlarged example of a general institutional experience. This was the typical model of state formation in early modern Europe, and most polities were forced to find ways to manage regional dissent over growing fiscal burdens that accompanied this process. In this context, reactions to British state formation in the Atlantic also reflected a common hostility to governmental militarism.[16] In the American setting, however, relatively weak integration between the centre and periphery of the polity created a series of constitutional disputes in which, unlike in much of Europe, regional elites were strong enough to obstruct military state-building. The American Revolution was distinctive in the fact that geographical conditions made it possible for regional notables to prevent the creation of a centralized military state (empire) and they were able to deploy for subversive purposes military institutions that the political (imperial) centre had created. To this degree, however, the American Revolution was not a nationalist or anti-colonial revolution, but a revolution within a common state-building process. The conflicts that ensued from this were not, or not exclusively, of an anti-imperial nature. On the contrary, these conflicts occurred within British institutions and reflected distinctive outcomes of a transnational process of societal militarization.

In its basic elements, the American Revolution originated in the British army, and it was rooted in organizational structures attached to the army. Clearly, military leaders in the American Revolution had acquired skills serving in the British army.[17] Yet, at a deeper level, the American Revolution expressed controversies over military obligations and related ideas of citizenship. As mentioned, through the Seven Years' War, some American colonies had experienced deep domestic militarization with extensive engagement of citizens both in militias and in the British army. As in Europe, militias tended to recruit soldiers from more marginal social groups.[18] After 1763, such militarization resulted in widespread disaffection as military performance was rewarded, not with strengthened citizenship rights, but with the

[16] See pp. 64–5, 76–7. One historian has explained that Britain and the colonies formed an extended transatlantic polity involving flexible sharing of functions within a broad cultural-normative order (Bilder 2004: 5).

[17] George Washington, Artemas Ward and Charles Lee had all served in the British army.

[18] See analysis of such demographics in Anderson (1984: 41), Knoblauch (1997: 171) and Ward (2006: 15).

perceived curtailment of rights normally obtained through military roles. As a result, one potent impulse for revolutionary change around 1775 was that the British imperial polity had promoted social militarization: it used the army as an organ of social coordination, and it had established potential citizenship roles through this process. However, the expansion of citizenship came to a halt after 1763, leaving a legacy of uncompensated militarization.

In some American colonies, militias assumed a significant role at the onset of the revolution. Militias were originally subject to the authority of royal governors and, as British citizens, their members were trained to defend British interests. However, in the 1770s, many militia members became actors in the revolution against Britain, so that the armed population was instrumental in shifting allegiance from Britain to the colonies. In some states, indicatively, British imposition of fiscal laws was unsuccessful because local militias refused to follow gubernatorial instructions to suppress the riots that such laws inflamed.[19] In most states, the early revolutionary period saw the arming of state militias in support of independence and many states reinforced existing duties of militia service.[20] Moreover, such mobilization extended beyond the regional level. Although originally opposed to standing armies, the Continental Congress, which was formed in 1774, recruited quotas of soldiers from different states. As in most societies marked by forcible recruitment, militia drafts triggered conflicting reactions, and some states saw high desertion rates and anti-enlistment rebellions.[21] Yet, in different ways, militia service formed an environment in which constitutional rights were established. In some states, the first constitutions, created during the break with Britain, were partly the work of state militias. In revolutionary Pennsylvania, broad military obligations were imposed on citizens after 1775 and militias formed the initial basis of state government. This meant that the army acquired an institutionalized political position and promoted a broad-based constitutional franchise.[22] In Massachusetts, the Suffolk Resolves of 1774 provided an early premise for constitutional self-rule and created an independent militia to protect this status. The New York constitution of 1777 was

[19] Mancke (2005: 94).

[20] One historian has estimated that in Virginia, more than half of all white men provided military service in the revolutionary wars (Kulikoff 1992: 163).

[21] Virginia saw major anti-conscription riots in 1781.

[22] See analyses of these points in Rosswurm (1987: 59, 66). One account claims that this period saw the 'convergence of military service and political activism' in Pennsylvania (Konouff 2004: 5).

introduced when the state was experiencing invasion, amidst a cluster of laws on militia service. It declared it the duty of every man who enjoys the protection of society to be prepared to defend it (Art. XL). Generally, in the early American Revolution, ideas of citizenship had been stimulated by military processes and attachment to militias played a key role in framing political expectations. This resulted in the creation of constitutions with relatively democratic electoral franchises, which assigned rights to citizens because of their military roles, so that soldiers or potential soldiers were endowed with political entitlements.

In these respects, the American Revolution centred around a conflict over citizenship, which was, in essence, a civil war converging with an intra-military split. Imperial war, finished in 1763, had formed the precondition for the intensification of citizenship. After this war, one part of the army turned against the regular army, demanding greater rights of citizenship, which resulted in revolutionary conflict. As such, this model anticipated many later civil wars. In other respects, further, wars waged by residents of British colonies were not clearly distinct from civil war; indeed, they included multiple civil wars. In strict terms, the essential conflict between elite actors in the American colonies and the British government was a simple case of civil war, reflecting rivalries caused by protracted military integration and divergent ideals of citizenship in the same polity.[23] The view that the revolutionary conflict was a civil war was widespread amongst Loyalist elites in the colonies and their Tory opponents used the concept of civil war unreservedly to describe the rebellion.[24] Of course, military actions of this time contained war, not only against the British, but between different factions inside the colonies, entailing violence between patriots (advocates of American independence) and subjects still loyal to the British crown. Moreover, advocates of independence in different states supported conflicting ideals of citizenship, and, beneath the shared commitment to sovereignty, different states displayed deep rivalry over their constitutional visions. For example, the first constitution of Pennsylvania

[23] One historian has observed simply: 'The American Revolution was a civil war. In proportion to population, almost as many Americans were engaged in fighting other Americans during the Revolution as did so during the Civil War' (Shy 1976: 183). For other accounts that classify the American Revolution as a 'civil war', see Nadelhaft (1981: 58), Tucker and Hendrickson (1982: 219–220), Marston (1987: 50), Higginbotham (1988: 124), Frey (1991: 45), Webb (1995: 270), McDonnell (2007: 13) and Horne (2014: x). One account describes the American Revolution as a 'triangular' sometimes 'quadrangular war' between rival groups (Neimeyer 1996: 161).

[24] Contemporary Loyalists described the American Revolution simply as 'the Civil War in America' (Stokes 1783: 16).

espoused a strong concept of civil participation. The constitution of Virginia was closer to a system of government by rural elites and it upheld existing electoral qualifications. Unsurprisingly, as in other regions, many states experienced draft rebellions amongst white citizens in the early revolutionary period. On each count, the independence wars were not simply wars directed against external enemies. They resembled multi-factional civil wars in which ideals of citizenship were contested by many military groups.

Also vital in this regard is the fact that parties in the American revolutionary wars were divided by attitudes towards slavery. The movement towards American independence was integrally determined by slavery and slavery partly defined colonial perceptions of British rule. On one hand, colonial elites, surrounded by the persons they enslaved, repeatedly used metaphors and images of slavery to describe British government in America.[25] However, one key reason for mobilization against the Westminster parliament was that, following the Seven Years' War, Britain was seen as increasingly hostile to slavery. The encroachment of the Westminster parliament on the civil freedoms of American citizens after 1763 was not restricted to new taxation regimes. Such encroachment was also felt in the threat that legislators in London might deprive American citizens of some of their most valued personal belongings – slaves. This danger became palpable in judicial rulings in England before the revolution. For example, in *Somerset v Stewart* (1772), it was declared that, unless authorized by a distinct statute, ownership of slaves was in breach of English law. This ruling induced alarm amongst slaveholders in America, and it was frequently seen both as heralding the statutory abolition of slavery and as intruding in essential personal interests of American citizens.[26] Partly for this reason, questions regarding slavery acquired both unifying and polarizing force during the revolutionary period in America and the revolutionary wars contained multiple conflicts over slavery.

At one level, controversies about parliamentary suppression of slavery motivated military hostility towards Britain and, among some factions, the war against Britain was conducted to uphold a system of common-law rights that authorized the possession of persons as chattels. Naturally, this meant that relations between Americans and slaves held in captivity were affected by the war and military loyalties were

[25] For analysis of how the sight of bodily thraldom amongst black inhabitants affected attitudes of white citizens towards Britain, see Holton (1999: 46) and Delbanco (2018: 49).

[26] See analysis in Wiecek (1977: 21).

partly conditioned by slavery. Moreover, this added a further front to the complex of civil wars in revolutionary America. This occurred because some slaves believed that the British army offered greater certainty of freedom than the American army.[27] In 1775, the governor of Virginia, Lord Dunmore, promised liberation to slaves who fought for Britain. As a result, the period of conflict witnessed the extensive flight of slaves into the ranks of the British army. One analysis argues that the British forces had access to an 'irregular "army" of refugees' because of Loyalist sympathies amongst black communities.[28] In states with large slave populations, the threat of slave revolt or conspiracy between slaves and the British army instilled heightened anxiety in the relations between slaves and their owners.[29] As a result, the volunteer tradition in American colonies was largely limited by racial lines and most American militias were not open to black inhabitants. Even in northern colonies, enlistment of black residents for state militias was banned at the onset of the revolution. Prohibition of military recruitment of black residents took place in New England in 1776. In New Jersey, black inhabitants were required to surrender their guns until the war was over. Through the pressures of enduring warfare, laws barring the recruitment of black Americans were sometimes relaxed and legislation allowing their mobilization was introduced in some states after 1777.[30] In some regions, however, the capacity of American colonies to mobilize militias and troops was restricted by the fact that militia members were required to discharge policing duties to prevent slave uprisings in support of the British.[31] In such processes, black inhabitants of revolutionary America became objects of singular hostility in a multipolar civil war. This meant that black residents were much less strongly integrated in the civil-political culture that emerged from the revolution, and, in most states, black Americans did not acquire voting rights after 1776. The military path to citizenship meant that the early American Republic was already shaped as a racially divided democracy, or a partial democracy.

[27] See the claim that the 'vast majority of slaves who actively participated in the Revolution' viewed the British occupation as 'a liberating moment' (Frey 1991: 118).

[28] Olwell (1998: 251).

[29] See discussion in Quarles (1961: 14–20), Nadelhaft (1981: 5) and Frey (1991: 56).

[30] On these points, see the classic discussion in Quarles (1961: 16–17, 54–55).

[31] Long before the American Revolution, some state militias had a duty to prevent slave insurrections (Higginbotham 1988: 116). See the account of related legislation in 1727 in Virginia in Hadden (2001: 30). The role of militias in policing slaves continued up to and beyond the revolution, and the deployment of militias against the British at times gave rise to slave rebellions.

In each respect, warfare in the American colonies after 1775 fluctuated between anti-colonial war and diffuse civil war in which military organizations in the British empire stirred multiple sites of violence in American society. These conflicts were not strictly distinct from hostilities in other state-building processes, and they centred on phenomena – especially unfree labour, taxation and military duties – that were contested in all contemporary lines of state formation. This was not a simple conflict between actors inside and actors outside national society; it was a war within an imperial nation, or an imperial civil war. In fact, in this context, the imperial state, Great Britain, promoted a more overarching construct of social membership than the polities that sought independence, so that, in some respects, the revolution formed a revolution against full national citizenship. The revolutionary wars left a conjuncture that reproduced many features of imperial society.

Alongside such conflicts, the revolutionary period gave rise to an additional mode of conflict in which American states reproduced more traditional aspects of imperialism. After the revolutionary wars, the newly independent American states soon began to act as expansionary polities. In fact, the revolutionary wars created military preconditions for the territorial enlargement of the former colonies and they consolidated identities and practices that directed the independent states onto an expansionary course.

Through the revolutionary period, the regions Americans inhabited grew dramatically in size. This growth began through British expansion before 1775. During the Seven Years' War, many British American citizens acquired land by violent expropriation as, alongside conflict with France, they engaged in conflict with different native populations.[32] After 1763, vast territories taken from France were added to the British American colonies. Before the revolution, the states soon to become the USA were already in a process of accelerated enlargement as their residents migrated to remote regions recently annexed to the British Empire. These processes continued after 1775, during the wars against Great Britain. For example, the military struggles during the wars of independence were partly directed against the British army, but they also imposed a system of internal colonization on regions where the Americans were victorious in war.[33] The wars

[32] See discussion in Ward (2003: 4).

[33] One historian states that the 'progress of the Revolution' was inextricably linked to 'the steadily mounting pressure on western lands' and Americans waged war against the British as part of a process of internal colonization (Hinderaker 1997: 199).

exacerbated fissures between settlers and native populations, expressed, for example, in war between Virginia militias and Cherokees in 1775–6.[34] These conflicts also brought a continued demographic shift, as residents of the original British colonies settled in new areas, leading to a significant increase in the territory inhabited by non-native Americans. One historian has explained that the independence wars were especially propitious for settlement and expansion as the decline of social order meant that land grabbing could be conducted in unchecked fashion.[35] One analysis also describes how, as in later European empires, such expansion was defined by particularly acute violence as peoples living in colonized regions were treated as inferior species.[36] The Seven Years' War was caused by conflicts over territorial claims in British colonies, and it ended as British Americans imposed colonization by force on a range of subjects. These conflicts were then perpetuated in a new form through the wars against Britain: Britain replaced France as the main adversary of the American colonies, and, in conflict with this new enemy, American colonial expansion continued in new domains. After 1776, British American subjects became American citizens, and, in this role, they immediately began to establish and populate an American empire, pushing back ethnic frontiers and subjugating prior population groups far more effectively than they had done while living under Westminster rule.[37]

At the same time, during the Seven Years' War, the British colonies, previously only diffusely connected, were increasingly united by military pressures, and they assumed the skeletal form of a large state. Plans for greater cohesion between states had already been expressed before the war in the Albany Plan (1754), but increased linkage with the imperial armies intensified this process after 1756. Initiatives for greater union between the colonies were then accelerated as they were pressed together in conflict with Britain. Before the onset of the revolutionary wars, the Continental Congress obtained powers close to those of a huge polity. Once connected by war, the American states established a de facto imperial order. In the Treaty of Paris (1783), the territories subject to the Confederation Congress doubled in size and the Congress assimilated much new territory that was not claimed by a particular

34 Neimeyer (1996: 101).
35 Griffin (2007: 150).
36 Gould (2012: 43).
37 One seminal work explains how, after 1776, population groups subjugated by the British confronted a political system whose expansionary features were largely unchanged (White 1991: 366).

state. At this time, the Congress also engaged in territorial disputes with Spain and Britain and conducted military actions against native groups. As early as the 1780s, illustratively, leadership elites projected an expansionist future for a unified American state. For example, James Madison began plotting annexation of the Mississippi region before the American Republic had been formed.[38] In 1780, Thomas Jefferson declared that the new republic would form an *Empire of Liberty*.[39] Later, Alexander Hamilton announced in *Federalist* 22 that the planned federal constitution for the American people, based in popular sovereignty, would provide a legal order for an 'American empire'.[40] Such expansionism was emblematically reflected in the Northwest Ordinance (1787). The Northwest Ordinance established the principle as law that the national government, at this stage still the Confederation Congress, could absorb new territory as a sovereign entity – not through the separate acts of individual states. As such, it provided a basis for the integration of large territories, many populated by native Americans, to the west of the states represented in the Congress. In other words, the Northwest Ordinance mandated continental colonization before the American Republic had been legally formed; it served as a colonial charter drawing new territory under the control of a sovereign state.[41]

Historians have often argued that the early American Republic was not inclined to militarism.[42] This claim may be substantiated by the fact that, unlike constitutionally ordered states in post-1789 Europe, the USA did not effectively impose conscription at the federal level. Conscription was notionally introduced in the Militia Acts of the 1790s, which gave the president powers to deploy state militias, but the national draft was not institutionalized until much later. However, once formed in 1787–9, the American Republic perpetuated earlier expansionist processes and from its origins it possessed attributes of a military empire.[43] This was clearly provided for in Article IV, Section 3, Clause 1 of the federal constitution (1789), which allowed Congress to integrate new states. The size of the nation doubled (peacefully) with the Louisiana Purchase in 1803, which secured trade through the Mississippi and would eventually create ten new states. By the 1820s, and then incontrovertibly by the 1840s, the

38 Egnal (1988: 328).
39 This expression is used in a letter to George Rogers Clark (December 25, 1780).
40 Madison, Hamilton and Jay (1987: 184).
41 On the constitutional status of the Ordinance, see Onuf (1987: 73).
42 Conge (2000: 138).
43 On the convergent formation of state and empire in this process, see Saler (2015: 17).

USA had become an elite member of the global association of empires. This was underlined in core declarations of foreign policy. Indicatively, the Monroe Doctrine, set out in 1823, implied that the USA had military primacy in the entire American continent.

In each respect, the constitutional revolution in the British colonies in North America reflects a complex, dialectical pattern of militarism. This revolution was both a war against an empire and a war within a nation, closely linked to the ongoing militarization of citizenship roles. Further, this revolution was a war that formed a nation whose policies were directed on a clearly imperialist trajectory and in which the formation of national citizenship was inseparable from trajectories of internal colonization. At the core of the republic was an uncertain distinction between nation and empire.

1(b): Imperial Civil War 2

On this basis, the American Revolution was a conflict between a range of factions, supporting diverse ideals of citizenship. Ultimately, in 1787–89, the American Republic was founded through a constitution that preserved an uncertain balance between divergent concepts of national membership, which reflected their origins in a fusion of national unification, civil war and imperialism. The constitution contained an awkwardly conflictual fusion of normative premises, combining ideas of citizenship based in the general expansion of rights and ideas of citizenship that privileged distinct groups, favouring coercive economic organization. Indeed, the governmental system of the USA was supported by two irreconcilable normative principles expressing two essentially different societies, so that, when constitutionally placed together, they gave rise to intense inter-societal conflicts.

As mentioned, the American Revolution possessed some features of a national revolutionary event and it expressed early democratic principles of equal and consensual citizenship, integrating all members of society in acts of political will formation. This can be seen in the political discourse surrounding constitutional organization in the revolutionary era. Before 1776, democratic principles were formulated by James Otis, who declared that supreme absolute power is '*originally* and *ultimately in the people*'.[44] Quintessentially, these principles were presented in the Virginia Declaration of Rights (1776), which announced that 'all power is vested in, and consequently derived from, the people'.

[44] Otis (1764: 12).

Later, these impulses became evident in the writing of the federal constitution itself. The federal constitution reposed on the primary idea that government extracts legitimacy from citizens who, compacted in a federal polity, are equally addressed by and implicated in the laws that sustain public authority. To support this, the founders of the constitution articulated a doctrine of constituent power and defined a constitution 'established by the people and unalterable by the government' as the source of all law.[45] As such, the constitution created a representative system with a relatively broad franchise, so that rights of political participation in the early American Republic substantially exceeded those guaranteed by previous representative systems. Many persons involved in writing and ratifying the constitution were little concerned with the extent to which such principles were applicable to slaves, and even the more egalitarian founders, such as Jefferson, clearly accepted slavery. Yet, in some regions, the longer revolutionary period witnessed the implementation of gradualist laws to abolish slavery and to consolidate minimal principles of legal autonomy for all inhabitants of American society. Initial plans to abolish slavery were proposed in Pennsylvania, New England, and New Jersey in the first years of independence. By the early 1800s, legislation eventually leading to abolition, albeit allowing for interstate repatriation of fugitives, was in place in the northern states.[46]

At the same time, the defence of involuntary labour that was prominent in the American Revolution meant that the wars of independence brought intensified enslavement. As mentioned, one purpose that motivated many British Americans to take up arms against Britain was to perpetuate the most insidious outgrowth of European imperialism – that is, the slow genocide of personal servitude. One commentary on the American Revolution has noted, simply, that, in the revolution, 'Americans bought their independence with slave labor' (Morgan 2003: 5).[47] To this extent, the wars against Britain possessed a manifest counter-revolutionary nature. As discussed later in this chapter, in many empires of the later eighteenth century, the consolidation of colonial rule was linked to the partial eradication of coercive production systems, and, by the 1770s, some imperial regimes were supported by constructs of citizenship in which involuntary labour was legally limited, although not abolished. By contrast, the revolutionary wars in America resulted in the

[45] Madison, Hamilton and Jay (1987: 327).
[46] See analysis in Zilversmit (1967: 122–123) and Tise (1987: 34–35).
[47] Morgan (2003: 5).

obdurate deceleration of legal moves towards the abolition of slavery.[48] The American Republic acquired form as a political entity that, in some of its parts, was committed to a harshly exclusionary citizenship regime protecting local economies and variable constructs of legal personality.

These contradictory elements of citizenship can both be linked to genealogies of imperialism. The more nationalist, integrationist model reflected concepts of citizenship that evolved in many empires after 1750, often linked to the need to mobilize populations for war. The more localist model remained rooted in earlier patterns of imperialism in which landed elites, with autonomous authority in regional economies, played the leading role in securing territorial dominion.[49] To this degree, the American Revolution was, not only a fusion of imperial war, national-revolutionary war and civil war – it also expressed a conflict between two rival systems of territorial integration. The tensions between these constructs were temporarily obscured during the period of revolutionary nation-building. However, the conflict between these principles was manifest in the 1789 constitution, designed to create a unified nation.[50] The constitution clearly endorsed a construction of shared citizenship and equal legal obligation. It declared in Article IV, Section 4, that the 'United States shall guarantee to every State in this Union a Republican Form of Government'. However, in Article IV, Section 2, the constitution preserved the institution of slavery. This was then given effect in the Fugitive Slave Act of 1793. This law made the federal government responsible for ensuring that some residents were barred from federal citizenship, so that one duty of the national government was to prevent the formation of a fully national society.

These divergent models of citizenship instilled two deeply conflictual dynamics at the heart of the American Republic. Clearly, these models endorsed different ideas of personal entitlement and national membership to support the constitution. However, these models projected different principles to sustain the territorial structure of the nation, and they reflected conflicting justifications for the acts of regional annexation that defined the early republic. Both models contained norms that, on divergent premises, determined the expansionary

48 See Sinha (2000: 7); Horne (2014: 7).

49 On the residues of feudalism in the southern states, see Olwell (1998: 3).

50 In implicit agreement with this claim, see Kulikoff (1992: 124). One historian explains how, during its ratification, the federal constitution was presented, depending on the state, both as a pro-slavery and as an anti-slavery document (Fehrenbacher 2002: 37).

trajectory of the USA, and both instilled an imperialist impetus in the new polity.

First, the principles of republican citizenship proclaimed in the revolutionary period promoted a distinctive premise to underpin the imperial enlargement of the new republic. In its nationalist aspect, the constitutional essence of the American Revolution was expressed in an idea of republican membership in which deliberate affiliations between citizens replaced coerced integration to form the substructure of political institutions. At the core of this idea was a definition of citizenship that immediately supported territorial expansion. The republican ideal of American citizenship was promoted to integrate populations previously connected by imperialism, and it established a normative basis for a polity able to expand into new territories. In particular, the fact that the polity was anchored in a constitution legitimated by ideals of popular sovereignty meant that the polity could extend its laws, validated by constitutional principles, into new terrains, and acts of territorial assimilation and enlargement could be easily conducted and justified.[51] One commentator has noted, tellingly, that the distinctive 'empire of liberty' imagined in the revolution built directly on pre-existing lines of British imperialism, and it 'yoked imperialism with republicanism'.[52] One observer has argued that the constitution of 1789 was a '*colonization constitution*' in which the exercise of popular sovereignty established a norm that permitted the imposition of national law on new domains and facilitated the expropriation of land from original inhabitants.[53]

Second, the early American polity reflected alternative ideals of imperialism, strongly marked by the rejection of uniform legal order and the protection of involuntary labour systems. Initially, in the longer revolutionary era, advocates of slavery supported less centralized political ideals than their nationalist counterparts, and their attitude to national constitutionalism was guarded. This was expressed, for example, by the Anti-Federalist Patrick Henry, who argued that ratification of the constitution would bring a form of government close to military occupation: it would create a 'great and mighty empire' implanting 'garrisons', 'magazines' and 'arsenals' in all the states and claim 'power of manumission' over treasured

[51] Hietala (1985: 191).

[52] Anderson (2000: 745–746). For closely related claims, see Marston (1987: 9). See similar analysis in Smith-Rosenberg (1992: 848), where it is argued that basic national-constitutional agency in revolutionary America was exercised by 'simultaneously postcolonial and colonizing subjects'.

[53] Dahl (2018: 18).

goods (slaves).[54] The early years of the republic were largely defined, politically, by conflicts between factions demanding greater centralization and factions intent on preserving local autonomy, often involving obligatory guarantees for slavery. As discussed below, however, the pro-slavery faction did not retain its reservations about national integration and territorial expansion for long. Following the consolidation of the federal system, advocates of slavery soon developed an imperialist strategy which defined coerced labour as the basis for regional and international expansion.

As a result, the early American Republic established conflicting constitutional principles of citizenship, one based in uniform citizenship, and one based in involuntary labour. Naturally, the new republic approached its greatest crises at moments when these two concepts of citizenship became tangibly contradictory, as legislation brought these ideals into discursive conflict. Illuminatingly, such moments of internal crisis occurred – primarily – when the government of the USA promoted imperial enlargement. Constitutional antagonisms regarding slavery induced most volatile lateral hostility in periods when the national government integrated new regions, which meant that the preconditions of citizenship were exposed, nationally, to critical pressure. As the American Republic acquired the form of an empire, it was confronted with its ill-balanced constitutional foundations and its internal constituents were militarized by external expansion. In this process, imperialism and civil war became integrally intertwined and nation-building and imperial expansion converged to induce deeply violent social contestation. In essence, the defining constitutional and military conflicts of the USA in the nineteenth century were conflicts in which the USA appeared, simultaneously, as an empire and as a nation, with uncertain distinctions between functions of a national character and functions of an imperial nature. These conflicts became most intense when the legitimacy of the polity was disputed in both dimensions at the same time.

These constitutional antinomies first gained expression in 1787 in the Northwest Ordinance. As mentioned, this Ordinance allowed the Confederation Congress to incorporate new states. In passing this law, however, the Congress added the proviso that states admitted to the republic through the Ordinance would be states without slavery, fixing an effective frontier (the Ohio River) between slave states and free

[54] These speeches are printed in Carpenter (1815: 23–27, 248).

states.[55] This Ordinance was not intended to abolish slavery; it allowed for forcible repatriation of slaves escaping into the integrated territories.[56] Yet it implied that, prior to the passing of the constitution, some limits were imposed on slavery and the legitimacy of slavery was called into question: the Ordinance indicated that the American empire would be one in which slavery was not exported into new regions. Nonetheless, after this, the expansion of the republic implicitly elevated the legitimacy of slavery. Several states – notably, Kentucky (1792), Tennessee (1796) and Louisiana (1812) – were admitted to the union after 1789, and all were slave states. In these decades, although importation of slaves was formally forbidden in 1807/8, federal troops were used to support military actions against escaped slaves in the USA and at its borders. Slave ownership induced further constitutional division during the admission of Missouri to the republic. In the Missouri Compromise of 1820, Missouri was allowed to enter the republic as a slave state, but limits were placed on slavery in other regions likely to become parts of the republic. However, by this time, opposition to slavery was losing ground and the moral tenor of the debate on the subject had become indulgent.[57]

Such controversies approached an apogee in the 1840s and 1850s. This was a period of intense imperialist expansion in the USA. In his inaugural address of 1853, indicatively, President Pierce stated that 'it is not to be disguised that our attitude as a nation and our position on the globe render the acquisition of certain possessions not within our jurisdiction eminently important for our protection, if not in the future essential for the preservation of the rights of commerce and the peace of the world'. At this time, territories taken from Mexico, parts of Oregon, Texas (a slave state) and California entered or were brought by force of arms into the federal polity.[58] This was also a period in which slave ownership was profoundly consolidated and slaveholders exercised great political power and ideological influence.[59] In other words – the

[55] Article 6 stated: 'There shall be neither slavery nor involuntary servitude in the said territory.' It also stated: 'That any person escaping into the same, from whom labor or service is lawfully claimed in any one of the original States, such fugitive may be lawfully reclaimed and conveyed to the person claiming his or her labor or service as aforesaid.'

[56] On this and other ambiguities, see Finkelman (1986: 368).

[57] One observer declares that after 1812, there was an explosive expansion of slave holding (Mason 2006: 130).

[58] It is estimated that the USA acquired nearly 800,000,000 acres of land during the presidencies of Tyler and Polk (Hietala 1985: 2).

[59] On this vision of slaveholding imperialism, see Morrison (1997: 14, 81) and Fehrenbacher (2002: 118, 126).

exponential growth of the American empire coincided materially with the growth of slavery.[60] In this period, the value of slave labour to the American economy increased sharply and imperial expansion was clearly driven by pro-slavery factions in the polity.[61]

In these occurrences, the USA evolved, both as an empire that favoured slavery within its own boundaries and as one that coercively imposed slavery as it extended outwards. Externally, slavery was exported to Texas through American colonization in the 1820s and 1830s.[62] Former American slaves residing in Mexico were exposed to the terrifying threat of re-enslavement through American colonization in 1846.[63] Opposition to the imposition of slavery in former Mexican regions was set out in the Wilmot Proviso (1846). This Proviso was intended to protect the interests of northern states by making military conquest in Mexico conditional on the prohibition of slavery in incorporated areas. The Proviso formed a statement of constitutional principles based in an understanding of citizenship as a state of shared individual freedom.[64] However, this Proviso was not adopted. At this time, Albert Gallatin Brown, Governor of Mississippi, expressed the simple desire that, along with parts of Mexico, other regions such as Cuba and Central America should be annexed to the USA in order to promote 'the spread of slavery'.[65]

Internally, attempts to limit slavery met with intractable resistance in the Fugitive Slave Act (1850). This law compelled federal agents to issue certificates of removal to slaves who had escaped into free states if their previous owners, residing in states that supported slavery, caught up with them.[66] This Act implied that residents of the USA could not be released from the terms of citizenship defined by the state in which they had originally lived, and federal expectations regarding citizenship could not prevail over categories of citizenship dictated at the state level. In effect, this Act rejected the principle that citizenship could be established at the federal level, denying the existence of the USA as a fully integrated nation. This Act also reinforced the horrifying

[60] On one estimate, the number of slaves increased from 400,000 to 4,000,000 between 1760 and 1860 (Hammond 2014: 264).
[61] Karp (2016: 1, 9).
[62] Campbell (1989: 32).
[63] Cornell (2013: 353).
[64] Morrison (1997: 54–6).
[65] This is quoted in May (1973: 9).
[66] This law is described as 'utterly one-sided, lending categorical federal protection to slavery while making no concession to the humanity of African Americans' (Fehrenbacher 2002: 232).

prospect for black Americans that they could not be free anywhere in the USA, and the fear of deportation into slave states (not always unfounded) became widespread. This Act even deprived suspected escapees from submitting evidence against certification of removal, and it subjected persons providing aid to escapees to criminal charges. Importantly, this Act meant that American territorial expansion could be advanced without dislodging the foundations of slavery, as slaves could not escape into newly incorporated states without fear of being forced into custody and returned to the states where they were born. This reality was reinforced by the *Dred Scott* decision of 1857. This decision denied the constitutional possibility of citizenship at the federal level, and it effectively sanctioned slavery as a national institution. This process was also strengthened by the Kansas–Nebraska Act of 1854, which weakened the provisions of the Missouri Compromise, effectively allowing slavery in newly integrated regions. In observing these phenomena, historians have noted that actions of the US government towards non-white population groups resembled those of a 'stereotypical empire'.[67] However, the USA differed from other empires of this period as, until the 1860s, it imposed an acutely tiered citizenship regime on internal citizens. The US government took shape as a polity that deployed extreme imperialist violence against selected members of its own population within the metropolitan segment of imperial society.

Through these events, the American Republic was formed as a polity that was beset by deep conflicts resulting from its original colonial history. The American Republic was born, paradoxically, through an anti-colonial revolution against an empire and an elite revolution against a nation-building process, which fused to form a multidimensional civil war. This revolution was both a revolution in favour of unified citizenship and, in effect, a counter-revolution intended to protect harsh residues of imperialism (slavery) and curtailed citizenship. Both aspects of this revolution contained implications for territorial expansion, and they projected conflicting premises to support the continental enlargement of the post-1789 state. This meant – in essence – that the American Republic centred around a latent civil war: the republic contained two ideas of nationhood supported by insolubly opposed constructions of constitutional citizenship. But the republic also centred around an inter-imperial war. The republic contained two distinct

[67] Go (2011: 53).

empires, and the consolidation of the USA as an imperial nation required the displacement of one imperial vision by a rival vision through inter-imperial civil war. Tellingly, one interpreter has observed that the two factions that made up the USA, expressing opposed constitutional visions, emerged 'as de facto imperial rivals' during the expansion of the federal government up to the 1860s.[68] In this regard, the distinction between nation and empire was uncertain, and the construction of national society depended on wars with national and international dimensions that possessed both.

Ultimately, of course, the conflicts over slavery in the USA caused a real civil war in the 1860s. Indicatively, each side in this civil war saw the opposing side as an empire. As the Confederacy was formed, the *New York Times* declared simply: 'The new empire is at last fairly launched.'[69] In the south, the Republican Party, operating as the executive of the Union, was perceived as a colonizing organization treating southerners as 'subjugated and craven people'.[70] By 1865, northern victory resulted in a process of citizenship formation in which a common stratum of norms was imposed across national society by acts of military occupation. This was reflected in the civil war amendments to the 1789 constitution. The Thirteenth Amendment (1865) abolished slavery and the Fourteenth Amendment (1868) stipulated terms of equal citizenship for all residents in the USA. The Fifteenth Amendment (1869) extended democratic rights of citizenship to black Americans. The first of these Amendments was passed through President Lincoln's use of war powers. During Reconstruction, armies imposed these new constitutional norms across American territories. As in earlier settings, in fact, citizenship was partly enforced for military imperatives. For example, the Thirteenth Amendment was directly connected to military recruitment processes; it coincided with new militia laws, and it reflected increasing enlistment of black soldiers.[71] During Reconstruction, northern occupation of the south after 1865 was partly conducted by black soldiers who had been released from slavery into citizenship, as Yankee armies needed more recruits to effectuate occupation plans. In each respect, the army was the basis for the recreation of the US Constitution in the 1860s, and military

[68] Hammond (2014: 287). For classic analysis of the ways in which territorial expansion uncovered the fault lines between pro- and anti-slavery groups and regions, see Graebner (1955: 185–187).
[69] *New York Times*, 'The New Confederacy' (11 February 1861).
[70] Fehrenbacher (2002: 296).
[71] See Lang (2017: 139).

recruitment played a key role in imposing a revised system of national citizenship across society. In key respects, the US constitution first became reality for national society as an *occupation constitution* enforcing a citizenship regime in which national and imperial elements coalesced. This brought a transition to a more vertical social order partly reproducing aspects of military state-building, against which American revolutionaries had rebelled in the 1770s.

Of great long-term consequence is the fact that, in the 1860s, the civil war led to the international solidification of the USA as an imperial power. A fully uniform citizenship regime was not legally imposed in the USA until the 1960s, and it was only in the aftermath of World War II that a (still incomplete) system of equal constitutional rights took shape. However, the civil war created social and constitutional premises that consolidated the American nation state as an integrational structure, and the inner colonization of the south laid the bedrock for further territorial expansion. Most obviously, as in other emerging empires, the civil war brought (short-lived) conscription laws, so that the population was partly mobilized and more directly linked to central institutions. After 1865, then, military expansion did not end and American territorial expansion continued apace. One historian has noted, intuitively, that the civil war and Reconstruction have a central place in the longer history of America empire-building and they created a domestic apparatus that supported later occupation strategies: this period appears as 'the dawning age of American wars of occupation'.[72] Similarly, one historian has explained that the civil war was a 'rite of passage' in the acquisition of 'great power status' by the USA (Edling 2014: 181). After 1865, the overseas territories of the USA did not rival those held by major European powers. Yet the USA embarked on successful inter-imperial wars with Spain, also a democratizing empire, in the 1890s, and it expanded its influence in the Caribbean. In parallel, the integration of internal regions in the polity accelerated rapidly. By 1900, the US government was able to dictate constitutional terms, not only to its citizens, but to citizens of neighbouring countries, and it began to instil a system of occupation constitutionalism outside its borders polities. Indicatively, Cuba and Panama came into being as independent states after 1900 under the tutelage of the USA. The terms of Cuban independence from Spain were agreed after the Cuban government constitutionally incorporated

[72] Lang (2017: 8).

the Platt Amendment (1901), which placed limits on its treaty powers and gave USA armed forces the right to intervene in Cuban politics. The USA occupied Cuba from 1906 to 1909. The 1904 constitution of Panama contained a clause (Art. 136) allowing occupation by the USA where this appeared necessary for American security interests linked to the Panama Canal.

2 France

The origins of constitutionalism in France can be found in a similar constellation. The later eighteenth century saw a substantial power change in Europe resulting from the Seven Years' War. Through this change, Britain became the dominant imperial nation and France entered a period of financial crisis because of war debts accrued through unsuccessful imperial conflicts. Owing to its parlous fiscal position, the Bourbon monarchy in France was exposed to numerous reformist pressures in different spheres. After 1763, the monarchy began to examine methods for improving fiscal extraction, and this involved greater consultation with groups in society able to produce more revenue. This occurred against a background in which the existing methods for raising taxes were ineffective as they partly depended on the sale of public offices. This also occurred in a context in which royal control over society was patchy and members of the nobility still possessed far-reaching authority in their domains, especially in judicial and fiscal functions. Although serfdom was disappearing in France, feudalism still shaped the structure of society and unfree labour limited the ability of the monarchy to generate revenue. Remedies to the fiscal weakness of government were often proposed by physiocratic theorists who argued that such problems should be solved by increases in revenue raised directly on agrarian products. Such theorists advocated far-reaching agrarian reform, explaining that 'agricultural advances' were vital for the 'production of tax' and 'the subsistence of all classes of citizens'.[73]

Monarchical weakness in France was strongly determined by problems of military administration, which also became the focus of reform policies. In the earlier eighteenth century, the French monarchy had avoided some problems experienced by other states with large armies as its dependence on entrepreneurs for supply of military personnel was limited. The French army developed a system of direct state commissioning from an early stage. This system did not avert problems of

[73] Quesnay (1768: 109).

military financing, but it reduced the external dependency of the monarch in military matters.[74] Nonetheless, the expenditures of the Seven Years' War challenged governmental capacity for raising troops in France. Further, through the eighteenth century, a militia system had been established that was extremely unpopular, creating hostility in society at a time when the government was fiscally vulnerable.[75] More specifically, the French officer corps, largely recruited from the nobility, was weak, partly because, like other offices, military commissions were transacted venally. For example, military captains typically purchased their commands and they were required to invest their own resources in maintaining their units. This often meant that captains limited their outlays in hiring soldiers, partly because they depended on expensive mercenaries, and the readiness of their troops for combat was questionable. The international power shift placed pressure on the French army, and the years after 1763 saw costly attempts at military reform. This was concentrated in policies enacted first by Étienne François de Choiseul and then by Claude-Louis Comte de Saint-Germain. These reforms entailed measures to subject military recruitment to stricter governmental oversight, to abolish private commands and to ensure adequate qualifications amongst ranking officers.[76] Central to these reforms was a decree of 1776 to prevent private acquisition of military office. However, such reforms had limited impact on the social structure of the army and, even in the 1780s, the status of the nobility as natural members of the officer class was not contested.[77]

On each count, in the aftermath of 1763 in France, a crisis in military finance and performance led to, or at least accentuated, a more general crisis of state. This crisis was then expressed in a series of constitutional conflicts which ultimately culminated in the revolution of 1789. The first conflict occurred in 1787–8, in tensions about fiscal legislation between the monarchy and Paris *parlement*, a judicial body with duties for authorizing new taxes. This ended as the monarch suspended the *parlement* because it refused to support his taxation plans. In parallel the Assembly of Notables was called to discuss the fiscal conditions of the monarchy in 1787, and a meeting of representatives of all political

[74] Parrott (2001: 366).

[75] On the origins of the militia service and its unpopularity, see Girard (1921: 163, 255). One earlier commentary describes the *milices* as the 'remote origin of conscription' while also underlying the 'extreme unpopularity' of militia service (Vallée 1937: 2–3).

[76] See commentary in Léonard (1958: 163–190), Corvisier (1964: 147–251) and Blaufarb (2001: 237).

[77] This is contained in the Édit de Segur (1781).

classes, the General Estates, was then convened in 1789. This occurred against a background in which, through the eighteenth century, representative assemblies had not been convoked at the national level. Disputes in the General Estates led to the formation of the revolutionary National Assembly in 1789, which declared itself an autonomous constituent body comprising representatives of all parts of France, who decided, initially, to create a constitutional order to frame the powers of the monarchy.

In the National Assembly, delegates of different regions immediately addressed the question of military defence, and a military committee was created in 1789. Initially, owing to the unpopularity of militia service, proposals in the Assembly to create a conscripted army were rejected and the army was organized on a professional basis. Yet, from the outset, some revolutionaries had in mind a plan for military reform in which offices in the army would be separated from existing social hierarchies, and the sociopolitical basis of the army would be fully reconfigured. These ideas were partly reflected in the *Décret sur la constitution militaire* (February 1790) in which the allocation of military functions reflected a distinct constitutional vision of the polity. In this decree, access to military office was guaranteed for all citizens (Art. 5) and military budgets were subject to control by the legislature (Art. 4). However, this decree moved beyond traditional designs for a professional army and began to propose a new conception of the military. For example, in Art. 3, it prohibited the use of foreign armies in France, at least without express authorization by the legislature. This advanced an ideal of a national army in which mercenaries were perceived as politically dangerous. The connection between nationhood and army was more strongly declared in Art. 7, which stated that a soldier who had served for sixteen years should acquire *active citizenship*, which, under the emerging electoral law of the revolutionary polity, entailed the right to vote. At this early stage, military service was presented as a distinct pathway to citizenship and the military allowed access to political rights. This was also expressed (1790) in legislation that declared that all active citizens had a duty to serve as members of the National Guard. This law was supported by the argument that the 'right to bear arms is inherent in the quality of the active citizen'.[78] In provisional manner, these documents expressed the principle that citizens earned political rights through military duties,

[78] This was declared by Edmond Louis Alexis Dubois-Crancé (1790: 22), the main military reformer in the earlier revolution.

so that political and military interactions were closely connected. From an early stage in the revolution, full citizenship entailed certain military obligations.

Of course, these military reforms were not isolated phenomena and they formed part of a wider process of social transformation. However, most laws of the revolutionary period had some military implications. For example, the military reforms followed revolutionary laws to abolish the remnants of feudalism and to liberate agricultural labourers from serfdom. Such laws established guarantees for equal legal personality amongst the population, for the suspension of seigneurial jurisdiction and for the abolition of tithes and duties that impeded free labour. In each point, these laws contributed to improving government capacity for raising taxation and for weakening aristocratic authority, partly for military reasons. Soon after the first military reforms, the Le Chapelier Law (June 1791) abolished all corporations so that economic production was subject to uniform laws. The revolutionaries in France also devoted particular attention to producing general law codes, which they introduced to eradicate the privatistic structure of the *ancien régime*. In each respect, new laws reflected a process of internal colonization in which revolutionaries used uniform legal orders to extend the reach of government power, penetrating into social domains traditionally under familial jurisdiction. A penal code was passed in 1791, and early codes of civil law were also drafted in the 1790s. This meant that citizens acquired increased proximity to the state in both the economic and military domains.

These military forces were then articulated in the construction of constitutional law throughout the revolutionary period in France. By 1791, the first revolutionary constitution reflected the fiscal problems of the Bourbon government, and it established a representative government, forming a more robust, consensual basis for public authority, including taxation. This was expressed in provisions for an elected legislature with control over taxation matters, based in the assumption that national representation is the central point of the sovereign state. This commitment to popular sovereignty was also reflected in the fact that the legislature was elected by an extended, semi-democratic male franchise, so that citizenship, electoral rights and fiscal contribution were connected. In fact, the franchise was constructed on a tiered design, in which men who made lower fiscal contributions had the right to vote only in local, communal and primary elections.[79]

[79] On one assessment, this group incorporated 60–70 per cent of men (Jones 1995: 224).

At a manifest level, the constitution of 1791 attached relatively marginal importance to military considerations. The constitution in its totality was shaped by a powerful anti-corporatist emphasis reflected in the declaration of rights attached to the constitution, which eliminated intermediary associations between the citizens and the state. This emphasis clearly implied hostility to the historical status of the military organizations as distinct corps, and it reflected anxiety about possible armed mobilization against the emerging constitutional polity. Indicatively, under the constitution, citizens were barred from exercising electoral rights if armed, and deployment of the army in France was subject to strict legislative approval. Any independent deployment of military force by the king was defined as treasonous, and, famously, it was declared that 'no armed body' could assume a legislative role (IV/12). On this basis, the constitution constructed the military as a public organization bound by public legal contracts, assuming an essentially subordinate position in the state. The constitution even dictated that the king's own guard had to be selected from soldiers who had already served in the regular army or from members of the National Guard. New laws on military discipline (1790) and a code of criminal law for the army (1791) were introduced in this period.

Despite this, the military assumed functions from 1791 that escaped such narrow constitutional demarcation. For example, the 1791 constitution contained public-order provisions allowing use of the army for suppressing domestic unrest. Indeed, the constitution was introduced at the same time as laws allowing declaration of the state of siege in France (July 1791). Military force was vital for the success of the revolution, and the constraints on its use were limited. As the 1791 constitution was enforced, then, the definition of the army was altered and the revolutionaries abandoned their initial objective of establishing a professional army. By late 1792, the revolutionary government, now organized in the elected Convention, revised its recruitment strategies and began to enlist more volunteers.[80] This reform coincided with the onset of war against different European monarchies, and it was partly caused by the simple need to extract more soldiers. As the revolutionary government confronted heightened military challenges, the fiscal system proved unequal to demands for military capacity and the government was forced to seek more recruits. However, this reform was partly

[80] One historian calculates that, in 1794, almost 50 per cent of officers had been recruited since 1791 (Lynn 1984: 48).

caused by the need to restructure the officer corps.[81] By this point, the polity was exposed to unsettling internal military threats. The king had tried to flee the country in 1791 and the loyalty of the army was precarious, as many officers appointed under the *ancien régime* left France, some joining anti-revolutionary armies abroad. Rebellion amongst the officer class had begun in summer 1790 as officers were stripped of noble titles. Indicatively, a decree of June 1791 placed officers under greatly increased surveillance. In fact, Robespierre, by 1792 a leading figure in the Convention, was known for his reticence to declare war, and this shaped his controversies with his opponents amongst the Girondins. One reason for his reticence to engage in war was that he thought that warfare increased the authority of unelected leaders and heightened the risk of military usurpation. This scepticism culminated in April 1793 as Charles-François Dumouriez defected while leading the *armée du nord*. In response to this, Robespierre declared that the war in Belgium had been caused by the Girondins for treasonous reasons, to create 'false popularity' and to sabotage elected government. He argued that military resources should be concentrated on defence, vested in the 'défenseurs de la patrie', and that protection of internal liberty should be the main object of military force.[82]

Military organization in the French polity changed further during Jacobin rule. This was intensified by the execution of the king in 1793, as the king had been designated head of the military in the 1791 constitution. From this point, the source of military obligation shifted discernibly towards the principle that military duties were rooted in national membership and the military was projected as the armed organ of the people. Under the Convention, new measures were implemented to increase the loyalty of the military and to reduce the autonomy of regional units, which were seen as potentially hostile to the revolution. Legislation of April 1793 established a system in which representatives of the people were sent to oversee armies and their leaders. This was partly designed to make sure that the armies were adequately supplied, but it also prevented treasonable behaviour. In May 1793, important legislation was introduced which established military tribunals for all armies. This law appointed a military prosecutor (*accusateur militaire*) to ensure the appropriate dispensation of military justice by judges. A new code of military penal law was also passed in 1793. At the same time,

[81] See Blaufarb (2002: 104).
[82] This is taken from Robespierre's *Discours contre Brissot et les Girondins* (1958: 383).

these measures were flanked by recruitment laws that modified the military basis of the polity. In February 1793, a large-scale recruitment drive was initiated. By August 1793, male citizens in certain age groups and social categories (bachelors, widowers with no children) were called up on a mandatory basis for military duties, initially for short periods of service in a *levée en masse*.[83]

This increase in military conscription was flanked by a changing concept of citizenship which unfolded through the Jacobin period. At the beginning of the revolutionary experiment, the association of citizenship with the army was only implied. From 1793, this association became stronger and citizenship was strictly bound to combat duties, so that the *soldat-citoyen* became a basic political unit. This link was seen in electoral policies, as the *levée en masse* coincided with the drafting of a new constitution in which voting rights were significantly expanded. The 1793 constitution was in essence a wartime constitution in which the mobilization of the population played a central role. This was declared in Arts 107 and 109 of the constitution. By October 1793, it was decreed that constitutional government would be suspended for the duration of war with other European states. This meant that all ministerial functions were placed under the direct control of the Committee of Public Safety, which served as an emergency executive with fused civil and military powers. Despite the anxieties of Jacobin leaders about arbitrary rule, the Jacobin interlude was close to a military regime. At a more conceptual level, citizenship was observed as a condition of military identity or common national virtue in which members of society were bound by mortal commitments to the republic. One commentator even observed that death in combat was a fundamental expression of republican 'equality'.[84] In military practice, further, the growing reliance on conscripted soldiers brought important changes in strategy as it meant that the revolutionary government could recruit large armies and was less concerned about losing soldiers in battle than previous regimes. It has often been noted that, before the revolutionary era, military leaders mainly adopted defensive tactics and they were often prepared to settle for less than total victory.[85] This was partly because they were concerned about losing soldiers, who were difficult to

[83] On one account this expanded the size of the army from 650,000 to 1,200,000 soldiers (Godechot 1993: 124).

[84] Billaud-Varenne 1794: 31.

[85] This is explained in Léonard (1958: 27). One analysis explains that *ancien-régime* armies were unwieldy and generals were often reluctant to commence battle, partly for financial reasons (Cénat 2010: 302–308).

recruit and expensive to train for combat. In the 1790s, such concerns gave way to strategies that relied on larger, more offensive deployment of troops intended to annihilate the enemy, often with high collateral costs. In 1794, the revolutionary *Comité du salut publique* declared that the 'general rules' of war dictated that the army should 'attack as a massed body', and 'take every opportunity to engage in combat by bayonet and to pursue the enemy until he is completely destroyed'.[86] The emergence of constitutional rule created more violent armies whose goals were more singularly focused on destruction.

At the heart of these processes was a transformation of human labour. In 1789, many French subjects were released from unfree labour regimes through early revolutionary legislation passed by the National Assembly. By 1793, many of these same subjects were reintegrated into an unfree labour regime as former serfs were forced to serve in the army and military engagement lost its voluntary dimension. The legislation of the French Republic accelerated the core trajectory of modern European society: it transformed the serf into the soldier-citizen in four years. This development was flanked by the accelerated political marginalization of the nobility, many of whose members were put to death at the point where their former serfs were incorporated in the army. The long-term process in which national governments penetrated their societies to obtain military capacity, at the constitutional expense of the nobility, came to a rapid conclusion in these events. Conscription laws were soon followed by education laws (November 1794) creating schools in which pupils were taught to read and write, to recite the rights of man, and to memorize heroic actions and military songs.

In revolutionary France, as in revolutionary America, the division between war and civil war was frequently unclear. At one level, military government in the Jacobin period was caused by the fact that France was engaged in warfare with European monarchies, who promised the restoration of monarchy in France, finding many supporters amongst French elites. As such, France's military opponents were potential occupying powers able to mobilize support amongst military actors within France. In this constellation, France's wars of the earlier 1790s were external and internal at the same time, and they were fought on two fronts. As mentioned, Robespierre was less enthusiastic about war than his disciples and adversaries. But in 1792, he declared that his

[86] This is recorded in Savary (1825: 126).

priority was to eradicate '*ennemis intérieurs*', and he saw internal purification of the body politic as a precondition for suppressing '*ennemis étrangers*'.[87] Alongside this, the revolution caused intense interfactional hostility between revolutionary groups, so that the prospect of an intra-governmental *coup d'état* was always present. Indicatively, the 1795 constitution contained a provision (Art. 69) that created a demilitarized zone around Paris to protect the government from insurgency. Moreover, the essential military form in which citizenship was imposed in French society induced intense resistance. The introduction of conscription in 1793 caused deep agrarian unrest, so that large parts of rural France entered a state of factual civil war. From 1793, conscription gave incendiary expression to the extended presence of the state and provoked numerous instances of dissent and insurrection. Such conflicts were conducted, in essence, by social groups who did not want to be citizens, and who did not want to be bound by direct obligations to the national government. In many settings, uprisings against the revolutionary government were also connected with religious controversies, as the revolution was strictly secularist, subjecting the church to a civil constitution as early as 1790.

In each respect, the French Revolution distilled an integrally militarized mode of citizenship. First, citizenship was intended to cement military attachments as the vertical premise for a new model of government allowing semi-democratic political rights for citizens but demanding high levels of obedience and duty. Second, this form of citizenship meant that lateral relations in society were charged with deep hostility and that the government, legitimated by the political will of its citizens, became an actor in a domestic war with multiple fronts. In both respects, citizenship was tied both to the deployment of external military force and to a process of intra-societal colonization in which the government used principles of citizenship to impose a single legal-political regime across society. National society was constructed around a thick set of norms that fused internal and external violence, and the fact that governments attached their power to citizens for external military ends also allowed them to regiment society internally. As mentioned, the early years of the revolution saw the intensified reconfiguration of all areas of law, including criminal law, agrarian law and civil law, and, in conjunction with military reforms, new legal orders were imposed by violent means. In fact, the writing of constitutions

[87] Robespierre (1954: 47).

itself was a process in which the national government dictated the preconditions of its authority, and it established the legal codification of citizenship by force of arms.

At the same time, the consolidation of citizenship norms in France did not only have implications for social integration and social obligations in domestic society. On the contrary, the revolutionary design of the French polity had profound international consequences. Advocates of republican citizenship during the revolution promised, initially, that the French polity would only engage peacefully with other states. Robespierre expressed this at an early stage, declaring in the assembly in May 1790 that 'the French nation, happy to be free, does not want to be involved in any wars and wants to live in that fraternity that nature has ordained'.[88] Related ideas were present in the 1791 constitution. This constitution contained a declaratory statement that the French nation would never act 'with a view to making conquests' and – perhaps ambiguously – it would 'never use its forces against the liberty of any people' (Title VI). In essence, this meant that, from its construction, the French republic symbolically renounced imperialism. These ideas were also linked to legislation (May 1791 and March 1792), which established legal equality for freeborn citizens with non-white skin colour.

Yet, from an early stage, the revolutionary government engaged in non-defensive war with essentially imperialist objectives. As mentioned, in April 1792, the republic entered war against hostile monarchies which involved territorial aggrandizement. This war was declared in anti-militarist diction; it was presented as a war for freedom conducted for the 'just defence of a free people'. However, such anti-militarism was not shared by all revolutionaries. Some Girondins identified war as a necessary precondition for government based in popular sovereignty. For example, Jacques-Pierre Brissot argued that war was a necessary baptism for a 'people that has conquered its liberty', claiming that a war for liberty was needed to regenerate the nation; he added to this the qualification that 'war whose goal is to conquer' was execrable.[89] At the same time, the revolutionary state integrated other territories. In the first instance, this took place through a sequence of reunions in which regions at the French borders were absorbed within France. By 1792, France had incorporated the papal domain of Avignon as well as Savoy.

[88] Robespierre (1950: 359).
[89] Brissot (1792: 3, 15).

By late 1792, France had imposed a revolutionary administration in some regions to the west of the Rhine. Such cases differed from conventional colonization as occupied territories were directly united with France and a general legal regime was enforced in all areas within the revolutionary state.

As early as 1790, legal thinkers close to the revolution suggested a constitutional doctrine to support revolutionary annexation. At this point, it was claimed in the Assembly that France could legitimately integrate external territories by showing that, in these territories, governments were not based in the sovereign power of the people, and they were not recognized by treaties established by self-legislating nations.[90] These theories acquired reality as the status of neighbouring territories was discussed in 1790–1, in reports concerning the reunion with Avignon. Here, military leaders argued that the revolution created a 'constitutional pact' that united all France and this legitimated the incorporation of territories that had not been at liberty to join the revolution.[91] From this moment, in effect, constitutional citizenship became an instrument for removing foreign governments. In December 1792, the Convention passed a decree to establish principles for the French administration of annexed regions, especially regions with strong attachments to France. Illustratively, the first article of this decree stated that annexation should be conducted by military generals. It stated that generals possessed the legitimate power to abolish all 'established authorities', all 'existing taxes and contributions', all 'fixed feudal rights' and the 'nobility and all privileges in general'. The generals should justify such acts by declaring to the conquered people that they were bringing 'peace, assistance, fraternity freedom, equality'. Such annexation was to be conducted 'in the name of the French nation' and for the 'sovereignty of the people', and generals effecting annexation should immediately convene representative bodies – 'primary or communal assemblies' – to express and vindicate their sovereignty. This decree was presented and explained in a report delivered by Pierre-Joseph Cambon to advise military leaders about their actions in conquered territories. Cambon declared that annexation was justified by the fact that, in incorporated regions, 'the people did not have the experience necessary to re-establish their rights'. Accordingly, the invading army

[90] This is the essential implication of a speech by Merlin de Douai in October 1790.
[91] Menou (1791: 32).

should declare itself a 'revolutionary power [*pouvoir révolutionnaire*]', and it obtained legitimacy as it brought rights to conquered peoples, who might otherwise struggle to achieve such rights. He declared: 'if we are the revolutionary power, everything that exists that is contrary to the rights of the people must be destroyed the minute we enter the country'.[92] Slightly later, Cambon argued that, as bearers of the *pouvoir révolutionnaire*, French military leaders had the authority to suspend all existing modes of administration in regions which they entered.[93] The *pouvoir révolutionnaire* was construed as an irresistible extra-territorial constituent power, creating the precondition for all law and all political sovereignty in annexed regions.

In such processes, the principles of citizenship that were used to unify France as a nation state were transposed outwards to integrate other domains into its structure. By the mid-1790s, leading figures in the revolutionary regime accepted an idea of France as a visibly demarcated territory lying between the Pyrenees and the Rhine, and they saw expansion within these limits as geographically justified. In 1793, Danton famously announced that the extension of the republic was legitimated by limits set by nature. However, the aforementioned decree of December 1792 implied that popular sovereignty itself formed an effective basis for imperialism, with some parallels to concurrent developments in the USA. That is, in this decree, the idea that government was legitimated by its direct attachment to the popular will was constructed to justify territorial colonization, and the claim of the government to draw legitimacy from the shared will of citizens allowed it to enforce order in new domains. Indicatively, where representative assemblies were established in annexed regions, the outcomes of elections were predetermined, as only voters who declared fidelity to revolutionary ideals were allowed to participate.[94]

Through these developments, the formation of citizenship in revolutionary France followed a deeply paradoxical course. The revolution was based in legal techniques to position citizens as holders of sovereign force in society and to form a strong accountable sovereign state on this foundation. However, revolutionary citizenship authorized external war. In its external effects, the revolution engendered multiple patterns of militarization in which ideals of citizenship used to unify France were employed to overthrow other social orders so that internal and external

92 These quotations are taken from Cambon (1793a: 7–8).
93 Cambon (1793b: 14–15).
94 Godechot (1992: 73); Lignereux (2023: 31).

integration appeared as parts of the same process. In annexed regions, the revolutionary army directly imposed French administration so that new domains were simply assimilated into France on the basis of generalized models of citizenship. In so doing, the revolutionary army enforced external occupation regimes in which resistance to French administration could be dismissed as reactionary subterfuge. Once created, revolutionary regimes outside France were usually marked by deep civil conflict, as revolutionary laws brought internal antagonisms to the surface of society in integrated regions.[95] In each respect, the revolution created a transnational military system in which revolutionary ideals of citizenship traversed the boundaries between the inside and the outside of different societies. The principle of popular sovereignty, used to found a constitutionally ordered nation, became the premise for the creation of an imperial nation and, both inside and outside France, nationalism and imperialism had closely related effects.

These tendencies continued under the more conservative regime led by the five-member *Directoire*, under the constitution of 1795. By 1795, the revolutionary constitutional order was centred on a model of citizenship designed to control the extremes of Jacobin terror. On one hand, government under the *Directoire* was based in a limited, indirect electoral franchise and the legislature had weaker functions. Alongside this, however, the constitution made citizenship contingent on military duties both in external and in internal military actions, so that political integration and military integration remained closely linked (Art. 279). The expansionist tendencies of revolutionary government also increased substantially under the *Directoire*. The Thermidorean regime that passed the 1795 constitution was already consolidating a more robust hold on territories outside France as the constitution assumed force. In late 1794, French armies passed through Belgium, reached Aachen and Cologne and crossed the Pyrenees. Holland was subject to French occupation at the same time. By 1795, therefore, the writing of the constitution was not easily separable from acts of external expansion, and the clauses it contained were at least partly focused on securing the internal preconditions of external enlargement. By a law of 1798, conscription quotas were imposed annually and on a permanent basis on single French men, so that the *levée en masse* became a fixed feature of the polity. This law was passed at a point of great imperial strength. It followed the Treaty of Campo Formio (1797) in which France's extended frontiers were

[95] See pp. 84–5.

internationally accepted and French dominance in much of Italy was cemented. This law was very different in motivation from the emergency levies approved in 1793; it was a conscription law clearly intended to serve concerted annexation. By this time, constitutional law explicitly sustained the internal and the external consolidation of government.

The military initiatives of the *Directoire* also brought Napoleon to prominence. In 1799, Napoleon used his military position to launch a *coup d'état*, and, from this point, the military construction of citizenship in France became integral to social order. In 1799, a constitution was passed that placed far-reaching powers in the hands of three Consuls, and – in particular – of the First Consul (Napoleon). This constitution tangibly weakened democratic commitments in earlier constitutions. However, under this constitution, government remained centred in a mixed system in which the power of the Consuls was partly limited by a legislature authorized to check and discuss legislative proposals. The constitution provided for a representative order, in which popular delegates were nominated by lists (Arts 7–8) and appointed by the Senate (Art. 20). It was the duty of the First Consul to promulgate laws (Art. 41), and the Consuls together formed the government with responsibility for proposing legislation and regulating fiscal policies (Arts 44–45), conducting foreign policy (Arts 49–50) and maintaining internal security (Art. 47). In key respects, the 1799 constitution formed a military constitution attaching citizens immediately to state organs for military purposes. It subordinated the army to civil power (Art. 84). However, it conferred special privileges (including pensions) on soldiers and it refined provisions for conscription; in March 1800, the conditions for conscription were specified, allowing some conscripts to use proxies and, in 1802, recruitment councils were established. In parallel, it initiated the formalization of administrative law, which became a defining feature of French law. It created a right of petition (Art. 83) and provided for the creation of the supreme Council of State (Conseil d'État, Art. 52) to edit draft laws and to 'resolve difficulties that may arise in administrative matters'. In this regard, the constitution illustrated the deep connection between individualization and militarization in modern society, as it was intended to regulate state institutions in their interactions with single persons while also binding citizens to the state in a security constitution, as soldiers. The development of administrative law progressed further as, by 1806, the functions of the Conseil d'État in matters of administrative law became more specialized. This constitution was then revised in 1802, as Napoleon became First Consul for life. By 1804, after the expiration of the Treaty of Amiens, which interrupted the long continuum of war, the constitution was replaced with an imperial constitution. This constitution retained the legislature and the Conseil d'État, but it abolished the Consuls, creating instead a Grand Council (Art. 36) and a Senate presided over by the emperor (Art. 37), which had important functions in military recruitment.

The Napoleonic regime retained some continuity with post-1789 constitutional ideals. Although curtailing political rights, the government Napoleon established was based in constitutional texts that established immediate channels of communication between government and citizens. For instance, the 1802 constitution introduced primary elections in different regional units which were convened to send representatives to electoral colleges. These colleges were initially based in broad suffrage, operating as organizational hinges between government and citizens, although their functions were limited to the nomination of candidates for legislative and executive roles.[96] Moreover, the Napoleonic regime continued to deploy models of national citizenship created in the revolutionary period to attach territories to the French empire. This was evident outside the strict domain of constitutional law. In 1804, the Code Civile passed by Napoleon formed a legal order that dictated principles of individual legal equality for all persons subject to it, and it was predicated on ideas of legal equality that gained appeal during the revolution. This Code was transplanted by Napoleon across Europe, and, wherever it was enforced, it induced far-reaching agrarian reform, capitalization of land and increased emancipation of serfs. In regions Napoleon had conquered, further constitutions were created that supported annexation, and, in many regions of Europe, Napoleon imposed the first modern constitutions as part of an imperialist occupation system. In most instances, these constitutions allowed the direct exercise of electoral rights by residents of annexed regions, so that submission to Napoleon brought many people closer to citizenship.

Napoleonic annexation took place in different ways, and Napoleonic constitutions acquired different functions and created different political entities. In some cases, Napoleon overthrew existing states. In northern Italy, Piedmont was invaded in 1796, became a satellite republic in 1800, and was re-annexed in 1802. However, many Napoleonic conquests were closer to inter-imperial capture, and they

[96] See the discussion in Coppolani (1980: 68, 110) and Crook and Dunne (2014: 665–666).

involved the absorption of regions that did not possess independent sovereignty. Outside Piedmont, parts of northern Italy conquered by Napoleon had been controlled by the Habsburg government in Vienna before Napoleon arrived. When placed under Napoleonic control, Italian regions were first formed as separate republics with distinct constitutional orders. For example, before Napoleon became First Consul, the Cispadane Republic was created in 1796, which was integrated in the Cisalpine Republic in 1797 with its capital in Milan. This gave way to the republic of Italy in 1802, also administered from Milan, acting as a semi-autonomous polity under French military control. This republic acquired a constitution that established Napoleon as president and contained a class-based electoral system in which different social groups were represented in different colleges. Then, the kingdom of Italy was formed in 1805, in which Napoleon was proclaimed king, so that much of Italy was placed in personal union with France. Other parts of Italy were formally assimilated in France at different points, and Italian regions eventually formed fourteen French departments. For example, Tuscany became part of France in 1808; the Papal States were incorporated in 1809–10. In Italy, unlike other regions, Napoleon created many states without clear historical foundations, and he imposed citizenship in warfare as the first step in national state-building. In parallel, the Polish region around Warsaw was occupied by Napoleon in 1806/7 following war with Prussia, which had colonized Warsaw only eleven years earlier. In this setting, Napoleonic rule was imposed with greater social support. In other areas – for example, Westphalia – new states were created by aggregating previously unconnected territories. The formation of Westphalia was, strictly, also the result of inter-imperial capture, as it was established after Napoleon dissolved the Holy Roman Empire. The 1807 constitution of the Kingdom of Westphalia established equality before law as constitutional norm (Art. 10) and it abolished legal privileges (Art. 12) and made serfdom illegal (Art. 13). It created an equivalent to the French Conseil d'État, whose function was both to resolve administrative disputes (Art. 21) and to produce draft legislation to be considered in final form by representative estates (Art. 25). As in France, the Conseil d'État initiated the development of administrative law, as it was charged with deciding when administrative officials should be subject to legal proceedings (Art. 27).

Across the Napoleonic empire, constitutions took root partly as instruments of state-building and partly as instruments of colonization, and they integrated emerging societies in a complex fusion of internal lawmaking and external violence. At this juncture, empire-building and national construction were essentially convergent phenomena. In each setting, the constitutions introduced in territories subject to Napoleonic rule were designed to extract military conscripts (mainly peasants recently liberated from serfdom) from subject populations. In most regions, the primary provisions of Napoleonic constitutions were concentrated on the mobilization of military personnel, and mechanisms facilitating political representation and legal inclusion were designed to enhance military capacity.

In the original borders of France, conscription increased and became more strictly regulated after 1804. Over time, a large administrative machine was put in place to enumerate young men liable for service, to draw up local lists of recruits, and to prevent evasion. This process was closely connected to the organization of elections under Napoleonic constitutional law. In January 1806, a decree was passed in France that established a civil register, and inscription on the register was obligatory for those wishing to vote for cantonal assemblies. This decree meant that local administrators were able to use electoral lists to identify potential soldiers in their region, so that political representation became a tool to augment military force. Through these structures, the Napoleonic system extracted soldiers much more effectively than the revolutionary armies. It is often noted that, to motivate recruits, the Napoleonic army adopted a technique for rewarding soldiers that reduced the importance of patriotism and republican virtue as sources of military loyalty, and it partly reverted to the distribution of honours and distinctions that typified armies before 1789.[97] However, conscription under Napoleon still relied on revolutionary ideas of military citizenship, and the convergence between legal and political status and military obligations was reinforced through this period.

This extractive function of constitutions was prominent in Napoleon's satellite states. These regions reproduced the revolutionary patterns of legal reform in which subjects were integrated into a system of citizenship rights and then directly relocated in the army. This aspect of Napoleonic government in Poland is discussed more fully below. In the different Italian states, conscription was imposed in different waves, alongside laws promoting legal equality and economic freedom. In the Italian republic under Napoleon, deep conscription was enforced from

[97] See discussion of this idea in Lynn (1989) and Forrest (2006: 98–99).

1802.[98] In Westphalia, the 1807 constitution dictated that conscription was a basic law of state (Art. 53) and recruitment of salaried soldiers was illegal; this coincided with the introduction of French civil law. The Confederation of the Rhine (1806) was formed through a treaty that secured many soldiers from confederated states. In each case, the Napoleonic system promulgated constitutions to establish parity before the law for all persons, in order, in part, to integrate persons into the army. In turn, integration into the army formed a crucial method of political socialization. Indicatively, in Piedmont, which was subject directly to French constitutional law, Napoleon reflected that it was only through conscription that the country could become French.[99]

Such enforcement of citizenship for stabilizing imperialism had deep implications for societal organization and in regions occupied by Napoleon. In fact, the strategy of military integration promoted by Napoleon gave sharp expression to the divergent implications of constitutional law, and it created societal orders that were militarized in two dimensions, vertically and horizontally.

On one hand, the societies where Napoleonic regimes were formed were subject to a vertically constructed military system. Manifestly, in regions governed by Napoleon, the extractive powers of government were dramatically extended and the army increased in size, largely due to conscription techniques. Moreover, military roles and offices became more central to the interaction between citizens and state, and military attachments to government remained powerful even after soldiers had completed military service. For example, the 1804 constitution made formal provision for military pensions. At the same time, the imperial government created after 1802 attached its legitimacy to outcomes of war, and the regime maintained its momentum as it was successful in military combat. In France, this meant that national integration, expressed through the abolition of privileges and the construction of a general legal order, occurred as the domestic effect of war.

In conjunction, however, Napoleonic governments instilled other military pressures in European society. Distinctively, Napoleonic armies were marked by a sharp distinction between their legitimational

[98] On one account, for much of the period 1802–14, conscription in Italy exceeded that in France by about 400 per cent (Zaghi 1986: 554). One observer comments that, using conscription, the French pursued 'the militarization of an entire society, a social and cultural transformation of Italian life' (Broers 2001: 252).

[99] This is discussed in Lignereux (2023: 155–157), who portrays conscription as the 'cement of the empire'.

claim and their actual nature. Initially, Napoleon's armies were based on the principle of national service in which military obligations flowed from social membership, rooted in revolutionary ideals of the *soldat-citoyen*. However, after 1802, Napoleonic armies began to resemble the diffusely assembled armies of the seventeenth century as they comprised multinational corps recruited from annexed territories. By the time the Grande Armée prepared for the invasion of Russia in 1812, less than half of Napoleon's soldiers were French, and many were pressed into service from Austrian, Prussian and Italian armies that Napoleon had previously defeated. Napoleon partly reversed the regulated nationalization of armies that began around 1700 and was placed on new footing during the French Revolution. Given the size of the imperial armies, further, soldiers usually survived by feeding off the land and by plundering, mirroring earlier military corporations.[100] More importantly, in many territories, Napoleonic occupation incited large-scale counter-mobilization in different forms. Most regions subject to Napoleonic control saw violent reactions against conscription such that military force was widely used against internal resistance to secure military capacity.[101] Occupied societies also devised distinct military techniques to combat Napoleonic occupation. Some states that had experienced defeat by Napoleon began to emulate military reforms introduced in revolutionary France to create a military apparatus able to instil national loyalty in soldiers, providing them with strong motivations to resist Napoleonic rule. Reforms of this kind were prominent in Prussia after 1806; conquest by France brought deep structural adjustments to the polity. Equally, some societies began to organize unregulated uprisings against Napoleonic rule. For example, some type of *levée en masse*, promoted in France in 1793, became an important mechanism for mobilizing societies against Napoleon, and the proliferation of small wars against France became frequent. This occurred in Tyrol and – most famously – in Spain, where spontaneously formed military units shaped the structure of government after Napoleonic invasion.[102] Even in Prussia, the possibility of mass uprising against Napoleon was considered in 1808. In such contexts, Napoleon's presence induced complex societal militarization,

[100] See the classical description in Morvan (1904: 23).

[101] On one account, conscription triggered a 'two-front war' in Napoleonic domains (Woloch 1986: 2011). Anti-conscription riots were frequent phenomena in Napoleon's territories, including large outbreaks in different parts of Italy.

[102] See pp. 115–6.

including regimented militarization for war and lateral mobilization for civil war. Such scenarios engendered types of guerrilla warfare more typical of the conflicts encountered by European empires at their peripheries.[103] In each respect, the Napoleonic military system brought a deep socialization of warfare, and the effects of war cut deep into regional societies and profoundly altered social structures. Over a longer period, the revolutionary militarization of society that served French expansion became a structural principle in societies occupied by France, so that some pattern of collective military mobilization became an experience on which nationhood and national citizenship were built. These outcomes of Napoleonic rule had ambiguous consequences which proved vital to the development of constitutional law, and indeed to the basic form of state sovereignty.

Through this diffuse militarization of European society, many states began to interact with their citizens with new intensity and vertical immediacy, and they were forced to entrust citizens with roles that would not have been imaginable before Napoleon. In particular, states that experienced conflict with Napoleon began to arm their populations, as new patterns of military mobilization were required to drive out occupying armies. In most contexts, this meant that states fighting Napoleon reproduced the convergence of agrarian reform, constitutional reordering and military conscription that had been pioneered in revolutionary France. During Napoleonic occupation, Bavaria, Prussia, Spain and Austria entered reform processes that led either to the drafting of a representative constitution or at least to the deep transformation of the state. In most cases, conflicts with Napoleon led to the liberation of subjects working in agrarian economies, as throughout Europe laws were introduced to abolish tied labour. Serfdom was abolished in Prussia in 1807, in Bavaria in 1808 and in other German-speaking states in these years same or shortly afterwards, although such legislation had limited effect in some Habsburg regions. In each case, the elevation of subjects into legally defined citizenship roles coincided with the imposition of conscription. Conscription was imposed in Bavaria in 1804–5, in Württemberg in 1806, in Austria in 1808 and in Prussia in 1813–14. In each respect, the military proximity Napoleon imposed between state and society led rapidly to generalized definitions of citizenship, and French legal forms of imperialism galvanized national reactions against Napoleon.

[103] Indicatively, General Bugeaud, responsible for French colonization of Algeria in the 1830s and 1840s, experienced anti-partisan warfare in Spain.

In many settings, however, the mobilization of populations against Napoleonic rule brought substantial internal risks, and the arming of populations was inherently perilous. Some regions, such as the Rhineland and parts of Italy, contained substantial groups that had sympathized with the revolutionary ideals announced in 1789. In some territories, support for Napoleon was strong and some elites drew clear benefit from Napoleonic government. Many states mobilized their populations for war against Napoleon after 1812, although their armies had fought for him after 1807. In such contexts, military loyalties were necessarily precarious. Overall, the construction of military citizenship against Napoleonic occupation had contradictory outcomes. Although it imposed unifying structure on national societies, it instilled acute potentials for civil conflict at the core of the nations it began to engender. The creation of national armies was a highly sensitive technique for promoting national integration, and it constructed national societies in a form with some similarities to external war.

In each point, the first mass transformation of subjects into citizens in Europe was inseparable from imperialism and military violence, and this had distinctive implications for political organization. In this context, states were required to initiate constitutional construction and enfranchisement in a military environment marked by cross-cutting pressures, and they began to extract legitimacy and sovereignty from citizens in volatile circumstances. Indeed, many states entered a situation in which they relied on their subjects for military purposes, to assert sovereignty, but the loyalty of these subjects, on which state sovereignty depended, was not guaranteed. This distilled the basic paradox of early constitutionalism: states accorded rights to citizens to stabilize their sovereignty, but citizens unsettled the sovereign form of the state that gave them rights. One consequence of this was that states began to deploy additional means to assure themselves of the loyalty of their citizens and to stabilize their sovereignty on reliable premises. In some cases, indicatively, states that promoted a *levée en masse* against Napoleonic occupation soon implemented regulated conscription laws, so that the spontaneous dimension of military enlistment was reduced. This had already occurred in France in 1793 and 1798, but the conversion of spontaneously armed troops into regimented armies remained a defining challenge for many states after Napoleon.[104] One further consequence of this was that, from the

[104] See pp. 128–9.

outset, governments took steps to control the national sentiments and loyalties that motivated citizens to join armies. As discussed in Chapter 2, nationalism was officially discouraged in most of Europe after 1815. Over time, however, memories of mobilization against Napoleon were frequently reconfigured to form the focus of reactionary political identities with a strong anti-revolutionary dimension. The fact that collective mobilization had been directed against France meant, from the outset, that other European societies were integrated by conservative national affinities. In some German settings, the wars of liberation slowly assumed a central role in national imaginaries, and gradualist ideas of organic nationhood moved to the centre of constitutional thinking. In reflecting on the relation between France and Germany, the great historian Ranke concluded that terror of the French Revolution was an example of the metaphysical strife that occurs when people are 'chained to ideas', allowing 'rational' constructions to prescribe the coercive form of 'legality'.[105] Many parts of Europe developed a reactionary brand of nationalism after 1815 which was framed, partly retrospectively, by hostility to Napoleon.

In each point, further, the Napoleonic period raised simple questions about the distinction between nations and empires, and it constructed models of citizenship that crossed the boundaries between these two political forms. In France, Napoleonic government imposed a dense, clearly national form on society as it extended outwards, and direct attachments between citizens and the state were intensified through external colonization. In this process, vitally, military constructs of citizenship deployed to integrate people in France were also used to absorb foreign territories, so that the empire was partly convergent in its internal and external dimensions. In fact, the actions of the imperial government towards persons resident outside France and to inhabitants of France were shaped by convergent motivations as military mobilization formed the core nexus between citizen and state in both domains. By 1812, following defeat in Russia, conscription increased rapidly in all Napoleonic territories. Indicatively, citizenship instilled parallel resentment in both the internal and the external parts of the empire. This process stimulated intense resistance outside France, and, inside France, Napoleonic rule was accompanied by common signs of hostility to military citizenship.[106] In both parts of the empire, citizenship was

[105] Ranke (1832: 86).

[106] For statistics on desertion and self-mutilation amongst French soldiers who did not wish to be citizens, see Pigeard (2003: 126).

often observed as an oppressive, partly annexationist regime. Consequently, France was formed internally as a nation by imperialism, but nation-building was also experienced as internal colonization. In occupied regions, conversely, Napoleonic imperialism acquired nation-building force, and it radically accelerated the lines of inner social construction that, more latently, had defined eighteenth-century Europe. Across Europe and Latin America, the impetus towards the realization of national citizenship resulted from Napoleonic administrative techniques, and most nations approached nationhood because, at least temporarily, they became parts of an empire. This meant that, from this point, empires formed a model for nation-building, and nations were configured through the construction of citizenship in semi-imperial fashion. This also meant that legal categories used to established nations could be made serviceable for empires, and empires increasingly patterned themselves on nations. After circa 1806, most empires began to organize their interactions with society through principles of citizenship borrowed from the French Revolution. In each dimension, further, the Napoleonic era had the outcome that states engaged with their citizens, primarily, as potential soldiers, and they relied for their sovereignty on citizens that constituted a threat to their essential sovereign form. As discussed in Chapter 2, the immediate reaction of most states to this condition became visible in the Congress of Vienna, when the link between national militarism and sovereignty was denied.

A distinct variant on the pattern of military constitutionalism appeared in the main example of anti-Napoleonic uprising outside Europe – in Haiti. In Haiti, originally a French colony with embedded slavery, the construction of national citizenship depended on complex interactions between the locus of citizenship, Haiti, and the imperial power, France, and it was driven by diffusely convergent military pressures. Large uprisings amongst slaves in Haiti began in 1791, caused both by local slaveholder repression and by revolutionary events in France. This mobilization acquired the form of an anti-imperial war and a civil war, as slaves directed their primary hostility towards local plantation owners. The uprising was partly successful because it coincided with war between the French Convention and Spain and Britain in the Caribbean. At this point, the colonial government on the island lacked military personnel to deploy French troops to campaign against rival empires in the Caribbean, and it was unable to suppress the anti-slavery protests in Haiti. As a result, a series of decrees were introduced to free Haitian slaves. This was partly intended to pacify the revolts in Haiti, but it also served broader military purposes. Some insurgent slaves had formed alliances with Spain, and emancipation was intended to separate Haitian slaves from the Spanish army and to promote their recruitment for France. By August 1793, the French commissioners abolished slavery in the north of the island, albeit with caveats and restrictions, and, by 1794, the Convention in Paris abolished slavery in all French territories. This meant that the revolts in Haiti stimulated general emancipation throughout the French Empire.

This conflict acquired a different character under Napoleon. By the onset of Napoleonic rule, military forces in Haiti were led by Toussaint Louverture, whose armies had a stronger focus on the assertion of independent sovereignty. Although a primary force beyond the abolition of serfdom in Europe, Napoleon's approach to involuntary labour outside Europe was less certain. The 1799 constitution placed French colonies under separate laws, and, by 1802, Napoleon sanctioned slavery in some colonial regions and legalized the slave trade again. He also reduced other liberties of black subjects. Such actions gave rise to the perception that Napoleon was intent on reimposing slavery in Haiti, which naturally affected attitudes towards France. These factors resulted first in the promulgation of a separate constitution for the colony, in 1801. Like other constitutions of the period, the constitution had a strong military inflection. The constitution permanently abolished slavery (Art. 3), but it placed supreme power in the hands of Louverture, who was authorized to use the army for public order purposes and to appoint his successor. It was also flanked by measures to impose military discipline on the rural production, so that labour and militarism remained connected.[107] Against this background, Napoleon sent an expeditionary forced to restore order in the island, which brought brutal multi-polar warfare. After the deportation of Louverture, the Haitian armed forces were led by Jean-Jacques Dessalines, who oversaw an intensified militarization of society with large-scale mobilization of guerrillas, resulting in the independence constitution of 1805. This constitution declared Dessalines the emperor of Haiti and placed the island under government by military divisions, with strong military control over civil and judicial functions. The constitution was supported by far-reaching conscription provisions. In key respects, the mobilization of society against French imperialism imprinted a persistent bias towards military hierarchy in Haitian society,

[107] This is documented in Dubois (2004: 239).

which was replicated both in government and in social organization. In fact, through and after the revolutionary period, military structures became embedded in economic practices, and strongly regimented production regimes were imposed on agricultural workers.[108]

3 Poland

A third line of constitutional formation in the late eighteenth century developed in Poland. This line acquired expression in several reforms, but it culminated in the short-lived constitution of 1791. This constitution was designed to reorganize the Polish body politic in order to prevent the occupation of Poland by rising dynastic empires based in Berlin, Vienna and St Petersburg, which commenced (formally) in the early 1770s. The constitution was shaped by a background in which Poland's sovereignty had been progressively reduced over a long period. This process in fact originated in the later seventeenth century, at which time Russia's international position was reinforced and the sovereignty of Brandenburg–Prussia, a marginal principality until 1648, was tangibly hardened, notably in the Peace of Oliva (1660). The 1791 constitution formed the central point in a long sequence of endeavours to strengthen the Polish polity, and imperialism, with strongly dialectical outcomes, was a defining impetus in these events.

Poland stands out in European history as a polity that was pervasively structured by different patterns of international expansion. In the early modern era, Poland itself was an expansionary state, and, following union with Lithuania in 1569, it incorporated large territories to the north and east of its original location. At this time, Poland was constructed as a Commonwealth, which, although centred around an elective monarchy, possessed strong republican features and was constitutionally committed to representative government and equal rights under law for all full citizens. The Polish Commonwealth was weakly centralized, and it was supported by an estate-based constitution, whose central organ was the bicameral parliament (*Sejm*), to whose sittings members were elected by a highly selective franchise. This constitution had an anti-absolutist emphasis. It originally expressed a balance between the interests of several social groups, notably of large magnates and the lesser nobility, and it protected their privileges by upholding regional administrations based in

[108] One important commentary argues that, by 1800, the military apparatus was engaged in enforcing agricultural laws, which limited the rights of freed slaves (Fick 2007: 410–411). See related comment on the implications of the *Loi concernant la culture* (1812) in Fatton (2007: 90–91).

patronage and serfdom. Individual regions in Poland possessed smaller representative parliaments (*Sejmiki*), whose delegates influenced legislation in the *Sejm*. The position of the *Sejmiki* was defined by the expansionary form of the polity. The *Sejmiki* were first established as representative instruments to link newly integrated regions as Polish rule spread in the north and east. Originally, they performed defensive functions in raising troops and upholding Polish rule in colonized borderlands. By the late seventeenth century, the *Sejmiki* had assumed far-reaching autonomy, especially in fiscal matters. Their role in providing military resources also increased greatly, so that they clearly checked the centralizing pull of the monarchy and the *Sejm*. By the eighteenth century, powerful magnate families acquired dominance in the constitutional order, using the regional *Sejmiki* to exercise control of government.[109] As a result, the Polish state was marked by low internal consolidation of governmental sovereignty. It acted in essence as a loose parliamentary confederation of regional power centres, partly dominated by large family oligarchies.

The powers of the Polish government were further restricted by a traditional constitutional provision – the *liberum veto*, which prescribed unanimity amongst delegates in the *Sejm* as a precondition for vital legislation. This meant that parliaments were often inconclusive and influential regional groups attached to *Sejmiki* could control legislation at the national level. The force of this provision was limited in 1764, after repeated plans to revise it. However, 1768 saw the publication of a corpus of laws defined as *cardinal laws*. This collection was very close to a modern constitution, written as the polity experienced internal war and was exposed to extreme external pressure. This collection set out norms concerning political representation and procedures for legislation, and it included the stipulation (Art. 17) that the *liberum veto* should be retained with full effect. Unsurprisingly, neighbouring states drew great benefit from the *liberum veto*, as it weakened the legislative power of the Polish polity and created internal dissent that provided pretexts for external acts of pacification.[110] Its retention in the cardinal laws of 1768 owed much to the influence of Catherine II in St Petersburg.

[109] On the increased authority of the magnates and the *Sejmiki* by circa 1700, see Olszewski (2002: 86, 117) and Strojnowski (2005: 319). One excellent analysis explains that the magnates assumed dominance between 1650 and 1700 because the lower gentry lost their wealth during the wars with Sweden. The magnates gained influence over other groups by distributing wealth and favours (clientelism) (Kłaczewski 1993: 8).

[110] Zielińska (2012: 592); Dukwicz (2015: 82).

One primary feature of the traditional Polish constitution was that it did not establish a strong fiscal system, not lastly because magnates viewed increased fiscal extraction as a pretext for military absolutism. In consequence, the military apparatus was not effectively centralized and regents routinely struggled to recruit and pay armies. Unlike many European states, Poland was only marginally affected by the Thirty Years' War, and the military system was not substantially reformed in the decades after 1648.[111] Moreover, Poland experienced protracted warfare between 1648 and 1720, both in and outside Polish territory, causing extreme devastation, territorial depredation and demographic depletion. At this time, Polish military resources were greatly stretched in wars with the Ottoman Empire, often conducted far from Poland. Like other states, Poland saw increasing professionalization of the officer corps in the eighteenth century. Yet the techniques promoted in other European countries to stabilize military funding and ensure official regimentation of armies were not permanently implemented.[112]

Through this time, Polish governments were dependent on different armies for military capacity. The army at the disposal of the monarch had multiple foundations, and Commonwealth armies, militia armies provided by the noble estates, and a range of mercenary units combined to form the total military force.[113] The composite nature of the army was partly a result of the size of the territories in the Commonwealth, which made concerted military mobilization difficult. However, it meant that the command structure of the army was complex and fractious. Poland and Lithuania had separate armies, each of which was led by military officials with high constitutional status (the *Hetmans*). The *Hetman* was a vital figure in the Commonwealth, possessing extensive duties in military and fiscal governance. However, the position of the *Hetman* was not defined in clear constitutional terms, and it varied over time. The *Hetman* was expected to raise and organize the army, but he controlled the army through webs of patronage, so that the Commonwealth army was partly recruited as a large entourage of the *Hetman*, reflecting older patterns of military recruitment through affinity.[114] Historically, the *Hetman* protected the interests of the high nobility, and the loyalty of the *Hetman* to the

[111] On the lack of standing armies in Poland, see Ciesieski (2009: 569).

[112] See Janas (1998: 16); Wimmer (2019: 20).

[113] On the composite nature of traditional Polish armies, see Łopatecki (2013: 579) and Wimmer (2019: 121).

[114] See important discussion of the private and personal patterns of military recruitment by the *Hetman* in Augustynak (2004: 34, 179, 259).

crown was frequently uncertain. However, leading noble families were often hostile to the *Hetman*, whose powers they saw as draining monetary resources for commitments inimical to their own.[115] The *Hetman* was able to station armies in noble domains, often with devastating material results for the owner.

The reliance of the Polish crown on multiple armies weakened the inner structure of the state, and it meant that leading families could act at a high level of political independence. In fact, at crucial junctures, families and other regional groups formed confederations which performed significant military, legislative and judicial functions, even developing autonomous fiscal systems. Such confederations were sometimes established to provide institutional order and domestic security in periods in which other political institutions were depleted.[116] For example, confederations acquired influence by performing state-supporting functions and guaranteeing military supply during interregna. By the eighteenth century, such confederations had become fundamental to the political system. They were formally recognized in constitutional doctrine as organs of the polity, separate from military associations or informal factions.[117] One account describes confederations as the 'dominant political form' in the eighteenth-century Polish constitution.[118] However, confederations provided an intrinsically uncertain basis for public order. At times, confederations acted as parts of government, appearing as formal organizations in parliaments and steering legislative initiatives in parliamentary assemblies. In parallel, confederations often pursued military objectives that were opposed to other organs of the polity, and they conflicted with the government. This had the result that the organic composition of the Polish state was informal and associational, and actors within the polity moved variably between systemic and subversive functions.[119] Periodically, the highest organs of state – including the *Sejm* itself – saw their functions usurped by confederations, and, in such contexts, parliaments acted, not as internal organs of state, but as conferences between rival military organizations.

For these reasons, the Polish constitutional system showed a repeated tendency to degenerate into civil war between internal groups.

[115] Rostworowski (1957: 28); Gawron (2010: 248–52).

[116] See Kriegseisen (1989: 118–119).

[117] In a leading eighteenth-century discourse, confederations were clearly distinguished from noble insurrections (see Lengnich 1746: 394–395).

[118] Stanek (1991: 226).

[119] This follows analysis in Stanek (1991: 183–199).

Conflicts recognizable as partial or full civil wars occurred frequently, notably in 1606–7, 1665–6, 1704–6, 1715, 1733–5 and 1768–72. In these periods, it was common for parts of different armies to form rebel confederations or several confederations at once. Fatefully, civil wars often coincided with external wars in which some domestic factions attached themselves to foreign powers. The loose territorial order of Poland meant that civil wars easily acquired an international dimension and fused with interstate wars as domestic unrest brought external actors into Poland. For example, the late 1760s saw de facto civil war between confederations with opposed international objectives, partly organized to resist Russian intervention. In such conflicts, nobles frequently formed alliances to oppose the monarchy, at times treating the monarchy as an alien military power. In fact, actions of the Polish nobility towards the monarchy often mirrored anti-imperial uprisings. For example, from the 1690s, Poland was intermittently ruled by the Saxon royal family. During this time, the Saxon monarchy stationed its army in Poland with implicit Prussian support, and it extracted fiscal contributions from the Polish estates much like a foreign occupying force.[120] Resultant opposition amongst the noble estates to the Saxon dynasty was expressed through military actions that formed a hybrid between civil war and interstate war. In such settings, noble confederations also operated in a form close to occupying regimes, and they extracted contributions from domains where they were stationed.[121] In different ways, government was rooted in violent contest over territorial occupancy, in which distinctions between national and external rule were unclear and the perceived legitimacy of central authority was low.

By 1720, the sovereignty of the Polish state was discernibly restricted and external powers had obtained a powerful hold on the political system. A key milestone on this process was a set of agreements reached by the *Sejm* in 1717. These agreements were partly engineered by Russia (officially declared an empire in 1721) after the *Sejm* had encouraged Peter I to intervene to control violence caused by noble uprisings on Polish territory. These agreements included (ineffective) reforms to prohibit confederations and to limit the number of soldiers in the army. These reforms curtailed the powers of the *Hetman* and restricted

[120] See Gierowski (1953: 39–40); Kriegseisen (1989: 19–22).

[121] One account explains how anti-partition confederations in the late 1760s created a legalized system of extraction, combining regular taxation and informal contributions (Szczygielski 1970: 178–181).

his involvement in domestic disputes, although they were also intended to weaken the military authority of the monarch. Importantly, this *Sejm* reduced the role of regional assemblies in providing revenue for armies; it coincided with provisions for regular payment of the Commonwealth's army.[122] By this time, however, Poland had relinquished vital attributes of sovereignty and it relied on external intervention to maintain internal order. From this time, elections were subject to Russian influence, with Russian troops often stationed in Poland or at the Polish borders. Russian soldiers and other armies travelled through Poland freely, repeatedly intervening in Polish conflicts and living off rural contributions. A perennial problem was that foreign armies used Poland as a recruitment region, meaning that Polish territories were subject to undeclared occupation and Polish soldiers were often integrated into armies of states arrayed against the Commonwealth.[123] This created an enduring role for Poland as a military supplier for foreign armies, visibly displaying that its government had limited monopoly over core political functions. By the 1740s, further, Russian engagement in Polish politics was accompanied by an increased threat from the western borders. Through the 1730s, Prussia intensified its system of military conscription, and it was able to mobilize armies of a magnitude disproportionate to its economic capacity. The annexation of Silesia by Prussia in 1740–1 brought long and brutal war between Prussia and Austria, with some Russian involvement, and it meant that Polish territorial integrity was imperilled on several fronts. By this time, the Prussian monarchy actively undermined attempts by the Polish government to reinforce its institutions through the implementation of new fiscal measures.[124] Further, as primary theatres of the Seven Years' War were close to the Polish borders, Poland became an access route to war for foreign troops at this time. One cause of the first partition of Poland was that other countries had concentrated military force around Poland between 1756 and 1763, and foreign troops stayed in Poland when the war was over.[125]

By the 1760s, Poland was close to becoming a vassal state. By this time, both Russia and Prussia actively intervened in Polish fiscal decisions, strategically obstructing planned reforms to the Polish constitution.[126] Poland had introduced a portfolio of indirect taxes in the seventeenth and

122 Olszewski (2002: 390).
123 On this crucial point, see Szymborski (2020: 26).
124 See Zielińska (2012: 338).
125 One classic account calculates that in the war about 60,000 Russian troops were stationed in Poland, financed by the Polish state (Szczygielski 1970: 36).
126 See Hoensch (1970: 360, 370).

early eighteenth centuries.[127] However, the Polish state lacked the independent fiscal instruments other early modern states used to stabilize their sovereignty. This meant that reduction of military spending, rather than increased taxation, was the only expedient response to fiscal shortcomings, and fiscal weakness was directly reflected in continued military debility.

Overall, a distinct pathology characterized the early modern Polish polity. The decentralized, loosely integrated structure of the state meant that it suffered from fiscal and military weakness. It was vulnerable to internal fracture as private armies were able to assert authority in some regions. In turn, this made it acutely susceptible to external depredation. Moreover, the depletion of state authority was exacerbated by the constitution, notably by the rights granted to the nobility represented in national and regional parliaments. The Polish nobility was numerically very large in proportion to the country's population size, and many of its members were not wealthy, so they were unwilling to sanction fiscal-military or agrarian reforms that threatened their material standing. The nobility defended the decentralized constitution for strict economic imperatives, to protect rural economies based in serfdom. These features of the Polish state were particularly damaging because, by the earlier eighteenth century, many other states, notably Prussia, had recovered from earlier religious and dynastic wars. Such states were rapidly expanding their armies. They owed their rise, internally, to the increased political regimentation of the nobility and the qualified restriction of serfdom. Externally, however, they broadly supported the anti-centralistic interests that unified large parts of the Polish nobility.

Ultimately, between 1772 and 1795, Poland was partitioned between Russia, Prussia and the Habsburg government in Vienna, and the Polish state lost full sovereignty until 1918. The final conditions of the Polish partition were cemented in the Congress of Vienna (1815) under international treaties between occupying powers. During the partition, some vestiges of statehood and self-government were upheld in Poland. However, Poland was the major victim of early continental imperialism in Europe.

(3a): Citizenship and Colonial Law

From 1772, occupying powers in Poland conducted a process of colonization, which initiated a new pattern of empire-building. For Russia,

[127] Nycz (2016: 56, 70).

indicatively, the partition of Poland was part of a wider course of imperial enlargement, forming one move in a sequence in which Russia challenged Ottoman dominance in South-East Europe. In this context, Poland was a victim of its own military success and expansionary actions. In 1683, the Polish king had helped defeat the Ottoman Empire in warfare, and this created a space for the growth of Russian power, which collaterally affected Poland.[128] The partition of Poland was central to a deep inter-imperial shift in which Poland and the Ottoman Empire, two essentially premodern empires, lost power to more systematically structured empires with more robustly organized armies and harsher recruitment systems.

Colonization in Poland was also marked by the distinctive fact that the process of partition brought reforms in Poland that enhanced the citizenship status of many persons living in regions exposed to colonization. Theories of national citizenship were already widespread in Poland before partition.[129] Practically, however, legally inclusive constructs of citizenship did not assume reality in Poland until it was exposed to external depredation. In key respects, the military annexation of Poland created an impetus for national constitutional formation and citizenship construction, and some normative designs used to secure foreign imperial authority in Poland served, equally, to fertilize national constitutional ideals. As in the USA, the development of constitutional rule in Poland was deeply embedded in experiences of colonization.

Before partition, Polish constitutional law was attached to a concept of political citizenship in which legally designated citizens were allowed to exercise political rights by electing delegates to the *Sejm* and the *Sejmiki*. However, the legal structure of Polish society was largely based in a patchwork condition of citizenship. Owing to the diffuse form of the polity, different regions possessed distinct legal structures. Legal and political privileges for the nobility were extensive and included important judicial immunities and personal powers over peasants. As a result, a variable citizenship regime was at the core of pre-1772 Polish society, and members of the nobility jealously protected their powers to sustain this regime. In some regions, peasants lacked formal legal protection and personality, and they were often not allowed legal representation independently of seigneurial lords. In this context, the first phase of

[128] See on this point Davies (2016: 243).
[129] See p. 100.

Polish partition led to the rapid extension of citizenship rights for many Poles, especially amongst the peasantry. At the onset of partition, some occupying powers had introduced or were introducing legislation in their traditional domains that promoted greater uniformity in citizenship rights, according increased legal protection to serfs. After partition, these laws were transferred to parts of Poland as part of a strategy for imperial occupation. The military encroachment of foreign states in Poland was reflected in the parallel incursion of new principles of citizenship into Polish terrain: imperialism and rudimentary concepts of citizenship formed a joint legal bloc imposed in Poland to sustain external military rule.

This was visible in Polish territories placed under Prussian occupation. By the 1730s, the Prussian monarchy had implemented reforms inside Prussia to increase military conscription, and these reforms were flanked by laws to limit serfdom. Through these measures, serfs were given increasing legal protection by the state and expectations of military service were intensified. As mentioned, serfdom was not fully prohibited in Prussia until 1807, and, within limits, it retained formal recognition in the great Prussian law code (*Landrecht*) of 1794. However, some measures to curtail the effects of serfdom were passed in different Prussian regions in the 1740s and 1770s. Naturally, some actors experienced such processes as a domestic invasion in which new principles of citizenship were used to hollow out noble institutions, especially in rural localities.[130] As Prussia occupied Habsburg Silesia in the 1740s, similar structures were progressively imposed in the colonized regions. Prussian military invasion of Silesia was followed in late 1748 by reforms to reduce the arbitrary aspects of feudalism, to improve the legal position of serfs and to enforce conscription.[131] Before the annexation of Poland after 1772, therefore, Prussia had a tradition of combining colonization, citizenship and military recruitment. Prussian colonization of Polish regions after 1772 also saw the gradual implementation of rudimentary citizenship laws, leading to the eventual abolition of servitude.[132]

More significantly, in the parts of southern Poland added to the Habsburg lands in the 1770s and the 1790s, reforms were introduced that significantly changed the legal position of peasants, extending

[130] See Gneist (1966: 120).

[131] One historian states that the imposition of the Prussian cantonal system in post-1740 Silesia caused an 'enormous increase' in its military force (Baumgart 1984: 104).

[132] See p. 123.

a wider citizenship regime across society. Habsburg colonization of parts of South Poland, later termed Galicia, in the 1770s involved coercive territorial settlement by German speakers and state-coordinated acquisition of land. In this respect, Habsburg partition of Poland was a simple act of violent annexation. Yet Habsburg occupation was flanked by legal policies in which many inhabitants – although not, in the first instance, the large Jewish population of Galicia – were integrated in a system of extended citizenship rights. This process began under Maria Theresia in 1772 as legislation was implemented to weaken the feudal dependency of peasants. These reforms led to a raft of laws to transform the legal position of the nobility, to reduce noble control of the law courts and to strip the nobility of fiscal freedoms and immunities. By the 1780s, Joseph II introduced a series of edicts (not fully enforced) that changed the relation between lord and serf in all Habsburg domains, including regions annexed from Poland. Notable amongst such legislation was the Serfdom Patent of 1781, applied in Galicia slightly later, which formally abolished serfdom in many Habsburg territories. This legislation was followed, in 1786, by legislation to regulate feudal duties; in 1787, by further restrictions on noble exercise of private jurisdiction; and in 1789, by laws to systematize agrarian taxation. These laws were largely driven by the goal of increasing fiscal revenue in the Habsburg Empire, following military defeats against Prussia. They were accompanied by educational reforms, reforms imposing religious tolerance, and by new currency and taxation laws, as the liberation of the serfs was intended to free productive labour on the land, to improve government finances. As a result, Habsburg occupation of southern Poland formed a process of territorial expansion in which heightened legal personality was conferred on Polish serfs, whose freedoms had historically been severely curtailed under the Polish social order.

The legal emancipation of serfs in the Habsburg domains was directly linked to laws regarding military recruitment, and, in the period 1770–81, intensified conscription laws were introduced through the Habsburg regions. In the years immediately after colonization, military recruitment in Galicia was limited, but it increased in the War of Bavarian Succession (1778–9). During this war, Prussia and the Habsburg Empire, although joined in the partitioning of Poland, were briefly in conflict once more. This meant that the demand for soldiers amongst partitioning powers was high, especially in Vienna.[133] Within two

[133] See on these points Michalski (1964: 19).

decades, the Habsburg government was able to penetrate Galician society to enlist soldiers, and Galicia became an important recruitment region.[134]

In these developments, the colonization of Poland was an early manifestation of the wider dynamic of military citizenship formation, which, by the 1790s, became fundamental to European society. No claim here implies that the partition of Poland was a benign occurrence. The partition reflected classical depredatory practices of imperialism. Each partitioning power enforced military expropriation of resources and state-sponsored occupation of lands under Polish rule. By the 1790s, Polish territories in Prussia were officially designated *colonies* and the Prussian monarchy adopted formal policies for colonial settlement, at times utilizing non-Prussian farmers to settle Polish lands. Moreover, many people experienced colonization as an intensely punitive condition. In Galicia during the early partition period, many peasants reacted to their new-found rights of citizenship by deserting the army, by hiding in the woods, by emigrating or by inflicting injuries on themselves to avoid military recruitment.[135] Despite this, however, Polish partition was also an event in which early constructs of generalized citizenship were imposed in Polish society. Foreign powers used these constructs to supplant the feudal institutions that Polish nobles and magnates deployed to underpin their socio-constitutional position.

On this basis, the external partition of Poland had two, rather contradictory results. First, this process eradicated the ancient constitution, originally based in selectively privileged citizenship. Second, it promoted new elements of citizenship and it instilled norms in Polish society more typically linked to nation-building constitutionalism than to colonization. Imperialism and national integration became dialectically interdependent, and imperialism began to promote patterns of individualization, legal autonomy and legal equality usually associated with nations. In a telling manner, then, the early period of partition stimulated new constitutional movements in Poland, which emulated some features of the regimes imposed by the occupying powers. By the 1770s, a number of Polish reformist groups became active, whose objective was to impede partition by promoting policies to reinforce the state and solidify its control in society. During partition, these reformers attached their plans for national reform, in part, to legal designs and models of citizenship that had been

[134] See Baczkowski (2017: 33).
[135] An outstanding discussion is found in Jewuła, Kargol and Ślusarek (2015: 271, 287–288, 293).

coercively enforced by colonizing powers. Norms used to support imperialism were transformed into the constitutional premise for anti-imperial polity formation.

After circa 1750, some Polish elites began to devise reform policies to consolidate the Polish commonwealth as a robust nation state. The middle decades of the eighteenth century saw (partly successful) reform policies in Poland. Central to this process was the reformist *Sejm*, convened in 1764 amidst civil conflict and Russian military presence, which elected Stanisław August Poniatowski king. This *Sejm* initiated reforms to the electoral system, and it was followed by legislation in 1767/8 that prescribed a procedure for organizing representation in the *Sejm*.[136] As mentioned, the armoury of taxes available to the government was curtailed because of external supervision. Nonetheless, important fiscal reforms were introduced at this point, including the creation of a new treasury commission in 1764, which brought an increase in fiscal revenue.[137] After 1717, controls of public expenditure were tightened, and by 1768, the Polish government had established an apparatus for planning and checking yearly national budgets. The reforms of the 1760s had limited effect, as they were drafted amidst civil war. At the same time, the background threat and then onset of external occupation triggered military reforms closely connected to taxation policies. In 1717, as mentioned, the reformist *Sejm* had greatly reduced Poland's military capacity. By the late 1730s, however, policies were tentatively envisaged to expand the size of the army. In 1764, a military commission was created, and military laws were introduced in 1775 to bring the army more fully under official control.[138] Government organs were then reformed through the establishment of the Permanent Council (1775–6), which survived until 1789. This Council included a specialized military department which performed executive and judicial responsibilities. The numerical depletion of the army remained a systemic problem despite these innovations. However, this Council assumed central authority for the military apparatus, and it was intended to separate military organs from traditional conflicts between monarch, *Hetman* and magnates.[139] In each point, a stricter institutional order was imposed on Poland through the onset of colonization.

[136] This was part of a longer process of electoral reform, which included further legislation in 1788–91 (Ilski 2022: 226–235).

[137] For analysis, see Hoensch (1970: 366) and Wóznicki (2014).

[138] On this process, see Organiściak (2002: 50) and Szczygielski (2009: 65–66).

[139] See excellent analysis in Bucholc-Srogosz (2007: 52–53).

This centralizing reaction to external imperial pressure was opposed by some domestic factions, for different reasons. In particular, the Permanent Council was perceived as an executive institution that conferred constitutional autonomy on the monarchy, and it caused great polarization, giving rise to conditions close to civil war. The Permanent Council met with hostility amongst the conservative nobility, whose members wished to preserve their privileges and resented the erosion of traditional military institutions, especially those attached to the *Hetman*. Yet the creation of the Council also drew strictures from progressive reformers, who supported state reform but proposed a stronger parliamentary model of centralization. Such opposition was stimulated, not lastly, by the fact that the Permanent Council was susceptible to Russian influence, and different opposition groups argued that it weakened the national army.[140]

Ultimately, Polish reformers of more progressive persuasion began to propose national military mobilization as a strategy to reinforce the state. In the longer wake of 1772, leading reformers argued that the creation of a national army was the most effective way to resolve systemic crisis without creating conditions favourable to absolutism. For example, Hugo Kołłątaj, who later drafted the 1791 constitution, emphasized the need to create a people's army committed to the public interests of the state.[141] Kołłątaj also favoured the creation of local militias to improve the military spirit of the nation. In fact, Polish reformists anticipated techniques for mass recruitment deployed in other European countries some decades later.[142] In Poland, the experience of colonization pre-empted the military construction of the citizen that was later intensified by revolution.

On one hand, military ideas of citizenship in Poland built on long-standing traditions. Polish peasants were not noted for military enthusiasm, and, by the eighteenth century, their unwillingness to sacrifice themselves for the commonwealth was almost proverbial.[143] However, partly owing to the fragmented basis of the army, the ancient tradition of popular recruitment in the face of invasion had disappeared more slowly than in other European counties. In the seventeenth century, obligatory popular conscription, both national and regional, remained

[140] For analysis of these rival opposition camps, see Strojnowski (2005: 35–55) and Piegzik (2016: 14).

[141] Kołłątaj (1954: 247).

[142] See discussion in Grynwaser (1951: 206) and Strojnowski (2005: 280).

[143] See analysis of reasons for this in Ratajczyk (1975: 105) and Łotys (2005: 115).

an important (although dubiously effective) recruitment technique. Even after 1648, substantial armies were raised through this method.[144] At the same time, progressive plans for popular military recruitment reflected broader doctrines of agrarian reform and peasant emancipation which had already been implemented by colonizing powers, especially in the Habsburg regions. As in other countries, exponents of physiocratic theories gained influence in partition-era Poland, and ideas for agrarian transformation shaped many discussions in the *Sejm*. Physiocrats declared at this time that the peasants formed the basic 'foundation of the population' whose 'liberation from recent oppression' was vital for the nation and its economic basis.[145] Such observers argued – first – that agrarian reform, including legal protections for peasants, was needed to increase tax revenues on markets for agrarian produce. Yet, importantly, observers endorsing physiocratic views claimed that the abolition of serfdom would strengthen the national army. Advocates of reform before the 1790s argued that peasants who performed military service should be emancipated from serfdom.[146] Such ideas met with strong opposition, and many nobles were prepared to accept partition in order to preserve their social position and privileges, which depended on involuntary labour. Indicatively, before 1791, some reform projects remained unimplemented because of noble opposition, on grounds that such reforms increased the legal standing and protection of peasants.[147] During the final stages of annexation, Polish nobles in Galicia even approached the rulers in Vienna with a plan for a new constitution, the Charta Leopoldina (1790), intended to preserve noble rights in a state under Habsburg sovereignty. In different regions, factions that supported serfdom played a complex, multifaceted role in the decline of Poland as a sovereign state. However, by the 1770s, agrarian reform was clearly perceived as a pathway to military reinforcement and the link between enhanced citizenship and military recruitment was publicly established.

In this context, experiences of imperialism in Poland began to promote an ideal of citizenship in which the emancipation of social

[144] There is illuminating discussion of this in Łotys (2005: 6–7), Wierzbicki (2011: 349) and Wimmer (2019: 22–27).

[145] This is the classical principle in physiocratic thought in Poland, expressed in the work of Popławski (1774: 47–48). Popławski stated that literacy and education were vital for the improvement of 'peasant citizens' (123).

[146] This is expressed in a speech by Andrzej Zamoyski in 1764, published in Michalski (1954: 77).

[147] In 1776, a legal code was drawn up by Andrzej Zamoyski, the *Kodeks Zamoyskiego*, which gave peasants some rights of legal personality. The code was not implemented.

agents from bonded labour formed the cornerstone of the national polity. This ideal was partly borrowed from partitioning powers, but it was intended to obviate further imperial incursion in Polish territory. Concepts arising in this context were articulated in the sessions of the Great Parliament (Sejm Wielki), convened in 1788. This parliament was convoked to reinforce plans for fiscal reform, and it aimed to expand the army through new recruitment strategies, including mandatory military conscription.[148]

These designs shaped the writing of the 1791 constitution. The constitution of 1791 was largely the work of reformist factions. However, it reflected a broad social compromise and it combined monarchical and parliamentary visions of political reform. It created a bicameral legislature with one elected chamber (Art. VI). It included provisions for a strong executive branch, concentrated in the person of the monarch (Art. VII), enacting the decisions of a sovereign parliament and bound by the will of parliament. It retained protections for the nobility (Art. II). It also contained provisions for popular military service, and it foresaw the creation of an army of citizens drawn 'from the general strength of the nation' (Art. XL), not based in mercenaries. This predated the first imposition of a *levée en masse* in revolutionary France by two years. In parallel, the drafters of the constitution advocated the restriction of serfdom, basing their arguments on notions of natural rights. While formulating the constitution, Kołłątaj set out principles of public order in Poland, supporting abolition of serfdom and declaring that persons in Poland were 'subjects of the law alone', not beholden to private holders of privilege.[149] However, although it reinforced the legal position of serfs (Art. IV), the constitution did not abolish serfdom for the majority of peasants, and it defended some core interests of the traditional nobility.

The 1791 constitution was accepted across a spectrum of social and regional groups.[150] However, it provoked violent opposition amongst some elites, and it was often decried as a military ordinance.[151] Within

[148] On these points, see Życiński (1992: 9, 21), Łotys (2005: 140, 156) and Drozdowski (2017: 158). In December 1788, the *Sejm* commissioned a new military budget to expand military recruitment. Historians argue that mandatory conscription was planned because fiscal income was inadequate for recruitment goals (Herbst 1983: 413–414; Bucholc-Srogosz 2007: 104).

[149] This view is expressed in Hugo Kołłątaj's treatise *Prawo polityczne narodu polskiego* (1790: folio 115).

[150] The constitution was subject to approval by regional parliaments and roughly 50 per cent accepted it (Szczygielski 1994: 362).

[151] Historians have described it as an effective *coup d'état* (Ratajczyk 1975: 53; Maciejak 2014: 104).

a year, more conservative groups in the Polish nobility took up arms to overthrow the constitution, and it caused a multipolar war combining elements of civil and interstate war. This culminated in the formation of a reactionary confederation, the Konfederacja Targowicka, in 1792. This was a league of nobles, who, in close alliance with Russia, mobilized against the constitution and advocated a reversion to earlier fiscal and military structures. This league briefly became the ruling national executive, and it was joined by the king himself. Subsequently, a rival military league, led by Tadeusz Kościuszko, was formed in 1794 to defend the constitution against the colonizing powers. This army was partly recruited through mass levy and it was proclaimed an army of national liberation. In the final throes of partition, military opposition to the occupying forces relied – in part – on the mobilization of a conscript army. Leaders of the reformist league showed greater support for uniform citizenship than was expressed in the 1791 constitution, and, in 1794, they issued a proclamation (unenforced) that partly abolished serfdom, tying liberation to discharge of military service in the national cause.[152] Even in this final attempt to mobilize troops, the nobility shied away from offering peasants full emancipation, although serfs serving as soldiers were released from duties while performing military service. Unsurprisingly, appeals for mass military support for the constitution often fell on deaf ears amongst Polish serfs and the endeavour to raise a national, anti-imperial army had limited success.[153] The transformation from serf into soldier-citizen that lay at the core of these reforms was often not accepted.[154] Indicatively, although the 1791 constitution provided for national military recruitment, popular militias were not used to suppress the noble revolt in 1792.[155] The fate of Poland was sealed in 1794, when military formations created to defend the constitutional state, based in mass military recruitment, were defeated.

The case of Poland throws clear light on the fact that, in its origins, constitutionalism formed a system of social organization that moved diffusely between national and imperial dimensions. In Poland, constitutional reforms were essentially promoted to prevent external occupation. However, they were partly rooted in patterns of citizenship

[152] This is expressed in the *Uniwersał połaniecki* (1794), printed in Inglot (1952: 227–228).
[153] See the analysis in Kowecki (1963: 193, 278) and Jewuła, Kargol and Ślusarek (2015: 136). One historian reflects that, during the 1794 uprising, many peasants decided not to fight for national independence. Instead, they 'drifted off to their homes' (Łotys 2005: 239).
[154] See p. 100.
[155] See Łojek (1986: 308).

construction devised by partitioning powers, which had been enforced to support colonial rule. Moreover, many groups in Polish society perceived such reforms as policies that imposed colonialism in revised form. Nation-building reforms expressed through constitutional rule engendered unmanageable lateral conflicts, culminating in civil war, which benefited external actors. The partition process occurred, broadly, as a combined experience of external annexation, internal colonization and hybrid civil–interstate warfare, splitting the military apparatus into openly hostile groups. The emergence of constitutional ideas in Poland was largely induced by imperialist pressures on the military system. From the outset, definitions of citizenship expressed deep rivalry between different ideas of military duty and different opinions concerning the social role of the army. Ultimately, however, Poland formed a constitutional context in which experiences of imperialism created patterns of intra-societal conflict that prevented the formation of a stable national constitutional order based in shared citizenship norms. The attempt at constitutional formation in 1791 reflected the fusion of imperialism and nation-building found in other settings, but the ability of the government to impose a robust national citizenship regime, anchored in nation-building through military recruitment, was too weak to support constitutional rule. The structural weaknesses that had earlier caused Poland's decline as an empire ultimately caused its disappearance as a nation.

The deep connection between imperialism, civil war and constitutionalism persisted in Poland after 1795. Indeed, the structure of Polish society remained profoundly shaped by the military emphasis of constitutionalism. In the longer wake of partition, the relation between constitutional formation and demands for military recruits again became visible during the Napoleonic interlude, when French armies occupied parts of Poland, mainly those already colonized by Prussia. Napoleon's defeat of Prussia brought the imposition of a constitution (1807) in the Duchy of Warsaw. This document introduced characteristic elements of Napoleonic legal order. It created a limited monarchy, connecting Poland to the royal house of Saxony and, with subsequent laws, it abolished some aspects of serfdom (Art. 4) and enfranchised some peasant farmers. In Art. 69, it imposed Napoleonic civil law and promoted the integration of citizens at the level of private interaction, a process that again met with resentment amongst the nobility.[156] This

[156] Grynwaser (1951: 54, 55, 73).

was flanked by legislation of May 1808, which imposed military duties on Polish citizens of the Duchy, and this ultimately produced a large army for Napoleon, maintaining the tradition of foreign military extraction in Poland. By 1812–13, the Duchy had moved towards independence as Polish leaders formed a general confederation during the war between France and Russia, which assumed some constitutional powers. This coincided with intense military mobilization and high military taxation. Nonetheless, the Congress of Vienna reinforced Polish partition and confirmed Russian, Prussian and Habsburg dominion in different regions. In 1815, the treaties drawn up in Vienna transferred the regions around Warsaw from Napoleonic to Russian rule, to form the Kingdom of Poland, and, in the manner of an inter-imperial accord, they placed powers of military, fiscal and constitutional sovereignty in the hands of the Russian tsar. As in previous experiences, this colonial polity was rooted in extended citizenship. It obtained a constitution largely written by Poles, which reflected earlier centralizing policies of the reform era.[157] This constitution created a complex system of national representation in which electoral rights were variably allocated to different groups of citizens (Arts 125–133). The polity was centred in a bicameral *Sejm* (Art. 86), but the constitution established chambers at different social levels. However, citizenship was closely correlated with political rights, and the proportion of citizens entitled to exercise political rights exceeded that in fully sovereign European countries. This constitution also imposed military recruitment for the Russian army on Polish citizens, and it created a regular army and supplementary militias (Art. 153). It allowed Polish solders to wear national uniforms, so that military roles were linked to national citizenship (Art. 156). After the anti-Russian uprising of 1830/1, constitutional rights of Poles were greatly diminished. In an imposed constitutional document of 1832, a new system was established, which was more fully subject to Russian rule, and the *Sejm* was dissolved – although local representation continued. The Polish army was fused with the imperial army, and, after 1832, military conscription continued in intensified form.[158] As analysed below, in regions controlled by Prussia after 1815, Poles were assimilated into the citizenship regime applied to Prussians. They also acquired electoral rights in Prussia after 1848 and again after 1871. Similar processes occurred in

[157] On the sources for this, see Gałędek (2017: 467–468).
[158] Caban (2001: 53).

the Habsburg regions. The region of Galicia, stretching from near Kraków to the Russian borders acquired some consultative organs after partition, with a reinforced representative assembly in Lwów (now L'viv) from 1861.

The fact that the occupying powers imposed conscription in Poland meant that many Poles acquired military experience, and the army opened professional opportunities for many Poles. Indeed, colonizing armies became important organizations for coordinating opposition to colonization in which Polish citizenship ideals could be articulated. Throughout the nineteenth century, Polish political culture remained characterized by informal confederations in which military bodies formed conspiratorial networks that mobilized against partition. This culture of conspiracy culminated in the first uprising in 1830–1, in which members of the officer corps established irregular units. During partition, the ideal of the partisan soldier, acting outside or alongside the regular army as an informal liberation fighter, became almost a cliché of Polish military and political diction. The linkage between citizenship and the army acquired greatest significance through the fact, discussed below, that the eventual acquisition of independent citizenship in by Poland was partly crafted by military agents whose formative experiences had been gained in imperial armies.

CONCLUSION

In these early cases of constitutional formation, constitutional law was strongly shaped by the pressures of imperialism on emerging national societies, exposed to imperial violence in different ways. Crucially, in each case, constitutions were designed to produce legitimacy for government in terms that facilitated military recruitment and stabilized the military apparatus in the state. In each case, constitutions articulated models of citizenship to link citizens to the state that originated in military organizations, so that national citizenship partly transferred affiliations already formed in armies to the governmental level. At the same time, armies were usually unable to stabilize a premise for a national constitutional system, and the militarization of the vertical relation between citizens and state was usually mirrored in complex patterns of lateral militarism, so that most constitutions engendered civil war, or many civil wars. Moreover, in most cases, the fact that constitutions imposed militarized definitions of citizenship on society induced a propensity for external expansion in government in which states reproduced techniques deployed to gain control of their own societies in their external actions. In these different respects, early national constitutions shaped societies in which social formation had a strong international dimension, and the spaces of integration within national, society were not clearly separated from the interstate domain.

CHAPTER TWO

CONSTITUTIONS AND THE PERSISTENCE OF EMPIRES

The Rise of Instrumental Citizenship

CONSTITUTIONS AFTER 1815

The primary claim in the previous chapter was that, in their first construction, constitutions resulted from imperialism, and, in turn, they perpetuated elements of imperialism in both the internal and external dimensions of constitutional states. By the 1790s, constitutions typically established principles of legitimacy for governments in which, by way of a public-law contract, citizens had some right to representation in lawmaking processes and governments were authorized to extract military force from these citizens. Through this bargain, constitutions imprinted militarized constructions of citizenship in national societies and societies were forged through identities with a partly military nature. As a result, the expansion of citizenship through society often reinforced the role of military organizations. The democratic aspect of constitutionalism, rooted in ideals of popular sovereignty, brought intergroup conflicts to heightened national prominence, and, for different reasons, this normally increased the use of military coercion. In some cases, constitutions attached governments to images of sovereignty and legitimacy whose realization presupposed military violence, internal and external.

After the revolutionary period, the constitutional-democratic experiment ended in most European countries by 1815. After 1815, states such as France retained a formal constitution which allowed very limited political enfranchisement. Basic patterns of constitutional rule survived in the Netherlands, in Norway and in semi-autonomous parts of Poland.

Yet, as mentioned, the constitutional interlude was terminated by an international legal order ordained by the Congress of Vienna. Convened at a time when France was under military occupation, the Congress formed an international organization whose main purpose was to prevent, or at least to control, interstate warfare.[1] It created the short-lived Allied Council to maintain diplomatic exchanges between constituent states and established a military apparatus with responsibility for ensuring public order in European societies. In pursuing collective security, the Congress proceeded from the principle that war could be best contained by a European system of public law based in single sovereign states, legitimated by personal or dynastic authority, and not constitutionally accountable to national populations. The policies of the Congress reflected the belief that, after 1789, war had been exacerbated by unmanageable convergence between international conflicts and popular interests and emotions, which had been caused by constitutional commitments to popular sovereignty. From this perspective, after 1789, traditional causes of war such as territorial conflicts inflamed entire populations, militarizing different social factions and fracturing usual state capacities for conflict management. Theorists close to the European restoration argued that states with republican constitutions were inevitably dominated by the 'military establishment'. Such theorists viewed constitutional states, legitimated by popular sovereignty, as dedicated to waging 'external warfare' involving 'terrible conflicts of peoples against peoples'.[2] For this reason, the main policy of the Congress was to eradicate the *soldat-citoyen* as a focus of governmental legitimacy. To achieve this, it sought to transpose legitimational principles for national governments from the domestic (constitutional) to the international level: to ensure that governmental power and legitimacy were separated from national populations and concentrated in the hands of monarchs, supported by the Congress itself. Indicatively, Arts 57–58 of the concluding resolutions of the Congress of Vienna (1820) regarding the German Confederation (Deutscher Bund) effectively prohibited democratic constitutionalism throughout central Europe.

In each respect, the Congress attempted to re-establish a definition of war as an event that simply occurs between sovereign states in which members of national populations are not constitutively implicated. As after 1648, further, the Congress tried to ensure that the exercise of

[1] See Schulz (2009: 51–70).
[2] Bonald (1818: 13–4).

sovereignty in the international domain was conducted through strictly controlled armies, and this commitment placed limits on the exercise of sovereignty in the domestic domain. Indicatively, the Congress endeavoured to end the patterns of military recruitment typical of the revolutionary and Napoleonic periods. Around 1815, many states in Europe reversed earlier conscription policies, or at least restricted recruitment for national armies, so that the connection between military participation and claims to popular sovereignty were weakened. The post-1815 period saw the emergence of governments with strong police systems, often partly militarized, which were deployed to supress internal radicalism. For example, in Prussia, legislation of 1820 authorized the use of the army in domestic conflicts. Similar powers were established in Spain.

Over a longer period, the idea that war should be confined to categorically legitimated sovereign actors provided the premise for the codification of international military law. Important commentators on the post-1815 international system interpreted the Congress provisions as implying certain laws of war, including the expectation that, during warfare, occupying forces could not arrogate powers of sovereignty in territories under occupation.[3] In later manuals on international law, it was stated that, under the law of military occupation, any 'change to the constitution' of an invaded state could establish 'no obligations' for the sovereign decisions of that state after the end of occupation.[4] This underlying attitude was later reinforced in the Brussels Declaration of 1874 (Art. 3) and reflected in the Hague Conventions of 1899 and 1907. Such conceptions of military law indicated that, in principle, members of national populations were relatively secure during wartime and occupying forces could not legitimately target private individuals or their belongings. In addition, legitimist ideas of war were conceived to make sure that, after war, states occupying other territories could not impose new sovereign institutions in conquered territories and that attributes of sovereignty could not be transferred from state to state in consequence of war. In the aftermath of 1789, monarchies felt deep anxiety in face of states presuming to derive legitimacy directly from the people, not last because revolutionary France had used this claim to justify the acquisition of sovereignty through invasion.[5] At a deep level, concepts of war

3 Klüber (1819: 400–4).
4 Heffter (1855: 312).
5 Kolla (2017: 121–4).

and sovereignty in the Congress were proposed to reject the notion of the *pouvoir révolutionnaire*: the belief that the people could assert a volitional title to sovereignty. Indicatively, the Congress justified its military intervention in France by distinguishing it from a war of peoples, describing it instead as a war against a 'revolutionary France' and 'military Jacobinism'. That is, the Congress explained its position as the result of a war that *reinstated* French sovereignty, implying that, in the period 1792–1815, French government had been imposed by military occupation.[6]

The anti-democratic policies of the Congress were reflected in the establishment of international military bodies, which were designed to reduce the reliance of national governments on their solders. For example, the German Confederation was allowed to deploy military force in matters with common security implications for member states, and it separated military mobilization from specific national commitments.[7] The Congress also reserved to itself the power to intervene in states where anti-monarchical uprisings took place. For example, Congress states intervened militarily in Naples and Spain between 1820 and 1823 to suppress national-democratic movements.[8]

The attempt to construct a collective security system in Vienna met with only partial success. In Europe, the decades after 1815 were a period of relative peace. Such peace was always fragile, punctuated by nationalist or constitutionalist uprisings often close to or escalating into civil war. Anti-legitimist movements erupted in Naples (1820), Madrid (1820), Turin (1821), Greece (1821), Paris (1830), Brussels (1830) and Warsaw (1830–1). Moreover, the reduction of conscription to avert social militarization was promoted only in Northern Europe. In the Ottoman Empire, the trend towards the creation of popular armies remained strong after 1815.[9] Russia and the Ottoman government were at war in 1828, and this coincided with military reforms in Istanbul. European imperialism also gathered pace again in the longer wake of 1815. The year 1815 hardened Britain's position as the leading imperial power, and, in the following decades, Britain increased military control over India. British imperialism gave rise to extensive violence outside Europe. For example, British presence in East Asia proved destabilizing

[6] This is taken from a speech by Castlereagh quoted in Capefigue (1864: 1676).

[7] The German Federation acquired a military constitution in 1821–2 which committed all German states to provide contingents for a confederated army. This integrated troops from regions recently assimilated in Eastern Europe.

[8] This was justified in the Troppau Protocol (1820).

[9] See pp. 272–6.

in that region, contributing to some of the worst wars in world history by the 1850s. France began the colonization of North Africa around 1830, and Russian colonization continued through this period, notably through wars with Persia in the 1820s.

For all these caveats, except in the Ottoman region, the interruption of constitutionalism after 1815 coincided with the absence of *large-scale interstate war* until the 1850s, which meant that primary determinants of constitutional formation were weakened. The interstate management of violence reduced the number of constitutionally ordered polities after 1815, and the external weakening of militarism restricted opportunities for national self-government based in the exercise of popular sovereignty. Nonetheless, in the decades following 1815, the thick attachment between constitutional citizenship, militarism and imperialism survived in different ways, in different contexts. Although the Congress system created in Vienna was intended to sever this nexus by establishing an inter-imperial balance, the effects of this nexus remained visible across Europe.

In the broad European context, post-1815 Spain exemplifies a polity in which the links between imperialism, war, civil war and constitutional formation enduringly shaped social life. After 1815, the Spanish polity had an uneasy relation with norms promoted by the Viennese Congress. In post-1815 Spain, international measures designed to limit warfare had relatively limited influence, and Spain continued to experience deep and multifocal militarization. This was strongly connected to the pressures caused by imperialism and the dissolution of the Spanish empire.

Like other European polities, Spain assumed more centralized form in the eighteenth century, in a context deeply determined by imperial transformation. Through the eighteenth century, the Bourbon monarchy in Madrid introduced reforms that imposed a more robust institutional order in its overseas territories, especially in Latin America.[10] After the Seven Years' War and the brief loss of Havana, the dynasty heightened its administrative penetration in the Spanish regions, promoting the intensification of metropolitan rule and stricter extraction of resources. One observer claims that it was only in this period that Spain fully became an empire, creating a 'new identity' and a 'different form of state' which conflicted with the traditional patronage-based

[10] On these processes, see Velazquez (1950: 97), Fisher (1970: 1), McFarlane (1993: 2), Kuethe and Andrien (2014: 353) and Eissa-Barroso (2016: 208). On the fiscal dimensions of these reforms, see Sánchez (2013: 283).

associations that connected Spain to overseas territories under Spanish rule.[11] The Bourbons accomplished this transformation by increasing their military presence in their overseas domains[12] and designing new military units to provide governance and defence.[13]

As in other empires, the reforms that the Spanish monarchy executed in overseas territories in the eighteenth century were not separable from domestic administrative designs. Importantly, Spanish territories in South America had a distinct status. These regions were not strictly colonies, but viceroyalties which nominally formed coequal parts of the Spanish polity. This meant that reforms in Spain and in the viceroyalties were closely linked elements of a common polity-building process, and the reordering of Spanish rule in overseas territories was not distinct from domestic reform. Spain had acquired greater domestic integrity through the War of Spanish Succession in the early eighteenth century. Moreover, Spain no longer had a system of forced labour (serfdom) in the eighteenth century. However, many regions in Spain were controlled by powerful families and their clienteles, who used informal dispensations to uphold their authority, which extended to the management of economic production. A clear consequence of this was that Spanish society was not strongly nationalized and its legal form was visibly shaped by feudal patterns of internal colonialism. As they initiated reforms outside Spain, therefore, the Bourbons also implemented reforms to modify the diffuse form of domestic society. For example, the Bourbons established a new system of administrative control, which was centred from 1718 around appointed inspectors (intendants) who policed local administrators and ensured their compliance with monarchical edicts. Similar policies were later replicated in Latin America. Whether such policies were effective is disputable. The Bourbon monarchy continued to operate within a territorial patchwork, and the transformation of Spain into a national society long remained incomplete. Yet the intensification of the state's internal structures was closely attached to external processes, and external colonization and internal colonization were closely linked.

[11] Almario García 2013: 49. One historical analysis describes the 'impotence' of the Spanish crown towards administrative bodies in the empire before circa 1750 (Burkholder and Chandler 1977: 72).

[12] One military historian calculates that before 1750 the entire Spanish Empire in the New World had been protected by only 14,000 soldiers (Vinson 2001: 8). For one example of new military directives, see the Ordenanza de Intendentes de Buenos Aires (1782), creating a body of intendants to administer royal functions.

[13] See pp. 221–4.

The attempt to harden royal authority in Spain and in the Spanish colonies was clearly reflected in laws regarding military appointments, by which military offices were brought more closely under monarchical control. Within Spain, one purpose of the Bourbon reforms was to establish centralized command structures in the army and to ensure that military agents in the nobility were subject to royal authority. These reforms were effected through ordinances introduced in the 1720s and in the late 1760s which regulated military recruitment. In 1768, military ordinances were passed to create a new disciplinary regime for military personnel, ensuring greater direct subordination of the army to the monarchy. Such policies had limited success, as persons with senior military roles were frequently allowed to subcontract recruitment functions, so that the military system remained dependent on clientelistic associations in the regional nobility.[14] Nonetheless, in this period, the army was increasingly structured as a system of rank and patronage, tying noble officeholders to the state.[15] The eighteenth century also saw the expansion of involuntary military service in Spain. As mentioned, militia laws imposed selective conscription on the population, notably in 1734 and 1766. This formed a response to fiscal pressures created by rising military mobilization, in which the government devised methods to find cheap soldiers. By consequence, the army began to obtain a fully national character. Military reforms and ordinances for militia recruitment in Spain were eventually mirrored in the Spanish overseas domains.[16] As discussed below, after 1763, the intensification of Spanish military administration in Latin America coincided with the creation of permanent militias, and, in both parts of the Spanish imperial system, military agents acquired new prominence and authority.[17] In each respect, empire-building, nation-building and military integration were closely connected. Distinctively, this process also involved the attribution of internal public-order functions to the army, so that the Spanish army played a role both in military and in civil institutional construction.[18] This was reflected in legislation

[14] See Castillo (2004: 43).

[15] This point is made in Andújar Castillo (1991: 156).

[16] One historian argues that the expanding role of the military in Spain created a militarized imperial polity (Kuethe 1978: 130). On the impact of the deployment of militias in the Spanish Caribbean and New Spain after 1763, see pp. 221–3, and analysis in Suarez (1984: 121–145), Albi (1987: 94–97) and Martínez (2014: 51).

[17] See p. 221. See also Velazquez (1950: 97) and Fernandez Marchena (1983: 9).

[18] González Calleja (2005: 95).

passed in the mid-1770s, when the Spanish army was accorded duties to protect 'tranquilidad pública'.[19]

The reconstruction of the Spanish military system was accelerated during the revolutionary period. In the first instance, Spain joined other monarchical powers in 1793 in fighting against revolutionary France. This event possessed great significance for the Spanish polity, marking an important experience of national military mobilization in which some parts of Spain were subject to French occupation. However, the decisive moment in the formation of the Spanish polity occurred through the partial occupation of Spain by Napoleonic troops from 1808. At this moment, the complex connection between imperialism, militarization, citizenship and constitution making became a core element in Spanish politics, persisting long after 1815.

The Napoleonic invasion of Spain led to the collapse of the Bourbon monarchy. In 1808, one Spanish king abdicated, a second king was imprisoned by Napoleon, and Napoleonic rule was enforced in most of Spain under Napoleon's brother. In areas of Spain not directly subject to Napoleonic government, this period was marked by intense revolutionary activity. In 1808, many Spanish cities and provinces witnessed the formation of independent military *juntas* subject to the notional authority of a supreme *junta* near Madrid, soon relocated to Seville, which formed temporary organs of government. These *juntas* usually comprised representatives of social groups with limited influence under the *ancien régime* who stepped into the administrative vacuum left by the collapse of the monarchy. The *juntas* explained their legitimacy as based in the emergency exercise of popular sovereignty, and they typically fused military and civil personnel.[20] One of their primary functions was to deploy military force for national defence and to organize popular mobilization, initially against Napoleonic occupation. In so doing, the *juntas* absorbed functions originally attached to the royal army, and they placed national defence on improvised public foundations.

The period of *junta* rule was flanked by the widespread establishment of national militias, which were often hostile to and partly supplanted regular units of the royal army. The formation of such militias was intended – to a large degree – to protect and consolidate the institutions created by the *juntas*, and the military assumed responsibilities for

[19] This is declared in a Royal Order (17 April 1774).
[20] See for analysis Moliner (1997: 43).

public order. The militia organizations, originating in recruitment patterns initiated during the Bourbon reforms, imbibed revolutionary ideas emanating from France and acted as cells in the construction of new citizenship regimes.[21] At the same time, the wars against Napoleonic occupation saw the appearance of other, less formal military units. As mentioned, resistance to Napoleon was partly organized by guerrillas and partisan groups who mobilized through spontaneous recruitment and patriotic appeals. The supreme *junta* passed a decree in late 1808 to regulate the guerrillas. However, informal armies, operating close to the population and reliant on patriotic sympathy, formed an important source of military capacity in anti-Napoleonic mobilization. Overall, in the period of partial Napoleonic occupation, the social foundations of the Spanish army were transformed. Enlistment in the military acquired popular or national dimensions and rapidly assembled militias and other more irregular units become forces in political life. This period was clearly defined by anti-imperial warfare against Napoleon. But such warfare shaded into civil war. Popular mobilization was conducted against the traditional ally of the Spanish monarchy, subverting domestic institutions built on the eighteenth-century alliance between the Bourbon dynasties. Such conflicts also created deep rivalries between the regular army and popular militias.

This complex bundle of occurrences was partly expressed in the Spanish constitution of 1812, which was drafted by delegates in the *cortes* in Cadiz beginning in 1810. This constitution was stimulated by Napoleonic intervention in Spanish politics, so that, literally, it formed a constitution for an occupied society. As such, it was shaped by highly militarized and contested experiences of citizenship in which military roles pervasively shaped collective self-comprehensions. However, it was established in a region outside full Napoleonic control, and it attempted to create a sovereign nation state with a fully national foundation able to consolidate uniform legal and political conditions across all Spanish society. This was made clear in Art. 3, which established national sovereignty as the basis of governmental legitimacy, and in Arts 244 and 339, which established a uniform judicial system and a common set of fiscal duties. In this respect, the constitution extended patterns of

[21] Different observers have described these militias, linked to the *juntas*, in similar terms – as the shock troops of the progressive bourgeoisie (Perez Garzon 1978: xiii), as the 'armed wing of the bourgeoisie' (Gay 1993: 82), as the 'most dynamic factor in the rupture with the *ancien régime*' (López Garrido 1982: 178) and as the 'armed force for the presentation of constitutional rule' (García Leon 1983: 165).

nation-building that had already begun in the eighteenth century. Significant in this regard is the fact, discussed in Chapter 4, that the constitution was intended both to reinforce Spanish nationhood and to resolidify Spanish rule in Latin America, so that it was also an imperial constitution. Inhabitants of Spanish dominions were defined in the constitution as members of the Spanish nation (Art. 1), and citizenship provisions covered all residents in Spanish territory (Art. 18). The constitution allowed the colonies rights of representation, and some colonies sent delegates to the *cortes* that prepared the constitution. These rights were declared in Arts 5, 28 and 29 of the constitution. However, the *cortes* in Cadiz also mobilized troops to suppress independence movements in Spanish America, and its military provisions were partly intended to re-enforce the lines of obligation between Spain and Spanish territories overseas.

The reformist plans expressed in the 1812 constitution contained important directives for military reform, reflecting the transformation of the army that had begun after 1808. In fact, strictly, the 1812 constitution formed a constitution for the army, and one of its main purposes was to place the military on new legal and organizational premises. To achieve this, first, the constitution aimed to reduce the immediate connection between civil and military authority, and it placed the military more strictly beneath civilian control (Art. 357). The military elite of pre-revolutionary Spain had formed a separate corporate estate bound to the monarchy by patronage. At this time, the army possessed partial judicial autonomy in the state and members of the military were subject to a legal order (the *fuero militar*) which protected their collective privileges.[22] This status was secured by royal decree in 1793, coinciding with war against France.[23] The Cadiz constitution did not abolish the *fuero* (Art. 250), but it restricted its reach and sought to terminate the privileges attached to military status.[24] In addition, second, the constitution drew on traditions of revolutionary recruitment seen in France and on experiences of spontaneous military engagement after 1808. All military officials were required to declare loyalty to the constitution (Art. 374), and formal status was accorded to the militias established after 1808 (Art. 362). The constitution also attached rights of citizenship to military obligations (Art. 361). In fact, in parallel, a constitution for the militias was

[22] See Burbano (1982: 18).
[23] See Royal Decree (9 February 1793).
[24] Blanco Valdés (1988: 359).

drafted which prescribed rules of recruitment and punishment for evasion, and unenforced legislation of April 1814 foresaw compulsory militia service.[25] In its military implications, the Cadiz Constitution marked a dialectical attempt to alter the political emphasis of the Spanish army. It separated the military from royal control, yet it invigorated the position of the army as part of strategy of national-liberal reform.[26] Central to this policy was the conviction that the army should stand as close as possible to the national population, making the military an immediate organ of the people. Also central to this was an idea of the army as an elevated representative of the national popular will such that the army could claim to embody national values and interests. In other words, the constitution was intended to depoliticize the army by intensifying its accountability to the people, yet it also acknowledged its privileged character role as a focus of national citizenship.

The 1812 constitution was suspended at the restoration of the monarchy, as the deposed king returned in 1814. However, the 1812 constitution created two constitutional principles that resonated through Spanish politics from that time. First, it expressed the assumption that constitution making is a military matter and that the military is a central object of constitutional organization. Second, it expressed the assumption that a constitution requires the support of the army and the army is an essential constitutional organ. On the second point, vitally, the constitution divided the army itself, and this meant that military loyalties were fractured by constitutional law. After 1812, some military groups were clearly committed to constitutional rule, and they derived benefit from the fact that the constitution diminished the status of the army as a bastion of corporate privilege.[27] During restoration, however, substantial parts of the army acted in support of the reestablishment of monarchical government. Indicatively, in 1814, militias were disbanded, and military force was reconcentrated in the regular army. Accordingly, a socio-institutional reality took shape in which commitments to constitutional principles split the army into different factions and different sectors in the army declared loyalty to rival constitutional visions. From 1812, constitutional rule instilled a deep military fissure at the core of society.

[25] See chapter IV of the *Proyecto de una constitución de las milicias nacionales* (1814), drafted by Vicente Sancho.

[26] On the dialectics of politicization and militarization in this process, see Ballbé (1983: 82).

[27] See Lawrence (2014: 22–3).

These conditions formed the background for the tradition of *pronunciamientos* that became a feature of Spanish society after 1812. Throughout the nineteenth century, military groups frequently intervened in civilian government, claiming authority, tenuously based on constitutional interpretation, to provide direction for state and society.[28] From 1812, Spanish history was punctuated by moments in which military leadership groups declared opposition to a particular governmental order, leading to its overthrow. These conditions also initiated a tradition of militia mobilization, as most moments of institutional transformation witnessed broad recruitment for radical militias, often constituting *juntas* as temporary governmental bodies. As a result, through and beyond the nineteenth century, the Spanish army played a distinct constitutional role and retained intermittent force as a constituent actor.[29]

This tradition was first expressed in the revolution of 1820. At this time, an interim government was formed by self-proclaimed military *juntas* who demanded the reimposition of the 1812 constitution. Prominent amongst the insurgents were soldiers commissioned to pacify territories claiming independence in Latin America. The revolution coincided with the final deployment of Spanish armies in Mexico, and it was closely linked to this imperial endgame. After 1820, new laws were passed in Spain to abolish noble privileges and seigneurial forms of ownership, and, in parallel, a military constitution was created as provisions for militia service, conscription and annual enrolment were reincorporated in public law.[30] Orders to form national militias had already been passed in 1820, with compulsory recruitment from August 1820. This period had certain similarities to a process of national annexation, as the military was recruited on a regional basis and used to enforce constitutional loyalty and public order across society. Decrees of February 1821 declared that any attempt to 'destroy or transform the constitution' would be subject to harsh penalty and established a special category of crimes to cover actions 'against the constitution or against internal and external security'. These decrees ordained that perpetrators of such crimes could be judged in military

[28] Article 356 of the 1812 constitution stated that the army should provide external defence and ensure domestic order. This power was amplified in the line of military coups that followed.

[29] For an analysis of the weak force of 'institutional norms' in defining military roles in post-1812 Spain, see Gómez (1990: 243).

[30] See Perez Garzon (1978: 25); Burbano (1982: 23). See Articles 2, 5 and 22 of the Ley Orgánica del Ejército (1821).

courts, making the army an immediate organ of constitutional implementation.[31]

The 1820 revolution was suppressed in 1823, partly by armies located in France. However, the early 1830s saw a renewal of constitutional rule. This followed the death of King Ferdinand VII in 1833 and the introduction of a new constitutional statute in 1834. The statute gave some limited governmental powers to the *cortes*, whose members were divided into two social estates, one elected and one nominated by the monarch. In design, this statute was observed as an important moment of political equipoise as the bicameral legislature encouraged some elite groups to accept constitutional rule.[32] However, the statute also contained military regulations reflecting the need to raise more revenue and soldiers for the army in a time when internal military conflict was escalating.[33] The implementation of the statute coincided with the mobilization of reactionary armies associated with *Carlismo*, who supported rival dynastic claims and were hostile to the emerging constitutional order. The 1830s saw deep civil war in Spain, exacting a terrible death toll, between constitutionalists and *carlistas*, who were committed to defending traditional social structure, to protecting the authority of the church and to ensuring the integrity of regional laws and privileges. Carlism was also fuelled by traces of imperialism as it reflected resentment for the recognition of former Spanish territories as independent states, most of which acquired sovereignty in the 1820s.[34] In regions where they enjoyed support, the Carlists created separate governmental institutions, using military organizations to construct an administrative apparatus similar to a regular state imposing police rule, education policies and far-reaching conscription laws.[35] The Carlist civil war of the 1830s was close to a war of unification, reflecting the deep fissures in Spanish society that became tangible after 1808. In this conflict, national military units, legitimated by constitutionalist visions of order, waged war against deep-rooted centrifugal forces and the state came close to fracture. Military units became primary governmental organs and *juntas* and local militias again acted as defenders of centralized political institutions; new military recruitment legislation was passed in 1837. Eventually, a liberal-progressive regime was

[31] These decrees are printed in the *Colección de los Decretos y Órdenes* (1821: 37–51).
[32] San Miguel (1836: 45).
[33] Monerri Molina (2019: 235).
[34] See analysis in Marichal (1980: 152) and Lawrence (2017: 142).
[35] See Lawrence (2017: 199). Discussing the Carlist war of the 1870s, one historian shows how the Carlists established a 'counter-state' in regions under their control (Canal 2000: 191).

consolidated in the late 1830s, under the 1837 constitution, passed during civil war, which was again replaced in 1845. Constitutional rule was progressively cemented after the end of the first Carlist wars. This system fell short of the demands of some radical military units, and it partly resulted from the ability of military leaders to tame volatile elements amongst their soldiers. It coincided with hardening of Spanish rule in its remaining colonies, as delegates from Cuba and Puerto Rico were expelled from the *cortes* in 1837. However, more than the changes in 1808–14 or 1820–3, the end of the first Carlist wars created a solid basis for the expansion of national representative institutions in Spain. After 1837, some form of representative government was broadly accepted.[36]

In these processes, constitutional citizenship was imposed in Spain by military units in a form other military units rejected. The creation of a constitutional system was inseparable from warfare, and, in effect, constitutional law formed a mechanism for territorial control and occupation with strong military support. This process was caused by Napoleonic invasion and the collapse of the Spanish empire, and by the emergence of the army as an independent source of political loyalties. Through this, the army became the site in which new definitions of citizenship were articulated, both extending and intensifying modes of nation-building that originated in the imperial era.

In other post-1815 societies, the link between imperialism and constitutional formation was expressed in a less volatile manner. However, this link remained evident in a range of contexts. For example, in post-1815 Prussia, the connection between war, imperialism and citizenship rights continued to shape society at a fundamental level. Prussia is not usually considered an empire, at least until 1864–71.[37] Yet before and after 1815, the Prussian state was clearly in a process of imperial expansion, externally and internally. In the years 1740–95, Prussia had absorbed large territories that had previously been subject to Habsburg and Polish rule, and it acquired the form of a continental empire containing large Polish-speaking communities in its border regions. Prussian expansion was interrupted by Napoleonic occupation from 1806. At this point, however, Napoleonic occupation intensified

[36] One historian claims that, from 1837 to 1923, sessions of both the Senate and the Chamber of Deputies were held each year (Marichal 1980: 131).

[37] One interpretation shares my account of Prussia as an empire, although it dates the advent of Prussian imperialism to 1772, later than the date of 1740–1 suggested in my analysis (see Lerp 2016: 20).

imperialist tendencies in Prussia, and Napoleon's administrative designs formed the premise for subsequent patterns of institutional construction and territorial integration in Prussia.

By the later eighteenth century, Prussia had conducted important reforms in the military and fiscal domains. However, before 1806, Prussia retained a composite administrative structure in which government institutions were still rooted in separate provinces. There had been numerous attempts in the eighteenth century to remedy the weak centralization of the state, but the autonomy of its regions, largely based in aristocratic authority, remained high. This limited centralization was a primary reason for the military vulnerability of Prussia in face of Napoleon. After defeat by Napoleon, the reformist plans of the eighteenth century were revived and a legal regime based in increasingly uniform citizenship ideals was constructed. This was enacted through a number of laws in the longer wake of 1806. This began with laws in 1807–8 to abolish serfdom and to reform urban administration, giving greater autonomy to Prussian towns. Through this period, the Prussian monarchy also established a more centralized administrative order which gradually removed provincial variations in Prussia. For example, in 1817, the Council of State was created to advise the monarch, and, in the years after 1815, separate ministries were formed to conduct government in different policy areas, with authority for all Prussian territory. Plans for a national constitution began in 1810, and, in 1817, a constitutional commission was established in the Council of State, although no constitution was written. These policies were also reflected in economic legislation. After 1815, customs borders in Prussia were gradually removed and the national economy was subject to uniform tax laws. Such reforms were accompanied by new military legislation and they connected citizenship to military recruitment. Indicatively, centralizing reforms were implemented at a time when the ranks of the army had swelled. In 1806, as mentioned, the military leadership considered declaring a *levée en masse* to combat Napoleon. By 1815, military recruitment was subject to stricter regulation through the creation of the conscripted *Landwehr* in 1813–14 and the imposition of universal military duties in 1814–15, which persisted after the Congress of Vienna.

Following the Congress of Vienna, Prussia absorbed substantial swathes of new territory, including regions originally in Poland, which Prussia had briefly acquired during partition and then lost to Napoleon. In this context, the centralization of Prussian government in traditional Prussian regions was effected as part of a process in which new domains were incorporated in the state, so that legal reforms were promoted both to solidify Prussian rule internally and to integrate regions previously outside Prussia. In predominantly Polish-speaking territories subject to Prussia after 1815, the government enforced integration by elaborating uniform models of citizenship. For example, serfdom was abolished in the Prussian-ruled regions of Poland in 1823, against the opposition of some Polish nobles.[38] Symbolically, the Occupation Patent by which parts of Poland were transferred to Prussia in May 1815 was accompanied by a royal declaration (not realized) promising that Polish citizens, like Prussians, would soon be subject to the new constitution planned for Prussia. As in earlier periods, constitutional law was explicitly envisaged as an instrument of occupation and equal citizenship was projected to simplify territorial control. Uniformly, these processes involved the continued imposition of military service. Prussian expansion meant that, after 1815, Prussia had a large direct border with Russia and its eastern borderlands were objects of military concern.[39] Prussian conscription laws were extended to newly incorporated Polish-speaking regions in 1816, often in the face of stiff hostility amongst conscripts.[40] For many Poles, military recruitment formed the most immediate connection with the Prussian government, and Poles became subjects of a foreign power and soldiers in a foreign army at the same time.

In these events, after 1815, Prussia acquired increasingly centralized internal form as it expanded externally. On one hand, it was only in the aftermath of 1815 that Prussian regions were structurally connected, so that Prussia became territorially unified. However, this process was not separate from the colonization of western Poland. Laws of citizenship used to colonize Poland were not distinct from those utilized to unify Prussia more widely, and the assimilation of parts of Poland reflected a more general line of Prussian nation-building.[41] In each respect, norms of citizenship produced a system of political authority in which nation-building and colonization overlapped, and both processes were supported by similar norms and obligations.

38 On these points, see Kozłowski (2004: 27).

39 One historian explains that, although rarely examined, these eastern regions possessed 'existential' importance for Prussia after 1815 (Jędrysiak 2014: 31).

40 This was enforced in the 1816 military constitution for Poznan (Kriegsverfassung Posen).

41 See Wąsicki (1980: 7).

1848: NATIONAL LIBERALISM OR IMPERIALISM?

The attempts at constitutional foundation that occurred in and around 1848 gave further expression to the conjuncture connecting national constitutions, military violence and imperialism. The occurrences of 1848–9 are usually viewed as emblematic manifestations of liberal nationalism in which early constructs of national democratic citizenship were devised to oppose existing imperialist governments. This view is particularly strong in the German context, where 1848 is identified as the historical moment at which liberal ideals of government were promoted to place the German polity on collective foundations, replacing the remnants of the Holy Roman Empire. This view is frequently linked to the claim that the groups seeking to create a representative constitution were thwarted by Prussia's imperial pretensions.[42] At a general level, an anti-imperialist element was pronounced in the movements of 1848. For example, uprisings around Venice in 1848 were directed against the Bourbon and Habsburg empires. Uprisings in Poznan were directed against Prussian rulers in Poland. Uprisings in Hungary had similar characteristics. To this degree, participants in such uprisings attempted (largely unsuccessfully) to utilize models of citizenship pioneered in the late eighteenth century to carve out political systems based in national representation. Yet, at the same time, the 1848 revolutions had more complex associations with imperialism. Most constitutions established at this point evolved through a two-stage process; although they first supported national autonomy, they soon reproduced dynamics of territorial colonization. One enduring legacy of 1848 is visible in the fact that, from this time, constitutional rule began to serve as a reflexive design for empire-building. After 1848, constitutional models of citizenship were consciously deployed to create societies with both national and imperial features.

Such phenomena are manifest in France. The revolutionary uprising in France in 1848 was initially a radical movement outreaching in its demands the constitutional revolution beginning in 1789. The 1848 constitution in France expressed a clear commitment to equal citizenship as the substructure of nation-building, and it abolished slavery in all French domains (Art. 6). It made provisions for a large electoral franchise (Art. 25) and some implied social rights, as the preamble defined protection of labour as a state duty and some limits were

42 See Wettengel (2022: 3).

envisaged on the use of private property (Art. 11). However, the imposition of citizenship had a coercive dimension. For example, the constitution utilized citizenship for expansionary ends as it transformed Algeria into French territory (Art. 109). Soon, the army assumed a central role in constitutional organization, and, by 1851, the republic was replaced by a renewed experiment in Bonapartism, the Second Empire, founded in 1851–2. The Second Empire took shape as a polity in which power was concentrated in the executive. However, the imperial executive was supported by a large franchise and regular elections were institutionalized, albeit in controlled manner. Although existing conscription laws of 1832 were not revised, military mobilization also formed an important source of legitimacy in the Second Empire as France engaged in conflict with other Congress powers, including Russia in the Crimea and Austria in Italy. Indicatively, the Second Empire saw the recommencement of French imperial expansion outside Europe. The abolition of slavery coincided with overseas military actions and the formation of a colonial army, the Tirailleurs Sénégalais, in West Africa in 1857, which was partly used to colonize the regions from which soldiers were extracted.

Analogies to this are evident in Italy. In 1848–9, Italian regions were witness to numerous national constitutional movements, some directed against external empires, some focused on the reorganization of political entities within Italy. Importantly, the only Italian constitution that proved enduring was the Statuto Albertino, applied in Piedmont and Sardinia. This was anything but a radical constitution. It was implemented by the Savoyard monarch, and its function was to stabilize a system of restricted political representation to bolster royal government, providing for a strong and undivided royal executive (Art. 3). It also had imperial origins as Sardinia had been acquired by Savoy in 1720, and the constitution was meant to place the composite dynastic state on shared normative premises, to strengthen its social and territorial substructure. This constitution foresaw the introduction of universal military service (Arts 75–76). It later became central to the unification of Italy under the Savoyard monarchy after 1859, when it was forcibly applied in integrated regions.

Similar developments are perceptible in the early unification process in Germany from 1848 to 1849. The endeavour to create an all-German constitution in 1848–9 took place in two quite separate dimensions, in both of which forces arising from imperialism acquired a substantial significance.

First, 1848 saw a collective impetus towards the unification of different German states in one national polity. Short uprisings in early 1848 led to the convocation of a constitutional assembly in Frankfurt in which delegates from different German regions assembled to project a representative system for a unified Germany, including regions under Habsburg rule where most inhabitants did not speak German. This marked the great rupture in the interstate system created in 1815. As a constituent body that incorporated many states subject to the agreements reached in Vienna, the assembly in Frankfurt deeply modified the international premises of European order consecrated after Napoleon. Reflecting this, the Frankfurt Assembly created a constitution in 1848–9 (not fully enforced) that possessed a strong national-democratic emphasis. It established a bicameral legislature, with one chamber elected by citizens possessing equal electoral rights, as the foundation for a democratic polity (§94). The proclamation of national or popular sovereignty that it contained was intended to promote the centralization of political authority, supported by unified system of citizenship for all Germany.

However, the constitution-making process in Frankfurt was closely intertwined with legacies of empire, and it did not envisage German nationhood as an entirely anti-imperial reality. For example, the construction of German nationhood was an extension of policies initially conducted by imperialist actors. In key respects, constitutional designs in 1848 served to complete the acts of intra-societal colonization that had begun in different parts of Germany a century earlier. The 1849 constitution contained clauses to remove the residues of feudal law and feudal jurisdiction and to imprint a uniform legal structure on society (§174). In such respects, constitutionalists simply gave public-legal form to techniques of territorial assimilation originally deployed by the monarchies in Prussia and Austria, and, with limited societal support, they imposed models of citizenship to cut through regional partitions in society. In addition, the 1848 plan for the creation of a German nation state was not, even in its initial form, separate from a deliberate strategy to promote German military expansion. The 1848 revolution coincided with war with Denmark, conducted by military units established under the German Confederation. Once formed, the Frankfurt assembly soon connected national citizenship to military service, and the constitution required persons with constitutional rights to provide military support to the emerging national polity (§137). On this basis, the building of a nation state was flanked by plans for military reinforcement in which the granting of citizenship was intended to build up German military capacity separate from the Confederation. Early policies in Frankfurt addressed matters of military strategy, prominent amongst which was the endeavour to create a unified army and to finance a German navy.[43] This was motivated, not last, by anxieties that revolutionary turmoil could lead to Russian intervention in German regions. The 1849 constitution established a German navy (§19), subject only to the unified state. In each respect, nation-building and empire-building were overlapping processes and the emerging German polity was both a nation and an empire. The 1849 constitution was intended in part to replace the international order of 1815 with a new national-imperial order. Indeed, the constitution was shaped by anti-Slavic attitudes amongst delegates in Frankfurt, who rejected national representation for residents of German regions who did not identify with German nationhood.[44]

Second, more enduringly, uprisings in Germany in 1848 led to the formation of a separate constitutional system in Prussia. The Prussian constitution, established in different texts between 1848 and 1850, acquired greater permanence than the planned constitution for Germany as a whole, and it remained in force until late 1918. Unlike the constitution in Frankfurt, the Prussian constitution was initially imposed by royal decree, following popular unrest in early 1848, and it was then modified in a more deliberated manner. Once in force, the constitution was revised so that it only granted limited rights of political participation, and it protected highly selective rights of citizenship. The final form of the constitution (1850) provided for a bicameral system of representation in which members of the second chamber were elected by a weighted franchise and the allocation of voting rights was calibrated in accordance with voters' personal income and fiscal category. The constitution thus instilled a tiered citizenship regime at the core of Prussian society.

The political order created in Prussia between 1848 and 1850 utilized constitutional ideals as part of a strategy to consolidate the geopolitical position of Prussian government. It did this in relation to internal actors within Prussia, by establishing uniform laws for all Prussian territories, and by centralizing the representation of elite interests in a new parliament in Berlin. However, it also did this in relation to

43 One interpreter argues that the nation-building plan of 1848/9 was driven by Prussian expansionism and anticipated later imperialist projects (Kamissek 2018: 267).

44 For example, despite early promises to the contrary, Poles in eastern regions of Prussia did not obtain specified political rights.

external forces, by dictating principles of citizenship that were closely linked to military service. This was set out in Art. 33 of the 1848 constitution, which created a regular army, a conscripted *Landwehr* and a militia corps. The constitutions of 1848 and 1850 both imposed universal military service (Art. 32 in 1848; Art. 34 in 1850). The years after 1848 saw extensive military reform in Prussia in which the army grew in size, notably in reforms of 1859. Moreover, the Prussian constitution was immediately tested in war as in late 1848, the Prussian government mobilized its army to suppress the Constitutional Assembly in Frankfurt, which resulted in Prussian occupation of German states loyal to the Frankfurt constitution. The multilevel experiment in constitutionalism that commenced in early 1848 collapsed into conflicts combining interstate war, civil war, war of national unification and imperial war. These conflicts involved wars between separate states that had recently attempted to forge a unified nation state and which were all members of the German Confederation. In these wars, Prussia, legitimated by a new constitution, defeated the armies gathered in parts of south-west Germany, legitimated by a different constitutional order, and the Prussian constitutions formed the basis for temporary military occupation. States in southern Germany that fought for the Frankfurt constitution also imposed high levels of conscription on their populations.

In essence, the inter- and intra-German wars of 1848–9 were fought between two rival visions of constitutional citizenship, both sustained by the construction of constitutional law as a means of mass military recruitment and territorial integration. Indicatively, constitutional attitudes in 1848 often polarized around attitudes to military service. Liberal or progressive constitutionalists of the 1848 era normally expressed support for a militia-based model of military obligation, influenced by memories of national mobilization against Napoleon.[45] Most liberal factions in 1848 envisaged constitutions as documents to which soldiers would swear loyalty, so that military duties would be discharged as expressions of constitutional affiliations. In the Frankfurt region, 1848 saw the introduction of urban militias in many cities, and soldiers who fought against Prussia swore loyalty to the all-German 1849 constitution.[46] By contrast, a more prerogative vision of military politics became pervasive through the years around 1848, which

[45] See the seminal expression of this in Rotteck (1816), whose influence on the 1848 generation was profound.

[46] Wettengel (2022: 104–7).

demanded that armies should be separated from representative organs and that military service should be imposed as a coercive integration regime. In the 1850 constitution of Prussia, for example, Art. 38 prohibited gatherings of military personnel not directly ordered by a superior, separating the military from all independent political functions. In Prussia, military service was only attached to uneven electoral rights. Different German constitutions written in the period 1848–50 reflected opposing attempts to solve the problem of the *soldat-citoyen*. The *soldat-citoyen* had come to life around 1789 and it had been partly marginalized, or temporarily suppressed, around 1815. But the *soldat-citoyen* became a vital figure again in 1848, and constitutions of this time were defined by constructions of the citizen as a military agent. Progressive factions at this time advocated the military mobilization of citizens as defenders of a constitutional ideal. Reactionary factions advocated the mobilization of citizens as more passive providers of violence.

Overlapping phenomena are perceptible in a different form in the Habsburg monarchy. At one level, Habsburg regions joined the endeavour to create a national, all-German constitutional order in Frankfurt. This necessarily complicated the claim that the new constitution was to be based in German nationhood, as some delegates sent from Habsburg territories to Frankfurt represented regions where the majority of the population did not speak German as a primary language. In parallel to this, however, in 1848–9, a separate constitutional order was created for the Habsburg monarchy in Vienna. This necessarily meant that, as in Prussia, Austrian constitutional designs rivalled the ideals proposed in Frankfurt. After the introduction of an interim constitution in 1848, the constitutional order for the Habsburg monarchy was formalized in an imposed constitution in March 1849. This constitution was mainly designed to limit the effects of revolutionary change, and it was suspended in late 1851. After 1851, a fully constitutional system was not reintroduced until the 1860s, coinciding with war between the Habsburg government and France over parts of Italy. However, the 1849 constitution was an important step in the consolidation of political constitutionalism in areas under Habsburg rule. In the strict sense, this constitution stood at the beginning of a constitutional tradition that was both national and imperial.

Although located in an empire, the 1849 constitution for the Habsburg territories was, in key features, a classical national constitution. The most enduring aspect of the constitution was that, at the societal level, it accelerated policies to clear away remaining local counterweights to monarchical power. Indicatively, this constitution permanently prohibited serfdom (§26) and abolished all noble courts (§100). In parts of the empire where feudal relations had survived, provisions to end serfdom were supported by the indemnification of landowners. Clearly reflected in this process, further, was the principle that a constitution must create a focus of political attachment for citizens, separate from regional obligations, and the constitutional organization of loyalty must intensify the willingness of citizens to provide military support for the state. The constitution declared that the military was subject to civil control (§113–115); this part of the constitution dictated that soldiers should swear loyalty to the constitution (§118). In conjunction, the constitution provided for the introduction of conscription and the creation of civil militias (§116, 119). These innovations acquired great symbolic importance in Vienna, as 1848 marked the beginning of the end of the Viennese interstate order. Ideas of European public law promoted in Vienna in 1815 still retained force after 1848, notably in norms regarding the laws of war and military occupation set out in the Brussels Declaration (1874) and later in the Hague Conventions. Yet the creation of a constitution for a Habsburg imperial nation meant that many underlying principles expressed in Vienna in 1815 lost force. In this context, the 1849 constitution implicitly indicated that the international pathway towards the stabilization of European states, charted in 1815, had been abandoned. The constitution was designed to secure the Habsburg empire in the form of a trans-regional nation, whose members, of all ethnicities, were bound together under constitutional law, with shared military duties. At the same time, however, the 1849 constitution was evidently an imperial constitution. One of its purposes was to hold together the Habsburg polity in the face of national separatism, and it was expected to stabilize citizenship at the basic social level in order to persuade different ethnic groups to retain loyalty to the empire. As in the 1770s, constitutional citizenship was enforced both as a source of national obligation and as a fulcrum for preserving a continental empire, so that the division between nation and empire became very slight.

In each setting in 1848–9, in sum, constitutions were created in environments in which interstate war and civil war were not clearly distinct, and they served purposes in which acts of nation-building and acts of empire-building converged. In central dimensions, the constitutional events of 1848 reinforced conditions created by imperialism, and constitutions acquired utility in creating societies with a partly imperial, partly national character.

First, as mentioned, the constitutional ideas expressed in 1848 often replicated norms of citizenship that had first gained purchase through previous processes of colonization. As discussed, principles of equal citizenship had initially been enforced in much of Central Europe through reform policies in the eighteenth century designed to release serfs and to recruit military personnel, and, in so doing, to extend imperial authority. Later, principles of national citizenship had been rearticulated in Napoleonic invasions and in the legal codes the Napoleonic armies left behind. It was in these over-layered contexts that demands for national citizenship, linked to processes of nation state formation, were expressed in 1848–9. Citizenship, originally constructed for imperialist ends, became a force to connect imperial societies in more national form. In these settings, clearly citizenship retained a strong military focus, and it was established to deepen social support for the state and to promote the formation of national armies based in national or semi-national loyalty. The constitutional movements around 1848 reproduced patterns of social administration originally used to create empires, and they embodied forms of citizenship pioneered in empires.

Second, the ideas of citizenship expressed in 1848 had long-term results for the organization of military violence in different social settings. Owing partly to their impact on the post-1815 interstate order, the 1848 revolutions marked the beginning of a long process of remilitarization in Europe. This was already clear in the military provisions of some constitutions written at this time. However, this became clearer in policies adopted after 1849. In the wake of 1848, many states began to promote widening conscription, and they relied on conscription to solidify national affiliations. In many societies, this was caused by the fact that the invigoration of nationalism in 1848 had incendiary results for relations between population groups in imperial societies, which in turn created antagonisms between empires. The Habsburg Empire experienced war in Italy, with French involvement, in the 1850s. Russia experienced disastrous war in Crimea in the 1850s, and the Ottoman Empire entered multiple military conflicts after 1850. In each context, war involved both external hostility and internal intergroup conflicts concerning ethnic or national membership, containing some element of civil war and some element of ethnic partitioning.[47] At this time, national constitutions assumed importance as they helped

[47] See discussion in Chapter 5.

states vertically to manage interstate tensions and to recruit soldiers for international or inter-imperial conflicts. However, constitutions were also turned inwards, and they were deployed to increase unity within national societies as a precondition for external military stability. Generally, 1848 was the moment in which the thread between domestic politics and international politics was retied. Of course, after 1848, military conflicts in Europe did not reach the same dimensions as after 1789 until circa 1912. Yet from 1848, constitutions were deployed as part of a strategic military calculus and they were used to balance both the external and the internal dimensions of national political systems in environments shaped by interstate tensions. In this context, constitutions were increasingly defined as instruments to structure domestic societies in a form likely to placate or repress lateral tensions between different domestic groups, so that nationalist and imperialist imperatives were densely interconnected in constitutional law. In some cases, as discussed below, constitutions were used to support internal colonization and external expansion at the same time, and management of internal conflicts formed a springboard for external incorporation. This dual function was the long-term, almost inevitable outcome of the French Revolution of 1789, which the Congress of Vienna had tried to suppress. However, whereas the anti-revolutionary reaction in 1815 involved a restriction of constitutionalism per se, the aftermath of 1848 was marked by the fact that governments appraised the military functions of constitutions more positively and they designed constitutions as mechanisms for creating imperial nations. Such constitutions were typically *post-imperial*, as they linked state institutions to national patterns of legitimation, but they did this for partly imperialist ends.

NATIONAL UNIFICATION OR NATIONAL COLONIZATION?

The elaboration of a system of national-imperial constitutionalism was a striking feature of the period starting around 1860. The years from circa 1850 to 1890 marked a deep caesura in interstate politics at the beginning of the era of high imperialism. This period saw the commencement of large-scale European expansion in Asia and Africa and witnessed intensified rivalry between empires in Europe, mainly caused by the incipient collapse of the Ottoman Empire. This was also the period in which constitutional rule became an international norm in Europe and beyond. During this time, most European states adopted constitutions and the constitutional impetus to democratic inclusion gained impetus. Some states moved towards universal male suffrage, albeit in constitutional frameworks that placed strict limits on legislative powers. For example, France, Switzerland, Greece, Spain, Bulgaria and Germany had reached or come close to universal male suffrage by approximately 1890. Most other states were conducting reforms to enlarge their electoral franchises. Typically, however, these conjoined processes of constitution making and increased democratization had a strategic emphasis. At this time, constitutional citizenship was modelled as the legal form through which states managed their reactions to imperialism. Indeed, many states used constitutions to promote national integration in order to extract military capacities required for empire-building, so that constitutions served as national and imperial documents simultaneously.

As discussed in Chapter 5, military citizenship formation acquired striking expression in the Ottoman sphere of influence.[48] The first Ottoman constitution of 1876 was introduced in response to military pressures. Post-Ottoman states in Greece, Serbia and Bulgaria developed constitutions on a parallel track. In Russia, the debacle in Crimea led to the introduction of reform policies which, although they did not create a full constitution, instilled basic norms of citizenship in Russian society. During the war, which concentrated more military violence in Russian territory than any previous war, military recruitment efforts had been patchy and calls to arms had been met with protest.[49] After this, the tsarist government reformulated its approach to its subjects, imposing a new system of military individualism on society. Post-1856 reforms created local assemblies for political representation, and they brought the abolition of serfdom, which occurred in 1861 in most Russian-governed territories. These measures established an informal constitutional order for rural society in Russia, attaching village communities more closely to the state. These policies were supported by far-reaching education reforms in 1864. Moreover, these reforms resulted in laws that increased conscription, so that, by the mid-1870s, Russia had extensive obligatory military service. Conscription was most robustly imposed on recently released serfs, who lacked the means to evade recruitment. In regions where Russian speakers were not the dominant group, the abolition of serfdom was strategically enforced

[48] See pp. 274–9.
[49] Kozelsky (2019: 118–9).

to create a stronger social foundation for imperial rule.[50] This internal concentration coincided with acts of colonization in Central Asia and mobilization against the Ottoman Empire.

Complex expression was given to this militarized fusion of imperialism and constitutionalism in Germany. By the 1860s, the impulse towards national unification in Germany had assumed a strong imperialist texture and German nation-building became almost indistinguishable from Prussian colonialism. Earlier patterns of Prussian expansion in Silesia (from the 1740s) and Poland (1772–95, after 1815) provided precedents for the eventual process of all-German unification, and the national reconfiguration of Germany, starting in 1864, reflected continuities with earlier colonization programmes.[51] The post-1848 path towards national unity was directed through war, and war became the galvanizing element for German citizenship. Through the 1860s, the Prussian government established modern Germany through a sequence of wars ordained by Bismarck – first with Denmark (1864), second with Austria (1866), third with France (1870–1). Through these wars, frontiers between separate German states were erased to incorporate all German regions in the same state under Prussian leadership. The Austro-Prussian War was a war between two core states in the Congress system of 1815, which had formed a joint army after 1815; Prussia dissolved the German Confederation in 1866. The final point in German unification was achieved as Prussia defeated France in the Franco-Prussian war. In the Prussian army mobilized against France in 1870, many soldiers were recruited or conscripted in German states outside Prussia, and Prussian soldiers fought alongside regiments from other German states, some of whom had been defeated in war by Prussia in the Austro-Prussian war only a few years earlier. This meant that many Saxons and Bavarians became German soldiers before they became German citizens. In each point, the integration of new regions in the German nation state occurred through multifocal violence, partly as nation-building, partly as colonization and partly as the outcome of civil hostilities.

German nation formation was consolidated, not only by military violence, but in acts of constitution making in which constitutional law served as an instrument for managing civil opposition and tying diverse social groups to the national imperial state. Through the different

[50] See p. 187.
[51] Others have noted that the invasion of Silesia initiated the unification process later completed by Bismarck (Bein 1994: 56).

stages of German unification, constitutional laws were created, redrafted and expanded, so that, as regions were integrated in the German polity by military actions, their inhabitants were subject simultaneously to a system of constitutional law. At the end of the Austro-Prussian war (1866), Bismarck drafted a constitution for the states already attached to Prussia, and this constitution granted extensive electoral rights to male citizens so that citizenship enabled political participation. In this system, as discussed in Chapter 3, the potential unpredictability of elections was always mitigated by the fact that the elected legislature had limited authority, so political rights were exercised in a condition of managed participation. This constitution, in slightly revised form, became the basis for the unified German polity in 1871. Both these constitutions contained conscription laws (Arts 57, 59) so that Germans acquired citizenship rights and formal political roles as they were subject to military duties. For many German men, unification involved the performance of military service towards a government clearly perceived as an invading empire in which citizenship, colonization and military coercion were not separable. Hostility towards Prussia in the German army remained a strong force until 1918, and the ability of the army to reconcile pre-national hostilities was limited.

A parallel, converse process can be observed in Vienna. After military defeats against France in 1859 and in the Austro-Prussian war in 1866, the Habsburg government conducted extensive constitutional reform. The period 1860–1 marked the beginning of a fresh line of constitution making, and 1867 saw the introduction of a liberal constitution granting certain formal rights to citizens and establishing an independent legislature. As in Prussia, this involved the construction of a citizenship regime in which manifest political results of citizenship were curtailed, as representation was initially based in a limited franchise with curial elections. In 1867, constitutional measures granted autonomy to Hungary and partial autonomy to other Habsburg regions, established through the *Ausgleich*. Arguably, this settlement marked the first construction of Austria itself as a national polity within the Habsburg Empire. These constitutional acts had a strong military focus, envisioning the imposition of military service. The *Ausgleich* was introduced in a context of deepening interstate militarization such that procedures for semi-federal devolution were designed to facilitate conscription in different parts of the empire. In 1868, conscription laws were introduced for most male citizens in Austria and Hungary. In subsequent decades, the expansion of electoral rights – which culminated in the granting of universal male suffrage to residents of the Austrian part of the Habsburg Empire in 1907 – was accompanied by deepening conscription. The classic constitutional balance between political rights and military service was rearticulated in this case through a process of de facto federalization, granting rights both to citizens and to regions in return for military quotas.[52] As Germany pursued a policy of constitutional centralization to mobilize troops, Austria, in part, pursued a reverse policy in which regional devolution was utilized to secure military recruitment and capacity. In this process, military integration was only partly successful, and conscription raised adverse reactions in many regions, so that recruitment yields were uneven.[53] By 1900, the government in Vienna began to promote separate military units in sub-imperial regions, which, as discussed in Chapter 3, eventually undermined the structure of the empire, creating a military foundation for new nation states.

By the 1870s, both Austria and Germany had formed hybrid polities containing aspects of imperial order and of national statehood. The wars through which they assumed their modern form were partly imperial wars, partly nation-building wars and partly civil wars. In each case, constitutions played a central role in managing complex relations of violence and they simultaneously served nation-building and empire-building ends.

Similar patterns of nation-building occurred in Italy. The integration of different parts of Italy in a unified governmental order moved towards completion through military conflicts in the 1860s. This process depended, on one hand, on anti-imperial war, as regions taken from the Habsburg Empire were incorporated into the emerging nation state. This process entailed experiences of informal military mobilization as, in some conflicts, partisan units supplemented regular armies. This process also depended on brutal intra-societal colonization, fusing civil war, international war and imperial coercion, as the Piedmontese army was deployed to suppress opposition to Italian nation-building (or imperialism), especially in the southern regions. Through the progressive unification of Italy, Piedmontese constitutional law was imposed on territories absorbed in the emerging nation state. This initially resulted in a system of restricted citizenship as few men were allowed to vote in

[52] See Pijaj (2003: 57).
[53] Hämmerle (2022: 20).

post-unification Italy. At the same time, from 1863, conscription laws already enforced in Sardinia were extended to Italians in other regions.[54] Obligations to the new government were imposed by armies, as persons finding themselves inside the changing geographical boundaries of the polity were immediately subject to military duties.[55] As in Germany, national citizenship was formed as a military condition, and, by 1875, Italy had universal conscription. Further, Italy developed on a pathway that combined national integration and external expansion. Italy established colonies in (formerly Ottoman) Eritrea between 1869 and 1882, where Italian forces recruited indigenous armies. Italy thus acquired imperial features before national unification was fully realized. After 1900, new laws brought deepening conscription (1907). This was followed by military intervention in Ottoman Libya (1911) and increased male enfranchisement (1912). Post-1870 Italy was persistently affected by the belief that the nation state had been incompletely unified as substantial Italian minorities remained under Habsburg rule.

The lines of citizenship formation in other major European countries were less clearly connected to national-imperial consolidation. However, the use of constitutions for national military unification was a common factor in most states. The foundation of the Third Republic in France (1870–1), following traumatic defeat and invasion by Prussia, occurred in a context in which the population had mobilized for war, in some cases through *levée en masse*. The republic was consolidated through the passing of new constitutional laws (1875), through the exercise of universal male suffrage in free elections (1871) and through the implementation of military reforms, including extended conscription (1872). Importantly, although the Third Republic was formed by war and occupation, it was consolidated through civil war and domestic military force. The governmental order of the Third Republic was stabilized progressively after the regular army had liquidated the Paris Commune in 1871, in which dissident officers of the Garde Nationale had established a radical republican government in the French capital. Some soldiers killed in the Commune were the same soldiers who months previously had mobilized spontaneously to liberate

[54] On one view, the unification of Italy was a civil war that prompted loathing for conscription – 11 per cent of recruits did not present for service (Rovinello 2020: 82–84). This account also stresses that, in principle, conscription determined who was and who was not an Italian citizen (123).

[55] One analysis explains how, after 1861, conscription led many Italian peasants to 'flee to the mountains' (Dal Lago 2018: 236). This same account describes how southern Italy was essentially placed under military rule during 'unification' (82).

the French nation from Prussian armies. This event demonstrated that the republic had its primary support in the regular army. The introduction of military service in 1872 was designed to incorporate citizens in the military in orderly fashion and to avoid unpredictable patterns of recruitment and mobilization; it followed the dissolution of the Garde Nationale.[56] Within a decade, the military played a leading role in advancing renewed imperial policies in France. Further, France came close to military coup in 1889. In Great Britain, the age of high imperialism did not see the introduction of conscription. However, the causal connection between political citizenship and imperialism was clearly visible in Britain. The acceleration of British expansion overseas, including the formation of the Raj (1858) and the invasion of Egypt (1882), were flanked by electoral reforms (1876 and 1884), which greatly increased male enfranchisement.

CITIZENSHIP TRANSFORMED

In each case, constitutional law after 1848 created states ambiguously positioned between nations and empires. At this time, only the British constitution was a strictly imperial constitution. Other constitutions with imperial functions, such as those in Germany and Austria, were constitutions of nationalizing empires or of imperial nations. They created a premise for government that combined nationalism and imperialism, adapting nationalism to serve imperialist objectives and vice versa. The constitution of France was the constitution of a colonizing republic. In each case, further, constitutional law promoted a new model of political integration which gave elevated expression to military aspects in citizenship formation. By the 1870s, European states became fundamentally reliant on constitutional modes of engaging with citizens, and few states did not have constitutions with strong representative elements. By this time, most European constitutions were created in environments marked by warfare or the threat of warfare, in which imperial war and civil war interacted fluidly. The period from 1870 to 1900 is frequently described as an era of prolonged European peace.[57] However, this was a period of rapid military expansion outside Europe. It was also one in which most states

[56] One observer has explained how the army acquired its socializing role in a space defined both by military defeat and by the revolutionary legacy of the Commune, and it assimilated young French men to address both internal and external risks (Roynette 2000: 23–24).

[57] Blainey (1988: 4).

adapted their constitutions to military exigencies, and it initiated long-term increases in military and military-related spending.[58] In fact, as they acquired constitutions, most states transposed military directives into all parts of public policy and much legislation was designed, directly or indirectly, to prepare societies for war. For example, many states began new infrastructural projects funding the building of roads and railways. These projects reflected military strategies as enhanced communication networks enabled the rapid mobilization of troops and industrial goods for military purposes.[59]

After circa 1860, the widening of constitutional law in much of Europe also had important political results. As their military utility became more palpable, constitutions became parts of a complex societal bargaining system (a security constitution) in many nations, and this system brought non-trivial benefits to the citizens integrated in it. By the late nineteenth century, subjects on the inside of imperial polities were almost invariably linked to government by increased legal protections, by some electoral rights and even by some material or economic rights. To this degree, militarism drove a hard constitutional bargain in many national societies, and external security threats brought clear increases in political enfranchisement and social protection after the 1860s. However, in these processes, the prominence of military pressures in shaping constitutional imperatives instilled strong strategic functions in national citizenship regimes, and constitutions that evolved at this point trended to follow a common instrumental model. Discernibly, constitutions of this period established sets of rights that enabled governments to integrate citizens in the vertical dimension so that citizens were subject to strong political duties, often of a military nature. Yet these constitutions were designed to avert, or at least to control, unpredictable expressions of lateral violence often resulting from vertical integration and mass inclusion. In other words, at this time, states gradually created constitutions to pursue democratic integration as part of a measured bargain. Constitutions were established that allowed governments to increase the integration of citizens

[58] Michael Mann (2012: 375) explains how the second part of the nineteenth century was a time in which the proportion of public spending devoted to 'civil expenses' expanded rapidly, easily eclipsing military spending in many states. This analysis is surely accurate, but it does not acknowledge how civil expenses (especially on education, social insurance and transport) were attached to military causes. It also does not consider the fact that, in states such as Germany, Britain, Spain and Austria, civil government had a military component.

[59] Military functions of railways were described in early analysis by Pönitz (1842: 110). These functions were recognized in the German constitution of 1849 (§28–29).

to preserve their sovereignty in their external interactions, and constitutional rights were protected to the degree that they secured military violence. But, in parallel, constitutions were encased in sociopolitical structures that prevented the popular exercise of such rights in a form likely to generate uncontrollable or systemically unsettling violence in society. In many cases, this meant that governments subjected their populations to robust executive control. From the 1860s, constitutions were increasingly devised as documents that augmented the military capacities of national states: they promoted vertical militarization. However, they also contained or were accompanied by mechanisms to mollify lateral hostilities or militarization, and they were enforced to insulate societies against the tendency of constitutional bargains to stimulate extreme violence in the horizontal dimension of societal interaction.

These functions became apparent, first, in the conditions under which constitutions granted political rights. By the 1860s, constitutions typically allocated electoral rights to citizens in a form that was easy to manage and that diminished the institutional risks mass enfranchisement caused. This can be seen – paradigmatically – in the constitutions created in the 1860s and 1870s, which established rights of citizenship for soldiers but positioned citizens in electoral regimes that limited their political influence. This was usually achieved through the construction of weak legislatures, in which powers of elected assemblies were balanced by powerful second chambers or executives, but it was sometimes achieved by simple franchise restrictions. Most constitutions that established large franchises created systems of representation that preponderately favoured executive organs, so that the rise of democracy also saw the growth of executive authority.[60] Through such devices, constitutions created legitimacy for government through some exercise of popular sovereignty. However, they controlled the procedures in which popular sovereignty was exercised, to avert lateral militarism or civil war.

These functions became visible, second, in the fact that, in most European societies, early constitutions coincided not only with the military organization of society and the consolidation of electoral rights, but with policies to increase public spending on social welfare, including public education. In the late nineteenth century, many states

[60] Examples of this in Spain and Germany are discussed in Chapter 3, but Bulgaria and Serbia can be added to this list.

began to invest in the promotion of welfare rights, and, as they allocated political rights to citizens, they established a broad social constitution, in which the legal-political constitution of state was embedded in a set of early (still very rudimentary) provisions for material welfare. This tended to weaken parallel dependencies in society, and it meant that the state displaced other welfare dispensers such as families and religious institutions. As a result, citizens experienced no negligible improvements in their material circumstances, and some protection for material well-being was a vital outcome of basic constitutional bargains. Yet the construction of welfare rights also served strategic military ends and played a central role in allowing governments to manage military capacity.

To illustrate this, most European states implemented education reforms as part of the process in which they developed political constitutions, and, in so doing, they extended educational rights to large numbers of citizens. However, such reforms were integrally linked to the need to increase military capacity, and they facilitated the imposition of military duties. This linkage between education of military integration was already apparent in the eighteenth century. For instance, Prussia introduced a nominal obligation for children to attend school in 1717, coinciding with early conscription laws. In Vienna, school attendance became obligatory in 1774, at the same time as military service was extended. In Sweden, the decades beginning after 1815 saw extensive education reforms, flanked, unusually for this period, by deepening military conscription. In Prussia, as discussed, governmental penetration in social life increased after 1814, largely owing to conscription, and this period saw the implementation of national education reforms. In fact, far-reaching education reforms began soon after the Prussian military collapse in 1806, and they were not fully separate from military innovations. After 1848, however, this linkage between education and militarism was strengthened and the influence of plans for raising military capacity on education reforms became explicit. At an immediate level, some education reforms were simply designed to improve the quality of soldiers. For example, Austria's defeat by Prussia in 1866 was publicly blamed on low literacy levels and poor cognitive adaptability amongst soldiers.[61] This defeat led, not only to a new constitution and new conscription laws, but to

[61] See Grawe (2020: 149). Grawe also explains that, in the reform legislation of 1869, even the ordering of lessons was shaped by military imperatives (156).

substantial school reforms. In France, education reforms were introduced in 1881, after the government had endorsed universal male suffrage, and as it recommenced imperial expansion; Tunisia became a French protectorate in 1881. In 1882, legislation was introduced to establish secular principles for French education. The Russian education system was also reconstructed after the Crimean War. Parallel processes in the Ottoman Empire are discussed in Chapter 5. In such examples, education reforms were often designed to inculcate national consciousness into populations, and their purpose was, in part, to establish social mentalities favourable to military service. As education became a national obligation, the content of national school curricula was increasingly shaped by nationalist imagery, and one function of education was to transmit nationalistic beliefs and pro-imperial convictions. In many societies, education reforms introduced some elements of physical education or military training in schools.

In parallel, after circa 1870, most constitutional states slowly promoted the expansion of healthcare policies and industrial insurance schemes. These measures also coincided with military recruitment laws, and they were aligned to military imperatives. On one hand, such laws were partly intended to reduce the number of conscripts not fit for service. In some states, welfare laws and protective measures for child workers were justified by the need to increase the number of high-quality recruits.[62] At the same time, such laws were designed to generate social rights for citizens in order to encourage them to accept national military commitments. By consequence, early welfare states formed central components in a system of military motivation and mobilization. Security researchers have often argued that the provision of economic protection for individual citizens is a relatively new tactic for intensifying military security.[63] However, from the outset, European welfare systems formed part of a social arrangement for organizing national security. As one striking example, in Austria, legislation of 1867 created the legal basis for a voluntary social insurance system, established in 1868.[64] As mentioned, 1868 was the year in which universal conscription was imposed. Similarly, Bismarck initiated social policies in Germany in 1881, and they were completed in 1889. Key

[62] For example, laws in Prussia (1839) to regulate child labour in factories are often attributed to concerns about military capacity. The fact that Germany had high levels of conscription meant that, by 1914, Germans had access to 'a fairly progressive set of labor protection laws' (Dörr, Grawe and Obinger 2020: 50).

[63] Buzan (1991: 234–5); Neocleous (2006: 364).

[64] This was the Allgemeine Arbeiter-Kranken- und Invalidenkasse, founded in Vienna in 1868.

elements in these policies, namely an insurance scheme to cover illness (1883) and a scheme covering invalidity caused by accidents, coincided with early policies endorsing foreign military expansion (1884). More progressive labour legislation was introduced in Germany in 1891, giving greater protection to workers, and this coincided with a formal commitment to imperial enlargement as a policy objective.[65] In France, the first legal protections for trade unions (1884) followed the approval of colonial budgets to support military expansion. In each case, the acceptance of social security policies occurred as national societies were exposed to rising pressures in the organization of military security. Early building blocks of the welfare state were laid in the UK from 1906 as military rivalry with Germany intensified. By 1900, in fact, some European governments were willing to risk alienating their own aristocracies by introducing land and inheritance taxes, which funded both increased military capacity and increased welfare investment. Both Britain and Germany suffered inter-class conflicts over inheritance tax in the decade after 1900, which at times made government unworkable. In Britain, this conflict led to a major democratizing reform as the impasse created by the House of Lords over taxation meant that its legislative powers were reduced in 1911.[66]

Third, the instrumental functions of constitutions in democracy from the 1860s were also displayed, in different contexts, by the elaboration of exclusionary models of citizenship, in which citizens not easily harnessed to military programmes became objects of vilification. As mentioned, the widening of constitutional law after 1848 was an occurrence in which constitutional law was redesigned as a structure for managing social violence: it formed a system for selective inclusion, offering incentives to citizens for the provision of military force, and controlling potential parties in civil war. Through this transformation, some states supported by ideals of citizenship began to impose military conditions on their own societies, especially where they identified some groups as marginal to sanctioned legitimation processes. At this time, many societies witnessed the emergence of two-level constitutional regimes in which some sectors were ostracized from full citizenship, so that provisions for increased inclusion coexisted with mechanisms for harsh exclusion.

65 One important analysis explains that imperialist ideology in Germany partly served to distract from support for social rights (Berlepsch 1984: 79).

66 Hew Strachan (2004: 64) links this conflict to war financing. Others see it as caused by increased welfare spending.

To give examples of this, from the 1860s, some European polities expanded general rights of citizenship while withholding full access to citizenship from designated ethnic groups. As discussed, for instance, unified Germany was based in extensive political enfranchisement from 1871. However, definitions of citizenship were promoted in the years after unification that limited the rights accorded to groups deviating from typical social profiles. The unification of Germany was solidified, at once, by deeply inclusive and by deeply exclusive concepts of citizenship. By the 1880s, hostility towards minority citizenship groups was focused on Poles and Roman Catholics, but it also included Jewish citizens. Waves of anti-Polish legislation were introduced from the 1870s and 1880s and then, yet more stringently, after 1900, reducing linguistic and religious freedoms for Poles. The year 1886 saw the creation of the Colonization Commission to promote German settlement in incorporated Polish regions.[67] Importantly, such policies were closely linked to military service. Conscription in Prussia was originally utilized as a method of strategic Germanization for Poles. By 1905, however, non-German soldiers received differential treatment in the army and the military reduced its integrational function.[68] In France, the promotion of military citizenship provoked strong exclusionary sensibilities concerning religious minorities, which became manifest in the major scandal of the Third Republic, the Dreyfus affair. Turkey formed an extreme case in this regard, as conscription brought visibility to ethnic differences, and religious groups deemed unreliable conscripts were at times exposed to extreme military violence.[69] In each instance, the military acted as the primary organ of integration, yet it also imposed status variations on different groups perceived as possessing dubious military loyalty.

Equally importantly, citizenship regimes established after the 1860s promoted exclusion for reasons associated with individual social status. As mentioned, most political systems created at this time began – very tentatively – to guarantee general electoral rights and welfare provisions for disadvantaged sectors of society. However, the allocation of constitutional rights to citizens was subject to strict limits, and it took place within the terms of an implied military bargain. Groups

[67] See on this process Trzeciakowski (1973: 193–197), Kozłowski (2004: 2000) and Volkmann (2016: 82, 132).

[68] One account explains how, from 1905, Polish recruits in the German army were marked with a 'P' and recruited to garrisons outside their home regions (Boysen 2008: 50–51).

[69] See p. 285.

of citizens that destabilized national integration functions were frequently marginalized from this process. Access to full citizenship was finely controlled for social sectors whose military utility was limited.

This is illustrated, most clearly, by the fact that many polities of the later nineteenth century checked political integration by establishing limited electoral franchises, so that many citizens were excluded from full citizenship on grounds of socio-economic position. In many cases, the depth of electoral enfranchisement was immediately contingent on the value of citizens as military actors. For example, Great Britain had a very restricted electoral franchise during the period of high imperialism. As late as 1918, working-class British men had curtailed political representation. This reflects a specific paradox in British constitutional history. By 1900, Great Britain had by far the largest empire in the world, but, by 1914, it had significantly lower enfranchisement than imperial states such as Germany, Austria–Hungary and France. A significant cause of this is that Britain had no immediate borders with hostile imperial powers, and the need to conscript soldiers for territorial defence was less pressing than in other states. In addition, British armies in colonial regions were largely enlisted from colonized populations, and colonial troops could be deployed in different colonies, so that full mobilization in Britain was not required. British defence was also based in naval power, which necessitated lower recruitment levels amongst the domestic population. Together, these factors meant that governmental dependence on the population was low. It is frequently claimed that, owing to the lack of an immediate military adversary, Britain developed on a relatively liberal or democratic pathway.[70] Strictly speaking, however, the opposite is true, as the absence of direct adversity was expressed in low military recruitment and low enfranchisement in Britain. Electoral inclusion in Britain progressed cautiously, and *full* male enfranchisement was not reached until 1918, following wartime conscription laws in 1916. In fact, *full and equal* male enfranchisement was not reached until 1950. This also had implications for social stratification, as the British aristocracy retained powerful social and political positions for longer than in other states. In Italy, working-class participation in elections was also low until 1912, and it increased as Italy began large-scale overseas expansion. Countries with deep working-class enfranchisement before 1914 usually fell into one of two categories. Typically, these states were smaller

[70] Hintze (1962: 52–83).

countries, such as Bulgaria, Serbia, Switzerland, Greece, and Norway, in which assimilation of different class memberships was usually facilitated by an integrational structure based in religion, cultural homogeneity or proximity to a large external empire. In other cases, such states were empires with large vulnerable external borders, such as Germany and France.

Those major states that accepted large-scale working-class enfranchisement before 1914 usually reacted to their complex internal structure through the violent exclusion of dissident groups. In France, as mentioned, full male citizenship, entailing the general exercise of voting rights in free elections, was consolidated in 1871. However, the openings for radical class-determined mobilization in France were curtailed by the memory of the Paris Commune. In effect, the Third Republic was founded through the mass murder of the political left, which enduringly weakened anti-systemic mobilization. Indicatively, political parties lacked full legal status in France until 1901. Although France was a republic, the government spent less on welfare than Germany or Britain before 1900.[71] In Germany, the integration of the political left was particularly challenging to the process of nation-building and citizenship formation. From 1867 onwards, as mentioned, the emergent national government in Germany allowed full enfranchisement for male citizens, at least for those aged twenty-five or above. Moreover, these citizens were soon organized in a large radical party, the Social Democratic Party (SPD), forming much the most important organization of the European labour movement. In this setting, conservative groups in Germany were strongly mobilized against the SPD and derided its members as insufficiently committed to German nationalism and military effort. The SPD was partly outlawed in 1878. After its renewed legalization, the German government promoted imperialist policies to unify all anti-socialist groups in parliament (*Sammlungspolitik*), so that external expansion was deployed to reinforce the domestic marginalization of organized labour.[72] By 1917, the SPD had split into two parties. One party had a strong anti-imperialist, anti-militarist emphasis. The other party endorsed policies that connected effective domestic integration of the workforce to successful military expansion, and it accepted warfare as a path to full political inclusion of the working class. The model of the

[71] See brilliant inquiry into reasons for reduced social spending in France in Weber (2010: 52). This analysis does not assess military causes of lower welfare spending in France.

[72] See Altrichter (1977: 191–2).

working-class citizen was here divided into two rival dispositions, both reflecting a different approach to imperialism.

What appears through these processes is that the extension of constitutional democracy in the period of high imperialism reflected a convergence between external and internal policymaking. Imperialism formed one part of a dynamic that promoted social integration in European polities. It generated constitutional systems based in complex social bargaining, bringing significant benefits for many persons on the inner, domestic/metropolitan side of imperial political systems. In such processes, constitutional designs were put in place to reduce generalized violence in domestic integration processes. In most cases, however, citizenship regimes arising from imperialism were limited, and they were at least partly designed to structure society for military ends. The constitutional inclusion of citizens formed a dialectical occurrence in which national governments used constitutional law both to gain military recruits and to control resultant social militarization. To manage lateral conflict, governments established provisions that softened material hardship amongst electors. But they also imposed conditions of low-level civil war on their populations, or on some parts of their populations. Many societies in the later nineteenth century were marked by deep fissures between social groups, and most states imposed formal or informal segregation on their own societies. This can be seen in the legislative actions of national governments. Until roughly 1900, most European states enforced discriminatory labour laws, which prevented effective exercise of citizenship by national labour movements. This can also be seen in the military functions of governments. Through the later nineteenth century, national armies often assumed domestic policing roles, and military organizations played a key part in domestic securitization. This was pronounced in France, which was substantially more democratic than other major states. Legislation of 1878 in France set out conditions in which a state of siege could be declared, allowing internal mobilization of the army. Many European constitutions contained powerful emergency clauses, which allowed governments to suspend constitutional guarantees deploy to suppress civil unrest.[73] In most constitutions, the inclusion of populations for external conflict meant that governments imposed managed citizenship regimes at the domestic level, such that some convergence existed between external and internal use of military force.

[73] See Art. 17 of the Spanish constitution of 1876, and Art. 68 of the 1871 constitution of Germany.

IMPERIAL SYSTEMS INSIDE AND OUTSIDE

By circa 1880, in sum, most European polities had begun to exploit the military attributes of constitutions to intensify their military capacities, in the system of inter-imperial competition. In most states, this calculus was effective in territorial terms, and the inner (national) solidification of citizenship usually led to outward (imperial) military expansion. As discussed below, this can be seen in the actions of smaller states, such as Serbia, Greece, Bulgaria and Romania, whose constitutional formation brought significant territorial enlargement. However, this was clearest in the actions of larger states. To illustrate this, as mentioned, Germany initiated a colonial programme in the 1880s, only fourteen years after its unification under a national constitution. Under the constitution of the Third Republic, France embarked on extensive overseas expansion after circa 1881, forming – in effect – a republican empire. This occurred in a period of persistent internal instability. However, the constitutional mechanisms supporting republican government generated a fiscal basis for French expansion and prominent constitutionalists passionately advocated colonial policy. The leading republican in the early Third Republic, Jules Ferry, was, from the early 1880s, a committed expansionist who celebrated the 'genius of the colonizer' in French imperial enlargement.[74] This fusion of military defeat, civil violence and constitutional redirection in 1870 created a formidable impetus for empire-building in France. Early constructions of citizenship in Russia took root during a period of accelerated expansion, as parts of Central Asia were colonized in the 1860s and 1870s. This brought increased rivalry between Russia and Britain, as imperial administrators in Britain feared Russian incursion in India. As mentioned, electoral reforms in the 1860s and 1880s in Great Britain coincided with the rapid increase in the number of territories subject to Britain.

In these processes, integration strategies inside colonizing societies differed qualitatively from the administrative techniques used by imperial governments towards subjects in colonized regions, especially in those separated by blue water from metropolitan heartlands. Importantly, societies in different parts of imperial systems were divided by the fact that, in most cases, members of societies subject to external colonization were not exposed to mandatory conscription, and, as a result, the bargaining structures that allowed metropolitan subjects

[74] Ferry (1982: 8). Ferry's conversion to imperial enthusiast is dated to 1881 (Ganiage 1968: 21).

to obtain constitutional rights were weak. Before and after 1914, armies in colonized regions did not – typically – conscript soldiers, and they mainly employed military personnel as professionals or mercenaries.[75] This meant that the integrational arrangements derived from the extraction of military force on the inside of imperial polities were not strongly developed in non-metropolitan imperial regions. Where imperial armies depended on involuntary labour in colonies, this dependency was normally not broad enough to create a constitutional bargaining position for suppliers of military force.[76] In some environments, indicatively, the citizenship status of external inhabitants of European empires improved slightly before and after World War I, as imperial subjects became useful as potential recruits for the war. In the French Empire, Algerian men were subject to extensive recruitment and localized conscription after 1914, at times fighting against fellow Muslims in the Ottoman region, and this led to the passing of the Jonnart Law (1919). This law partly enfranchised Algerian men, although it fell short of promises of citizenship offered to soldiers in the war. In other colonies, notably Senegal, campaigns for enhanced citizenship were based on demands for recognition for military sacrifice, as conscription was introduced in some French colonies in West Africa after 1914.[77] In the British Empire, 1919 saw the enfranchisement of soldiers who had served in the army in World War I in some colonial regions – notably in the Punjab, which had provided a high number of recruits.[78] In such cases, patterns of integration in colonies converged, to a partial degree, with those in metropolitan regions. Generally, however, material imbalances between the inside and the outside of imperial systems meant that, in colonized regions, military force could be procured in a form that did not necessitate the granting of political rights.

Both before and after 1914, therefore, the administration of colonies was conducted in much more violent fashion than administration in societies where colonizing states were centred. In fact, the day-to-day control of colonies was often entrusted to military units, whose role in society was largely coercive. The accelerated wave of European

[75] Major British colonial armies were mercenary armies (Callahan and Marston 2021: 204). French colonial armies were mainly mercenary until 1912, although Ottoman-era conscription laws were retained in Tunisia after 1881. France imposed colonial conscription in other parts of Africa by 1912 and again in 1919.

[76] For related claims, see Koehler-Derrick and Lee (2023: 269).

[77] Thomas (2005: 26–7, 65–73).

[78] See Yong (2005: 258–9).

colonization beginning around 1870 had a strongly militarized nature, and armies usually established the governance regimes in occupied regions. In 1857, the major Indian rebellion against British presence was a military mutiny that was suppressed by the army, and, after the formation of the Raj, the Indian army was frequently portrayed as the 'Sword of the Raj'.[79] The suppression of the uprising led to the dissolution of the East India Company and the direct imposition of British authority in India, in which the British government absorbed the armies maintained by the company. Slightly later, France conquered Indochina by a 'war of pacification', in which regular armies fought against local guerrillas.[80] In such contexts, colonized societies were governed in partly exceptionalist fashion, as imperial institutions often operated outside common rule-of-law provisions and depended on the legally sanctioned use of violence. In Namibia in 1904, the German government suppressed internal Herero uprisings by applying Art. 68 of the national constitution, which was reserved for the state of war. The Code de l'Indigénat, imposed by France in Algeria in 1881, contained aspects of a military code. It created a variable system of colonial jurisdiction according to which non-French residents were at times subject to arbitrary punishments. In addition, opposition to colonial rule in European empires was frequently channelled through irregular military units, whose soldiers were not identifiable by rank, office or uniform, which deeply challenged the powers of colonizing states.[81] In such settings, patterns of informal mobilization amongst colonized populations stimulated interstate war and ethnically rooted civil war. Where colonized subjects undertook military actions to demand independence, colonizing governments launched wars of horrific intensity, anticipating the later exterminatory wars that occurred in the twentieth century.[82] Importantly, colonial populations were not recognized in the European inter-sovereign agreements regarding conduct of warfare, and they fell outside the normal laws of war.[83]

[79] Marston (2014: 43).

[80] See Brocheux and Hémery (2001: 55).

[81] This phenomenon is evident in different empires. On the German Empire, see Pesek (2005: 198), comparing colonial war to civil war; see Zollmann (2010: 56), comparing colonial rule to a police state; see Bley (1968: 314), interpreting colonialism as a precursor of totalitarianism.

[82] The Cuban war of independence can be seen as an example of this, in which Spanish troops killed about 10 per cent of the Cuban population (Stone 2006: 223).

[83] On these points, see Lindner (2011: 190–192). The General Act of the Berlin conference (1884/5), which regulated trade in colonial Africa, only made legal provision for war between colonizing states (Art. 11). It did not recognize colonies as sovereign actors. One leading international lawyer of this period observed that 'the sovereignty of a European state over an

In fact, although World War I improved citizenship norms in some colonial regions, the wider militarization of global society at this time was strongly felt in many colonies. Many historians have observed that colonial repression and police control became more acutely militarized after 1918. This was partly due to wartime use of martial law, and partly to the easy accessibility of arms after World War I. However, it was partly caused by the fact that independence movements became stronger in many colonies as their members had, directly or indirectly, experienced warfare. In many settings, after 1918, colonial rule was often intensified, and it acquired the form of an asymmetrical interracial civil war.[84] For example, as mentioned, Britain recruited many Indians to fight in World War I, and this temporarily formed part of a classical constitutional bargain – the secretary of state for India declared in August 1917 that Britain's objective was to establish institutions to facilitate Indian self-government. However, this did not prevent large-scale use of military violence against India nationalists in Amritsar in 1919. The Rowlatt Act passed in this year gave exceptional powers to the police. This Act was implemented at the same time that the Government of India Act (1919) was passed in Westminster, allowing colonial subjects greater participation in local government.[85] Additional emergency laws were passed in India through the 1920s and 1930s. Such fusion of military and policing powers remained in force even as some colonies became mandate territories after 1918, and colonial administration often became more repressive in the death throes of colonialism, around 1945. As discussed in Chapter 6 below, some convergence of civil and military rule was prevalent in major European colonies after 1945.[86]

In these features, imperial rule in colonized societies was largely imposed as a protracted system of emergency government in which core aspects of citizenship were withheld. This revealed an acute asymmetry between the constitutional bargaining position of citizens inside colonizing societies and that of persons subject to the external enforcement of colonizing authority. In broad terms, empires developed as two-sided integration systems in which subjects on the inside were integrated more fully and less coercively than those on the outside. In

uncivilised region' was not a matter for treaty law, which uncivilised peoples were not qualified to sign; this meant that territories of Africa were subject only to treaties between European states (Westlake 1894: 145).

84 Thomas (2012: 41).

85 Ahmad (1985: 16).

86 See pp. 357–9.

central respects, clearly, the material integration of persons on the inside of imperial systems was causally reliant on the material exclusion of those on the outside of the same system.

Despite this, nonetheless, the military emphasis of constitutional rule within Europe meant that the separation between the internal and the external functions of imperial polities was at times less than absolute. In some respects, the partition between different dimensions of imperial polities was fragile, and, under some circumstances, it could be suspended. In both dimensions, empires operated as political systems defined by violence, and no domain was completely exempted from this characteristic. In some functions, European governments acted towards their own populations in a fashion that reflected their operations in colonized zones, and governments replicated some colonial administrative techniques in their domestic actions. Illustratively, for example, in Germany, the first acquisition of overseas colonies in East Africa (1884–5) fell between the domestic prohibition of the SPD (1878) and the targeted Germanization of Polish regions (1886).[87] After 1870, use of the French army to suppress domestic social unrest became less frequent, partly because of military conscription.[88] As discussed, however, the army had clearly defined itself as the guarantor of public order in 1871, and deployment of troops against industrial protests repeatedly occurred, even after 1900. During the Dreyfus affair, some citizens perceived the army as a hostile internal force which conducted war of attrition against the population.[89] Around 1900, France experienced the development of an anti-militarist brand of syndicalism whose representatives used industrial mobilization to oppose the army. The syndicalists defined their position as actors in a *guerre sociale*, strongly committed to domestic reform and anti-imperialism. Historians have noted that the basic geography of France bore a strong military imprint from the 1870s. From this time, soldiers enlisted under new conscription laws were housed in a growing number of garrisons, which altered provincial environments, and the country was divided into military regions, close to an occupation system, in which military hierarchies penetrated everyday life.[90] In Spain, the years after the loss of Cuba saw increased governmental violence towards marginal social and

87 On connections between nationalism and imperialism in Germany see Walkenhorst (2007: 226). On the confluence of German expansion in Europe and in Africa, see Kienemann (2018: 98).
88 Roynette-Gland (1997: 38).
89 Gohier (1899: v).
90 See illuminating discussions in Doise (1994: 10) and Chanet (2006: 41).

economic groups, often supported by the army. A particularly acute example of military repression, the Tragic Week in July 1909, involved military mobilization against groups protesting against conscription for colonial missions. In each process, military units were used within imperial society to ensure regimented citizenship. As discussed in Chapter 5, by 1908, national and external techniques of military repression in the Ottoman Empire were difficult to disentangle. In these points, citizens on the inside and citizens on the outside of imperial polities were exposed to governments with strong military features. At the most fundamental level, societal spaces on the inside and the outside of imperial systems were connected by the fact that citizenship was based in an instrumental calculus, of an essential military nature. In both domains, citizenship was linked to colonization, and the degree of citizenship allotted to social agents depended – largely – on their utility as providers of violence.

Overall, in the longer wake of 1848, constitutions were widely formed as elements in an imperialist bargaining system. As such, they created acute status disparities between subjects on the inside and subjects on the outside of empires. Most constitutions managed to integrate populations on the inside of this divide, and they brought benefits to them through an implied security contract. Yet some continuity existed between governmental systems in metropolitan states in Europe and the systems installed in the colonies occupied by these states. It became a feature of constitutions that they allowed states to include citizens to obtain external violence, but they also devised violently exclusionary means to monitor the internal effects of this strategy. In both dimensions, government resided in military constructions of citizenship, overarching different parts of imperial polities. In both dimensions, constitutional states developed – in part – as *occupation systems*, whose primary function was to assert territorial control domestically and externally, albeit with much softer coercive functions in the domestic domain. National citizenship always contains elements of colonizing violence, and national society was structurally linked to imperial society.

THE EMULATION OF INSTRUMENTAL CITIZENSHIP

As discussed in Chapter 5, the discovery of the instrumental potentials of constitutional citizenship acquired vital functions in the geographical margins of European imperialism, and constitutions were widely emulated for military purposes in the Ottoman region. However, the link between nationalism and imperialism in constitutional law shaped many societies, and many societies outside Europe reproduced the constitutional designs for violent ends. The most direct resonance of the relation between constitutional law, imperialism and warfare was felt in Japan, where the instrumental essence of constitutional law acquired deep structural force.

By the later nineteenth century, Japan was locked into a global imperial system, and this had a profound impact on its inner institutional structure. This process began in the 1850s as Japan became vulnerable to the threat of foreign invasion. From 1853, American naval personnel demanded access to port facilities in the Japanese mainland, which had previously been closed to foreign traders. Although not strictly acts of imperialism, these developments were backed by threats of military occupation, and, subsequently, the Japanese government was forced to sign commercial treaties with the USA and with European powers, which imposed unfavourable import conditions on Japan. As such, this process involved non-negotiable incursion on Japanese territory by foreign military agents; it also brought foreign arms into Japan and foreign actors established ties with different factions in Japanese society.[91] The opening of Japan then induced a long period of internal conflict between factions with opposed attitudes to foreign intervention.

Up to the 1860s, Japan was subject to the Tokugawa regime in which power was vested in the shogun, supposedly acting in the name of the emperor, who governed indirectly in an acentric order close to European feudalism. In this regime, regional control was exercised by daimyos, who were similar to large magnates, and they discharged some fiscal and military duties towards the emperor. Notionally, the Tokugawa system was intended to maintain national military capacity as daimyos raised armies of samurais which provided trained military forces. However, the Tokugawa system lacked central military resources. Moreover, before the 1850s, Japan had experienced a long period of peace. Many samurai had abandoned their military duties for administrative work, and samurai violence was primarily directed against internal groups. The fact that Japan operated in largely peaceful external environment meant that government was loosely coordinated, and daimyos operated almost like separate governments. Like many

[91] Totman (1980: 215).

premodern states, military mobilization was impeded by the fact that the state did not arm the people because it was afraid of attack by its subjects.[92]

In the first instance, the opening of Japanese ports showed that Japan was not adapted to the increasingly violent external landscape imposed by imperialism, European and American, and its sovereignty was under threat. Accordingly, reforms were initiated to modify the Tokugawa system, focused on transforming the fiscal apparatus and centralizing the administration, with a view to averting colonization and loss of sovereignty.[93] By 1868, the shogunate was replaced by a military coup, restoring direct rule by the Meiji emperor. The restored imperial regime was precariously constructed, but it was based in a commitment to centralization and institutional reform. Importantly, the restoration brought an immediate constitutional pledge, as the restored emperor swore a 'Charter Oath' to integrate different social castes in the political system, to promote educational communication, and to establish 'public discussion' as the basis for government.[94] The government created a national assembly, albeit without an electoral franchise.

In key respects, the Meiji restoration mirrored state-building processes in other settings, as it was intended to transform a diffuse feudal system into a more concentrated national polity. Indeed, like other such processes, it was framed by multiple patterns of warfare involving overlapping external and internal violence. The restoration occurred amidst conflict between reformist samurai and some Tokugawa elites in 1868, and it later met local resistance in the Satsuma Rebellion (1877), close to a samurai Fronde. Military actions to consolidate the restoration were discharged by co-opted military units, as there was no national army. In some respects, these conflicts formed a war of national unification conducted in rapid time. In some respects, they formed a civil war, as they centred around hostilities between traditional and reformist factions. The 1868 restoration reflected a split in the military class; leading actors who supported the restoration were samurai, although samurai factions were also primary opponents of restoration. However, these conflicts had some features of an imperial war, as the restoration was put into effect by military leaders in two powerful regions, the Chōshū and Satsuma regions, in western Japan, so that

92 Ravina (2017: 17).
93 For accounts of late Tokugawa military reform, see Jaundrill (2016: 52). For general discussion, see Ravina (2017: 83, 115).
94 This is summarized in Umegaki (1988: 53).

national integration brought increased dominance of distinct regional elites.[95] As a result, the restoration also constituted an act of invasion.[96] The centralization process induced repeated regional resistance, as before and after the restoration groups with stronger local attachments mobilized against it.

The completion of the restoration brought significant military and structural changes in Japan, as the samurai class was abolished and the daimyos were dissolved and replaced with prefectures. As in eighteenth-century Europe, this revolution involved far-reaching land reform, starting in 1873, in which daimyo control of peasants was reduced, and some daimyos initially lost holdings, as farmers obtained private titles in their land.[97] At the same time, daimyos were prohibited from assembling separate armies. Remarkably, these land reforms coincided with the early development of zaibatsu – that is, of large industrial conglomerates – which rapidly acquired important functions in military production. In parallel, the restoration was followed by a series of laws which, under European influence, began to impose military conscription. The first of these was enacted in 1873, and it was followed by further measures in 1879, 1883 and 1889. As in Europe, this meant that the state penetrated more immediately into national society. This also brought dramatic change in rural communities, as the military released rural populations from traditional associations.[98] As in Europe, this process gave rise to extensive conscription revolts, although the actual proportion of the population conscripted was initially small. In each respect, Japan embodied, in accelerated form, the pattern of convergent national integration and civil war that typified the construction of other states. Initially, French military advisers were recruited to assist in this process, although, after 1871, German advisers acquired higher prestige. Within a short period of time, other measures for national consolidation were deployed using European models. The restoration of 1868 led to extensive education reforms, and, within four decades of 1870, school attendance in Japan increased from less than 30 per cent to more than 90 per cent of children.[99] Electoral laws were also introduced from 1878, so that the state acquired its first footing in concepts of political citizenship.

[95] For background, see the analysis in Craig (1961: 200, 311).
[96] See an excellent analysis in Lewis (2000: 1–3).
[97] On these reforms, discussing the privatization of land and lifting of restrictions on personal mobility of farmers, see Waswo (1977: 12).
[98] Humphreys (1995: 4).
[99] Weiner (1991: 14).

As in Europe, these processes resulted in the writing of a constitution, the Meiji constitution of 1889. Drafted with the assistance of German and Austrian jurists, the constitution was designed to establish an instrumental balance, or a system of managed citizenship, at the core of government. On one hand, it founded an imperial Diet and marked the beginning of a sequence of reforms that expanded electoral participation. However, the constitution only permitted very limited enfranchisement. It provided protection for a national oligarchy as Tokugawa elites retained dominant positions in the new system. This was reflected in the fact that the Diet had two chambers or Houses, in which the Upper House, dominated by oligarchs, was much the more powerful. On the other hand, while sustaining elite protections, the constitution reinforced some nationalizing reform policies, especially in the military domain. The constitution prescribed mandatory military service, and it was accompanied by laws that imposed much deeper conscription in society. It followed a period in which the military share of the budget had expanded substantially, and, like other constitutions, it was intended as a cautious bargain to obtain cheap soldiers, owing to fiscal pressures and security risks caused by imperialism.[100] Accordingly, the constitution created an obligation-based citizenship regime in which national affiliation was based in military duties. The constitution was equivocally worded in the position that it assigned to the military command, but it allowed the army to operate as an autonomous organization with national reach. As in other contexts, the army had already been brought to prominence through wars and unification and civil wars, and it formed a key national institution before the state was ordered in constitutional form. In the longer restoration period, the army was used, in effect, as a device for domestic colonization and integration, and, from the outset, the emerging regime relied on military groups for social control.

Striking in the Japanese case is the fact that the construction of the Meiji system, culminating in 1889, was immediately flanked by a tendency towards territorial expansion, such that, once formed, the government used the military functions secured by the constitution to mirror the behaviour of European states. As in other cases, nation-building and empire-building were hardly separable. For example, Japanese military interest in Korea began as early as 1875, when

[100] On one calculation, in the mid-1880s, the military share of state spending increased from 2.2 million to 3.5 million yen (Drea 2009: 56). A different analysis argues that the years of constitution making brought a 'revolutionary change' in military conscription as most men were subject to some military duties (Jaundrill 2016: 177).

Japan was itself still in a process of internal transformation. Major Japanese intervention in Korea took place in 1894, and the resultant Sino-Japanese War altered the traditional balance of power in eastern Asia, with Japan emerging as more powerful than China and able to restrict Russian influence in the Pacific region. By 1909–10, Japan had dissolved the Korean army and Korea became part of Japan. In 1904–5, pivotally, the Japanese government registered unforeseen military success against Russia, which required deep mobilization of national citizens and resources. This event added extraordinarily powerful global symbolism to constitutional organization as a state-building technique, as it signalled that, using constitutional means, a recently consolidated non-European nation could defeat the world's largest imperial military. This event induced constitutional reform in many different locations. Obviously, it resulted in reform in Russia in 1905–6. Within a short time, it was followed by constitutional experiments in countries exposed to frequent military conflict with Russia, such as Turkey and Iran. In Japan, the aftermath of the war with Russia brought stronger moves towards the democratization of the polity, following classical patterns. The franchise was first extended between wars, in 1900. In the longer wake of 1905, a universal suffrage bill cleared the Lower House only to be blocked by the Upper House (1911). One important account describes how external colonization was constantly linked to domestic policies of population concentration, as, in parallel to external expansion and internal franchise reforms, governments moved citizens into border regions to stabilize national frontiers.[101] Alongside these processes, continued military expansion brought further conscription laws, notably in 1906. By 1914, Japan also declared war on Germany. Japan was one of the great victors of World War I, which brought substantial territorial gains in the Pacific and parts of China.

Less immediately, the military functions of constitutional law were echoed in China. Like Japan, China became increasingly integrated in the global imperial system in the nineteenth century, which also took place, in part, through military interactions with European states. Unlike Japan, China was a major regional empire before its military encounters with western states, as the Qing empire had been built through Manchu conquest in the eighteenth century. China of course had an ancient imperial tradition. Yet from the seventeenth century China was governed by the Qing dynasty. Many Chinese subjects viewed the Qing

[101] Duus (1995: 297).

dynasty as a foreign occupation regime, implanted in China by Manchu invasion. In the nineteenth century, the political order in China still displayed typical weaknesses of pre-modern imperial systems, as central rule had patchy social penetration and colonization was still incomplete, especially in western regions. However, by this time, the empire had also been weakened by lack of external conflict. Military resources in China were primarily used to impose order on regions and social strata inside the empire, so that intra-imperial civil war was the dominant mode of conflict. By 1800, the empire was exposed to great strain because of regional uprisings, caused by weak governmental control. The tendency towards violent interregional fragmentation was exacerbated by early military engagements with European powers. For example, the Opium War of the 1840s, resulting in one-sided victory for Britain, stoked domestic conflict in China, and, from this point, external and internal wars often partly converged.

The discrediting of the imperial government through defeat in war with Britain was one cause of the warfare that erupted in China in the Taiping rebellion or revolution (1850–64). The Taiping rebellion, led by religious revolutionaries, was the worst amongst a series of uprisings against the Qing dynasty around 1850, and, as far as can be established, it caused a number of deaths that vastly exceeded all the casualties in the Napoleonic wars in Europe. Apart from the intrinsically catastrophic nature of this event, the Taiping rebellion intensified the already advanced depletion of the imperial government as the revolutionaries were only suppressed because the government co-opted local and regional elites for the war effort by allowing them to mobilize their own militias. This fact meant that, in effect, the civil war was partly conducted as an inter-militia conflict, as many rebels had their origins in communal militias and they were conquered by members of rival militias attached to the empire. Moreover, this fact meant that, even in victory, national military resources remained decentralized, and national control of the military apparatus depended on regional attachments. In fact, the suppression of the rebellion partly relied on foreign intervention, as British and French military provided forces to combat the rebels to maintain imperial strongholds. The period after 1850 saw China follow a trajectory counterposed to that of Japan, as China witnessed deep societalization of military violence and state authority depended on external military units.

In the aftermath of the Taiping disaster, the imperial government in China adopted policies to consolidate state capacity, partly using military reforms as a means of bolstering governmental authority. Attempts were made to build a modern military apparatus in China, including strategies for improved military education, for advancing military technology and for the development of naval resources. However, initiatives for Chinese military reform were undermined by the changing imperial environment as, from the 1870s, China became vulnerable to Japanese power. China's sovereignty was already gravely threatened by European depredation before this point. Yet the emerging power of Japan posed an additional threat. This meant that the effective sovereignty of the imperial government was exposed to multiple internal and external threats and military reformers were confronted with conflicting challenges. The imperial government was placed in a complex position in which external imperial pressures demanded centralization but regional forces, reinforced by the Taiping uprising, were hostile to centralizing policies, which could not be achieved without their support. This created a context in which polarized patterns of citizenship emerged and measures to secure the sovereignty of the empire were difficult to implement without alienating powerful internal factions. As mentioned, attempts to stabilize the empire were undermined by the fact that many Chinese elites saw the Qing dynasty as an occupation regime, and their willingness to accept its further reinforcement was qualified.

Meiji Japan had been reformed as Japanese elites copied institutional and military designs used by hostile powers, and, on this basis, they replicated European patterns of behaviour towards other Asian states. By the 1890s, the deployment of external templates to conduct domestic reforms was emulated in China. During the Sino-Japanese War of 1894–5, the imperial government began to develop a modern drilled army. The following years saw increased external intervention, notably with German incursion on the Chinese coast. The Boxer Rebellion beginning in 1899, led by Chinese groups mobilized against foreign military organizations, was suppressed by an alliance of European armies, and, in its aftermath, a strong foreign military presence remained in Beijing. By this time, Chinese emissaries were sent to Japan to observe strategies for institutional modernization. After 1900, Japanese influence in Chinese military politics increased and Japanese officials assumed consultative positions in military reform processes.[102] The aftermath of the Sino-Japanese war saw the creation

[102] Powell (2015: 161).

of the more fully national New Army in China, in which official ranks were increasingly professionalized, and which assumed external and internal security functions. Reforms of 1900–1 brought changes to military education, establishing provincial military schools and reserve lists.[103] In parallel, leading Chinese reformers promoted policies that extended beyond the strict military domain, and reformist factions noted how constitutional instruments employed in Japan and Europe could serve military reinforcement. The emperor initiated a series of brief institutional reforms in 1898, and the New Army pressed for constitutional reform at this time.[104] As early as January 1901, the empress dowager, who had assumed a powerful political role, issued an edict committing the empire 'to scrutinize Chinese and Western governmental systems' especially as means 'to expand state revenues' and 'to revitalize the military'.[105]

It was the Japanese victory over Russia in 1904–5 that reinforced modernizing imperatives in China, partly because the war was fought in Manchuria, which implicated Chinese sovereignty. This war led to military reforms that partly reflected standard designs for imperial consolidation. Some reforms were realized through the Commission for Army Reorganization (founded 1903), which began to establish standing armies in different provinces, separate from regional militias, and it drew up policies for education and manpower supply.[106] At the same time, the war gave new impetus to plans for constitutional reorganization, and some reformists agitated for the implementation of a constitution. The constitutionalist movement attracted support from different social factions, and it was promoted for various reasons by different groups. Amongst the imperial elite, the move towards constitutional rule was linked to the strategic belief that a constitution would place the empire on new administrative foundations and placate potential opponents, especially those who resented the Qing dynasty. In addition, this constitutional turn was connected to the fact that, after 1905, the semi-autocratic system governmental system in Russia lost advocates outside Russia, as it appeared vulnerable if confronted with mobile national armies, supported by constitutional measures.[107]

[103] Fung (1980: 14).
[104] This is discussed in Esherick (1976: 91–92).
[105] This is printed in Reynolds (1993: 13).
[106] Fung (1980: 20).
[107] One historian reports that, in 1905, the Chinese press declared that 'Russian defeat eliminated the last powerful argument for autocracy in China' (Price 1974: 138). For similar analysis, see Fung (1980: 41).

Accordingly, constitutional constructions of citizenship were explicitly conceived as instruments to bolster Chinese sovereignty. For example, the leading constitutional thinker, Liang Qichao, presented a theory of citizenship to strengthen the Chinese nation against depredatory foreign interests, and he saw constitutional rule as an essential support for state-led integration.[108] Indeed, the emperor issued a decree in 1905 to send commissioners to other countries to assess mechanisms for government able to sustain effective military systems, to support reform in China. In September 1906, the empress dowager passed a decree containing a commitment to introduce constitutional reforms. This was centred in the declaration that a constitution should be created in which 'supreme authority shall be vested in the crown, but all questions shall be considered by a popular assembly'.[109] This was followed by a set of constitutional principles promulgated in 1908, leading to the establishment of provincial assemblies and ultimately of a national assembly with consultative functions (1910). This coincided with the creation of a new ministry for war (1906) with integrated planning functions. As in other countries, this period also witnessed education reforms, coinciding with constitutional reforms and military reforms as part of a broad plan for social transformation. In each point, the constitutionalist movement reflected the dialectical link between imperial transformation, militarism and internal integration through the construction of citizenship.

Unlike in Japan, however, in the Chinese case, the construction of citizenship as a nation-building principle did not weaken the tradition of societal militarization. The reconstruction of the army was not able to create a uniform national military system, and, over time, it induced increased military discord. For example, the growing force of the army was flanked by increased revolutionary activity in military units, as educated soldiers attached themselves to revolutionary nationalism. At the heart of this problem was the fact that different factions promoted military reform for divergent reasons. The elite bloc around the emperor saw the army as an instrument of imperialist regime stabilization, promoting military reform and unification to cement the existing socio-institutional order. By contrast, many groups in the army were

[108] In his *Discourse on the New Citizen*, Liang Qichao saw citizenship as serving to reinforce the 'centripetal force of the nation' and observed that without 'the qualifications of a citizen, it is absolutely impossible for your country to continue to exist in the world' (Qichao 1916: 10). I thank Chuxi Zhang for the translation.

[109] Extracts from this are published in Cameron (1931: 103).

driven by anti-imperialist ideals, and they were committed to overthrowing the Qing dynasty and preserving local autonomy. This meant that the army was an unreliable focus for regime security. These fissures converged with fissures in the constitutionalist movement, which was also supported for diverse motives by different groups, and which did not produce a unifying ethic of citizenship. At the imperial level, as mentioned, constitutional plans were designed to broaden social support for the imperial state. However, for many, constitutionalism was a military cause, and the army had special responsibility for leading political reforms, to advance anti-Qing republicanism, perceived as an anti-imperialist sentiment. After 1900, Sun Yat-sen, later the provisional president of the Chinese republic from 1911 to 1912, developed a concept of constitutional rule in which the army was presented as the primary embodiment of citizens' interests. He argued that the army was required to effect regime change by imposing military law across Chinese society. The imposition of military rule, he explained, would be the first stage in a three-stage process of constitutional formation, replacing the Qing empire to create a republic. Constitutional ideas were thus sharply divided between imperialist and nationalist objectives, containing correlated ideals of citizenship.

Ultimately, the imperial order was overthrown in 1911–12, leading to the creation of a republic. This was initiated by a military uprising in Wuchang, and officers trained through the reform period acquired central roles in this process, so that the revolution was, at least in part, a military coup. During the collapse of the Qing dynasty, previous modernizing policies were extended, and 1911 saw the promulgation of constitutional articles. After the abdication of the emperor (1912), a provisional constitution was introduced (1912), which, in Article 53, stipulated that a national parliamentary election was to be held within ten months, by early 1913. This initiated a short experiment in representative rule in which government was established through elections, albeit with a small franchise. A full constitution was drafted in 1913, although it was not enforced, and parliament was dissolved in early 1914. At this point, Yuan Shikai assumed a dominant position in state, governing on the basis of a revised constitution, with a presidential bias. Through this, the revolution brought military figures into prominent roles, both at the national and the provincial levels. Yuan Shikai was leader of the Beiyang army, which he had developed using western models and Japanese teachers, and he had previous served as reformer of the imperial military. Most provincial governors came from the army, which meant that civil control of the military was uncertain.[110] In this respect, the typical military features of constitutions founded amidst imperial conflicts became very pronounced. At the same time, this transitional period was marked by deep conflicts between different regions, as the polity was not fully unified and government was partly imposed as military occupation. In each point, the early republican period was marked by a mixture of military unification, internal colonization and civil war.

By 1915, China experienced a civil war in which a military coalition was founded to avert the restoration of imperial rule by Yuan Shikai. From 1917, government was contested between the Beiyang government in the north of the country and a rival government with a rival army based in southern China. Importantly, from 1917, different governments expressed different attitudes to external imperial forces, as the official Beiyang government, dominated by the military, was formally supported by outside powers. However, neither government possessed strong claim to real sovereignty, as from 1916, civil war assumed endemic character, and military leaders or warlords, many coming from the Beiyang army, replaced national government officeholders as bearers of political authority. By the 1920s, the spread of warlord power had given rise to a complex civil war with ideological and regional variations, in which nationalists and Communists briefly united to suppress the warlords. Military integration was a central force in the provisional nationalist constitution of 1931, which created an interim authoritarian system based in the claim that a period of political tutelage was required to prepare the people for elected self-government. Later in the 1930s, as China experienced partial occupation by Japan, civil war again abated, albeit temporarily. Military mobilization against Japan after 1931, involving informal recruitment, partisan activism and military socialization, became an important determinant of national consolidation at this point.[111]

In these respects, China clearly represents the wider phenomenon of military isomorphism in constitution making. Like Japan, China experienced an impetus towards citizenship formation partly because of deep inner conflicts and partly because of potential loss of sovereignty, and the long constitutional transformation of subjects into citizens was pressed into society by imperialism. Accordingly, the development of constitutionalism was driven by external military

110 McCord (1993: 83, 159).

111 I thank Guoshu Yang for advising me and providing material for the preceding three paragraphs.

pressures, especially after 1905, and it was initially expected both to stabilize the government in relation to internal actors and to harden the position of the state in the international setting. China eventually joined World War I on the side of the Entente powers, although it only provided labour recruits. Equally, the constitutional experiment in China was driven by factions in the army, and a split within the military was a cause of constitutional transformation beginning in 1911. Largely for this reason, early republican China saw numerous attempts to stabilize a constitutional regime, mainly dominated by military figures.[112] However, in important ways, China fell outside the strict family of constitutional states. The constitutional experiment immediately induced harsh lateral militarization which was not resolved by constitutional means. Contestation over the dominant form of national government released conflicts that constitutional law did not control, and some aspect of military rule remained a constant feature of government. This continued under the Communist Party after 1949, which frequently used military means for social consolidation.

CONCLUSION

The nineteenth century saw a deep, but often unperceived transformation of constitutional law in which the functions of constitutions were adapted to changing interstate environments shaped by the global rise of imperialism. This transformation gained momentum after 1848, when governmental reactions to constitutional movements differed substantially from those expressed in 1815. In the decades that followed 1848, constitutions were frequently designed as measured instruments of social bargaining. In such instruments, governments allotted certain political and social rights to citizens, and citizens acquired significant benefits from this arrangement. However, the exercise of such rights was strictly controlled for military ends (vertical integration), and constitutions were typically designed to stabilize the sovereignty of constitutional states in their external actions. To realize this strategy, constitutions allocated political rights within an administrative structure, with both pacifying and coercive features, in which the potential for mass political inclusion through rights to generate institutionally destabilizing or counter-systemic effects (lateral violence) was reduced

[112] On one count there were seven attempts at creating a constitution in China from 1911 to 1923 (Zhao 1995: 21).

by strong executive agents. One outcome of this was that, as imperialism imprinted a stringent form on constitutions, imperial nations showed some convergence in their inner and outer dimensions, and, in both domains, they were oriented towards the maintenance of violence. This created a global constitutional model, which states affected by the promotion of imperialism as a universal political form were, in essence, forced to emulate. Different polities at the perimeter of European empires adapted to pressures of imperialism by using constitutional law to transform themselves into imperial nations.

CHAPTER THREE

IMPERIALISM AND GLOBAL CIVIL WAR

In the discussion in previous chapters, modern constitutions acquired permanent social functions by promoting a concept of citizenship to stabilize sovereign institutions in societies affected by imperialism. In the late nineteenth century, constitutions were used to consolidate a political system based in managed citizenship, allowing governments to integrate their populations for potential external conflict (vertical militarism) without exposing themselves to internal disorder (lateral militarism). Fundamental to this process, however, was the fact that constitutions were never fully successful in eradicating the potential for lateral militarism from emerging national societies. The constitutional construction of the citizen that emerged after 1848 initially held civil conflict at a point of strained latency in national society. Yet, after 1900, the intensification of interstate tensions meant that demands for military recruitment increased. In turn, this meant that many states extended the scope of citizenship to new social groups, which they used a complex bargaining apparatus, usually flanked by education and welfare laws, to pacify. This process of political integration always increased the risk of political destabilization (low- or high-intensity civil war); typically, it strengthened the repressive functions of national states and, frequently, it brought the military into play as a civil actor. By 1900, governments legitimated by constitutional constructs of popular sovereignty often encountered their citizens in conflictual interactions, and many bargaining arrangements put in place to integrate citizens were unsettled by this.

These propensities became most vividly perceptible in Europe after 1918. Prior to 1914, European states remained moderately effective in managing the instrumental balance at the core of post-1848 constitutional law. Of course, this period was overshadowed by the warning, audible in Russia in 1905–6 and the Ottoman Empire in 1908, that deep vertical militarization of society was likely to have profoundly unsettling results in societies faced with defeat in war. Yet most pre-1914 states were still able to integrate their populations in reasonably settled procedures. After World War I, however, the violent consequences of external militarism became less controllable.

As in earlier settings, political transformations after 1918 were directly connected to the administration of imperialism. The years after 1918 witnessed, notionally, the establishment of a new international order, mirroring some aspects of the interstate security arrangements that developed in 1648 and 1815. The post-1918 order was founded through the League of Nations, which, like earlier international systems, was designed to manage state power in a broader context defined by imperial transformation. The years around 1918 saw the dissolution of continental empires in Europe, especially the Habsburg Empire, the Ottoman Empire, the Russian tsarist empire (in part) and (in part) the Prussian/German Empire. In each setting, new states were created with new constitutions strongly influenced by ideals embodied in the League of Nations. Indeed, the League of Nations was partly intended to regulate interstate relations by connecting the constitutional laws of newly founded states to international law. First, this system gave expression to the norm, declared by Woodrow Wilson in 1918, that national self-government should be the basic form of the legitimate polity. This principle influenced the peace treaties finalized around Paris in 1919, in which new post-imperial states, attached to delineated national populations, acquired recognition. In parallel, second, this system was rooted in the precondition that national sovereignty should be exercised in a humane manner. In the League of Nations, weight was placed on the assumption that states should avoid violence towards minority groups residing within the frontiers of national societies, so that rights of minorities formed a primary constraint on national sovereignty. This was expressed in minority treaties agreed near Paris in 1919–20, and in territorial settlements in Sèvres (1920) and Riga (1921). This was also implied in Art. 14 of the Covenant of the League of Nations, which established the Permanent Court of International Justice for mediating international conflicts. Importantly, Art. 12 of the

Polish minority treaty (1919), set a crucial precedent declaring that the protection of minorities in Poland should be placed under guarantee of the League of Nations and could give rise to proceedings before the Permanent Court. This two-level construction of sovereignty was conceived as the political form required to replace imperialism and to manage the transformation of empires and colonies into nations. Third, this system placed a (nominal) taboo on the acquisition of territory by military occupancy. While protecting the sovereignty of new European states, the Covenant of the League of Nations created a mandates system (Art. 22) for states outside Europe. In this arrangement, states formerly subject to Ottoman rule were subsequently placed under the tutelary protection of leading imperial states (mainly France and the UK), who were then expected to guide them towards sovereignty. In each respect, like earlier security systems, the post-1918 order was designed to limit warfare and to avert the diffuse societalization of military violence typical of empires.

Against this background, most European populations underwent a process of democratization around 1918 in which constitutional provisions allowing citizens to exercise political rights were greatly expanded. The nature of this transfer was varied, and, with a very small number of exceptions, populations experienced democratization in processes that can be divided into three distinct categories, each with specific features. First, in some societies, usually those that emerged on the victorious side or that had remained neutral in World War I, existing constitutional provisions for political enfranchisement were increased. This occurred in Great Britain, Italy, the Netherlands, Belgium and some Scandinavian countries. In France, this was less pronounced as France had been strongly democratized before 1918; however, the French Communist Party was formed in 1920, so that the veto on the radical left was weakened. Second, in some societies, typically those not victorious in the war, new constitutions were created that established greatly enlarged franchises and stronger provisions for legislative authority and executive accountability. This occurred in Germany and Austria. Third, in societies that gained independence through the dissolution of continental empires around 1918, entirely new constitutional polities were established. In most such cases, constitutions were designed to establish national democracy, enfranchising populations that had previously been subject, either partially or completely, to external rule. This occurred, with clear variations, in constitutions created in Czechoslovakia, Poland, Yugoslavia (named such in 1929), Hungary (with strong caveats), Finland, Lithuania, Estonia and Latvia. Some societies such as Russia and Turkey experimented briefly with constitutional rule, but they did not establish democratic systems.

In each category, constitutions that evolved around and after 1918 were determined by experiences of war, and – either expressly or more indirectly – by experiences of imperialism. After 1918, the British empire retained a clearly imperial constitution. Through the post-1918 arrangements, the British empire reached its maximum extent as British mandate territories were formed in former Ottoman regions. At the same time, the British electoral franchise underwent its largest single extension as all men and some women were given the vote in 1918, with some privileges for soldiers. However, most European constitutions created or reformed after 1918 were post-imperial constitutions. Most new states emerging after 1918 had a fully or partly post-imperial character. In parallel, German and Austrian nation states were founded in the shrunken shells of imperial polities. At this time, Germany lost its character as a European empire and forfeited its overseas territories. By 1914, Germany had the third largest overseas empire in Europe, built rapidly after 1884. However, Germany was stripped of its overseas colonies in the Treaty of Versailles, and German control of many Polish-speaking regions exercised from 1772 to 1815 was terminated. Parts of Silesia taken by Germany after 1740 also became Polish following a plebiscite in 1921. The polity that emerged in Germany after 1918 was, in two distinct ways, a classical post-imperial state. It surrendered its imperial status through the loss of its colonies and the enforced reduction in size of its army. Further, as it was placed on constitutional footing, the imperial dominance of Prussia over other German territories was effaced so that other German states became equal actors in the constitutional order.[1] Even Italy, whose territory was marginally expanded through the integration of Tyrol and Istria from 1918, entered a new phase of imperialism. Italy's anticipated enlargement in the Adriatic and the Balkans did not materialize, and the expansionary process released by unification came to a temporary end. The Spanish constitution was created later, in 1931, but it also belonged to the category of the post-imperial constitution.

The post-imperial character of post-1918 constitutionalism became most visible in questions of institutional design and popular legitimation

[1] See p. 179. For one historian, the Weimar Republic was a 'postcolonial state surrounded by ongoing imperial powers' (Wempe 2019: 158).

and integration. After 1918, as mentioned, states obtained constitutions that were much more democratic than those before 1914, and they ensured that national populations were more fully included in legislative processes. In so doing, they designed provisions to subject instruments of violence to publicly agreed norms and to ensure that executive agents, especially those with military offices, could not operate in unaccountable fashion.[2] In each respect, most states moved away from the imperialist model of managed citizenship, in which vertical integration was not correlated with strong representative procedures and executives acted at a high level of autonomy.

Although shaped by the shift away from imperialism, however, most constitutions formed around 1918 remained rooted in concepts of citizenship strongly defined by military organization. As such, they reproduced earlier bargaining systems for generating political rights and constructing legitimacy used in pre-1914 polities, but they partly released the lateral outcomes of integration from executive control. In most cases, these constitutions formed political-democratic contracts drawn up to compensate military personnel for sacrifices in World War I, and they were utilized to reintegrate large, demobilized armies in the polity. In some cases, constitutions were expressly utilized to consolidate military capacity (e.g. Turkey, Poland). Further, most post-1918 constitutions expanded the electoral rights of citizens because citizens assumed new relevance as providers of violence. In these points, many post-1918 constitutions brought deep-lying patterns of conflict to the surface of society, intensifying collective experiences of violence. In fact, many constitutions attached social conflicts to patterns of violent interaction experienced in World War I, so that political contests assumed intensified military characteristics. Further, many constitutions quickly reproduced imperialist government models in their societies, and they framed states that embarked (successfully or otherwise) on expansionary policies towards other states. As discussed in this chapter and in Chapter 5, these problems were partly caused by the fact that, after 1918, warfare persisted in much of Europe. In some areas, war continued in broadly typical form, as interstate or at least inter-regime hostility. But war also continued in distinct form as militarized actions between intra-societal groups became a dominant political phenomenon.[3] Even post-1918 wars that possessed classical features,

[2] See examples at pp. 198, 212–3.
[3] See discussion of the 'civilianization of collective violence' at this time in Winter (2022: 4).

such as those between Turkey and Greece and Russia and Poland, involved conflict between groups that would have been classified as protagonists in civil war only a few years previously. Moreover, most constitution-making situations after 1918 were affected by the intense ideological and geopolitical polarization that followed the Bolshevik Revolution (1917) and the harrowing realities of the Russian civil war (1918–22). In post-1917 Russia, militarism penetrated deep into civil politics. During the civil war, the long-term process of constitutional transformation in Russia, linked to agrarian reform and military conscription, came to an end.[4] This war resulted in a political system dominated by the Bolsheviks and the Red Army, in which the partition between political parties and military units was often unclear. This system was centred on a deep fusion of political and military notions of citizenship, and soldiers acquired privileged status in the regime apparatus created by the Bolsheviks. The Russian civil war spilled into other parts of Eastern Europe, and its ideological polarities led to acute political polarization, strongly articulated through organized political violence in all Europe and beyond. This reality of convergent internal and external conflict framed constitutions in much of Europe, and many constitutions exacerbated this condition. In general, this period saw a rapid re-emergence of military constitutionalism, in which lateral violence became a dominant social feature, in turn stimulating increased vertical militarism.

The post-1918 tendency towards military constitutionalism was clearly demonstrated in polities whose post-1918 form was built on earlier constitutions, such as France and Belgium. After 1918, these polities were based in a parliamentary constitution dating from long before 1914. In fact, France provided the model for parliamentary rule in many new states in post-1918 Europe. In the longer aftermath of 1918, however, these polities struggled to preserve institutions whose accountability to democratically integrated citizens was upheld. By the 1930s, both these polities relied on elements of military governance, and they increasingly introduced legislation using procedures that had been tested during World War I. By the 1930s, core legislation in France and Belgium was frequently introduced through the use of *pleins pouvoirs*, which gave great latitude to the executive. From 1938, key acts of legislation were passed by decree under Daladier. By 1931,

[4] See discussion of this background at p. 133.

additionally Britain was governed by an emergency regime, with precarious democratic mandate.

This militaristic tendency was visible in more extreme form in many new national polities, which used constitutional law to separate their structures from pre-existing empires. For example, democratic provisions introduced in 1918 in Hungary were not fully enforced, and territorial war with Romania meant that government was subordinated to military leadership from an early stage. After independence, Lithuania had a series of temporary constitutions, but, by 1922, the Lithuanian polity was based in a fixed constitution that (notionally) established a strong parliament alongside a relatively a weak presidency. However, after 1918, Lithuania experienced an extraordinarily high degree of militarization caused by mobilization for military conflict with Poland and Russia. Even when Lithuania functioned as a parliamentary democracy, much of its territory was subject to martial law. The parliamentary constitution was suspended by Antanas Smetona's military coup in 1926 and replaced in 1928. The political system established in Yugoslavia in 1918, initially based in the existing Serbian polity, was marked by pervasive military interference throughout the 1920s, with democracy being suspended in 1929. In Austria, democracy was ended in 1933 by an authoritarian bloc with strong military support. In most contexts, democratic governments were replaced by regimes dependent on military authority, with partly fascist dispositions. Of all new democratic polities established after 1918 in Eastern, Central and Southern Europe, only Czechoslovakia did not become authoritarian through internal forces. Czechoslovakia was annexed and divided in 1938–9 by Germany, and a highly authoritarian government was imposed that recruited some domestic support.

In different ways, these lines of constitutional collapse were caused by the background of imperialism. New constitutions after 1918 were mainly conceived as parts of a post-imperial constellation following the collapse of major empires. However, the relation between these constitutions and imperial legacies was precarious. On one hand, many post-1918 constitutions placed the construction of legitimacy for government on democratic premises, defined by full political integration. That is, they attached legitimacy directly to popular elections, largely separated from earlier military instrumentalism typical of empires. In so doing, post-1918 constitutions endeavoured to establish a legitimational system that was not strategically focused on military extraction, allowing differences in the horizontal dimension of society to acquire stronger articulation through the political system. Yet constitutions of this time were deeply shaped by military prerogatives, and they were largely designed by war. Moreover, these constitutions framed governments that operated in a singularly unsparing system of international rivalry, intensified by the rise of Bolshevism. At the same time, constitutions organized political systems in which intra-societal tensions that typify imperialist societies persistently shaped political practice, and controversies over primary questions of societal ownership had not been settled. In such contexts, constitutional constructs of citizenship typically gave rise to political systems in which lateral conflicts were violently expressed. Through these processes, a form of government became widespread in which the capacity of pre-1914 governments to insulate themselves against lateral violence lost strength. In turn, this brought militaries into central political roles. Soon, many states displayed renewed features of imperial government, using selective citizenship norms to suppress intra-societal conflicts and greatly intensifying the military aspects of government that typified pre-1918 regimes. By the late 1920s, many states relied more openly on military violence to integrate their populations and they re-established some form of occupation system for their societies in which the distinction between the external and the internal acts of government was eroded. Such endemic crises became especially tangible after the onset of the Great Depression starting in 1929, when social conflicts were intensified by material deprivation. In each point, most constitutions created after 1918 failed to open a path out of imperial governance towards a condition of national citizenship, and the advent of democracy increased the deployment of military bodies for managing national integration.

As distilled expressions of the post-1918 dialectic between citizenship, imperialism and war, three lines of national constitution making can be specifically isolated. In each line, constitutions proved unable to move states away from imperial patterns of coercion and a close convergence persisted between national and imperial society. These cases are the constitutional orders created in Germany, Poland and Spain.

1. GERMANY

As discussed, patterns of constitutional formation in Germany were, from the outset, integrally linked to imperialism. As examined, the German Empire (*Kaiserreich*), founded in 1870–1, introduced universal male suffrage, albeit for a legislature (*Reichstag*) with limited powers. As such, it sanctioned national citizenship as a principle of controlled social integration. This constitution also imposed military conscription on all men allowed to exercise citizenship rights. Further, it ensured that Prussia remained the hegemonic state within the imperial nation. This was achieved through the creation of a federal council in which Prussian power was predominant (Art. 6). The federal council acted with the *Reichstag* as a central decision-making body, and, through this, Prussian interests partly dictated the content of legislation. In addition, this constitution created an institutional system in which the holders of executive power were not subject to robust constraints. In particular, Art. 15 conferred executive powers on the chancellor, nominated not by the *Reichstag*, but by the Kaiser, which meant that the accountability of highest officeholders was limited, and even that the executive was able to control legislative processes. Over a longer period, the position of the chancellor proved pivotal to the constitution as the chancellor played a leading role in initiating legislating and in organizing coalitions in the *Reichstag* to support draft laws. In each respect, as discussed, the constitutional order of Imperial Germany was designed to moderate social integration by extracting the instruments of geographical expansion (military force) from citizens without admitting them fully to the realm of political conflict.

Subsequently, the connection between imperialism and citizenship remained prominent through the *Kaiserreich*. After unification, as mentioned, Germany entered a course of imperial expansion, and, by circa 1890, imperial success was often proclaimed a vital indicator of Germany's prestige on the world stage. Indeed, reformist thinkers in Imperial Germany often supported constitutional modernization because they saw the deepening integration of citizens as a precondition for effective external expansion and colonization. Weber himself advocated representative democracy as he thought it would improve the quality of German political elites, who would then support effective German expansion. The promotion of citizenship rights thus had a clear instrumental bias. This view was often expressed by politicians who declared enthusiasm for social welfare policies.[5] On this basis, pro-empire factions in the *Kaiserreich* endorsed institutional designs to promoted vertical integration for military ends while obviating internal conflict.

These trajectories in Germany reached an interim apogee in World War I, at which point both the interdependence of national citizenship

[5] Both these arguments appear in quintessential form in Naumann (1900: 142).

and imperialism and the use of citizenship norms to manage internal conflict and to sustain military force were strongly expressed. First, during World War I, the experience of external war, not easily separable from imperialism, intensified constructions of German national membership. Externally, the German war effort had varied features. Although conducted as an attritional interstate war in the west, in the east, it developed into a war of colonization. By 1915, German presence was cemented in areas in Poland previously ruled by Russia and parts of the Baltic region were placed under military administration with frequent exploitation of forced labour. Internally, the war formed an environment in which tensions between German political factions were temporarily put to one side. In 1914, a policy of inter-factional reconciliation was declared for the duration of hostilities, and the war created a cross-party front in the *Reichstag*. This policy was presented as the *Burgfrieden*, initiated as the SPD agreed to support credits to finance the war. Strictly, the term *Burgfrieden* described the declaration of peace inside the walls of a castle during times of siege or war. But this term also contained a clear reference to civil war (*Bürgerkrieg*), and it implied a domestic condition in which internal conflict was suspended because a society was mobilized against an external enemy. In 1914, this term was employed to suggest that external war, symbolically, had instilled a unified experience of national belonging in German society. The period of *Burgfrieden* was framed by laws that heightened the military aspect of the national government, dramatically expanding governmental force for the vertical integration of society. This began with the declaration of a state of military emergency in July 1914. This law transferred powers to the military executive, and, by the late stages of the war, Germany was in essence a military dictatorship. However, the period of *Burgfrieden* gave rise to laws that extended the reach of citizenship rights. In 1916, the Auxiliary Service Law mandated forcible recruitment of labour and organization of production for military purposes. Yet this law contained provisions that, on condition of their discharge of military functions, gave increased recognition to trade unions, even incorporating them in the legislative process. By 1917, these policies were accompanied by official pledges for constitutional reform. At Easter 1917, even as military power grew, the Kaiser promised revisions to the existing constitution to increase the authority of elected deputies and to limit regional counterweights to national democratization. These policies promoted full sociopolitical integration (equal citizenship) as a platform for military victory, embodying emblematically the construct of the imperial nation.

The relation between militarism, imperialism and democratization at the heart of German constitutionalism acquired further expression as the imperial regime collapsed in 1918 and a new constitution was created in 1919. First, the end of the imperial government was caused partly by military defeat and partly by the threat insurgent German soldiers posed to public order in late 1918. After the Kaiser abdicated in early November 1918, an interim council government was appointed, comprising representatives of factions formerly belonging to the SPD. At this point, the basic elements of post-imperial government were not consolidated, and the future of Germany was contested by rival military organizations. In November 1918, semi-demobilized soldiers remained, for a short time, important players in the German political system, and radical revolts amongst soldiers created an atmosphere close to civil war, especially as some soldiers supported pro-Bolshevik movements. In response to this, the foundation for the post-1918 polity was put in place through a pact between the SPD leadership and the military (Ebert–Groener-Pakt), so that the army became a guarantor of liberal capitalist democracy. Through this pact, the SPD agreed to oppose Communist revolution and the military accepted a constitutional-democratic transition. From this moment, military leadership elites deployed the armed forces to suppress pro-Communist insurrection. Importantly, German military engagement outside Germany did not entirely cease in late 1918. Some German units were still deployed in anti-Bolshevik combat, mainly around the Baltic coast and in border conflicts with citizens of the emerging Polish state, primarily in Silesia. As a result, paramilitary organizations continued to exert influence after armistice, and they were co-opted by the (nominally) revolutionary interim government to suppress Bolshevik agitation inside Germany. This continued – in part – because of the abolition of military conscription in Germany, dictated by the Treaty of Versailles, which meant that paramilitaries acquired elevated appeal for militarized young men.

Against this background, second, a constituent assembly was convened in Weimar in early 1919 to write a new constitution for Germany as a post-imperial nation. In dialectical fashion, the constitution established in 1919 was, in some respects, a military constitution designed to configure wartime experiences of nationhood as the substructure for a democratic polity. This constitution was centred in the assumption that, before 1914, Germany had only been incompletely unified as a nation state. That is, it reflected the conviction that, after 1870, the full unification of Germany had been impeded by two factors: first, it had been impeded by class divisions in society; second, it had been impeded by the limited force of national territorial citizenship since unification had been imposed, in essence, by Prussian annexation. The declared intention of the architects of the 1919 constitution was to soften intergroup conflict in both the economic and the territorial dimensions of social life and to promote a model of citizenship based inter-sectoral bargains strong enough to bring cohesion to national society, creating a conclusively sovereign nation state and a conclusively integrated societal order. This objective was deeply determined by conditions in Germany during World War I. Architects of the constitution envisaged that national citizenship could be reached if they replicated the cross-party unity (*Burgfrieden*) instilled in German society by the war as the basis for post-1918 democratization. The main author of the constitution, Hugo Preuß, expressly claimed that the war had conferred a new, politicized form on the German people, enabling it to gain identity, finally, as a national constitutional entity.[6]

These purposes were displayed in the fact that the 1919 constitution re-established some of the economic legislation introduced during the war, formalizing rights for trade unions and consolidating social rights and principles of labour law to integrate working-class organizations in the polity (Art. 165). This emphasis was not uncharacteristic for this period, as the 1917 constitution of Mexico established social and labour rights (Art. 123). These purposes were also evident in the fact that, although it created a strong legislature, the constitution placed highest national authority in the hands of a president, who was given broad freedom to enforce emergency legislation and to take measures to secure public order in states of exception (Art. 48). Both the economic legislation and the emergency provisions in the 1919 constitution were designed explicitly as parts of a collective nation-building process. Clauses establishing labour rights meant that constitutional roles were assigned to a range of economic organizations, including trade unions, which were expected to promote the relative pacification of class relations, reinforcing citizenship as a fully national-political experience.[7] Preuß expressed this point in paradigmatic terms, stating that democracy could acquire reality only as a 'synthesis' of 'political

[6] Preuß (1915: 186–7).
[7] For a similar point, see Voßkuhle (2011: 255).

equality and unified citizenship', overcoming the typical 'antithesis of capitalists and proletarians'.[8] Likewise, the emergency provisions in the constitution were conceived as legal clauses that could be used to override separatist impulses in different states, forming a final backstop for the structural integrity of the nation. The president, who was authorized to enforce these provisions, was elected by plebiscite. Drafters of the constitution conceived plebiscitary elections as a means of ensuring that presidential authority was legitimated by the nation in its entirety, so that emergency powers were enforced as an intense crystallization of the national will.[9] The nation-building purposes of the constitution were also evident in the fact that important parts of the text restricted the power of Prussia (Art. 13). Indeed, Art. 18 implied that, under certain circumstances, the territorial boundaries of Prussia could be redrawn by an elected government.[10] The emergency clauses in the constitution allowed the president to impose imperial law immediately in states that deviated from the national constitution; it was envisaged that such clauses would be effective against Prussia. In each point, basic provisions of the 1919 constitution were expected to ensure that the (still) unconsolidated German nation could acquire reality.

At a primary level, the 1919 constitution was based in the understanding that it was forged by a militarized constituent power, and it was conceived as a text that would reconfigure the role of warfare in forming national legal order. As such, it projected a dialectical constitutional strategy for moving government beyond imperial rule, opposed to other post-conflict constitutional designs. On one hand, the 1919 constitution was deliberately distinguished from the 1871 constitution of Germany. The 1871 constitution had mainly been designed to consolidate territorial conditions resulting from war, and, on this basis, it had imposed de facto imperial rule (an occupation system) through German national society. On the other hand, the 1919 constitution was distinguished from the Bolshevik system created in Russia in 1917, where the path away from imperial warfare led into and through civil war. In contrast to both these situations, the 1919 constitution of Germany was conceived to capture constituent experiences of war by extending experiences of citizenship thickened by war to furnish a consensual legal form for post-war society. The German constitution was intended

[8] Preuß (2008: 147).
[9] This was Max Weber's (1921: 424) main contribution to writing the constitution.
[10] See Schmidt (1927: 211).

to build on social convergence arising in World War I to create a distinct post-imperial order, transforming wartime conditions into a legal-political structure that pacified rival social factions, and citizens occupied national territory as a shared social domain. In each respect, the 1919 constitution was expected to continue the vertical integration functions of war to form a unified citizenship regime. Yet it was expected to achieve this by founding a democratic polity in which the military would lose its status as the primary source of cohesion, and in which lateral integration would be managed by arrangements for economic moderation, also originating in war. In this regard, the constitution reflected a deep insight into the relation between imperialism, war and citizenship. It aimed to construct national citizenship in a form that, although concretized through war, placed society beyond war and pulled all parts of society together in a politically and materially unified order detached from imperial legacies. The emergence of a nation of German citizens was envisaged as the result of a collective decision in which, by means of distributive rights, exceptionalist authority and interregional balance, constitutional laws originating in war were to frame a condition of civil peace, distinct from imperialism and from civil war.

Manifestly, the attempt in 1918–19 to unify German society by non-imperialist techniques and without civil war was unsuccessful. It became rapidly apparent that the constitutional devices intended to underpin national unification in 1919 were unreliable. In fact, the specific clauses in the Weimar constitution designed to promote national unity in Germany typically had the opposite effect. Despite some early initiatives, first, the labour law clauses in the constitution were not fully enforced. The welfare regime put into effect under the constitution soon caused resentment amongst economic leadership groups, instilling deep fissures between business elites and trade unions at the heart of the polity. These clauses proved incendiary for civil conflict, leading to extreme constitutional crisis in 1929–30. At this point, controversies over public spending brought the collapse of the ruling coalition and the powers of government were placed in the hands of the president, who established an unelected anti-welfare executive. In parallel, second, the emergency clauses in the constitution were often used beyond their original scope. Different presidents applied these clauses to enforce spending policies and to cut public debts. After 1930, these clauses were employed as a constitutional substructure to prop up the executive after the suspension of the elected coalition, and they provided hard legal support for anti-labour policies.[11] Extensive use of these clauses for regular legislation weakened the procedural order of the state, intermittently bestowing heightened powers on the army, and their deployment facilitated the insertion of Hitler in government in 1933. Most paradoxically, the constitutional clauses that reduced Prussian imperial influence proved disastrously counterproductive. By the late 1920s, Prussia was the most democratically committed state in the German polity, and it formed the main defence for the ideals of citizenship spelled out in the 1919 constitution. Eventually, the independent power of Prussia, the last stable block of German democracy, was destroyed in 1932 as the government used emergency laws to suspend the Prussian parliament. This step eradicated the primary counterweight to the increasingly repressive imperial executive, and it initiated the concerted destruction of democratic institutions (*Gleichschaltung*). In a bitter paradox, this meant that laws created to protect the German nation from Prussian imperialism were used with military support to suspend Prussia's role as a bastion of democracy, allowing Germany to slide into extreme authoritarianism. Overall, the elements of the 1919 constitution intended to direct German society towards national democracy had outcomes that contradicted their primary design. In different ways, the clauses expected to consolidate unified citizenship militated against political stabilization, and they played a vital role in the polarization of German society. Clauses whose purpose was to capture and control potential sources of violence signally failed to achieve this, such that German society eventually moved towards deep civil conflict after 1930.

Ultimately, the political system in Germany was reconsolidated in the 1930s in a form that violently rearticulated its origins in imperialism, war and civil war, in which an alternative strategy of military integration was enacted. This involved – paradigmatically – the redirection of social integration from welfare-based organizations towards military units, of different types. The assumption of power by Hitler's National Socialist German Workers' Party (NSDAP) in 1933 was, in key respects, an act of civil war, overthrowing the political order created in 1919. There was no factual civil war in Germany prior to the Nazi take-over. However, 1933 marked the end of a process in which the NSDAP had mobilized its members – in effect – as a private

[11] The key example are the emergency decrees of November 1932 to cut wages.

army, deploying paramilitary units (*Sturmabteilung* [SA]) to stimulate street-level violence to dislodge the constitutional system, creating conditions that threatened civil war. The NSDAP leadership was first installed in power in 1933 by a cabinet comprising many figures linked to the traditional military hierarchy, partly to avert full civil war. Once in power, then, the NSDAP forcibly suspended democratic procedures and imposed a regime close to a wartime control system. Indicatively, the regime was strongly supported by the army (the *Reichswehr*), which formed a core pillar of the system. In 1933, Hitler obtained support from *Reichswehr* leaders, who despised the Weimar Republic because of the conditions imposed upon German military forces in the Treaty of Versailles. Members of the *Reichswehr*, reformed as the *Wehrmacht* in 1935, were required to swear allegiance to Hitler in person. Through this, the regime assumed control of the military apparatus and the army became a subordinate organ of the party-state.[12] After 1935, the reintroduction of military service and huge investment in the army became a primary determinant of governmental integration. From the outset, further, Hitler's system was propped up by irregular troops whose function was to obliterate opposition to the government, so that military units acquired domestic policing roles. After 1934, the party paramilitaries (*Schutzstaffel* [SS]) acquired a more formal role in the governmental system. Parts of the SS were transformed into a hybrid military police unit (from 1936, financed from the national budget), which meant that Hitler was able to mobilize armed forces to prevent domestic opposition. In this regard, although not originating in a military takeover, the NSDAP regime developed as an ideologically charged military dictatorship supported by a militarized party and the regular army. The SS also formed special units in the *Wehrmacht*, so that the separation between common military units and paramilitary bodies was erased; by 1939, the SS and the SA were subject to military law. This was encapsulated by Heinrich Himmler, who, in 1937, declared that the SS was responsible for the 'theatre of war within Germany'.[13]

Through these processes, the basic order of German government depended on the intense militarization of society, in which the distinction between units responsible for external violence and units responsible for internal violence was weakened. This dual militarization

[12] One observer claims simply that the 'Reichswehr was without doubt a National Socialist organization' (Toppe 2008: 275).

[13] See on this and Himmler's plans to fuse the SS and the *Wehrmacht* (Förster 2007: 138).

culminated, first, in the citizenship laws of 1935, which, shortly after the reintroduction of mandatory conscription, imposed a tiered structure of national membership on German society, reducing rights for some subjects. These laws were mainly directed against ethnic minorities, especially Jewish citizens of Germany, but they included measures to weaken legal protection for regime opponents. This formed a moment of state-declared civil war involving the imposition of 'exceptional law' (*Sonderrecht*) to exclude political opponents and ethnic minorities from the national citizenship regime.[14] Through this, the NSDAP consolidated a system of internal coercion that was very close to imperial government in which interstate war, civil war and imperial administrative repression all merged. In fact, the NSDAP addressed citizens of Germany in procedures very close to those traditionally deployed by occupying armies, and the partition between actions typical of the inside and actions typical of the outside of national society lost some strength. This was centrally determined by the fact that the NSDAP saw itself as an actor in a protracted two-front global/civil war against Bolshevism in which internal mobilization and repression were legitimated as acts of war in a universal conflict.

Of profound significance in this respect is that the external wars Germany conducted from 1938 onwards were military programmes in which the patterns of civil war released inside Germany were transplanted, in horrifically intensified form, into other domains. Military conflicts initiated by Hitler's government involved a process of brutal administrative annexation in which modes of internal violence deployed in Germany provided a premise for external colonization. In this process, the tiered citizenship regime already imposed in Germany was reconsolidated in ultra-violent form outside the geographical terrains that, up to 1938, were classified as parts of Germany. In Eastern Europe, this was linked to the fact that some annexed territories contained substantial German populations whose presence was used to justify occupation. These population groups were often (speciously) presumed to be in ethnic conflict with other groups in the societies where they lived. Their members identified as Germans after invasion were integrated into the German army. By consequence, German invasions starting in 1938 often created governmental regimes in which the division between the invading power and the invaded society was placed outside customary understandings of military occupation. In most scenarios, the

[14] Majer (2002: 34).

NSDAP imposed administrations in occupied regions that fused civil and military government, usually establishing variable structures of citizenship to sustain this. This was seen in the division of Czechoslovakia and the creation of the Protectorate of Bohemia and Moravia in Prague in 1938–9. This tendency became acutely visible in the renewed partition of Poland, which took place after September 1939.

In occupied Poland, areas that had been subject to German rule before 1918 were reintegrated directly in the *Reich* from 1939 onwards. In Polish areas, including Krakow and Warsaw, which had not been in the pre-1918 *Reich*, a new administrative order was introduced in 1939. This was known to those who imposed it as the *Generalgouvernement* and to most of those subject to it as *Generalne Gubernatorstwo*. This administrative system was clearly distinct from institutions normally established for military occupation. It liquidated existing Polish political structures and transferred exclusive territorial sovereignty to the *Reich*.[15] Legal spokesmen for the Hitler regime proposed a theory of *debellatio* to explain the status of regions belonging to Poland before 1939. This theory stated that, by 1939, Poland had been fully consumed in war, and German laws could be immediately applied to all occupants of former Polish territory.[16] As a result, the *Generalgouvernement* was created through the imposition of a sui generis organizational system. Governmental force was placed in the hands of administrators, strongly backed by the *Wehrmacht* and the SS, who were appointed both to control the Polish population and to manage genocidal inflows of Jewish citizens and other minorities from different European countries. At the core of this process was a horrific system of constructed citizenship in which many Poles were transformed into enslaved subjects of the *Reich* without authentic national affiliation. This meant that any Polish insurrection against German troops in the *Generalgouvernement* was treated, legally, as a domestic matter. A specific judicial system was established for Poles, so that military opposition to German invasion was regulated by internal criminal law.[17] One objective of this was to deny to insurgent Poles the status of partisans and to classify those who took up arms as simple criminals. More implicitly, this indicated that

[15] On the legal distinctiveness of this system, see Seidel (2006: 29), Toppe (2008: 392) and Mielnik (2020: 111). One historian states that the *Generalgouvernement* constituted 'no-man's land in international law' (Roth 2009: 67). The legal status of this system remained unclear in war crimes trials after 1945. Representatives of Poland claimed that German officials formed an occupation force and were subject to international law (Klafkowski 1946: 75, 78).

[16] Best (1940: 117).

[17] Mielnik (2020: 11).

the German occupying forces viewed war against Poles as an extension of citizenship policies implemented within Germany, so that war against Poland formed part of an imperial civil war, carrying the German civil war beyond Germany itself.

This fused internal/external aspect of German warfare was intensified after the end of the Hitler–Stalin pact. From 1941, German conduct of war was defined expressly as a global civil war against Bolshevism in which unrestrained violence against Communists was declared a legitimate military act. In this context, the understanding of war as legally circumscribed conflict between separate sovereign states was renounced. In this environment, military violence escalated in staggering fashion, as it flooded beyond the basic constructions of statehood. This was made clear by Nazi apologists. Before 1941, leading theorists of international law in interwar Germany had described war with the Soviet Union as the expression of 'existential enmity'.[18] Accordingly, this war embodied the 'absolute form' of war, in which normal rules of interstate obligation lost force.[19] This implied that policies of moral extermination could be used against Soviet citizens because the war conducted against them was not a regular war between sovereign states, but an imperial civil war without fixed territorial location. Unsurprisingly, Soviet citizens reciprocated this by conducting partisan warfare against German soldiers, and the Soviet military response was organized as total societal mobilization.[20]

In each respect, military violence in Eastern Europe after 1939 assumed the form of a fluid global civil war in which war, imperialism, civil violence and genocide were not fully distinct. This cataclysmic explosion of violence began in Germany as a German civil war. It then extended outside Germany. However, war constantly spilled back into German society as domestic opponents and military defeatists became targets of escalating state terror.[21] Here, Germany reproduced in extreme form the traditional convergence between nation and empire, as national formation proceeded through overlapping internal and external violence. More importantly, Germany formed an extreme

[18] Bockhoff (1937: 227).
[19] Gürke (1937/8: 210–1).
[20] The German invasion of Russia was attempted colonization (Pohl 2008: 284). Stalin declared partisan war in 1941, and German soldiers were ordered to execute partisans (see Hartmann 2010: 5).
[21] One account of this process also emphasizes the delimitation of violence in Nazi-occupied areas as the manifestation of hybrid war, following such delimitation in Germany itself (Thalhofer 2010: 164).

manifestation of a democratic constitutional system that failed to direct imperial patterns of integration onto post-imperial foundations. The post-1919 system was designed to separate vertical integration from war and to embed democratic conflicts in a consensual framework. Yet it generated intense lateral conflicts that brought military organizations to the centre of society, ultimately reattaching national integration to extreme imperial violence.

2. POLAND

The interwoven relation between imperialism, war and national constitutionalism was strongly displayed in post-1918 Poland. From 1795 to the foundation of the Second Republic in 1918–19, Polish experiences of citizenship were closely attached to military forces. Distinctively, up to 1918, elements of national citizenship in Poland were crafted through deep traction between military organizations at different levels in the imperial polities that incorporated Poland. Rights of citizenship emerged partly through regimented military experiences and partly through informal military actions, in both of which military organizations inside and outside (pre-1795) Polish territory exercised influence. This meant that the social bedrock of Polish constitutional law, which was established after 1918, was the product of multiple imperial pressures, and it contained a deep and diverse military emphasis. This also meant that attempts to build a sovereign sociopolitical order in Poland faced intractable challenges, and military units, of very different kinds, retained prominence in this process. Through the first experiment in Polish democracy that commenced in 1918, the primary division between the external and the internal dimension of society was not strong.

As discussed, in parts of post-1795 Poland controlled by Prussia and the Habsburg dynasty, Polish residents were initially assimilated in a citizenship regime which governments in Berlin and Vienna had established to integrate their own populations. In parts of Poland ruled by Russia, principles of citizenship were, at first, less consolidated than in other Polish regions, at least until 1905. For example, serfdom survived in Russian-ruled Polish regions until 1864. In fact, serfdom was abolished in the Polish-speaking parts of the Russian Empire three years after its abolition in most other parts of Russia (1861), and abolition was not favoured by the Polish nobility.[22] The liberation of Polish serfs eventually occurred against

[22] Szumski (2002: 245).

a complex background of military conflict in which different actors contributed to the formation of a system of citizenship for Poles.

In the years before abolition, first, Polish regions subject to Russian government were marked by strong divisions between peasants and the gentry, and peasant uprisings occurred across Polish regions in 1861. On the eve of abolition, then, the Polish regions witnessed a major nationalist uprising against Russian rule (1863–4), partly caused by hostility to conscription in the Russian army. The leaders of the uprising created an interim military executive, the National Government, which promised to emancipate the peasantry, issuing proclamations to this effect as early as January 1863.[23] Such declarations were integrally tied to military recruitment plans. The uprising was led by irregular units whose leaders looked for instruments to transform partisan soldiers into a regular national Polish army. The conscription of peasants was promoted for this purpose, and serf soldiers who participated in the uprising were offered freedom and land. Later, the National Government declared that all members of society, without regard for status, were required by 'duties of citizenship' to join nationalist military units.[24] In these respects, Polish citizenship in Russian areas can be traced to specifically national patterns of anti-imperial mobilization.

Importantly, however, the Polish uprising of 1863–4 was suppressed by the tsarist government, which immediately introduced laws to abolish serfdom throughout Polish territories, ensuring that many peasants gained possession of their lands and farms. This policy was guided by imperialist designs in St Petersburg as tsarist elites had noted the low support for Polish nationalism amongst the peasantry. As a result, they tried to weaken attachments between different sectors in Polish society and to destroy the Polish gentry by strengthening the legal position of Polish peasants.[25] The liberation of Polish serfs was accompanied by policies that reduced local political representation of the Polish gentry.[26] These measures were flanked by judicial reforms (1864) in which a uniform court system was established in Russian-governed parts of Poland, permitting peasants increased access to law. One anti-Russian commentator observed how the abolition laws bought a 'phalanx of officials' with ad hoc

[23] The deep connection between the reform of rural society and military emergency in Poland is examined in Kukulski (1995: 114).

[24] *Dekret powołujący do walki wszystkich obywateli polskich* (14.5.1863) (printed in Halicz et al. 1986: 119).

[25] This strategy is clearly noted in Groniowski (1963: 30).

[26] Jurkowski (2001: 447).

powers into local administrations.[27] The years 1861–4 also saw education reforms resulting in increased peasant education, mainly in Russian. As in the 1770s, therefore, policies of citizenship formation were partly imposed in Poland by external actors in order to extricate Polish peasants from traditional agrarian regimes, as these policies subordinated both the peasants and the territories on which they lived to the administrative structure of the Russian empire.

The liberation of Polish serfs from feudal tenure in Russia was deeply connected to intertwined military pressures, and it reflected the intensification of Russian imperialism at this time. After the uprising in 1863–4, the Polish regions in Russia were more invasively colonized. This meant that military obligations of Poles were intensified and conscription increased markedly after the abolition of serfdom.[28] Legislation of 1874 brought near universal conscription in much of the Russian Empire. These developments followed Russian military disasters in the Crimean War, which, as discussed, led both to military reorganization and to agrarian reform. In fact, the enforcement of citizenship norms across Russia coincided with renewed expansion of the empire. This expansion did not only occur in Poland. It also occurred in Central Asia, whose annexation to Russia was very advanced by 1867–8. As discussed below, Russian involvement in the Balkans and eastern Armenia also increased through the 1870s, causing large-scale military conflict with the Ottoman Empire. By the mid-1880s, the Russian Empire had almost reached its full magnitude. In Central Asia, the tsarist government presented itself as the embodiment both of military force and of free citizenship. Slavery, including of Russians, still existed in conquered regions in Central Asia, and the Russian government used this fact to justify military annexation.[29]

In these processes, the Russian empire assumed a presence in Polish territories as an entity that simultaneously imposed colonial rule and stimulated conventional nation-building dynamics. First, as discussed, traditional elites in Poland often opposed general constructions of national citizenship, and, by the 1860s, the Russian government was more willing to establish uniform citizenship norms for Polish subjects than the Polish-speaking gentry. National citizenship for Poles was partly constructed by Russian officials as an element of empire-building policy linked to strategies for Russification. In consequence, the consolidation of shared rights of

[27] Ochimowski (1919: 348).
[28] See Caban (2001: 82); Legieć (2013: 50).
[29] See discussion of this in Brower (2003: 17) and Morrison (2021: 316).

citizenship in Poland was not originally the expression of a national constitutional will. On the contrary, it was stamped into society by external forces designed to undermine Polish social structure. It contained elements of colonization and elements of civil war, and it resulted – in part – from intergroup rivalry amongst Poles, from which the imperial government in St Petersburg drew advantage. At a sociological level, second, Russian laws introduced to solidify imperial rule created the deeper social bedrock for the emergence of stronger national citizenship for Poles. The imposition of conscription after 1874 in Russia meant that Polish peasants who were recruited for the army moved more widely through the country, encountering social groups outside their own localities. Moreover, as they assumed military duties, former serfs acquired increased literacy, gaining access to political literature and to the press – a primary vehicle for forming national consciousness. Military reforms, promoted to instil Russian identity in Polish peasants, had the paradoxical outcome that they increased nationalism amongst sub-imperial communities. This formed a classical process of citizenship formation through military-economic individualization; the longer aftermath of 1864 saw the opening of village communities to capitalist economic practices, the erosion of traditional weaknesses in collective political organization in Poland, and the intensification of military service.[30] The loosening of local and familial ties caused by Russian military recruitment played a vital role in the emergence of a national social domain, which proved conducive to constructions of citizenship separate from the empire in which military recruitment was imposed.

This complex convergence of imperialism and citizenship formation also became visible in the fact that, by circa 1900, many acts of national mobilization in Polish territories ruled by Russia were not exclusively national. On the contrary, the integrated position of Poland in the Russian Empire meant that the struggles of Poles overlapped with conflicts in the empire more widely. This acquired greatest salience in the 1905 revolution in Russia, which, in classical fashion, was caused both by rising military conscription and Russian military defeat in the war against Japan and by long-term conflicts over agrarian reform. The period around 1904–5 saw uprisings against the tsarist government throughout Russian territory involving radicalized former peasants,

[30] Jan Molenda (1999: 58, 111) notes that the year 1904 saw the formation of the first political association for peasants in Russian-governed regions of Poland, indicating growing national consciousness. The increasing military role of peasants in pro-independence movements before 1914 is observed in Hampel (2008: 8). One illuminating analysis discusses the widening of social horizons caused by military service, claiming that conscription for the Russian army was the 'essential experience' for young Polish peasants after 1864/74 (Mędrzecki 2002: 62).

industrial workers and – to some degree – soldiers. This meant that a multi-front war took shape in Russia in which the Russian army fought with Japan, with Russian citizens in Russia, with residents of Polish and other incorporated regions and, in more isolated cases, with mutinous groups of its own members. By 1906, this constellation led to the transformation of Russian citizenship at the national or imperial level, affecting all residents of Russian territory. Yet these events had distinct outcomes for Polish speakers and created new political configurations, whose implications for Polish society at least equalled those of earlier national uprisings, led solely by Poles. In 1905, a range of groups acquired new political prominence in Polish parts of Russia. For example, the revolutionary period saw school strikes among young intelligentsia demanding educational use of the Polish language. As it culminated in large-scale industrial agitation, the revolution crated avenues for the mobilization of workers and peasants, at times in organized political parties with paramilitary wings.[31] Generally, the 1905 revolution brought rapid, semi-militaristic politicization of organized labour in Polish industrial centres. Moreover, the revolution strengthened the conviction amongst conservative nationalists that Russia was a declining empire, opening the path to increased Polish autonomy.[32] The groups who came to prominence in this setting were often deeply hostile to each other, but, despite this, 1905 created a vital revolutionary space for Polish nation-building commitments.

One result of 1905 was that, in 1906, a constitution was introduced for the Russian Empire. This constitution defined powers assigned to the Duma in St Petersburg, founded in late 1905, and it established a first political franchise for Russian citizens, clearly tied to military duties. The constitution did not offer equal or direct participation for all citizens in electoral processes.[33] However, unlike earlier national uprisings, the events of 1905 were not disadvantageous for the consolidation of political rights for Poles; uniquely, 1905 was a moment of uprising in which the political representation of Poles increased. The Duma allowed representation for

[31] On the consequences of 1905 for non-elite political consciousness in Poland, see Kiepurska (1974: 96), Brodowska-Kubicz (1986: 14), Samuś (2013: 76, 307) and Marzec (2016: 90). On the increased militarization of politics around 1905, see Karwacki (1975: 72).

[32] In 1908, Roman Dmowski (2021: 86) argued that the Russian weakness displayed in war with Japan was partly caused by the Polish question, as hostile relations with the Polish population in the Russian empire undermined the empire's strength.

[33] The electoral system was based in limited indirect voting. On one account only roughly 14 per cent of the population of Warsaw could vote (Kiepurska 1974: 288). Polish representation was further reduced in 1907.

Polish parties, and this benefited, in particular, some national conservative organizations. In these respects, the Russian revolution of 1905 created a conjuncture of citizenship in Poland that set the parameters for the move towards full independence that occurred in 1918–19.

This convergence of imperialism, war and national citizenship retained importance in Poland up to World War I. Before 1914, war between different powers involved in partitioning Poland became increasingly probable. This was primarily due to the rapid dissolution of the Ottoman Empire, which caused tensions between Russia and the Habsburg government in the Balkan regions. This reality brought opportunities for Polish independence movements as fissures between partitioning powers meant that Polish nationalist groups acquired new utility in the foreign policies of the empires that governed them. Before 1914, the growing threat of war between Russia and Austria–Hungary meant that the Habsburg government became more sympathetic to Polish insurgents in Russia. Austrian support for the uprising of 1863 in the Russian regions was strong. After 1900, the Austrian army promoted the training of Polish partisan units within its own military structure, with the plan to use them to infiltrate Russia or to provide manpower in case of war. Although their military influence was very limited, such units became foci of nationalist elite formation in Poland.

This role of imperialism in shaping Polish national citizenship culminated in World War I. At this time, war impacted Polish society in a very unusual fashion. In fact, the consequences of World War I in Poland can be divided into three separate categories, elements of which shaped Poland's constitutional form. At one level, the war tragically intensified the fragmentation of Polish-speaking populations in the tripartite occupation system. As Poland was partitioned into distinct imperial citizenship regimes, each partly based in military service, many individual persons who might have considered themselves Poles fought in opposing imperial armies after 1914. As many Poles fought for the Russian Empire, self-identifying Poles often entered combat against other self-identifying Poles, who were forced to fight for Germany or Austria-Hungary. In the Polish context, by consequence, World War I was a hybrid conflict entailing both international war, in which Poles fought against other nations, and civil war, as many potential Polish citizens killed each other in warfare, especially in regions now in Ukraine.[34]

[34] On the close relation between war and civil war in the Polish experience of World War I, see Volkmann (2016: 273).

At a different level, second, the war intensified experiences of Polish national distinction and induced patterns of shared resistance and affiliation. In the early months of the war, German and Austrian forces combined to defeat the Russian army in Polish-speaking regions, and Poles formerly subject to Russia were placed under Austrian/German military administration. This administrative system imposed harsh requisitioning laws on persons subject to it and, in some areas, forced labour regimes were implemented.[35] Such wartime conditions reinforced modes of behaviour traditionally directed towards occupying powers. For example, Polish opposition to military service in the partitioned zones was pronounced, and the direct experience of warfare and the presence of foreign armies on Polish soil brought feelings of national membership to the surface of society.[36]

In this respect, third, the war also shaped Polish nation-building in a more positive manner. The administration created by German and Austrian armies initially had two separate governmental centres, respectively in Warsaw and Lublin. However, this joint administration connected Poles in former Russian regions with Poles in other regions subject to German and Austrian military rule. For the first time since the partition, the war gave rise to a government with overarching reach in Poland, imposing unified political experiences on the inhabitants of (pre-1795) Polish territory. By November 1916, ultimately, the German military command created a partly self-legislating government in Warsaw called the Kingdom of Poland, in which Polish politicians assumed important, although still subordinate roles. One reason for the formation of this system was that the Central Powers believed that selective concessions of governmental autonomy to Poles would stimulate production for the war effort in Polish regions, even increasing the willingness of Poles to fight as recruits in the German and Austrian armies. One leading contemporary commentator observed that Polish institutions established in late 1916 were designed to reinforce 'the call to conscription' issued by the German military command.[37] The traditional exploitation of Poles for foreign military service was intensified through this strategy of quasi-national institution building. Nonetheless, whatever its motives, in the latter stages of the war a specifically Polish governmental system was formed. The institutions

[35] Przeniosło (2003: 28).

[36] On the growth of Polish national consciousness, especially amongst non-elite groups, during the war, see Molenda (1999: 281–289), Przeniosło (2003: 7, 167) and Hampel (2008: 27–29).

[37] Berezowski (1934: 37).

in this system acquired substantial competence and drafts for an independent constitution for Poland were presented as early as mid-1917. This system initially centred on the Provisional Council of State, which was later replaced by the Regency Council. Edicts of September 1917 and January 1918 established the institutional form of the Council, which included the Council of Ministers with separate portfolios, whose president was designated the head of government in Poland.

Through such conditions, World War I produced a military situation in Poland in which colonial occupation, resistance, civil war and the beginnings of national unification were inextricably interwoven. This situation laid the foundations for the independent Polish state, the Second Republic, which was formed in November 1918 as the empires that had colonized Poland from 1772 to 1815 collapsed between early 1917 and late 1918.

Strictly, the first independent Polish administration after World War I was the short-lived commissarial government that was created, through Russian-influenced insurrection, in Lublin in early November 1918. By mid-November 1918, however, the institutions the German army had established during the war formed the basis for the new republic. The Regency Council had in fact announced independence in October 1918, declaring that this decision expressed the 'clear, firm and unanimous will of the Polish people'. Alongside this, rudimentary components of a Polish army had been formed during the war. One reason Polish leaders had been willing to work with the Regency Council was that it promised to establish a military apparatus for Poles. The unenforced draft constitution of 1917 of the projected Kingdom of Poland provided for a Polish army with mandatory conscription (Art. 138). Before full independence had been reached, then, the Regency Council issued decrees in October 1918 which created a Polish army with compulsory military service, and a command structure was designed for the independent armed forces.[38] By the end of the war, distinct Polish military units existed in most parts of the country, as new military organizations emerged from different imperial armies.[39] In these respects, the essential building blocks of Polish nationhood

[38] See the temporary law of late October 1918, Dz.U. 1918 nr 13 poz. 28. On the process in which the Council acquired leadership in the army, see Marszałek (2011: 99–100). On the formation of new military offices, including a chief of staff, before the end of the war, see Winnicki (2017: 257–259).

[39] See discussion of these parallel processes in Wyszczelski (2006: 15–19) and Tomaszewski (2019: 200–205).

had been consolidated during the war. The institutional and economic infrastructure of much of Poland was devastated between 1914 and 1918. Yet the war imprinted some skeletal institutional unity on Polish society. The independent government created in November 1918 already presided over substantial military force.[40] In addition, Poland possessed an organ for international representation before it had achieved independence. A national committee linked to Polish emigrants in the French army was established in 1917.

From late 1918, the basic institutional structure of the Polish national polity resulted, to a large degree, from military imperatives. The first decisive step in the formation of an independent Polish state was the appointment (November 1918) by the Regency Council of Jozef Piłsudski as interim head of state and commander-in-chief of the Polish army. Piłsudski, born a Russian citizen, had previously worked as a military activist linked to the partisan wing of the socialist movement, eventually leading Polish military units in the Austro-Hungarian army. Before his appointment as head of state, he had been interned by the German government in Magdeburg. At his appointment, the form of government in Poland had not been defined. However, on assuming power, Piłsudski passed laws to declare Poland a democratic republic, to create a provisional government, and to formalize his position, assuming strong powers of executive authority and legislative oversight.[41] After gaining formal independence, then, the Polish government existed in a precarious territorial space. The collapse of the empires in which Polish lands had been situated meant that borders were uncertain, subject to conflicting claims. Moreover, the Russian civil war caused deep uncertainty along the eastern frontiers of the emerging state. The Russian civil war entailed typical hostility between domestic political factions. However, this war was not only a civil war. It was in part an anti-imperial war as it entailed mobilization against defenders of the tsarist order. Yet, at the same time, it was an imperial war; it involved the Russian reconquest of some regions, especially in Central Asia, and it converged with territorial conflicts in border regions, including eastern Poland. In this acutely insecure environment, Piłsudski's government embarked on a series of military conflicts over national territory and borders which closely resembled the unification wars in Italy and Germany in the 1860s. After 1918, the Polish

[40] Marszałek (2011: 124).
[41] This was decided in decree laws of 14 and 22 November 1918. Piłsudski's opponents saw him as a dictator (Komarnicki 1922: 51).

government was involved in a war with Lithuania over territorial disputes and the international status of Lithuania. Even before it was formed, the Polish government was involved in a territorial war with Ukrainians in East Galicia; the West Ukrainian army was also composed in ad hoc manner, largely deploying military personnel from the Austrian army.[42] In parallel, the Polish government engaged in smaller border conflicts with Czechoslovakia and in armed hostilities with militias coordinated by German communities in Silesia. By 1919, Poland was involved in a major war with Soviet Russia which threatened the existence of the new state. This war was initiated by territorial conflicts in areas occupied by informally mobilized German troops until 1919. Some of these wars were fought between soldiers mobilized by the emerging government of Poland and soldiers who had very recently lived within the same territorial and electoral spaces as Poles. In conflicts with Ukrainian soldiers and Lithuania, the Polish government conducted war with peoples who had resided in the boundaries of Poland before 1795 and who now claimed independence for themselves. In such contexts, war was very difficult to separate from civil war or even from intra-factional conflicts in different armies. In many cases, military units on both sides contained irregular soldiers. The borders of the Polish state were not finally agreed until 1922–3.

In this international context, Poland was rapidly transformed into a state, ostensibly with one of the most democratic constitutional systems in the world. The transition to democracy was initiated by a decree in late 1918 which announced national elections for January 1919 in which all citizens, male and female, were allowed to vote. Steps were taken at this point to separate the political process from ongoing military violence as serving soldiers were excluded from electoral participation. The transition was then placed on more formalized footing in a shortly worded set of constitutional provisions implemented in February 1919. This text established a governmental system with, in principle, a strong parliamentary bias in which executive power was to be used under parliamentary control and within defined obligations towards appointed ministers.

Despite its declared democratic emphasis, the new Polish state remained deeply determined by military pressures. Piłsudski's office was defined as the Provisional Commander of Government (Tymczasowy Naczelnik Państwa), which recalled leadership titles in earlier partisan

[42] Krotofil (2002: 163).

movements.[43] Edicts of January 1919 established provisions for emergency rule, which allowed deployment of the army for domestic public-order purposes – as a police force.[44] A state of emergency was briefly imposed at this point. Use of emergency military courts was also widespread after 1918, even in civil matters, and the unification of military courts formed an important moment in the consolidation of the state more generally. Further, the first months of the republic witnessed the reimposition of obligatory military service in which defence duties were transferred from occupying powers to the new national government.[45] Moreover, the 1919 elections created structural friction in the polity. Although Piłsudski was originally attached to the left, the first elections produced a legislature with a strong national-conservative bias. This meant that inter-branch tension, in which the re-established *Sejm* was the more conservative organ, formed a pressing constitutional problem for the early republic. The army was controlled by the head of state, who was not aligned to the political majority in parliament. In early 1920, then, the Council of National Defence of the Republic was established, led by Piłsudski and comprising a small group of politicians.[46] This Council was authorized to introduce emergency legislation with instant effect, and it briefly assumed primary executive and legislative duties, at one point assigning civil authority to the army.[47] This period also saw new legislation for the enforcement of states of siege.[48] From late 1918, in short, the new Polish state was close to a military democracy. During its consolidation, Poland was formed both as a state guaranteeing far-reaching rights of citizenship and as a state rooted in military power: these two attributes were closely connected.[49]

On entry into force, the provisional constitutional text of 1919 was applied in uncertainly shifting geographical terrains as border changes were dictated by the fortunes of war, especially in war with Soviet Russia. The constitution was imposed on inhabitants of Poland amidst

[43] See the discussion of this connection in Kaczmarczyk-Klak (2018: 62).

[44] See Decree Dz.P.PP. 1919 Nr 1, poz. 79; Decree Dz.P.PP 1919 Nr 1, poz. 80; Law Dz.Pr.P.P. 1919 nr 61 poz. 364. These powers were enforced in some regions in 1919.

[45] Dz.Pr.P.P. 1919 nr 22 poz. 234.

[46] Dz.U. 1919 nr 53, poz. 327.

[47] See Dz.U. 1920 nr 64, poz. 427. One expert argues that the Council was the primary government body from July to October 1920. With parliamentary approval, the Council issued roughly ninety legal acts in this time (Marszałek 1995: 175–176). Essentially, this period saw government by a constitutionally authorized military dictatorship.

[48] Dz.U. 1920 nr 69 poz. 460.

[49] On these conjoined processes, one account claims that, within a year of its formation, the Polish state committed 75 per cent of taxation to war (Wrzosek 1988: 66–69).

military violence, and constitutional law was extended across the emergent map of Poland as the army asserted powers of military occupation. Indicatively, many residents of prospective Polish territories were not registered to vote in the parliamentary elections of 1919 as national boundaries had not been settled. As residents of contested regions were integrated into Poland, then, the fact that they became Poles meant immediately that they were subject to military duties, so that the experiential frontiers of Polish society were defined by membership in the army. The war with Russia (1919–20) brought extensive military recruitment in Poland amongst both men and women, and conscription greatly exceeded levels during World War I. Harsh requisitioning techniques and forced labour regimes were used to run the war economy at this time. Naturally, many social groups perceived the new constitutional order as a system of military repression that simply reproduced in more acute form governmental structures earlier imposed by empires.[50] These conditions were accompanied by the militarization of police activity in which policing units were deployed to enforce recruitment laws. From the outset, despite constitutional guarantees to the contrary, the army interlocked densely with civil institutions and assumed far-reaching societal functions. This was especially the case in eastern regions marked by interethnic strife and Bolshevik infiltration.[51]

These military contexts integrally shaped Polish citizenship laws. The first law on Polish citizenship (1920) created a strong tie between citizenship and military service.[52] A second decree on citizenship provided for deprivation of citizenship for persons evading military service.[53] This decree specified that the refusal to discharge military service would be evidenced if a potential recruit (i.e. a citizen) left or remained outside the borders of Polish territory during warfare.[54] In parallel, deserters from other ex-imperial armies were entitled to Polish

[50] One historian has explained how in war after 1918 members of the working and peasant classes reproduced their earlier behaviour by deserting from the army. Concentration camps were created in Warsaw to detain deserters (Kania 2019: 287–288, 299). One more patriotic historian argues that, during the Polish-Russian War, desertion reached 40 per cent in 1920 (Szczepański 2000: 104). On widespread anti-militarism in post-1918 Poland, see Stankiewicz (1963: 174) and Stawecki (1981: 111–113). Matters relevant to recruitment and war economics are brilliantly discussed in Podolska-Meducka (2011: 114, 126, 203, 225).

[51] This is explained in discussions of military operations around Lviv/Lwów in Ostanek (2019: 9, 136, 289).

[52] Dz.U. 1920. 7.44.

[53] Dz.U. 1920. 81.540.

[54] Malec (2015: 90).

citizenship if they joined Polish military units.[55] Through such measures, citizenship became a device for recruiting soldiers and for preventing foreign recruitment in Poland. Importantly, similar militarization was evident in states bordering on or at war with Poland. In Russia, the Red Army was formed through conscription and soldiers acquired privileged citizenship status. As mentioned, the construction of independent statehood in Lithuania induced intense militarization. In each case, the form of national citizenship was defined in military conflicts in which civil war and external war overlapped. Indeed, citizenship was often defined as a legal form to separate civil war from external war and to attach military organizations to clear national flags.

Eventually, a formal and, in conception, permanent constitution was passed in Poland in 1921, after the worst period of military conflict. To some degree, this constitution reduced the military emphasis of the polity. It established a strong parliamentary order in which the *Sejm* had control of all legislation, including laws regarding the military (Arts 3–5), and it formalized full male and female enfranchisement (Art. 12), excluding soldiers on active service. It created a relatively weak presidency; the president had the power to issue decrees, but all such ordinances needed to be countersigned by the Council of Ministers (Art. 44), so that ministers had primary authority in key executive domains. Presidential control over the armed forces was also limited (Art. 46). As such, the constitution was intended to obviate the exercise of unmandated power by Piłsudski. This was reflected in the provision that the size of the army depended on parliamentary approval (Art. 5). By 1923, Piłsudski temporarily renounced political office. However, the 1921 constitution retained some military elements. For example, it was a decidedly national constitution, and it was drafted as a counterpart to federalist or even ethno-federalist constitutional projects that had been proposed before 1921.[56] It thus subjected Polish regions to a centralizing regime based in primary loyalties. Further, after 1921, the government remained at least intermittently on emergency footing. Moreover, Polish society continued to be highly militarized. After 1921, the army retained crucial sociopolitical functions, and nation-building strategies were linked to military service and the ideal of the *soldat-citoyen*. This was reflected at the level of constitutional law. Like the German constitution, the Polish constitution

[55] Kania (2019: 294).
[56] For contemporary reflections on early federal constitutional plans, see Komarnicki (1922: 195).

contained provisions for emergency rule (Arts 123, 124). In Art. 91, it imposed universal conscription. Supplementary conscription laws were introduced in 1924. These laws stated (Art. 1) that the army was the defender of national liberty and (Art. 2) that the soldier was a citizen whose duty was to give his (or her) life for the republic.[57]

In post-1921 Poland, military service assumed social functions beyond the sphere of military conflict, and it became a defining mechanism for reinforcing national citizenship and consolidating state control of national territory. For example, the army assumed duties for providing educational resources and combating illiteracy.[58] Moreover, the army played a structural role in social and regional solidification. Owing partly to the stabilization of Bolshevik rule to the east, the Polish government devised citizenship policies that included plans for agrarian reform in which land was to be removed from large estates and given to citizens. These plans began soon after World War I, as legislation of 1920 provided for enforced purchasing of some landed estates.[59] Eventually, such policies were tied to the principle that soldiers should have privileged entitlement to public land; legislation of late 1921 promoted the allocation of land to demobilized servicemen, such that military loyalty became a qualification for inter-class redistribution.[60] In these respects, some radical policies in the early years of the Second Republic reproduced the correlation between military citizenship and landownership that had characterized earlier policies for agrarian reform and peasant emancipation.[61] Lands allocated to soldiers were usually positioned in border regions, often devastated by war, where the presence of loyal soldiers was expected to stabilize national frontiers.[62] In fact, these policies were introduced before Polish borders were formally settled.

The enforcement of military service acquired additional importance in post-1918 Poland because Polish territory was inhabited by many different population groups. Approximately 30 per cent of the population belonged to Ukrainian, Lithuanian, Russian, German, Czech,

57 Dz.U.1924 nr 72 poz. 698. At this time, a conscript army was widely observed as essential for democracy. See, for instance, Haller (1926: 8–11). For comment on the symbolic status of the military citizen, see Kęsik (1998: 29).

58 The role of the Polish army in constructing citizenship was linked to education. It integrated Poles in the republic both as soldiers and as persons with literacy skills (see Wyszczelski 2006: 236).

59 Dz.U. 1920 nr 70 poz. 462.

60 Dz.U. 1921 nr 4 poz. 18.

61 On this similarity, see Landau and Tomaszewski (1967: 164).

62 See Kacprzak (2009: 44–5).

Jewish and other minorities. Like Poles, many of these people had seen their hopes of national independence increased (and disappointed) by World War I. Poland emerged, therefore, as a society that was at least as intensely divided along ethnic fissures as the empires that it replaced. The terms of Polish independence were agreed through a series of international treaties in which the rights of societal minorities were protected. This was expressed both in the Treaty of Versailles, in clauses addressing Poland (Art. 93), and in a separate treaty regarding the status of minorities in Poland, also agreed in Versailles in 1919. This was expressed again in the Treaty of Riga (1921). These principles fed into the 1921 constitution, which contained guarantees for linguistic and cultural rights for minorities (Arts 109–110).

At different stages in the Polish Second Republic, governments promoted measures to address the status of minorities and potential ethnic centrifugality. Initially, such measures had a partly pluralistic tone based in protections for minority linguistic and educational rights.[63] By the 1930s, however, coercive integration procedures became more frequent.[64] Moreover, the army played an important role in enforcing integration. Throughout the republic, military conscription was central to government policies regarding ethnic minorities, and the army assumed vital functions in the management of different populations. The assimilatory functions of military organizations varied over time, and military laws struck a balance between forcible integration and the recognition of ethnic pluralism. In its first years, the army held religious services for different faiths. Later, conscription laws of 1924 allowed soldiers in minority religious groups to swear different military oaths. However, by the later 1920s, the army began to operate as an organ of Polonization intended to inculcate Polish culture into soldiers. From 1922, indicatively, conscription laws forced recruits to serve in the army outside their native regions, so that the army was used to connect Polish citizens from different territories.[65] The land reform programmes, in which soldiers were offered land in return for service, were often intended to locate politically committed and integrated citizens into communities with divided ethnic loyalties.[66]

Vital in the Polish context, however, is that, as in other contexts, the strategies for constructing citizenship failed to establish a strong system

[63] Dz.U. 1924 nr 79 poz. 766.
[64] On these variations, see Chojnowski (1979: 23, 41, 92, 234) and Paruch (1997: 269–281).
[65] Śleszyński (2007: 160).
[66] Wyszczelski (2015: 83–6).

of democratic integration. As in the colonial period, the association of citizenship and military duties often met with resistance in the form of periodically high levels of desertion.[67] More generally, in interwar Poland, two deep fissures obdurately blocked national integration. The 1930s saw increased eruptions of anti-Polish violence amongst minorities, particularly in Ukrainian-speaking regions. Through the 1930s, official ethnic policies became more authoritarian, and the role of military actors in their imposition was intensified.[68] At the same time, interwar Polish society was marked by deep divisions between social classes. By the mid-1920s, the reformist policies projected after 1918 had been palpably diluted. After 1926, the governmental system was broadly committed to the defence of the existing economic order, at least partly owing to international economic pressures. In this context, the Polish government presided over a society marked by extraordinarily deep economic cleavages, often partly overlapping with ethnic divisions.

The limited force of national citizenship in the Second Republic was reflected in 1926, when the constitution was substantially revised. At this moment, the tendency towards military citizenship, which was always pronounced in the republic, gave rise to more overtly violent patterns of social integration. In 1926, Piłsudski and his followers launched a military coup supported by a broad insurgency movement (Sanacja), which promoted national renewal and anti-corruption policies. Following this, the military became an effective organ of the executive and renounced its constitutional neutrality. This was accompanied by a process of military cleansing in which anti-Piłsudski elements were purged from the army and the military leadership lost independence. By late 1926, Piłsudski assumed office as prime minister. Before this, the government implemented decrees and constitutional measures to reinforce the executive against the legislature, reducing parliamentary veto rights and allowing the president to pass legislative acts without parliamentary authorization.[69] These reforms curtailed parliamentary control of the army, enabling the president and the army to assume a conjoined directive position.[70] These changes were followed by emergency laws in 1928 that authorized the head of the

[67] Kasprzycki (2016: 93).

[68] The army played a heightened role in shaping ethnic and internal security policies after 1935. For analysis, see Zaporowski (1992: 153), Nowak (2007: 230) and Ostanek (2019: 316).

[69] Dz.U. 1926 nr 78 poz. 443.

[70] See Dz.U. 1926 nr 79 poz. 445.

army to impose a state of emergency[71] and permitted deployment of the military to secure public order.[72] In this process, Piłsudski resumed his position as de facto leader of the republic, occupying several offices with limited constitutional authority.

The post-1926 regime was initially tolerated by parties of the political left, who resented conservative dominance in the *Sejm*. The post-coup regime was not initially a full dictatorship, and it had unusual features. For example, Piłsudski advocated increased rights for ethnic minorities; officials in the post-1926 system initially supported conciliatory interethnic policies.[73] Yet by 1928, Piłsudski had become affiliated to a notionally cross-party political bloc (Bezpartyjny Blok Współpracy z Rządem), which created a diffuse social power base to support the regime.[74] In parallel, the regime recruited many supporters of the traditional right,[75] and, by the early 1930s, it had acquired highly repressive dimensions, emulating, or prefiguring, methods of the European ultra-right. The government stabilized its hold on power by intimidating political opponents and by instigating violent repression against organized labour, banning some parties of the left. At different junctures, regime opponents were placed in prison or forced into exile, and outcomes of elections were controlled. The regime's support base was attached both to the regular military and to organized paramilitary groups, often comprising former servicemen with experience in World War I. These groups threw their weight behind Piłsudski in election campaigns and promoted mobilization in a pro-government reserve army. Unlike in Germany after 1933, such internal militarization was primarily oriented towards national defence. Despite this, the regime depended on a diffuse military coalition in which military units acquired functions usually reserved for political parties or police forces.[76] Illustratively, the national-conservative figurehead, Roman Dmowski, reflected on the increasing militarization of politics at this time (1934).[77] He claimed that Poland had not undergone full

[71] Dz.U. 1928 nr 8, poz. 54.

[72] Dz.U.RP 1928 nr 32, poz. 307.

[73] Chojnowski 1979: 24.

[74] On Piłsudski's general relation to the left, see Ajnenkiel (1972: 304–307), and on his move towards the radical right see Ajnenkiel (1980: 290–291). On the proximity between Sanacja and the ultra-right, see Kulesza (1985: 231, 261).

[75] Dz.U. 1928 nr 8 poz. 54.

[76] See enlightening discussions of how paramilitaries supported Piłsudski in Niewęgłowska (2011: 87, 131).

[77] Dmowski (2020: 317).

pacification after 1918, and 'military formations, created by secret political organizations' had retained vital structural roles.

After 1926, work began on a new constitution, initially entailing input from different parties. This was mainly designed to reduce the powers of the parliament, justified by the perception that parliamentary governments had been damagingly unstable. The resultant constitution was approved in 1935, and it greatly strengthened executive authority. It gave the president powers to control key appointments and endowed him with vital military competences (Art. 12). It also reduced parliamentary authority in countersigning laws (Art. 14) and made stronger provisions for exceptionalist government (Arts 78–9). Piłsudski died before this constitution could assume force. However, it created a short-lived regime that moved close to a full military dictatorship; it was committed to expansion of the military and the army was assigned a role in economic coordination. In 1936, a long-term plan for reinforcement of the army was announced. Importantly, this was accompanied, in 1937, by further laws regarding agrarian reforms which set favourable conditions for ex-soldiers to obtain land. The historical connection between military recruitment, transformation of agricultural production and internal colonization was again articulated.[78]

In each point, Poland experienced challenging integration processes as it transformed into a national polity under constitutional rule. This process was strongly dependent on affiliations mediated through the army, which had served as a core promoter of national citizenship in the period of Poland's colonization. Originally, the army formed part of a democratic order. As in Germany, however, military organs acquired increased centrality with functions that reached deep into society. In this condition, citizenship was not fully demilitarized, either in the vertical or in the lateral dimension. The post-1926 regime transferred social control permanently to the army and the government acquired features close to these of a military occupation regime.

3. SPAIN

As discussed, the legacies of imperialism gave rise to a distinct conjuncture of violence in nineteenth-century Spain, often resulting in open civil war. After the 1820s, Spanish military spending on the regular

[78] Dz.U. 1937 nr 77 poz. 556.

army was relatively low, and Spain was not engaged in extensive colonial initiatives. However, the army retained a strong domestic position. Civil conflicts beginning in 1808 were rearticulated through much of the nineteenth century as changes in constitutional rule were directly connected to rivalries between military factions. This gave rise to renewed conflicts in the 1860s and 1870s, in which the army again played a central role in defining constitutional form.

The late 1860s witnessed a radical political experiment in which, initially, the army and national militias embarked on a progressive constitutional transformation which resulted in the establishment of a new constitution (1869) and the overthrow of the monarchy and the proclamation of the First Republic in 1873. The 1869 constitution had an ambiguous relation to its military background. On one hand, it contained articles to curtail military powers. These articles prevented unwarranted detention and police intrusion and guaranteed judicial rights, setting out strict constraints on public-order legislation (Arts 2–13). In Art. 31, the constitution delineated the limited circumstances in which such rights could be suspended. On the other hand, aspects of constitutional citizenship were partly determined by military factors. The constitution imposed military duties on citizens (Art. 28). Moreover, universal male suffrage was briefly introduced. This was implied in Art. 16 of the constitution and reinforced by an electoral law of 1870. This period also saw, in 1870, the introduction of the Moret Law, which began the abolition of slavery in Cuba, the main remaining Spanish colony. This law had a strong military emphasis, and it was closely linked to imperial pressures. In Cuba, a war for independence began in October 1868, immediately following the regime change in Spain. This war was fought by an army in which large numbers of slaves and former slaves were recruited, and its leaders supported abolition. Accordingly, the war contained elements of civil war as plantation owners in Cuba often opposed the liberation of enslaved workers. This war soon resulted in the declaration of a republican constitution for Cuba in 1869. Article 24 of this constitution stated that 'all inhabitants of the republic are entirely free' and Art. 25 stated that all citizens were 'soldiers of the liberation army'. In this context, the Moret Law in Spain was intended to regulate the end of slavery in non-revolutionary manner, and it promoted free citizenship to quell the Cuban revolt, to avert civil war in the colony and to preserve imperial authority. In each point, constitutional change in Spain was connected to violence in Spanish territories outside Spain. Radical factions that emerged in

Spain after 1868 favoured abolition throughout all Spanish domains. However, slavery was not fully abolished until after 1874, and the First Republic preserved a model of republican imperialism, extending citizenship norms as part of an imperial strategy. The laws addressing colonial relations incited intensified conflict in Spain. The Moret Law met with deep hostility amongst residual Carlist factions, who utilized the party-political apparatus created by the republic to raise volunteer units to sabotage the government.[79] In some respects, the onset of the Cuban war created a two-front civil war in which external conflicts between Spain and Cuba created new citizenship policies in Spain, which in turn stimulated internal hostilities. The end of the first Cuban civil war (1878) followed renewed regime change in Spain.

By early 1874, the Spanish First Republic was overthrown by the army, which restored the monarchy. This occurred in conditions of partial civil war and armed working-class mobilization. At the cessation of hostilities, a restoration system was initiated, which established the basis for Spanish government for almost fifty years. In key respects, the restoration reflected a compromise between factions engaging in conflict in Spain since the revolutionary interlude that began in 1808. Initially, although it re-established the monarchy, the institutional structure of the restoration system was based in the partial, selective realization of constitutional ideals. The restoration constitution (1876) created a public order in which legislative power was shared between the monarch and a bicameral parliament, which comprised an elected House of Deputies and a Senate, containing, among others, relatives of the king, military leaders, and large property owners (Art. 21). The electoral law of 1870 was initially replaced in 1877. However, the restoration arrangement saw the introduction of regular elections, and elections were conducted with an increasingly large franchise.

Despite this, the restoration constitution preserved much of the pluralistic structure of Spanish society. Importantly, it was supported by an electoral agreement in which the rotation of governmental office was organized through peaceful negotiations between parties, and under this arrangement local bosses (*caciques*) played a key role in distributing influence and managing access to power.[80] This system, known as *caciquismo*, was intended to avoid any deep politicization of society and to maintain elite positions in rural economies. Local

[79] Canal (2000: 178). On the importance of slavery in the move towards Cuban independence, see de Montaud (2000: 48).

[80] Ortega (1977: 357).

patterns of authority remained relatively untouched by the new constitutional order, and some actors who had previously contested constitutional order were placated by the preservation of their social privileges. One contemporary constitutionalist characterized this system as the opposite of parliamentary government. He portrayed it as an arrangement in which parties acted not to facilitate national self-government, but to uphold illegitimate power monopolies in which the executive acquired dominance owing to lack of electoral competition and the social basis of the state was constructed through 'a new type of feudalism'.[81]

Under the restoration, the military again acquired an important role in defining the constitutional form of the state. At one level, the restoration marked the final triumph of civilian government in Spain, contested since 1812. The 1876 constitution separated the state from the army and accorded to the *cortes* far-reaching powers over the military (Art. 88). Through the first decades of the restoration, direct military engagement in politics became weaker and the preponderance of civil power tangibly increased. Indeed, the techniques used for the informal rotation of government were intended to avert the militarization of society. The restoration compromise softened the attitudes of some military elites, so that counter-systemic forces in the army became less disruptive.[82] The placatory impact of the restoration was felt, vitally, in the fact that it reduced the appeal of Carlism, meaning that open civil war abated. However, the restoration system still relied on military support. The restoration leader, Cánovas, styled himself as a military figure, and he was careful to secure the support of the military, stabilizing the polity by integrating military leaders through selective allocation of military office and by allowing the army to control military appointments.[83] Conscription was strengthened in laws and decrees of 1877, 1878, 1882, 1885 and 1896. In the early restoration, laws were introduced that authorized the army to assume core functions in guaranteeing public order. For example, legislation on military organization in 1878, the Ley Constitutiva del Ejército, stated (Art. 2) that the most important mission of the army was to protect the state from internal and external enemies. As a result, the army obtained important duties in civil policing and in the suppression of civil disobedience.

81 Azcárate (1892: 103).
82 See Nuñez Florencio (1990: 5–6); Balfour (1997: 172).
83 One historian argues that civil government in Spain after 1874 was a 'brilliant illusion' – the system 'always required the army to make it work' (Stone 2006: 104).

The restoration of the 1870s initiated a period of equipoise – or a 'tacit pact' – between the progressive-nationalist and the localist-reactionary visions that had polarized Spain since 1808.[84] This was also the moment in which the constitutional alliance between radical-reformist sectors of the middle class and progressive sectors in the military lost force. To some degree, from 1876, both partners in this alliance showed increased support for the governing regime.[85] From this time on, Spanish society began to experience large-scale industrial agitation and, less immediately, agrarian unrest, often exacerbated by hostility to conscription. Both the progressive middle class and the army acquired new, collaborative functions in holding such tendencies in check, which meant that the army accepted a role in helping to avert social politicization and to stabilize the constitution.

In these respects, restoration Spain formed a distinctive example of a polity whose constitutional order was defined by the need to manage military pressures. In the restoration period, the Spanish government imposed representative government and conscription together. At one level, Spain promoted military service as a political duty. Recruitment laws of this time were based in the assumption that 'modern armies are the loyal expression of the nation'.[86] As in other countries, further, the government passed laws to extend electoral participation, which were strongly shaped by pressures caused by imperial collapse and increasing interstate tensions. By 1890, Spain was a European frontrunner in the promotion of the universal male franchise. However, the effects of such electoral laws were balanced by the fact that the alternation of government was predetermined, and candidates for election were usually hand-picked from local elites. The arrangement typical of *caciquismo* was constructed to avert the inner fragmentation of the polity caused by the convergence between political interests and the military, but still to preserve a broad political structure for national society. This system clearly reflected the core constitutional paradigm of the late nineteenth century, in which governments created electoral rights to acquire military force (vertical militarism), but then hedged these rights within measures to avert acute social conflict (lateral militarism).

Nonetheless, to a greater degree than in other major European states, the relation between civil and military power in Spain continued to resonated in unsettling form through society, and the restoration system

[84] Pro Ruiz (1998: 175).
[85] See discussion in Christiansen (1967: 153), Perez Garzon (1978: 507) and Lleixa (1986: 60).
[86] This is taken from a draft law of 1887, printed in *Gaceta de Madrid* (23 April 1887), p. 204.

struggled to unify its constituent groups. Initially, this was connected to overseas conflict. The stepwise loss of Cuba and other colonies, completed in the Cuban war of independence (1895–8), induced broad internal hostility to the restoration system. By 1898, approximately 200,000 Spanish conscripts were engaged in unsuccessful wars in Cuba and the Philippines, suffering very high mortality rates.[87] The Cuban war was marked by extreme brutality as Cuban civilians were uprooted and detained as prisoners in camps and Cuban armies suffered devastating death tolls. In Spain, military losses occurred against a background of deep aversion to conscription, not lastly because, before new recruitment laws were passed in 1909 and 1912, wealthier families could evade enlistment. The political left largely opposed the Cuban war, and martial law was imposed in Madrid to quell the factional unrest the conflict caused. Ultimately, imperial conflicts fed into conflicts of a domestic nature. The aftermath of 1898 saw increased militarization of industrial conflict and repeated regional use of martial law to suppress organized labour. As mentioned, extreme military violence was used in 1909 to suppress protests caused by conscription. At the same time, after 1898, some army factions returned to core ideological positions, advocating political ideals clearly at odds with the constitutional order. Powerful groups in the army imagined a role for the military as a key force in a wider vision of Spanish regeneration, identifying the reconsolidation of Spain's military prestige as the path to robust political order.[88] One outcome of this process was that the military acquired stronger influence in the national political system. This culminated in the passing of the La ley de Jurisdicciones (1906), which heightened the political autonomy of the military. By 1911, the army was mobilized again as part of Morocco became a Spanish protectorate in 1912.

In central points, the final collapse of the Spanish empire in 1898 pulled against the loose compromises that supported the restoration system, weakening the perceived legitimacy and centralizing force of the polity.[89] Tangibly, moreover, the geographical structure of the Spanish nation came under strain through these occurrences as the loss of Cuba reinforced Catalan separatism, not lastly because the Catalan bourgeoisie had strong commercial ties with Havana.[90] As mentioned, most polities that lost wars after 1789 experienced regime change led by

[87] Balfour (1997: 92–3); Stone (2006: 97).
[88] Ortega (1977: 319).
[89] See Balfour (1997: 63).
[90] See on this Nuñez Florencio (1990: 357) and Balfour (1997: 137).

military actors. In Spain, the loss of Cuba did not immediately cause constitutional transformation as the restoration system persisted for a further two decades. However, the Cuban war engendered social fault lines that led to the eventual collapse of the restoration regime, which occurred between 1917 and 1923. Indeed, the Cuban war articulated a conflictual opposition between factions, partly linked to the military, whose hostility would define twentieth-century Spanish politics.

The tensions between constitutional government and militarism became especially acute in Spain between 1914 and 1918. Although Spain was not formally a belligerent power in World War I, the war deeply affected social relations in Spanish society. The war intensified economic conflicts by stimulating demands for Spanish industrial goods and modernizing productive sectors. The war also exposed Spain to transnational ideological conflicts, and the population was sharply divided by rival affiliations. Towards the end of the war, the Bolshevik Revolution acquired deep impact. During this time, the underlying bargains that supported the restoration regime fractured, and intergroup competition increasingly destabilized the foundations of the polity.

Pressures resulting from World War I culminated in the sharp militarization of different social factions, which brought the restoration system to effective collapse in 1917. This militarization was reflected in the actions of organized labour as a general strike with large-scale violence was organized in 1917. This militarization was also expressed immediately through military units, which presented a decisive challenge to the system. In 1916, sections of the army began to form independent *juntas*, whose purpose was to advance the prerogatives of the army, to restore military prestige, still weakened by 1898, and to increase military influence in civil politics. One demand of the *juntas* was that the army should be organized by meritocratic principles and privileges for members of the army serving outside Spain should be abolished. As such, the *juntas* formed a military coalition strongly opposed to the colonial army in Morocco, declaring resentment at the relative autonomy of colonial soldiers. The regular army was divided in its attitude to the *juntas*, and the position of the *junteros* vis-à-vis the traditional political-military establishment was uncertain. On one level, the *juntas* took shape within a context of general political insecurity, and they exacerbated the threats posed to the restoration state by unambiguously revolutionary organizations. Some elements in the *juntas* expressed a democratic military spirit, insisting that military ranks should be attached to genuine service. However, in envisaging a more political role for the military, the *juntas* found allies in the regular army and reactionary social factions. The mobilization of the *juntas* led to the resignation of the liberal premier Prieto, and his replacement by a more conservative, pro-military premier, Eduardo Dato, who legalized the *juntas*. Count Romanones, periodically prime minister during World War I, was a strong advocate of military reform.[91] He perceived the democratization of the army and the imposition of universal conscription as key constitutional hallmarks of a strong nation state. Most importantly, the emergence of the *juntas* signalled that the army had not been fully integrated into the restoration polity, and it again began to assume a role in mediating larger social conflicts.[92] The army was extensively deployed to suppress industrial insurrection in 1917, and it assumed responsibility for securing public order. The influence of the army was reflected in legislation in 1918 designed to assuage military sensibilities.[93]

The restoration settlement was finally terminated in 1923 by a military coup led by Primo de Rivera, attached to the radical right and supported by the monarchy. This coup ended the instability caused by intra-factional antagonism during World War I, and it was cemented by the imposition of martial law and the transfer of civil offices to the army, especially in local government. The early years of the regime saw the expansion of the military court system, allowing military tribunals to hear public-order cases. In particular, the regime used the army as a bulwark against social radicalism as it suppressed traded unions and prohibited opposition parties. The coup was deeply shaped by international conditions. It coincided with the Rif war in Morocco, where the army experienced disastrous losses in 1921. It was partly supported by conspirators in Morocco, who complained about poor political management of the conflict and especially about the government's willingness to establish supremacy of civil rule in the protectorate.[94] The regime effectively remobilized troops in Morocco in 1925, and it was strongly legitimized by prestige extracted from imperial military victories.[95]

[91] Romanones (1920: 26).

[92] One historian states that the Restoration system was partly brought down by 'its inability to reform the army' (Alpert 1982: 96).

[93] The Ley aprobando las Bases para la reorganización del Ejército (1918) contained provisions to regulate military promotions. It also contained provisions for the regulation and promotion of industrial production relevant for war, giving the army a more central role in society.

[94] On the role of the African troops in the coup, see Calbet (1987: 57).

[95] See Calleja (2005: 117).

Institutionally, the regime of Primo de Rivera was built as an alternative to the oligarchical system of the restoration. In intent, it imposed a more fully national administrative form on society and deployed the army as an instrument of centralization, replacing traditional *caciques* with soldier-bureaucrats. As in other cases, this nationalizing policy was reflected in educational reforms as the military regime reached into society to construct citizens. For example, in rural areas, illiteracy declined markedly in the 1920s and the number of university students increased rapidly.[96] Such centralizing policies were accompanied by measures to suppress separatist groups, especially in Catalonia, as crimes 'against the security and unity of the nation' were subject to military jurisdiction.[97] In these respects, the Rivera regime formed a system of military integration in which the will of the army and the will of the people were seen to converge and the army was deployed to force a structure of national citizenship on the country through institutional invasion. At the same time, however, the dictatorship did not efface informal, localized patterns of governments and, beneath the veneer of national unity imposed by military organization, the ancient political contours of Spanish society remained palpable. The military acquired an integral rule in propping up local authority, using military officials to link localities to the state. Moreover, the regime did not touch the economic basis of society. Primo de Rivera eventually convened a body to draft a constitution (made public in 1929, but not implemented), which was intended to create a cautiously pluralistic system with representation through corporatist chambers.

In these different ways, the Primo de Rivera regime established a distinct condition of military citizenship in Spain. By 1917, the informal balance between local and central power resulting from the restoration had been eroded as it lost sustainability in the face of the ideological conflicts resulting from defeat in Cuba and World War I. After 1923, then, the army arrogated new functions in promoting a construction of national citizenship. This construction was imposed, in effect, as a process of social colonization: it cut through the equilibrium of the restoration and linked local regions more tightly to the governmental centre. However, at the same time, the army ensured that the reinforcement of citizenship was achieved in a manner that avoided intense politicization of social divisions. In this respect, Primo de

[96] Tusell (1977: 300).

[97] *Gaceta de Madrid* (19 September 1923), p. 1146.

Rivera's polity reproduced some aspects of the restoration; it was, at its base, designed to avert intense articulations of intergroup conflicts and to structure a path toward nationhood without encountering controllable antagonism, mitigating the polarizing political effects of nation-building. Nonetheless, the military character of the regime meant that it disrupted the local structure of Spanish society, and, as a result, it ultimately brought embedded conflicts to the surface of society, inducing more conflicted expressions of national citizenship. Owing to this, the regime had effects similar to those of World War I in other contexts, as the militarization of citizens gave rise to deep lateral antagonisms. Moreover, as the army was used to regulate society, existing cleavages in society were charged with potential military volatility, and military partitions once again converged with social partitions.

These factors were reflected in the process in which the constitution of the Spanish Second Republic, founded in 1931, was written. The Second Republic was inaugurated after the collapse of the Primo de Rivera regime in 1930, which was followed by the abdication of the king in early 1931. At one level, the transition that occurred in 1931 had limited military implications, and it differed from previous regime changes in Spain in that it was not led by the army. The transition began following municipal elections, which led to a largely non-violent institutional transformation, and the republic even obtained some support amongst members of the army.[98] At one point, the interim government thanked the army for its peaceful behaviour.[99] Eventually, the constitution of 1931 was conceived in antithesis to the regime established in 1923, and it was designed to imprint a unified structure of citizenship on society without military organizations. This was reflected in reforms to the army conducted before the constitution had been promulgated, after the end of the military regime. During this time, the interim minister of war, Manuel Azaña, passed decrees that redefined the institutional position and self-comprehension of the army. These decrees included measures that limited the scope of military tribunals and stripped captains of their judicial powers, and measures that offered retirement on good terms to high-level military figures, thinning out the well-paid and politically obdurate senior ranks. The Ley de Jurisdicciones was also suspended, and the leading military academy was closed by decree. These reforms were driven by the

[98] Barajas (2016: 103).
[99] *Gaceta de Madrid* (23 April 1931), p. 286.

republican conviction that the army should be loyally subordinate to legislative power, and that the military should assume functions exclusively related to war.[100] At the beginning of the reforms, Azaña renamed the Ministry for the Army the Ministry of War to stress this narrow functionality. Also central amongst these acts was a decree of April 1931 stating that all soldiers should swear loyalty to the republic. This was based in the classical revolutionary principle that the 'army is the nation' and 'the army is the nation governed for self-defence'.[101] Azaña had earlier authored a book on military politics in France, where he affirmed policies to democratize the army.[102] A decree of June 1931 abolished regional recruitment zones to reinforce central control of the military. At the same time, the government endeavoured to break the link between colonial politics and domestic insurgency as he attempted to demilitarize the Moroccan government.

Against this background, the constitution of Spain introduced in 1931 clearly rearticulated the traditional principle that an effective constitution for the army was the precondition for an effective constitution of state. To achieve this, the constitution reduced some conventional implications of the military for citizenship formation. Indicatively, Art. 6 prohibited imperial warfare – although, fatefully, this period did not see the withdrawal of the Spanish army from Morocco. Article 77 stated that any declaration of war had to comply with international norms. Article 95 created a unified judiciary, which reduced the independence of military courts. At the core of the constitution was an attempt to create a semi-parliamentary system, which conferred important powers on the president yet imposed checks on the use of executive power by actors able to recruit military support. For example, the constitution created a split executive in which a president and a president of the government discharged distinct functions. In this system, the president was obliged to submit decrees for ministerial approval (Art. 76c). However, the president retained important functions regarding 'the defence of the integrity or the security of the nation' (Art. 76d). Article 80 allowed the president to introduce emergency laws if the congress was not assembled, and, under Art. 81, the president was permitted to dissolve the parliament. Article 42 authorized the government, not the president, to suspend constitutional guarantees where public security was threatened. This partial weakening of the

[100] *Gaceta de Madrid* (27 April 1931), pp. 349–350.
[101] *Gaceta de Madrid* (23 April 1931), p. 286.
[102] Importantly, Azaña (1918: 146) saw the republican army as an organization serving the 'creation of the individual'.

executive was linked to the weakening of the army, as the army was subject to parliamentary control (Art. 37). At a more structural level, the 1931 constitution showed certain parallels to the Weimar Constitution. Although not produced directly by war, it was designed to reorder a society historically dominated by the army. Importantly, it established clauses to protect social rights. Article 44 stated that all wealth was subordinate to the interests of the national economy and the state could intervene in economic production in the public interest. Article 46 placed labour under special protection and foresaw the introduction of welfare laws and provisions for economic co-determination. As in Weimar, the constitution imposed a system of welfare citizenship on society, expecting that the increased economic role of the state would stabilize its sovereignty and direct social integration from military functions to social welfare functions. As in Germany, this was informed by the idea that only a robust model of material citizenship could supplant military force in linking together different regions and groups.

Like the Weimar Constitution, however, the 1931 constitution did not provide an effective constitution for managing military violence, and it did not redirect social integration away from military emphases. In fact, as it was intended to project an overarching definition of citizenship, the constitution brought social divisions to renewed articulation, and it soon attached these divisions to military factionalism.

Significant in this respect, first, is the fact that, from its inception, the constitution was enforced in conjunction with military law. Martial law was imposed in parts of Spain in May 1931, partly because of radical violence against the Roman Catholic Church. This meant that the army immediately became a prominent political actor. At the same time, new public-order laws were implemented, the first being the Law for the Defence of Republic in late 1931. Although introduced by the progressive constituent assembly, this law provided a robust armoury for organizations charged with protecting public order before the constitution had been passed. The powers it established soon became instruments for shoring up a strong executive system in which the traditional fusion between executive force and military authority was reconsolidated. The enforcement of such provisions acquired critical dimensions after 1933, when the original reformist coalition of 1931 was replaced by a reactionary pro-military coalition. Provisions for public-order powers were expanded in the Law of Public Order of 1933, which established new, variable provisions for enforcing states of emergency, and it created distinct tribunals to address public-order offences. From late 1933, very extensive regional and national use was made of emergency powers throughout the republic, and some deployment of exceptional force was almost invariably the order of the day. These institutional tendencies were dramatically reinforced in October 1934, when a militarized strike was organized by miners in Asturias. This strike was brutally suppressed by the army after the declaration of a state of war lasting in which military units were able to act with a high level of autonomy. At this point, political factions on the left and the right polarized acutely, and emergency laws were used for suppressing political opponents of the regime. This led to significant revisions of Azaña's army reforms, restoring some military privileges. In 1935, the ministry of war was placed under the authority of José María Gil-Robles, who used his position to appoint reactionary figures to leading military offices. Importantly, one historian has observed that the failed insurrection in Asturias brought a change in the functional definition of the army as the military was once again perceived as a force designed for 'the occupation of territory', used to subordinate Spanish regions to the power of central government; in fact, a special military command system was installed in Asturias. It is also noted that the suppression of the uprising relied on military techniques previously deployed in counter-insurgency warfare in Morocco.[103] After Asturias, leading politicians in the conservative bloc defiantly connived with military leaders, and the prospect of a reactionary coup was frequently considered. The elections of 1936, in which a leftist coalition, the Frente Popular, triumphed, were conducted in an atmosphere of open violence.

In parallel, one characteristic of the Second Republic was that, as in Germany, the constitutional provisions intended to establish a thick order of citizenship in society proved counterproductive. In the early period of the republic, reformist measures were implemented to address primary antagonisms in Spanish society, especially conflicts over land, which had been partly obscured by previous compromises. These reforms began in 1931 with decrees to weaken seigneurial control of rural labour markets and culminated in the Law of Agrarian Reform (1932). Although hardly revolutionary, this law provided for some redistribution and some expropriation of land held by hereditary title. Other reforms included laws that abolished bonded labour, laws that limited the freedom of landlords in employing labourers, and laws that

[103] See discussion in Madariaga (2002: 137).

co-opted workers to sit on commissions with responsibility for labour-market regulation.[104] Together, these laws formed part of the wider assault on rural patronage and *caciquismo*. These laws were flanked by rural activism, as 1931 and 1934 saw numerous strikes by rural workers. In these contexts, tradition patterns of agrarian violence, caused by the penetration of government authority into rural economies, occurred with particular intensity, and conflicts over land tenure formed an axis of conflict that ran through the republic. Many aspects of these reforms were undone by the rightist coalition after 1933/4. Frequently, military forces were used to control potential rural conflicts.

Overall, the Second Republic formed a polity which was built upon a declared endeavour to solidify a citizenship regime without mobilizing the army as an immediate focus of integration. This was a crucial stage in a longer-term shift towards vertical integration rooted in national constructs of citizenship, which had historically been contested by factions in the military, and it was intended to direct integration from military organization to cross-class solidarity and welfare provision. This process was backed by a narrowed understanding of the army as a republican institution used for national defence and presupposing popular loyalty to the constitution. However, the reforms used to instil national citizenship in society opened intense conflicts over the terms of citizenship, and the constitutional penetration of government immediately militarized rivalries that had remained partly latent during the restoration decades. As in previous periods, this meant that opposed social factions became linked to different military groups and political parties converged with military organizations. Eventually, during the civil war that started in 1936, the army was largely deployed as an organ for asserting government control of society, imposing a harsh peace on protagonists in political conflict. In some respects, the civil war reflected a process of social colonization by military means, intended to reconstruct the imperial form of society. On one hand, in the regime Franco created through civil war, the army was responsible for social control, and it formed the primary national organization. However, the army served to defend strong local interests, and it contained elements of tiered citizenship preserved by military force. The revolt against the republic that caused the civil war was led by troops under Franco, who were stationed in Morocco, and the conduct of the civil war mirrored a colonial war, using counter-insurgency methods aimed at renewed

[104] Decreto de Términos Municipales (20 April 1931). This decree later became a statute.

colonization. This was visible in the fact that the war was often conducted in rough terrain, often between groups with uncertain attachment to political flags, and in circumstances in which classical laws of war had limited effect. This was also the case because Franco's forces were only able to defeat republican armies as they could access German and Italian military hardware, and they were aligned to foreign ideological directives, so that the war formed one scenario in a global civil war.

CONCLUSION

The three polities addressed here reflect, diversely, paradigmatic crises of post-imperial constitution making. From 1870, Germany was formed both as an empire and as a nation. From 1918, it obtained a constitution designed to create a post-imperial nation. Nineteenth-century Poland was the main European victim of imperialism. It obtained a constitution through the collapse of European empires in 1918–19. In Spain, constitutional rule was consolidated as the Spanish empire collapsed, and it was beset by antagonistic forces linked to the legacy of imperialism. In each setting, constitutions were used to stabilize government in society, to integrate populations as post-imperial collectives and to promote models of deeply rooted citizenship. In Germany and Spain, this marked a conscious attempt to create a bargaining system in which military responsibility for social integration was limited. This endeavour triggered profound lateral tensions, and the constitutional attempt to stabilize society by means of a national citizenship regime failed. In each case, acute constitutional crisis was caused by the fact that constitutional identities were not detached from militarism and constructs of citizenship recurrently militarized intra-societal partitions, causing extreme civil violence along class or ethnic lines. In each case, governments again displayed imperial attributes and replicated military modes of coercion that usually typify imperial policies, with some proximity to occupation regimes. Government was formed at the end of an experiment in nation-building in which national citizenship had been separated from its imperial origins. However, government was shaped by convergence between internal and external violence, and government resumed a colonizing form.

Such patterns are most clearly observable in Europe. However, outside Europe, the interwoven relation between democratic inclusion, civil war and renewed imperialism was manifest. In Japan, similar tendencies became evident. As in Europe, World War I induced significant social and political change in Japan. This was partly caused by Japan's military engagement, but it was linked to the fact that international demand for Japanese industrial products increased, leading to intensified industrialization. The decade after World War I then saw deep material transformation of the Japanese constitution as rule by the imperial oligarchy was modified to allow full male enfranchisement, implemented by 1925. As in other settings, World War I released a push for democratization, albeit in non-revolutionary fashion. In fact, democratization was part of a continued strategy to preserve military force as the victory of the Entente discredited the German model of systemic modernization initially favoured in Tokyo.[105] As in other settings, this development also stimulated new modes of political activism. The 1920s were marked by an increased articulation of labour conflicts. This began with food strikes in 1918, but it continued through the period. In the first instance, World War I led to the granting of increased protection to industrial workers. For example, a health insurance law was passed in 1922. By the later 1920s, legislation was put in place that was more permissive to trade union activities, aiming to defuse industrial conflict by supporting moderate unions.[106] This was reflected in the creation of an industrial dispute settlement system in 1926–7. Through this process, Japan followed a classical trajectory in which social integration was redirected from military functions towards welfare functions. Indeed, the early 1920s saw deep cuts in military personnel.

At the same time, military organizations did not lose influence in Japanese society. After World War I and through the 1920s, membership in reservist military organizations increased with the support of military elites, so that rural population groups were widely connected through a web of military associations.[107] Moreover, liberalizing measures were introduced in a form that elevated the potential influence of the military. Alongside changes to the franchise, military service reforms were introduced in 1927, and the Peace Preservation Law was passed in 1925, which permitted mass arrests and heightened the public-order duties of the army. In these points, mass integration after the war was not fully detached from the army, and the army retained

[105] See the very illuminating discussion in Dickinson (2013: 86–87).
[106] I am relying on the account in Garon (1987: 66–112).
[107] See discussion in Smethurst (1974: 182). One historian calculates that the reservist association had 2.3 million members in 1918 (Young 1998: 133).

key responsibilities for social administration. The continued prominence of the army was also connected to the external position of the military. For example, after 1918, the Japanese government acquired former German colonies in the Pacific and preserved garrisons in China and a substantial army in Korea, where it was exposed to nationalist mobilization in 1919.[108] In 1918, the Japanese government had also engaged in ineffective military intervention against Russia. Against this background, as in Europe, the mobilized working class was divided between a radical and a nationalist wing, and parts of organized labour became aligned to conservative political groups linked to the military and supportive of imperialism. This gravitation became stronger after the onset of economic recession in 1929, when the army assumed greater importance as an integrational organization. The course of domestic politics in Japan was then decisively shaped by imperialist actions, as Japanese intervention in Manchuria in 1931, initiating a period of war that lasted until 1945, meant that military actors acquired increased autonomy. Through this event, conservative factions in government became stronger, and, by the mid-1930s, the army was able to shape government policy through threats of military intervention. The authoritarian governments that followed the assassination of the prime minister in 1932 had a strong emphasis on military policy and defence. Illuminatingly, by the late 1930s, the regime, now largely based in the army, passed a broadened national health insurance law (1938), so that the army became an organ of welfare provision.[109] This coincided with the passing of the National Mobilization Law (1938), which imposed conscription and measures to control public opinion, and some branches of trade and production were subject to political control. As in European societies, these events reflected a process of social formation in which citizenship construction had begun in the army and national integration had been promoted through imperial nationhood. Eventually, attempts to guide citizenship away from the military were unsuccessful and a societal order was created in which internal and external policies were closely convergent.

[108] See discussion in Humphreys (1995: 24). This account also explains how public perceptions of the army improved after the earthquake of 1923, when the army also participated in violence against minorities (52–54).

[109] One analysis states that the reforms were intended to ensure 'healthy soldiers' (Sugita 2019: 105).

CHAPTER FOUR

IMPERIAL NATIONS IN LATIN AMERICA

Early constitutions in the Iberian region were created in a context defined by patterns of governance in which military organizations became more prominent, both at the imperial centre and in overseas territories. As mentioned, this was especially evident in the Spanish Empire, where, through the eighteenth century, the Spanish Bourbons subjected dependent governments to stricter vigilance. For instance, metropolitan authority was enforced through the creation of a viceroyalty in Nueva Granada (now Colombia, Panama, Ecuador and Venezuela) in 1717 and again in 1739–40. Later, following the end of the Seven Years' War (1763), the viceroyalty of Peru was divided into new administrative units. Beginning in Havana in the 1760s, a class of intendants, characteristic of Bourbon governments, was also appointed to oversee regions subject to the Spanish crown. The primary goal of these reforms was to consolidate the institutions that organized fiscal extraction and military control in Spanish overseas territories, reflecting the fact that the defence of colonies had become more demanding.[1]

In Spanish-speaking Latin America, the Bourbon reforms were perceived as renewed colonization, *Reconquista*, in which the premises of Spanish government were redefined. Indicatively, one purpose of administrative reorganization was to ensure that senior colonial offices were assigned to Spaniards. This policy altered conventional assumptions

[1] On one account, by circa 1800, the population of Mexico paid 70 per cent more tax per capita than residents of Spain (Marichal 1999: 92).

amongst elite officials in the colonies, and, arguably, it unsettled an informal constitutional order in which colonial notables controlled administrative bodies, often using venal or clientelistic means to distribute powers and offices.[2] The effects of the Bourbon reforms were not uniform, and different regions experienced variations in the translation of reform policies into actual practice. Nonetheless, these reforms provoked strong constitutional reactions across South America, including occurrences close to revolution in some areas. The onset of these reforms gave rise to the *Comunero* revolt in Nueva Granada in 1781, in which hostility to new taxes and defence of elite privileges amongst the urban patriciate converged.

One relatively general result of these reforms was that, while the composition of the imperial bureaucracy became more Spanish after 1763, the imperial military became less Spanish. Together, the expansion of armies and the rising costs of imperial defence meant that new, potentially cost-saving patterns of military recruitment were required to secure military force in the empire. These measures relied on the increased recruitment of local soldiers for units in Spanish overseas territories. An exception to this pattern was in senior military ranks, as non-Spanish participation at the command level was limited until the 1790s.[3] As part of this process, the years after 1763 saw the introduction of new laws for recruiting militias in many Spanish domains, starting in Cuba (1769) and spreading by the 1770s to many Spanish territories. Such militia recruitment was subject to variations, and different administrators adopted distinct approaches to the formation of militias. In some parts of the empire, militias temporarily lost importance in the 1780s as imperial policy was directed towards creating a stronger professional army with larger quotas from Spain.[4] Yet, through the later eighteenth century, enlistment in militias became more significant and militia membership was opened to new groups as governments used local manpower to maximize military capacity.[5] These developments had far-reaching implications beyond the purely military sphere. For example, as militias became more important, the traditional domination of militias by elite members of colonial society was qualified, and militias provided new opportunities for non-elite social groups to

[2] Phelan (1978: 17); Rodríguez (2012: 19). See commentary on this administrative 'reconquista' in Garrido (1993: 116) and Pearce (2014: 147).

[3] Archer (1977: 193–8).

[4] On this policy in Mexico, see Archer (1977: 28–32) and Depalo (1997: 5).

[5] Kuethe (1978: 25).

assume public roles.[6] Indicatively, militias allowed recruitment from different ethnic populations, and they established corporate memberships that overarched different social communities. By the 1780s, multi-ethnic militias had been established, such that military organizations created cross-sectoral affiliations. This meant that, during the reform era, both the social and the ethnic fabrics of the Spanish army in Latin America were transformed. The regular army was more fully incorporated in local society, as more elite members of colonial society sought military positions.[7] At the same time, the militias created new routes to professional status and social mobility for black residents of Spanish domains, with obvious interregional variations.[8]

The militia laws introduced in Spanish regions contained the provision that persons recruited for militia service would be bound by a corporate legal code (*fuero militar*), forming a separate judicial system for those subject to it. In a society in which most corporations contained their own legal order, the *fuero militar* was an important source of legal distinction and protection for militia members. It had originally been reserved for members of the regular royal army, placing soldiers directly under royal protection. The extension of the *fuero militar* to militias made it possible for serving *milicianos* to claim special status in certain matters of criminal and civil law. From the 1760s onwards, the social effects of the *fuero* were significantly altered, as, in order to increase recruitment, new legislation extended the *fuero* to all military personnel, regardless of ethnic provenance.[9] By design, the grant of the *fuero* created strong incentives for minority groups, especially black residents, to join the militias, and affiliation to the militias became an important source of prestige and social mobility, helping to widen both the base of the army in society and the spectrum of royal support.[10] Widening access to the *fuero militar* necessarily meant that military

[6] One analysis of Mexico states that 'changing rules of eligibility for military service during the late eighteenth century' acquired vital nation-building force, linking inhabitants of disparate regions together decades before the push for independence (McEnroe 2012: 142).

[7] See statistical data on the numbers of Spanish soldiers in oversees regions in Fernandez (1983: 300–301).

[8] On this, see Helg (2004: 100) and Munévar (2008: 208).

[9] Royal ordinances regarding militia formation in Spain dictated that the *fuero* should include 'any individual in the militias' (Real Declaración 1767: 167–168). The code for the militias in Cuba, which formed the basis for militia organization in the Spanish New World, declared (Chapter IV, Art. 1) that 'Each soldier in the militia will enjoy the *fuero militar*' (Reglamento para las milicias 1769: 16). Vital in this process in the colonies was the edict passed in Mexico in December 1767, which extended the *fuero* to citizens of different ethnicity.

[10] See for comment on these processes Fernandez (1982: 376), Suarez (1984: 52), Vinson (2001: 227), Helg (2004: 103).

organization acquired greater autonomy in society. Moreover, it reinforced the common professional identity of militia members at the expense of inherited status roles. The military became an important channel for accessing certain rights of citizenship amongst minority populations, and free black soldiers acquired increased social protection by these means.

These military reforms engendered a complex social reality. One result of these policies was that the presence of military units grew significantly in the regions under Spanish rule, so that, over decades, the army, alongside the Catholic Church, became the primary pillar of Spanish government. Prior to the reforms, colonial society was not deeply militarized, and the imperial army merely formed one corporation among others. One further result of these policies was that military units in Spanish territories became ethnically more diverse, more rooted in local fabrics of obligation and more inclined to induce and express local divisions.[11] In crucial respects, the expansion of military duties was promoted by the government in Madrid to bind administrative organs more closely to Spanish institutions and to weaken the privileges and autonomy of colonial administrators. As in eighteenth-century Europe, increased military recruitment brought the broadening of citizenship rights in Spanish territories, which undercut the authority of local notables and intensified the centralization of society. In many settings, the rising importance of military units altered the structure of social life, upsetting existing personal hierarchies, and it caused positional conflicts between groups favoured by the army and members of traditional oligarchies.[12] From the outset, the generalization of citizenship norms was a military process conducted for imperial purposes, and it elicited antagonistic reactions. The hostility to the assumption of the *fuero* by black soldiers amongst traditional elite groups is widely documented.[13]

Such developments were less pronounced in the Portuguese empire. Portugal's military position was fundamentally determined by the fact that it was allied with Great Britain. During the eighteenth-century wars, Portugal operated – in essence – as a client empire bound by treaties to avoid conflicts with Britain and receiving some military protection in return. This meant that Portugal was not a major

[11] For this point regarding Colombia, see Chaparro (2010: 60–61).
[12] Chaparro (2010: 63).
[13] Lasso (2007: 21). One commentator notes that these reforms 'subverted the order' of a society that previously possessed a strongly 'hierarchical structure' (McAlister 1957: 5).

participant in international warfare in the eighteenth century, and military exigencies penetrated less deeply into national and colonial society. In fact, this had enduring impact on social structure in Portugal and its colonies, especially in Brazil, which persisted through modern history. Nonetheless, parallels existed between Portugal and Spain in the eighteenth century. For example, in the Seven Years' War, Portugal was invaded by Spanish troops in 1762 and became involved in inter-imperial border conflicts with Spain in South America, both of which stimulated military reform. Brazilian regions were more fully unified as a Portuguese viceroyalty from 1763 to 1775. The Portuguese military compelled some soldiers in Brazil to discharge mandatory duties, especially in the Corpos de Ordenanças, which recruited residents for local defence. New recruitment laws were introduced in Portugal in 1764. In 1766, military reforms placed recruitment of black residents of Brazil on more formal footing.[14] From 1776, auxiliary corps were founded that abandoned racial distinctions, so that military recruitment gave rise to new social affiliations. Militias were created in 1797 in Brazil which incorporated black soldiers.

The restructuring of military organizations from the 1760s onwards had great importance in the eventual transition of Spanish-speaking domains towards independence. In Spanish regions in Latin America, the Napoleonic occupation of Spain in 1808 initiated a process of state construction in which military bodies acquired unprecedented influence, and national citizenship practices largely emanated from the army. In many settings, 1808 marked the beginning of a period of military dominance, in which traditional actors in society saw their authority diminished, and military units, often defining themselves as organs that expressed and enforced the popular will, became agents of constitutional change. In Mexico, for example, the viceroy was replaced in 1808 by the army, creating a short-lived royalist regime protecting the interests of Spanish elites. This regime was overthrown by a multi-ethnic guerrilla army in 1810, followed by the short-lived reassertion of Spanish rule. In much of Latin America, military organizations became core pillars of transitional government, and, typically, persons brought to prominence by armies assumed leadership roles.

The linkage between military pressures and the realization of independent citizenship regimes across Latin America needs to be observed

[14] For accounts of earlier ad hoc patterns of black recruitment in militias and *corpos*, see Costa (2006: 156) and Silva (2013: 128).

in a global context. Except in parts of the Caribbean region, the path to constitutional rule in South America involved far less military violence than in the USA or in Europe. Hilda Sabato's claim that observers often exaggerate the intensity of sociopolitical violence in South America is surely accurate.[15] As discussed below, further, the institutional effects of military violence differed from region to region. Some polities emerged after 1808 with relatively stable military systems, which provided a solid foundation for government, so that states integrated their citizens in citizenship regimes in relatively controlled form. This can be observed in Brazil. Moreover, some armies recruited far more heavily than others during and after liberation. For example, areas now in Argentina had very high recruitment, proportionate to population size.[16] Yet, despite such variations, the governments that took shape after 1808 had foundations in the military transformation of society that began in the colonial era. After 1808, military conflict reverberated through many regional societies, and different social cleavages acquired specific military articulation. In the first instance, such militarization was linked to relatively binary political strategies, involving parties fighting for and parties fighting against independent statehood. However, militarization found amorphous reflection in society, coalescing with conflicts of local nature and with violent disputes about exclusion and social membership.[17] As in other settings, acts of anti-imperial mobilization expressed identities and antagonisms originating in the colonial era, and they converged with civil war. The deep dialectical interaction between imperialism, civil war and constitutional order was reflected diversely across the region.

This chapter addresses these phenomena by focusing on two states that embody such processes in divergent form – Colombia and Brazil. These polities are selected as counterposed examples of the consequences of imperialism for constitutional law in Latin America. Colombia occupies the region where the first constitutions in the Spanish-speaking world were created. This regional space was strongly militarized in independence wars after 1808, and the path to representative government was punctuated by extreme, very diffuse violence as increased democratization triggered intense and persistent lateral

[15] Sabato (2018: 121).

[16] On one account, by 1816, 5 per cent of the regional population was in the army (Rabinovich 2012: 34–35).

[17] On the general convergence of different types of conflict during independence, see Adelman (2010: 318–319).

conflicts. However, Colombia is also a polity where direct military intervention in government has been relatively infrequent and the army has historically been weak. By contrast, Brazil is a polity where independence wars had lower impact on social structure, and in which, at key junctures, spurts of democratization were conducted without high mortality rates. Yet, despite (or because of) this fact, the Brazilian military frequently engaged in civil politics, and, by the later nineteenth century, it played a key role in constitutional formation. In both cases, imperialism forged a society in which citizenship was shaped by military organizations, and military attachments pervaded post-imperial society. In both cases, the construction of constitutions reflected conflicted processes of internal colonization in which principles of citizenship were defined by the army and military conflicts over citizenship formed the dominant interaction in society. In both cases, the distinction between violence of an external nature and violence with an internal character was frequently unclear and governments appeared as external violent actors in their societies, creating new variants on the constitutional form of the imperial nation.

COLOMBIA

The origins of modern Colombian statehood lay in Nueva Granada, a geographical location that underwent many administrative transformations after 1808, but most of which became Venezuela and Colombia. The emergence of state institutions in this region can be traced to multiple patterns of militarization, and the early rise of national government in Colombia reflected a close interaction between imperialism, militarism, citizenship formation and constitutional law.

As in Spain itself, the collapse of Spanish government beginning in 1808 forced local actors to assume political authority across Latin America, and this led to the formation of *juntas* in many cities, which operated in the absence of royal power. Initially, these *juntas* were intended to preserve political order on a temporary basis, acting in the name of the Spanish monarch, Fernando VII. As such, they extracted a mandate to govern from a legitimist position, envisaging their own suspension in case the rightful monarch should return to power in Madrid. The composition of such *juntas* varied greatly, but they generally assumed important military functions. In some cases, *juntas* quickly obtained responsibilities that exceeded a simple placeholding role, and they began, either expressly or de facto, to assert claims to independence.

The *junta* in Bogotá replaced the government led by the Spanish viceroy. Through this process, *juntas* became central administrative units in small states, increasingly understanding themselves as sovereign actors.

By 1810, Nueva Granada had seen the emergence of several *juntas* that assumed the power, albeit notionally still subject to Spanish rule, to draft constitutional orders for the cities or provinces in which they were located. In such contexts, *juntas* established constituent assemblies more rapidly than in Spain, and parts of the Spanish Caribbean had acquired free-standing constitutional orders before this occurred in Spain.

These early constitutions were founded as military actors moved into central social positions. At this time, military bodies acquired unprecedented prominence, as previously, with the exception of coastal cities, imperial armies had penetrated only lightly into much of Nueva Granada. By 1810, different types of warfare had begun to characterize the region, initiating a long sequence of multifocal militarism. In these circumstances, some militias originally formed in the Bourbon empire became core institutional cells, and militia members played important roles either in creating *juntas* or in providing support for them. This was not a universal phenomenon. In some areas, militias mobilized to defend imperial interests. Nonetheless, in some Caribbean regions, militias acquired great importance during the transition away from empire, and military memberships formed in the colonial period constructed an institutional thread that shaped emergent independent states.[18] Moreover, constitutions were created as new regional governments were exposed to diverse military challenges and they were forced to raise armies in rapid time. In such settings, military obligations became strong determinants of political integration, and constitutions created around 1811 attached citizenship to military duties. The link between citizenship and military duties was programmatically stated in the constitution of Cundinamarca (1811). Here, rights of citizenship were closed to men not enlisted for military service (IX, Art. 7), so that the population was subject to a continuous *levée en masse* (IX, Art. 3). The citizen was defined as the 'soldado nato de la patria' (IX, Art. 2). Similar principles were repeated in other provincial constitutions. Such concepts of citizenship were echoed across all Spanish America at this point.[19] In

[18] On this process in Mexico, see Martínez (2014: 279); on Colombia, see Helg (2004: 147) and Thibaud (2005: 52). On the dilemmas confronting military figures in this process, see Chaparro (2010: 113).

[19] In 1811, the *junta* in Buenos Aires declared that 'all citizens will be born soldiers'. This declaration is printed in Domínguez (1898: 31–33).

these respects, the *juntas* intensified membership patterns already sanctioned by colonial militaries. Before independence, citizenship rights had increasingly been attached to military recruitment, and this connection acquired greatly increased force after 1808.

These conditions meant that the first constitutions created from 1811 had a complex, partly military relation to the constitutional order established in Spain in 1812. As mentioned, the Cadiz Constitution (1812) was written as a document to be enforced across all Spanish domains, and it was intended to impose constitutional rule on regions in South America that were already approaching independence. It was designed to incorporate residents of Spanish overseas territories as citizens of a trans-regional constitutional order (an imperial nation), and representatives of the overseas territories were involved in its drafting.[20] Where enforced, the Cadiz Constitution provided for representative elections based in a large male franchise, and it embodied a spirit of progressive monarchical constitutionalism. To this degree, it established a model of imperial citizenship. However, the impact of the Cadiz Constitution outside Spain was ambiguous. Some constitutions in Latin America created before 1812 were more democratic than the Cadiz Constitution. The Cadiz Constitution also contained strong exclusionary provisions regarding access to citizenship, and subjects of the Spanish Empire of African origin were accorded full citizenship only in cases of special merit, including military service (Art. 22).[21] In addition, the normative appeal of the Cadiz Constitution was questionable for political constituencies in Latin America. Plans for a reconquest of Spanish colonies began under the liberal government in Cadiz, at a time when Spain itself was largely under Napoleonic occupation and engaged in military mobilization against external armies. The *cortes* in Cadiz, mainly comprising liberal delegates, passed legislation to deploy troops in Latin America, to suppress the growing independence movements. At this time, the Spanish government in Cadiz was both a colonized and a colonizing power, and it mobilized troops both to resist annexation and to re-annex other regions. This meant, inevitably, that the promotion of constitutional rule in Spain, legitimated by mobilization against France, had conflicting outcomes when transposed to Spanish colonies. Indicatively, Spanish troops were more willing to mobilize to defend

[20] See discussion in Rieu-Millan (1990: 147–152) and Lasso (2006: 344).
[21] See analysis of the background to this in Rieu-Millan (1990: 152–153).

the empire against independence movements than to defend Spain against Napoleon.[22] Members of independence movements in Latin America expressed hostility to Spanish liberalism, and many independence fighters perceived Spanish constitutionalists as inherently imperialist.[23]

The military disposition of constitutionalism in Latin America was increased by the fact that, in 1814, with the aid of the regular army, the Spanish monarchy was restored and suspended the Cadiz Constitution. At this point, Spanish mobilization for the reconquest of Latin America gained impetus. By 1815, the termination of constitutional rule in Spain meant that populations in Latin America mobilized against Spain, not only for the formal assertion of sovereignty, but to claim constitutional rights that had been abrogated in Spain. In this context, loyalties naturally remained divided, with variations from region to region. Moreover, the intensity of the fighting showed great regional differences. Such conflict reached its most vicious expression after 1815 in regions now in Venezuela and Colombia, where Spanish rule was briefly re-established in 1816. Generally, however, the Spanish restoration in 1814 had the result that constitutionalism became an object of military conflict.

One notable characteristic of this situation was that the first wave of constitution making in Latin America occurred in a setting in which warfare proliferated in often uncontrolled fashion and political questions divided populations into various hostile groups. The move towards independence articulated deep inter-elite fissures in Spanish territories, and the strongest military opposition to independence often emanated, not from Spain itself, but from loyalist groups in colonial society. In Nueva Granada, as Clément Thibaut has explained, the beginnings of the independence era stimulated highly variable patterns of warfare.[24] These included aspects of civil war and inter-municipal war in which interests that had little to do with independence motivated hostilities. One classic study of Venezuela in the early years of independence declares simply that 'the war of independence was a civil war'.[25] The harshest conflicts in Venezuela were those conducted between Simon Bolivar and the royalist José Boves in 1813. Boves

[22] See Costeloe (1986: 116). On colonial perceptions of the liberal Cortes in Cadiz as an organ of imperialism, see Damas (2010: 113) and Montoya (2014: 11).

[23] See Damas (2010: 113).

[24] Thibaut (2005: 20–4).

[25] Lanz (1961: 11).

was declaredly supportive of the Spanish monarchy, but his military aims were of a radical nature; he recruited his army from rural and non-Hispanic populations, appealing directly to marginal groups, and he began to abolish slavery to increase the size of his army.[26] In this environment, the relation between the soldier and the civilian was also unclear, and war led to the acute militarization of civil life, such that the 'armed citizen' became the formative unit of national society.[27] Military hostilities were often concentrated in rough terrain, fought at times by a mixture of royal troops, counter-revolutionaries, republican patriots and militias, foreign mercenaries, local conscripts, released slaves and guerrillas.[28]

Independence became more secure in Colombia after 1819. From this point, however, the military remained the primary constitutional actor. By 1819, political force in Colombia was concentrated in loosely assembled revolutionary armies, mobilized for military conflict little different from civil war. These armies created the constitution-making situation from which Colombia emerged. The basic legal structure of the modern Colombian state can be traced, first, to the Fundamental Law of 1819. This law was passed by the Congress in Angostura, Venezuela, which had established a constitution for Venezuela in August 1819 – shortly after a decisive victory in the independence wars. The Congress in Angostura was partly elected by Bolivar's soldiers, and it drafted a constitution for Venezuela that differentiated between passive and active citizens, conferring active citizenship (the right to vote) on soldiers who had fought for independence (Title 3, Section 1, Art. 7). The Fundamental Law of 1819 bound together Venezuela and Colombia as one country, Gran Colombia, providing for the convocation of a constituent Congress for Colombia as a unified independent nation (Arts 8–9). This law clearly resulted from military actions, and it was accompanied by a decree that placed civil authority in the hands of military commanders.[29] This reflected Bolivar's

[26] This is encapsulated in the description of Boves' army as embodying 'insurrection of a different type', beyond the dichotomy of patriotism and royalism (Figueroa 1985: 246). One historian argues that Colombia saw civil war in 1812–13 and 1814. The first was caused by expansive attempts to centralize political power in Cundinamarca. The second involved the conquest of Cundinamarca by federalist forces and its integration into the federation (see Villa 2010: 103–107).

[27] Conde Calderon (2014: 25).

[28] In 1813, Bolivar declared a war to the death against royalists, defining all Spaniards not committed to the quest for independence as an 'enemy' (Bolivar 1961: 6). On Bolivar's government as 'commissarial dictatorship', see Damas (2010: 88). One interpreter claims that this war 'turned the war for independence into a true civil war' (Thibaut 2005: 98).

[29] Bolivar (1961: 173).

enthusiasm for military centralization as a cornerstone of independent government. It was made possible by a series of peace treaties between the rival armies such that, from the outset, national polity building overlapped with international military accords. Through these accords, a constitution for Gran Colombia was drafted and put into effect in 1821, which established, briefly, a unified state in regions now in Colombia, Ecuador, Panama and Venezuela. This was directly linked to the collapse of the restoration in Spain; as mentioned, the 1820 coup in Spain led to the renewed proclamation of the 1812 constitution in Madrid, and this opened a new constitution-making opportunity in the Spanish overseas territories.

Generally, the period of liberation in Spanish-speaking Latin America was one period in which military necessities determined the construction of citizenship, and constitutions reflected this background, allocating rights to different social groups partly for military reasons. This was reflected, most generally, in the fact that Latin American constitutions created in the independence era, especially those introduced before 1820, created large electorates, as the need to raise armies forced governments to negotiate with large sectors of society. Military needs instilled broad constitutional bargains in society, and this was reflected in the rapid widening of political rights. Moreover, the military expansion of citizenship intensified the tendency, originating before 1808, to create ethnically inclusive modes of citizenship as the conferring of citizenship on marginal ethnic groups was vital for the nationalist military effort. In some settings, wars of independence were conducted by military leaders who promised to emancipate slaves if they took up arms in support of independence. Except for Chile, where the number of slaves was small, the institution of slavery survived the immediate independence period in every country in Latin America. Polities such as Brazil and Cuba, whose elites were economically dependent on slave labour, were much more resistant to abolition than polities such as Colombia, where there were few slaves. Nonetheless, the move towards independence led to the widespread mobilization of slaves and the intensified integration of slaves in military citizenship regimes.

In Nueva Granada, slaves were mobilized both for and against Spain after 1808. In some areas, many slaves were recruited to fight against the armies of nascent republican polities.[30] However, across this regional

[30] One historian describes how in Venezuela, thousands of slaves were motivated to fight against the young republic (Thibaut 2005: 94).

space, the independence period witnessed an increase in emancipation, and military engagement improved the social position of many black inhabitants. In Cartagena, new militias were formed during the break with Spain, and substantial parts of the black population were immediately armed.[31] Financially independent black residents (not slaves) in Cartagena were offered full citizenship in the first revolutionary interim (1810–12).[32] Following his war with royalist armies in 1813–14, Bolivar acknowledged the value of mobilizing slaves. In 1816, he passed a decree offering liberty to slaves willing to fight for independence, preserving servitude for slaves who would not fight.[33] The war for independence thus became a national undertaking linked to the construction of full national citizenship.[34] These processes partly continued after independence. For example, a decree was passed in January 1820 that gave liberty to slaves who had fought for independence. Laws of July 1821 initiated a universal abolition process, determining that, on reaching eighteen years of age, all slaves were to be freed. Many factions reneged on such implied contracts, and the years after 1821 reflected deep ideological cleavages relating to slavery, with repeated attempts to rescind manumission laws.[35] It took three decades until abolition was fully completed in Colombia. In the 1832 constitution, created after division of Colombia and Venezuela and the formation of Nueva Granada as a separate state, slaves were not accorded full citizenship (Art. 5). However, anti-slavery laws acquired broad penetration, and they were implemented by public commissions (*juntas de manumisión*).

Through the longer period of its constitutional stabilization, military factors continued to play a central role in forming the Colombian polity and in consolidating political affiliations in Colombian society. This military emphasis was partly evident at an express legal level. For example, the constitution of 1821 contained clauses laws that – implicitly at least – conferred military competences on the president. Article 128 of the 1821 constitution provided for use of emergency powers by the executive. In a decree of October 1821, the congress

31 Helg (2004: 147).

32 The edict of December 1810 that initiated this process is cited at length in Monsalvo Mendoza (2013: 180).

33 Bolivar (1961: 55–6).

34 The decree of June 1816 passed by Bolivar promised 'libertad absoluta'. This is printed in Bolivar (1961: 55–56). See discussion in Figueroa (1985: 348).

35 On the various attempts to weaken the laws of 1821, see Tovar Mora and Tovar Pinzón (2009: 33–34).

established that the president should be assigned extraordinary authority if required for military success, which, in some areas, meant that the government was only subject to nominal limitations. This law gave the president, initially Bolivar himself, the power to take personal control of the army, to raise military contributions and to impose punishment on an ad hoc basis. By 1828, these provisions were linked to public-order provisions which allowed the president to use special powers to guarantee 'tranquilidad interior'.[36]

Alongside this, the military emphasis of Colombian constitutionalism remained palpable at a deeper structural level, expressed both in the institutional and normative dimensions of the polity. First, this was manifest in the allocation of electoral rights. Initially, the right to vote in the elections that created the constituent assembly in 1821 was partly tied to military duties. This assembly contained armed soldiers, and soldiers who had fought for independence were given the right to vote for its members in primary elections, even if they did not satisfy the property qualifications that otherwise determined access to the franchise. The right to vote was still, in this regard, part of a set of military bargains, and it reflected the idea, inherent in the *fuero militar*, that military participation was a source of social status.[37]

In some regions, the *fuero militar* had remained in existence through the independence period; it was upheld in the 1812 constitution of Cundinamarca (Title VI, Section 1, Art. 1), including for *milicias* (Title VI, Section 1, Art. 31). Under the 1821 constitution, the privileges originally attached to the *fuero militar* were reduced. However, military bodies continued to act as a source of distinct identities and affiliations, and military membership remained a channel for political integration. Later in the 1820s, protection of the right to vote for solders was called into question and measures were adopted that began selectively to disenfranchise the army.[38] The constitution introduced for Nueva Granada in 1832 did not establish a right for soldiers to vote. Yet, despite this, soldiers were awarded sufficient pay to qualify for electoral rights in primary elections on grounds of income. By these means, military attachments remained a line of access to political rights.[39] In

[36] Decreto 1 de 1828 Nivel Nacional (27 August 1828).

[37] See the discussion in Cardoso (2006: 236) and Almarza Villalobos (2019: 22). One observer explains that in the first Colombian citizenship law of 1819 the right to vote was 'part of the *fuero militar*' (Deaquiz 2021: 138).

[38] Bushnell (1954: 270–271) describes how, in 1828, lower-ranked soldiers were excluded from voting.

[39] On these points, see Pinzón de Lewin (1994: 20–21).

the years after 1821, the army continued to act as a core institution in defining national citizenship in society.[40] This was reflected clearly enough in the 1821 constitution, which expressed an understanding of citizenship that was tied to military obligations (Art. 5). The link between citizenship and the army was reinforced in conscription laws of August 1821 and in legislation providing for the creation of a national militia in 1826. This link was also evident in the aforementioned laws that began the abolition of slavery in July 1821; these laws made special provisions for indemnification for slaves that had served in the army. In each respect, the army formed an organ of citizenship.

The link between military roles and citizenship in Colombia after 1821 had dialectical dimensions. Although military membership shaped citizenship laws, laws were also passed to place political rights on non-military premises. For example, the passage of the 1832 constitution coincided with the purging of the higher military ranks and the concerted attempt to separate civil offices from military offices, symbolically linked to the end of the Bolivarian legacy.[41] Nonetheless, military policies remained attached to the idea that the army possessed a central role in citizenship formation. In 1833, José Hilario López, later president but at this time the secretary of state for the army and the navy, explained that military service should bring an entitlement to rights of citizenship. However, he also explained that the military should be subject formally to state control, and the legal apparatus of the army should be subordinate to the regular legal system.[42] In this outlook, national citizenship was seen as related to military involvement. Yet privileges obtained by the army could not be distinct from the national legal order, and military service acquired political value as part of the national constitutional system. Importantly, this statement was made at a time in which the reach of the *fuero militar* had been curtailed. Under the 1832 constitution, soldiers only assumed distinct judicial status when they were on military campaigns (Art. 172). Such arguments implied that military service was a core premise of citizenship, but that rights acquired by soldiers needed to be fused with rights of a general nature, such that the exclusive corporate focus of such rights was weakened. The implication of this was that, ultimately,

[40] One historian has argued that the military served as an organization that circulated 'liberal principles' through society, forming a 'legitimating element' in the republican system (Cardozo 2006).

[41] See discussion in Chaparro (2010: 227–237).

[42] López (1833: 11–3).

rights of national citizenship, which resulted from military engagement, had to converge with political rights of a broader, national character.

In addition, second, the military emphasis of Colombian constitutionalism remained visible because of persistent civil conflict in Colombia. Before the drafting of the 1821 constitution, Colombia had witnessed military conflicts of varied nature. The main conflicts were conducted between Colombian and pro-Spanish armies, but this period also saw violence between different groups in Colombian society, supporting distinct visions of the eventual character of the polity. In 1811, these problems had been temporarily addressed by an act of confederation to connect different regions. However, the longer independence period was marked by the rise of divergent factions, some of which advocated more centralized government for Colombia and some of which were committed to protracting local liberties, such that the military path to independence generated subsidiary conflicts over the form of national citizenship. Such interregional rivalries partly replicated conflicts typical of the imperial period, but they acquired increased urgency through the growing nationalization of government after circa 1815. In this context, as in the imperial period, an important unifying function was accorded to the army. The attempts in the 1821 constitution and in subsequent legislation to construct military roles as the basis for national affiliations were, in part, an endeavour to solidify the army as a national institution, and to use the army to weaken local groups and affinities, committed to defending local authority. At times, the military was used to cement a more coercive structure for national society. As mentioned, 1828 saw the passing of an organic decree that supported a short-lived dictatorial regime. This decree made the head of state responsible for internal and external security (Title 1, Art. 1(1)) and gave him control over military justice (Title 1, Art. 1(9)). By 1830–1, Gran Colombia split into separate states in which most of what is now Colombia was incorporated in Nueva Granada. From 1832, then, the army was organized on a dual model comprising a permanent army and the National Guard, subject to military ordinances, which had defensive functions and responsibilities for preserving public order.[43] In some cases, the National Guard assumed roles that extended beyond military defence, and it played an important role in educating citizens and promoting identification with the republic.[44] On this basis, the army was intended both to solidify the

[43] See an analysis in Prado Arellano (2019: 155).

[44] On the socializing and educational role of the national guard, see Flórez Bolívar and Solano (2014: 607).

national substructure of the state and to draw on traditions of military citizenship manifested in the independence wars.

In each respect, however, it is manifest that, factually, the plan to create a national army strong enough to promulgate an ethos of citizenship was merely a fiction in the Colombian polity. Associations through the army did not establish deep foundations for national citizenship, Colombian society remained enduringly localized, and attempts to centralize the polity misfired. After independence, Colombia had a very high national debt and an ineffective taxation system which impeded military investment and state construction more broadly. A longer-term policy objective of early national governments was to reduce military expenditure, and this was accomplished by the 1840s. Moreover, from 1821, citizens were divided into separate categories, with different electoral entitlements based in property and education, which meant that political representation became concentrated at the local level, and elections were often coordinated by local notables or dignitaries.[45] For these reasons, local actors acquired powerful social positions, and they often developed their own military bodies. This meant that military attachment became strongly focused around local commitments and organizations, and military units cemented strong intra-societal cleavages as local military bonds often prevailed over national duties. Indicatively, from independence, Colombia was repeatedly fractured by civil wars, or by domestic conflicts close to civil war. This occurred, notably, in 1839–42, 1851, 1854, 1860–2, 1876–7, 1884–5 and 1899–1902. Colombia was also engaged in external conflicts at this time; Colombia was at war with Peru in the late 1820s. Nonetheless, the military affiliations that defined the Colombian polity were created, not in interstate war, but in civil war – or in an amalgam of civil war and other semi-latent military conflicts, usually reflecting fault lines that appeared in the first years of independence. This tendency was connected to the fact that the national army was not fully unified, and military leaders in different social locations mobilized for different purposes. Distinct groups in the army tended to reflect divergent views of the overall character of the Colombian polity, with some groups favouring a compact, nationalized construction of the state and other groups favouring a loosely decentralized polity.

[45] See discussion of Colombian citizenship as 'hybrid citizenship' in Uribe de Hincapié (1996: 75). The 1821 constitution differentiated between voters in primary elections and electors, so that many citizens possessed reduced status (Art. 22).

These problems were expressed to the fact that leading regional actors refused to accept the centralization of government in Bogotá, and they consolidated deep partitions in Colombian society. After the creation of Nueva Granada, new or reformed constitutions were introduced in 1832 and 1843. These constitutions rejected the system of military rule and the institutional centralization initially advocated by Bolivar, but they retained a centralist governmental order. However, this period witnessed growing civil conflict over the form of government in which different social and regional groups mobilized against each other. Through the 1840s, Colombian society acquired a strongly bipartisan character in which different political factions began to converge with military organizations. In this context, primary fissures appeared between factions designated as liberals and factions designated as conservatives. The liberals typically supported greater popular participation in government, greater decentralization and abolition of the regular army. By contrast, the conservatives endorsed strong attachments between church and state, increased political centralization and a stronger national army.[46] Originally, persons seen as liberals were associated with regional oligarchies, and they were motivated partly by the defence of secular political institutions and partly by the preservation of local political monopolies.[47] From the 1840s, effectively, different national constitutions were imposed as documents that reflected the given balance of military force between these factions in Colombian society, and each constitution resulted from military conflict. Eventually, a reformist constitution was passed in 1853 which expressed an anti-centralist vision of the polity. Although notionally unitary, it established far-reaching autonomy for provincial legislatures (Arts 50–55) and allowed provincial governments to define their own constitutional orders (Art. 48). It also provided for a very broad electoral franchise. These federalist tendencies were then more strongly expressed in subsequent constitutions, passed in 1858 and 1863, after different regions had promulgated separate constitutions, essentially operating as autonomous states. In 1858, Colombia became a confederation of states, and in 1863, it became a federal polity. This period initiated a secularist republican experiment, with greatly increased electoral participation, persisting until the 1880s.

In this context, clearly, unifying conceptions of citizenship expressed in early constitutional texts found limited echo in social life in

46 For variations on this scheme, see the account in Park (1985: 19), explaining how some conservatives at times also favoured decentralization.

47 See for discussion Llano (1988: 21).

Colombia.[48] Citizenship grew out of a military environment, but it did not penetrate deep into society, partly because military organizations were weakly articulated at the national level. Recurrent lateral militarization became a dominant societal feature. First, over time, the leading political factions in Colombian society developed their own military capacities. In fact, this was the almost inevitable outcome of a society produced by militarization, marked by deep constitutional conflict, yet unable to establish a centralized army, rooted in central institutions. Second, Colombia entered a condition in which, when installed in power, different factions deployed existing military resources against their rivals, meaning that the army became a shield for protecting embedded interests. In both respects, the military apparatus became tied to the bipartisan structure that marked Colombian society more broadly, and the separation between military units and political interest groups lost clarity. Through and beyond the nineteenth century, the distinction between regular political processes and civil war was not categorically established, and elections at times spilled over into military conflict. Moreover, military policies adopted by different governments were shaped by defensive strategies vis-à-vis rival parties. Indicatively, the constitution of 1863 had a strongly federal character, and it was designed to distribute power between the central government and the regions. This constitution effectively created two separate armies (Art. 26), a national army organized at the federal level, and national militias organized in the states. In case of war, members of the state militias could be called up to the national army. However, the national government was not normally authorized to influence military units established in the states (Art. 27). This followed a period in the 1850s in which the government had reduced the size of central armies to enhance the security of regional elites.[49] Such provisions reflected the fact that different factions viewed the army in different ways, and parties committed to federalism were anxious to avoid a build-up of central military force that could be deployed against them. Third, it became characteristic of Colombia that groups located outside government tended to mobilize informal troops against sitting regimes. Over a longer period, the deployment of guerrilla units became a common aspect of political life in Colombia. Especially outside urban centres, the capacity of

[48] On hatred of conscription in post-independence Colombia, see Bushnell (1954: 71), Herrera (2003: 55) and Thibaut (2005: 362).

[49] See Cruz (2001: 134–5).

political institutions to assert a monopoly of the means of military violence was very restricted throughout the nineteenth century.

These factors were articulated in the constitutional constructions of the state that took shape through the middle part of the nineteenth century. At this time, it was increasingly acknowledged that the Colombian polity was an atypical entity, and it was unable to stabilize a dominant position in society above and separate from rival social groups and political factions. In fact, the state itself was constitutionally represented as a scenario of conflict between groups with divergent understandings of national citizenship. By the 1860s, a distinctive constitutional definition of the Colombian state was proposed which construed it, in effect, as an inter-party congress whose function was to preside over hostile factions in society. This idea was expressed in constitutional texts as, by the 1850s, written constitutions increasingly formed hybrids between classical documents of public law and treaties between antagonistic military organizations. In key points, these texts implied that Colombian society was a militarized zone that could not be stabilized by common sovereign means.

Under the constitution of 1863, the central organs of Colombian government were weakly constructed, and the primary locus of sovereignty was placed in the separate states, which were brought together in a compact by needs of security and mutual defence (Arts 1–2). Although it provided for a federal army, as mentioned, military force was mainly organized in the states, and military units retained a high degree of autonomy. In parallel, the national government was constituted in partial analogy to an international organization, acting as a body that mediated between subnational polities. Indicatively, the constitution gave to the federal government the power, under certain conditions, to declare war on constituent states (Art. 19). Moreover, in some respects, the 1863 constitution came close to admitting a condition of belligerence in Colombian territory. In Art. 91, it declared that international norms should be applied in addressing civil conflict within Colombia. This implied that the duties of the national government had a peacekeeping dimension and, in cases of intergroup and interregional conflict, principles of international military law should be enforced domestically. This meant that the state acquired some obligations for intra-societal pacification.[50] More centralist critics also noted that this

[50] One constitutionalist has explained that, in the 1863 constitution, international humanitarian law (still in its infancy) was part of the 'constitutional hierarchy' (Villa 1991: 145).

provision conferred unusual legitimacy on insurgents.[51] In 1867, public-order legislation recognized a condition of civil war in Colombian society and stipulated that the federal government should assume a neutral position in case of conflict between the states.[52]

Following the civil war of 1876–7, international military law was utilized as an organizational form in Colombian society. Indicatively, a military code was introduced in 1881 that contained a clear definition of civil war, and it provided legal directives regarding governmental behaviour in such circumstances. This code also stipulated (Art. 1054) that legal principles governing armed conflict, contained in the Declaration of St Petersburg (1868), should be enforced as domestic military law in cases of civil conflict. Like other legal codes concerning armed conflict, this code denied to guerrillas any formal recognition as soldiers, but it set out basic moral rules for treatment of informal combatants.[53] By inference, such provisions suggested that the national state could only acquire and demonstrate legitimacy as truly national if it separated itself from military factions in society and if agents in the state reduced their own military loyalties. At this point, the national government's main role was to maintain peace between sovereign regions.[54] These provisions indicated that wars within Colombia were not simple civil wars, but, instead, they formed hybrid wars, combining civil war and interstate war, with uncertain boundaries between the internal and the external domain.[55] However, such provisions also implied that the national state itself was a potential hostile military organ acting in analogy to an occupation regime, whose military power in society had to be checked by international law. Implicitly, the functions of the central government were defined in terms that reflected the laws of military that gained significance from the 1860s onwards. The Colombian national government was expected simultaneously to enact and to comply with laws that were later applied to states that occupied foreign territories, and, on this basis, political dissidents – or guerrillas – acquired some recognition as actors distinct from regular criminals. The state itself, in other words, was defined as an actor in

51 This was influentially argued in Samper (1886: 302).

52 Law 20 (16 April 1867).

53 See *Código militar* (1881: 78, 166–167).

54 One interpretation argues that the 1863 constitution established a theory of 'double sovereignty' between the states and the federal union (Uribe de Hincapié and Lopera 2008: 49).

55 This view is shared by Borja (2010: 265), who argues that wars in nineteenth-century Colombia fell between civil war and interstate wars. Likewise, Abad (1992: 4) claims that such conflicts were marked by the 'quasi-internationalization of the interior political-military space'.

a hybrid or semi-colonial war, and its actions were subject to a constitution partly based in laws of military occupation.

Over a longer period, the consolidation of Colombia as a nation state was promoted through constitutional laws that weakened centrifugal tendencies in society. This was cemented by the constitution of 1886, which consolidated a more centralized political order, depriving the states of their residual sovereignty. Although curtailing some basic liberties and reducing the number of citizens allowed to vote, this document initially provided a framework for a relative moderate governmental alliance, drawing support across the political spectrum. Above all, it was conceived as the centrepiece in a long project of national moral consolidation and concerted territorial unification – *regeneración*. This constitution established a strong presidency (Art. 121), it created a national army (Art. 166), and it stipulated that every citizen had military duties (Art. 65). In Art. 170, it protected the special status of soldiers by maintaining the *fuero militar*. Under this constitution, obligatory conscription was introduced, in Ley 167/1896. By the final years of the nineteenth century, extensive measures were introduced to reinforce the position of the army and to weaken its attachment to informal organizations and particular parties. Foreign expertise was imported to achieve this, and military advisors from Chile and later from Germany were employed to place the army on secure professional foundations. In this process, the army was seen – in effect – as an organ of intra-societal annexation, and the expansion of military order was promoted as a technique for securing the sovereign authority of the national government in society. The Colombian army was deployed outside Colombian territory during the wars, which combined aspects of civil and interstate warfare, leading to the loss of Panama in 1903. However, its main function after 1886 was to enforce domestic order.[56]

Despite the attempted centralization in 1886, the attachment between national citizenship and lateral military violence remained the dominant source of instability in Colombian society. As discussed below, the proliferation of internal armed conflict persisted throughout the twentieth century.[57] One state-building strategy that became pronounced by the later nineteenth century was the concerted depoliticization of military personnel, which was viewed as a precondition for robust national formation. By the 1870s, the argument that soldiers

[56] See analysis in Esquivel Triana (2009: 277).
[57] See further discussion in Chapter 8.

should not be allowed to vote acquired support. Of course, this was not unique. Yet in Colombia, such policies had particular importance for national pacification. A law to prohibit soldiers from voting was drafted in 1913. These policies were not put into effect until 1930, when legislation abolished the vote for serving soldiers. The attachment of soldiers to the bipartisan structure of society meant that the exclusion of active soldiers from full citizenship was deemed essential for the consolidation of a national polity.

In each point, Colombia forms the paradigm of a society in which the military configuration of citizenship, carried over from the imperial membership structures, was vital to the first emergence of the nation state. However, the state proved unable to extract stable, vertically installed foundations from this construction, and it was not able to hold together the hostile internal forces released by imperial collapse. The state itself evolved both as an entity with similarities to a party in civil war and as an entity with some features of an empire so that, on both counts, it did not acquire a comprehensively nationalized shape. This formed a particular variant on the paradigm of the imperial nation. It was not until the 1950s that the army was formed as a fully national political actor able to sustain concerted state-building. This initiated a period of national government by the Frente Nacional (1958–74), which temporarily weakened bipartisan conflict. This period saw the reinforcement of the army and the increasingly effective assertion of military dominance by the state. Even this consolidation was short-lived, and society again fractured into military rivalries through the 1970s and 1980s. As examined in Chapter 8, the 1991 constitution was intended as a remedy for the military fragmentation of citizenship, and, like earlier constitutions, it was part constituent act and part peace treaty between warring parties.

BRAZIL

As mentioned, Brazilian history embodies a relationship between constitution making and the military that deviates sharply from the case of Colombia. Nonetheless, after independence, constitutional models in Brazil were enduringly marked by aspects of imperialism, and society as a whole was configured by rival military visions, often rooted in intra-military partitions. In both cases, constitutions were formed by agents attached to the army, and constitutional formation took place as a variant on colonization or imperial nation-building.

The differences between Brazil and Colombia were established during the first independence period. Unlike Colombia, Brazil did not experience full-scale military conflict as a precondition of independence. Most importantly, Brazil retained a monarchical form as it approached sovereign status. After 1808, Brazil became home to the Portuguese royal family, which took flight across the Atlantic to escape Napoleon and established a royal court in Rio de Janeiro. This meant that Brazil developed a centralized military order while still a colony, which remained largely unchanged through the transition. The Portuguese monarchy immediately created the Supreme Military and Justice Council in Rio de Janeiro, reproducing techniques of military control used in Portugal. In May 1809, a military division of the Royal Guard was created, forming the first step in the emergence of a military police force (*policía militar*) to enforce order across Brazilian society. Brazil's first move towards independence occurred in 1815 as it obtained recognition as part of the United Kingdom of Brazil and Portugal. Brazil then acquired status as a fully independent polity (1822) through a division in the Portuguese royal house in which one prince, Dom Pedro, separated himself from the main branch of the dynasty in Lisbon, claiming title in Brazil as an independent monarch. The nature of this transition had a series of distinct consequences for the emerging Brazilian polity.

The dynastic origins of Brazil were reflected, first, in the fact that the premises of Brazilian government were formed in broad continuity with the imperial regime. For instance, the first independent constitution of 1824 was founded through a procedure that was less open to popular contestation than in other regions in Latin America, and it preserved a constitutional monarchy. Initially, a constituent assembly was convened to create the constitution in 1823. The assembly was dissolved in late 1823, and the constitution was imposed through intra-elite agreements in a royal council. The 1824 constitution was not simply a restoration constitution, and it established a state containing some republican elements. From 1824, in fact, the polity was defined as an empire. By the end of the Napoleonic era, this term had acquired a specific valence. It implied a polity combining a mixed system of government in which fundamental laws determined the political order and executive power was exercised in the name of the population.[58] This distinct emphasis can be seen in several provisions in the

[58] See analysis in Slemian (2009: 93).

constitution. For example, the constitution emphasized the principle that government should be a based in a system of balanced powers with organs to temper disputes between legislative and executive branches. Representative government was then reinforced through the opening of a general assembly in 1826. Despite this, the organization of the new state had limited basis in popular decisions, and the constitution was introduced without comprehensive change in the government. Once created, the constitution established a small franchise in which electoral rights were partly exercised by indirect vote, with passive and active citizens (Art. 90). It assigned far-reaching prerogatives to the emperor, who was placed at the head of the executive (Art. 102). The emperor was also accorded the status of a *moderating power*, which included the right to appoint and dismiss ministers, to nominate members of the Senate, to approve laws, and to prorogue the parliamentary chamber (Art. 101). The constitution retained the centralistic design of the Portuguese empire. It established economic chambers at the municipal level (Art. 167), but it did not provide for autonomous governmental bodies outside the main organs of state.

Second, the fact that the independent state was built on dynastic foundations meant that the independence era did not bring military units to the surface of society to the same degree as in other regions. To be clear, Brazil did not become an independent polity in peaceful manner, and military engagement played an important role in the first construction of Brazilian citizenship.[59] Like other parts of South America, Brazil experienced wars of independence against the imperial power, Portugal. These wars began in 1820, following a liberal military coup in Lisbon, and they lasted until 1822–3. Initially, Brazil sent some deputies to the *cortes* in Lisbon, but differences regarding the extent of Brazilian autonomy proved irreconcilable, inducing military hostilities.[60] These years saw the creation of temporary *juntas* in cities and provinces. In addition, conflicts at this time articulated strong regional divisions as different states in Brazil displayed varying enthusiasm for independence. Indicatively, the longer independence period saw an attempt in north-east Brazil (1817) to create a republican polity separate from the Portuguese government in Rio de Janeiro, and it witnessed military conflict between loyalists and separatist factions in other eastern areas (Bahia). Further, after independence, the military

[59] Neto (2019: 627).
[60] See Berbel (1999: 194).

was used to consolidate territorial control in the Amazon, and, in 1825, it engaged in warfare with Argentina over regions now in Uruguay. The transition from Portuguese dominion to independent polity was – in short – not an event that passed without violence, and it exacted a not negligible toll on the Brazilian population. These military conditions were clearly reflected in the 1824 constitution, which devised a new administrative structure for the army and prescribed to citizens a notional duty of military service to defend the empire and maintain its integrity (Art. 145). These provisions were based in wartime legislation of July 1822, which had set out norms for military recruitment, creating obligations of service (with many exemptions) for many single white men and freed black citizens. As in other constitutions, the army's functions were limited to a passive, obedient role (Art. 147).

Nonetheless, in key respects, the transition to independence was less strongly shaped by military violence than in other parts of Latin America. The independence wars in Brazil did not result in a complete transformation of the political system. The social fragmentation usually induced by civil and anti-colonial warfare was not as comprehensive as in some contexts, and, in material terms, the number of casualties and the percentage of the population recruited to the army were lower. This was due to the fact, not lastly, that Portugal was a weak empire, and, owing to its client status, it was less militarized than the Spanish Empire and less capable of mobilizing troops for colonial reconquest.

The relatively low intensity of warfare in Brazil as it gained sovereignty had several implications for the development of Brazilian society. For example, these conditions were reflected in the institutional design of government. On one hand, Brazil was originally formed as a unitary state after 1824, and the formal institutional structure of the polity followed a centralistic design. In this respect, the Brazilian state was unusually centralized in independence-era South America. In key respects, this resulted from the fact that independence had not brought deep war, and it had not induced loyalties that were divided across regions. Beneath the formal-institutional level, however, society did not converge around a strong definition of national membership, and legal bonds emanating from ideals of citizenship were weak. This also reflected the fact that armies had not forced citizenship ideals into the fabric of society, and it mirrored the limited role of the military in state formation. Indicatively, the centralistic design of the 1824 constitution was soon modified. By 1834, an Additional Act was inserted in the original constitution that gave new powers to provincial governments, creating legislative assemblies in the provinces and establishing foundations for provincial fiscal regimes.[61] This revision was in some respects part of a liberal movement against the imperial centre. It followed the creation of a regency, after the abdication of the emperor in 1831, as the army had intervened to prevent a build-up of power at the political centre. The unitary design of the state thus remained largely nominal.

These conditions were reflected further in the fact that, after independence, the Brazilian government continued the territorial consolidation that defined the imperial era. At one level, the absence of a protracted multipolar war meant that the territorial structure of Brazil remained largely unaltered during the independence period, and the boundaries of the country were not marked by military contest. The army did not act as a geographical nation-building organization, and the convergence between the physical delineation of territory and military actions was limited. Instead, the Brazilian army defended existing territories and frontiers, and its main tasks did not greatly differ from functions of colonial oversight in border regions that had been discharged by the Portuguese army.[62] Indicatively, the major insurrections that the Brazilian government confronted were related to border regions and territorial disputes. In the mid-1830s, a separatist uprising took place in Rio Grande do Sul, whose leaders recruited slaves as soldiers and whose suppression required significant military mobilization in Rio de Janeiro. In such initiatives, the army was deployed in a form not obviously distinct from that of a colonial army. In the Amazon, the army continued to conduct an incomplete process of geographical incorporation. To the extent that the army assumed nation-building functions, these were concentrated on territorial absorption in which social assimilation and citizenship formation played a marginal role. The post-independence army remained focused on the preservation of an imperial space.

In addition, these conditions were also reflected in the social dimension of nationhood. Importantly, military conflicts did not pierce deeply into traditional regions of elite influence through the independence period, and the structure of Brazilian society, condensed around

[61] One important interpretation explains that this created a balance between centre and provinces which was vital for the co-option of regional elites in the imperial system (Dolhnikoff 2007: 19).

[62] See Pimenta (2006: 192).

regional economies controlled by powerful families, remained largely unaltered. The absence of extensive warfare meant that patterns of social affiliation and rural administration typical of pre-revolutionary Europe persisted in the sovereign polity after 1822. Above all, the underlying order of the independent polity was defined by a deep intra-elite commitment to the maintenance of slavery. After 1822, the main institutions in Brazil remained tied to the production of key crops – sugar and coffee – which was administered by leading families, strongly attached to an inherited oligarchical order. Such production systems relied on the intense consumption of involuntary labour, and they were not fundamentally disrupted by revolutionary warfare. During the period of military conflict around 1822, some slaves were recruited in Bahia for the nascent Brazilian military and subsequently liberated. At the same time, plans were drawn up for separate battalions of black soldiers.[63] However, the demand for military recruits that had placed pressure on slaveholding economies in Nueva Granada was less pervasive in Brazil, so that the transformation of slaves into soldier-citizens was not widespread.[64] Slavery continued in Brazil longer, and in a less controversial form, than in other independent states in Latin America.

Beyond the independence era, the military became closely aligned to the protection of slavery and the authority of regional oligarchs. After 1824, central control of society remained patchy and the government sustained cohesion through loose accommodations between central institutions and regional families. Indeed, the political system was underpinned most fundamentally by an informal arrangement between the imperial court and local slaveholding elites in which the dynasty helped to preserve the liberties of oligarchs in organizing production in their provinces, with limited intervention. In this context, the role of national military units was necessarily restricted, as bodies with security duties mainly served local interests. By 1831, public-order responsibilities originally performed by militias and auxiliaries were transferred to the National Guard, whose members were typically associated with provincial families. Through the formation of the National Guard, the role of the military in linking government and society was weakened. At this point, military force was strongly tied to local status positions, as regional *senhores* used the National Guard to transmit patronage and consolidate regional authority. In addition, the National Guard

[63] See Kraay (2002: 112–3).

[64] On the commitment of the imperial state to preserving slavery, see Rohloff de Mattos (2017: 240).

acquired an important role in upholding regional economies based in slavery, and its public-order functions involved control of local production systems.[65] The longer independence era saw many slave uprisings supressed by military units. Initially, members of the National Guard were exempted from regular military duties.

Owing to these factors, the military in Brazil in and after the independence-era did not affect national citizenship to the same extent as in some other post-imperial regions.[66] Initially, the army had a relatively marginal role in society, and military units were filled with persons such as prisoners, criminals or vagrants, who were excluded from regular professions. Military organizations were renowned for the poor treatment of servicemen, and rebellions in military and naval units were frequent. Partly by consequence, military pressures did not shake existing hierarchies and oligarchies established in the colonial period survived into the independence period. This in turn preserved privilege-based concepts of citizenship. Here, the Brazilian case contrasts strikingly with that of Colombia. In Brazil, society was not fundamentally unsettled by independence-era conflict, and this obstructed the formation of a unified citizenship regime; in Colombia, military conflict at the lateral level of society proved too intense to permit robust state formation.

Despite these circumstances, over a longer period, the more typical relation between the military as a centralizing force and holders of local and familial authority was partly reproduced in Brazil. Incrementally, for a range of reasons, the military began to promote a conception of national society and obligation that curtailed local authority, tending to imprint a more integrated form on society.[67] Through the decades after independence, Brazilian society was constructed around the process of internal colonization which characterized some European societies of this period. In this context, the army began to effectuate dynamics of nation formation that had remained weak after independence. By approximately 1850, the army took responsibility for

[65] On these points, see Motta (1971: 16), Santos (2003: 97) and Werneck Sodré (2010: 149). In some areas, the National Guard was intended to police borders.

[66] One classic study supports this claim by stating that, as in Brazil military authority was attached to seigneurial corporations, the 'politicization of militias' that formed citizenship practices in other parts of Latin America was weak (Uricoechea 1978: 86).

[67] One observer argues that the centralizing administrative role of the army increased after 1840 (Saes 2013: 19). The same account states that military centralization was initially promoted in a form that served to 'avoid the abolition of slavery' as slavery remained protected at the local level (20).

imprinting a cohesive structure of citizenship on society, and it presented itself as the main organ of the sovereign national people. By 1850, the position of National Guard had been revised and it lost some autonomy as it was directly subject to the Ministry of War. Military reforms of 1850 established more meritocratic structures in the army, and the army became increasingly professionalized and less closely enlaced with personal patronage at the local level. At the same time, many leading officeholders in the military expressed a commitment to increased national unification, and, on this basis, the military became increasingly hostile to slavery. After circa 1850, military figures frequently declared that the formation of Brazil as a fully integrated nation was obstructed by local oligarchies, possessing powers bolstered by coerced labour regimes, and enthusiasm for the abolition of slavery became pronounced amongst military elites.

This transformation in the military was partly driven by rising tensions in relation to other polities, and the social position of the army changed significantly during the Paraguayan War, or the War of the Triple Alliance (1864–70). This war was a devastating conflict conducted against Paraguay by the united forces of Brazil, Argentina and Uruguay. The Paraguayan War clearly fits the definition of a post-imperial war. It was fought over territories disputed during the fragmentation of the Spanish and Portuguese Empires, and it was caused by territorial ambitions on all sides. Under the dictatorship of Francisco Solano López, the Paraguayan government had adopted an intensified pattern of military nation-building, with aggressive intentions towards surrounding states. Although its population was small, Paraguay recruited a high proportion of its citizens for the army, and it resembled states created in militarized inter-imperial landscapes in Europe. However, this war was also a simple imperial war. By this point, Brazil was widely perceived as a hegemonic power in the region, strongly attached to European (British) financial interests and committed to re-enacting colonial modes of government.[68] Brazil's hegemonic position was consolidated after the victory of the alliance in 1870. Moreover, like many wars in regions undergoing imperial reconfiguration, this war was not solely a war between separate sovereign entities. It contained clear aspects of civil war as it was partly fought over land whose political attachment was uncertain. In its effects, then, the Paraguayan War also resembled the wars of unification, fusing interstate war and civil war,

[68] See Bandeira (1995: 148).

which occurred in Italy, the USA and Germany in the same decade. Illuminatingly, a later geopolitical strategist observed that the Paraguayan War was for Brazil a war of physical colonization, as it was fought in remote areas which the government had previously not penetrated.[69] Many soldiers died of sickness on the way to the battlefields because national territory was not linked to military theatres by secure communication routes, so that such regions were physically annexed to the national polity because of the conflict. This war had a decimating impact on Paraguay, killing an extraordinarily high percentage of its male population through combat and disease. This war also transformed the societies of the belligerent powers, as both Paraguay and Brazil implemented laws inducing high levels of military mobilization, which enduringly defined national integration.

In the Brazilian context, extended military mobilization in the Paraguayan War had a deep impact on perceptions of national citizenship. During the war, pressures for increased recruitment meant that the army assumed new salience as an organization that engaged directly with national citizens. In this context, military duties fell disproportionately on the black population, so that the army acquired increased integrational importance at a moment when it incorporated a large number of black citizens. Recruitment of ex-slaves or released slaves became a vital means for generating military personnel in the war; this was partly the case because oligarchical elites avoided military responsibilities, especially in the latter states of the war, as mortality rates increased. However, wartime recruitment was impeded by the fact that military pressures did not bring about the wholesale liberation of slaves. Slaves could usually only enlist in the army if their owners were indemnified for monetary loss, and even escaped slaves seeking to serve as soldiers were often returned to their owners.[70] On these grounds, recruitment pressures in the war converged with existing pro-abolition attitudes in the army, as the functions of the army could only be effectively discharged if more slaves were liberated.[71] After 1870, the army assumed a vanguard role in the abolitionist movement. In fact, after the Paraguayan War, a range of sentiments combined to shape antipathy to slavery amongst military office holders. These sentiments included support for industrialization, seen as essential for national

[69] Mattos (1975: 47).

[70] See comment in Doratioto (2002: 272) and Santos (2003: 99).

[71] On one account, military officials 'participated in the abolitionist campaign from its beginning', and military educational establishments were in the vanguard of abolition (Castro 1995: 77).

development, which necessitated hostility to provincial oligarchies. These sentiments included antipathy to the National Guard, which had performed poorly in the war, and supported the maintenance of slavery.[72] Most importantly, military leaders claimed, not unreasonably, that slaveholding weakened national military capacity such that effective national defence presupposed equal citizenship for all groups.[73]

In Brazil, in short, the Paraguayan War caused several important changes in the position and outlook of the military. First, the army was required to reach further into society to recruit soldiers, and its status as a nation-building organization was reinforced. Second, recruitment demands meant that the enlistment of black soldiers and former slaves grew, augmenting the already important link between the army and the abolitionist cause. Third, the centralizing, nation-building commitments of the army contradicted the interests of local oligarchs. On each count, fourth, the army came into conflict with the imperial government, which was strongly invested in upholding slave-based agricultural production and in obviating the spread of national citizenship norms. One historian argues that an abiding legacy of the war was that a gap was opened, 'fatal for the destiny of the empire', between armed forces and political institutions.[74] In this environment, the military viewed the persistence of monarchical government, with its foundation in regional oligarchies and the protection of slavery, as the strongest check on its modernizing functions. This brought two military visions of the polity, based in diverse residues of imperialism, into sharp contradiction.

The Paraguayan War did not immediately establish a new citizenship regime in Brazilian society. However, after 1870, the army did not surrender its new-found prominence, and the constitutional momentum arising from the war remained palpable. Internally, the military was galvanized by its successful engagement in warfare. It began to appear as a more unified and meritocratic organization, with increased awareness of its function as a guarantor of institutional stability in the state.[75] Through the decades after the war, controversial questions regarding the sociopolitical role of the army – grouped together as the Questão

[72] On the weakening of the National Guard after 1870, see Fertig (2010: 291).

[73] For a discussion of these factors, see Soares (2020: 4). This account states that abolition linked to the army was the mainspring for transition away from the empire (2).

[74] Costa (1998: 144).

[75] Nascimento (2009: 13).

Militar – occupied an important place in public debate, and relations between civilian and military institutions were openly contested. Through this period, the military increasingly asserted itself as a counter-systemic actor. Indeed, the oppositional role of the military was intensified by the fact that, after victory in 1870, public expenditure for military purposes decreased. The self-image of the army gained through victory was not matched by official recognition, and it was perceived in military circles that pre-war deprecation of military personnel remained pervasive.[76] From the 1870s on, further, the social self-comprehension of the military was insolubly connected to the question of slavery, and other military grievances became tied to the abolitionist cause; it was commonly claimed that an truly national army could not evolve in a slave-based economy.[77] Through this linkage, the post-1870 era saw a conjoined process in which more encompassing ideals of national citizenship were promoted, and these were linked to the expansion of military obligations. The first laws to abolish slavery were introduced in 1871, with legislation to ensure that no person could be born into slavery. In the 1880s, Joaquim Nabuco, a leading abolitionist, described this law as a vital attempt by the state to restrict seigneurial relations in rural communities – that is, as 'an act of national sovereignty'.[78] The year 1874 saw the introduction of an early lottery-based conscription law. Importantly, this law remained unenforced because it met with resistance amongst social groups worried about loss of labour, reflecting the anxiety that military service would fall heavily on slaves or ex-slaves.[79]

In these respects, political realities in Brazil in the 1880s were very close to those in some European states at the same time. Through the Paraguayan War, Brazil entered a trajectory through which it was progressively transformed from a residually imperial polity into a nation, so that war induced an accelerated transition from lateral to vertical integration in the polity. This did not involve a strict declaration of national unification as the territorial space occupied by Brazil was not redefined. Yet this was a process in which a more strictly constructed national polity began to emerge at the core of the empire. This polity separated itself from the inherited empire by promulgating specifically national concepts of citizenship able to cut across regional

[76] This point is made in Coelho (2000: 59) and Ferreira (2000: 73).
[77] Werneck Sodé (2010: 185).
[78] Nabuco (2003: 79).
[79] Castro (2012: 55).

divides and displace traditional foci of rural authority. As in other contexts, the form of the nation first took shape within the military, and the army radiated an ideal of national citizenship through society because of military pressures and through military directives. Indicatively, Benjamin Constant, the minister of war following the end of the empire, was a strong advocate of military citizenship. He saw the future of Brazil as dependent on a mobilized class of *soldados-cidadãos* defined by military patriotism. Other leading reformists proclaimed that social change was to be carried forward by two forces – 'the army and the people'.[80] As in other nationalizing societies, the push for a deepened linkage between citizenship and militarism was endorsed by educational reformists, and it was accompanied by an expansion of national education. This was reflected in the growing number of military publications at this time, which found a relatively broad readership. Such journals played an important role in promoting military ethics and military education in society, and they frequently presented distinctive constructions of citizenship, stressing the formative role of the army.[81]

The culmination of these processes can be observed in a sequence of revolutionary occurrences that took place in the late 1880s and the early 1890s, which led to the overthrow of the empire and the creation of a republican polity in Brazil. These events were not solely driven by military objectives. Historians have explained that, in the years after 1870, Brazilian elites developed an increasingly internationalist disposition which both influenced constitutional legislation and proved propitious for liberal reform.[82] This situation was shaped by changes in international trade linked to increasing industrialization and the end of slavery in the USA. It also reflected the rising power of the urban economy around São Paulo, which began to grow rapidly before 1900. However, the nation-building role of the military played a causal role in several transformative developments in the 1880s and 1890s.

First, the abolition of slavery was completed in Brazil in 1888. This process entailed a redefinition of the patterns of loyalty and citizenship that underpinned imperial society. Quite expressly, abolition did not bring an extension of political rights for released slaves.

[80] Antônio da Silva Jardim expressed this view in late 1888 (1978: 237).

[81] One example is a short article in the *Tribuna Militar* demanding the right to vote for army volunteers. This is printed next to articles on military schooling and amateur poetry (23 October 1881).

[82] Preuss (2012: 109).

The abolition laws were preceded by electoral legislation, the Lei Saraiva of 1881, which redefined electoral entitlements and abolished indirect elections imposed by the 1824 constitution. However, in this law, the direct vote was opened only to men who satisfied a literacy qualification, which excluded much of the population. Given the lower education levels amongst unfree workers, this law meant that the path to political citizenship for slaves was blocked before they were emancipated. As in Europe, a strict framework of managed emancipation was instituted, designed to reduce the politically unsettling effects of the liberation of labour.[83] Nonetheless, the abolition legislation weakened traditional sources of support for the imperial system, and it had striking political results. As slavery was abolished, the regional elites that had traditionally drawn benefit from the empire became alienated from it, and one of the key justifications for the empire – the fact that it upheld slavery – disappeared. This in turn meant that the traditional bastions that had supported the empire became less inclined to defend it. One consequence of this was that the centralizing objectives of the army could be much more easily enforced. The abolition laws strengthened the position of military elites in the polity, as they gave legal force to military ideals of citizenship and decreased the willingness of members of traditional oligarchies to resist military political plans.

Owing to these factors, second, the end of slavery, advocated by the army, marked the beginning of the end of the empire as the monarchy was overthrown by a military coup in 1889. This coup was originally supported by an interim decree of 15 November 1889, which declared the existence of a republic, and, from the outset, it abandoned the unitary form of the empire, stipulating that the new republic would have a federal design. The role of the military in the passage from the empire to the republic was always ambiguous. Members of the military elite were pivotal in the ending of the empire. First, Deodoro da Fonseca presided over the early transition, and he dissolved the transitional congress by decree (autogolpe) in late 1891, using emergency laws to create a short military regime. Then, the initial stabilization of the republic was achieved by Floriano Peixoto, who, also supported by the military, remained in power until the elections of 1894. However, the military acted largely without violence in the transition; military figures had strong civilian support, and they were not fully detached

[83] See pp. 138–40.

from political groupings in society.[84] From 1889, the army appeared in effect as a temporary power which emerged in the institutional space left through the weakening of oligarchy and the fragmentation of lateral attachments between monarch and society. The interim decree that created the republic stipulated that a new constitution would be introduced by general suffrage, providing for the establishment of a constituent assembly (Arts 4 and 7). Even during the military interim, figures very hostile to military rule helped to write the constitution for the republic. Republican government was created by civilian actors placed in constituent positions by military actors.

Despite this, the constitution of the new republic, which was enforced in 1891, bore a military imprint, and it displayed constructions of nationhood that had discernibly military origins. The interim government introduced a new criminal code for the army before the constitution entered force.[85] Then, in Art. 87, the 1891 constitution created a federal army, to which both the federal union and individual states were obliged to commit troops, some recruited through lottery-based conscription procedures. Article 34 established a reinforced national congress with heightened fiscal powers, including powers to regulate military spending and dictate the size of the army. In Art. 34(20), the congress was given authority over the National Guard. Article 34(21) contained provisions for the imposition of a state of emergency or a state of siege, in which the congress was allowed to mobilize military force to respond either to external threats or internal insurrection. Under certain conditions, the constitution permitted the executive to impose a state of siege (Art. 48(15)). These provisions were introduced despite opposition from leading politicians, notably Ruy Barbosa, who viewed them as an expression of 'military tyranny'.[86] Importantly, the clauses concerning state-of-siege powers meant that the federal union could prevail over the regions in matters of urgent national interest. This meant that the union itself appeared in constitutional form as a military actor with specific military competences vis-à-vis the regional states. Accordingly, the essential form of national citizenship was concentrated in the army, and the terms of such citizenship could be enforced by the military. In these different respects, the constitution reflected a military understanding of national

[84] Castro (1995: 176).

[85] On the modernization of military law under Constant, who sought to align military order to 'modern principles of law', see Bandeira (1919: 189–190).

[86] Barbosa 1892: 7.

membership. The military powers of the republic were immediately tested in civil war. A revolt against the republic broke out in southern Brazil in 1893, which resulted in warfare that on some calculations killed more than 10,000 people.

At the same time, the impact of military attachments on the 1891 constitution was limited by certain factors, and the constitution did not fully embody the ideals of nationhood circulating in some military groups. The presumption in favour of civilian rule expressed during the transition was clearly demonstrated in the constitutional text. Article 14 reiterated classical liberal principles regarding the position of the army, stating that the armed force must be 'essentially obedient' and should act only within the 'limits of the law'. Moreover, only a minority of delegates in the constituent assembly that drafted the 1891 constitution supported a fully centralized alternative to the unitarism of the empire.[87] As a result, the final constitution had a strongly federal character, establishing a federal order in which individual states acquired far-reaching powers, including the right to alter their territorial structure or to fuse with other states (Art. 4). The federal quality of the polity was supported by a regionalized pattern of organization carried over from the empire, which scarcely touched the social position of oligarchical families. This continuity was reinforced by the electoral system adopted under the constitution. As mentioned, literacy qualifications that determined the right to vote prevented the trans-sectoral expansion of political citizenship. The conditions for the exercise of electoral rights were extensively discussed in the constituent assembly, and commitment to a limited franchise that excluded some people on literacy grounds was reaffirmed.[88] In addition, however, the electoral system in the republic was subject to manipulation and access to office was managed by large families, so that connections between centre and periphery ran through familial channels. The term *coronelismo* was widely used to characterize the post-1891 political system. This term described an organizational structure in which large landowners aggregated votes and secured political influence in regions that they controlled in return for favours dispensed to different groups living in these localities. Importantly, the term referred to persons holding senior ranks (*coroneis*) in the National Guard, whose initial purpose was to act as protectors of public order – the electoral system implicitly incorporated some functions of a policing apparatus designed to maintain social

[87] Carvalho (2011: 150).
[88] Lynch (2011: 313).

stability. Through the consolidation of *coronelismo*, the transition from empire to republic was conducted without deep disruption of the pre-national oligarchies. In some respects, the system replicated earlier techniques for colonization rooted in patronage and commercial interests linked to familial control of different regions.

Together, these compromises meant that, in vital areas, the 1891 constitution upheld many features of the pre-1889 imperial system. Indeed, many aspects of the empire that nationalists in the military criticized continued to exist, often in strengthened form.

In the longer wake of 1891, then, the position of the army in the Brazilian social order reverted to some of its traditional features. The centrifugal structure of society was reproduced, and, concurrently, the army was required to play a role in upholding this social order and the bargains on which it reposed. Indicatively, the civil-political functions of the army were expanded in the years after 1891. At this time, the republic saw repeated use of provisions for enforcing the state of siege in cases of insurrection, such that emergency rule, enforced by the army, became an important component of government. One historian calculates that, during the republic (1891–1930), the state of siege was declared eleven times, and Rio de Janeiro was placed under emergency rule for 17 per cent of the entire period.[89] Through these developments, the military was expected to fulfil harsh repressive responsibilities, and the republic acquired a form close to that of recently unified states in Europe, based in low effective social integration and strategic use of military force. In other words, after 1891, the army increased its powers of social coercion but its integrational functions remained restricted. These facts meant that the military occupied a precarious and unsettling constitutional position. After 1891, the military served as a vital pillar of the government, as it had been instrumental in creating the republic. However, core factions within the army were motivated by ideals of citizenship that contradicted the underlying definition of the republic. As a result, the republic instilled a partition in the army between groups with different allegiances, split between nationalist and pro-oligarchical sympathies. After 1891, many of the uprisings that were suppressed by emergency laws originated in the army itself.[90] In key respects, the republic had its foundations in a division inside the armed forces. Members of elite military strata were

[89] Lynch (2011: 300).

[90] One contemporary account shows how the imposition of the state of siege, conducted by military actors, was typically used to suppress military mobilization (Fonseca 1916: 97).

accommodated in the political system, but regular members of the professional army were alienated from it, and their attachments to the nationalist ideals that predated 1889 remained strong.

Also important in this regard is the fact that, after 1891, civil–military relations were often critical. Although the army had helped to found the republic, the social perception and institutional order of the military caused persistent dissatisfaction amongst soldiers. Despite attempts to increase conscription, military service remained in essence a form of punishment, often serving as a substitute for incarceration, and standards of professionalism in the army were not high. This did little to enhance the army's social prestige. This situation was exacerbated by the fact that, from its origin, the republic was marked by a conflict between the army and the navy. The navy enjoyed greater prestige than the army, and naval careers were preferred by elite groups attached to the landowning class.[91] Moreover, protests amongst members of the military and naval forces about employment conditions were frequent. Such protest culminated notably in an attempted military coup in 1904 and a naval uprising in 1910, which partly reflected hostility to increased conscription.

Under such conditions, the historical conflicts between the military and the political establishment retained powerful social force in post-1891 Brazil. Such conflict was reflected ideologically in the renewed emergence of military factions that identified the army as the primary unit of the nation, advocating increased engagement of the military in national formation. After 1900, demands for military reform in Brazil grew in intensity, often closely linked to demands for political reform. These demands gave rise to the passing of a military service bill in 1908, which was not implemented until 1917. This law was partly designed to improve the standing of the army, and its supporters in the military imagined that it would connect the nation and the army more fundamentally.[92] As in many European countries, this period also saw a wider militarization of society, with the proliferation of shooting clubs and informal military associations.[93] The year 1913 saw the founding of the journal *Defesa Nacional*, committed to modernization of the army. The officers promoting such reform were directly influenced by contemporary events in the Ottoman Empire, and they were often branded Young Turks. Self-evidently, the frequency of emergency government

[91] See Motta (1971: 52).
[92] Castro (2012: 56).
[93] See on these points McCann (1984: 746).

practices in the republic meant that political opposition in the army became a matter of great sensitivity. The military became more assertive and more strongly engaged in national politics in a period in which governmental deployment of the army assumed a vital role in domestic security and social control. The reliance of the government on the army for management of civil violence instilled a persistent contradiction in the centre of the polity, as the state was dependent upon the mobilization of violence by units with partly conflicting ideological dispositions.

These tendencies reached new articulation during World War I. Amongst Latin American states, Brazilian involvement in World War I was unusually high. Brazil entered war on the side of the Entente powers in 1917, although it saw limited deployment of troops. Its main functions in the war related to the seizure of German goods and to the prevention of German shipping in the South Atlantic. However, World War I had a discernible impact on Brazilian society, and it released processes like those seen in European polities. The war left an imprint on the basic infrastructure in Brazil, enhancing the building of railways and other infrastructural facilities. The war also added force to long-standing attempts to impose mandatory conscription, and it saw the final implementation of laws that – notionally – obliged all men to serve in the army. This period saw the dissolution of the National Guard (1918), so that the union assumed intensified responsibilities for military command. Moreover, on entry into the war, the government enforced constitutional mechanisms like those used in much of Europe, and a state of siege was imposed domestically in late 1917.[94] As in other countries, wartime emergency laws fitted into a broader pattern of legislative practice, and it was not exclusively stimulated by warfare. As actual military conflict did not penetrate far into Brazilian society, such legislation mainly served to intensify constitutional means available for social repression.

As in Europe, World War I affected Brazilian society by inducing a climate of intergroup conflict at a general level. This period witnessed increased industrial activism and radical insurgency, evidenced in the general strike in São Paulo in 1917. Rapid industrialization and economic growth in the São Paulo region discernibly altered the economic basis of the polity, creating an enlarged urban proletariat; the Communist Party was briefly legalized in 1927. However, the period beginning in World War I was also marked by a distinctive social

[94] Decree 12.716 (17 November 1917).

process in which military units gave expression to conflicts that had run through Brazilian society since the 1860s. These conflicts were largely concentrated around rival visions of citizenship, which were in turn attached to different concepts of the appropriate political role of the army. It was a particular feature of Brazilian politics after 1918 that structurally defining conflicts were largely vocalized by the army, and their convergence with ideological motives and antagonisms in society as a whole was not always apparent. To some degree, these conflicts reflected divisions between rival military groups whose ideological stances had become polarized through the military politics of the republic. As a result, controversies between factions in the army had an unusually high impact on the political landscape in society at large.

Conflicts incubated in the army acquired clear social resonance in the early 1920s. This period was punctuated by a sequence of uprisings led by young officers, notably in Rio de Janeiro in 1922 and in São Paulo in 1924, with the purpose of overthrowing the government. The officers who initiated the revolts in the 1920s were typically associated with the movement known as *tenentismo*, concentrated amongst dissidents in the middle ranks of the army. These revolts were not well coordinated, and their ideological background was not clearly pronounced. They were partly fuelled by complaints specific to the military profession focused on poor working conditions and facilities.[95] However, these revolts reflected deep-lying ideological commitments in the army, and they re-expressed outlooks that had initially shaped the formation of the republic. First, the military revolts of the 1920s placed the concept of the *soldado-cidadão* in the centre of political organization, claiming that the militarized citizen, or the politically engaged soldier, should form the structural basis of the national political system. These ideas implied that soldiers were authorized to act against groups that held back national integration. *Tententismo* was especially hostile to the traditional oligarchy, which survived the military takeover of 1889. Its protagonists saw themselves as committed to imprinting a national form on society by forcing a fusion of party and state, based in examples found in Turkey, Italy and Russia.[96] On this basis, further, insurgents associated with *tenentismo* promoted a regenerationist outlook which incorporated ideological elements from different points on the classical political spectrum. As mentioned, ideological perspectives in the army had traditionally

95 McCann (1984: 764); Seidenfus (1985: 7).
96 This idea was expressed in 1933 in Santa Rosa (1976: 106).

contained progressive egalitarian components, not lastly because of their hostility to slavery. However, by the 1920s, such views were fused with alternative stances which were dismissive of conventional democratic procedures, tending to replicate, for different objectives, aspects of the exceptionalism promoted by the government.[97] A common position in the military by this point was that the army constituted the nation in its most condensed, authentic nucleus, such that, under certain circumstances, the army had an urgent responsibility to intervene in civil politics, regardless of democratic procedure.[98] *Tenentismo* was a broad political movement based in a volatile mix of nationalist, militarist and anti-oligarchical perspectives. Through the revolts of the 1920s, *tenentismo* moved military politics onto new terrain as parts of the army were prepared to act against the political system without the approval of the military leadership.

Given the threat posed by the military after 1918, successive governments in Brazil viewed increased consolidation of emergency laws as a vital instrument for protecting the state. At this time, Brazil saw recurrent debate about the legitimate use of such laws, and leading politicians endorsed the strengthening of clauses in the 1891 constitution concerning the declaration of the state of siege. One historian observes that the federal order of the state retained robust structure only because of the 'constitutional use of means of force', supported by emergency legislation.[99] Intensified enforcement of exceptional provisions began in 1917, when the Federal Senate conducted a debate about the correct definition of the state of siege in which this concept was defined as strictly separate from war, such that war was not a precondition for extended declarations of siege.[100] These debates continued in the earlier 1920s, and the promotion of emergency legislation figured prominently during the presidency of Artur Bernardes (1922–6). Bernardes incorporated this question in his election campaign, and he began to introduce reforms in 1924 focused on executive reinforcement.[101] One historian calculates that Bernardes imposed a state of siege for a total of 1,287 days during his presidency.[102] These developments culminated in 1926 when, in parallel to analogous tendencies in Austria, Germany, Poland and Portugal, the Brazilian constitution was revised to expand

[97] See Borges (1992: 112).
[98] See an analysis of this principle in Drummond (1986: 86).
[99] Rosenfeld (2020: 2).
[100] This was set out by João Luís Alves (1917: 18), senator for Espírito Santo.
[101] See on these points Ribeiro (1967: 74) and Castro and Santos (2022: 127).
[102] Paula Marques (2013: 355).

facilities for emergency rule and to harden executive power. The 1926 revisions extended federal powers against the states, and it brought important restrictions to habeas corpus rights. In a change to Art. 6, these amendments authorized the federal government to intervene in the states to declare and impose a state of siege in one or more areas, in response either to 'aggression by foreign forces' or 'internal commotion'.[103]

In these processes, the Brazilian political system acquired increasingly repressive features, and the army was accorded some praetorian duties. However, the army was not a reliable praetorian guard. Prominent factions in the military opposed the government; some factions advocated intensified nationalization of society by means of increased military control of the federal executive. These intra-military contradictions then came to a head in October 1930. At this point, a military coup brought down the republic, following elections in March 1930 and ensuing unrest across the country. The leaders of the coup dissolved the congress, deposed the elected president and replaced him with Getúlio Vargas, who initially governed with military support using federal troops to occupy many states during the consolidation of his rule.

The revolution of 1930 had support beyond military groups, and the regime that it created was not a full military dictatorship. Government was first conducted on premises set out in a transitory decree which protected some provisions of the 1891 constitution.[104] Although it suspended the activities of congress, it provided for the convocation of an assembly to draft a new constitution, implying that military and civil leadership functions should be separated. The period following 1930 was marked by conflicts between military leaders and advocates of civil government in which soldiers only intermittently obtained dominant positions.[105] However, the initial period of Vargas's rule instilled a strong executive bias in government. The transitory decree created a provisional government fusing legislative and executive powers (Art. 1) which was authorized to maintain public order and security throughout the country (Art. 13). These measures strengthened central governmental control over the states, and they foresaw increased federal invention in the internal functions of the states, implicitly on a prerogative basis (Art. 4). In these decisions, the interim government

[103] Constitutional amendment (3 September 1926).
[104] Decree 19.398 (11 November 1930).
[105] Silva (1969: 29); Borges (1992: 191).

gave expression to the creed of executive nationalism adopted by dissident sections of the army.

Both ideologically and institutionally, further, the coup of 1930 was partly attached to the *tenentismo* movement, and it reflected ideals of the *soldado-cidadão*. Reflecting this, some leaders of the revolution presented their role in the coup as a duty of citizenship in the face of a government that had failed to integrate society. Leading military participants stated that their objective was, inter alia, to express 'progressive tendencies in social and political government', and to provide 'representation of classes and associations of collective interest'.[106] This was based in a broad understanding of the role of the army, defined as an organization with duties covering 'all manifestations and activities of national life', including – naturally – public order functions.[107] At the same time, Vargas gave support to informal military legions, similar to Fascist *squadristi* in Italy and to Piłsudski's cross-party bloc, which operated in the margins of government, acting as pro-regime militias. The regime also enforced military education polices, creating a new curriculum that involved physical training.[108] After 1930, a series of laws were introduced that expanded the military obligations of citizens. In 1933, it was decreed that public office could be assumed only by persons who had performed military service, and, by 1935, the Ministry for Military Service and the Reserve Army had been established.[109]

Alongside this, the Vargas government was designed to confront the *coroneis* and the regional oligarchs, aiming to relocate power from regions to the central state. It used the army to curtail the spheres of autonomy previously occupied by oligarchs, creating new mechanisms of political engagement and mobilization that cut through local power monopolies.[110] This strategy was reflected in the fact that Vargas gave much stronger material substance to policies of national integration than earlier governments, and he promoted policies of citizenship formation intended to penetrate spheres of oligarchical authority, not only through military measures, but in wider social provisions. From the outset, the Vargas regime was built on the precondition that national unification could be achieved only if it were cemented both in the political dimension and in the economic dimension of society. For

106 Monteiro (1934: 99–100).
107 Monteiro (1934: 163).
108 Decree 19.890 (18 April 1931).
109 Castro (2012: 81).
110 For one observer, simply, 1930 marked the first moment in a process of redesign and redefinition of the Brazilian state, creating new 'forms and means of political action' (Da Silva 2006: 45).

example, the Vargas government established a strong system of labour law, to increase labour rights for employees, which was intended to connect citizens in different parts of society in their productive activities.[111] At the same time, laws were introduced to create the Ministry of Labour, to regulate economic conflicts, and to establish a syndicalist order for trade unions. At one level, these policies were designed to offset risks of radical revolution. The year 1932 saw large-scale revolts against the Vargas regime around São Paulo, demanding the return to constitutional rule. In response to this, Vargas embarked on a strict anti-communist course in which the placatory protection of labour rights played a central role. However, the creation of a body of labour law was a conscious nation-building strategy in which a ramified corpus of social rights was used to link groups in different locations in Brazilian society to centralized institutions. From this moment, although the actual welfare system created by Vargas remained narrow, a new symbolic pattern of national citizenship began to acquire shape. This was partly based on models of military attachment. Yet it assimilated elements of material citizenship, so that a line of national construction was promoted that combined strong executive leadership, tied to the army, and extensive social integration in the sphere of economic activity.

These policies were reflected in the constitution introduced under Vargas in 1934, partly caused by the 1932 revolts in São Paulo, which placed the regime on legal foundations. In prominent respects, the 1934 constitution was a democratic constitution. It was drafted by a constituent assembly, and it established political institutions typical of liberal constitutional orders. The constitution contained a commitment to the separation of powers. It also placed a term limit on presidential authority, so that it checked dictatorial tendencies. It established a catalogue of rights, including broad-based electoral rights. Electoral rights remained subject to restrictions as some persons were excluded from voting because of their economic status, and persons who could not read or write were not permitted to vote (Art. 108(a)). However, other rights had universal applicability. Moreover, although it expanded central authority, the constitution provided for a federal system with strong partitions between central and state responsibilities (Art. 12). As such, the constitution attracted the hostility of some members of Vargas's camp, who advocated more radical-nationalist solutions to the fragility of state structure.

[111] See Decree 19.671-A (4 February 1931).

Indicatively, Francisco Campos, the main author of the 1937 constitution, argued later that the 1934 constitution had been residually 'based in classical models of liberalism'. Bitingly, he added that the authors of the 1934 constitution were 'more preoccupied with false regional interests than with the authentic interests and aspirations of the nation'.[112]

Even in its liberal components, however, the 1934 constitution deviated from classical models. It emulated aspects of the post-liberal constitutions created in Mexico in 1917, Germany in 1919 and Spain in 1931, and it formalized a series of social rights. In Art. 121, it established a protective order for rights of workers, including a minimum wage and remedies for unfair dismissal. The same article envisaged state intervention in agriculture. In Art. 122, it created a system of labour tribunals. The constitution was also conceived as the centrepiece in a developmentalist programme which connected nation-building functions with strategic promotion of economic growth. For example, it contained a series of transitory dispositions, one of which – Art. 16 – foresaw the implementation of a project for national economic reconstruction. It dictated that the union should devise a national education plan (Art. 150(a)), with appropriate fiscal support. In this regard, the constitution committed the state to the active promotion of national citizenship, providing directions for the government to integrate citizens in the economic dimension of society. It also contained guarantees that citizens who had worked productively on a piece of land for ten years without legal challenge could claim possession of it (Art. 125). Moreover, despite its checks on presidential authority, the constitution reinforced the powers exercised by the union and reserved certain legislative matters to the union. These matters included electoral law, civil law, penal law, appointment of judges and establishment of legal norms to regulate rural labour, welfare assistance and legal assistance (Art. 5). The constitution also conferred extensive public-order duties on the president (Vargas). In Art. 175, the president was empowered to impose the state of siege. These powers were cautiously defined, and the president was obliged to justify the imposition of a state of siege to the legislature and to subject such measures to legislative approval, allowing the legislature to suspend the provision. The president was also subject to criminal liability.

The 1934 constitution provided for a permanent national army with the power to perform public-order functions in some situations

[112] Campos (2001: 45–6).

(Art. 162), recruited in part by mandatory military service (Art. 163). It provided for the creation of the Superior National Security Council (Art. 159). Before the constitution was enforced, military service was made an effective condition for persons seeking nomination to public office.[113] Moreover, outside the strict domain of constitutional law, the early Vargas years saw far-reaching military reforms introduced by law and decree to increase professionalism in the army. These measures established new rules for military promotions (1934) and new institutions for military education (1933), and the Law for the General Organization of the Army (1934) was passed, which regulated civil–military administrative interactions. The Law on the General Organization of the Ministry of War (1934) was introduced, which centralized all military power in federal command structures (Art. 1).[114] Importantly, Art. 167 of the constitution established the military police as a reserve organ of the regular army, so that the military retained formal policing functions.

In these points, the 1934 constitution was linked to the plan for the national transformation of society initiated by the coup in 1930. Although tempered by liberal qualifications, it was designed to continue this revolution in several social and institutional domains: that is, in the army, in the political system, in the education system and in the national economy. Importantly, the more liberal aspects of the constitution were weakened soon after it took effect. By 1935, the constitution had been deeply transformed through the introduction of additional security legislation that defined a new set of crimes against the state.[115] A decree of December 1935 gave the president special authority to extend the state of siege across all parts of national territory in response to perceived threats to public order.[116] Further emergency measures were enforced in 1936, to suppress radical opposition movements, which imposed a state of martial rule on all national territory, suspending a range of constitutional guarantees in the process.[117] By 1935, the army had become a leading actor in the state, and core provisions in the constitution were revised to suit the prerogatives of the army. In 1936, the National Security Tribunal was established to

[113] Decree 22.885 (4 July 1933).
[114] Decree 23.976 (8 March 1934).
[115] Law 38 (4 April 1935).
[116] Legislative Decree 8 (23 December 1935).
[117] Decree 702 (21 March 1936).

prosecute persons accused of posing a threat to the external integrity of the country, including crimes against military institutions.[118]

These measures formed the background for a second coup by Vargas, launched in 1937, as he imposed a state of war on Brazilian society.[119] This coup transformed the state, in design at least, into a military-corporatist dictatorship, the Estado Novo. This second coup gave rise to a new constitution in 1937 (never fully enforced), partly based in the Polish constitution of 1935, with a strong focus on executive power. Article 180 authorized the president, in some circumstances, to introduce prerogative laws in all matters under the competence of the union. This constitution moved the government, temporarily, close to European fascism. At one level, the constitution prohibited opposition parties, including rival parties of the ultra-right.[120] At the same time, the military, although subordinate to the president, was placed in the centre of society. This military emphasis was evident at a sociocultural level. The constitution imposed universal military service (Art. 164). The author of the constitution stated that military service should form a 'permanent preoccupation' of every citizen, and all society should exist in 'intimate connection with armed forces'.[121] This was especially important as active soldiers could not vote (Art. 117(b)), so that military service was presented as a political attachment that was stronger than electoral participation. However, this military emphasis was also perceptible in provisions for national security. The constitution contained a separate section on security. This created the National Security Council and additional emergency organs (Art. 162). Article 166 also allowed declaration of national states of emergency in cases of internal disorder, and judicial control of state acts was suspended (Art. 170). Article 111 partly limited the legal accountability of the military, recognizing the army's separate judicial status. As in earlier constitutions, the expansive role of the army in galvanizing citizenship was established in conjunction with provisions for economic coordination. Article 136 of the constitution proclaimed labour a social duty, and, elsewhere, it set out norms on collective contracts, salaries and employment conditions (Art. 137). It also created a labour court to adjudicate in industrial conflicts (Art. 139). Article 57 created the National Economic Council, modelled on corporatist chambers existing in

118 Law 244 (11 September 1936).
119 Decree 2.005 (2 October 1937).
120 Decree Law 37 (2 December 1937).
121 Campos (2001: 134).

Italy and Portugal in the 1930s, with authority to co-opt and regulate trade unions (Art. 61(b)). These provisions were flanked by strong material protections for citizens, ultimately set out in a new code of labour law. In these respects, the 1937 constitution in Brazil connected two integrational axes that had coexisted in different constitutional polities prior to that point. Most constitutions had implicitly linked military integration and welfare integration, at least since the 1870s. The second Vargas constitution brought these two principles together in explicit fashion, and it envisioned a social order in which citizens would be bound to the state directly by military duties and welfare rights, with political rights playing a subordinate role. In this context, citizenship was imagined as a condition of material and military existence in which social agents were tied to the state in both dimensions. This ideal was closely shaped by the sense that, owing to its imperial past, Brazil had not become a national state, and the fully national integration of society presupposed a new social or military–economic order. This ideal contained clear elements of imperial nationalism, as military force, close to second colonization, was required for the final construction of national citizenship.

CONCLUSION

The two cases examined in this chapter show how, in diverse manner, constitutional systems in South America developed from military organizations, often with roots in the colonial era. In both cases, the attachments that underpinned constitutional order originated in affiliations forged in military units. In each setting, these factors meant that military organizations assumed and retained central positions in society, and the promotion of national citizenship and national unity per se was strongly attached to the army, so that the army remained a vital constituent force. Until the later twentieth century, the army was an important source of political rights, and, in different ways, military organizations often engaged in the allocation of rights to citizens. In other democratizing polities, political parties often used military conditions to increase their success in political bargaining. In Colombia and Brazil, by contrast, military units pursued political interests more immediately, and constitutional forms were established through direct military influence. In Brazil, the army repeatedly gained control of the state. In Colombia, different military units acted like parties competing for a share in the power of the state. These factors meant that the army militarized conflicts in society, and the promotion of national affiliations tended to militarize lateral associations. One outcome of these factors was that constitutional integration was often imposed on society by military means, so that the construction of citizenship had some similarities to a process of military annexation. In both Brazil and Colombia, citizenship was imposed to eradicate structural remnants of imperialism, and it occurred through processes that originated in colonial rule as nation states were founded and consolidated through acts of social annexation similar to those performed by empires.

CHAPTER FIVE

MILITARY CONSTITUTIONS IN AND AFTER THE OTTOMAN EMPIRE

Many major wars and militarized conflicts in the twentieth century took place or originated in regions that either were or had at some point been parts of the Ottoman Empire.[1] Moreover, many such conflicts resulted from social phenomena that became manifest in the Ottoman period – that is, from interethnic partitions, religious contests and disputes over borders and territorial ownership. These conflicts include both major interstate wars that began in the empire – for example, the Balkan Wars, the Italo-Ottoman War (1911–12), World War I, the Greek-Turkish War (1919–22) and later post-Ottoman wars between Israel and Egypt – and arguably between Russia and Ukraine (2022–). These conflicts include civil wars, as far as these are categorically distinct from international wars such as interethnic conflicts in Ottoman regions before 1922 and civil wars in Greece in the 1940s, in the former Yugoslavia in the 1990s and in Libya after 2011. These conflicts also include foreign military involvement – for example, the French and British occupation of parts of Turkey from 1918, the consolidation of British and French mandates in Palestine and Syria in the 1920s and later international interventions in Kosovo, Iraq and Libya. In addition, these conflicts include military dictatorships repeatedly established in the region such as Ottoman governments after 1913; Greek dictatorships in the 1920s, from 1936–41 and in the 1960s; Nasser's regime in Egypt; and military governments in Turkey (after 1923), Syria and Libya.

[1] This section owes much to conversations with Stephan Stetter in 2022.

All these regimes are difficult to comprehend without consideration of military conditions in the Ottoman Empire. Importantly, further, regions in the Ottoman Empire were marked by an unusual trajectory of post-imperial state-building. The Wilsonian nation-building strategy that began in Europe in 1918 had limited effect in the Ottoman region. Here, except for Turkey, composite parts of the empire that had not achieved independence before 1918 did not immediately approach sovereign statehood. Some regions, notably Armenia, were soon assimilated into the Soviet Union. Regions such as Lebanon, Syria, Iraq and Palestine became mandate territories of Britain and France. In parallel, many regions that had previously belonged to the Ottoman Empire, such as Romania, Bulgaria, Serbia and Greece, became expansionist as soon as they became fully independent, and they grew rapidly before and after 1918. In the post-Ottoman region, the transition from imperial to constitutional rule was fraught by conflicts, with uncertain distinctions between empires and nations, so that a stable basis for sovereign authority almost invariably proved difficult to consolidate.

Nonetheless, the Ottoman region has seen many experiments in democratic constitutionalism, and few parts of the region lack a constitutional tradition. In key respects, the Ottoman region forms an exemplary case of the links between constitutionalism, imperialism and military violence. Most constitutional lineages in areas that belonged to the Ottoman Empire brought military actors to prominent positions as organs of integration; in many cases, armies acquired vital roles in creating nations from inside empires. The pacification of such societies remained elusive as militarization had a broad effect on society at both the vertical and the horizontal levels. In different ways, constitutional processes were closely attached to uncertainties about territorial occupancy and the conditions of legitimate residency in different localities, a problem that became acute through the fragmentation of the empire. For this reason, constitutions often contained claims to reorder geographical attachments, and they often imposed vertical citizenship regimes that contradicted existing local memberships, so that constitutional organization was experienced as a process of internal and external colonization. Many constitutions implemented citizenship regimes as part of imperial nation-building. Indeed, in many constitutions, armies retained strong governmental influence because of imperial pressures, and they propelled states onto expansionary pathways.

The prominence of military influence in the post-Ottoman region is often attributed to distinct factors in Ottoman society.[2] However, militarism in this region was not the result of an entirely sui generis causal chain. The analysis that follows isolates the specific ways in which imperialism, militarism and constitutionalism interacted in polity-building processes in the Ottoman context. It places such developments on a continuum with constitution making as a more general phenomenon, and it explains constitutional organization in the Ottoman region as an intensified expression of tendencies that are widely inherent in constitutional order.

TANZIMAT REFORMS

The beginnings of modern state formation in the Ottoman region were determined by the fact that, by the later eighteenth century, Russia had emerged as an imperial power that at least rivalled the Ottoman Empire in conflicts over territory. This placed increasing pressure on the northern borders of the Ottoman Empire and created anxieties amongst other states in Europe. By the 1780s, in fact, the Ottoman Empire appeared to be heading towards a fate like that of Poland. Poland and the Ottoman Empire had been military adversaries in the late seventeenth century, but, within a century, they were both at risk of external annexation. The partition of the Ottoman Empire was openly considered by Catherine II and Joseph II during the partition of Poland.[3] As the partition began in Poland, Russia detached the Crimea from Istanbul. The ensuing Treaty of Küçük Kaynarca (1774) was interpreted to imply that foreign empires could intervene in internal Ottoman matters in order to protect Christian subjects.

Like Poland, the Ottoman Empire was weakened by the fact that its military apparatus was not fully subject to central control. The imperial army, a formidable organization up to the later seventeenth century, was led by a private elite corps, the janissaries. The janissaries originated in a caste of slave soldiers, captured and assimilated in Christian regions conquered by the Ottomans, and they formed an example of an early standing army. This army occupied a distinct position in the legitimational system of the empire. On one hand, the empire extracted legitimacy from its claim that the sultan was both imperial ruler and

[2] See the claim that the Ottoman state was a 'garrison state', creating a military bias in the Ottoman social order (Aydinli 2004: 102).

[3] This is discussed in Bitis (2006: 21) and Vovchencko (2016: 41).

caliph, so that the imperial order embodied divine authority for Muslim subjects. Yet the empire also extracted legitimacy from the military, concentrated in the janissary corps, which extended the caliphate and centralized imperial power around the sultan.[4] By the late eighteenth century, however, the tight bond between the sultan and the janissaries had become unsettling. By this time, the janissaries formed a corporate group with distinct status claims, linked by alliance with other social groups and able to mobilize independently against legislation that threatened their position.[5] Faced with hostile powers with increasingly nationalized armies in the eighteenth century, the janissaries lost their effectiveness and their actual involvement in war was sometimes limited. Reformist sultans increasingly viewed the janissary corps as an impediment to their military success, and they attempted to abolish it. However, the janissaries were able to deploy substantial force against their sultans, and they staged military revolts to prevent reforms to erode their corporate position. Alongside the janissaries, traditional recruitment patterns in the Ottoman army, reliant on household troops, troops mobilized by provincial actors and irregular militias, were less effective than methods used in rival empires, especially Russia.[6]

The decline of the empire was also connected to the territorial and legal-cultural structure of Ottoman society. Although governed by a Muslim administrative elite, the empire contained multiple ethnicities, and it developed a complex order to manage different population groups. Different religious groups, such as Jews, Orthodox Christians (mainly Greeks) and Armenians, were subject to separate legal and cultural-institutional systems with distinct administrative orders and leaders, defined as *millets*. These millets mainly served to regulate Ottoman subjects who were not Muslims, as Islam was the dominant religion. However, Muslims were also connected across different parts of the empire by shared attachment to communities based in religion. Millets provided rules in religious and many civil matters and accorded variable legal status and privileges to distinct populations, such that particular communities existed in structured, partly self-contained trans-regional legal orders. This mode of social organization meant that the activities of different communities were easy for the central

[4] Ágoston (2005: 22–3).
[5] See Yaycioglu (2016: 31–2).
[6] On the beginning of the 'rebuilding of the military' after this point, see Aksan (2007: 169).

government to administer and control.[7] However, it also meant that the millets existed in a mediated relation to imperial institutions, and it diluted the obligations that attached non-dominant religious groups to the empire. The empire integrated different ethnicities on separate grounds and for different purposes, which instilled a segmentary form at the core of society, so that the legal convergence of society was low. In addition, some semi-feudal patterns of territorial rule persisted into the nineteenth century. Some Ottoman regions possessed semi-autonomous status with separate military resources. Overall, such conditions proved very unpropitious for the techniques of centralization and citizenship formation on which, by the early nineteenth century, modern states and empires relied.

Unlike Poland, however, the Ottoman Empire survived conflict with other European empires, and it (briefly) outlived its rivals in St Petersburg and Vienna. The period of confrontation with Russia gave rise to policies for military reform, beginning in the 1790s, which decisively shaped Ottoman politics up to the 1920s. In the first instance, this confrontation resulted in the creation by Selim III of a limited professional army, although this did not avert loss of territory to Russia. Plans for military modernization gathered pace in the first decade of the nineteenth century, especially after the Napoleonic invasion of Egypt and increased Russian pressure in the Balkans. These policies included failed attempts to abolish the janissary corps, which caused a military revolt in 1807 and the murder of Selim III (1808). After 1807, reforms partly stalled as the empire was exposed to the Napoleonic threat. These years saw the drafting of the semi-constitutional Deed of Alliance or Deed of Agreement (1808), which continued projects for army reform, providing for the drafting of state soldiers by regional dynasties.[8] However, the first effective push for modernizing military reform took place in the 1820s. This context was influenced by experiences of mass mobilization in the revolutionary period and by the nationalization of regional armies in the Ottoman region, demonstrated by the success of the Greek military in the bid for independence. The centrepiece of this reform was the decision to abolish the janissaries in 1826, during war with Greek separatists and before renewed war with Russia. This decision caused violent insurrection that led to the deaths of thousands of janissaries. This decision

[7] This point is made in Antaramian (2020: 17).
[8] Yaycioglu (2016: 209).

replaced the janissaries with a class of officers that was more formally trained and selected, albeit still largely drawn from court elites. In key respects, this process began to alter the legitimacy of the sultanate, as it separated imperial power from its attachments to a private army. These measures did not create a fully professional military apparatus, and military organization remained weak, partly because recruitment duties were persistently linked to local status groups.[9] After this point, however, the military was established as a separate institutional organ, a new officer class was created that became an important social group, and new military schools were founded.[10] A reserve corps similar to the Prussian *Landwehr* was then created in 1834.

On this basis, the principle became increasingly accepted in the Ottoman Empire that the army was not a distinct corporate organization in society, but a part of the state, bound by certain official rules and performing duties directed towards a public community. In the ensuing decades, this organic construction of the army was followed by reforms of a more general nature designed to establish a distinct Ottoman polity, built on foundations that traversed different regional and ethnic groups, to which individual persons could declare loyalty. As in parallel cases, a system of political membership with similarities to nationhood began take shape at the core of an empire, modifying the basic premises of imperial control and directing the integrational axis of the empire away from its segmentary form. By the late 1830s, the Ottoman government had embarked on a general process of institutional reconstruction, the Tanzimat reforms. These reforms modified a range of public functions and offices. For example, they altered the size and composition of the civil service, and they began to formalize the legal system, which meant that secular ideas of legality acquired new importance and the personal authority of the sultan was partly reduced. They also contained taxation reforms and early educational reforms. As in other polities, however, such reforms were at least partly impelled by military pressures in the empire. This resulted partly from external challenges, but it was also the outcome of civil wars or internal/external wars, caused mainly by the fact that Egypt pursued military modernization under Mehmed Ali in the 1820s and 1830s. With a large and forcibly recruited conscript army, Egypt briefly threatened to become a separate Muslim power within the empire.[11]

9 Moreau (2007: 22).
10 Turfan (2000: 60–3).
11 On organized resistance to conscription in this case, see Fahmy (1998: 430–1).

The first central pillar in the Tanzimat reforms was the Rescript of 1839, coinciding with moves to resist the Egyptian conquest of Syria. This legislation was accompanied by an admission of imperial crisis, so that reforms were justified by the need to increase taxation and strengthen military capacity.[12] The Rescript established some formal legal procedures for the use of public authority by the sultan, and it also created stricter norms for acts of public administration and the protection of subjects in their personal security. Indicatively, this period saw the implementation of codes of criminal law and land law, starting in 1840. The Rescript also promoted an implied ideal of Ottoman citizenship which brought all subjects of the empire under a shared legal order. This legislation did not establish equal legal recognition for Christians and Muslims. Further, it was hardly a secularist document; it recognized sharia law and it advocated reinforcement of Islam as a path to reinforcing the empire. However, by promoting formal legal reform, it marked a first step towards the definition of imperial membership as a legal condition with potentially secular foundations. This law had complex results. On one hand, this law began to redefine the basis of imperial loyalties as duties and obligations were framed by general principles distinct from the caliphate, and the religious element of imperial legitimacy was weakened. On the other hand, this law unsettled the millet system.[13] In dissociating political affiliations from religion, it created conflict between millets and the imperial government, as some members of millets with separate religious identities rejected overarching constructs of citizenship. Moreover, it meant that millets forfeited some of their functions as specifically religious administrative orders, as they gained greater importance as centres of ethnocultural identity.[14] The incipient secularization of government was promoted to impose a system of vertical integration in society, but it partly reinforced religious attachments at the lateral level, and the administrative segments on which the empire had relied acquired new features. The Rescript also foresaw an increase in military conscription, referring regulation of recruitment to a military council, so that the construction of secular legal attachments was closely shaped by plans for military

[12] See Koçunyan (2018: 66).

[13] See long discussion on these points in Davison (1963: 114–130). Note the claim that the reforms encouraged the 'consolidation of conflicted ethnic and religious identities' in Barkey (2008: 278). One outstanding analysis shows how the reforms impacted millets by transforming questions of millet membership into a distinction between minorities and majorities in the empire (Karpat 1982: 163).

[14] Berkes (1964: 153–4).

recruitment.[15] On each point, the pressure towards vertical integration caused by external militarism dislodged, simultaneously, the military apparatus, the symbolic and religious foundations of the state and the pluralistic structure of society, such that early notions of citizenship had much more challenging implications than in other empires.

Subsequently, the Tanzimat reforms included legislation to build a conscript army. This commenced with regulations providing for mass recruitment in 1843–6, realized in 1848, which quickly drew a high percentage of the Muslim population into the army. A further key step in these processes was the Reform Decree of 1856, which coincided with the end of the Crimean War, initiating a second reformist epoch. This law widened access for Christians to roles in state service and extended conscription to non-Muslim imperial subjects, a practice already encouraged in the Crimean War. Most non-Muslims remained exempt from military service until laws imposing universal conscription were passed in 1909, and arguably until 1914, when intensified conscription laws were implemented.[16] However, conscription provisions were reinforced in the period 1869–70, followed by further measures in 1886. By the 1870s, military measures were strongly influenced by Prussian designs and, by the 1880s, military education in the empire was modelled on Prussia.[17] Importantly, the early Tanzimat period involved forcible internal colonization, and the consolidation of citizenship, led by external pressures, brought increased internal repression. The government in Istanbul launched military campaigns to reduce the autonomy of Kurdish communities in the eastern regions.[18]

In these developments, the policies to reinforce shared citizenship, including the increased allocation of rights to Christian subjects, formed a clear case of enforced integration in face of external security risks. However, the granting of such rights was strongly shaped by expectations of Western powers, whose alliance with the empire against Russia in the Crimean War brought increased foreign presence in Istanbul. In particular, the Reform Decree of 1856 began a process in which Western directives were internalized in Ottoman legislation, and, at this time, external support became contingent on domestic

[15] Hacısalihoğlu (2007: 268).

[16] On one calculation, before 1914, exemptions reduced imperial military capacity by up to 30 per cent. Exempted groups included Christians and Jews, inhabitants of certain regions (Mecca), breadwinners and nomads (Fawaz 2014: 163). A different historian calculates that group-specific exemptions reduced the recruitment base by 40 per cent (Zürcher 2010: 65).

[17] See background in Moreau (2007: 22–100).

[18] See discussion of this process in affected regions in Ungor and Polatel (2011: 21).

legislation to guarantee rights for Christians.[19] For example, the Treaty of Paris (1856) contained an agreement stipulating that Western powers would guarantee the territorial integrity of the Ottoman Empire, and it recognized the empire as part of the Concert of Europe. However, this agreement came with strings attached; on one account, it contained an 'indirect right to intervene' for foreign governments seeking protection for Christians in the empire.[20] The year 1868 also brought the formation of a separate Ministry of Justice and the initial promulgation of a civil code. By 1869, the reforms also included the Nationality Law, which established universal and equal rights of nationality for all imperial subjects. Later international treaties, such as the Berlin Treaty (1878), effectively prescribed universal models of citizenship for the empire, insisting that Christians and Muslims should have equivalent treatment under the law (Art. LXII). Central to these reforms was the fact that, by the 1850s, the Ottoman Empire was partly dependent on Great Britain, and British politicians pushed for laws to protect Christians in the empire in return for military support against Russia. Indeed, the fact that the empire became dependent on other empires for survival meant that, initially, the military assumed less prominence amidst elite groups than in other empires.[21] Indicatively, full mobilization of Ottoman society only took place in the early twentieth century, after the alliance with Britain had ended.

This distinctive character of Ottoman politics was reflected in formal constitutional processes in the empire. At one level, as in other polities, the establishment of constitutional law in the Ottoman Empire began as the imperial government was forced to expand its military capabilities, and constitutional roles were allocated to citizens to preserve the position of the empire in the international security landscape. Indicatively, the secular law-bound order that was promoted in the Tanzimat era eventually gave rise to a formal constitution. In 1876, a civil-military alliance brought about the deposition of Sultan Abdulaziz and the brief enthronement of a new sultan, Murad V, who established by edict the first constitution for the Ottoman Empire. This constitution reflected internal conflicts, and it was drafted at the same

[19] One account links this decree to the influence of the British Embassy in Istanbul (Karpat 2001: 75–76).

[20] Akçam (2004: 23).

[21] One historian has argued that, after circa 1850, the empire depended more on diplomats than soldiers (Findley 2012: 60).

time as uprisings in the Balkans, especially in Bosnia and Bulgaria. The constitution was also influenced by international pressures, and it was partly designed to avert international intervention in the empire.[22] It was passed before the beginning of the Constantinople Conference, where representatives of foreign empires deliberated the territorial future of Ottoman regions. This constitution obtained support from different ethnic elites, and it reflected wider integrational objectives. In key respects, this constitution was a classical imperial constitution. For example, it vested supreme sovereign power in the sultan, so that limits on his power were mainly symbolic (Art. 3). However, although it endorsed state religion, it was conceived as a document that would express a notion of Ottoman citizenship able to include all members of the empire (Art. 8) and to avert internal fragmentation. It gave recognition to non-Muslim religions (Art. 11) and established a (weak) representative chamber, based in European parliamentary models (Art. 42), which functioned for two years. In these provisions, the constitution was conceived as a plan to reinforce imperial authority by placing it on a broader social basis, effectively reconfiguring the legal premises of empire to strengthen its solidity. At the same time, the constitution preserved the explicit religious basis of the sultan's powers (Arts 3–5). This constitution had limited immediate impact. It was disregarded after 1878, following the beginning of the Russo-Ottoman War, when the empire lost about half its Balkan territories. This turn away from constitutional rule was legitimated by military exigency, and it resulted in an era of more authoritarian government under Abdul Hamid II.

In each point, the Ottoman Empire was and subsequently remained an unusually clear example of a polity that was colonizing, in that it asserted control over diffuse regions, but that was also colonized, in that it was subject to incursion and legislative intervention by other powers. At each stage, the Tanzimat reforms were part of a strategy of *defensive imperialism*. The reforms were designed to stabilize intra-imperial authority and to resist external depredation, and they were driven by two overlapping modes of imperialism – Ottoman imperialism inside the empire and rival imperialisms outside the empire. As in other empires, these reforms were intended to recruit more soldiers and to establish a secure basis for military mobilization. As such, they increasingly tied all subjects directly to the imperial state, regardless of their ethnicity, establishing some

[22] On this point, see Devereux (1963: 21).

unifying bonds of nationhood within the imperial space. By the early twentieth century, ethnic groups loyal to the empire spoke out in favour of conscription as a mechanism for promoting interethnic communal ties.[23] However, the military pressures that shaped reform and determined laws in favour of Ottoman citizenship had a more existential, conflicted character than in other empires.

THE RESULTS OF REFORM

Strikingly, the Tanzimat reforms largely failed to create a broad base for Ottoman identity, and they did not bring structural cohesion to the empire. This was not invariably the case, and the earlier reform period in the empire saw an increased level of integration for some groups. For example, one historian describes how the Crimean War markedly expanded intergroup integration. At this point, many members of non-dominant communities supported the war, even requesting to serve in the army. This provided enhanced recognition for such communities, evident in the fact that more licenses were issued for the building of churches and synagogues.[24] However, deepening integration in the empire was not the dominant experience during the reform era, and the promotion of imperial citizenship tended to militarize population groups against imperial rule. Throughout the nineteenth century, for example, the progressive projection of imperial citizenship coincided with a process in which the Ottoman Empire lost territory at crucial junctures. This began with independence movements amongst imperial minorities, usually supported by Russia, which eventually acquired territorial independence. This commenced in Serbia, where the separatist movement began in 1804, achieving autonomy in 1817–30 and independence in 1867 and full international recognition in 1878, and in Greece, which began in the 1820s, achieving independence in 1830. This loss of territory occurred in parallel to foreign sequestration of Ottoman regions; notably, the reforms fell between the French invasion of Algeria (starting in 1830) and the Russian colonization of parts of the southern Caucasus (1878). Eventually, Bulgaria embarked on a pathway to independence, initially as a de facto Russian protectorate following war between the Ottoman empire and Russia in 1878, a process completed in 1908. This event had symbolic significance for the empire, as it

[23] Beşikçi (2013: 554).
[24] Badem (2010: 346).

showed that Russian influence could dislodge an ethnic Slavic state from within imperial territories. Moreover, the construction of citizenship to extract military force from society exacerbated antagonisms between domestic populations, and, as mentioned, it transformed the millets into sites of oppositional citizenship and minority separatism. In each point, the attempt to imprint convergent identities on imperial society confronted powerful counterweights, partly running along religious lines, which were hardened by the selective imposition of military duties. By consequence, the reformist impetus in the Tanzimat era often had results that were diametrically opposed to its intention, and, in seeking to solidify internal membership, it accelerated the fragmentation of the empire. Expressed schematically, the more the imperial executive sought to extract something like a vertically ordered, secular body of citizens from its multi-structured population, the more this population dissolved into separate, ethnically defined memberships.[25]

Critically, one persistent weakness in the empire was that, at different points, Christian citizens, especially those residing in Armenia and Bulgaria, expressed some solidarity with Russia, and they provided support – either military or moral – for the Russian army during inter-imperial conflicts. For example, many Bulgarians joined the Russians in the Russo-Ottoman war (1878), and the risk that Armenians would join Russian military forces was a source of enduring anxiety for the imperial government in Istanbul. This meant that the empire often fought wars that crossed the boundaries between the inside and the outside of its own territory, and adversaries of the empire recruited troops on both fronts. These solidarities presented an acute peril for the empire because many pro-Russian populations had separatist ambitions, and they profited from war with Russia to reinforce their own separatist claims. As a result, periods of warfare, in which other states consolidated their internal structures, tended to intensify the partitioning Ottoman society into hostile segments with distinct religious convictions. Imperial society as a whole was, in some respects, susceptible to an unusual pattern of militarization in which externally determined integration was weak and external conflicts were sharply reproduced in domestic contests. In fact, inter-imperial conflicts always raised questions about the internal legitimacy of the Ottoman government and its claims to societal ownership.

Like other parts of the longer reform process, the constitutional order created in 1876 also had paradoxical consequences for the imperial

[25] This is supported by claims in Berkes (1964: 326).

system. The constitution promoted generalized citizenship, and it reacted to external military pressures. However, the constitutional design for the imperial polity was established in the context of sub-imperial fragmentation, and it was mirrored, for counterposed purposes, in the composite parts of the empire. One result of the Tanzimat reforms, in specific terms, was that some millets developed separate constitutions which were increasingly attached to sub-imperial religious or cultural identities. For instance, a constitution for the Armenian millet was introduced in the years 1857–63 and the Jewish millet obtained a constitution in 1865. As a result, the 1876 constitution was imposed in a context in which constitutional subjectivities had already displayed their force in many sub-imperial contexts, as imperial populations seeking or acquiring independence had utilized constitutional mechanisms to promote separate patterns of social integration. Indeed, before 1876, several Ottoman populations had founded constitutions that granted very extensive rights to their citizens, in some cases even before full independence had been established. The first example of this is found in the Greek independence movement of the 1820s, which was consolidated in a constitution of 1822 and culminated in the creation of a political system with a very democratic constitution (1864). Serbia embarked on a constitutional pathway in 1808; from 1830, Serbia was an autonomous domain, and, as a vassal state, it passed constitutions in 1835 and 1838. It acquired full independence between the 1860s and the 1870s, and a further constitution was passed in 1869, with important provisions for political rights. By 1888, Serbia had a constitution that eventually, after revisions in 1903, created a representative system with far-reaching male enfranchisement. Romania obtained a constitution in 1866. After the drafting of the Ottoman constitution in 1876, Bulgaria established a constitution in 1879, before it was unified with Eastern Rumelia (also part of the Ottoman Empire) in 1885. This constitution was written under Russian occupation and with strong Russian input, after the exodus of Turks and Greeks in the Russo-Ottoman War, and it was based in almost complete male suffrage.[26] In each setting, the projection of constitutional ideals at the imperial centre occurred at an unpropitious moment, and it lacked sufficient force to countervail rival patterns of constitutional formation.

[26] On one account, it was vetted by Tsar Alexander II and the Foreign Ministry in St Petersburg (Vinkovetsky 2018: 762–763).

Importantly, the constitutions established by minorities seeking independence in the empire usually imposed heavy military obligations on their populations. This was partly the case because, on reaching independence, most post-Ottoman states were established as constitutional monarchies whose monarchs lacked obvious dynastic legitimacy, and military integration provided a vital indicator of their authority. However, this was also caused by the fact that new national populations were strongly galvanized by conflict with Istanbul, and they accepted constitutional affiliations that both replicated and opposed the construction of societal membership dictated at the imperial centre. Armies frequently became central constituent agents in post-Ottoman polities, even before they were fully independent. Constitutions passed in Serbia in 1869 (Art. 35) and Bulgaria in 1879 (Arts 11, 71) contained laws imposing deep military service. Both constitutions contained clauses to ensure that the state possessed sovereign control of the army, and the role of the military in politics was strictly controlled. Yet, in each case, the military frequently intervened in government. In Bulgaria, the 1879 constitution was soon suspended by a *coup d'état*, and far-reaching powers were temporarily given to the monarch. Later, Serbian officers murdered the king in 1903. In each context, these states replicated the fusion of external and internal violence at the core of the Ottoman polity. In each case, constitutions were consolidated as instruments for anti-Ottoman militarism, and sub-imperial citizenship regimes were formed through an intricate balance of interstate war, civil war and military integration. As in other settings, in fact, the promotion of citizenship in the empire gave rise to post-imperial states that declared war on each other; the first major case was the war between Serbia and Bulgaria in 1885, fought before Bulgaria was fully sovereign.

Overall, the Ottoman Empire embodied the convergence of interstate war, civil war and constitutional formation that typified imperial polities of the nineteenth century more generally. Constitutional reform was enacted create a society that had national and imperial features. However, the Ottoman Empire also formed a partial reverse image of other lines of European nation-building, in which the constitutional ordering of national institutions was directed against external military threats, and constitutions instilled cohesion within national societies in such environments. Across Europe, this model underpinned, diversely, the emergence of geographically stable states, such as France and the UK, but it also supported the transformation of empires into nations, as in the case of Italy and Germany. In such examples, the constitutional organization of society triggered a certain degree of lateral militarization. Yet, at least up to 1914, its primary impact was to solidify national society. In the Ottoman setting, exposure to external conflicts induced analogous processes and led to attempts to establish unifying citizenship regimes based in constitutional law and to impose military service on integrated citizens. However, this process was less successful than in other settings, and many characteristics of nation-building that occurred in other societies exposed to imperial warfare did not take place – or they took place only in partial form. In many parts of Ottoman Empire, the endeavour to create a robustly integrated imperial state miscarried, and it resulted in acute intra-societal fragmentation and lateral or segmentary militarization in which external and internal conflicts were often inseparable.

First, the reform processes, culminating in the short-lived 1876 constitution, led to increasing separatism and centrifugalism in the empire. As mentioned, the years after 1876 were years of intensified sub-imperial nationalism, and the strategic attempt to create imperial citizenship had limited overall impact. To be sure, identification with Ottomanism took root amongst some groups, and the Tanzimat project was not entirely without effect. Some groups – for example, Jews, who were not strongly attached to foreign powers – benefited from the reforms and experienced greater social recognition and political participation.[27] Yet the integrational force of the reforms was restricted. This was most clearly reflected in the Balkan regions, partly because of Russian intervention and pro-Russian sentiments amongst some ethnic and religious (Christian) groups. However, this was also reflected in imperial regions with large non-Turkish populations, such as Armenia and Syria. The wars with Russia starting in 1877 were not only fought in the Balkans. Armenia became an important theatre of war, and the Russian empire invaded parts of Anatolia, claiming an entitlement to protect Christian communities subject to Ottoman rule. Significant in this respect is the fact that other methods of imperial citizenship formation were also largely ineffective. As in other societies, the government in Istanbul introduced education reforms at the same time as military reforms, which were intended to promote Ottoman affinities, separating education from the millets. In fact, education reforms began with the creation of military schools in the 1830s. One historian argues

[27] See the very interesting discussion in Karmi (2010: 76–85).

that military conscription and education reforms formed the conjoined 'centerpiece' of 'Ottoman Modernization'.[28] The constitution of 1876 placed all schools under imperial control. Education reforms included a state education law (1869), and they were intensified after 1878 to promote national political consciousness.[29] In many cases, however, these reforms intensified separate cultural and ethnolinguistic affiliations, and they provided a basis for educational strategies in sub-imperial regions that favoured separatism.[30]

Second, the use of the army as a vector of citizenship in the Ottoman context was not effective.[31] From the 1840s, it was repeatedly argued in reformist circles that military conscription should be universally enforced. However, this did not approach reality until the eve of World War I.[32] This weakness was partly caused by the fact that conscription policies were not universally applied, and many groups obtained exemptions. In particular, Christians were largely exempted from military duties, and the army mainly served as a fulcrum of citizenship for Muslims. Indeed, conscription laws often inflamed civil violence arising from ethnic diversity. The first imposition of general conscription triggered popular rebellion in some areas, notably around Aleppo, and it remained extremely unpopular. Avoidance of conscription for the Crimean War was widespread across sub-imperial groups.[33] As mentioned, the military loyalty of some groups – for example, Kurds, Armenians, Serbs and Bulgarians – was often unclear. This proved a deeply unsettling factor in the later history of the empire, and it meant that recruitment of some ethnic groups was discouraged for fear that they might present an internal military threat. Alongside this, as conscription of sub-imperial groups intensified after 1912, non-Muslim soldiers were often reviled in the army and blamed for military defeat. In some wars, different ethnic groups fought separate local conflicts, and members of some population groups, supposedly mobilized in external warfare, used the military situation to perpetrate military violence against each other. For instance, some Muslim soldiers used the Crimean War to commit

[28] Provence (2017: 15). One historian declares that late Ottoman higher education was 'essentially a branch of the army' (Cronin 2014: 30).
[29] Karpat (2001: 291).
[30] See Evered (2012: 197).
[31] On the reasons for this, see Reid (2000: 115, 451) and Beşikçi (2012: 96).
[32] On the widening reach of conscription through legislation of May 1914, see Beşikçi (2012: 97).
[33] Ma'oz (1968: 50). On anti-conscription attitudes in Jewish communities, see Cohen (2014: 14). Even Albanians rebelled against conscription in 1871 (Karmi 2010: 101).

military acts against non-Muslims.[34] In the Russian-Ottoman War, Kurds committed mass murder against Armenians (Bloxham 2005: 45–46). In such occurrences, warfare frequently spilled into patterns of violence close to civil war, in which membership in a regular army did not dictate clear military loyalties. One further reason for the weakness of the army in instilling citizenship loyalties was that the army itself was not fully unified, and different regions, even those seemingly faithful to the empire, had separate military units. Private contingents retained significant roles in the Ottoman army until World War I.

This situation was exacerbated, third, by the fact that constructions of citizenship were partly responses to international directives, which made the empire vulnerable to further external encroachment. In fact, attempts to galvanize the population internally through constitutional laws usually occurred in situations in which external intervention increased. In such settings, typically, external powers imposed settlements that exacerbated the internal problems of the empire, so that the empire became caught in a trap of structural depletion. Following the war with Russia in the late 1870s, for example, the territorial, demographic and legal structure of the empire was partly regulated by foreign powers. On one hand, the Berlin Congress of 1878 imposed a post-war settlement on both Russia and the Ottoman Empire. This settlement recognized the independence of Serbia and Montenegro and the autonomy of Bulgaria. To justify this, the treaty adopted an ethnicity-based ideal of territorial sovereignty and declared that membership in different ethnic groups should determine the frontiers between sovereign states. This process cut to the heart of Ottoman constructions of legitimacy, as it implied that groups assuming similar ethnicity could, by this fact, lay claim to national sovereignty, and it politicized ethnicity to a new degree. In fact, it induced large-scale violence in regions affected by border claims or separatist movements. In addition, as mentioned, the Berlin Treaty (1878) prescribed certain norms for domestic legislation in Istanbul; it was designed to protect Christian minorities from violence, and it prescribed equal 'civil and or political rights' as a principle of Ottoman citizenship (Art. LXII). At one level, this treaty forced the imperial government to elevate the uniformity of citizenship laws. Yet it also legitimated the rejection of citizenship amongst some groups. In effect, this meant that the treaty prevented

[34] See Reid (2000: 447).

the empire from integrating its population to secure its own sovereign form. Moreover, by the 1870s, earlier Ottoman allies such as Britain and France had turned against the empire. Leading empires in Western Europe had mainly supported the empire because it formed a buffer against Russia. However, as the empire began to dissolve, it lost utility for other European empires, and, by the 1880s, they also carved away Ottoman territory. This was reflected in 1882, when Egypt, still nominally part of the empire, was transformed into a British dominion. The same period saw the formation of a French protectorate in Tunisia (1881). By circa 1900, the empire was subject to annexation by other European empires, whose attitude to the Ottoman empire differed markedly from their attitude towards other (Christian) empires. Finally, the ranks of imperial powers keen on invading Ottoman lands were enthusiastically joined by Italy in 1911.

Most importantly, fourth, the weakness of Ottoman citizenship was evident in the fact that, as citizenship was selectively militarized, military conflicts extended beyond actual periods of warfare and relations between some population groups existed in a condition with features of a permanent multifocal war. Some element of interethnic civil war became a constant feature of imperial existence, and this obstructed wider endeavours to design an Ottoman model of legal-political affiliation. This intensification of civil war became visible before and after the Russo-Ottoman War, when intergroup conflicts, articulated to inter-imperial antagonisms, resulted in genocidal attacks by imperial troops on Bulgarians and Armenians. The mass murder of Bulgarians in 1876 had fateful consequences for the empire, as it meant that the strategic support of Western European empires was reduced.[35] This exposed the empire to further territorial depredation and gradually pushed it into alliance with Germany. This intensification of civil war was also manifest in the fact that, as new nations emerged in the Balkan region, national populations and their citizenship regimes were consolidated in highly repressive, homogenizing manner. That is, newly emerging post-Ottoman states were often constructed through acts of ethnic partitioning in which some cultural, religious or ethnic groups were excluded from the territory occupied by emerging states, such that coerced population transfers become core elements of state- and nation-building. In many territories occupied by new nations, Muslims were forcibly uprooted and

[35] Gladstone's famous diatribe against the Ottomans was expressed six years before the invasion of Egypt.

compelled to live in parts of the empire with majority Muslim populations. This began in the eighteenth century, but it gained impetus in the Crimean War, when Russian Tatars were driven in large numbers into Ottoman regions. The systematic exclusion of Muslims from their traditional homelands became a frequent phenomenon, and the episodic cleansing of Muslim populations, mainly from the Balkans, accompanied the dissolution of the empire and the emergence of new states.[36] Such patterns of external post-imperial state formation necessarily resonated in state-building trajectories within the empire. Population inflows changed ethnic composition of whole regions, as some territories absorbed large numbers of displaced persons, and ethnic purification and interethnic hostility became a determinant of social life in these places. The mass resettlement of ethnic groups was legally restricted by imperial decrees in the 1880s, but it became a common form of population management.[37]

Overall, a cyclical conjuncture of violence characterized late Ottoman society. At one level, this period reflected wider tendencies in European history, as formal citizenship regimes were structured around the need to manage military violence and to strengthen military capacity. As in other cases, the constitutional definition of citizenship had volatile military outcomes. The militarization of citizenship inflected other social relations in unpredictable fashion, triggering the militarization of lateral attachments in society that at least rivalled in intensity the militarization of vertical obligations. This resulted from the fact that military constructs of citizenship presupposed national affiliation and required the intensification of nationalist sentiments, which had unsettling consequences in the multi-ethnic landscape of the empire. As in other polities, militaries formed core political actors, performing functions of external mobilization and internal integration. Unlike other settings, however, social militarization in the Ottoman Empire created many armies, attached to different ethnic groups, with hostile positions in the imperial polity. To a greater extent than in other imperial zones, the social environment in which early constitutional roles were consolidated was defined by external warfare and by multipolar internal war, so that the inside and the

[36] The displacement of Muslims is less well researched than the uprooting of Christians, but waves of depopulation occurred after the Crimean War, in the 1870s and during the Balkan Wars. This was often abetted by tsarist population policies driving Muslims out of Russia. One historian summarizes this by claiming that, between 1821 and 1922, about 10 million Ottoman Muslims were either forcibly uprooted or killed by war, starvation or disease. (Cagaptay 2006: 5).

[37] This was set out in separate decrees in 1884, 1887 and 1888.

outside of society possessed convergent features. As discussed below, this had crucial implications for the Ottoman Empire in 1914. At this point, other empires embarked on external warfare as a relatively isolated event for which their domestic populations had been prepared through national trajectories of integration. For the Ottoman Empire, World War I was one moment in a continuum of internal/external violence at a time when the empire was approaching a high degree of lateral militarization.

1908–1918: THE MILITARY IN POLITICS

The increasing prominence of militarized conflicts in the Ottoman landscape gained expression in 1908, when a group of reformist activists, the Committee of Union and Progress, sometimes known as the Young Turks, launched a revolutionary coup, beginning in uprisings in Macedonia. The Committee had its origins in student movements, but by 1908, it had strong military attachments and support. It had acquired political authority in some regions, before the coup was conducted, and it mobilized paramilitary units to flank and support its political actions.[38] The immediate result of the coup was that the Committee established a strong position to influence government and partly took control of the army. From this position, it forced the sultan to re-enforce the 1876 constitution. The Committee then initiated systemic reform with the longer-term goal of modernizing the empire. This coincided with several international military events that partly directed the reforms. It occurred against the background of the Russo-Japanese war, in which Japan had demonstrated that rapid constitutional organization could create a polity able to defeat Russia.[39] However, it also coincided with the final loss of Bulgaria and Crete to the empire, and with the annexation of Bosnia by Austria, flanked by rising volatility in the southern Balkans. In this environment, 1908 formed a militarized constitutional revolution, using constitutional means to react to imperial crisis.

The primary impetus of the reforms the Young Turks implemented after 1908 was to consolidate the external sovereignty of the empire and to shore up its authority internally, as a precondition for its external stabilization. To achieve this, the reforms aimed to establish a meritocratic state administration and to improve political culture

[38] See on these points Hanioğlu (2001: 279–286).
[39] One very important analysis stresses the impact of the Meiji restoration in Turkey in 1908 and emphasizes the 'nation-building' functions assigned to constitutional rule (Sohrabi 2011: 75, 133).

more widely. This involved several measures to promote unifying patterns of citizenship to support the constitution, so that, as in earlier contexts, constitutional ideals were utilized to construct a broad Ottoman identity for vertical integration and imperial reinforcement. Initially, the policies of the Young Turks looked back to the reformist ideals of the Tanzimat era, and the Committee endeavoured to apply constitutional law to stabilize the empire and to bind different groups to it. For example, after the coup, the parliament was reconvened and elections were held in late 1908. These hotly contested elections were based on earlier electoral laws, and they allowed a wide franchise, as qualification for participation depended on tax contribution, with a relatively low threshold. These elections also permitted representation for different sub-imperial groups, so that, in the first instance, the post-1908 regime promised to strengthen minority rights, it led to a brief reduction of anti-imperial violence in some areas, and it was warmly approved by some minorities. Then, the elected assembly modified the constitution in 1909. These changes reinforced the powers of the legislature, increased the accountability of the sultan to the General Assembly (Arts 3, 53–54) and narrowed the prerogatives of the sultan (Art. 113). Despite the secularist impulse behind the Young Turks, the 1909 amendments were partly drafted by religious authorities and reflected religious motivations amongst opponents of the sultan.[40] Central to Young Turk policies, further, was an emphasis on education, and the first years of the regime saw a remarkable expansion of publishing and press activities. These measures had strong military backing and reflected a deep commitment to military citizenship. From 1908, the military apparatus was rapidly modernized, with new conscription laws in 1909, and the military assumed increased salience. This military emphasis of the regime was then reinforced after a short and violent counter-revolutionary coup in 1909, leading to the deposition of the sultan, who was accused of conspiracy. At this point, the Committee still shared power with other actors, and constitutional rule was not renounced; in fact, some new measures enhanced the autonomy of the legislature. Nonetheless, opposition publications were banned, powers of government were vested in the military and martial law was imposed in some regions.[41]

[40] Gunasti (2016: 98).

[41] On these processes, see Ahmad (1969: 51–52), Erickson (2001: 2) and Sohrabi (2011: 265–258).

A further military-led regime change was imposed in Istanbul in 1912, as opponents of the Committee of Union and Progress took power and disbanded the cabinet. Then, in January 1913, the Committee launched a counter coup, overthrowing the government at gunpoint. From this juncture, military units linked to the Committee asserted greater control in the political system, marginalizing other political groups and creating a regime close to a military dictatorship. Actors in the army acquired increased influence through military challenges caused by Italian aggression in 1911 and by the Balkan War in 1912, as the empire was exposed to huge loss of territory and sovereignty – in essence, to rapid colonization. These events meant that military figures with revanchist intentions gained more significant roles in government, weakening the democratic aspect of constitutional rule. This also provided an occasion for far-reaching military reforms, influenced by German consultants, through which the composition of the army was altered, creating a corps of officers sympathetic to the Committee. The Young Turks then remained in power from 1913 to 1918. From 1913, a single-party regime was institutionalized through constitutional reforms that weakened the parliament and imposed martial law in some areas.[42] Increased military monopolization of public offices was flanked by the deepening militarization of society, in which the Committee partly exerted social control through use of paramilitaries. From the outset, the authoritarian bias of the regime was also linked to labour discipline, as, in 1909, laws to restrict strikes and other industrial action were introduced.

Once securely installed, the Young Turks imposed ideals of uniform citizenship more robustly than previous reformers, and the enforcement of such policies was conducted by increasingly prerogative means. Moreover, citizenship was progressively defined in more compact terms than in previous reforms, and it was designed to reduce ethnic deviation from a standard model. At the beginning of the Young Turk government, the regime was committed to preserving the empire and had limited space for exclusionary nationalist doctrines. Yet, as early as 1909, the government began to devise strategies to weaken subimperial affinities, and it passed the Law on Associations, which threatened to close organizations based in ethnic denominations. Such laws did not amount to a formal policy to endorse Turkish nationalism to the exclusion of other ethnic affiliations, but they were hostile to

[42] Kansu (2000: 404–408).

movements promoting parallel nationalism. Subsequently, outlooks amongst the Committee moved in part towards an ideology close to Turkism, isolating and prioritizing Turkish national membership as the dominant integrational focus of the empire. Nuance is required in treating this question.[43] In key respects, as mentioned, the Young Turks originally envisioned an ideal of citizenship that overcame the limitations of citizenship law in the Tanzimat era. Indicatively, in 1909 and 1914, they imposed conscription laws that were, in principle, applied to all citizens, which meant that minorities could bear arms. In this sphere, the Young Turks intensified earlier policies intended to reconstruct the empire as a union of citizens, abolishing laws that had sustained unequal citizenship. However, in other domains, many policies implemented after 1908 privileged people of Turkish ethnicity, against a background of ongoing ethnic partition. Such outlooks were distinct from the multicentric ideals of Ottoman integration characteristic of earlier reforms, and, in some respects, they aimed to correct the failure of previous reforms to solidify imperial citizenship.[44] For example, education policies led to the enforcement of Turkish as a state language. Population policies concentrated on protecting Turkish groups, especially those transferred from other imperial regions during the Balkan Wars. Even the reconvening of the parliament in 1908 contained an exclusionary dimension as it weakened religious channels of interest articulation and prioritized the Turkish language as a means of political communication.[45] Accordingly, the early years of the second constitutional period saw both the generalization and the restriction of citizenship, which conferred formal rights on all citizens, but also imposed more coercive integration on persons of non-dominant ethnic origin. Schematically, this period began to establish a military-nationalist concept of citizenship to support state legitimacy, finally supplanting the diffuse, residually religious premises of government that had been weakened in the nineteenth century.

During the post-1908 period, the imposition of military citizenship ideals again failed to stabilize the political system, and it continued to induce acute internal and external conflict. After 1908, the endemic problems of Ottoman government were intensified and the connected

[43] On divisions between members of the movement, see Ahmad (2014: 6).

[44] See Moreau 2007: 287–315.

[45] See the comment on the use of elections to create a 'politically integrated society' in Kayali (1997: 83). Close to my analysis, one historian describes this period as marking the 'transition away from a traditional empire toward a nation-state, or more accurately, toward an imperial nation state' (Sohrabi 2018: 844).

tendency towards the promotion of imperial citizenship, the militarization of government and the production of extreme lateral violence was reflected in different parts of the empire. For example, the reforms gave rise to intensified separatism in the Balkan regions. These conflicts remained inextricably connected to inter-imperial rivalry owing to strategic Russian support for Balkan states. In this process, Albania became independent in 1912; Albania had traditionally been a supporter of Ottoman rule in the Balkans, but this support was ended by attempts in Istanbul to harden the imperial government and promote Ottomanization in the region, involving the use of martial law in 1910. Bulgarian independence was finalized in 1908. At the same time, Italy's imperial aspirations led to the invasion of Libya in 1911. By 1912, the outbreak of the Balkan Wars, partly caused by Italian interventions, moved the continuum of violence that characterized the late Ottoman Empire into a new dimension. The Balkan Wars turned earlier intra-imperial conflicts into external wars, as the empire fought and experienced devastating defeat by its former constituent regions in the southern Balkans. These wars often fused different modes of violence, with irregular troops frequently engaging in conflict. Such external militarization reinforced the position of military units in government in Istanbul, and government was increasingly conducted on exceptionalist premises. Martial law was almost constantly in force in Istanbul from 1909, and it was imposed through the empire during World War I. At the same time, imperial military units experienced mutinies and insurrections, so that the assertion of political command by the military also induced civil conflict.

The assumption of power by the Young Turks in 1908 was, in part, an epochal and direction-changing event in modern history. This event clearly foreshadowed patterns of military intervention in civilian politics that became frequent in the twentieth century. At the same time, however, this process did not deviate categorically from constitutional lineages in other settings, and it brought wider constitutional tendencies, characteristic of the entire post-1789 era, to extreme, but still paradigmatic articulation.

From the first advent of constitutional democracy, governments that were unsuccessful in warfare usually experienced dramatic constitutional transformation, and this was typically enforced by organizations either linked to the military or brought to prominence by military circumstances. Although the Young Turks were not immediately brought to power by military defeat, the origins of this movement lay in disaffected military units, and they were shaped by long histories of military humiliation. In this respect, the Young Turks gave exemplary expression to processes that were more diffusely manifested in other constitutional settings. As mentioned, the transformation of Russia that started in 1905 formed an immediate precedent for the Turkish revolution. As Russia and the Ottoman Empire were linked by enmity, the revolutionary reaction to military catastrophe in St Petersburg found resonance in Istanbul. Moreover, the events after 1908 reflected the more general fact that attempts to construct unifying definitions of citizenship frequently brought military actors to the centre of politics. At one level, the Young Turks came to power because of the imperial citizenship reforms of the nineteenth century, which had been conducted to impose vertical integration processes on society, and their objective was to realize in a more committed fashion the unifying objectives of these reforms. However, the ideological position of the Young Turks was determined by the fact that the imposition of unifying citizenship norms had released intensely conflictual forces in society. This meant that the Young Turks claimed legitimacy as an organization able to contain lateral militarism and to impose a uniform stratum of citizenship norms across society. As in earlier examples, this process was conducted by military means, and the deployment of military force by the Committee of Union and Progress was legitimated by the fact that earlier reforms had led to violent social polarization. For this reason, the military became the leading organization in post-imperial nation-building, enacting policies with some clear elements of internal colonization.

The Young Turk revolution also reflected wider tendencies in the fact that, from the late eighteenth century onwards, constitutions had frequently been implemented to cement patterns of intra-societal control to sustain imperial authority. As discussed, most constitutions effected a process in which citizenship was imposed internally, in coercive fashion, to sustain the means of violence externally. The most essential distinction between the Young Turks and modes of constitutional government established in other nineteenth-century states was that the Young Turks led a regime that was exposed to multipolar violence in which internal and external violence converged with particular intensity. As mentioned, this was caused by the fact that the nationalization of citizenship was much more contested in the Ottoman region than in other areas. In other contexts, governments were typically able to declare legitimacy by unifying all members of a nation against external actors (vertical integration), and they exploited this process to generate military force for external military actions. Their domestic military force was typically used to suppress either relatively marginal ethnic groups or – more typically – organizations that mobilized against the government on anti-systemic grounds, usually linked to organized class interests. In such contexts, constitutions sustained patterns of simultaneous internal and external occupation, but internal occupation was relatively easily accomplished. In face of the conflictual ethnic landscape of the Ottoman Empire, however, the Young Turks were forced to engage in a unique process of bifocal occupation in which they were required to stabilize military rule over external and internal populations, often in settings where the demographic difference between the inside and the outside of imperial society was hard to determine. The period of government by the Committee of Union and Progress was a period of external militarization as the Ottoman region experienced major wars. But this was also a period of intense internal militarization in which, to a greater extent than before 1908, the governmental bloc legitimated its authority by promoting the interests of one ethnic group in the empire over others. This militarization was primarily expressed in the rising hostility of the Young Turk government to irredentist or potentially irredentist subgroups, notably Armenians and Greeks. New outbreaks of mass violence against Armenians coincided with the failed coup of 1909. During the Balkan Wars, large numbers of displaced ethnic Turks entered the empire, which added new hostility to inter-population interactions; such displaced groups had no strong motive to be sympathetic to Christians. By this time, policies of the Committee towards non-Turkish groups became decisively repressive. In these respects, the line between external warfare and internal warfare became almost vanishingly thin, as the late Ottoman government often faced similar conflicts both within and beyond its territorial limits. This was expressed in several legislative processes designed to promote Turkification.[46]

This particularity of the Ottoman system became most acutely manifest during World War I. At one level, World War I was the continuation of earlier wars and conflicts, as it again centred on the long-standing hostility between rival empires in St Petersburg and Istanbul. In this conflict, the Ottoman Empire was forced into alliance with Germany, as other

[46] On these processes, see Karpat (2001: 349) and Kayali (2021: 274).

belligerent empires had manifest designs on Ottoman territory. During World War I, Ottoman military force was naturally directed outwards, and Ottoman armies suffered very high death rates. However, the war also protracted existing patterns of violence inside Ottoman society, and the military assumed internal functions of institutional reinforcement which converged with and duplicated patterns of external violence. Military units were deployed to consolidate Ottoman government within the empire itself, which meant that many Ottoman citizens were subject, by their own governments, to a condition very similar to military occupation. In many regions, Ottoman government after 1914 formed a hybrid between domestic rule and foreign occupation.

To exemplify this, the Ottoman government imposed a system in Syria after 1914 that was very close to an external occupation regime. After 1914, Syria was placed under the rule of Cemal Pasha, and it became the site of an experiment in accelerated military citizenship formation. Under this regime, Syrians were subject to compulsory enlistment in the army, and organizations mobilized in external warfare were used to control the domestic population, brutally suppressing Arab dissidents.[47] Most traumatically, such propensities were reflected in acts of violence towards Armenians, culminating in the mass atrocities beginning in 1915. Many Armenians had been conscripted to fight for the Ottoman empire in 1914. Soon, however, doubts were raised about their loyalty and (often justified) fears existed that they may collaborate with Russia, which meant that they were disarmed. Many Armenians lived in areas settled by incoming Muslims from the Balkans, who had been uprooted from their homes. In many cases, Armenians were first attacked by local groups without governmental support. However, officials of the Young Turk regime soon supported these assaults and helped to drive Armenians from the regions where they resided, dispossessing them of lands and compelling many to join deadly forced labour battalions.[48] This policy of enforced population control (ethnic cleansing) resulted in genocidal acts against the Armenian community in which approximately a million Armenians died. In this process, the Ottoman government presented itself as an actor engaged in a multipolar war against external enemies and against a segment of its citizens. Largely unarmed Armenians were treated, in effect, as foreign military combatants in their own country, where they

[47] On this, see Çiçek (2014: 79) and Kayali (2021: 37–48).

[48] These were battalions for minorities not trusted to serve in the regular army (see Üngör 2011: 60).

lacked the protection under laws of war that would have applied to protagonists in interstate hostility. Illustratively, one historical account describes this both as a process of brutalized 'internal colonization' and as a strategy to extract capital from dispossessed communities for military ends.[49]

At different levels of terror, the Ottoman Empire was mobilized after 1914 on two fronts, and it deployed military force both against internal and external adversaries, in simultaneous acts of interstate war and civil war. In these processes, the simple distinction between a nation and an empire lost value. Through the nineteenth century, the Ottoman government intermittently sought to impose the features of a nation state on the empire, rooted in vertical citizenship laws and uniform constitutional rights. After 1908, as in other polities, this constitutional process was strongly attached to the army, and nation-building finally converged with the military imposition of citizenship. However, the transformation of the empire into a nation did not succeed. As it acquired constitutional form, the empire integrated its subunits in increasingly violent fashion, usually in procedures that reacted to external violence. In so doing, however, it transformed existing membership groups into hostile minorities, which it regimented through extreme acts of military violence. This simultaneous process of citizenship formation and lateral militarization became traumatically visible during World War I, when the empire imposed control across its territories in a form significantly more brutal than regular warfare. At this point, attempts to consolidate citizenship in the face of external violence created a constant surplus of violence inside imperial society, and war spilled diffusely between the internal and the external domains.

MILITARISM AFTER 1918

The military construction of citizenship in the Ottoman regions around 1908 produced a model of constitutionalism that was emulated in different regions, including Europe and, as mentioned, Latin America. In the Middle East, this model found echoes within and outside the Ottoman region, and military citizenship became a common feature in societies in this region, especially through the transformation of imperialism that began in World War I. One important parallel to the Ottoman case is the historical formation of constitutional law in Iran, formally known as

[49] Üngör and Polatel (2011: 65, 166).

Persia until 1935. By the 1920s, the military dictated primary terms of citizenship in Iran, reflecting features of the Ottoman trajectory in which legitimacy was transferred from religious to military sources. The key milestones in this process were the military coup led by Reza Khan (later Pahlavi) in 1921 and the deposition of the last Qajar shah in 1925. These events marked critical points in a longer constitutional sequence, beginning in 1905–6, when a revolution was conducted in Iran by a diffuse alliance of businessmen, official religious scholars (*ulama*), intellectuals and administrators, intending to frame royal power in a system of political representation. This revolution partly mirrored developments in the Ottoman domain, as it occurred in a polity deeply unsettled by the imperialist ambitions of Russia and Britain. It was closely connected to events in Russia, as it was made possible by the fact that Russia was debilitated in 1905, and it was partly encouraged by Britain.

Initially, the revolutionary alliance established a constitution (1906) that limited the powers of the shah and established a parliamentary assembly to sit alongside the monarchy. These reforms were strengthened by supplementary fundamental laws of 1907, which gave powerful expression to ideas of national sovereignty and individual rights. From the beginning, the Iranian constitution was designed to instil unity in society, in a situation deeply structured by imperial depredation. One of the main purposes of the constitutional faction was to counteract the territorial interests of Russian and British armies and to prevent the use of foreign militias by the shah. The year 1907 saw the Anglo–Russian Agreement, which effectively divided Iran into zones of control. Accordingly, Art. 106 of the 1907 supplementary legislation prohibited the internal use of foreign armies.[50] The constitution also reflected long-standing attempts to establish a national army and plans were made for the introduction of conscription in 1911.[51] As in Turkey, the revolution did not immediately reflect any weakening of religion in the state.[52] On the contrary, in the 1907 legislation, the *ulama* retained responsibility for ensuring that laws accorded with Islam (Art. 2). The parliamentary constitution was subject to repeated assault by the monarch, and it was suspended from 1908 to 1909, with Russian support, under conditions of civil war. Parliament was reopened in 1909 after

[50] One historian notes how 1906–7 saw a rise in popular militancy as citizens began military exercises to support the constitutional state (Matthews 2013: 127).

[51] Bayat (2020: 271–2).

[52] Different historians have noted how some *ulama* were hostile to the Qajar dynasty (see Algar 1969: 250–252).

the shah had been replaced by his son. However, Russia invaded northern Iran in 1911, putting an effective end to the transformation. Parliament was convened again in 1914, but its operations were chronically disrupted by World War I. During this time, Iran experienced partial external occupation by Britain and Russia, and, at the end of the war, the country was devastated by famine caused by external intervention, with extraordinarily high population loss.[53]

In 1921, Reza Khan's coup marked both the end and the manifest articulation of constitutional ideas elaborated since 1906. Khan's takeover was supported by parliamentary authority, and, on assuming power, he did not finally suspend the constitution or the parliament and his assumption of power was justified by a constitutional revision. He was finally crowned monarch with military support in 1926, having ended the Qajar dynasty, using parliament to secure the abdication of the shah. However, his government was based in a reordered military fusing different security units and designed to promote national centralization and security by military means. He imposed martial law in 1924 and large-scale conscription in 1926; up to that point, military force had been largely extracted from rural magnates.[54] The beginning of his dynasty brought a more decisive a shift to political secularism, and it was followed by a series of legal reforms that reduced the legal role of clerics and established a more formalized legal system.

After 1918, militarized citizenship also remained a core feature of government in the immediate Ottoman region. In fact, after 1918, military constitutionalism was strongly attuned to geopolitical realities in this area, and citizenship formation took place in environments marked by overlapping military conflicts.

Other European continental empires involved in World War I came to an abrupt end from 1917 to 1918. By contrast, the dissolution and eventual partition of the Ottoman Empire was a more prolonged process. Here, the continuum of violence starting in the nineteenth century was not immediately concluded. In the first instance, the Ottoman Empire was saved from complete external annexation by the Russian Revolution of 1917, which led to the dispersal of Russian troops in Anatolia. Subsequently, the Entente powers did not succeed in imposing a peace settlement in the empire, and the terms of peace were partly defined by politicians in the emerging Turkish state. The Treaty of Sèvres (1920)

[53] On the constitutional origins of the Gendarmerie, see Cronin (1997: 17).
[54] Abrahamian (1982: 131–2).

remained unratified by the Turkish government and the Entente powers lacked the military infrastructure to enforce its provisions. However, Ottoman territory experienced multiple temporary and permanent partitions from 1918. First, Istanbul was subject to military occupation by Entente governments from 1918. At the same, time, Turkey was involved in war with Greece, which lasted until 1923. The Greek army, supported by the Entente powers, invaded Ottoman territories in 1919 with the objective of unifying Greek communities across the Ottoman region in order to form an ethnically homogenous Greek imperial nation. The Greeks conducted a brutal war in which civilians were murdered in large numbers and political figures linked to the Committee of Union and Progress were especially targeted. From the Turkish perspective, these wars were partly wars of imperial consolidation, as Turkey defended territories forming part of the Ottoman Empire. But these wars were partly wars of liberation, in which Turks defied Greek imperialism. These wars were also partly a continuation of the inter-imperial conflicts in World War I, as Turkish armies were confronted with armies of the Entente alliance. Naturally, these wars were similar to civil wars. They mobilized ethnic groups against each other who, in many cases, had coexisted in the same polity for hundreds of years and who had been co-citizens until a few years previously. In these wars, the Turkish units recruited soldiers of many kinds, including irregular units.

International parties engaged in warfare with the Ottoman Empire in and after 1918 continued their habit of treating the empire as a semi-sovereign entity. The first attempt to establish final post-war terms was the Sèvres Treaty (1920) following the San Remo Conference. This treaty was instigated by the Entente powers, as Istanbul was still under Entente occupation, although it was approved by the sultan. It redefined the borders of Ottoman regions. It placed Turkey, now described as such in the treaty, in a position of restricted sovereignty, as the contracting parties set out a series of norms with which the Turkish government was required to comply in matters normally subject to internal jurisdiction. For example, the treaty prescribed conditions concerning minorities in Turkey and stipulated that all inhabitants of Turkey should enjoy 'the same civil, and political rights' (Art. 145). The treaty created a Commission in Istanbul, with British, French and Italian members, to draft provisions for self-government by minorities in some regions (Art. 62), reserving the right to impose political and territorial reforms if these norms were not respected

(Art. 36). The treaty also forced Turkey to recognize Armenia as an independent state (Art. 88), following partial reannexation of Armenia by Turkish troops in 1920. Further, it foresaw the transfer of Arab regions – for example, Syria, Mesopotamia and Palestine – to mandatory powers (Arts 94–5). This was agreed despite the fact that representatives of some Arab regions had initiated their own constitution-making process in 1919–20. The mandate system eventually brought a partial return to colonial rule for groups in the process of detaching themselves from Ottoman power, and it was often imposed through war between mandate powers and irregular armed forces. In addition, the treaty recognized British or French rule in Sudan, Egypt and Morocco. Importantly, it imposed a change of citizenship on Turks living outside the redrawn borders of the state, and it allowed non-Turks to leave Turkey to live in countries to which they claimed ethnic affiliation (Arts 123, 125). In the military domain, the treaty placed a limit on the size of the Turkish army and prohibited conscription (Art. 165). In each respect, the Sèvres Treaty had much in common with a colonial document, and it was designed to prevent the transformation of the Ottoman Empire and its constituent regions into sovereign nation states.[55] This coincided with the Russian Civil War and the ensuing construction of the Soviet Union, in which Russians invaded Armenia in 1920, which, by 1922, became a founding state of the Soviet Union. Overall, the conditions of decolonization that shaped constitution making after 1918 possessed particular complexity in the Ottoman sphere as the empire itself became an object of external imperial depredation, and it remained an actor in extremely violent post-imperial warfare.

In this context, military forces retained deep influence on polity building and constitution writing, both in Turkey and in successor states to the Ottoman Empire. At this time, the emerging post-Ottoman environment continued to give intensified expression to the paradigm of military constitutionalism in different social domains.

First, this can be seen in Turkey itself. After the collapse of the Central Powers, the parliament in Istanbul was dissolved in late 1918, and the sultan again began a short period of personal rule. The Committee was dissolved in 1918 before the parliament was reopened in late 1919. As Turkey remained at war after 1918, however, military

[55] On one account, this treaty was motivated by depredatory policies and it 'aimed to stabilize British and French imperial power in Middle East' (Baba and Winter 2022: 357).

leaders continued to exercise prominent political functions. In this setting, Mustafa Kemal, previously attached to the Committee, became the central political figure, acquiring an important position in the nationalist movement that came to the fore through war between Turkey and Greece, and through military conflicts with France. During these wars, Kemal helped to create a separate nationalist congress in Erzurum, eastern Turkey (summer 1919), which was committed to defending Turkey's territorial integrity. This congress distanced itself from the Committee, which was held responsible for the war and military defeat.[56] However, Kemal extended key policies of the Committee. In the first instance, Kemal's political designs were conceived to consolidate Turkish integrity by promoting fully national models of citizenship. Central to this were plans to abolish the sultanate and to establish the polity as a secular nation state. At the same time, Kemal promoted a governmental order based in militarism and political representation. The parliament in Istanbul suspended its activities in March 1920 in protest at restrictions imposed on its legislation by the Entente powers; it had just approved a national pact inspired by Kemal. After the dissolution, Kemal convened a new representative body, the Grand National Assembly, in Ankara. This Assembly was presented as the centrepiece in a new post-imperial polity committed to the representation of the interests of the Turkish people in the former Ottoman Empire, to the full restitution of Turkish sovereignty and to the expulsion of foreign military units from Turkish territory.[57] The Assembly acquired immediate significance as an organ of national military unification, and many of its first functions were designed to solidify national military resources. The assembly engaged externally in multipolar war with Greece and French occupying forces. The assembly was also involved in hostile conflict with internal groups. Accordingly, its first task was to expand the army. Military reforms required both the reorganization of the imperial army and the integration of informal military bodies, as militia organizations had proliferated through society after the surrender of the regular army. Conscription was reintroduced in June 1920, in breach of the Sèvres Treaty. By August 1921, faced with the prospect of a Greek military victory, Kemal became the commander-in-chief of the army as well as the head of government, so that he approached a dictatorial position.[58]

[56] On Kemal's renunciation of his attachment to the Committee, see Gingeras (2016: 239).
[57] Gawrych (1988: 326).
[58] This was decided in the notorious Law 144 of 5 August 1921.

In this setting, Kemal introduced a new constitution in 1921. Perhaps more than any earlier constitution, this formed an organic law that was intended to create and galvanize nation-building in a multidimensional military environment. The constitution established a parliamentary assembly (nominally elected) which combined executive and legislative powers (Art. 2). It intensified earlier processes of imperial centralization and reduced the administrative autonomy of provinces (Art. 14). Unlike earlier constitutions, it did not subject the legislative body to any external constraint, so that the will expressed through the Assembly was fully sovereign as the Assembly was an immediate organ of the Turkish nation (Art. 1). The fact that Kemal was the head of the army meant that the military was not separate from the assembly, and it formed an adjunct to the polity. At one level, this constitution was an anti-colonial constitution, as it was designed emphatically to reject the principles imposed in the Sèvres Treaty. However, it was also a post-imperial constitution, as it was intended to solidify Turkey's dominant position in a territorial space defined by ongoing war with Greece. It also had some aspects of a civil war constitution. It was intended to cement the power of the nationalists over other factions in society. In some areas, society was characterized by extreme lawlessness, caused by different wars of different types, and the consolidation of a national army was a key moment in internal pacification.[59] In each respect, the constitution displayed characteristic aspects of imperial nation-building.[60]

Kemal's nationalist policies formed the basis for a new republic, which was declared in 1923 following the abolition of the sultanate in late 1922 and before the abolition of the caliphate in 1924. Importantly, the foundation of the republic coincided with a new international treaty that concerned the terms of Turkish sovereignty, the Treaty of Lausanne (1923), agreed as the military position of Greece, Britain and France was becoming weaker. The Treaty of Lausanne was a tangible success for Kemal. It reflected many of the core demands for which Kemal's nationalist movement had mobilized, and its provisions were approvingly commentated in his speeches. For example, the Lausanne Treaty renounced many of the provisions of the Sèvres Treaty. It recognized Turkey as a sovereign state with redrawn boundaries, incorporating Anatolia. It did not impose restrictions on

[59] Metinsoy (2021: 106).
[60] One important analysis contains the claim that the republic entailed a 'project of the nation' based in a 'repetition of the project of the Empire' (Meeker 2002: 395).

the size of the Turkish army.[61] It established some norms to protect minority groups in Turkey. For example, it set out protections for the rights of non-Muslim citizens of Turkey regarding freedom of movement, emigration and general civil and political rights (Arts 38–39), defining these as subject to guarantees of League of Nations (Art. 44). However, this treaty established harder linkages between citizenship and ethnicity in the former Ottoman space. In Arts 31–32, it made provision for the removal of ethnic groups from one state to another in the former imperial territories. Most importantly, it included a convention of January 1923 agreed between Greece and Turkey that foresaw the large-scale transfer of ethnic Turks residing outside the newly determined Turkish borders into Turkey and the reciprocal transfer of non-Turkish population groups living inside Turkey into states in which their (putative) ethnicity was preponderant.

These provisions brought an intensification of the ethnic concentration that had characterized the last decades of Ottoman imperialism. For example, these provisions partly perpetuated aspects of the millet system. They also partly perpetuated elements of ethnic purification and repression that marked the decline of the empire. In principle, under the Lausanne Treaty, directives regarding population transfers implied that ethno-religious minorities were not entitled to secure citizenship except in the territories in which persons associated with a similar ethnicity and/or religion formed a majority. Accordingly, the treaty enshrined in international law a racial definition of citizenship, stating that Ottoman residents had a primary right to live in regions populated by persons of similar ethnicity. In establishing this principle, the treaty initiated the vast displacement of self-identifying Greeks from Turkey into Greece and brought a counter flow of Turkish refugees from Greece into the new Turkish state. This occurred at a time when large refugee communities were already on the move in the Middle East. In many cases, the actual ethnic affiliation of displaced persons was questionable. Many populations in the Ottoman Empire formed ancient cultural islands with far closer ties to the surrounding populations than to the bearers of (supposed) common ethnicity, residing in relatively new, often geographically remote nation states. At the same time, the treaty created the premise for a distinct post-imperial order, as it implied that the ethnically homogenous nation

[61] Kemal expressly noted these points in his famous speech of 1927 giving account of his achievements (Kemal 1929: 614–15).

state was the essential unit of sovereignty and personal protection. This gave a new intensity to Wilsonian ideals, as it indicated that self-determination of sovereign citizens presupposed *racial unmixing*, so that nationality and ethnicity became exclusively congruent. This meant that ethnic cleansing was imagined as an alternative to colonization – regions freed of multiple ethnicities were separated from their imperial past and their populations were incorporated in new nations. Paradoxically, in turn, this meant that principles enunciated in the later stages of empire became the foundation for new nations, and nations were anchored in affiliations that had become prominent through intra-imperial violence. Nations thus rearticulated patterns of violence typical of late imperialism and reproduced in intensified form patterns of citizenship forced into society by imperialism.

As a substructure for the new republic, Kemal introduced a new constitution in 1924 with notionally strong provisions for basic rights and popular sovereignty, which remained in force for nearly forty years. Materially, the constitution was flanked by reformist laws that solidified national attachments to secure the republic. For example, the Kemalist reforms included legislation of 1924 that eliminated religious schools and unified all school education, so that national doctrine had protected position. In 1926, the constitution was amended to make school-level education obligatory. Later, in 1928, it was amended to include a commitment to secularism, and, in February 1937, this principle acquired elevated protection. Eventually, the constitution was used to promote a construct of citizenship that at least overlapped with definitions promoted in later, ultra-authoritarian states in Western Europe. In 1926, posts in the civil service were reserved for Turks. By 1932, discriminatory citizenship laws were imposed which ensured that certain professional opportunities were open only to Turks, forcing employers to release non-Turkish staff.[62] In 1927, Law Nr 1041 created an instrument to strip persons of citizenship who had not fought for Turkey in the independence wars. In 1934, the Resettlement Law imposed a policy of forced population management and deportation in some regions.

The military assumed a key position in such policies. Formally, it was fundamental to Kemalism that the army should play no immediate active role in politics. A law of late 1923 stated that army officers could not run for elected office. The Military Penal Code of 1930 prescribed harsh

[62] Cagaptay (2006: 70).

prison sentences for soldiers who banded together for political purposes. However, the army was a forceful presence in early republican politics in Turkey. A large number of Kemalist politicians had military backgrounds. Alongside this, national conscription was retained even after demobilization following victory over Greece; conscription was imposed again in 1927. The army was also expected to promote primary obligations of citizenship, and the Kemalist party described military service as 'the most sacred of all national duties'.[63] Moreover, government was conducted in semi-militarized fashion. The Kemalist system did not develop into a democracy and early republican institution building revolved around the hardening of the political executive. In this process, the military was constitutionally separated from the executive. However, the military played an important in maintaining public order and suppressing dissent and opposition, and it acted as an auxiliary force in the authoritarian regime. This was framed by the Maintenance of Order Law (1925), which allowed for the use of force against organized labour and regime opponents. By the 1930s, the government had prohibited strikes and established a corporatist economic order in which the labour movement was closely marshalled. One historian has observed how schools absorbed semi-military socialization functions, determining dress codes and promoting secular ideals of behaviour. The same account stresses how, in this context, military organizations discharged pedagogic duties, including physical discipline and even the education of teachers in rural areas.[64] In these different respects, military and national ethics converged, and together they created a political culture in which the army formed a core bastion of the government. This was reflected in the ongoing promotion of military violence against some minorities whose status had not been secured under the Lausanne Treaty. Through the interwar period, military force and martial law were used against Kurdish minorities, which were also subject to forcible resettlement under laws of 1934.

In some dimensions, the constitutional underpinnings that emerged in Turkey after 1922–3 reconfigured the circumstances of imperialism in the Ottoman setting. At the core of the republican order was a greatly intensified reconsolidation of the model of citizenship first devised in the Tanzimat era, in which political membership was progressively separated from the historical form of the empire and placed on secular premises as a vertical integration structure. The translocation of citizenship from

63 See Section 8 of the 1931 party programme (quoted in Parla and Davison 2004: 231).
64 Yilmaz (2013: 52–3, 156).

religion to the army coincided perfectly with the translocation of citizenship from a segmentary to a vertical form of societal integration. However, after 1923, citizenship was promoted in an ethnically restricted definition tightly linked to service for the national army. In this regard, the army was expected to perpetuate its original modernizing and nation-building function, but it acquired policing responsibilities in managing lateral conflicts in society attached to both class and ethnic affiliations. This culminated in 1941, as the European war escalated; at this point, the government conscripted all non-Muslim males, partly to avoid political subterfuge. In each respect, the formation of a national polity entailed the specific – although selective – reproduction of techniques used to consolidate the Ottoman Empire in its final decades.

PERSISTENT IMPERIALISM AFTER 1918

In much of the post-Ottoman region, the years after 1918 saw the persistence of patterns of constitution making shaped by imperialism in different ways. Some regions that had not been sovereign before 1918 briefly approached independence at this time, often in settings where armies remained central actors. However, in most contexts, imperial authority remained a dominant force. This was evident in Syria. Syria briefly declared independence in late 1918 under Faysal, and an independent constitutional convention, the Syrian General Congress, was convened in 1919 before France was installed as mandatory power from 1920 to 1923. A new constitution was drafted in Syria following elections of 1928, which set out principles of limited government within the terms of the mandate imposed by France. This constitution was originally vetoed by France but was promulgated in 1930. A Syrian government then operated with increased autonomy from 1936. In parallel, Egypt became notionally independent in 1922, and a constitution was introduced in 1923 after civil uprisings at the end of the war in 1919. The post-1922 system in Egypt was marked by multiparty electoral competition under a constitutional monarchy. However, British involvement in Egypt deprived the government of full autonomy. From 1922, Britain retained reserved powers in Egypt. The Egyptian constitution was temporarily abrogated in 1930 and replaced by a constitution with a reduced franchise, and military supervision of political practice became common. Under a treaty of 1936, British troops were garrisoned in Egypt to defend the Suez Canal, and Sudan remained under joint British-Egyptian administration. More widely, the mandate system created in Versailles meant that most non-sovereign regions emerging from Ottoman control were governed by force of arms, as civil bodies were subordinate – directly or indirectly – to military rule. This gave rise to repeated large-scale insurgency in regions subject to mandate rule, in which nationalist movements recruited informal fighters. Some regions reached partial autonomy under the mandate system and established partly independent constitutions. This occurred in British-controlled Iraq in 1924; Iraq then became an independent monarchical state in 1932, with a notionally parliamentary constitution. This occurred in Lebanon in 1926.

At the same time, alongside Turkey, Greece evolved along a militarized constitutional pathway through the 1920s. Greece was intermittently democratic after 1918. However, many traditional aspects of Ottoman constitutional politics were mirrored in Greece. From circa 1910, the primary democratic party, which was led by the progressive republican, Venizelos, had its ideological origins in regenerationist doctrines promoted by military units. In fact, Venizelos had come to power in 1909–10 following a coup led by the Military League. This coup was in part a reaction to Turkey's defeat of Greece in 1897, which had great symbolic importance in Greece. This defeat was seen to threaten the realization of a persistent vision in Greek society, the Great Idea – namely, the creation of a Greater Greece unifying all ethnic Greeks in a single imperial nation.[65] From its foundation, Greece was a state with expansionary tendencies, and its territory increased significantly in 1881. Such aggrandizement accelerated dramatically through the Balkan Wars, in which Greece was led by Venizelos, and again after 1918. As a result, the defeat by Turkey in 1897 created a fissure between the Greek army and the government as the government appeared unable to provide material preconditions for the realization of Greek neo-imperial goals. The coup of 1909, influenced by the 1908 coup in Turkey, resulted in a revised constitution (1911), which protected political rights and certain social rights and enhanced the emergency powers of the government. This provided the basis for military success in the Balkan Wars.

After 1909, some aspect of military rule became commonplace in Greece. During the Balkan Wars and World War I, martial law was widely enforced, and new emergency powers were established in 1912. From 1915, political factions in Greece were strongly divided by attitudes to World War I, as different groups favoured different alliances, split

[65] For this point, see Gürsoy (2017: 54–55).

between pro-Venizelos factions who wanted an alliance with the Entente powers and pro-monarchical sectors who preferred to placate the Central Powers by adopting a policy of neutrality. This constellation initially created deep civil strife as the state was divided into two geographically separate governments and the parliament was suspended – a condition terminated only through British and French intervention. Venizelos again assumed powers of national government in 1917, after the king had temporarily gone into exile, as he joined the Entente side in the war and imposed heightened military duties on Greek citizens. Through this long sequence of warfare, the army expanded in size. After 1918, moreover, political competition was deeply connected to military force, and military coups remained a primary mechanism for alternating government. As in other states, acts of external mobilization often coincided with acute conflict at the domestic level, and, after 1919, the fortunes of the Greek army in Turkey were reflected in internal conflicts between progressives and royalists. This culminated in the revolutionary regime change of 1922, following military defeat in Turkey, which created a brief anti-Conservative government under the pro-Venizelos Plastiras. The leaders of this coup oversaw the summary execution of six leading Royalists who were held responsible for military failure. The abolition of the monarchy in 1924 followed a failed reactionary coup, and it was decided by plebiscite.

Owing to the post-1923 population transfers, Greece became an ethnically very homogenous country in which divisions between displaced Greeks from Turkey and long-term residents in Greece formed the dominant polarity.[66] However, Greece was enduringly defined by the endemic militarization of social conflicts in which the army, whose prominence had first been reinforced by ethnic antagonisms, became the central actor in intergroup disputes over state obligations. By 1925, democracy was overthrown by a military coup in which governmental hostility was directed against political radicals. In 1925, the Pangalos dictatorship, with strong support amongst former soldiers, made the Communist Party illegal and introduced repressive public-order laws against the left. This regime was itself brought down by a coup in 1926, leading to the implementation of a republican constitution in 1927. Eventually, Greece was subject to longer military rule during the Metaxas regime, beginning in 1936 after the monarchy had been re-established. The Metaxas regime met most definitions of a fascist state.

[66] See Mavrogordatos (1983: 183).

The government was rooted in the military, and it ruled by imposing a civil war ideology in which regime opponents were construed in military terms. The regime drew legitimacy from imperialist ideas, and, like Mussolini's dictatorship, it sustained domestic authoritarianism by invoking myths of greater Greece and by fostering ideas of a new Greek Empire in the Mediterranean.

After 1918, other former Ottoman states developed on similar patterns. Most independent Balkan states that had previously belonged to the Ottoman region gained territory during the final phase of the empire, and this instilled an expansionist dynamic in their formation. For example, Serbia gained large new territories in the Balkan Wars, indulging imperialist dreams of regional dominance in Belgrade. Serbia became the core state in a new multipartite state in 1918, known as Yugoslavia from 1929, partly founded because of Italian territorial claims. To form the state, Serbia fused with regions previously in the Habsburg Empire (now Croatia, Bosnia and Slovenia). The incorporation of Croatia in Yugoslavia after 1918 was decided in a national council in Zagreb, but it also reflected the dominant regional position of the Serbian army at this time. Through these two stages, Serbia lost its original homogeneity, a primary trigger for earlier uprisings against Ottoman rule, and national citizenship was imposed for more violent purposes of internal solidification. The post-1918 Yugoslav state was initially founded as a democratic constitutional monarchy, with a constitution passed in 1921, largely based in the 1903 constitution of Serbia, which provided for extensive male suffrage. This unified state was based in formal demilitarization, as soldiers were excluded from voting in Art. 70. However, resultant governments rarely institutionalized democratic procedure, and royal control of the legislative process was strongly protected. During the early post-1918 period, the military exercised vital administrative powers, which were established under the Law for the Protection of Public Security and Order in the State (1921).[67] In key respects, the new state centred in Belgrade reproduced conflicts between national and regional constructs of citizenship that had typified the Ottoman Empire, and hostility to the dominant Serbian population was widespread outside core Serbian regions. By 1929, the army took over as a leading actor in a royal dictatorship. This dictatorship was focused on promoting an all-Yugoslav concept of

[67] For an analysis of its provisions, which included the death sentence for persons deemed to threaten public peace, see Nielsen (2014: 170–171).

citizenship, and it created a coercive educational and cultural organization to achieve this. Indeed, one strategic mandate of the military was to promote unifying ideals of citizenship. The severity of resultant regimes varied over time, and competitive elections were restored in 1935 after the assassination of the king. However, by the late 1930s, the government moved close to fascism under the Germanophile premiership of Milan Stojadinović.

Parallel tendencies can be observed in Bulgaria. After 1918, Bulgaria remained a constitutional monarchy reliant on frequent use of martial law. In 1934, the government was brought down by a coup in 1934, which the monarchy utilized to launch an autocoup, creating a military regime, which was very close to fascism, especially after alliance with Nazi Germany. By circa 1940, many laws in Bulgaria concerning conditions of citizenship and employment were modelled on those introduced in Germany. Subsequently, Bulgaria's alliance with Germany enabled it to obtain substantial territory at the expense of Yugoslavia.

IMPERIALISM AFTER 1945

After 1945, the dynamics of decolonization that, to varying degrees, shaped the post-Ottoman region were partly reproduced. At this point, Bulgaria fell into the Russian sphere of influence, whose renewed power in the Balkans reproduced its pre-1917 geopolitical strategies. At the same time, military legitimation remained a powerful factor in Yugoslavia. During World War II, Serbia experienced multipolar warfare: this included partisan mobilization against Nazi occupation, against Croats who had formed an independent puppet state and between different Serbian partisans. In these conditions, military units made an important contribution to the formation of the post-1945 state. One result of this was that Yugoslavia retained an autonomous military system detached from the Soviet Union in which some military actors assumed core roles in the state. Partly because of this background, the leadership around Tito initially harboured ambitions for Balkan hegemony despite Russian opposition. Tito of course established a profile as a campaigner against colonialism amongst leaders of non-aligned states in the Cold War.

In parallel, after 1945, many post-Ottoman states that had been ruled as mandate regions after 1918 became fully sovereign. Between 1943 and 1951, Syria, Libya, Lebanon, Jordan and Israel became independent states. Each of these states developed separate constitutional orders, reflecting different systemic features. Across the region, however, each constitution reproduced aspects of the constitutional conflicts entrenched in the Ottoman period. Each was marked, at an essential level, by the construction of legitimacy in military terms, in which military units diversely assumed primary organizational and representative functions.

The ongoing reproduction of military constitutionalism was visible in the states divided by the core Ottoman conflict, Turkey and Greece. As in Yugoslavia, the experience of World War II in Greece was not entirely distinct from civil war. Fascist occupation of Greece, first by Italy and then by Germany, was conducted at a time when Greece was already subject to near-fascist government. After the defeat of Germany, the conflicts between social groups that had resulted in the installation of Metaxas reappeared in the form of civil war, conditioned by the onset of the Cold War and debates about Greece's position in the post-1945 global security system. Up to the 1970s, Greece saw periods of constitutional stability, but the military did not disappear and took control in 1967. New constitutions in 1968 and 1975 were marked diversely by strong military influence. Indicatively, the 1975 constitution finally separated civilian from military authority, but Art. 4 clearly linked basic legal rights to the obligation 'to contribute to the defence of the Fatherland as provided by law', still according integrational functions to the army. Simultaneously, the role of the military in Turkey was weakened after 1945, and the Kemalist Republican People's Party endorsed multiparty elections in 1946 and 1950. However, the army remained a core political actor. In 1960–1, the post-1945 system was overthrown by the army, claiming a reformist pro-democratic mandate, and the army created a new constitution in 1961. Although influenced by Kemalist ideas, the 1961 constitution established a pluralist party system closely aligned to post-authoritarian constitutions in other countries after 1945. It established far-reaching protections for individual rights (Arts 14–34) and expressed a deep commitment to welfare spending (Arts 41, 45), including provisions for nationalization (Art. 39). Under this constitution, nonetheless, the army retained immediate political influence. This was partly guaranteed by the National Security Council (Art. 111), but it was also based in the Internal Service Law (1961), which gave the army a central role in guarding the state. The army supported a Kemalist change of government in 1971. The year 1980 then saw a further coup, after which fuller powers were given to the army, and the army was also mobilized for acts of internal colonization in Kurdish regions.

Outside this core partition, different models of military constitutionalism appeared across the post-Ottoman region after 1945. In such contexts, armies explained and organized their constitutional functions in distinct ways, responding to specific threats or challenges, usually arising from post-imperial constellations. However, in each case, military actors were accorded a primary role in the administration of the state, in promoting social integration and in connecting government to popular sources of legitimacy. Variants on this primary process are outlined later in this chapter.

After 1945, Syria displayed a strong impetus towards military rule. Previously, Syria had a weak tradition of militarism. For example, the constitutional initiatives launched in 1919 had elicited harsh opposition in society because Faysal imposed conscription. Under the French Mandate, the army was not a powerful political actor.[68] In the first years after Syria became independent (1944–5), however, uncertainty over sovereignty and multiple military pressures brought the army to a central position so that the army became the primary locus of power. In 1949, government was overthrown three times by military coup, and the constitution written under the French mandate (1928/30) was terminated by the army. This coincided with the war in Palestine, where defeat destroyed confidence in the post-independence order. After the second coup in 1949, a new republican constitution was written by an assembly established through elections in which some women voted. Before the constitution was approved, a new coup took place, but the constitution became law in 1950. Although drafted at the instigation of the military leadership, this constitution created a national parliamentary system backed by provisions that enforced conscription (Art. 30) and established an extensive catalogue of social rights, with particular focus on education rights (Art. 28).[69] After this, the military did not fully retreat from power, and a full military regime was installed in 1951, also supported by a short-lived constitution (1953). Parliamentary power was partly re-established in 1954, led by a coalition that included Ba'ath Party factions sympathetic to pan-Arab socialism and union with Egypt (effected 1958). This was strongly linked to military pressures caused by the Suez Crisis. In 1961, one section of the army terminated the union with Egypt, and a new interim constitution was written. Following a transformative coup in 1963, the army, at times converging with the

[68] See Khoury (1987: 628–9).
[69] I rely on the meticulous presentation of this sequence in Atassi (2014: 137–162).

Ba'ath Party, formed the central axis of the state, allowing rising social groups to articulate with government. Domestic policy from this point increasingly focused on the material promotion of national concentration, and the provisional constitution of 1964 established far-reaching social rights, including free universal education. From 1945, Syria saw exponential increased in military spending and rapid increases in educational investment.[70] In each step, internal constitutional decisions were strongly affected by the external late colonial environment, and the contested consolidation of national sovereignty in this context elevated the army's role as an organ of national integration.

One further variant on this trajectory is evident in Egypt. Under Ottoman rule, Egypt was the site of highly effective anti-Ottoman military modernization. However, after British occupation in 1882, Egypt lacked powerful military institutions. Following independence in 1922, the monarchy possessed limited autonomy, and Egyptian military units were mainly adjuncts to the British army until the mid-1930s.[71] Even the Anglo-Egyptian Treaty of 1936 maintained a large British military presence in Egypt. However, this treaty established Egypt's military sovereignty. After this point, the army assumed a more central political role, applying martial law for much of the period from 1937 to 1952. Through World War II and the war in Palestine, the army became a central institutional actor, as the monarchy was discredited because of its close British ties and the institutions rooted in the 1923 constitution were unsettled by military misfortunes. By 1952, a military coup was conducted in which the Free Officers took power and overthrew the monarchy, claiming a constitutional mandate to rule and committing to a new constitution in 1953. One of the leaders of the Free Officers, Gamal Abdel Nasser, was named prime minister by 1954, later becoming president. The military movement in Egypt was determined by external hostility, primarily with Israel. Early conflicts with Israel were immediate triggers of militarization.[72] However, military goals also focused on full conquest of Egyptian territory, not lastly as one of Nasser's key acts was to nationalize the Suez Canal (1956), shortly after the final withdrawal of British military presence in Egypt. As a result, Britain and France launched a failed attempt to overthrow Nasser's government. Nasser also sought union with Syria based in a conjoined military regime. In

[70] See Hinnebusch (1990: 50).
[71] See Gordon (1992: 39).
[72] See Barnett (1992: 13).

this context, the army embodied a spirit of progressive nationalism, defined as a praetorian defender of national interest and a robust protector of national institutions. Nasser implemented a short-lived constitution in 1956, which was endorsed by plebiscite. This constitution contained provisions for a strong presidency, for economic developmentalism (Art. 7), for welfare and universal education (Art. 49) and for compulsory military service, defined as a 'sacred duty' (Art. 58). In this setting, the construction of an independent state institutions was intrinsically linked to the army, and internal and external militarization lay at the core of the postcolonial political order. These principles were consolidated further in the Charter of National Action (1962) after Syrian secession from union with Egypt.

Military constitutionalism also became characteristic in Israel after 1945, where state formation reflected models of militarized citizenship that looked back to traditions of citizenship in nineteenth-century imperial contexts. The foundations of modern Israel lay in early acts of settlement by Jews who migrated from Europe in Ottoman-ruled Palestine before 1914. Such migration was largely driven by growing anti-Semitic violence, especially in Russia. Israel then began to acquire political form through changing inter-imperial relations. This was punctuated by the Balfour Declaration of 1917 and the establishment in 1922 of the British mandate after Versailles and the San Remo Conference (1920). These events enabled the increasingly formal occupancy of British mandate territories by Jewish émigrés, to establish the Yishuv, which was supported by British colonial force. In this context, the consolidation of Israeli citizenship was shaped by multiple modes of military organization, many of which were typical of integration processes in late-imperial and post-imperial locations.

First, the initial stages of Jewish state-building in Israel were defined by the construction of nationality in military terms that characterized late Ottoman society. At this time, settler communities engaged in intermittent conflict with pre-existing populations towards the end of Ottoman rule, so that interethnic rivalry law was a cored feature of territorial occupancy. This occurred in a context that was deeply shaped by ethnic partitioning, which, as discussed, imposed separations on religious and regional groups throughout the Ottoman empire and the post-imperial region. The settlement of lands by population groups violently displaced from the regions that they originally inhabited was not unique to the Jewish communities who took flight to Palestine; it was a common mode of territorial settlement in late Ottoman society. As in other contexts, further, Jewish settlement was partly coordinated by paramilitaries, the Haganah (founded 1920), which again mirrored regional colonization in other Ottoman domains. By the 1930s, Jewish military bodies were partly professionalized. In the later 1930s, conflicts with some Arab groups intensified. In 1936, Arab rebellion, including large-scale communal violence alongside anti-Jewish and anti-British actions, was suppressed by the British army using harsh counter-insurgency policies. This followed the growth of the Jewish diaspora after the surge in European anti-Semitism starting in 1933. Early Jewish settlement in Palestine was partly underpinned by socialist commitments to regimented ownership and shared labour, and many early settlers traced their origins to socialist movements in Poland and Russia. However, early settlement also reproduced military models in Eastern Europe, where territorial consolidation by military personnel was common. As discussed, the trading of military service for land had been common in the border landscapes of European empires and in post-imperial regions that emerged after 1918. This fusion generated a tendency to labour militarism at the origins of Israel.

Second, after 1945, the existing Jewish militias were transformed into a regular army as the state acquired independence.[73] Jewish military organizations had cooperated with the British during the war, preparing for resistance in case of eventual German annexation of the mandate area. These and other informal units formed the basis for the national army, the Israel Defense Forces (founded 1948), which meant that the regular army had a deep connection with society more broadly. After 1945, military units conducted acts of insurgency against the British. From late 1947, war was fought with Palestinians, supported by Egypt and Jordan and other states, who rejected proposals for the partition of Palestine presented by the United Nations (UN). This conflict involved colonizing war, international war, civil war and, less obviously, anti-colonial war, as it marked the end of British presence in Palestine. On a small scale, in fact, these multi-featured wars mirrored earlier wars of national unification in Germany, Italy, Poland and Turkey, in which imperial regions were transformed into nations and soldiers cleared the ground for a national citizenship system. During the formation of the Israel state, military organizations played an important role in coordinating population influxes caused by genocide in Europe,

[73] See Ben-Eliezer (1995: 269).

assuming regulatory roles that extended beyond simple military functions. As in other regions in Eastern Europe and the post-Ottoman space, armies acquired important roles in the socialization of migrants, so that militaries effectively imposed the structure of citizenship on new arrivals. In this, Israel reproduced a common feature of post-imperial state-building. Indicatively, Israel exported military education to other African states during decolonization, including to Ghana under Kwame Nkrumah.

Third, the transitional government in Israel established an administrative order, with some features of a constitution, that again reflected elements of interwar constitutionalism in Eastern Europe, sustained by high levels of social militarization. On one hand, unlike some states in the Middle East, a functional partition existed in Israel between the government and the army. However, the military formed a key organ in the construction of state and society, and it played a social and political rule that sat uneasily in a system committed to the supremacy of civilian institutions. Amongst the first laws of state, an ordinance was issued that authorized full military conscription in emergency situations.[74] In 1949, the state acquired drafting powers in the Defense Service Law, and, by 1950, citizens were called up for reserve service. Military recruitment cut very deep into the population, and it found broad support, intentionally building on existing paramilitary traditions.[75] At this time, national boundaries were uncertain, and external conflicts generated extreme tensions between settlers and prior population groups. The military thus assumed external and internal functions at the same time, as external war and civil war were not clearly distinct. Subsequently, the government reproduced the historical nexus of military inclusion and welfare spending; alongside conscription, the government promoted policies committed to high (ethnically selective) democratic enfranchisement and high welfare spending and employment security, promoting deep integration of the national population. Indicatively, leading military figures argued that Israel's relative military prowess after 1948 was due to the fact that it had a stronger democracy and stronger welfare system than the Arab states. From this standpoint, Israeli 'social democracy' served as the basis for the 'fullest mobilization, both physical and moral, in times of national crisis'.[76] This system of mobilization imposed a strategically differential dimension on Israeli citizenship. For example,

[74] Defense Army of Israel Ordinance, Nr 4 of 5708 (1948).
[75] On one account, 18 per cent of the population was recruited by 1949 (Barnett 1992: 170).
[76] Allon (1970: 63).

Arab citizens of Israel had diminished rights in some areas of society, and access to citizenship for persons displaced by territorial conflict was reduced, even after the Citizenship Law of 1952. Arabs were generally not called upon to perform military duties, a fact that reflected traditional Ottoman anxiety in the face of armed minorities.[77] This gave further reflection to the conventional link between political integration and military duties. In fact, it is documented that Druze communities, who were conscripted from 1956, experienced higher integration levels than other Arabs.[78]

Alongside this, fourth, the Israeli state took shape as a constitutional order in which military regulations assumed an important role. The Israeli Declaration of Independence (1948) promised the introduction of a formal constitution, and the first (Polish-born) prime minister, Ben-Gurion, was originally elected to a constituent assembly. This was prescribed by the UN resolution that established Israel's independence. However, Ben-Gurion decided not to draft and implement a constitution. Instead, the Transition Law (1949) was passed, which established the unicameral Knesset as the legislature, ensuring a Westminster-style government monopoly of legislation. In this system, the use of prerogative and emergency powers was frequent, and reliance on military violence was routine. The Law and Administration Ordinance (1948) created substantial powers for the Provisional Council of State to declare a state of emergency in cases of public security threat and, on this basis, to override parliamentary legislation (Section 9). These powers were directed outwardly towards formal military adversaries. Yet exceptional powers were also pointed inwardly. Military government was imposed in some Arab lands until 1966, which restricted key basic rights. This was partly supported by the Emergency Regulations (Security Zones) Law (1949), which gave military officials administrative control in some regions. Moreover, prerogative laws were used to authorize the expropriation of land in regions inhabited by Arabs.

In these acts, Israel resembled, in intensified form, the paradigm of a society defined by imperialism, and it developed in a form close to that of an imperial nation. Population groups entered Israel from militarized societies in which imperial patterns of violence were endemic, and they entered Israel as a militarized society. Inside Israel, military violence was directed in two ways, outward towards military enemies and inward

[77] See on these points Peri (1983: 23) and Frisch (2011: 38).
[78] Krebs (2006: 65).

towards citizens, so that the division between war and civil war blurred. Emergency powers were used as external and internal instruments at the same time, as they were deployed to consolidate incomplete colonization of national territory, often reproducing exceptionalist measures deployed by the British mandatory power.[79] By 1967, of course, exceptional powers were used for more expressly annexationist purposes, as Israeli territory grew exponentially, and Israel revived the behaviour of other Ottoman states that grew from the Ottoman Empire, which also used national citizenship as a springboard for belligerent occupation. At this point, Israel placed originally external territories under a classical occupation regime in which residents were deprived of citizenship rights. In each dimension, the military was structural to the design of the Israeli state and Israel citizenship. The state took shape as an independent governing order that replicated primary aspects of imperial rule through inward and outward militarism.

CONCLUSION

The Ottoman Empire distilled the paradigm of military citizenship in which constitutional regimes were founded as military pressures imposed vertical integration processes in society, which were strongly articulated with lateral antagonisms. Constitution making began as military imperatives, resulting from intensified imperialism, began to form a nation at the centre of the empire, restructuring religious and local attachments to project a new set of obligations between government and society. Of central importance in this is the fact that the rise of armies was often part of a trajectory of secularization in which national militarism replaced religion as a source of political legitimacy. The post-Ottoman region then remained deeply structured by the constitutional effects of imperialism. In this region, citizenship was typically constructed through patterns of nation-building driven by armies, linking national government directly to international conflicts, often originating in imperial and post-imperial hostilities. As a result, many nations took shape through the rapid elaboration of military capacities, and the army frequently acted as a centre of social integration. Many constitutions translated military directives into public law, and, in many cases, citizenship was formed by military obligations. Frequently, this reproduced processes of citizenship

[79] This point is made in Robinson (2013: 35).

formation in the Ottoman period. Many regional polities remained rooted in intra-imperial conflicts in which the distinction between internal war and external war was not fully clear. In many cases, constitutions were imposed to sustain positions obtained through military actions, and they underpinned regimes partly designed to impose regional occupation.

CHAPTER SIX

WORLD LAW AND OCCUPATION CONSTITUTIONS

PERSISTENCE OF WAR

The continuation of military constitutionalism in post-Ottoman regions after 1945 embodied a continuing tendency after World War II. After 1945, the global onset of decolonization meant that the number of states in the world expanded rapidly, and warfare continued to determine constitutional organization. By the 1950s, decolonization was integrally shaped by global conflicts and pro-independence movements often positioned themselves around global ideological fault lines. As after 1918, further, many states that took shape through the transitions away from empires were marked by the intense militarization of intra-societal fissures. On each count, the post-1945 context reproduced central aspects of earlier patterns of citizenship formation, and the prominence of military units in government remained a dominant constitutional feature.[1] In new post-1945 nations, citizens were not normally formed from unfree labourers, but they were formed from colonial subjects, who often resembled unfree labourers in fundamental characteristics. As in earlier settings, many postcolonial states possessed limited infrastructural control of society, and new democratic institutions were built on the remnants of colonial institutions. In such circumstances, constitutions proclaimed ideals of sovereignty that placed military organizations in central roles, often reproducing imperial power structures. This has been discussed in Egypt and Syria.

[1] On the spread of military interventionism after 1945, see Perlmutter (1969: 382).

However, this can be observed in many cases of attempted democratic consolidation after 1945.

One emblematic example is Pakistan, founded as a democracy under the provisional constitutional order of 1947, which perpetuated the Government of India Act (1935), introduced as Pakistan was still part of the Raj. The origins of the state lay in the Muslim League in British India, but, after the war, the Pakistani army acquired a central governmental position. This was partly due to conflict with India during partition and in Kashmir, and it was partly caused by the fact that the departing British powers had left military structures that were stronger than other institutions. Under the Raj, the Punjab, much of which was transferred to Pakistan through partition, was home to some of the 'martial races'. Punjab served as an important source of military personnel for the British administration, and military careers had opened channels of social mobility in this region, so powerful elites had strong military attachments.[2] By 1953, the Pakistani military had monopolized key government functions and substantial parts of the country were subject to martial law. The first Pakistani constitution, introduced in 1956, was overthrown by the army in 1958 before it was effectively implemented. This constitution had a strong religious content, stating that all laws must confirm to Islamic law (Art. 198(1)). Then, the constitution of 1962 was accorded explicit nation-building functions. It established a presidential system flanked by controlled local representation, termed the Basic Democracies, introduced in 1959. This constitutional order also gave the army an important role in civil government.[3] By 1969, the army again imposed martial law, purportedly to facilitate elections. The imposition of military rule brought to the surface conflicts over national membership, as it heightened separatist tendencies in East Pakistan, later Bangladesh.[4] Elections in 1970 created a majority for residents of East Pakistan, led by a party whose campaign was based in a list of constitutional demands to the government, a six-point plan for regional autonomy. In response, the military refused to accept the election results and imposed a non-elected prime minister. This triggered civil war in East Pakistan, which was, in a strict sense, a constitutional war, fought because of disputes about regional autonomy and the extent of national obligations. This war brought

[2] Ali (1988: 110, 242).
[3] For analysis of these points, see Ziring (1971: 26–29) and Shah (2014: 99).
[4] One historian explains that martial law was enforced in East Pakistan as an intensified moment in a longer history of 'internal colonization' (Basu 2023: 111).

India into renewed military conflict with Pakistan in 1971, so that internal and external war converged. In each point, the prominence of military actors in government intensified antagonisms between the composite regions of the state, and with India. Yet the national army lacked the means to hold the territories together. The civil war led to a territorial transformation in Pakistan, resulting in the formation of Bangladesh. This ushered in a period of more consolidated democratic government under Zulfikar Ali Bhutto, who was eventually brought down by the army.

By the early 1960s, postcolonial state-building frequently occurred in settings where departing colonial powers transferred power to organizations with constitutionally formulated authority, which were replaced by military units without any conduct of elections. In such contexts, military supremacy was often consolidated in societies with multi-ethnic populations, in which the sovereign people was difficult to solidify and national institutions had limited integrational reach. This occurred, for example, in Ghana, the flagship postcolonial state in Africa, where Nkrumah tried to utilize the army as a nation-making unit to support his government. This experiment ended as he was overthrown by a military coup in 1966. The most important example of this is Nigeria. In post-1960 Nigeria, a republican constitution was formed in 1963. However, the army quickly rose to constitutional prominence, and, after a failed coup, it ruled from 1966 to 1979, suspending the 1963 constitution in 1966 and ending the regional system created to balance ethnic interests.[5] Before it took power, the army was small and tightly linked to the British colonial military, serving partly as an instrument of internal repression.[6] By 1967, the military takeover caused civil war, and the army was deployed to suppress the Biafra secession, so that military rule and territorial solidification became inseparable. The size of the Nigerian army increased exponentially at this time. The nationalization of military roles also meant that the army straddled and internalized deep ethnic cleavages, and military violence frequently resulted from conflicts between factions in the army.[7] In this period, the army became the main constituent organ, and it initiated the drafting of the 1979 constitution, supposedly forming the basis for democracy.

[5] This was effected through the Unification Decree (24 May 1966).
[6] Ejiogu (2007: 102).
[7] Siollun (2009: 180).

India requires separate analysis in this context, as it formed an important, partial exception to the prevalence of military constitutionalism in postcolonial societies after 1945. From 1947, the modern Indian polity was partly built on military bargains, and, to some degree, national citizenship was constructed around contracts and military attachments like those that supported other post-imperial states. In the Raj, the Indian army, unified from the East India Company's armies in 1893–5, formed a relatively autonomous professional or mercenary body. It was largely selected from certain 'martial races', mainly based in northern India, partly because the British deemed that a narrow ethnic focus would help to avert insurgent nationalism amongst military personnel. Indeed, Indian nationalists observed that Indian national spirit was under-evolved because Indians were not required to discharge military service.[8] India was taken into World War I and World War II by Britain, and enlistment remained essentially voluntary. However, in both war and peace, the proportion of the governmental budget allocated for defence of the Raj was high. Moreover in 1914 and 1939, wars shaped a relatively standard military constitution-making scenario in India in which military imperatives partly defined constitutional realities.

In World War I, Indian soldiers fought in Europe and other regions, and a substantial percentage of soldiers in the British military came from India. As recruitment increased during the war, a territorial quota system was introduced in 1917, which meant that the army's typical recruitment fields extended, and new regimental depots were established in regions where previously the army had not penetrated.[9] World War I also led to the creation of an Indian officer corps after 1919. The aftermath of World War I was marked, as in Europe, by growing political agitation, and by the increasingly violent mobilization of British authorities to supress Indian nationalism. At this time, the Indian National Congress, an oppositional, largely Hindu representative body committed to independence, adopted an increasingly conflictual stance towards the British and drafted an Indian constitution in the Nehru Report (1928). However, in parallel, this period witnessed increased self-government in India. The 1919 saw the consolidation of a colonial representative system, with the Government of India Act (1935). The constitutional effects of military pressures were clearly

[8] Kundu (1998: 38).

[9] Marston (2014: 14). One account explains that the war forced the British administration to explore 'new districts and classes' to obtain soldiers (Omissi 1994: 38–40).

reflected in the Government of India Act. This law formed an important basis for the independence constitution of 1950. It created a federal system for British India and the princely states, and it established some representative organs for colonial society, devolving important powers to provincial legislatures, elected by limited franchise. Plans for this law were partly driven by security demands, as they were drawn up as India was subject to emergency government. This law contained special national security provisions, allowing the transfer of executive power to the imperial governor-general in cases of security risks (Art. 102(1)). However, the plan for political self-government was based in the assumption that national defence should be transferred to Indians, partly as imperial defence costs were high. Drafters of the Government of India Act declared that the creation of an 'Indian nation' presupposed general military service, and it was impeded by the disproportionate recruitment of 'martial races'.[10] By 1937, the Congress began to assume limited representative powers at the regional level, forming part of an imperial constitutional system. Given its nationalist focus, the Congress was opposed to the 1935 Act, which it saw as pandering to particularistic interests of princely states and creating a system of effective indirect rule.

In World War II, the British army again utilized India as a source of soldiers, and this had complex consequences. As in other wartime environments, the army increasingly formed an integrational vector, as soldiers from different regions fought alongside each other in different conflicts, and deepening recruitment saw increased mobilization of lower-caste soldiers.[11] By 1943, the army had put more than 2 million soldiers in the field, despite the absence of conscription. As in other societies, however, war deepened existing fissures in society, and it contributed to the end of the Raj. Different regions saw large-scale rioting against colonial rule during the war. The early failings of the British army in Burma led to the creation of an Indian national army, mainly recruited from prisoners, which fought for Japan. Early in the war, further, the Congress resigned from its co-opted role in local government, and leading figures in the Congress sought to exploit British reliance on Indian servicemen to establish a pathway towards independence. This was expressed in the Quit India Movement, a large campaign of civil disobedience that resulted in the imprisonment of

[10] This is set out in *Joint Committee on Indian Constitutional Reform* (1934: 89–90).

[11] Barkawi (2017: 51, 68).

Congress leaders. These conflicts affected the British war effort, as they diverted military personnel from external conflict, as Japan moved close to India's borders. This resulted in the plan, presented by Stafford Cripps in 1942, for the creation of an Indian constituent assembly and the recognition of India as a dominion. Such plans had limited impact. In fact, the Indian army was deployed as a repressive instrument to support British violence against pro-independence activists, and paid soldiers proved very useful in helping to incapacitate Congress leaders and to keep down the Quit India Movement. Despite this, however, the path towards independence after World War II was strongly affected by patterns of military participation, and the traditional force of military engagement in constructing rights of citizenship was clearly palpable. War brought more people into the army, and it created increasingly robust bonds between colonial subjects in different regions. Nehru himself stated after 1945 that he would have welcomed war on Indian territory to 'harden the fibre of the nation' against the British.[12] Moreover, institutionally, the growth of the army created important openings for nationalists. By 1945, access to ranked offices had become easier for Indians, and officers often supported national independence.[13]

With an enlarged army, the Indian polity approached independence in 1947 through a transition punctuated by extreme violence. At one level, this took the form of communal violence, accompanying the partition with Pakistan, which on some estimates killed up to 2 million people. Partition brought deep ethnic separation in Indian society, and it echoed post-imperial experiences that had previously occurred in Ottoman regions. Even after partition, violence radiated below military and political command structures. After 1947, state formation took place amidst civil war of intense, partly genocidal ferocity, in which home-guard units or other informal military bodies were mobilized against local elites and ethnic minorities. At the same time, however, military force was also used for more regular state-building functions, as the national army was deployed to unify the nation. Indicatively, the status of the princely states was strengthened in 1947, as the Independence Act recognized them as entities distinct from India. This gave rise to military conflict, as, for example, the Indian army was mobilized to annex the state of Hyderabad in late 1948, an event marked by mass atrocities. After 1947, national military

[12] Nehru (1951: 443).
[13] Omissi (1994: 191).

policy also focused on using the army for nationalizing purposes, and leading generals and politicians advocated wider recruitment across all regional and religious groups.

Overall, two dimensions of military expansion – the nationalization of the army in warfare and the civil violence at the local level – converged to create the constitution-making situation in post-1945 India. This situation formed a de facto war of national unification, which transferred an imperial domain onto national premises, showing strong features of hybrid war typical of such processes.

It was in this context that the Constituent Assembly was convened (late 1946), to create the Indian constitution, which came into force in 1950. This Assembly comprised delegates elected through the narrow colonial franchise. During this formative period, some non-dominant ethnic groups refused to take part in constitution making, and it was widely suspected that the Assembly perpetuated the interests of the colonial Congress, placing Hindu elites at the centre of the polity.[14] Moreover, the princes who had benefited from the Raj took up marginal positions, and many established their own constitutions.[15] Against this highly contested background, the new constitution declared equal citizenship and popular sovereignty, with full and free elections, as the source of government (Arts 325–326). The constitution retained the federal structure established in 1935. Yet the assembly, largely centred around the Congress, created a much more unified polity than had existed under the Raj, and the constitution levelled out the patchwork structures resulting from the British techniques of indirect rule. In fact, electoral rolls for a universal national franchise were prepared before the constitution took effect. This nationalizing plan was backed by the list of Directive Principles in the constitution, which foresaw a welfare structure to support national citizenship. The constitution also established far-reaching emergency powers for the president to act against regional governments. Indicatively, the princely states were rapidly integrated in India, so that the model of citizenship in the constitution facilitated territorial incorporation.

Against this background, after 1950, some characteristics of postcolonial military politics were not displayed in India. In particular, the army proved relatively immune to fracture under pressures of political

[14] See related claims in Kapila (2021: 10).

[15] I am following the discussion of 'multiple constitution-making processes' in Re and Shani (2023: 10–13).

violence, and it provided a reasonably stable basis for the interim government.[16]

On one hand, the post-independence elites in India managed successfully to insulate the political system against potential threats of military involvement in politics. Indian military capacity and spending remained relatively high after 1945, especially owing to the increased pressure from China in the late 1950s. Yet, as prime minister, Nehru restricted the power of the army and initially he endeavoured to check the socio-political effects of wartime mobilization. Generally, Nehru maintained the military structure of the British Empire, in which the army operated as a professional corps with relative autonomy in society. A clear motivation for this was that he wished to ensure that the military did not become entangled in conflicts between ethnicities, religious groups and castes, which would have threatened the integrity of the new nation. In addition, Nehru attempted to insulate the political system as a whole against potential social volatility. To do this, he promoted a model of constitutional stabilization that relied on the relative social detachment of the political leadership, so that the mandate for rule was based in the management of personal and regional relationships, to avoid the politicization of social divisions left behind by imperialism. This strategy was linked to the role of the Congress under Nehru, which had deep roots in the colonial era. The Congress constructed a platform for government around strong intra-elite and clientelistic ties designed to avert deep political mobilization and to limit political conflict.[17] Until the 1960s, the Congress operated as a dominant party, successfully closing the political arena against other factions This strategy also had manifest military implications, as the Congress used patronage techniques to prevent processes of mass inclusion commonly stimulated by wartime militarization, and to avoid violent political articulation of religious differences arising from the partition. After 1947, Congress policies were committed to institutional secularism. For example, the constitution promoted national constructions of citizenship, distinct from religious affiliations, as the premise for state duties. This was set out in Arts 15(1), 25(1), 28(1), 29(2) and 325 of the 1950 constitution. However, the Congress also reduced Muslim participation in government and public officeholding.[18] In both respects, the post-1947 system was

16 Marston (2014: 278).

17 Roy (2007: 20).

18 On Nehru's disapplication of proportionality provisions for Muslims, see Wilkinson (2004: 102–113).

structured around an attempt to manage the political effects of societal conflicts and to limit the extent to which such conflicts converged with military politics. In this respect, the Congress government was organized against a background of civil war, but it was stabilized above such conflict through controlled social integration and strategic avoidance of militarism.

In the decades after 1950, however, this postcolonial political balance was unsettled. As he limited the role of the military, India became vulnerable to external conflict and wars with China (1962) and Pakistan (1965) led to renewed prioritization of military investment. Through this, the military leadership acquired a more central role as the army expanded in size. During the war with China, the government enforced emergency powers under Art. 352 of the constitution. Increased authority had already been given to the army in the Armed Forces Special Powers Act (1958). In parallel, the role of the Congress as the dominant political organization was weakened, as external militarization generated increased volatility in domestic politics. Through the mid-1960s, indicatively, political competition intensified, reflected in increased popular engagement in elections and escalating hostility between different parties. This occurred against a background of intermittent rising social violence and deadly rioting. In this context, it became apparent that secularist policies had not established thick constructs of citizenship in India, as ethnic fault lines between Hindus and Muslims became more sharply articulated. Hindu nationalism, expressed through religious parties, acquired louder voice.[19] Perhaps inevitably, as the post-1945 government had focused on controlling political participation, the 1960s showed that the state was built on shallow foundations and ethnic hostilities weakened its institutional structure. In 1969, the premiership of Indira Gandhi brought a split in the Congress, so that the cornerstone of democracy was dislodged.

Importantly, the increasing volatility of national citizenship affected the role of the Indian army. For example, Indira Gandhi was prepared to engage in war with Pakistan in 1971 partly because she saw war as an opportunity to secure India's position as a dominant post-imperial power in South Asia. However, she also did this because she thought that victory would bolster support for the fractured Congress, so that

[19] This link between the weakening of the Congress, increased party competition and social violence is assessed in Brass (2011: 220–225). This analysis compares the logic of rioting to insurrectionary war and civil war (356).

war served purposes of internal integration.[20] The Indian army deployed against Pakistan recruited soldiers from a range of social classes, and marginal social groups were strongly represented in it. Alongside these developments, the use of irregular military units proliferated in the 1960s. A core characteristic of Indian military politics in the 1960s was that the government deployed a range of paramilitary bodies in different states and spending on paramilitaries increased.[21] One of these, the Central Reserve Police, was created by the British before World War II to suppress insurgency. Under Art. 355 of the constitution, these paramilitaries were required to discharge internal security functions and to manage intergroup relations, limiting internal deployment of the regular army.[22] In many cases, the paramilitaries became enmeshed in webs of internal violence, and they supported state repression against Muslims.

In these processes, in total, the nation-building role of the Congress in India was diminished from the 1960s, and this deepened social militarism. Eventually, through the 1970s, Indira Gandhi tried to reassert political authority by new means, using prerogative or quasi-military methods. Through the early 1970s, Gandhi drew support from social groups (castes) that had been marginalized by previous incarnations of the Congress, and she committed the government to policies aimed at wide social transformation, strongly legitimated by the Directive Principles in the 1950 constitution. As early as 1969, she introduced policies to nationalize some banks. In 1971, changes to constitutional provisions concerning property law were justified by referenced to the Directive Principles. As part of this programme, she consistently arrogated power to the federal executive using a special constitutional instrument, Art. 356, to reduce the power of state governments. Then, in 1975, she declared an emergency regime, which echoed exceptionalist provisions earlier introduced in war, using Art. 352 of the constitution to limit political opposition, silence dissidents and suspend procedures for oversight of legislation. These policies were facilitated by the issuing of arrest warrants under the Maintenance of Internal Security Act (1971) and the Defence of India Act, dating from the war with China in 1962.[23] This security

[20] Sisson and Rose (2000: 208).

[21] One calculation is that spending on paramilitaries in India increased by circa 600 per cent from the 1960s to the mid-1970s (Misra 1980: 376).

[22] Wilkinson (2015: 25–31).

[23] My analysis is influenced by the brilliant discussion in Prakash (2019: 169–175).

legislation showed remarkable similarities to laws with analogous functions implemented under British rule. The centrepiece of Gandhi's authoritarian shift was Amendment 42 of 1976, which curtailed judicial powers and increased the freedom of the prime minister to change constitutional law. This also involved the insertion in the constitution of Art. 257-A (later rescinded) that allowed government to mobilize military force in the states. Measures imposed at this time included mass incarceration of opposition politicians and enforced mass sterilization of the poor for purposes of population management. This implied a distinctive remilitarization of welfare policies as exceptional bodily control was imposed as a means to regulate poverty. Institutionally, as mentioned, this process resulted from the weakening of the Congress in the 1960s, after which Gandhi attempted to consolidate a more populist basis for the party, using more polarizing means. However, this also resulted from the trajectories of militarization caused by interstate conflict in the 1960s, as military build-up changed the position of the army and brought intergroup conflicts to the political centre. Even under emergency rule, the army did not acquire governing authority. Yet the regime relied on police power and deployment of paramilitary forces laws to quell counter-systemic activism. The effects of this were brought to light by subsequent inquiries led by the Shah Commission. The emergency period also triggered a long period of violence as marginal social groups sought increased political integration. The emergency coincided with further laws to abolish involuntary labour, the Bonded Labour System (Abolition) Act (1976), so that exceptionalist policies expanded rights for some sectors.

After the end of emergency rule, there was no simple return to dominant-party politics in India. The emergency period effected a widening of the political system, and rights of political representation were claimed more fully by different social groups. At one level, this was transmitted through judicial politics as through the 1980s, the Supreme Court endeavoured to promote a mode of transformative constitutionalism, strongly articulated with international norms, to effect social change by non-prerogative means. Yet politics in India retained a militarized character as the demise of elite-led consensus politics brought religious differences to heightened articulation. The 1980s saw increased ethnic conflict and communal violence, triggered partly by the assassination of Indira Gandhi in 1984 and resultant hostility towards Sikhs. This initiated a period in which more exclusionary nationalist parties linked to Hinduism acquired greater presence in the political system, partly fuelled by military conflict in Kashmir. After 1998, the Bharatiya Janata Party, rooted in Hindu nationalism, frequently entered government, and it possessed features of a semi-militarized faction. Notably, it supported, or least acquiesced in, the perpetration of ethnic violence, and it promoted militarized citizenship patterns, indicatively through selective education policies.

The history of India since 1945 embodies elements of emergency politics that characterize imperial and post-imperial societies. India can be seen as a society, formed partly by military integration, in which experiences of violence imprinted a multicentric order of citizenship in society with strong proclivities for lateral militarism. In this context, the federal state at times acquired a semi-military position in relation to lateral manifestations of violence, and it actively allied itself to specific groups. The legacies of colonial rule remain clearly visible in the relative high dependence on emergency laws at the federal centre.

Across these examples, since 1945, the propensity for imperial legacies to generate military violence has been manifest, albeit variable. Nonetheless, with all appropriate caveats, it is not accurate to portray militarism as a dominant governmental form after 1945.[24] The period after 1945 was the first time in history that a number of states became constitutional democracies and then enduringly remained democratic, so that democratic institutions were not enveloped by violence – internal or external. After 1945, the number of democracies did not increase across the globe in continuous fashion. Yet, unlike after 1918, many post-1945 democracies did not become authoritarian, and some fitful increment of democracy became visible. As discussed in what follows, several divergent trajectories in democratic formation emerged after 1945, most of which were linked to militarism and reflected the legacies of imperialism. However, after 1945, the constitutional organization of democracy largely depended on techniques for controlling traces of imperial violence and for reducing imperialist modes of legitimation. Democracies that survived after 1945 were typically based in a constitution of violence drawing experience from previous democratic crises, and they were stabilized by instruments that reshaped the relation between constitutional inclusion and warfare. After 1945, constitutions that remained democratic generally preserved the rights for national citizens that had originally been engendered by warfare, and they solidified the bargains that states had entered for

[24] For a counterposed account, see Saull (2001: 70).

security reasons. However, such constitutions secured these rights and these bargains by severing them from their military basis, so that political rights became less prone to induce and condense military conflicts.

CONSTITUTIONAL LAW AND THE NON-MILITARY CITIZEN

After 1945, political rights in democratic constitutions were partly formed through the emergence of a transnational democratic culture in which democracy was advanced, not as part of a political bargain, but as a guiding principle. After 1945, clearly, political rights were still linked to warfare; the years after 1945 often deepened the connection between military force and the expansion of constitutional rights. Indicatively, most democracies created after 1945 retained high levels of military conscription, and citizenship remained closely associated with military obligations. In some states, notably the UK and the USA, military duties imposed during war were enforced for much longer than in previous historical eras. In the USA, political enfranchisement closely tracked military mobilization. For example, many black males in the USA were not enfranchised until 1964–5, as they were sent to kill and die in Vietnam. The Fourth Republic in France developed both as a highly democratic and as a highly militarized polity, and it was largely terminated by military conflicts. The French constitution of 1958 was influenced by military actors, and it was introduced in an exceptionalist environment following the imposition of a state of emergency in Algeria (1955), legally part of France, and a *coup d'état* in Algiers. This constitution contained provisions with a clear military emphasis, focused on the expansion of executive power (Arts 16, 36). Yet, despite these tendencies, the immediate impact of military pressures and military bargains on national constitutional law was commonly reduced after 1945. In crucial respects, constitutions evolved in which democratic inclusion relied less on procedures to integrate populations for war, likely to induce acute internal conflict.

This redirection can be seen, first, in the fact that, following 1945, democratic constitutions were often erected on foundations not resulting from an explicit democratic decision. After 1918, of course, many democratic states, such as Austria, Germany and Poland, resulted from undemocratic acts of foundation as they acquired constitutional form after deep systemic change. After 1945, the creation of constitutions by formal procedures, lacking clear democratic authority, became more widespread. For example, democratic constitutions in Japan and West Germany created after 1945 were written by bodies appointed without democratic mandate under foreign supervision, and the West German *Grundgesetz* was signed into force by a non-elected body. The constitutions of Brazil, France and Italy, which were eventually approved by democratically elected assemblies, originated in electoral laws lacking democratic mandate. The constituent assembly for the Brazilian constitution of 1946 was created after a military coup in 1945, when Vargas was deposed. On one calculation, the elections to the assembly expanded the number of Brazilian voters by more than 500 per cent.[25] Elected delegates were authorized to vote on a new constitution, after which they served as members of a regular legislature.[26] In France, great pains were taken to create deep democratic legitimacy for the 1946 constitution. This constitution was written by a national assembly elected by universal suffrage, and a referendum was held to permit the assembly to write the constitution, which was finally approved after a previous document had been rejected. However, even here, the decision for democracy was not originally democratic, and the constitution-making situation was determined by actors with limited democratic legitimacy, who acquired authority during the war.[27] In each case, constitutions were established on a broad democratic basis, but the decision to create a democracy was not the outcome of collective democratic demands.

This redirection can be seen, second, in the fact that, after 1945, democratic constitutions extended political rights beyond groups with obvious utility for warfare. Social groups whose access to electoral rights had historically been blocked by the link between war and democracy found themselves in an improved negotiating position. For instance, after World War II, constitutions or electoral systems that did not include women became exceptions, and women were usually enfranchised without a democratic vote to support this process. The enfranchisement of women in emerging constitutional systems in Japan (1945) and Italy (1945) illustrates this, as women gained the vote before the governments for which they would vote had acquired

[25] Nogueira (2005: 101).
[26] Law Nr 13 (12 November 1945).
[27] One excellent analysis explains how the constitution drew on ideas amongst members of the Résistance, illustrating how the return to democracy had an authoritarian basis (Bougrab 2002: 199–244, 257).

sovereignty. In the case of France, the enfranchisement of women was agreed in late 1944, by the exile government under de Gaulle when France did not exist as a fully sovereign entity. France had a long tradition of deep male enfranchisement. However, the explicit military bargain that supported enfranchisement had obstructed the attribution of political rights to women. Even after 1918, plans for female enfranchisement in France had been blocked by the Senate, notably in 1922. In post-1945 Europe, Belgium was a rare case in which women were enfranchised by laws introduced through a fully democratic legislative procedure. In parallel, the enfranchisement of women became prominent in societies far removed from centres of global military conflict, such that, in such contexts, war also lost force as a determinant of electoral rights. For example, women obtained the right to vote in Argentina in 1947 and in Colombia in 1954/7. After 1945, further, universal democratic inclusion was promoted in societies that had not existed before 1945. Full enfranchisement became a core part of legitimation processes attached to decolonization. Israel was a pioneer in this process, as the acquisition of independence coincided with the enfranchisement of women. Pakistan established (unenforced) voting rights for women in 1947, in a militarized environment. India played a vital role in this regard, as India created the world's largest female franchise in 1950. By the onset of African decolonization, the enfranchisement of women was commonplace, and political rights for women were proclaimed in some decolonization constitutions, including Algeria and Congo. In most African constitutions, as in much of South America, such rights were short-lived, as democratic procedures were widely abrogated by the 1970s.

Such processes imply that, by 1945, democracy was increasingly structured around a model of constitutional inclusion, whose causal attachment to social groups that negotiated bargains because of warfare was attenuated. War itself – manifestly – formed the background for the first wave of constitution making after 1945. However, the dense structure of political rights through which constitutions historically secured their legitimacy was separated from experiences of social integration caused by war. Broadly, these phenomena indicate that, in many societies, enhanced democratic representation became less connected to intra-societal political agency. In most cases, constitutions were shaped by a transnational culture of democratic inclusion, and constitutional order was frequently established on premises defined outside national society.

The case of the USA is very illuminating in this regard. As mentioned, it was not until 1965 that the USA secured a system of basic political rights for all citizens; the Voting Rights Act of that year, following the Civil Rights Act (1964), finally meant that black Americans in the southern states could exercise political rights attached to citizenship. Rights of black Americans had been violently disputed in a sequence of wars. Electoral rights of black men had been contested in the civil war of the 1860s, and recruitment of black men had contributed to the (formal) enfranchisement of black men in the Fifteenth Amendment (1869–70). World War I had intensified expectations among black men that they would gain guarantees of electoral participation in return for military sacrifice.[28] Then, World War II had formed a key moment in the emancipation of black Americans as, after 1945, black men demanded civil rights as political recognition for service. Federal desegregation gained impetus in the US Army under Truman's Executive Order 9981 (1948). Yet, although wars played a part in pressuring governments to enfranchise black men, wars had not exercised sufficient force to establish black suffrage in conclusive form. Ultimately, it was, not the domestic effects of war, but reaction to international expectations, that brought the full enfranchisement of black Americans in the mid-1960s. In particular, the perception that, in the context of the Cold War and decolonization, newly liberated Africans might find greater appeal in Moscow than Washington was a vital determinant in the introduction of electoral reforms inside the USA. It was left to an unelected president, Lyndon Johnson, to enshrine universal political rights in the Civil Rights Act. Johnson justified this in part by declaring that the granting of such rights was an act of compliance with international requirements, using this to weaken the symbolic attraction of the Soviet Union.[29] Here, norms set out in the international arena broke domestic resistance to the granting of political rights more effectively than warfare, and rights usually obtained through wars were established through the strategic endorsement of international cultural expectations.

In each respect, a process of profound significance for constitutional law occurred after 1945. Historically, the fabric of rights in national constitutional constitutions had been configured by military pressures and contracts. After 1945, democracies remained enduringly shaped by

[28] See the discussion in Williams (2010: 245, 264, 287).
[29] See Johnson's address before the General Assembly of the United Nations (17 December 1963).

warfare, and early post-1945 constitutions strengthened the rights that had been built up through long histories of military bargaining, and they explained their legitimacy through such rights. But, around 1945, war engendered an international consensus that framed national constitutions. This consensus meant that military imperatives were frequently *less directly* transmitted into constitutional law, and governments were able to integrate citizens on premises not materially defined by war.

WAR AND PEACE: INSEPARABLE REALMS

In key respects, the development of democracy after 1945 reflected a profound dialectic at the core of constitutional law. After 1945, democratic constitutions preserved the basic substructure (political rights) that they had acquired as parts of a global military system. Post-1945 constitutions shaped governments by reinforcing some rights that citizens had obtained as they were integrated through long histories of war. However, constitutions developed the capacity to define such rights in a form that insulated them against militarism, and, as discussed later in this chapter, they achieved this by borrowing different elements of law from a global military system. Democracy took shape as a relatively permanent order as constitutions evolved two layers of military law, one guaranteeing basic rights, and one framing these rights in an additional set of rights, also rooted in experiences of war, which weakened the tendency of democratic inclusion to assume violent form or to provoke further militarism.

This dialectic of military law became visible in the fact that, after 1945, constitutional law reflected a heightened concern with individual rights and their protection, such that human rights law, which had scarcely existed in consolidated form before 1945, became an almost universal aspect of national constitutions. After 1945, both international law and constitutional law were marked by the assumption that the exercise of state power should show proportionate recognition of the rights of individual persons. In international law, the following documents approved by the UN fall into the broad category of human rights law and, as such, they shaped democratic constitutional emphases: the UN Charter (1945), the Universal Declaration of Human Rights (1948), the Genocide Convention (1948), the Geneva Conventions (1949) and the Refugee Convention (1951). Later, these documents were supplemented by the Human Rights

Covenants of the mid-1960s and the Convention on the Elimination of All Forms of Racial Discrimination. At the international level, the UN did not initially develop an apparatus to establish meaningful protections for individual persons in national societies. The rise of human rights law sat alongside the presumption, also expressed in the UN Charter, that sovereign states were the main actors in international law, and that non-interference in domestic decisions of nation states was a guiding rule of international society (Art. 2(7)). In the years following 1945, however, many national constitutions integrated elements of international law through internal provisions. Many constitutions extracted basic rights clauses from international documents, such that international laws were frequently transformed into elements of domestic legal systems.[30] This can be seen in the new constitutions that assumed force after 1945, such as those instituted in Japan (1946), Italy (1948), West Germany (1949) and India (1950). Each of these constitutions contained distinctive recognition for the rights of single subjects, and, over time, they provided for institutions to protect such rights. For example, most new constitutions created powerful apex courts, with some express responsibility for scrutinizing legislation to ensure its compliance with protections for basic rights. This began with the reimplementation of the Austrian constitution, largely dating from 1920, in 1945. Subsequently, courts began to develop jurisprudence that aligned national laws to international laws, expressing presumptions in favour of global protections for human subjects. From the late 1950s onwards, the reinforcement of human rights protections was extended by the fact that, in Europe and Latin America, regional human rights systems developed. In these settings, the convergence between national legal systems and wider constructions of human rights law was promoted, first, by supranational commissions, and, later, by courts with transnational reach, assuming direct effect in national societies. Such regional organizations came to offer much greater protection to human rights than was afforded by bodies attached to the UN. However, initially, regional human rights systems echoed principles promulgated in the UN.

Together, these factors meant that, after 1945, an international legal system took shape that supported individual protections, presenting a model of exogenous legitimacy for national polities, in relation to which governments began to formulate their responsibilities. This

[30] See pp. 353–4.

marked the fourth stage in a longer systemic process of global legal formation. It followed earlier attempts to establish a transnational legal order able to manage the actions of sovereign states, which had been conducted in 1648, 1815 and around 1919–20. The post-1945 international order reproduced some motivations that guided earlier patterns of systemic formation. For example, this legal order was self-evidently the result of war; it was created partly as a reaction to the societalization of war and the atrocities caused by military actions beginning in the 1930s. Like the Viennese system of 1815, it was intended to project a model of state legitimacy that avoided the diffuse militarization of national populations. At its core was the idea that states demonstrated legitimacy, not by integrating national populations for war, but by reflecting the status of citizens as individual agents. This legal order was also profoundly concerned with imperialism and the patterns of territorial enlargement related to it. As in earlier contexts, the post-1945 international legal system was intended to manage a global process in which empires were placed on new foundations. It was defined by the collapse of Fascist empires in and before 1945. It was created partly as a response to the onset of decolonization in Africa and Asia, marking, primarily, the global contraction of British and French imperial power. It was also shaped by the fact that the world's post-1945 superpower, the USA, was (nominally) committed to ending European imperialism and to establishing post-imperial state structures. Unlike previous international endeavours to manage the exercise of state sovereignty in conditions of imperial dissolution, however, the system that emerged after 1945 was not based in a primary antinomy between international law and constitutional law. This legal system was based, at least in part, in the convergence of these two legal orders around shared normative expectations – especially around individual-legal protections for human rights norms. At this juncture, as mentioned, national constitutional law gave greater force to norms spelled out in international law than the bodies responsible for overseeing the global implementation of human rights law. This meant that a legal system evolved in which national and international laws palpably coalesced.

The development of human rights law was connected to a modified understanding of the apparatus required to regulate warfare. On one hand, the key clause of the UN Charter, Art. 2(4), prohibited aggressive warfare, and, unlike earlier documents designed to manage warfare, this prohibition entailed the classification of colonization as an act of war. In parallel, the post-1945 legal system contained provisions, both international and national, that addressed military violence in new ways, defining violence as an amorphous condition, which could not be limited to actions perpetrated between states and occurring outside national societies. The post-1945 legal structure reflected the assumption that control of interstate antagonism should address the ways in which states interacted internally with their citizens, ensuring that such interactions did not induce military violence. This assumption implied that external and internal militarism were causally connected and that the internal regulation of societies was vital for preventing war. Human rights entered national constitutions to reduce the violence inherent in constitutional interaction. Against this background, human rights norms gradually framed the actions of national governments in four distinct ways.

First, human rights law was designed as an international framework that transposed interactions between governments and citizens onto premises not created by war. This was evident in the Refugee Convention and the Genocide Convention, which established norms of individual protection to be applied even amidst extreme violence. However, this was expressed in provisions in the UN Charter for trusteeship arrangements during decolonization (Art. 76(c)), in which such arrangements were supposed to uphold human rights in territories where they were implemented. In these principles, interactions between governments and citizens originating in military occupation were subject to higher-order protections.

Second, human rights law began to prescribe specific patterns of interaction between national governments and their citizens, so that the protective duties of governments were heightened. Importantly, this process was enforced in legal spheres not strongly defined by political mobilization or express political bargaining. This was mainly visible in administrative law. In this domain, governments established new principles to regulate the actions of executive bodies towards citizens, and executive power was increasingly increased in accordance with individual protections. For example, in the USA, several states introduced administrative law reforms during World War II.[31] At the federal level, a major overhaul of administrative law was implemented in 1946, following the expansion of public agencies in the New Deal

[31] For example, in 1943, Uniform Administrative Procedure Acts became statutes in Ohio and Wisconsin. In 1945, the Administrative Procedure Act was introduced in California. One commentator observed in this 'the beginnings of a codification movement that will sweep throughout the country' (Blythe-Stason 1946: 802).

era. Parallel processes occurred in the UK. The period after 1945 saw the rapid growth of administrative tribunals, whose judicial function was acknowledged.[32] Important changes were also registered in UK administrative law through 1960s. Here, the regulatory powers of courts were cemented, and, over time, administrative law reached beyond its original function as a guarantor of the adequate enforcement of parliamentary statutes, and it was applied as a more formal measure of the exercise of public power.[33] In the Federal Republic of Germany (FRG), the principles of administrative law also changed, and administrative law internalized protections for subjective rights in constitutional law.[34] In Brazil, the post-war period saw important innovations in administrative law. Both the 1946 constitution and subsequent legislation of 1951 expanded the power of citizens to initiate individual claims (*mandados de segurança*) against public agencies.[35] This legislation was based in provisions in the 1934 constitution and in an earlier law of 1936, whose scope was curtailed in 1937, and it was intended to simplify the assertion of individual rights against acts in abuse of 'public power'.[36] In each instance, administrative law created a new legal structure for the public interactions of citizens, which reinforced individual protections and state responsibility towards individuals. In Europe and the USA, this occurred at a time when executive bodies had expanded rapidly because of warfare, so that the growth of rights-based administrative law was – in strict terms – intended to protect citizens from acts of public organs whose authority was rooted in war.

Third, more generally, the impact of human rights became visible in the legitimational dimension of government, as states separated the production of legitimacy from mobilization attached to warfare. Historically, as indicated, states constructed basic rights, usually centred in rights of electoral participation, as integrational structures in which they were able to motivate their citizens. Most constitutional states experienced patterns of democratization in which the expansion of rights mirrored the intensification of military threats – electoral

[32] See discussion of this in the *Franks Report on Administrative Tribunals and Enquiries* (1957).

[33] The case *Ridge v Baldwin* (1964) directed English law away from *ultra vires* as the basis for judicial review.

[34] Before 1945, subjective rights were mainly defined in German private law. By 1951, leading commentators observed that 'all basic rights' in the constitution created a 'subjective right', such that administrative bodies were bound to 'act in accordance with them' (Bachof 1951: 74).

[35] This was addressed in Arts 101, 104, 119, 120, 121 and 141 and in Law Nr 1.533 (31 December 1951).

[36] This theory was set out clearly in Nunes (1956: 75).

rights were normally allocated before or after warfare. After 1945, democratization was again intensified by war, and most enduring democracies created immediately after 1945 were unified by war, and war hardened the sets of rights that citizens could exercise. However, at a direct causal level, constitutional rights were detached from warfare. In these aforementioned instances, individual rights acquired increasing force in interactions between citizens and government. More broadly, most constitutions written shortly after 1945 established basic rights that placed limits on the degree to which governmental legitimacy was defined by the simple representation of popular majorities. For example, constitutions established in the FRG, in Italy, in Japan and – more implicitly – in India constructed human rights as entrenched elements of public order which could not be dislodged by momentary popular choices. This was clearest in the 1949 *Grundgesetz* of the FRG (Art. 79(c)). Yet in each case, rights articulated suprapositive principles of legitimacy, which governments did not have to create for themselves by expressing sporadic interests of the people. This necessarily mediated the relation of governments to citizens, and it meant that governments could construct and signal legitimacy without deep inclusion of their electorates. In each case, basic rights were largely modelled on international law.

In central dimensions, this rights-based legal order was meant to replace the legal order instilled in national societies by imperialism. Before 1945, as discussed, imperialism structured national societies internally and externally, creating a global domain in which states organized their actions in response to imperial pressures. This meant that the vertical integration of citizens for military functions was a dominant feature of national society, leading to deep interpenetration between the inside and the outside of national societies. The post-1945 legal order redirected global society towards new normative premises. Through this legal order, states were required to integrate citizens on increasingly individualized premises, and states displayed legitimacy by establishing protections for single subjects, especially in relation to executive acts. In principle, this meant that states began to engage with citizens on premises not originating in military conflict, as the terms of interaction between governments and citizens were defined, not by bargains relating to military integration, but by internationally defined rights.

In such developments, the underlying origin of post-1945 constitutional systems can be attributed to a deep alteration in the ways in which constitutional law reflected its most ancient source: *the military*. The post-1945 legal order implicitly recognized that both the internal and external acts of states were components of a global military system, and that the interaction between these parts had generated violence that national constitutions, and nation states more generally, could not contain. In particular, this legal order detached the production of legitimacy from acts of popular integration, as it allowed governments to explain the validity of laws as norms proportioned to the protection of overarching individual rights. Through this process, states preserved the rights originally generated by war. Yet the role of constitutional law in granting political rights as part of a military bargain were altered, and the legitimational dominance of groups with military utility was reduced. In each respect, the application of human rights law also meant that the functions of vertical integration performed by constitutions were less strongly correlated with lateral violence. As discussed in Chapter 7, the period of democratic consolidation after 1945 was generally marked by the increasingly pacified integration of domestic political organizations. One reason for this was that states were able to legitimate their acts in terms that did not rely solely on the enactment of momentary popular commitments.[37]

Fourth, in many cases, human rights law directly addressed the constitutional role of the military, and it was specifically designed to manage military violence. As mentioned, the corpus of international norms created after 1945 included, not only human rights declarations, but rules regarding state actions in war and during military occupation, parts of which were later identified as international humanitarian law. Many commentators on international law claim that humanitarian law and international human rights law were formed as separate bodies of law with distinct spheres of application.[38] This is usually claimed because the main attempts to formalize humanitarian law after 1945, the Geneva Conventions, were initiated, not directly by the UN, but by the International Committee of the Red Cross. This view is also connected to the fact that human rights law did not originate in the laws of war, and it was not expressly extended to war zones until the 1960s; it was only at this time that the UN Security Council began to consider military conflicts as occurrences with human rights

[37] See pp. 384–94.

[38] See for this view Kolb (1998: 409). For a recent definition of human rights law and humanitarian law as 'two wholly independent systems', see Provost (2002: 274). For an alternative view, see Fortin (2012).

implications (Weiss 2004: 136).[39] However, the claim that there is a strict dichotomy between human rights law and humanitarian law is difficult to sustain. In their original conception, the Geneva Conventions drew on assumptions that were being promoted in human rights law after 1945, and they were observed as a human rights system for warfare.[40] One of their architects, Jean Pictet, argued that the UN should be responsible for their enforcement in wartime situations.[41] Moreover, like human rights law, post-1945 humanitarian law acquired great resonance in national constitutional law.

The body of international humanitarian law established after 1945 looked back to classical laws of armed conflict, expressed in the Brussels Declaration (1874) and the Hague Convention (1907). As mentioned, some elements of modern humanitarian law had already been implied in the principles that supported the Congress of Vienna. However, post-1945 humanitarian law established norms that were distinct from the classical positivist premises of the laws of war. The growth of humanitarian law after 1945 was shaped by emerging concepts of international criminal law, from which it absorbed some principles. Indicatively, early international criminal law expressed the strong presumption that violations of some laws of war, including laws of military occupation, could be subject to criminal sanction. Because of this, after 1945, principles of individual liability were reinforced in laws regarding military violence, and bodies with jurisdiction in enforcing international law acquired scope beyond interstate actions. After 1945, different allied states established military tribunals to hear claims against German military personnel, and these addressed the treatment of prisoners and civilians, covering matters partly pertaining to humanitarian law. These cases were not officially defined as cases in which humanitarian law was applied, but they had manifest humanitarian implications. Moreover, these cases addressed a range of actions perpetrated in a range of settings, not all of which were conventionally covered by international law.[42] For example, such cases included proceedings against German citizens for violent actions in German territory. They also included proceedings for actions against partisans in

[39] Weiss (2004: 136).

[40] In 1952, Hersch Lauterpacht (1952: 362) described the Geneva Conventions as a 'universal declaration of human rights' for warfare.

[41] Pictet (1960: 545).

[42] See the trial of Erich Heyer and Six Others ('The Essen Lynching Case') (1945), the trial of Wilhelm List and others (1948) and *United States of America v. Otto Ohlendorf et al.* (Einsatzgruppen case) (1948).

locations where German military administration had asserted sovereign power.[43] German military actors were prosecuted for actions towards residents of Polish territories, which had been formally stripped of sovereignty.[44] In each respect, such cases – in principle – established common norms for state and individual actions in circumstances in which military organizations had very different positions. Against this background, the Statute for the Nürnberg Tribunal expressed the conviction that human persons were bearers of rights and duties in all circumstances, and certain obligations existed that could not be suspended, regardless of territorial location. In the Nürnberg Trials, legal principles used to assess the actions of German officials towards their own subjects and towards the subjects of other states were analogous, if not wholly identical.[45] In 1945, then, the occupying powers directly enforced international criminal law in German territory, under Control Council Law 10, which established domestic penalties for crimes against humanity and violations of the customary laws of war (Art. II).

These developments meant that a body of law evolved after 1945 in which the uncertain dividing line between criminal law and the law of armed conflict almost vanished. Most importantly, these developments modified the classical distinction between war and peace, or between the outside and the inside of national society, which had informed the historical canon of international military law. In these examples, military tribunals were created after 1945 to enforce the laws of war and related aspects of criminal law. However, in doing this, they extended their jurisdiction to settings where war had technically ended or not yet formally begun.[46] In some cases, it was indicated that the laws of war were not solely applicable to societies in a state of belligerency, declared or recognized by sovereign states. This implied that the decision to end a war is not solely the decision of a sovereign state, and informal military actors may legitimately protract warfare against the will of an occupying power. Prosecution of Germans for crimes committed outside military zones – for example, in concentration camps – extended

[43] See the trial of Franz Holstein, The Permanent Military Tribunal at Dijon (1947).

[44] Special proceedings were initiated, amongst others, against Arthur Greiser and Amon Leopold Göth (1946) for war crimes during occupation, before the rulings in Nürnberg.

[45] By 1950, the International Law Commission endorsed the following principle, arising from the Nürnberg Trials: 'The fact that internal law does not impose a penalty for an act which constitutes a crime under international law does not relieve the person who committed the act from responsibility under international law.'

[46] The Charter for the International Military Tribunal, agreed in London in August 1945, gave the tribunal jurisdiction in cases of crimes against humanity committed 'before or during the war' (Art. 6(c)).

this definition still further, suggesting that war may be a phenomenon that occurs inside and outside national societies.[47] The prosecution of such persons implied that international law could have effect in all domains of a militarized society, and that victims of war were not defined in territorially or temporally limited categories. Many perpetrators of such atrocities did not have conventional military status, and many perpetrators strictly were not acting in war zones subject to international law.

In the years after 1945, the Geneva Conventions (1949) solidified some of these principles. It is often observed that, at least insofar as they were applied to combatants, the Geneva Conventions did little more than restate principles of military law already defined in the Hague Conventions.[48] There is much truth to such observations. The actual ground-level protection offered to residents of war zones after 1949 was not greatly increased. Yet in their normative-conceptual dimension, the Geneva Conventions contained several innovations, creating new principles to regulate military actions and military occupation, which had a deep impact on subsequent legal history.

Innovations in humanitarian law after 1945 reflected experiences of military occupation, as until a few years previously, most of Europe had been under military occupation of some kind. This period of military rule had witnessed the proliferation of new modes of warfare and new patterns of combat, partly because the legal status of territories occupied by Fascist armies and their allies was often unclear. As discussed, the Nazi administration in Poland presented itself as a simple sovereign government. In other parts of Europe, Nazi administrations were defined as protectorates and commissariats, and their status as occupation systems was not clear. One reason for this, of course, was that in some cases, notably Poland, Czechoslovakia and Ukraine, the Nazis justified occupation either by claiming that they had reacquired territory lost in Versailles or that they had released foreign territory from a rival empire – the Soviet Union. Many regions under German and/or Italian occupation experienced multiple conflicts, partly between regular armies, partly between regular armies and partisans or insurgents. Poland, Greece, Yugoslavia and the post-1941 Soviet Union all saw convergent conflicts of this kind. Accordingly, after 1945, the status of

[47] See the Zyklon B case (1946), leading to death sentences for gas suppliers to Auschwitz. International military laws were used as a basis for the proceedings, as the accused (civilians) were charged with acting in 'violation of the laws and usages of war' to 'supply poison gas'.
[48] Toppe (2008: 80).

partisan fighters, who were not acting under formal colour of law yet took up arms against occupying forces, was a question that acquired great relevance. In many wartime environments, further, military conflict entailed aspects of civil war. As in more classical empires, occupied populations in World War II were often divided by their attitudes to and degrees of complicity with occupying forces. In many parts of Europe, including France, Ukraine, Yugoslavia, Italy and Greece, German occupation led to protracted civil war alongside external conflicts.

The Geneva Conventions mirrored these conditions. They did so, in general terms, because they altered the basic orientation of the law of military occupation. The conventions promoted a subject-based understanding of warfare and its effects, and they declared relatively high-threshold obligations for occupying powers towards individual persons living under occupation regimes. One commentary has even declared that this displayed a 'change of paradigm' in military law in which the axis of legal obligation was moved from the relation between states to the relation between state and subjects living in war zones.[49] More specifically, the conventions re-accentuated the established assumption, implied in the Congress of Vienna and expressed in the 1907 Hague Convention, that occupying powers were required to respect the basic sovereignty of public bodies in occupied zones. The conventions made clear that public institutions could not be obliterated by military occupation, and persons living in areas under occupation lived in a state in which basic elements of sovereign self-government were merely suspended.[50] In addition, the conventions provided some recognition for the rights of soldiers who took up arms against occupying forces. From the 1870s, documents that formalized laws of war had established a grudgingly minimalist definition of the protections afforded to spontaneously recruited military personnel.[51] Indicatively, the Hague Convention (1907) contained limited guarantees for persons engaged in a *levée en masse*.[52] Before 1949, however, legal protection for soldiers was almost exclusively granted to members of national armies bearing arms for sovereign states. The law of armed force was fixed on a construction of war as an event that occurred outside

[49] Kolb and Vité 2009: 3.
[50] See provisions for the maintenance of the pre-conflict legal order in Geneva Convention IV, Arts 47, 51, 53, 58, 64, 67.
[51] See Brussels Declaration (1874), Art. 10.
[52] See Regulation 2, annexed to Hague Convention IV.

national societies, between sovereign states, such that legal regulations for warfare had minimal consequences for the internal military acts of sovereign states. Through the Geneva Conventions, however, the principle was established, albeit still tentatively, that war could give rise to legal entitlements for combatants inside belligerent societies, or at least within territory subject to military control by hostile sovereign states after war had finished.

The authors of the Geneva Conventions expressed the view that the informal combatant should be identified as a figure in law, and persons engaged in military mobilization against occupying forces, even if they lacked sovereign authorization, should be accorded some recognition. In Art. 4A(2), Geneva Convention III stated that persons claiming international legal recognition could be members of 'resistance movements' and – crucially – members of resistance movements acquired some legal protection even when operating inside occupied territories.[53] This recognition was also implied in Common Article 3. To be sure, such recognition would not have provided great reassurance for partisans in real-time military situations. Yet these provisions contained principles of some significance. First, these provisions implied that the laws of war could reach beyond the authority of sovereign states, and the points at which laws of war came into and lost effect could not be exclusively controlled by sovereign states. As Jonathan Gumz has explained, the Geneva Conventions moved on a fine line. In attempting to create 'islands of protection' for partisans and civilians in wartime situations, they came close to recognizing war as a pervasive and contingent social fact, which was not solely defined by declarations of states.[54] Second, these provisions suggested that some types of warfare not acknowledged by sovereign states could be subject to international law. In doing so, they generated rights for actors implicated in different categories of war, so that individual subjects not directly acting for sovereign nation states could assume protected legal subjectivity in military conflicts. This second principle did not cover civil war, but it referred to some conditions of military occupation in which interstate war and civil war were not fully distinct. Third, these provisions implied that the partition between war and peace was not an absolute distinction, and violent acts perpetrated in times when sovereign states have terminated military actions could be classified as legitimate acts of war. The expression of

[53] On the distinctive nature of these provisions, see Clarke (2005: 16–18) and Stuke (2017: 220–221). For more cautious early interpretation, see Schmid (1956: 143).

[54] Gumz (2018: 657).

these principles was striking in the post-1945 global context, in which members of emerging national liberation armies in Africa and Asia had clear similarities to anti-Fascist partisans in World War II. Notably, by the late 1960s, the UN invoked the Geneva Conventions to define the position of anti-apartheid fighters in South Africa.[55] In Indochina, India and Pakistan, decolonization after 1945 also induced irregular multipolar warfare, often causing huge loss of life. These scenarios extended some tendencies seen in occupied territories in pre-1945 Europe.

Underlying these principles was a revised understanding of military occupation. In essence, this revision indicated that, in some circumstances, domestic law could be placed on a certain continuum with occupation law. That is, it implied that states could not unilaterally decide which matters were merely domestic questions and which were not, so that the beginning and the end of war was not a matter to be determined by states alone. Through this process, international law began, in outline, to articulate a *new constitution of military occupation*. On one hand, it constructed a constitution for military violence in which occupying powers were subject to stricter regulation and their freedom to alter existing structures was limited. Yet it also produced a legal order in which states could – at least potentially – be perceived as military actors towards persons defined as their subjects, so that the constitution of war contained some norms for interstate war and some for civil violence. The need for this legal order had acquired visibility in the theatres of violence in Europe from the late 1930s. Yet this emergent system reflected a deep insight into the historical convergence between national government and imperial government.

The channels along which international human rights law entered constitutional law are not difficult to find. Such influence was commonplace after 1945, and it affected both states whose constitutions were based in existing democratic traditions and states that constructed their constitutions on new premises. The migration of principles of humanitarian law into constitutional law is less easy to chart. Broadly, however, international law shaped constitutional formation in two dimensions after 1945, in both of which it moved national societies

[55] See UN General Assembly, The Policies of Apartheid of the Government of South Africa, 21 November 1969. In Resolution 2396 (XXIII) of 2 December 1968, the General Assembly declared that opponents of Apartheid in South Africa were 'freedom fighters' engaged in 'legitimate struggle', entitled to full protection under the Geneva Conventions. See also General Assembly Resolution 2444 (XXIII): Respect for Human Rights in Armed Conflicts (19 December 1968), and General Assembly Resolution 2675 (XXV): Basic Principles for the Protection of Civilian Populations in Armed Conflicts (9 December 1970).

away from their traditional military foundations. First, international human rights formed a general environment for democratic formation, and it contributed to promoting post-imperial constitutionalism by separating constitutional law from war and creating heightened protections for individual subjects. Second, a more diffuse body of law emerged combining law of armed conflict (humanitarian law), human rights law and international criminal law, which together shaped national constitutional law. In particular, the presumption in humanitarian law that war is a legally unsettled phenomenon, which crosses the divide between national and international society and may require regulation in both domains, played an important role in shaping post-1945 constitutional law. With varying degrees of intensity, human rights and humanitarian law combined to create a legal form in which states were observed through a new constitutional lens. This form implied that states were potential military actors outside and inside their societies, engaged both in external war and in diffuse civil war, so that legal norms applied to these domains were not absolutely distinct. In this process, constitutions increasingly attached their legitimacy not to the simple integration of citizens, but to the management of the societal and subjective effects of violence. One function of constitutions, after 1945, was to delineate paths from imperialism to nationhood that did not replicate traditional military results of constitutional citizenship in which internal violence was accepted as a condition for external security. In this regard, a constitutional order took shape in which state powers were framed in a new transnational constitution of military law, and national governments were subject to a new *occupation constitution* to protect citizens from internal and external military actions. In some settings, national constitutions internalized a second tier of military law which dialectically reduced their original military functions, and democratic systems developed through the use of international military law to pacify state functions.

THE CONSTITUTION OF OCCUPATION LAW: POST-IMPERIAL STATES 1

Processes of this kind are observable in the simple fact that, after 1945, many new constitutions were established in societies that had previously promoted imperial rule but were now subject to foreign military control. Such societies gave extreme expression to new constitutional paradigms, and the relation between democracy and the organization of internal and external violence assumed specific visibility in these settings. In Japan, West Germany and Italy, this meant that states that had engaged in intense imperial expansion from the 1930s were now themselves governed under laws of military occupation. In key respects, these states developed new constitutions through a process in which occupation law, imposed by external military forces, was configured to as the basis for domestic public law. In these contexts, military law reflected a dialectical movement. As stated, constitutional law originated in military law. After 1945, military law again served as the basis for constitutional law. However, this took place, not because military law was constructed by internal actors promoting military mobilization for the external defence of sovereignty, but because it was used to control the use of military violence inside national society. The scope of military law was widened as it was imposed as the basic order for legal formation, but the traditional thread between military law and constitutional law was partly severed.

The most important example in this regard is post-1945 Germany under occupation by the Western Allies. In the immediate aftermath of World War II, the legal status of the German *Reich* was disputed. Hans Kelsen argued that, like Poland after 1939, Germany was in a state of *debellatio* as the devastation caused by war was so great that Germany had ceased to exist as a legal entity.[56] Other commentators argued that Germany should be classified as occupied territory, such that former German territory was subject to laws of military occupation, but it did not renounce residual sovereignty.[57] In this legal condition, the occupation regime the Allies imposed had complex constitutional results. To some degree, Allied occupation in Germany reproduced legal techniques used by Germany before the collapse of the *Reich*. Manifestly, in 1945, Allied occupation of Germany did not have the genocidal consequences Germany had inflicted on other states before 1945. Yet the fact that Germany was subject to forcible regime change meant that the Allies acted in manifest breach of the international laws of war set out in the 1907 Hague Convention.[58] In this setting, however, the Allies also began to redesign occupation law. They organized military occupation on normative premises that pre-empted later developments in

[56] Kelsen (1945: 521).

[57] See Schlochauer (1948: 200); Schmid (1948: 124).

[58] See Art. 43 of the Regulations annexed to Hague Convention IV. For comment on this principle, see Graber (1949: 68–69). On this principle in post-1945 Germany, see Benvenisti (1993: 91) and Waibel (1996: 63). See further discussion of Germany in Carcano (2015: 62).

constitutional law, and revised elements of occupation law set the foundations for a global process of constitutional redirection.

As mentioned, important legal measures the Allies adopted in Germany fell into the category of international criminal law, used to cover grave violations of humanitarian law or extreme acts of violence against individual persons. These measures were applied retroactively to address historical crimes in German-controlled war zones, including in Germany itself. At the same time, however, judicial practices the Allies adopted were intended to perform a pedagogic function. That is, they demonstrated to German citizens that, except in the prosecution of extreme criminality, the Allies would adhere to established conventions in enforcing an occupation regime: they would respect international military norms determining the behaviour of military personnel, and they would limit individual damage caused by occupation.[59] Before the war was concluded, the Allies closed German courts in occupied regions and established strict controls for judicial actions, requiring judges to swear a special oath. The US leadership installed a legal division in occupied territories with responsibility for rebuilding the German legal order, committed to providing democratic legal education.[60] This was linked to the growing consciousness of the symbolic value of human rights law. By October 1945, the Allies issued a proclamation regarding the foundations of the legal system in occupied German regions, stating that basic rights inherent in the 'democratic concept of the state' should be placed at the core of the legal order.[61] Through this, the Allies imposed a distinctive system of occupation law in Germany which included aspects of criminal, military and human rights law. Germany emerged as a technical laboratory of international law in which different elements, still not strictly separated at the international level, were applied as a framework for social and constitutional organization.

In each aspect of these processes, German society was construed as a location saturated with war, and the laws of war were applied to crimes committed in Germany in terms that did not strongly differentiate between actions in the national and in the interstate domains. In this setting, in turn, influential figures in post-1945 Germany began to redesign German institutions by using norms inherent in the occupation system to which Germany was subject. In the first instance, tentatively, this was reflected in the fact that some German judges

59 Waibel (1996: 78).
60 Raim (2013: 24).
61 *Kontrollratsproklamation Nr. 3: Grundsätze für die Umgestaltung der Rechtspflege*, II(4).

and legal practitioners replicated norms promoted by the Allies, and German legal institutions internalized normative aspects of the occupation system. Indicatively, Control Council Law 10, based in international criminal law, was at times directly applied by German courts in the British zone, although many judges and jurists resented its implications and qualified its effects. As mentioned, Control Council Law 10 placed emphasis on individual accountability for actions contrary to the laws of war, and it covered actions by German citizens against other German citizens (Art. III). Control Council Law 10 was enforced by a German court in the final hearing of the *Heinrich Tillessen* case against the perpetrator of political assassination in the 1920s.[62] This ascribed higher-order status to some aspects of international criminal law in occupied Germany, implicitly projecting criminal law back in time in German history.

These developments had a more enduring effect in the process, beginning in 1948, which led to the creation of the constitution in parts of Germany under the rule of the Western Allies, later the FRG. This process involved a technique of constructive signalling in which the drafters of the constitution acknowledged that, in Germany, as an occupied territory, international law had high authority and provided a normative structure both for occupying forces and German politicians themselves. The 1949 constitution was framed by international law, and, during its drafting, some of its authors suggested that German citizens should be immediately subject to international human rights law.[63] The constitution itself and subsequent judicial practice did not endorse this principle. However, the constitution established openness to international law as a core aspect of German constitutional interpretation (Art. 25). It also prohibited actions promoting military aggression (Art. 26(1)). This reflected a background in which Germany was already subject to international law and the German legal structure was rebuilt through norms embedded in an occupation regime. As mentioned, the regime in Germany from 1933 to 1945 had some relation to an occupation regime under a militarized political party. The 1949 constitution acquired a dual relation to occupation law as it was imposed under foreign occupation but designed to create a governmental order that was categorically distinct from internal military violence.

[62] My analysis here follows Raim (2013: 596–604). One contemporary commentator declared that, as it elaborated international *ius commune* and reflected general human rights law, this law integrated international norms into German criminal law (Lange 1948: 192).

[63] This was expressed in a speech by Carlo Schmid in 1948.

Important analogies in this regard can be found in Italy. The Italian constitution of 1948 was written after 1945 in a setting in which Italy's sovereignty was still qualified, and which was marked by regional civil war, re-enacting some conflicts that had typified Mussolini's regime. In this context, pre-1943 supporters of Mussolini used violence against their political opponents and exploited criminal laws Mussolini had introduced to combat them.[64] Against this background, the Italian interim government was more independent than its equivalent in Germany, and the 1948 constitution was less invasively shaped by directives issued by the Allies. Yet the constitution was written as Italy remained technically under the jurisdiction of the Allied Control Council, and the international treaties that detailed the terms of Italian sovereignty were agreed in the same year that the constitution was drafted (1947). Importantly, the treaty that returned sovereignty to Italy imposed a series of legal preconditions for the independent exercise of governmental powers. This treaty stated in Art. 15 that Italy must 'take all measures to secure to all persons under Italian jurisdiction ... the enjoyment of human rights and of the fundamental freedoms'. Moreover, in Art. 16, it established protective guarantees for partisans who had supported Allied attacks on German occupying forces and the remnants of the Italian Fascist government after 1943. These preconditions crossed the spectrum between criminal, humanitarian and human rights law. As in Germany, these norms were designed as a constitution for internal war in which domestic society was perceived as an inherently warlike space.

It was on these conditions that the Italian constitution, framing the powers of an independent sovereign state, came into force. These external norms of government were not enduringly recognized. Fascist parties began to re-emerge in Italy after 1945, and they became influential by the 1970s. Nonetheless, occupation law formed the premise for constitutional formation, and government was constructed in 1947–8 using principles that grafted together elements of occupation law as the substructure of the polity. These provisions then became partly embedded in constitutional law. The Italian constitution also developed a constitutional system focused on the protection of individual subjects, in which subjective rights were defined as primary values in the constitution. It contained provisions to avert the militarization of political life (Art. 18) and to prohibit aggressive warfare (Art. 11).

[64] On the 'legal vacuum' in which Italian partisans found themselves after 1945, see Ponzani (2011: 129–130).

Some parallels can be found in circumstances regarding the detention and prosecution of war criminals in Japan after 1945. The charter for the military tribunal established in Tokyo in 1946 set out an extended definition of war crimes for which Japanese military personnel could be tried. This definition included common crimes and crimes not of a specifically military nature, such as murder. In addition, the tribunal established the crime of waging unlawful war as a ground for prosecution, which extended basic norms of humanitarian obligation. As in Germany, prosecutions of Japanese war criminals frequently addressed crimes committed outside Japan, in imperial warfare against China and Mongolia. In China itself, a law was passed in October 1946 to provide jurisdiction for the trial of Japanese war criminals. This law defined war crimes in broad terms including not only acts of physical violence, but the perpetration of thought control and administration of narcotics. This law made international criminal law directly enforceable in China, and it fused such law with domestic provisions. War crimes trials in Japan necessarily involved questions of colonial responsibility as some crimes had been committed in Korea, formally annexed by Japan in 1910. Such questions were only marginally raised in the trials in Tokyo and other locations in East Asia, and the question of Japanese responsibility for colonial aggression was not addressed. The trials only heard cases relating to crimes perpetrated after 1928, so imperialism was clearly not treated as a crime. Yet the rulings of the tribunals were not without relevance for imperial violence. Cases covered the treatment of Koreans by Japanese military personnel, implying that actions against subjects in colonial domains were subject to laws of occupation. This process coincided with a mass repatriation of Japanese citizens living in former colonies, so that the imperial project was geographical reversed at the same time as Japanese citizens were charged under military law.[65]

As in Germany, questions of criminal law ultimately fed back into the ordering of national constitutional law in Japan. The constitution of post-war Japan formed a classical occupation constitution. First, the constitution was created by occupying forces, and it was designed to pacify Japanese society. The constitution did not abolish the Japanese empire. However, Art. 9 renounced war as a state prerogative, and debates during the drafting of the constitution foresaw the comprehensive demilitarization of Japanese society.[66] In addition, it indicated that

65 See the illuminating discussion in Watt (2009: 1–3).
66 See for an account of these debates Hellegers (2001: 577–579).

Japanese government had acted as an occupation regime towards its own citizens, and it was intended to eradicate the social premises of imperialism from society. At one level, the constitution heightened protections for individual rights. However, it was accompanied by legal reforms that imprinted individual rights more deeply in society. These reforms included land reforms and family law reforms, and reforms that reduced the force of large military complexes. As such, the formal constitution formed one element in a broader constitution for war based in the implication that eradication of war required a legal structure that regulated state action internally and externally.

In these contexts, constitutions for new democracies were based in a legal system in which some variant on occupation law formed the premise for authorizing constitutional norms. In each example, constitutions expressed the perception that national societies were military spaces in which national governments had some proximity to occupying regimes, with a propensity for military aggression towards their own citizens and towards other states. To steer society towards democracy, constitutions were enforced as part of a global military system intended to control violence both within and beyond national boundaries. Manifestly, this was intended to alter the vertical dimension of social integration in national states, as it reduced the force of external violence in the formation of political institutions. Less manifestly, this also altered the lateral dimension of social integration as it instituted heightened protections for single political actors. This was based in a two-level system of military law in which international military law was used to encase the military potentials of national constitutional law.

THE CONSTITUTION OF OCCUPATION LAW: POST-IMPERIAL STATES 2

Variations on these processes can be found in societies in Africa which in converse fashion had also embodied imperialist governance techniques, and where imperial rule was terminated after 1945. In this context, states again devised occupation constitutions for their functions. Under the emerging UN system, as mentioned, territories that were transferred from imperial control to trusteeship arrangements were immediately subject to international human rights law.[67] This

[67] For example, the UN General Assembly recommended in 1950 that former South African mandate territories should be placed under international trusteeship, partly to protect the

reflected the principle that, in regions under external control, human rights law should be applied instead of classical occupation law, and human rights law was presented as an alternative to extraterritorial regimes based in military force. Alongside this, some states constructed occupation constitutions in militarized scenarios, and they used military law as a formative constitutional element to escape imperial domination. In these settings, military law was used as a design for occupation constitutions to delegitimate imperial power.

The impetus towards decolonization in Africa was often peaceful, and many postcolonial governments were established without extreme violence. Militaries then came to the fore through post-independence coups or civil wars. However, in some cases, independence was realized by insurgent groups whose legal position raised questions like those posed in occupied regions in World War II. This was visible, for example, in Kenya in the 1950s and, more protractedly, in South Africa from the 1960s to the 1990s. In some cases, notably Algeria, devastating warfare was required to reach independence, and the construction of a distinct constitutional system to regulate occupation was vital to the transition to independence.

Across a spectrum of states, the death throes of European imperialism were characterized by the fact that many imperial governments refused to recognize anti-colonial insurgents as actors engaged in war with a claim to separate legal status. Instead, governments claimed that colonial rule was a system of regular civil government, and persons taking up arms against imperial regimes were perpetrators of civil violence – essentially criminals bound by colonial criminal codes. This approach was evident in Kenya during the Mau Mau uprisings against British rule, which the British did not recognize as having an international or interstate dimension. This was formal policy in the French Fourth Republic where the war in Algeria in the 1950s was not acknowledged as an interstate war: Algeria was, in the French understanding, part of France, which had never been a separate sovereign nation, and French military engagement there served purposes of *pacification*, to preserve public order. As a result, independence activists in Algeria, who defined themselves as fighters against illegal military occupation, were perceived as perpetrators of civil disobedience.[68]

rights of their inhabitants. See General Assembly Resolution 449 (V) B (1950). These principles were greatly reinforced in 1966, in resolution 2145 (27 October 1966).

[68] See legal and historical commentary in Bedjaoui (1961: 212), Fraleigh (1971: 181), Klose (2009: 152) and Branche (2016: 120).

In such cases, the denial of interstate war implied that colonial rule was not military occupation, and it meant that colonial powers could refuse to apply the Geneva Conventions to their adversaries.[69] In such settings, colonial powers often used extraordinary violence for purposes of state repression, effectively accepting protracted asymmetrical civil war as the price for avoiding international recognition of combatants. In Algeria, a militarized legal regime was supported by civil and military tribunals, and the French governments mobilized national courts as effective instruments of war.[70]

Over a longer period, however, anti-colonial insurgents in Africa began to assert a legal personality separate from imperial criminal law, and they were able to promote a perception of colonial rule as a system of military occupation. This occurred largely because actors in these zones positioned themselves in relation to international humanitarian law, gaining some recognition by this means. Indicatively, in Kenya during the Mau Mau era, insurgents invoked humanitarian law to explain their position and objectives.[71] By the later 1950s, anti-colonial factions in Algeria had begun to identify with groups protected in the Geneva Conventions. Despite the refusal of the French government to recognize them, Algerian revolutionaries attached to the Front de libération nationale (FLN) worked with the Geneva Conventions in two ways, culminating in the publication of a white paper in 1960, which set out these policies. First, members of the FLN claimed recognition as military actors with a provisional government engaged in regular warfare between sovereign states. On this basis, they asserted that certain rights and entitlements accrued to their soldiers, especially if captured or imprisoned. Importantly, they argued that, under the Geneva Conventions, the French government was not authorized to determine the circumstances that qualified as a state of international conflict. Second, they declared an intention, as military organizations, to act in accordance with the Conventions, and they announced that they would ratify the Conventions, implicitly claiming status as persons in international law through such voluntary compliance.[72] In these practices, insurgent movements used laws of occupation to attract support for their cause and to demand recognition of colonialism as

[69] Justification for this is set out in Touscoz (1963: 958–959).
[70] See the excellent analysis in Thénault (2001: 51).
[71] Klose (2009: 161).
[72] See for these points *White Paper on the Application of the Geneva Conventions of 1949 to the French-Algerian Conflict* (1960: 15–24).

an illegitimate system of military coercion. By the 1960s, similar principles were included in handbooks promulgated by national liberation armies. In Ghana, Nkrumah wrote a manual for liberation fighters prescribing strict adherence to international humanitarian law.[73] In each case, anti-colonial actors demanded recognition as constitutional actors by extending the constitution of war into national society.

The outcomes of such tactics were mixed, and they did not usually provide a pathway out of militarism. The Mau Mau uprising did not lead immediately to independence for Kenya. However, within a short period of time, Kenya was an independent state, and the importation of international human rights law played a key role in this process. The 1963 constitution contained a strong body of human rights law patterned on international law (Chapter 2). By contrast, military insurgency in Algeria was effective in promoting independence, in part, because it came close to inducing civil war inside France. The French declaration that the Algerian conflict was strictly a civil war meant that the implications of the conflict were deeply felt in France's domestic politics, and the state almost fractured because of post-imperial overreach. The war led to a sharp militarization of French political groups opposed to Algerian independence, whose acts within France were not far from civil war mobilization. This brought to intense articulation conflicts between left and right, in which the military was strongly politicized, so that decolonization became vital for regime stability in France. Eventually, civil war in France itself was averted through the Gaullist compromise of 1958, expressed in a constitution with strong presidential features which eventually limited the direct political role of the military. The war partly persisted beyond 1958 in France, as French soldiers and police murdered many Algerians, culminating in the political massacres in Paris in late summer 1961. The war in Algeria continued until separate referenda were held in France and Algeria and peace was formalized in the Evian Accords (1962). Both Algeria and Kenya were subject to one-party rule or military rule by 1969.

Through these processes, nonetheless, the question of legal recognition for national liberation movements acquired important consequences for both international law and national constitutional law. By the early 1960s, the UN General Assembly began to issue declarations to the effect that national liberation movements should not be criminalized, and they should be viewed as legitimate military

[73] Nkrumah (1968: 112).

combatants.[74] By the 1970s, this had hardened into the conviction that colonial systems in Africa were simply occupation regimes originating in military violence. This implied that military mobilization against the government could be legitimated under the UN Charter, as defensive warfare. This also implied that insurgents against colonialism could obtain the same recognition in international law as members of regular armies. This clearly relativized claims to sovereignty made by imperial states. It also involved the suggestion that military actors could acquire legal status without attachment to a sovereign state, such that some military causes generate their own legal justification. Most importantly, this moved away from strictly positivist understandings of war, and it recognized the principle that states could not categorically dictate which social conditions should be characterized as war. These principles were ultimately reinforced in the Protocols Additional to the Geneva Conventions of 1977. The Protocols provided much greater protection for insurgents in colonial regions, essentially expanding the concept of international conflict to cover anti-colonial war (Protocol 1, Art 1(4)). In so doing, they subjected sovereign states to a more robust constitution of warfare.

These events eventually became important in the dissolution of the apartheid system in South Africa. Initially, the sitting supremacist regime in South Africa followed the line of earlier colonial governments in denying that anti-apartheid insurgents could claim military status, and all steps were taken to avoid legitimating regime opponents by admitting a state of belligerency in the country. This occurred despite mounting international acceptance that South Africa formed an invasive system of occupation whose opponents had some claim to recognition. By the late 1970s, however, the main anti-regime forum, the African National Congress (ANC), adopted tactics earlier used in Algeria. That is, its leaders attempted to gain international acceptance by declaring that compliance with the Geneva Conventions was one of its commitments. This was backed by reinforced UN Declarations supporting the military position of the ANC. By 1981, the UN declared South Africa, which it defined as organizations conducting legitimate 'armed struggle' to resist 'foreign domination' and emphasized its 'strong support' for national liberation movements.[75]

[74] See note 55 at p. 349.

[75] General Assembly, Implementation of the Programme for the Decade for Action to Combat Racism and Racial Discrimination [1981] UNGA 9; A/RES/36/8 (28 October 1981).

Before the end of the apartheid system, beginning in 1991, the ANC found only limited legal recognition as a military organization inside South Africa. In fact, the 1980s witnessed the effective transformation of South Africa into a military state. Military engagement in wars in Angola, in Mozambique and with independence fighters in Namibia, followed by a domestic state of emergency from 1985, stretched the capacity of the South African army. By the mid-1980s, the army focused intensely on internal functions, serving to uphold white minority rule in domestic society. These processes were flanked by rapidly deepening conscription amongst white men as citizenship laws of 1984 attached citizenship to military obligations, degrading the status of ethnic groups excluded from service.[76] This also led to broad hostility to military service, which further challenged military capacity. However, some judicial acknowledgement of the role of the ANC as a political agent became visible in the 1980s. Legal observers have shown how in pre-transitional South Africa, international humanitarian law provided some basis for official engagement with the ANC, and this formed an important background to the process of constitutional opening in the 1990s.[77] In the 1980s, some judges in South Africa gave partial effect to international humanitarian norms in cases concerning the ANC, such that, before the beginning of democratization, liberation fighters claimed implied personality in international law.[78] By the late 1980s, the ANC had begun to appear as a constitutionally recognized faction, and its leadership played a key role in setting out the normative frameworks within which the post-apartheid constitution-making process began. The eventual constitution of South Africa, created between 1993 and 1995, was designed as a document that construed all participants in its drafting as potentially hostile powers. Certain norms, rooted in international human rights law, were agreed prior to the drafting of the constitution to ensure that actions of all parties could be subject to certain basic principles. Once created, the constitution gave high authority to international law as a basis for establishing legal rights (Art. 39(a)) and formed a framework for socially transformative judicial culture.

In these developments, societies determined by histories of imperialism approached constitutional form after 1945 as they constructed

[76] See discussion in Cock (1989: 2–3).
[77] Murray (1987: 145).
[78] Cases cited by Murray are *Sagarius en Andere* 1983 (1) SA 833, 836 (SWA); *S v. Buthelezi and Others* (D&CLD), 22 September 1982 (unreported). This is noted in Boister (1991: 79–86), extending Murray's argument to *S v Masina and Others* 1990(4) SA 709(A).

patterns of political recognition by extracting norms from international military law, especially international humanitarian law. This was not a uniform process as, in some settings, the application of international humanitarian law did not effect a transition from military rule. In territories occupied by Israel in 1967, for example, occupation law was enforced under a number of military proclamations, the third of which, in Art. 35, stated that international humanitarian law should be used as a basis for legal practice in occupied zones. After this, humanitarian law was used in some relevant legal cases, and some Israeli courts acquired an unusual position as organs giving direct domestic effect to laws of armed conflict.[79] In this context, humanitarian law served as a surrogate for citizenship, creating a minimal protective order for subjects living under occupation, yet also weakening the claims of such subjects to full citizenship rights.[80] In many post-imperial contexts, nonetheless, governments were framed by an extended constitution of war. This process rested on the principle that national societies were part of a transnational military system in which the inside and the outside of society could not be clearly separated. This system altered the vertical dimension of social integration, as it constructed state actions around protective norms. More generally, this system implied that political integration of citizens depended on the prior construction of the state as a military actor whose internal and external actions were bound by military law. Normative systems of this type became most prominent in societies where political integration had historically been limited by imperial violence. In such contexts, however, the line of constitutional development that supported democracy more generally became most clearly visible.

PERSISTENT CIVIL WAR: DIALECTICS OF INTERNATIONAL SOCIETY

Despite this, one striking feature of democratic formation after 1945 was that the aforementioned patterns of constitutional transformation had only partial reach. In many societies, it remained impossible to separate government from military violence. The insight that democratization presupposed a constitution for military action, implying that war is both a national and an international condition, was not

[79] See as leading examples the *Beit El* case (decided 1979) and the *Targeted Killings* case (2006) in the Supreme Court, sitting as the High Court of Justice.

[80] This argument is skilfully made in Shafir (2017: 20).

universally internalized. In Europe, traditional propensities for militarism were partly checked, arguably, by the simple fact that the USA retained a substantial military presence on the continent. Over a longer period, however, the emergence of the USA as the main global power tended to divert traditional geopolitical hostilities towards ideological conflicts. Through this process, actual interstate military violence, historically linked to imperialism, became less frequent. Yet ideological antagonisms reflecting Cold War polarities became central to government and created new propensities for civil conflict in most environments. As a result, global ideological splits became a salient determinant of military violence and control. In some settings, as discussed, governments moved away from violence by linking their functions to a global military system that acknowledged the convergence between internal and external military processes. By contrast, some governments inverted this process, and they placed themselves in a global military system to legitimate the coercive use of authority. One frequent phenomenon after 1945 was that governments attached internal conflicts to international conflicts because this allowed them to claim greater legitimacy in using violence in domestic policies. In such cases, the convergence between the military dimensions of national society and the military dimensions of international society was presented, not as a means to control internal violence, but as a means to justify, to protract and to intensify it. On this basis, two parallel systems of global military law developed, with highly conflicting consequences for constitutional rule.

These tendencies became visible almost immediately after 1945, as, in some contexts, decolonization converged with harsh ideological conflicts, creating wars that moved between the external and the internal domains. In particular, the end of French colonial government in Indochina formed an environment in which military hostility was placed in a global constellation. During World War II, French colonial administrators in East Asia were loyal to the regime in Vichy, and, from 1940, they were partly controlled by Japan, which became the governing power in Indochina in March 1945. The French empire remained in Asia during World War II, and, as it was part of the Vichy regime, it was close to a Fascist empire. Yet, after the liberation in France, the left-leaning republican government in Paris sought, with the complicity of the British army, to restore colonial rule in Indochina, so that France was transformed abruptly from a violently governed colony to a violently governing empire. The reassertion of colonial rule in

Indochina occurred after Vietnamese nationalists declared independence and initiated a national constitution-making process, resulting in the progressive democratic constitution of 1946. The first planned national constitution of Indochina was rooted in French republican ideals and it established a system of representative democracy, with equal rights in all fields for all citizens, with a strong focus on social and educational rights. It also imposed military service (Art. 5). The constitution was an avowedly anti-colonial text, containing no mention of France. In parallel, de Gaulle and later French leaders declared that Indochina could become a federation within a French union but rejected demands for its independence. From 1946, this dispute induced anti-French mobilization in different parts of Indochina, which encompassed multiple forms of warfare, initially at a relatively low level. These wars reflected a traditional hybrid of civil war and interstate war that typifies anti-colonial conflict. After the success of the Chinese revolution in 1949, these wars incorporated civil war between Communists and anti-Communists, which became more intense as the USA increased support for France. In this context, Communist units in Indochina used military force in seeking to restructure all society.[81] The French military was confronted with highly mobilized societies, which fought in part through irregular units, operating with the help of the resident population.[82] The French army also recruited irregular units skilled in anti-guerrilla tactics to support its operations and preserve colonial rule.

Together, these factors raised a question, often faced by the military forces of imperial states in colonial environments, concerning the distinction between combatants and non-combatants and the nature of the war that their adversaries were waging. This question was addressed by leading military thinkers connected to the French army. For example, Jean Nemo described such conflict as socially embedded warfare in which military combatants were not manifestly different from civilians.[83] Later, Roger Trinquier described such war as a mode of subversive combat in which 'weak armed elements', inferior to regular military units, gained support of the local population, with the goal of 'overturning the established order'.[84] On this basis, the French

[81] For an illuminating account of the informal militias in Vietnam in 1945, which were gradually integrated in the regular army by 1946, see Marr (2015: 188).

[82] See Logevall (2012: 241).

[83] Nemo (1956).

[84] Trinquier (1961: 18, 71).

colonial military adopted a strategy of observing anti-colonial fighters as participants in a *revolutionary war* – that is, as actors who were part soldiers and part revolutionaries, subject to Soviet and Chinese influence, and whose military acts had sociopolitical objectives.[85] This conception was derived from Mao Tse-Tung, who viewed guerrilla warfare as an integral part of political mobilization and as a preliminary to large-scale deployment of military force.

These classifications assumed more central importance in the Algerian war, where the French army was again confronted with loosely organized irregular units. In the Algerian context, the linkage of anti-colonial movements to Communist ideology was less explicit than in Indochina, but the reliance on informal mobilization retained fundamental significance. Here, the French army explained its role as an actor in a revolutionary war, engaged in military conflict of an encompassing political nature, not fully distinct from civil war, so that all society was construed as a militarized space.[86] This embracing concept of war was also used to legitimate techniques that were illegal under international laws of war, including torture.

Clearly, the concept of revolutionary war marked a shift away from strategies of high-intensity warfare common before 1945. At one level, this concept implied that warfare took place in many forms and with many purposes, and it often entailed conflict with internal enemies, who lacked the full legitimacy of parties in an interstate war. As a result, it implied that, in such conflicts, war and civil war were not fully distinct as revolutionary war contained elements of both. This also implied that armies were inherently political actors operating partly as organizations with political goals, not limited to interstate war. At the same time, French military officials used the concept of revolutionary war to characterize a condition of global ideological hostility – a war against Communism, in which they perceived themselves as front-line protagonists. This meant that the French army could explain its actions in Indochina and Algeria as something more than the violent imposition of colonial occupation, as anti-colonial uprisings were presented as one amongst many political sites in a global civil war. In consequence, military agents hostile to the French regime could be placed in a distinct legal zone, as irregular fighters or guerrillas, in which highly repressive measures were easily justified. In reaction to such actors, the

[85] On this concept in Indochina, see Branche (2016: 154).

[86] See the brilliant analysis in Rigouste (2009: 81). One historian explains that revolutionary war is located between war and dictatorship (Rubenstein 2022: 165).

French military developed new tactics, involving guerrilla mobilization, counterpropaganda and psychological warfare.[87] In some cases, this meant that military personnel assumed functions of infiltration and influence, which gave military leaders a certain autonomy in relation to regular politicians.[88] In each respect, a construction of war as global reality was adopted that strategically reconnected international and domestic conflict, deliberately legitimating conflict as one point in a transnational revolutionary war or a global civil war.

By the 1960s, the doctrine of global civil war became fundamental to the international role of the US Army, which fused French doctrines more closely with anti-Communist ideology. The Greek civil war, starting in 1946, had already convinced observers in the USA that all wars were tied to ideological partitions defined by the Cold War.[89] This war, which also involved large-scale guerrilla mobilization, continued in altered form the global civil war of the pre-1939 era, and Western governments reacted to it as one site in a transnational conflict. The theory of global revolutionary war became more pronounced through the USA's involvement in Vietnam, beginning with Truman's decision to support France in 1950 – an unlikely act for a state committed to the end of colonialism. This initial intervention was closely linked to the ascendancy of Mao's troops in the Chinese civil war, as it followed Ho Chi Minh's requests for Mao's support. By the mid-1960s, the Vietnam War was partly conducted by the USA as an interstate war and partly as a diffuse asymmetrical irregular war in which the army of the USA fought, not strictly against a state, but against a society in a condition of total, primarily informal mobilization. In this context, psychological warfare in rural areas played a crucial role, and it was used to minimize local support for insurgents. Large-scale deployment of American troops in Vietnam was supported by increasing promotion of counterinsurgency tactics in the US Army.[90] In salient respects, the concept of a multipolar *war without fronts*, which developed in Vietnam, was also applied in greatly softened form within American society, as this period saw the militarization of domestic reactions to anti-war movements and the acute intensification of intra-societal conflicts.

[87] Leroux (2014: 529).

[88] This was one reason why de Gaulle later tried to weaken units committed to waging *guerre révolutionnaire* (Pahlavi and Ouellet 2009: 142).

[89] David Galula, who refined his theory of revolutionary war in Indochina and Algeria, had observed the Greek civil war.

[90] See Krepinevich (1986: 103).

In South America, the doctrine of revolutionary war, linked to global civil war, proved particularly resonant, although it was used for quite distinct purposes. During and after the Cuban Revolution that ended in 1959, French military theories were widely applied to describe political realities in South American states. The doctrine of global revolutionary war was deployed in many contexts to induce alarm about imminent revolution, suggesting that the imposition of revolutionary communism was a general threat after Castro's victory. As a result, this doctrine was transposed from real wartime situations in Indochina and Algeria into settings in South America in which there was no war, nor any real probability of war. In this situation, the doctrine of revolutionary war penetrated deep into the thinking of different military organizations, especially in Brazil and Argentina, who used it to replace more traditional defence-based understandings of their domestic functions. National military organizations in Latin America began to adopt the belief that the Cold War was an undeclared global revolutionary war traversing borders between national and international society. This idea was presented to explain and justify measures taken to establish national security at the domestic level. Through this process, the concept of the global revolutionary war was employed, not to support the deployment of force in warzones in colonized societies, but to vindicate repressive actions of national militaries, implying that their public-order functions could be authorized on international military grounds. In effect, this meant that some governments invoked the idea of total global war as a premise to conduct military actions against their own populations.

In the case of Brazil, this constellation led in 1964 to the overthrow of President Goulart, who was forced out of office by a military coup strongly backed by the US government, which trained military units in Brazil to enforce regime change. This event is compelling evidence against the theory that democracies do not declare war on other democracies.[91] In 1964, the USA and Brazil were both incomplete democracies, but both were more democratic than at any previous point in their history; full enfranchisement in the USA was achieved in the same year as external intervention in Brazil. This coup against Goulart was conducted in a setting marked by street-level mobilization by paramilitaries and by conspiracy amongst soldiers, and both groups justified their intervention against the elected government by claiming it was part of a global revolutionary war. Military advocates of the

[91] See pp. 33–6.

revolutionary war doctrine claimed that Goulart was implicated in ideological hostility declared by the USSR, and he was denounced as a 'co-author' of global civil conflict.[92]

After 1964, the Brazilian military established a system that in effect enforced the security directives of the USA in a semi-colonial military order involving interstate and civil war at the same time. In 1965, the government implemented new prerogatives to extend the authority of military courts in matters of national security.[93] By 1967, the Brazilian military regime had acquired highly repressive features. A new constitutional instrument, presented as a bona fide constitution, was introduced to solidify the dominant position of the army. This document accorded expanded powers to the government to impose the state of siege and to guarantee national security (Art. 8, II, III, IV); these powers were concentrated in the office of the president (Art. 58, I). These provisions allowed detention of persons seen as threatening public order and enabled comprehensive censorship of the press. In the same year, further repressive legislation conferred special powers on the military police.[94] Together, these laws created a national security regime focused both on external and internal domestic threats; they applied the idea of the revolutionary war to justify intensified state mobilization against Brazilian citizens, designated as internal and as external enemies, situated physically and ideologically both inside and outside national society.[95] Core pieces of national security legislation legitimated repression by using the diction of revolutionary war.[96] The origins of these policies lay in colonial environments, and they transposed the logic of colonial war to intra-societal conflict. Several leading figures in the military regime, including the first dictatorial president, Castello Branco, had received their education in a French military mission.[97] Further, Brazilian national security policy was strongly influenced by the Higher School of War (founded 1949), where teachers promoted a totalizing concept of national security, reflecting experiences of colonial war.[98]

92 Pinto (1964: 57).
93 Ato Institucional Nr 2 (27 October 1965).
94 Decree-Law 317 (13 March 1967).
95 See also Decree Law 898 (29 September 1969).
96 Decree Law 314 (13 March 1967) stated that 'revolutionary war is an internal conflict' inspired by an external ideology whose purpose is the 'subversive conquest of power for progressive control of the nation'.
97 See Araujo (2012: 40).
98 The School presented a developmentalist ideal of national security intended to turn Brazil into a great power, incorporating 'demographic, economic and financial' policies in the definition of security (Sardenberg 1987: 9–10).

By the 1960s, doctrines of revolutionary warfare were strongly represented there.[99] Further laws of the late 1960s also subordinated parts of the state police force to the Ministry for the Army, essentially creating a military unit to pacify and occupy domestic society.[100]

In Brazil, concepts of citizenship extracted from imperial environments created an impulse for civil war in a society whose level of pacification was otherwise high. Indeed, the doctrine of revolutionary war was specifically employed to authorize civil war. Similar justifications were used during the military takeover in Chile in 1973, which, like Brazil, was in a state of rapid, essentially peaceful democratization. These doctrines were also used in Argentina in 1976, where the military was more closely involved in politics. The Peronist government in Buenos Aires that was overthrown in 1976 had strong historical links to the army, and it was challenged by rising rightist terrorism in the early 1970s. Before the 1970s, military rulers had already used militarized concepts of national security to stabilize their regimes. This was clearly illustrated by the Onganía regime in 1966, which created a national security council and a national security planning system to control the domestic political arena.[101] In post-1976 Argentina, leaders of the military justified extreme armed repression by claiming to be engaged in conflict with infiltrated enemies who mobilized through domestic agents. This involved the assertion that conflicts in Argentina were sites in a global revolutionary war in which combatants operated outside normal legal constraints. In this conception, the army imagined itself as an occupying force taking control of domestic society as enemy territory in a global civil war. This could also be traced to the impact of French military doctrine, which accompanied the ideological transformation of imperialism after 1945.[102]

CONCLUSION

The period after 1945 witnessed two counterposed tendencies in constitutional law, both linked to warfare and to the complex residues of imperialism, and both of which reflected constructions of global society as a military system. This period was the first time in global history that

[99] For varying accounts of this translation, see Lewandowski (1985: 214) and Martins Filho (2008: 41).

[100] Decree Law 667 (2 July 1969).

[101] Ley de Defensa Nacional 16970 (1966).

[102] On the background to such Argentine theory in French colonial warfare, see Ranaletti (2010: 55) and Pontoriero (2012: 152).

many states acquired democratic constitutions that remained enduringly democratic. Where this occurred, military pressures remained original determinants of constitutional formation. For example, such democratic constitutions preserved in peacetime form legal provisions for democratic enfranchisement and the full exercise of political rights that had historically resulted from war. Yet, typically, constitutional acts that created democracy presupposed the existence of a normative system enabling polities to detach their interactions with citizens from military imperatives. This took place in different ways, partly mediated through human rights law, and partly mediated through humanitarian law or the law of military occupation. In some cases, states established democracies by identifying their societies as social locations that at least partly converged with warfare, and they subjected their societies to normative orders based in military law. Some societies that underwent democratic demilitarization after 1945 obtained constitutions expressing the principle that domestic society was part of a global military system: a civil-military zone that required pacification through international norms, applied directly both to state agents and to individual subjects. This understanding implied that national and global social domains were inherently connected, and democratic formation presupposed the management of violence in both dimensions. Societies that experienced remilitarization after 1945 also promoted models of citizenship reflecting the assumption that domestic society was a part of a global military system where national and transnational conflicts converged, such that each subject was an actor in a global struggle. This positing of a global revolutionary dichotomy created militarized governments of different kinds – it led to hybrid imperial/civil wars (Vietnam), and to military regimes close to civil wars in most of South America. In each case, political institutions were built around overlapping, yet also counterposed understandings of the position of war in modern society, and counterposed attitudes to the legacies of imperial violence. One outlook used a global construction of law to reduce internal military violence; one outlook used a globalist perspective to legitimate it as part of a transnational civil war. Of course, in many states, these visions of political order jostled for constitutional force, and many systems, notably in France and the USA, contained elements of both.

In this balance, after 1945, elements of a system of *world law* began to take shape in some polities which was able to uphold constitutional democracy, even in environments where democracy had been historically precarious. *World law* means here a systemic legal structure, connecting national and international spheres of interaction, establishing a normative order to soften the production of violence in national societies. Where features of this system developed, basic constitutional goods originally arising from warfare were secured: constitutions emerged in which individual rights were protected, especially rights regarding electoral participation. Yet, dialectically, such rights were secured as they were detached from their military origins. As discussed, national constitutions first developed as military law for promoting military contracts with populations. They gradually consolidated democratic government as they were integrated in a system that pacified their military purposes, partly using a second constitutional tier, also resulting from war, to achieve this. In essence, this means that, in much of the globe, democracy was built through a double security constitution. In this constitution, rights originating in war in the security constitutions of national societies were consolidated in a secondary constitutional system, also originating in war, which separated these rights from military purposes.

CHAPTER SEVEN

THE OCCUPATION CONSTITUTION II

Changing Security Constitutions

The foregoing discussion assessed how, in some post-1945 polities, the role of warfare in creating constitutional law was transformed, resulting in a partial separation of constitutions from their military origins. This separation was manifest in the fact that constitutional provisions were often created on external premises, partly integrating states into a transnational system of norms. Frequently, constitutional rights were disconnected from the military bargains in which they originated, and their tendency to inflame intra-societal conflict was reduced. This separation was also manifest in the fact that states began to reorder their interactions with individual citizens, identifying themselves as actors in quasi-military scenarios. In extreme cases, international law was applied directly to reduce military violence in national society. The previous analysis focused mainly on interactions between state and citizens in the field of political rights. However, after 1945, the differentiation between constitutional law and its military premises also became visible in laws addressing social rights, which, in most polities, became a legal domain that was either integrated in or closely attached to the constitution of state. After 1945, the design of constitutional law was profoundly shaped by the pacification of societal interactions to which social rights were linked, so that such rights also mitigated the effects of vertical integration processes caused by war. In vital examples, this formed through a dialectical process similar to that shaping political rights: rights originally established through war acquired more secure form as they fused with a secondary legal order, which also originated in war, which partly separated them from military imperatives. Through this, social rights became a second key component of a system of world law.

SOCIAL RIGHTS AND WAR

As constitutional law became more fundamental to social organization in the nineteenth century, most constitutions established a corpus of social provisions, and social rights rapidly acquired protection in or alongside constitutional law. In most legal systems, guaranteed social rights were not initially formalized as constitutional responsibilities. However, periods of constitution making that widened political rights almost invariably led to the expansion of social legislation as, through political bargains, groups who sought distinct provisions for social well-being and personal security were admitted to the franchise. As a result, the development of early welfare-state institutions was a central outcome of the expansion of constitutional law in the later nineteenth century. Illustratively, as discussed, one characteristic of the second wave of constitution making concentrated in the 1860s and 1870s was that, under such constitutions, laws were introduced that covered basic social rights such as provision for national school-level education and some protection for citizens affected by injury or ill health. In the 1880s, legislation in some European countries established statutory guarantees for health insurance and protection against unemployment. By 1918, as constitutions allocated rights to larger electorates, some constitutions included formal catalogues of social rights, elevating social protection to the rank of a constitutionally protected entitlement. As discussed, this was evident in the Weimar Constitution, which contained a separate section on the 'organization of economic life', which set out a corpus of economic rights. This tendency was reflected in the 1931 constitution of Spain and in the 1934 constitution of Brazil. In societies where such principles were not given formal constitutional status, the years after 1918 saw substantial welfare state development, and national governments internalized deep welfare obligations.

As indicated, the construction of social rights, forming preliminary elements of the modern welfare state, was deeply linked to warfare.[1] Like political rights, social rights were usually elaborated – at least in part – as blocks in a bargaining system which enabled governments to extract military force from society, and such rights served to pacified groups from which such force was obtained.

[1] For analysis of 'the compensation of conscription by the provision of social rights', see Obinger (2020: 17).

This connection was often evident in the right to education. In most societies, as discussed, provisions for the expansion of education constituted a core part of nation building.[2] Almost invariably, reforms expanding rights to education were introduced in times of military modernization. This began before the advent of democratic or semi-democratic constitutions. However, the link between militarism and education became pronounced through the rise of constitutional law in the later nineteenth century when the allocation of constitutional roles to citizens was usually flanked by the growing formation of education systems with broad penetration. By this time, most states in a process of militarization developed constitutional systems, and the right to education assumed particular importance in improving the supply of soldiers for government. By the later nineteenth century, most constitutional states had introduced national school education, and the duties of state-sponsored schools reached beyond the promotion of cognitive skills. In many countries, national schools did mot only impart cognitive skills. In addition, they enforced physical education and even semi-military training, to increase the physical aptitude of students for war. In fact, education was often designed to promote pro-imperial attitudes amongst schoolchildren, and it had clear motivational content.[3] One striking pronouncement on the attachment of education rights to military pressures is found in debates in the constituent assembly that created the 1891 constitution of Brazil. Here, in discussing the terms of military service to be imposed by the constitution, one delegate claimed simply that Brazil was a country where the 'people were completely heterogonous' and 'where there was no national education' and 'only a tenth of the population was able to read and write'. For this reason, the delegate stated that it was not feasible to establish a military recruitment system in which the people could be expected to act as 'servants of the fatherland'. Few people, he concluded, were sufficiently well educated to be 'willing to die for their country'.[4] Access to education was projected as a precondition for patriotism, instilling in citizens the virtues required for death in combat.

By the earlier twentieth century, the right to education was frequently enshrined in constitutional texts, so that the political education of citizens expanded further. At the same time, the understanding of education was explicitly broadened beyond formal learning, and it was attached both to cultural and physical improvement and to moral

[2] See pp. 71, 133, 140–2, 156, 162.
[3] See p. 142.
[4] This is recorded in Roure (1920: 218–219).

socialization. The Weimar Constitution created a right to public school-level education (Arts 143, 145) and Art. 148 stated that all schools must provide 'moral education', to instil 'civic mentality' and 'personal and professional proficiency' in pupils. The Weimar Constitution was of itself a document with pronounced national pedagogic functions, and it was intended to elevate the population towards a uniform national consciousness. One of its authors, Friedrich Naumann, who led the left-liberal faction in 1918–19 and assumed responsibility for writing the section on fundamental rights in the constitution, expressed the wish that parts of it should be used as a popular catechism to instil national values into the electorate. Under the 1921 constitution of Poland, education reforms flanked military reforms so that, as they became soldiers and citizens, all Polish citizens were obliged to go to school and were given access to free education (Art. 119). Like the Weimar Constitution, the 1921 constitution had a pedagogic dimension as all parents were expected to educate children in the rights and duties attached to citizenship (Art. 94). Although the constitution protected minority rights, these provisions were partly devised to instil a cohesive national consciousness in a socially and ethnically diverse society. The 1934 constitution of Brazil placed great emphasis on the right to education (Art. 149), and it committed the federal union to creating 'a national education plan' (Art. 150(a)). Education was connected to the promotion of national integration, and the government even acquired the duty to promote 'eugenic education' (Art. 138(b)). Leading Brazilian constitutionalists stated that modern constitutional law is required to frame a mass of social rights, including the right to public 'services and goods', the right to work, the right to security in face of 'the hazards and misfortunes of life' and the right to 'a reasonable standard of living'. This was tied to the claim amongst members of the regime's elite that education should be seen as the most important of all social rights, and it should be expanded to cultural and physical education.[5]

Across these examples, the deep interwovenness of citizenship, militarism and education was evident, and citizens who obtained constitutional rights for military purposes acquired educational rights for related functions. Similar observations can be made about other social rights. Initially, before the growth of modern constitutional law, national armies provided welfare resources for soldiers and their dependents,

[5] Campos (1942: 309–19).

and the prospect of material support in case of invalidity was an important incentive for poorer recruits to join the army.[6] By the nineteenth century, armies were often leading welfare providers, and they established provisions for the material security of soldiers standing alongside other mechanisms for providing social care, usually administered locally or by religious organizations. This function of the military was already formulated in the French constitution of 1799, Art. 86 of which stated that, in the name of the *nation française*, pensions would be provided for all people wounded in defence of the homeland, as well as for the widows and children of soldiers who died in battle. Parallel phenomena have been observed in the USA, where veterans were, after 1865, recipients of welfare resources with broad coverage.[7] By the later nineteenth century, some European states reinforced welfare provision at the national level, which meant that the army lost some importance as a welfare provider. At this point, in many states, central governments assumed responsibilities for public welfare that superseded or complemented those exercised by the military, and this coincided with the universal imposition of military conscription and the increasing organization of education rights. As mentioned, this was pioneered in Germany by Bismarck's social legislation, and, from the 1880s onwards, German men were covered by overlapping insurance policies in their professional lives and in their lives as military recruits. The construction of the German welfare state took place through the 1880s, as Germany embarked on its first imperial programmes. After the 1880s, welfare expenditure increased in most European states, and this coincided directly with rising interstate tensions. France remained an important exception to this rule as France saw lower social spending.

By the late nineteenth century, social rights were constructed in a twofold relation to military pressures. In some settings, welfare protections were simply devised to increase the physical robustness of potential soldiers. As discussed, conscription was universally enforced in most European societies by the final decades of the nineteenth century. However, in many contexts, conscription was only nominally universal. Many potential recruits were deemed unfit for service on health grounds, so that the physical deficiencies of the population restricted national military potential. Many healthcare reforms were

[6] See an analysis in Meyer (1983: 82).

[7] Skocpol (1992: 59). On one account, exposure to military violence created 'a military welfare state' in the USA (Obinger, Grawe and Dörr 2020: 497).

implemented for these reasons.[8] Prior to this, important social reforms, such as laws limiting child labour, had also frequently been justified by the need to ensure the military value of young men.[9] In parallel, social rights were also constructed as part of the wider political bargaining system that shaped the modern constitutional order. Citizens typically acquired welfare rights as one component in a political-military contract to motivate them to accept military risks and governmental security imperatives. This formed a central moment in the process of internal integration that supported national military efforts. As mentioned, governments accorded political rights to citizens for military reasons. However, as also discussed, the allocation of such rights created fissures in society that could not be wholly placated by coercive means. By the late nineteenth century, in consequence, many governments began to allocate social rights to citizens in order to control the lateral militarization caused by the collective exercise of political rights. Welfare states began to take shape at the national level, broadly, at historical junctures where external militarization and internal political enfranchisement rapidly increased, and conflicts between social groups in domestic society were intensified because of this. In most contexts, early welfare states evolved as institutions to manage this process. That is, organizations protecting social rights were created to insulate national polities against the domestic effects of external militarization, producing incentives for social groups to channel their military propensities, not against domestic adversaries, but against external enemies. In fact, the function of social rights in softening the lateral effects of military integration was spelled out in semi-official doctrine. After circa 1880, the doctrine of social imperialism became a common intellectual currency in some polities. The core implication of this doctrine was that, externally, states could only successfully promote imperialism if, internally, they committed to deepened integration by co-opting the socially compliant elements of their own working class, likely to be achieved through welfare policies.[10] Exponents of this outlook stood at different positions on the political spectrum in their polities, and this view was not monopolized by thinkers on the right. In this outlook, social investment in national populations appeared as a vital precondition for effective territorial defence and external expansion.

[8] Obinger (2020: 13–4).
[9] On this link in Prussia, see Berlepsch (1984: 227).
[10] See p. 175.

To be sure, other immediate factors shaped the growth of social rights in the later nineteenth century. Clearly, early welfare provisions were often established at critical points in the history of European labour movements, and they responded both to the rise of organized labour as a political force and to increasing industrial hostilities between business and trade unions. In most countries, the formation of welfare states was eventually supported by social compacts in which organized labour acquired a more structured role in the political system, and the slow integration of trade unions was central to the establishment of welfare policies. In key respects, however, the role of trade unions in shaping welfare states was also attached to military pressures. Over a longer period, European governments identified trade unions as possible partners in the coordination of domestic societies for war, and they frequently reacted to the risk of warfare by giving enhanced recognition to trade unions. In the first instance, this can be seen in early laws that legalized the activities of trade unions. In France, legal recognition for trade unions was established as France embarked on large-scale imperial enlargement, in 1884.[11] Further recognition was then granted in 1901. In Prussia, trade unions acquired basic rights of legal recognition in 1869, during the process of national unification and before major military mobilization against France, in laws that were soon transferred to the unified German state.[12] In this case, membership in trade unions was protected as an internal part of a process of external military annexation flanked by mandatory conscription laws. In most of Europe, the period prior to World War I saw increasing recognition of trade unions. As discussed, the rising mobilization of national populations was partly reflected in hostile labour relations and class conflicts. However, this period also saw the political co-optation of the more moderate sections of organized labour, and different governments passed laws to soften industrial hostility, especially in conditions where they were exposed to military conflict.

These processes became most striking in and after World War I. During World War I, trade unions acquired an expanded role in policymaking in most belligerent polities. The role of trade unions in wartime societies was partly regulated in coercive manner, as laws were often passed to prohibit strike action.[13] But, by this time, representatives

[11] See the Waldeck-Rousseau Law (21 March 1884).

[12] Criminalization of union membership was forbidden in §152 of the Gewerbeordnung für den Norddeutschen Bund (1869).

[13] See, in the UK, the Munitions of War Act (1915); in Germany, the Hilfsdienstgesetz (1916); and in Austria, the Streikverordnung (1914), which prohibited industrial action in the public sector.

of organized labour possessed new utility for national governments, which were willing to make concessions to them to secure their services for military economies. In many polities, World War I created a system of partly coercive and partly voluntary labour integration, from which trade unions drew benefits for their members. In Germany, as mentioned, the war brought reforms that expanded the bargaining position of the trade unions. In the UK, representatives of the Labour Party entered government without specific electoral mandate before the end of the war.

After 1918, then, social rights were greatly widened in most constitutional systems through constitutional norms, legislative packages or both. Importantly, the widening of social rights was driven by war as a general factor as state institutions were transposed onto more democratic footing after 1918 and governments were required to integrate new sectors of society in the political system. However, such widening of social rights was driven by warfare for more specific reasons. During the war, the guarantee of material security for soldiers who survived the war and for families of those who did not was often presented as a moral imperative, such that state obligations for welfare provision formed simple contractual recompense for military service.[14] After 1918, the first welfare laws were usually introduced for soldiers and their dependents, and protective measures for persons affected by war formed the first institutional elements of post-1918 welfare states. In Poland, the Ministry for Public Health, Social Care, and Labour Protection was established before Poland formally regained independence in 1918. Germany saw the introduction of welfare legislation from 1919 whose purpose was to provide for injured soldiers and the dependents of fallen soldiers.[15] Similar legislation was passed in Austria, where a complex judicial system was created to address claims for benefits amongst ex-soldiers and dependents.[16] In the USA, where military recruitment was much lower, Congress established new benefits for veterans in 1917 and the Veterans Bureau in 1921. In addition, the widening of social rights was strongly informed by international military and ideological antagonisms, as states in Western Europe promoted social rights to reduce the appeal of Bolshevism; the new Soviet government introduced a

[14] See the assertion that conscription and welfare provision were 'inseparable concepts' in Marchet (1915: 27).

[15] In Germany, a series of laws covering persons affected by the war was passed: the Gesetz über die Beschäftigung Schwerbeschädigter (1920), the Reichsversorgungsgesetz (1920) and the Gesetz betreffend die öffentliche Krüppelfürsorge (1920) (Prussia).

[16] See the Austrian Invalidenentschädigungsgesetz (1919) and the Invalidenbeschäftigungsgesetz (1920).

protective Labour Code in 1922. This was especially significant as, as mentioned, the first insurrectionist movements in Europe at the end of World War I were concentrated in military units. In many cases, social measures were introduced in 1918–19 to prevent further radicalization amongst soldiers, as demobilization posed a threat of revolutionary unrest.[17] The widening of social rights often coincided with the implementation of repressive public order laws, so that welfare provisions formed one part of a design for social regimentation.[18]

In these examples, the social rights secured in many national constitutions, or in laws sanctioned under national constitutions, developed slightly later than provisions for political rights. No societies developed advanced welfare states before 1914, and few possessed welfare states with general social coverage before 1945. However, in staggered sequence, the formative logic in the construction of social rights mirrored the security imperatives that propelled the elaboration of political rights. The first great leap forward in the protection of social rights occurred after 1918, and this was connected to the fact that international military pressures had forced national governments to integrate their populations more deeply. At this point, states stabilized their sovereignty by allocating political rights to citizens. Because of this, governments were required to provide some guarantees of material security to instil loyalty in their citizens and to discourage their citizens from using their political rights for counter-systemic affiliations. Social rights thus became core elements in vertical integration in which states secured sovereignty through the internal allocation of rights.

What ultimately became visible in these phenomena is that, in the longer aftermath of 1918, key sets of welfare rights – education rights, healthcare rights and social security rights – did not lose their connection to their original military background. Like political rights, in fact, social rights remained attached to military pressures and purposes. In their initial construction after 1918, social rights became intense vectors of intra-societal militarization, and, like political rights, they acquired destabilizing outcomes for the constitutions that protected them.

These outcomes can be in several ways. First, in post-1918 polities that promoted education rights as instruments of social consolidation, such rights often intensified intra-societal hostility. Most markedly, in

[17] See an excellent discussion of Germany and France in Weber (2010: 187–188).
[18] See p. 31.

societies with complex population structures, education rights led to increased national consciousness amongst groups that exercised them, and linguistic and religious questions became highly divisive. This was already the case in multinational empires that existed before 1918.[19] However, this also proved undermining for many interwar polities, and authoritarian techniques of population management became commonplace to address resultant social fragmentation.[20]

Second, the promotion of income support and healthcare rights after 1918 created a harsh matrix of social militarization as many governments struggled to pacify the conflicts between different groups that obtained public entitlement to a stake in social wealth because of such rights. At this time, most constitutionally ordered societies experienced deep hostility between political sectors with different dispositions towards welfare provision. Many constitutional systems in Europe and Latin America were brought to crisis in the 1920s and 1930s by conflicts between political organizations that channelled class-related hostilities, typically concentrated around competition for material goods. In most societies, the termination of democracy was effected by parties who were committed to eradicating welfare organizations or placing welfare provisions on authoritarian foundations.[21]

In such developments, military factors often played a vital role. On one hand, in most constitutional systems formed after 1918, military associations remained prominent actors in the competition for welfare resources, and, in different societies, ex-soldiers formed organizations to assert claims for a share in the allocation of material goods. In some cases, associations of veterans came into conflict with other groups committed to negotiating resources for their members – for example, with trade unions. This took place in different ways. In some societies, of course, veterans were largely pacifists. In other contexts, veterans were displaced into marginal social positions, and authoritarian or military leaders often sought to appeal to former soldiers.[22] In more volatile environments, veterans gained representation via less institutionalized movements, and Fascist and semi-Fascist parties that came to

[19] See discussion of Turkey and Poland at pp. 189, 284–5.

[20] This was discussed in the section on post-1918 Poland. In Yugoslavia, under the dictatorial regime starting in 1929, education reforms were immediately implemented to instil national unity, involving regime control of teachers as organs of nation-building (see Troch 2015: 47, 190).

[21] See cases examined in Chapter 3.

[22] On the marginalization of veterans in Germany, see the brilliant discussions in Kienitz (2008: 93). One important analysis explains how military regimes in interwar Greece were sustained by welfare arrangements for veterans (Makris 2023: 260).

power recruited strongly amongst groups that had served in the armed forces.[23] In these respects, competition over welfare, which became more acute after the onset of the Great Depression in 1929, took a form in which military identities remained live.

On the other hand, more generally, conflicts over welfare after 1918 created a constellation in which military organs reacquired dominant integrational functions. As mentioned, in many states, military organizations initially acted as primary promoters of welfare state construction. In fact, by the 1870s, the integration of national society through the army and the integration of society through the welfare state were often closely conjoined, or even interlinked parts of the same process. As discussed, this did not preclude the extensive use of military force against organized labour; broadly, the military was both a driver of social welfare and an organ of violence for limiting its scope. This conjunction was at times strategically rearticulated after 1918, as military attachments remained vital sources of material integration. After 1929, however, the link between military integration and welfare integration was rebalanced, usually to the detriment of welfare provisions, and many governments opted for policies in which welfare investment was reduced in favour of military integration. In some cases, military integration and welfare integration advanced together in authoritarian form, as regimes linked citizens to the state through armies and welfare programmes at the same time; this was exemplified by Brazil under Vargas. More typically, however, military violence was used to reduce welfare provisions, and elite groups who supported the retrenchment of warfare states deployed military units, either formal or informal, to impose welfare cuts: welfare provision became – literally – a field of multipolar conflict. These processes were visible in post-1930 Germany and post-1934 Spain. In some instances, as discussed, such conflicts redirected state policy towards external militarism. By 1940, some form of militarized anti-welfarism was institutionalized across virtually the entire European continent, as well as much of Latin America.

In each respect, many constitutional systems after 1918 promoted social rights legislation linked to warfare – both to its memory and to its preparation. Welfare states were commonly designed in essence as an internal apparatus to absorb the social shocks of war, closely

[23] See the discussion of Germany and Poland in Chapter 3. On this aspect of interwar politics in Yugoslavia, see Newman (2015: 189–199).

connected to the purposes of constitutional law. However, controversy over social rights often created conflicts in which military organizations acquired direct roles in the state. Moreover, such rights opened national society to international polarities, as internal contests over welfare were generally aligned to policies relating to the Soviet Union, in Europe and Latin America. Like political rights, the different sets of social rights formed after 1918 often incubated propensities for lateral violence in society, and they created social conditions in which military functions of social control and administration remained prominent.

WELFARE STATES AND THE SECURITY CONSTITUTION

One of the key factors in post-1945 democracies is that national governments showed an increased ability to separate social rights from their military origins, and they devised mechanisms to weaken the pressures on governments transmitted through social rights. These processes cannot be seen in exclusively constitutional terms as they reflected patterns of transformation shaping global society in its entirety. However, as in the domain of political rights, most democracies that developed after 1945 were stabilized through a trajectory in which social rights resulting from warfare were, at the same time, both consolidated and partly detached from military imperatives. This process cannot be presented as a completely uniform model, and it took place in many variations. However, few democracies did not secure their foundations by placing social rights on new premises, and, in most contexts, democracy was stabilized around welfare systems that did not generate unmanageable social antagonisms. In most cases, this was connected to a process in which military determinants of social integration were weakened.

After 1945, constitutionally ordered states showed a marked tendency to expand social rights in core areas of the welfare state, such that the process of welfare state construction that had gained momentum after 1918 was substantially reinforced. At this time, most constitutional states increased social transfers to citizens through healthcare investment, through the introduction of national pensions and through the administration of schemes for income supplements. Crucially, post-1945 patterns of welfare-state construction converged most universally around provisions for social transfers via subsidized national education systems. In some contexts, subsidized education is not viewed as a core aspect of the modern welfare state.[24] However, public education is surely a primary social transfer, and the right to education belongs to the cluster of social rights that underpin modern welfare systems. After 1945, increases in access to education were closely attached to other aspects of welfare state formation, and increased provision for education rights closely mirrored the development of other rights. In these developments, social rights were sometimes established after 1945 at an express constitutional level. For example, social rights were strongly protected in the preamble to the French constitution of 1946; in Arts 20(1) and 28(1) of the constitution of the FRG; in Arts 32, 35, 36, 38 of the Italian constitution (1948); in Arts 145–7, 157 of the Brazilian constitution of 1946. This was also a prominent feature of postcolonial constitutions; as mentioned, welfare commitments formed Directive Principles in the Indian Constitution (Arts 38–39). In other contexts – for example, the UK and the USA – social rights were not covered by formal constitutional guarantees, but they progressively became primary elements of public law and were subject to protection under public law.

In different spheres of welfare state formation, war remained a dominant impetus after 1945, and the expansion of welfare systems reflected traditional linkages with experiences of war. This traditional linkage was visible in the fact that, as in previous eras, military personnel were often privileged recipients of social rights, and the expansion of these rights was driven by interests established and recognized in war. In many countries, the first welfare packages introduced around 1945 targeted ex-soldiers and dependents of former soldiers.[25] In some countries, ex-soldiers received social benefits designed to enhance, not only their physical health, but their educational opportunities and prospects for social mobility. One key example is the G.I. Bill of Rights (1944) in the USA, which created social opportunities for many ex-servicemen. The Employment Act (1946) was also intended to ease the integration of citizens exiting military roles. In more general terms, the expansion of welfare provision after World War II was determined by the fact that, in many settings, the essential capacities of national government had been augmented by war and public authorities had assumed wartime powers of material distribution that persisted into peacetime. This is starkly reflected in fiscal statistics for many belligerent states, in which high levels of taxation and public spending during warfare were only

[24] For summary of this divergence and claims similar to mine concerning the need to classify subsidized education as part of the national welfare effort, see Obinger (2020: 9).

[25] See as a key example the Bundesversorgungsgesetz (1950) in West Germany.

partly reduced after 1945. In most democracies, with variations, public outlays were at least partly transferred from military expenditure to social investment after 1945, giving rise to sustained increases in welfare spending (including education).[26] In some societies, further, societal experiences of war necessitated social investment. World War II caused social devastation in many belligerent countries that could be remedied only by large-scale redevelopment, through appropriate planning bodies. Wartime experiences of aerial bombing, extensive civilian casualties and mass population displacement all required the formation of government institutions to engage with welfare-related challenges such as rehousing, healthcare and infrastructural development. In addition, post-1945 governments were forced to demobilize vast armies, many of whose members were injured or ill. The socially indiscriminating nature of these experiences meant that rebuilding processes led by national governments covered all social spheres.[27] Furthermore, the environment after 1945 was hardly one of global peace. By 1950, state investment in welfare provision was again linked to ideological conflict in the context of the Cold War, as, once again, Western governments used public spending to reduce the appeal of Soviet communism. In some post-1945 societies, sympathy for communism was high, and the maintenance of public attitudes required to support the Cold War was not straightforward. In the USA, welfare spending increased dramatically in the 1960s, which was closely tied to intra-societal militarization and increased conscription for ideologically driven warfare in Vietnam.

This traditional linkage was apparent in the fact that education investment remained, in part, tied to military experience. After 1945, many governments reproduced traditional patterns of citizenship formation in which military policies played an important role in promoting educational advancement for citizens. This was manifest in states in the process of decolonization, where education reproduced the nation-building functions it had performed in earlier national societies. In post-1945 Africa, most new governments prioritized investment in school and university education.[28] At the same time, some African states imposed military duties on their newly liberated citizens. There was no general template for conscription in Africa in the decades

[26] I am using data provided by Ortiz-Ospina and Roser (2016).

[27] See analysis of this in Dryzek and Goodin (1986).

[28] On one calculation, after 1945, the number of universities grew globally by an annual rate of nearly 6 per cent. In Africa, proportional growth was highest, from a very low base (Zeleza 2016: 3–6). For broader systematic discussion, see the analysis linked to the Stanford School in Ramirez and Ventresca (1992).

after imperialism. In some societies, it did not exist, and, in others, it was weakly enforced. In some settings, governments were reluctant to introduce conscription for fear of reinforcing military cadres who could easily turn against civilian governments. Moreover, where conscription existed, it served different purposes. In Egypt, for example, conscription was closely linked to serious external threats. In other contexts, it was imposed as a force to diminish the lateral effects of intra-societal loyalties and to reduce tribalism. In post-1957 Ghana, Nkrumah endorsed the idea of the citizen-soldier, and he encouraged national service and youth mobilization. In South Africa, which ultimately had deep conscription, military service supported an exclusionary model of citizenship designed both for external military actions and internal conflict management. Generally, however, African states that imposed conscription also established broad education rights. In some cases, military duties were inseparable from education rights as citizens who obtained certain qualifications were required to perform military service. This is evident in the National Youth Service Corps created in Nigeria in 1973. In Nigeria, access to school-level and higher education increased sharply after the civil war of 1967–70, during military rule, as schools were brought under direct state control.[29] In fact, in some lower-income societies whose governments did not impose conscription, less impressive educational reforms were reached. For example, India saw huge educational expansion after 1950, yet the government placed less emphasis on the abolition of child labour, so that levels of literacy remained relatively low.[30] In most Western societies, in parallel, the years after 1945 saw an expansion of educational provision which coincided with continued mandatory conscription. The growth of education reflected conventional ideological prerogatives, and the content of school-level tuition after 1945 was focused on reinforcing national loyalties and cognitive capacities in the context of the Cold War. This was reflected in school curricula at different points in the global system, but it was clearly visible in the USA.[31] In some South

[29] On one account, the military governments in the 1970s promoted centralized control of university education as a tool both to facilitate access for different social groups and to forge greater national integration (Anyanwu 2011: 107).

[30] Weiner (1991: 4).

[31] By the late 1940s, the Educational Policies Commission set down guidelines against employing communist teachers in schools in the USA. Some universities coerced professors into rejecting radical views through 'loyalty oaths'. Note further the introduction of the National Defense Education Act (1958) in the USA, designed to improve technological education to match Russian advances.

American polities, rights to education were intensified as the military extended its role as an education provider. As mentioned, education rights were reinforced in post-1945 Brazil. At the same time, a new military academy was created, the Escola Superior de Guerra, which identified education as a core terrain in the ideological conflict with communism and defined the military socialization of national elites as one of its functions.[32] Ultimately, some Brazilian universities played an important role in training anti-communist paramilitaries before the coup of 1964.

Despite these traditional tendencies, the expansion of welfare investment after 1945 contained impulses that altered such formative links. In different contexts, primarily in countries historically located on the metropolitan side of imperial systems, a model of state construction became widespread in which welfare protections were augmented because of World War II, but social rights were also separated from military force. This causal detachment appeared in different ways. Most obviously, this was reflected in the fact that increased social spending became a broadly universal feature of democratic states, and it was not integrally correlated with military engagement in World War II. At this time, as mentioned, the traditional welfare bargain was reproduced in some settings as military personnel gained material recompense for their services. However, commitment to welfare investment became a central part of public policy in most states after 1945, regardless of the impact that the war had had on their population. For example, states engaged in decolonization usually promoted social investment after 1945, although they had not existed as sovereign entities before 1945. Moreover, states that had been neutral in the war, in both Europe and Latin America, implemented deepened welfare policies. Across polity types, further, social spending was strongly connected to the emergence of an international consensus in favour of welfare investment, and it was prompted by attachments to the UN, the International Labour Organization and emerging regional human rights systems.[33] Perhaps most notably, many states began progressively to define welfare obligations in universal or near-universal terms, such that entitlement to welfare was not intrinsically related to the social position, the professional history, or – vitally – the gender of its recipients. As a result, in the decades after 1945, many governments began to distribute material

[32] Decree 25.705 (22 October 1948).
[33] See on this process Strang and Chang (1993: 239).

benefits to all citizens, proportionate to need and regardless of military utility. In particular, access to education was typically construed as a universal right which crossed gender and social divides, such that the strategic ideological value of education was diminished.

In these respects, after 1945, national polities constructed social rights in terms that weakened the convergence between welfarism and militarism. World War II clearly intensified the construction of social rights, but these rights were placed on foundations in which militarism lost some effect in framing the bargains that created such rights. From this point, many states began to establish welfare systems that insulated all social groups, to some degree, from extreme material hardship. Most importantly, the weakening of the attachment between welfare and violence meant that welfare states partly lost their historical connection to domestic hostility, and the protection of social rights engendered less lateral conflict in society. After 1945, the move towards broader welfare provision was shaped by the fact that an increasing cross-section of social groups favoured welfarism, so that commitments to material distribution were separated from entrenched political positions at the domestic level. Naturally, this was not an even or uncontested process, and clear fault lines persisted between approaches to welfare as parties at different points on the political spectrum favoured different attitudes to public spending. Yet, after 1945, policies for welfare provision became markedly less incendiary in their impact on lateral social interaction. For this reason, the traditional tendency of welfare states to incubate intense inter-factional conflict was, in part, reduced.

This latter aspect of welfare state formation became perceptible in the fact that, immediately after 1945, political parties that had traditionally represented social groups opposed to welfare investment adopted manifestos that cautiously endorsed welfarism. In Germany and Italy, for example, the first post-1945 elections saw the emergence of Christian Democratic Parties which recruited from interwar right-of-centre constituencies but now supported relatively high social spending.[34] In much of Europe, welfare investment became a policy feature that traversed historically ingrained political fissures, and some commitment to social rights became a general part of the political landscape. Ultimately, many European welfare states were primarily

[34] For example, in West Germany in 1949, the main centre-right party presented its economic plans in the first free elections in the Düsseldorfer Leitsätze, which contained a strong notional commitment to social justice.

built by parties of the moderate right. Whereas after 1918 the fear of communism usually drove conservative parties to the right, after 1945 the same fear typically drove them towards the left. For example, Germany, Austria and Italy developed substantial welfare states after 1945. Parties of the left did not hold highest governmental office in these countries for at least twenty years after their re-foundation. The British welfare state was founded by the Labour Party after 1945, albeit using the Beveridge Report as a template, which had been commissioned by a largely Conservative wartime government. Yet many key social policies in Britain, such as housing and education provisions, were put into effect by the Conservative governments of the 1950s. In France, the welfare state was first established in the radical years of the early Fourth Republic, but its inspirations were partly conservative.[35] Moreover, the French left lost much influence from 1947 and parties of the left had no central governmental role from 1958 to 1981, which did not prevent a rise in social spending.

Significant in this respect is the fact that, over a longer period, the expansion of social spending triggered a more diffuse process of norm formation in many societies, in which patterns of social affiliation became more variable. This meant that democratic constitutions acquired a complex bedrock in society that gradually reinforced the normative individualism that, after 1945, became pronounced in constitutional law. For example, the growth of welfare investment after 1945 typically created a societal conjuncture in which traditional economic organizations lost some of their traditional roles, and individual citizens experienced weakened material dependence on class-based or large sectoral associations. In many settings, this period saw broad social disaffiliation from traditional left-oriented parties as it became clear that material security could be accessed without party activism.[36] At one level, further welfare states tended to stimulate increased membership in professional organizations and trade unions. For example, after 1945, trade union membership increased in most democracies. Yet, at the same time, the function of trade unions became more limited as they were gradually narrowed to bargaining for single constituencies.[37] Because of this, the number of general strikes decreased rapidly, so that collective class mobilization lost

[35] Nord (2012: 24, 188).
[36] See Bartolini (2000: 279–80).
[37] Ritter (1991: 219).

importance as a union activity. In parallel, national societies with strong welfare arrangements developed a fabric in which other collective dependencies were diminished. For example, owing to the rise of welfare spending, many societies entered a condition in which family life and familial reciprocities lost relevance as sources of protection and coercion. In the years after 1945, many national governments developed policies that displaced social power from familial structures, locating familial roles and modes of authority on state-defined public premises. As illustration, the increasing role of national states as distributors of welfare meant that divorce laws could be relaxed, that the standing of women vis-à-vis male family members was transformed and that – later – guarantees for the autonomy and well-being of children were reinforced.[38] Over a longer period, governments that designed welfare states promoted policies regarding sexual rights, which reduced the force of traditional gender roles and sexual identities, often linked to familial and religious expectations.[39] Through the same process, the structural influence of religious organizations was diminished, and the social weakening of the family usually coincided with the reduction in the power of churches.

Such developments brought profound transformation in the role of national governments, in which, both at the vertical and at the lateral level, the historical effects of government integration were modified. As discussed, in the first instance, national states began to acquire form as organizations that reached into social domains traditionally organized by families and religious bodies. In so doing, they dislodged the authority of powerful oligarchies, religious officeholders and other non-political institutions. Initially, national governments did this primarily to impose military duties on individual members of their populations. This formed the basis for the constitutional calculus at the historical core of modern democratic states: vertical integration was required for military purposes, and such integration reduced the role of families and local and religious organizations, transferring basic social duties to the state. After 1945, democratic societies normally experienced an

[38] In the UK, the liberalization of divorce laws began in 1958. These laws provided for payment to ex-wives by former spouses, constructing a welfare order for divorced women. In West Germany, 1971 brought reforms to divorce laws which protected the material well-being of mothers. France saw related reforms in the 1970s.

[39] The legalization of homosexuality occurred in the UK and Germany in the 1960s. In France, homosexuality had been criminalized under Vichy, but not earlier. In the USA, the publication of the Model Penal Code (1962) gave significant impetus to the decriminalization of homosexuality.

exponential intensification of this process. Indeed, governments acquired increased infrastructural power, reaching into a growing number of social domains and forming immediate connections with individual citizens in many different functional domains. By this stage, however, the levelling out of family and religious life around the state was caused by the fact that national governments reduced the dependence of citizens on organizations linked to families and churches, not by enforcing military duties, but by allocating welfare resources directly to individual citizens. Through this, individual citizens entered a relation to state institutions that was based on individual interests and needs, in which the extraction of military force played a reduced (although still not negligible) role. Incrementally, this induced a process of institutional formation and social integration that was diametrically opposed to the developmental logic that first shaped the rise of the modern nation state. After 1945, the convergence of society around national state institutions increased sharply. This was evidenced in rising taxation and public spending and in the extended production and societal penetration of legislation. Yet this convergence took place through a process in which citizens were not, or not primarily, attached to the state because of military imperatives. Instead, the growing distributive role of the state meant that the separation of citizens from collective groupings in society was a largely voluntary or self-interested process, as citizens were integrated into national societies on individual choice-based premises linked to the acquisition of public material support. As mentioned, the individualization of subjects in society had originally been driven by armies or by military organizations that attached local communities to the state, so that societies acquired general form as individual subjects were removed from family milieux and placed in military or semi-military collectives.[40] After 1945, democratic societies usually had the characteristic that social individualization was greatly intensified, and it was sustained by welfare states which established social rights that allowed individual social actors to enter trajectories of integration without re-entering new coercive collectives. Welfare thus became the new substructure for democracy, placing the state on new vertical integrational premises. This replaced military organizations as primary drivers of social integration, and it placed the bargains at the core of democracy onto less conflicted, more individualized foundations.

[40] See discussion at pp. 17–8.

This new mode of welfare-driven democratization also meant that, in many cases, national societies were reconfigured in the lateral dimension, and lines of attachment between different groups were altered. At a fundamental level, as mentioned, the process of individualization in post-1945 constitutional states had the result that social groups became less likely to bargain with governments through class-based organizations. At the same time, social actors became more likely to articulate interests through multiple associations as pathways to rights were opened through a broad spectrum of organizations. The rise of the welfare state coincided with the emergence of more pluralistic movements in society, and it created a social environment in which citizens pursued a variety of individual rights, extending beyond classical interests in political and social rights. Indicatively, by the 1960s, contestation over questions of sexuality and gender status often replaced conflicts specifically attached to social class or ethnicity. By this time, rights relating to practices traditionally covered by non-political organizations – for example, sexuality, the family and reproduction – had become objects of rights-based mobilization. As analysed, the early growth of nation states linked citizens directly to military units, and citizens bargained with governments through organizations that had some military utility, usually creating rights for powerful (male) collectives. As discussed, this often had a militarizing effect on intergroup relations in society, primarily along class-related or ethnic lines. In the longer wake of 1945, societal conflict itself assumed a more individualized character, and the tendency for national societies to divide along relatively binary class fissures was reduced.

Perhaps the most important aspect in such transformation of social affiliations became evident in the field of education. In most post-1945 polities, widening access to education was central to the process in which rights of citizenship were increasingly universalized, and the formation of school systems based in equal entitlements formed a policy commitment even under governments with weaker welfare states. As mentioned, in some cases, educational expansion was tied to developmentalism, and it was linked to military programmes. However, in most democratic societies, some traditional functions of education were modified, and widening access to education had a deep impact on patterns of social formation and integration.

At an essential level, increased access to education coincided with the wider multiplication of social identities that occurred after 1945 as schools and universities became centres in the promotion of new modes of social attachment. The separation of individual subjects from traditional communities was strongly supported by access to education, and education often meant that persons at different social positions were able to move from inherited roles and milieux. Persons obtaining access to higher education were necessarily removed from local organizations and dependencies. At the same time, in the decades after 1945, access to education became strongly (if temporarily) linked to anti-systemic attitudes, and institutions offering higher education became important sites of political protest. Importantly, student radicalization in the 1960s was often attached to questions connected with war; in Germany, student movements focused partly on their parents' complicity in the Nazi regime; in the USA, student activism was directed against the Vietnam War and the draft; in South America, where not suppressed by military regimes, student mobilization was linked to American political and military encroachment. In such cases, increased access to education severed the traditional linkage between military integration and the expansion of education rights, and experiences related to warfare often induced individual radicalization amongst recipients of education rights.[41] In this respect, notably, education also formed a primary driver of patterns of internationalization that became prevalent after 1945. Of course, this occurred in different ways in different regions. Yet the expansion of education after 1945 was a global initiative, and it reflected transnational convergence between subjects in educational environments.[42] Expressions of radical behaviour in universities were widely emulated across national borders, and transnational protest communities developed that connected Paris, Frankfurt, Mexico City and Berkeley. Through this, education became an important means of transnational communication, and universities created cognitive settings that were partly replicated in different countries. As educational expansion coincided with welfare investment, further, societies with higher levels of education tended to create educational environments in which post-traditional identities developed along transnational lines. Across most democracies, for example, the politicization of traditional gender and family roles occurred at roughly the same time, and universities were primary sites for debates on these questions.

[41] In the USA, sociologists reported that most campus activists had upper-middle-class backgrounds (Flacks 1967: 65).

[42] See the classical sociological account of this in Meyer, Ramirez, Rubinson and Boli-Bennett (1977: 251).

In different spheres of welfare provision, the post-1945 era stimulated a societal structure that transformed the original premises of the nation state. As examined, the promotion of social rights was initially very closely attached to military functions. It supported a process of vertical integration that removed persons from traditional communities in society, in part, for military purposes, and it tended to militarize different factions in society. After 1945, however, expanding access to social rights redirected this process. On one hand, it separated rights from military obligations, and it meant that bargaining for rights showed reduced dependency on external military pressures. On the other hand, it modified the intra-societal results of vertical integration. The circulation of social rights continued to weaken traditional attachments in society, but it tended to integrate recipients of social rights in environments in which simple patterns of social polarization were less pronounced.

CHANGING DISCOURSES OF SECURITY

These occurrences revealed a significant change in basic understandings of national security, which formed a central point in social and political organization after 1945. The original development of the modern political system took place as increasing interstate hostility drove the formation of national constitutional law. As discussed, constitutional law was originally based in the allocation of political rights, but, as soon as national constitutions acquired enduring effect, it usually included provisions for social rights. In broad terms, the political and social rights contained in most modern constitutions formed connected parts of a *security constitution*. That is, citizens obtained rights in society as constitutions allowed states to galvanize their societies in face of external security risks, and constitution established rights for citizens because rights were expected to motivate citizens to accept security risks created by interstate rivalry.

This correlation between military security and constitutional ordering was partly reinforced after 1945. In the context of the Cold War, national security often acquired new constitutional importance, and security policies exerted deep impact on the form of national states and the interactions between states and citizens. This was observable across a range of polities in different global positions. Obviously, core states in the Cold War developed institutional architectures and spending programmes in which conventional national security imperatives assumed great force, both domestically and externally. Both the USA and the USSR experienced intensified governmental centralization after 1945 because of their expanding military budgets. Military pressures stimulated technological innovations in both societies that increased levels of governmental control. In both contexts, security pressures defined the internal structures of states. In the USA, this process was solidified in Truman's National Security Act (1947), which connected the armed forces more closely to the executive, creating new resources for domestic surveillance and intelligence. In the aftermath of 1945, further, the USA witnessed a substantial widening of the concept of national security, and the remit of national security policies was extended beyond classical functions of defence.[43] In this period, both in the USA and in other states, a definition of national security was promoted that covered, not only aspects of military defence, but social provision, national development and domestic social control.[44] This altered framing of security coincided, by the late 1950s, with increased American involvement in regime formation outside the USA, notably through NATO and military interventions in Latin America that served American security designs.[45] In fact, a broad concept of national security had been repeatedly articulated in security legislation in Brazil in the late 1930s, as Vargas designed security policies for the suppression of regime opponents.[46] As a result, the classical imperial correlation between external conflicts and internal policy formation was partly replicated in the USA after 1945. Over a longer period, this coincided with increased welfare investment, so that, as in earlier contexts, the national security state and social security state grew side by side in the USA.

In some new states undergoing decolonization, strong emphasis was also placed on national security, and military spending reached high levels. This occurred partly because of external risks, and partly because postcolonial institution building required policies of national integration that conferred central roles on the military. In such contexts, military governments often promoted a distinctive commitment to

[43] In influential research, this has been as seen as a process that first institutionalized national security policies promoting the 'multisectoral, long-term mobilisation' of American society (Buzan and Waever 2003: 283–284).

[44] The use of the term 'national security' is often seen as building on the ideas behind Roosevelt's Social Security Act of 1935 (Neocleous 2006: 375).

[45] See analysis in Leffler (1984: 356). For an important analysis of earlier use of the term to replace conventional concepts of defence, see Schulman (1999: 291).

[46] See pp. 266–7.

social rights, and they endorsed state-led developmentalism as a strategy of national consolidation. Developmentalist states in postcolonial societies were usually formed as political elites attempted to unify national populations around central government bodies by expanding government involvement in industrial production and by strengthening the position of national economies in international systems of competition. In such polities, national security and social security were closely interlinked as governments viewed industrial investment and increased productivity as a precondition for military security and regime stability. Accordingly, many regimes created in Africa from the 1960s promoted developmentalism as a policy priority. The first Charter of the Organization of African Unity stated that one of its purposes was to 'harness the natural and human resources of our continent for the total advancement of our peoples in spheres of human endeavour'. As mentioned, the Nigerian military regime in the 1970s was a strong promoter of developmentalism, especially in education. Military developmentalism became prominent in Latin America at the same time. In Brazil, the military coup of 1964 created a setting in which the military was defined as an agent in the promotion of social rights. One theorist of national security in the Brazilian military defined policies to protect social rights not as 'activities parallel to national security', but as means to 'obtain more security'.[47] In this example, a military regime took shape that presented welfare and military security as overlapping and interdependent policy objectives.

Despite such phenomena, in the longer wake of 1945, the primary emphasis on security as a military phenomenon was mainly confined to states that abandoned democratic constitutionalism. In most democracies, the period after 1945 brought changes in the understanding of security, which partly detached it from its military focus. Many researchers addressing welfare and security have claimed that welfare states deepened national security regimes, extending security concerns into all parts of social life.[48] In certain respects, to be sure, post-1945 welfare states performed functions analogous to or converging with military control, and, as examined, they served to defuse domestic social dissent and to co-opt potentially counter-systemic organizations. In much of post-1945 Europe, welfare state formation coincided with the entry of states into a major international security alliance, NATO,

[47] Pessoa (1971: 317).

[48] See for diverse examples Buzan (1991: 234–235) and Neocleous (2006: 364).

so that social spending and military spending increased together, and the reinforcement of social provision was part of a broad security nexus. Yet, in the longer aftermath of World War II, the construction of welfare democratic regimes led to a diversification in concepts of security, which – in part – removed welfare provision from its historical military premises and reduced the immediate prominence of military considerations in welfare allocation. Through this process, security became a multifocal field in which citizens were able to claim security in an increasing number of social domains in relation to multiple threats.

On one hand, changes in the conception of security became manifest at the legitimational level of government action. The growth of the welfare state was accompanied by a programmatic reorientation amongst national governments and parties, in which political manifestos were partly focused on material distribution. Through this process, governments legitimated themselves through multiple security commitments, in which the provision of military security was merely one, increasingly non-dominant concern amongst a range of security obligations. Through this, rights first generated through national security obligations were rearticulated and placed on complex redefined foundations, so that rights arising from war became structural to peacetime societies. In some post-1945 polities, in fact, campaigns to reduce poverty were compared to military initiatives, so that military security and material security were symbolically linked, and welfare regimes replaced war as the basis of societal solidarity.[49] In some cases, basic ideas of national sovereignty that lay at the heart of government became attached to welfare provision, and governments conceived their sovereignty as the result of cross-class distribution. This was expressed by leading theorists of the post-1945 welfare state. In England, T. H. Marshall argued that the welfare state brought to completion the construction of a society of national citizens. In Sweden, Gunnar Myrdal declared simply: 'Planning is national. It is a manifestation of the nation state, which is everywhere becoming stronger.'[50] This move entailed a significant switch in the construction of sovereignty from defence to welfare, with clear implications for the production of legitimacy.

[49] In 1945, the British Labour Party campaigned for government by claiming that its programme was 'a practical expression' of 'the spirit of Dunkirk and of the Blitz', albeit 'applied to the tasks of peace'.

[50] Myrdal (1960: 130).

On the other hand, changing conceptions of security became more tangible at the interactional interface of government institutions. Historically, as discussed, states had built up their obligations to citizens around bilateral security contracts, in which citizens gained certain rights as members of national security communities linked to military defence. In the longer wake of 1945, these contracts became more strongly focused on questions of individual security in which the aim of mobilizing society around national security prerogatives became less pronounced – although surely not unimportant. Through this tendency, the essential comprehension of security was altered, and security became strongly tied to preserving the preconditions of individual autonomy. At a broad level, government policies in new welfare states were committed to preserving 'social security', which implied the securitization of individual people against economic hardship. In most post-1945 democracies, government policies also placed emphasis on 'income security', which meant that governments assumed some obligation to insulate members of society against catastrophic loss or diminution of income. Uniformly, welfare states also provided increased 'age security' to reduce the loss of individual self-reliance in face of imminent death. Pension reforms were a widespread feature of emerging welfare states, regardless of the structural capacity of the state. For example, important pensions benefits were secured in India in 1952. Most importantly, investment in public education was closely connected to new concepts of security, as laws to widen access to education endowed a larger sector of society with enhanced capacities for individual choice making and for flexible career orientation. Education was clearly expanded as a primary means to offer individual persons improved security options in their exposure to social contingencies.[51] Through these processes, democratic states began to arrange a spectrum of security instruments in which the complex securitization of individual persons, traversing multiple social domains, became a dominant factor. At the core of this process was a deep trajectory of social individualization in which single persons were released from collective protection systems (families, churches, unions) and the state legitimated itself by softening experiences of insecurity caused by this process. This expansion of state functions necessarily meant the government executives engaged with citizens in a wider range of activities in multiple roles related to multiple insecurities. As a result, governments

[51] One excellent early sociological analysis of welfare state formation underlines the deep 'connection between education and security' (Kaufmann 1973: 351).

interacted with citizens on a more individualized basis, and this proximity led to a changing legal construction of the terms of this interaction. As mentioned, in many societies, this process coincided with the formalization of administrative law, and, as state competences expanded, executive agents addressed citizens as persons endowed with subjective rights.

These changes in security provision also involved a moment of deep redirection in the basic process of modern sovereign state construction. Historically, the growth of state functions had been integrally connected to warfare and to the provision of military security against external actors. Through the development of welfare states, state expansion was incrementally attached to the provision of security for individual persons in a range of social environments and in face of many causes of insecurity. One defining consequence of this alteration was that the lines of articulation between state and citizens changed and the social affiliations created by governmental actions acquired a new character. As discussed, interactions between states and governments had historically tended to press citizens into collective memberships. Above all, governmental engagement with citizens had constructed citizens as members of nations bound together by strong national loyalties. But, as a secondary feature, the concentration of social affiliations around nationhood had tended to split national societies into hostile social groups (classes or ethnicities), the antagonism between which was usually inflamed by the military emphasis of citizenship. Indeed, under states that promoted external security at the expense of individual security, collective organizations attached to class interests necessarily acquired broad responsibilities. In such contexts, individual security depended to a large degree on the membership of citizens in collective organizations not controlled by the state – such as families, religious organizations and trade unions. As examined, this frequently resulted in intense lateral militarization, often destabilizing the state itself. Through the construction of welfare states, governments expanded their functions in society, assuming deepened roles in many spheres. In so doing, they began to isolate individual persons as recipients of security, addressing the individual person as a subject exposed to multiple risks. This meant that governments constructed more immediate relations between public agencies and individual persons, filling the gaps left by traditional collective bodies with protective security functions. In addressing multiple insecurities, governments accepted obligations that single organizations could not perform, and they placed themselves in direct relation to social subjects in many life-spheres. The reduction of personal insecurity became the essential premise for the increased social role of the state, which was discharged in diffuse individualized fashion. The initial formation of states with attributes of sovereignty had begun as states created security constitutions to mobilize citizens for war. The formation of sovereign states approached a new level of stability as states developed alternative, multifocal security constitutions concentrated on protecting individual citizens from unbearable personal risk. As states established their sovereignty through welfare-based definitions of security, they weakened lateral militarism in society and reinforced their own sovereign foundations.

Critical observers of the post-1945 welfare state often argued that it distorted the essential quality of the modern state and eroded the fundamental constitutional premises of state sovereignty. In the FRG, for example, Ernst Forsthoff argued from a conservative standpoint that, if formed as a welfare state, the state was simply 'instrumentalized' by social groups seeking a share of the resources which it distributed.[52] On this account, the privileged position accorded to collective organizations such as trade unions and employers' associations in the bargaining systems supporting national welfare systems undermined the formal sovereignty of the state, and it deprived the state of its authentic character as the embodiment of overarching societal needs. By the 1960s, a similar view appeared across the political spectrum as observers on the left defined the welfare state as a clearing house for group interests which could not give expression to the sovereign will of the people.[53] By contrast, an alternative critical view of the welfare state eventually emerged amongst more libertarian groups. By the 1970s, a body of conservative reflection on the welfare state emerged in the USA and Europe that identified the welfare state with a crisis of individualism, arguing that welfare policies weakened individual self-reliance, falsely compensated people for their own deficiencies and reduced vital economic liberties.[54] Across this spectrum, it was argued that the welfare state lacked legitimacy either because it imposed a false particularism on the state or because it eroded the particularism of society.

Each such line of argument is deeply inaccurate. In most societies, the welfare state augmented both the sovereignty of state institutions and the individualization of society as a whole. In key respects, the rise

[52] Forsthoff (1968: 163).

[53] Habermas (1990: 292).

[54] This line of thought is well characterized as based in the principle that the 'power of government to limit the choice field of the individual . . . is the single power source in society to be feared' (Kuenne 1993: 47).

of the welfare state was an institution-building process in which interactions between governments and citizens were transformed. At the core of this, first, was an orientation of government policy towards *multiple securitization*, so that security legislation was increasingly focused on the needs of individual subjects. Through the rise of the welfare state, state agencies penetrated much more deeply into society than previously, and they increasingly attached their functions to individual persons. Through this, states extracted legitimacy from personal exchanges, they addressed persons outside collective interaction systems, and their tendency to induce deep lateral conflicts in society became weaker. As such, the growth of the welfare state formed a core element in the formation of an individualistic constitution, both for government and for society. At the same time, the growth of the welfare state reinforced the sovereign capacities of the state as its promotion of individualization meant that it could perform acts of vertical integration without generating lateral violence, and it regulated societal problems in relatively controlled form. In short, societal individualism and the construction of the state as a sovereign organization emerged as two elements in the same process. The increased sovereignty of government was acquired, unprecedentedly, through a relatively robust partition between the military and the social functions of government, through which individual security prevailed over military security as the primary line of communication between state and citizen. As mentioned, the formation post-1945 welfare states remained linked to a wider interstate security constitution. However, the welfare state placed individual interactions between state and citizens on new foundations so that violence between internal social groups was reduced and the translation of external security objectives into extreme internal coercion became less frequent.

WELFARE STATES AND INTERNAL COLONIZATION

Historically, many societies developed extensive welfare states at the same time in which they moved away imperialism, so that welfare organizations often occupied an institutional and symbolic space created by the decline of imperialism. In the UK, the construction of the welfare state coincided with the granting of independence to India, and its expansion accompanied the decolonization of Africa. As discussed, France engaged in two major imperial wars between 1945 and 1960, but the building of the French welfare state largely paralleled the dissolution of the French Empire. In Germany and Italy, welfare policies became key commitments after the catastrophic collapse of their empire-building endeavours in the 1930s. In most European societies, in short, welfare states were created as primary governmental policies were directed away from foreign expansion towards domestic social investment. In most postcolonial systems, further, early welfare policies were introduced at the beginning of independence. This was seen in India, where a commitment to welfare policies was expressed before the constitution was enacted.[55] This was also expressed in the developmental policies implemented in other new states.

In some respects, the growth of welfare states filled this post-imperial space at a strict legitimational level. As mentioned, some post-1945 constitutions specifically promoted an idea of citizenship based in material security as an alternative to the military constructions of citizenship that had previously prevailed. However, the growth of welfare states also filled this post-imperial space at a more functional or geographical level. In some cases, the rise of welfarism brought towards completion patterns of national territorial integration that had originated under imperialism, so that welfare states acquired intra-societal functions analogous to those previously performed by empires. Typically, the rise of welfare states increased the fiscal capacities of national governments, and it meant that public spending conducted by national government increased relative to that of regional or local governments. In this regard, welfare states directly replicated the earlier processes of internal institutional convergence initiated by investment in national armies. In fact, in polities such as Germany, Brazil, India and the USA, the historical unification of federal systems had necessitated extreme military violence. After 1945, welfare investment became a core line of communication between national governments and regions, and shared understandings of social rights connected different parts of national polities to governmental centres. In some polities with overseas empires, commitment to welfare immediately replaced commitment to expansion as a primary source of internal obligation connecting governmental centres and regional administrations within domestic society. For example, in the UK, the welfare state quickly developed as a shared nation-building project, binding together different subnational regions, and it replaced the symbolic functions of the British

55 See the Employees' State Insurance Act (1948).

empire before 1945.[56] In polities formed by imperialism, such as Germany, welfare spending and the promotion of social rights formed a core linkage between government and regions. Although, in the FRG, social regulation and educational policy were partly devolved to individual states, the federal government set basic levels of social spending, and, over a longer period, federal institutions stipulated minimum thresholds of well-being for national citizens. This was supported by high-level judicial rulings that established a constitutional duty for the government to provide welfare payments.[57] In the USA, the development of welfare policies occurred in a context in which social integration through the army remained high, so that integration linked to welfare was not fully separate from integration through the military. However, after 1945, the federal government acted as a primary provider of funds for social welfare projects, and, by 1950s, the federal government initiated new policies in medical insurance, disability compensation and pension reforms.[58] Importantly, across polity-specific variations, after 1945, the grammar of social rights became a framework in which national governments interacted with subnational bodies, and public policies were phrased in relation to social rights. This period saw a general growth in the share of national budgets allotted to central government.

In this range of cases, the growth of the welfare state after 1945 again formed a process in which the structural trajectory at the core of modern society was realigned. Integrational functions traditionally attached to the military were transferred to organizations with responsibilities for implementing welfare and educational policies. In many cases, the consolidation of welfare states brought towards completion histories of institutional centralization and territorial occupation that commenced as imperial projects. As mentioned, central to this redirection was a focus on individual citizens, not – or not primarily – as potential soldiers, but as recipients of social provision. This meant that the basic construction of citizenship around which states had legitimated their functions was partly reconfigured. As a result, state control was asserted through a legal learning process in which integrational force was directed away from military organizations towards individualized subjectivities. Before this process, states had asserted

[56] This view is widely expressed in the UK, and it is solidly supported in Béland and Lecours (2008: 95–105).

[57] 24.06.1954 (BVerwGE 1, 159).

[58] See Berkowitz and McQuaid (1988: 147).

basic control of their societies through techniques of extraction that originated in military pressures, determined by internal and external imperial forces, and they possessed some similarities to occupation systems. As in other aspects of the post-1945 legal order, the rise of the welfare state altered the basic *occupation constitution* in which governments previously operated.

CONCLUSION

Naturally, it is not possible to extract a universal model of constitutional formation from the analysis presented here. Yet after 1945, welfare states and constitutional democracies usually developed together. Few polities stabilized constitutional democracy without embarking on a process in which they softened their propensities for civil conflict by directing their constituencies towards a corpus of social rights. Such rights typically were established on a design that generated legitimacy by placing governmental functions on relatively pacified foundations oriented towards individualized protections. Like the formation of political rights after 1945, dialectically, such constitutions preserved rights that had been historically constructed by war. Social rights originated in the military bargains examined earlier in this chapter, but, after 1945, the generalization of such rights was a largely peaceful process, and it was underpinned by experiences of societal individualization, which were themselves supported by social rights. Social rights were clearly intensified and generalized by World War II, but they were secured in a legal apparatus in which their direct attachment to warfare was weakened. In this respect, welfare systems formed an important part of a system of *world law* in which democratic polities ordered their functions. The first dimension of world law was formed by international human rights law, which pacified the basic form of government. The second dimension of world law was formed by social welfare law, which pacified interactions within national societies. In both dimensions, world law was constructed through a process in which states built their legal orders through war and military bargains, but they located these legal orders and bargains onto new premises, distinct from war. In each respect, states altered the relation between the inside and the outside of the societies that they governed, so that, through world law, states abandoned their status as military actors in their own societies.

CHAPTER EIGHT

THE OCCUPATION CONSTITUTION III

Constitutions without War

In the period after 1945, it remained a defining political experience that constitutions were created in conditions shaped by warfare, frequently combining the effects of interstate war and civil war. After World War II, as discussed, military actors often retained powerful roles in establishing constitutional law, and many constitutions reflected interests brought to social prominence during warfare. Despite this, many constitutions that emerged after 1945 proved more effective than earlier constitutions in managing the violence to which they owed their origins, and they stabilized constitutional rights in a form that diminished democratic volatility. In the longer aftermath of 1945, then, constitution making began to acquire features in which the military dimensions of constitutional law receded. By the late 1970s, a fifth wave of constitution making commenced in which constitutions emerged in social environments in which the military had only limited significance. By the 1980s, many polities in Europe, Latin America and Africa entered a process of constitutional restructuring in which, unprecedentedly, the impact of military pressures on governmental form was restricted. As discussed in this chapter, this does not imply that security concerns were without constitutional influence in these transitions. However, security prerogatives defined constitutional form in new ways, and war lost some significance as a direct determinant of constitutional integration.

This reconfiguration of constitutional law occurred in different ways, and, in some cases, military organizations continued to influence constitutional formation. Many democratic transitions in Latin America were transitions away from military dictatorships. This began with transitions in Ecuador and Peru but culminated in Argentina in 1983 and Brazil in 1985. The Brazilian constitution of 1988 acquired particular prominence amongst the transitional constitutions written at this time, and it charted an occasionally ambiguous path towards full civilian rule. In Colombia, a new constitution was created in 1991, in a more conventional military environment. This constitution was designed to end the ongoing civil conflict which had intermittently been the dominant feature of Colombian society since the nineteenth century. By the 1980s, the Colombian conflict had resulted in an enduring state of emergency. Although the drafting of the new constitution was initiated by popular movements, mainly groups operating at universities, one of its functions was to establish peace between rival groups, serving as an intergroup accord both for democratic institution building and for social pacification.

In the constitutions written in Eastern Europe following 1989 and the dissolution of the Soviet Union in 1991, military actors were typically less immediately engaged in the construction of constitutional systems. This statement should not in any way diminish the importance of military conflicts that occurred in the Soviet sphere of influence in the 1990s. For instance, Tajikistan experienced deep civil war through the 1990s. Afghanistan repeatedly saw civil war after the withdrawal of the Soviet army. In this same period, smaller wars occurred in Georgia and other parts of the Caucasus and then a larger civil war was fought in Chechnya. At this time, further military circumstances immediately affected some constitutions, especially after the fragmentation of Yugoslavia. Yugoslavia had a distinct position in Eastern Europe as the state had originally been founded, with limited Soviet influence, by internal military actors, which meant that it possessed strong independent military capacities. However, a unitary system of citizenship had not developed in post-1945 Yugoslavia, and the government was supported by an ethno-federalist order. These factors meant that Yugoslavia was susceptible to violent fragmentation during the geopolitical restructuring that started in the 1980s. In this environment, the constitutions of Croatia, Bosnia and Serbia were marked by a background of military violence, and they reflected a post-imperial civil war shaped by the distant collapse of the Ottoman and the more recent waning of Soviet influence. In Serbia, the first post-1989 constitution impeded democratization and blocked the move towards independence amongst the constituent republics of Yugoslavia. In Croatia, the 1990 constitution, introduced while Croatia was not yet independent, linked constitutional citizenship to the 'millennial national identity of the Croatian nation' and led to secession from Yugoslavia. In much of Yugoslavia, the emergence of a constitutionally autonomous definition of citizenship induced extreme interethnic violence. In Bosnia and Herzegovina, constitutional law was closely linked to international state-building initiatives, as constitutional rules for ethnic coexistence after the Bosnian War were prescribed in the Dayton Accords (1995). In this setting, the allocation of constitutional offices and functions was internationally regulated, leading to a highly diffuse and decentralized governance system. This system was based in strong partitions between ethnic groups, and it provided for a legal order in which international human rights law had direct effect and some judges were appointed by international authorities.

Nonetheless, the case of the former Yugoslavian states was an exception to the general constitutional pattern in the Eastern European transitions, and most constitutions were created without extreme violence. Distinctively, although some constitutional transitions were shadowed by acute military violence, military conflict was not typically the cause of constitution making or of constitutional claims to citizenship. This period saw an exponential rise in the global quantity of democracies, and few constitutional transitions in Latin America and Europe in the 1980s and 1990s were the immediate results of war.

In parallel, from the early 1990s onwards, many African countries experienced processes of democratization, often temporary, and here too the constitutional role of military organizations was less pronounced than in earlier settings. In addressing this, nuance is again required. Clearly, many constitutions implemented in Africa in the 1990s reflected military backgrounds and directives. In the early 1990s, the constitutions introduced in Benin and Ghana were initiated by military leaderships. The South African constitution of 1996 evolved, as discussed, against a background of civil conflict which required social pacification. In 1999, Nigeria saw a constitutional transition away from military rule in which the redefinition of the political functions of the army was a tortuous process. The 1999 constitution was introduced by military decree and partly drafted by military officials. In this context, continued unrest and insurgency, subsequently linked to Boko Haram, meant that society persisted in a state of localized civil war and lateral conflicts between militia units continued in different regions. This reflected a familiar pattern of democratization in which the reinforcement of democracy led to increased violence. In addition, some constitutions created in the 1990s simply established a new legal basis for extended authoritarian rule; this was most striking in the 1995 constitution of Ethiopia. These facts mean that strong caveats are required in descriptions of African constitutional transition as peaceful events. Yet from the 1990s on, constitutions acquired an enduring reality in some African states, and this coincided with the separation of governments from military organizations. As a rule, post-colonial constitutions created in the 1960s were soon replaced by military governments or other dictatorial regimes in which control of governmental power was mainly alternated by military coup or by changing relations between military factions. From the 1990s, decisions regarding the allocation of powers in government were removed from the army in some African polities, and popular elections became a frequent means for establishing the authority to rule.

Despite the reduced role of military agents, constitutions created from the 1980s did not renounce the essential design of constitutional law formed after 1945, and they served to detach constitutional law from its primary military origins. Many constitutions were constructed around the principle that national societies exist in a hybrid condition between peace and war, and that external norms were required to pacify national society. In different ways, constitutions that developed in democratization processes beginning in the 1980s again enacted elements of an occupation constitution in which the ordering of military violence within domestic political arenas formed the precondition for democracy and its legitimation. In different regions, the use of international law as a system in which military impulses in national democracy were dialectically both preserved and controlled became widespread. On one hand, constitutions created at this point usually secured electoral rights for all citizens, and they implemented measures to prevent governments from undermining political rights. Frequently, however, new constitutions were created in security environments that altered the historical attachment between political rights and security imperatives. Many democratizing states constructed their legitimacy by aligning their actions to an international normative order, and external principles became vital to constitution making. In different settings, in fact, states promoted such alignment to external norms partly because this allowed them to reorganize their security functions, forming part of a deep security strategy. Quite generally, in the constitution-making époque starting in the 1980s, the role of national security commitments in constructing governmental legitimacy was altered, concrete military bargains between citizens and government lost some force as a source of constitutional law, and international military law became an overlying meta-constitution for national polities. In certain cases, this resulted in the creation of constitutions that observed national government as a system of occupation, and which directed the source of legitimacy away from national society to pacify the functions of governments.

HUMAN RIGHTS LAW AND IMAGINED WARFARE

By the 1980s, most states that developed democratic constitutions were influenced by regional human rights systems. In most cases, democracies proved enduring when governments committed to the recognition of human rights law, and acceptance of such law became the most reliable indicator of democratic stability. Initially, the assimilation of human rights norms in national constitutions was strongly shaped by security imperatives, and human rights law acted, either directly or indirectly, as part of a transnational constitution of military violence. Indeed, in some contexts, human rights law assumed a clear military function as compliance with such law allowed states to change the security system to which they were aligned.

At one level, human rights law imposed an immediate constitution of violence on some transitional societies. For example, some Eastern European states had experienced the protracted imposition of martial law before 1989, so that the association between constitution making and the end of military repression was very strong. Indicatively, in Poland, martial law had been imposed in 1981, and this shaped the path towards democracy. In summer 1985, a long meeting was held at the Polish Academy of Science, which proposed that international law should be more formally integrated in Polish law.[1] As early as 1989, constitutional changes were introduced in Poland that placed limits on governmental powers to enforce exceptional legislative orders.[2] A declaration of early 1992 stated symbolically that the 1981 enforcement of martial law had been illegal. Polish ratification of the European Convention on Human Rights (ECHR) in 1993 was shaped by this context. Later, the Polish constitution of 1997 contained strict rules concerning the subordinate position of the army (Art. 26). It also

[1] Daranowski (1989: 41).
[2] Dz.U. 1989 nr 19 poz. 101.

included important articles covering emergency laws. Article 228(6) placed limits on the legal and institutional changes that governments could enforce in states of emergency.[3]

In parallel, the transition to democracy after 1989 in Eastern Europe was very strongly linked to the ambition amongst transitioning states to enter a geopolitical setting outside the Soviet sphere of influence. In such cases, transitions were also motivated by the long-term policy of seeking European Union membership. For both purposes, the assimilation of human rights law became part of a trajectory of strategic repositioning. European Union membership required membership in the Council of Europe, such that recognition of international human rights law served as a precondition for economic realignment. Moreover, human rights law was expressly associated with changing security regimes before the transitions commenced. For example, interstate bodies in the Warsaw Pact system had begun to signal commitment to human rights compliance in interstate and domestic action before 1989, to deescalate conflict with NATO.[4] To this degree, human rights law formed part of a transnational security constitution that accompanied transitions; notably, states in the Warsaw Pact that transitioned after 1989 experienced major structural change with low levels of violence. During transition, then, most post-Communist states showed a willingness to comply with the ECHR and citizens were immediately constructed as persons with a legal personality that could reach beyond national level. Indeed, some governments, notably in Hungary, achieved structural reform by simply aligning their constitutions to regional human rights norms so that citizens acquired democratic rights directly from international law.[5] Through these processes, states that converted to rights-based democratic constitutionalism also utilized human rights law to campaign for membership in pro-USA security organizations. Indicatively, the main Western security organization, NATO, embarked on a (notional) process of redefinition at this time, and it included the protection of human rights amongst its collective security functions. This was expressed in the London Declaration (1990), in the new Strategic Concept agreed in Rome in 1991 and later in the Founding Act of 1997, which was intended to

[3] One commentator observes that rules regarding the state of emergency belonged to the 'most important' questions addressed by the authors of this constitution (Eckhardt 2012: 63). This article extended provisions for the state of war in the 1935 constitution of Poland (Art. 79(2)). For analysis, see Mażewski (2010: 256–257).

[4] Bílý (2022: 367).

[5] See p. 460.

deepen cooperation between Russia and NATO. In 1995, American policy advisors advocated NATO membership for former Soviet satellite states because this would help strengthen democratic institutions and elevate transnational protection for human rights.[6]

In each respect, human rights law formed part of a new security system. In this system, human rights law reproduced developments after 1945 as governmental orientation towards human rights law meant that basic elements of national constitutional law were detached from national political decisions. However, after 1989, human rights law was used to create democracies in societies where largely there had been no war and the typical preconditions of constitutional formation were not organically manifest. To some degree, international security directives acquired surrogacy power in defining national governmental systems, and human rights law created an international security constitution in which explicit bargains between governments and citizens over national security agreements no longer generated constitutional norms. For many states, the recognition of individual rights opened a quick route to full constitutional autonomy, which governments accepted as part of a regional security switch. This meant that military pressures retained their traditional force in driving processes of democratic individualization. However, it also meant that democracy was severed from its historical origin in military experience and resultant vertical integration. Indicatively, in locations formerly subject to Soviet rule where governments were not integrated in new security communities, democracy remained unconsolidated and military pressures reinforced authoritarianism. For example, under President Karimov, Uzbekistan adopted a policy of military balancing or non-alliance which formed the cornerstone for a highly repressive governmental system largely focused on maintaining internal security.

In Latin America, the situation was rather different, and human rights law had less explicit security functions. However, the states that embarked on democratic transitions in the 1980s were gradually encased in a system of norms for the management of violence, and this altered their basic constitutional design.

The onset of the transitions in Latin America coincided with the consolidation of the Inter-American Human Rights system. This human rights system had originally been represented by the Inter-American Commission on Human Rights, which was first founded in

[6] MccGwire (1998: 24).

a period of relative democratic consolidation (1959). This system soon lost traction, partly because its establishment coincided with the Cuban revolution, which initiated intensified US intervention across Latin America. Yet this system was later reconsolidated through the creation of the Inter-American Court of Human Rights in 1979, charged with enforcing the American Convention on Human Rights, which was written in 1969 and took effect in 1978. The Inter-American Court had varying outcomes for democratic formation. At one level, it ascribed general prominence to human rights norms, which served as a stimulus for democratic formation across the region. Indicatively, the end of military rule in Argentina in 1983 was partly the outcome of transnational mobilization around human rights law, drawing impetus from the reinforcement of the inter-American system. After 1983, Raoul Alfonsín's government in Buenos Aires legitimated itself through reference to human rights law, and external human rights law partly replaced the military as the legitimating pillar of governmental authority.[7] More specifically, the Inter-American Court began to hear contentious cases in the mid-1980s, and its caseload increased through the broadening process of constitutional transition. Accordingly, many Latin American polities on a trajectory of democratic reorientation were subject to critical scrutiny by the court as their constitutional orders were formulated and entrenched. As discussed later in this Chapter, early rulings of the court often addressed the abuse of power by militaries. Through this process, individual citizens began to acquire a conjoined legal personality, and they assumed rights both at the national level, frequently before national constitutions had been drafted, and at the international level, under the jurisdiction of the Inter-American Court.

Across Latin America, the role of international human rights law in supplanting militarized governments showed striking variations, and military officials performed different roles during transition. With distinctions, however, constitutions created in Latin America from the 1980s fit the model of the occupation constitution, and they reflected the sense that national societies could not be fully separated from military zones. In key respects, constitutions established in Latin America in the 1980s and 1990s were defined by the thick convergence of national constitutional law and international military law in which

[7] Alfonsín was a member of the Permanent Assembly for Human Rights that existed through the dictatorship. This Assembly then played a prominent role in prosecuting military crimes.

a stratum of international law was constructed as the basis for democracy. In each case, this was supported by the assumption that state agents engaged in warlike activities in their internal and external functions, such that the basic construction of democracy required a military constitution.

In Brazil, the military retained a position of influence during the early period of democratization after 1985, so that the formation of a constitutional system for the army was subject to certain limits. In fact, Brazilian military leaders were protected from punitive legal sanction after the end of the military rule, and the immunity of military officials was carefully preserved. The first move towards transition had been initiated under the military regime and it broadly coincided with the passing of a pre-emptive Amnesty Law (1979), which, at that time, was applied both to military officials and to some political exiles and regime opponents. This law created a basis for democratization; it meant that military leaders were prepared to engage in democratic reform on condition that they would not be retroactively indicted for criminal acts perpetrated during the military dictatorship. This law was not removed from the statute book, and legislative attempts to suspend it were struck down by the Supreme Court as late as 2010.[8] Importantly, in the 1988 constitution (Art. 142), the Brazilian military was assigned internal duties for protecting law and order. Despite this, the partial recognition of a right to truth for victims of military crimes was recognized in 1995.[9] By 2008, human rights programmes implemented by the government facilitated investigation into military abuses. In 2011–12, a truth commission was established to investigate crimes committed during the military regime.

In Chile, Pinochet's military system, created by coup in 1973, survived in part after 1988–90, and the regime was not ended by a full constitutional transition. Amnesty legislation was introduced in 1978 by Pinochet and partly integrated in the 1980 constitution, as questions of amnesty were placed under the authority of the Senate (Art. 62). Although amnesty laws initially found judicial support, the Supreme Court qualified the validity of amnesty provisions in 1998, using the Geneva Conventions to support this. The court argued that the military regime had formed a state of war, creating a strong presumption in favour of state liability, which triggered the internal application of

[8] ADPF 153 (*Federal Council of the Order of Attorneys of Brazil v. President of the Republic*) (29 April 2010).

[9] Law 9.140 (4 December 1995).

international humanitarian law.[10] Formally, the amnesty laws were not fully rescinded. Eventually, however, in 2004, provisions in the constitution that safeguarded military personnel were modified through the use of international laws governing warfare. At this point, the Supreme Court invoked the Geneva Conventions to overturn some existing impunity provisions and authorized the prosecution of certain crimes committed under military rule.[11] In Uruguay, the military regime ended in 1985, and amnesty laws covering some regime crimes were passed in 1986, which were not fully revoked until 2011.[12] In 2000, a lower court used international law to establish an imperative for the government to investigate crimes committed under the military regime.[13] Amnesty laws were then declared unconstitutional by the Supreme Court in 2009.[14] Such rulings often addressed cases of forced disappearance, which were observed as acts of war in which both victim and perpetrator were placed outside recognized legal structures.

In Argentina, the transition of the 1980s occurred against a background in which the armed forces were more fully discredited as the number of violations under the military regime was higher than in neighbouring states. In Argentina, as mentioned, democratization was strongly propelled by international organizations which used international norms to mobilize opposition to the military. At the beginning of the transition, international human rights law formed the basis for a policy of concerted prosecution of military leaders. Amnesty provisions were introduced by the military government in 1983 and then suspended after the end of the regime later in the same year. These provisions were partially reinstated in 1986, and they were annulled again in 2003. Through these variations, however, rights-based accountability assumed deep legitimational importance in the process of institutional redirection. By 1994, important constitutional amendments had incorporated Argentina's obligations under international treaties directly in national constitutional law, which meant that amnesty laws could be challenged on grounds provided by international human rights law. Ultimately, the Supreme Court ruled that amnesty

[10] Rol No 469–98 (9 September 1998).
[11] Rol No 517–2004 (17 November 2004). See analysis in Lafontaine (2005: 470).
[12] Law 18831 (27 October 2011).
[13] Almeida de Quinteros Maria del Carmen c/Poder Ejecutivo (Ministerio de Defensa Nacional), Amparo, Ficha 216/99 (10 May 2000).
[14] My analysis here follows Mallinder (2016: 652–654).

laws were unconstitutional.[15] This followed legislation of 2003 that outlawed amnesties. This law was flanked by legislation that imposed a new regulatory order on the military.

At a manifest level, such innovations imposed legal accountability on politicians in military dictatorships by establishing principles of criminal liability for military agents. Decisions to revoke amnesty laws were typically enforced to ensure that all actors in society, including all bearers of public authority, were subject to uniform legal norms. However, such decisions also possessed important constitutional implications. One of their implications was that domestic society should be constructed in analogy to an arena of military conflict. As in earlier cases, laws abolishing impunity for military officials reflected an understanding of national governments as entities with a certain proximity to occupation regimes in which military conflict and civil war were fluidly interrelated. Indicatively, in the 2004 ruling of the Chilean Supreme Court that overruled earlier amnesty laws, it was indicated that, from 1973 to 1989/90, Chilean society should be observed legally as a militarized zone.[16] In Pinochet's coup, on this analysis, the army had used military instruments to take hold of the means of government, and, in so doing, it had initiated an internal armed conflict. This suggested that, in the face of military rule, international laws of war must acquire immediate effect, and such laws were enforceable against actors engaged in the internal armed conflict. On this basis, the court declared that some provisions of the Geneva Conventions, especially Common Article 3, could be used to suspend immunity in cases of grave breaches of international humanitarian law, even by agents of domestic government. In Argentina, the primary judgment in favour of the suspension of amnesty laws had similar implications. This ruling was supported by the assertion that, owing to the constitutional reforms of 1994, a 'necessary connection between internal law and international humanitarian law' existed in Argentina, and that Argentine public law contained 'a constitutionalized humanitarian law'.[17] This ruling placed limits on the power of the government to issue amnesties for violations of such law.[18] In both settings, the pattern of constitutional reorganization initiated in the 1980s created a diction of legitimacy which

[15] Argentine Supreme Court, Simón, Julio Héctor y otros s/ privación ilegítima de la libertad, etc. Causa N° 17.768 (14 June 2005).

[16] Rol No 517–2004 (17 November 2004).

[17] Simón, Julio Héctor y otros, p. 156.

[18] Simón, Julio Héctor y otros, p. 254.

literally accepted the self-understanding of military dictatorships, beginning in the 1960s. As examined, military rulers in Latin America declared that they were actors in global war, and that they were at war in or with their own societies. Following the collapse of the military regimes, legal rulings that used humanitarian law to suspend amnesty agreements endorsed this extended construction of war. Such rulings accepted the convergence between intra-societal and international military conflict as a principle to establish accountability for members of a peacetime government, essentially constructing domestic society as a war zone. This meant that violent actors could not hide behind national law and that the differentiation between the inside and the outside of national society lost legal force.

These constructions were not exclusive to national courts. In parallel, the principle that national government could be subject to laws regulating military occupation was reinforced by judicial bodies attached to the American human rights system. To explain this, it is important to underline the fact that the main judicial organ of the American system, the Inter-American Court of Human Rights in San José, oversees implementation of the American Convention on Human Rights in states under its jurisdiction. Accordingly, this court does not have strict responsibility for the enforcement of humanitarian law or laws of armed conflict. As in other jurisdictions, the distinction between human rights law and humanitarian law is essential to the functions of the court, as Art. 62(3) of the American Convention clearly limits the functions of the Court to the interpretation and application of the Convention. Many societies in which the court has authority experienced intergroup conflict or violent military intervention in government. However, few experienced manifest states of war. As a result, the court is – in essence – a peacetime court intended to regulate interactions between public agencies and citizens in non-exceptional social conditions, under the sovereign force of national polities. In some contexts, nonetheless, the court developed lines of jurisprudence that constructively interweave human rights law and international humanitarian law. In some rulings, it applied humanitarian law as a *lex specialis* to ensure that exceptional circumstances involving intra-societal hostility between military or quasi-military actors did not lead to the depletion of human rights protections.[19] One observer claims that, from circa 2000, the Inter-American Court

[19] This theory has been advanced in Gárate (2016: 340).

became an 'indirect mechanism' for the enforcement of international humanitarian law as part of domestic legal systems.[20]

In cases concerning states in which a condition of de facto belligerency exists – for example, Colombia – the Inter-American Court expanded the scope of its jurisprudence to give effect, in specified cases, to principles of international humanitarian law.[21] This is addressed more extensively later in this chapter.[22] Even in societies where there was no manifest belligerency, however, the court devised a system of human rights law that construed some societies as existing in an indeterminate condition of military conflict, with some proximity to warfare. In circumstances of this kind, the court promoted a constitutional structure based in human rights to address acts of military organizations and to regulate exchanges of a military nature. In so doing, the court used human rights law to provide remedies in contexts close to warfare, grafting together human rights law and humanitarian law to form a sui generis legal order applicable to the grey zones between war and peace.[23]

Indicatively, the revocation of amnesty laws that occurred in parts of Latin America through and after the 1990s was strongly supported by jurisprudence of the Inter-American Court. The earliest cases heard by the court in the 1980s gave rise to the insistence that states had a duty to punish perpetrators of military violence.[24] Later, the Inter-American Commission began to address specific instances in which governments had issued amnesties for human rights abusers, notably in *Mendoza et al. v. Uruguay* (1992). This question was then taken up by the Inter-American Court, which, incrementally, placed limits on the power of governments to establish impunity for crimes under military regimes. Initially, the court focused on cases in which military violence had been unpunished because politicians in military regimes had issued 'self-amnesties' – that is, laws that pre-emptively stipulated that their actions could not create causes of action following regime change. In such early cases, the court made a clear distinction between amnesties of this kind and amnesty laws commonly accepted as preconditions for

[20] Ibáñez (2016: 197).

[21] See an early example of this in *Las Palmeras v. Colombia* (Judgment 4 February 2000). Here, the Colombian state submitted objections that the court was not authorized to apply humanitarian law. The court accepted restrictions on its authority but stated that human rights law and humanitarian law may converge to form a unified international 'corpus juris' (para. 7).

[22] See pp. 427–8.

[23] For broad discussion of this approach, see Burgorgue-Larsen and Úbeda de Torres (2011).

[24] *Velásquez-Rodríguez v. Honduras* (1988).

peaceful democratization.[25] Subsequently, the court restricted the validity of amnesty laws more broadly, which it construed as obstructions to the application of core rights set out in the American Convention. For example, in a 2001 case against Peru, the court decided that amnesty laws exonerating perpetrators of state-sponsored military massacres contravened Convention provisions regarding the right to life and due process.[26] This ruling was accepted by the ombudsman in Peru in a formal resolution, stating that all amnesty laws were unconstitutional.[27] This ultimately provided the basis for reparation payments to victims and their relatives and for the indictment of President Fujimori, who was held partly responsible for the massacres. By 2011, in a case against Uruguay, the Inter-American Court judged that all obstacles to justice for victims of human rights violations should be removed. This ruling effectively declared amnesty laws, in relation to certain crimes, as in violation of the American Convention, and the court used international humanitarian law to make this claim.[28] Importantly, in a case against Brazil decided in 2010, the court stated that amnesty laws cannot provide protection for actors guilty of violations of certain rights protected in the Convention.[29]

In developing its reasoning regarding military regimes, the Inter-American Court asserted, implicitly, that national governments are subject to a military constitution. That is, in certain circumstances, governments could be seen as entities that imposed military violence on their own populations. When this happens, vitally, the court indicated that governments could not decide which legal protections should be suspended and which retained. Moreover, when acting as military organizations, governments could not assume full sovereignty towards their subjects, and they did not possess the power to decide when the military action stops: a legal order exists which overarches the form of state sovereignty, and it authorizes sanctions against actions of a military nature. In this regard, the court implied that, in some settings, national society must be treated as an extension of international society, and legal principles traditionally applied to war zones were applicable to citizens in domestic society – even where there is no war. At one point, emblematically, one judge declared

[25] See discussions in *Castillo Páez v. Perú* (1997).
[26] *Barrios Altos v. Perú* (2001). This case referred to Amnesty Laws 26479 and 26492.
[27] Resolución Defensorial Nr 019–2001/DP (30 May 2001).
[28] *Gelman v. Uruguay* (2011).
[29] *Caso Gomes Lund e outros v. Brasil* (2010).

that 'grave violations of human rights and international humanitarian law' should be observed as 'two faces of the same coin'.[30] In proposing this argument, the court indicated that military actors were bound by human rights law, and warfare could not invalidate human rights provisions. At the same time, it implied that government bodies were bound by humanitarian law in their domestic actions, and they were liable for internal breaches of humanitarian law. It thus created an overlapping constitution for war and peace, securing democracy within an overarching military constitution. In a special opinion, one judge argued that 'international humanitarian law and international human rights law are founded on their common concern for safeguarding human dignity', such that they applied equally to all locations. In this opinion, it was also decided that the Geneva Conventions establish an 'underlying principle of the prohibition of inhuman treatment', which implied that human rights norms could be used to reinforce humanitarian law.[31]

These principles were established in rulings regarding amnesty provisions in states with histories of military government. As discussed, the limitation of amnesty laws reflected the principle that military actions were subject to higher law, and that military operations do not take place in an open legal space. Over time, these basic principles were applied by the Inter-American Court to create a more extended constitutional order for national military bodies. This constitutional order was based on norms regulating state actions in past military regimes, but it was broadened to determine the duties of military actors in polities with democratic features. Accordingly, the court used its jurisprudence relating to past military crimes to configure a larger constitutional system in which the entire national security regime of the states accountable to it was subject to heightened regulation.

This tendency was reflected, first, in the fact that the Inter-American Court imposed strict duties on states regarding the actions of military personnel. To do this, it enlarged common rules of state liability, declaring that governments had responsibility for all actions possessing military qualities with ensuing obligations in cases in which military agents violated human rights law. In leading cases, the court declared that states have liability for the actions of soldiers even when soldiers are not actively discharging military functions. This principle was set

[30] *Barrios Altos v. Perú* (2001) (Opinion Cançado Trindade, para 13).
[31] *Plan de Sánchez Masacre v. Guatemala* (2004) (Opinion Cançado Trindade, para 19).

out, for example, in *Masacre de Santo Domingo*, decided in 2012, which related to military violence perpetrated in Colombia in 1998. Here, the Colombian state challenged the jurisdiction of the court by submitting that it could not be liable for crimes under international humanitarian law (which it defined as the law of war), and it could not be imputed responsibility for human-rights violations committed by private military personnel, not acting under formal command.[32] The resultant ruling against Colombia stated that national governments possessed a positive duty to ensure that military personnel acted in accordance with human rights law. Ultimately, this principle was interpreted to imply that states were obliged to offer fully effective remedies for victims of crimes perpetrated by the army. In related cases, court rulings demanded the revision of national laws, to ensure that military actors were subject to the same principles of criminal law and human rights law as other citizens. In a case filed against Mexico, the court issued an injunction that obliged the state to transform the national legal system, subordinating military courts more fully to general procedures and giving higher prominence to human rights law in the entire constitutional order.[33] In Argentina, the case *Rodolfo Correa Belisle v. Argentina* also led to far-reaching reform of the military justice system, in 2007–8.

This tendency was visible, second, in jurisprudence regarding forced disappearances, typically perpetrated under military regimes. On one hand, the court accepted that decisions regarding national security pertained to the vital powers of sovereign states. The court clarified at an early stage in promoting such jurisprudence: 'Without question, the State has the right and duty to guarantee its security.' Yet the court qualified this provision by explaining that, even in security matters, 'the power of the State is not unlimited, nor may the State resort to any means to attain its ends'.[34] This restriction on national security policy was construed as applicable in particular to cases in which government agents had perpetrated or were complicit in the perpetration of kidnappings or the forced disappearance of regime opponents. Naturally, the court found such practices in violation of several Convention rights, including the right to fair trial, to protection from arbitrary arrest, to humane treatment and to protection from torture. But, from the outset, cases of forced disappearance provided a setting in which the court expanded its basic jurisprudence. In such cases, it cited humanitarian

[32] *Masacre de Santo Domingo v. Colombia* (2012), paras 16–17.
[33] *Rosendo Cantú y otra v. México* (2010).
[34] *Velásquez-Rodríguez v. Honduras* (Merits) (1988), para. 154.

law to determine that surviving relatives of persons who disappeared under military rule had a right to expect that governments will fully investigate cases.[35] It explained that states could be deemed in violation of the Convention, not solely in cases where public agents had contributed to the perpetrated disappearance of opponents, but in cases where such disappearance resulted from private actions. In such examples, it decided that states may be found in breach of the Convention for lack of diligence.[36] This implied that states had a positive obligation to promote human rights and to ensure that, even in militarized conflicts, national security concerns were bound by strict norms.

This tendency was evident, third, in legal decisions of the court regarding the state of emergency. In this context, the court typically addressed questions regarding the suspension of rights in circumstances in which exceptional public-order legislation had been enforced. In cases concerning the state of emergency, the court has not strictly differentiated between contexts, such as those in Colombia, which are marked by acute civil conflict, and conditions of more localized exceptionalism imposed by governments outside actual military scenarios. On these grounds, the exceptionalist jurisprudence of the court suggested a certain proximity between warfare and regular state functions, indicating that certain thresholds of protection for individual rights should be upheld in both scenarios.

The basic principles determining these matters are established in the American Convention, which allows executive agents some derogation from certain human rights in states of war, emergency or manifest public risk. However, the Convention sets out a list of rights that cannot be suspended in any emergency. These include the right to life, to political participation, to freedom of conscience and to legal personality. Expanding on this, the court proposed a basic set of rules for regulating the declaration of states of emergency; these rules included the expectation that the state of emergency should be imposed for a specified and appropriate duration, that it should be proportionate to the threats experienced by the state and that institutions must be protected that are able to monitor the measures imposed by the state.[37] Such restrictive provisions included the vital stipulation that, in emergencies, judicial mechanisms should be upheld to allow citizens to

[35] *Masacres de El Mozote y Lugares Aledaños v. El Salvador* (2012).
[36] *Velásquez-Rodríguez v. Honduras*, para. 172.
[37] Advisory Opinion oc-9/87 (1987), para. 36.

access such rights.[38] From an early stage in its activity, the Inter-American Court used these provisions to impose robust limits on executive action during states of emergency of different kinds. In essence, this jurisprudence was meant to show that states of emergency could only have a partial quality, and even the most acute emergencies could not eradicate the basic legal structure from society. In turn, this implied that national governments could not presume to possess full authority over their own societies, and they were not authorized to exercise territorial power in fully militarized fashion. To illustrate this, in an early advisory opinion (1987) solicited by the government of Uruguay, the court declared that judicial guarantees in states of emergency should be amply construed and that judicial remedies for violations of rights contained in the American Convention and in national constitutional law could not be abrogated.[39] Accordingly, the court concluded that any measure introduced 'by virtue of the state of emergency' that resulted in the suppression of such guarantees should be treated as legally invalid.[40] In many instances, the court established such protection during states of emergency to limit the executive force of military organizations and to ensure military bodies could not assume greater latitude than other public bodies in complying with legal norms. In later jurisprudence, the court sought to restrict the powers of military courts in states of emergency, claiming that 'an international consensus' existed supporting the prohibition of use of such courts.[41] The court explained that military tribunals operating under emergency laws in Peru did not satisfy Convention norms prescribing due process and judicial independence.[42]

This tendency became tangible, fourth, in the fact that the court created an extended rights regime for subjects affected by violence. For example, the court ruled that all persons subject to military violence, including refugees and internally displaced persons, possessed certain rights supported by *jus cogens* principles, including rights of non-discrimination and equal treatment under law. In this respect, the court indicated that, in cases of military action, international law created immediate rights and protections for individual subjects. Such rights, it declared, formed components of a general 'international

[38] *Neira Alegria et al. v. Peru* (1995).
[39] Advisory Opinion oc-9/87 (1987), para. 23.
[40] Advisory Opinion oc-9/87 (1987), para. 26.
[41] *Castillo Petruzzi et al. v. Peru* (1999), para. 125.
[42] *Castillo Petruzzi et al. v. Peru* (1999), para. 132.

public order', whose purpose was to bring security to persons in conditions of extreme vulnerability, which was partly independent of the location of the subjects to which it was applied.[43] In such decisions, the court came close to identifying an international rights-based constitution for militarism in which human precariousness generated immutable entitlements, separate from single states and applicable within national territories. This construction was based in a wide interpretation of *jus cogens* rights in which the court ascribed to itself the authority to define new rights with *jus cogens* standing, effectively extracting such rights from treaty law and applying them as laws of individual protection.[44]

Two constitutional innovations stood at the core of these developments. First, these constructions entailed a change in the basic structure of constitutional law. These principles altered the relation to security commitments in conventional constitutional law. They implied that constitutional law obtained legitimacy only within an overarching security constitution in which external laws regulated military policies deployed by governments. This security constitution was not defined as the outcome of concrete bargains between governments and citizens, but as a transnational normative order, with the power to frame national executive processes in a rights-based set of obligations. Second, these constructions implied an understanding of military violence that rejected the simple separation of war and peace, which observed domestic governmental actions as de facto military acts, and which presented a security constitution for all society. Important in this respect is the fact that, in its jurisprudence relating to armed conflict, the Inter-American court crafted rights that were not expressly incorporated in the American Convention, and it promoted a jurisprudence of rights expansionism in scenarios marked by militarism. For example, it decided that the relatives of victims of military violence should be classified as victims, so that the category of subjects affected by war should include persons not directly engaged in conflict.[45] In such cases, the court strengthened the presumption that many societal acts and experiences existed in a condition with some analogies to a military zone. Together, these norms created a legal order

[43] See judicial opinions in *Plan de Sánchez Massacre v. Guatemala* (2004).

[44] See again arguments in *Plan de Sánchez Massacre v. Guatemala* (2004), claiming that *jus cogens* is an open category.

[45] See the analysis of *indirect victimhood* in the reasoning in *Bámaca-Velásquez v. Guatemala* (2000).

in which states were subject to limits in acts of vertical integration, as the extent to which they could claim legitimacy by and for the use of military violence was constrained. However, this legal order imposed strong checks on lateral violence in society, and it attached governmental legitimacy to the mitigation of such violence.

THE CASE OF COLOMBIA

In some aforementioned cases, the Inter-American Court generated broad constitutional protections for persons exposed to military violence, at times linking human rights law and humanitarian law.[46] However, it has normally shown restraint in using military vocabulary to describe national security questions in the societies subject to its jurisdiction, and it has typically avoided designating intra-societal military conflicts strictly as examples of war. Yet in relation to Colombia, a society marked by long-standing multipolar civil violence, judicial and semi-judicial organs in the American human rights system adopted a different approach.

Unlike other polities in Latin America, Colombia was not subject to protracted military dictatorship in the twentieth century. In the 1950s, Colombia experienced a short-lived military regime under Rojas Pinilla, but, generally, some features of democracy remained institutionalized. However, despite an experiment in power sharing from 1958 to 1974, Colombian society remained a theatre of diffuse civil war whose protagonists were the government, the army, leftist insurgents, guerrillas and, at times, ultra-reactionary paramilitaries. The conflict reached greatest intensity after 1945 and from the mid-1980s. This conflict was mainly concentrated in rural areas, and, like many constitutional contests, it had deep origins in questions about landownership and peasant duties. This conflict both reflected and exacerbated the primary weakness in Colombian society examined earlier – namely, that central institutions had weak penetration in society outside large cities. During the conflict, rival organizations, controlled by informal military units or insurgents, replaced government bodies and assumed political and administrative functions in different areas. In each point, the conflict had its origins in structural problems evident in the early post-colonial era, which were exacerbated by the bipartisan character

46 My thanks are due to Juan Barrero Berardinelli for reading and providing material for the following sections.

of the polity. The conflict also created a situation in which democracy was undermined by humanitarian catastrophes, including not only high mortality amongst belligerents, but large-scale displacement of citizens affected by war.

From the later 1980s, the view became prevalent in Colombia that civil war could only be ended through democratic re-foundation. This led to the establishment of a new constitution to pacify hostile groups in 1991. This constitution was, in a strict sense, an emergency constitution. It was written against a background of exceptional legislation; in fact, the decree that convened the assembly that wrote the constitution in August 1990 also established that Colombian society was in a state of emergency. As mentioned, the constitution was partly designed as a peace treaty, and it was drafted by a constituent assembly including different parties in the civil conflict. But it was also conceived as the cornerstone in a more inclusive democratic order. The constitution set out protective rights for vulnerable subjects, promoting active rights of political engagement for marginal groups (Art. 40), and it established an extensive catalogue of social rights (Arts 42–77). The constitution gave high authority to international law, with provisions to ensure that international human rights law was respected in emergency conditions (Art. 93). It was also committed to a policy of institutional reinforcement, extending the societal reach of political organizations, and to enhanced recognition of regional and municipal bodies (Art. 286). On each count, the constitution promoted the legal regulation of violence as the only path to democracy, and, in key respects, it formed a constitution for war. In Art. 22, the constitution declared that it was intended to promote the right to peace.

After the enactment of the constitution in 1991, civil war in Colombia did not abate. Even though parties engaged in creating the constitution declared a commitment to democracy, military actors intensified their use of violence under the constitutional system. This was made worse by the fact that factions in the conflict developed links with the narcotics industry (serving supply chains in the USA), and by the increased mobilization of paramilitaries shadily attached to the regular army. As a result, the constitution did not create an effective legal order to support democracy, and the need to devise means to promote pacification remained central to the new constitutional system. After 1991, the expansion of a constitutional order for warfare was central to democracy, and state organs began to design constitutional norms to stabilize social violence. This was partly conducted by judicial bodies that oversaw the implementation of human rights law, which was accorded very high status in the constitution and was immediately used to protect victims of war. Most importantly, judicial institutions also began to enforce humanitarian law inside Colombia, and this use of international law acquired deep constitutional importance.

Humanitarian law assumed a constitutional role in Colombia because its application by judicial actors meant, in effect, that the political branch of the government was denied the power to claim a monopoly of political authority, or exclusive sovereign control of society. Indeed, such judicial actions clearly implied that vital decisions regarding the existence of a state of belligerency in Colombia partly exceeded the authority of government. After 1991, different presidents denied that the military conflict in Colombia should be classified as war. This position was originally rather ambiguous, as, before 1991, President Virgilio Barco Vargas declared that state actions against drug traffickers formed a type of war.[47] Between 1998 and 2000 President Pastrana Arango also tried to negotiate with guerrilla insurgents in the FARC, effectively admitting some level of internal belligerence. However, successive presidents were reluctant to accept the principle that military adversaries in Colombia could be classified as belligerents. This denial was meant to limit the extent to which international agencies could intervene in Colombia, and it implied that domestic institutions possessed full sovereign authority in addressing civil violence. This denial also meant that legal protections for individual insurgents were restricted, and governments were able to engage with military conflicts as matters of domestic criminal law, or – at most – as questions of human rights law. After 2002, President Uribe denounced regime opponents as simple narco-terrorists and dismissed the suggestion that an armed conflict existed in Colombia.[48] This classification was intended to augment Uribe's authority within the conflict scenario and to gain international support in the context of global antiterror initiatives. This denial of belligerency was ultimately qualified by President Santos, who accepted the existence of an internal conflict. Santos passed legislation in 2011 to provide remedies for persons in Colombia affected by 'violations of international humanitarian law', which were defined as occurring in the context of an 'internal armed conflict'.[49] Before this point, however, the insistence that Colombian

[47] For related analysis of different types of violence in Colombia at this point, see Abad (1989).
[48] See on this Tickner and Pardo (2003: 64).
[49] Law 1448 (2011), Art. 3.

society was not a war zone meant that the inclusive commitments of the 1991 constitution had limited force and political positions were largely consolidated by exceptional military actions.

Despite such constructions, Colombian society was gradually subject to a warfare constitution in which both national political organizations and informal military actors were construed as subjects of international humanitarian law. This was closely linked to attempts by judicial institutions to give full effect to the provisions of the 1991 constitution. Gradually, the constitutional recognition of war in Colombian society emerged as a core legal question in the process of constitutional entrenchment, and international humanitarian law was consciously utilized to reinforce the political objectives of the constitution.

At one level, the establishment of a warfare constitution in Colombia was driven by Colombia's growing integration in the American human rights system, as judicial bodies outside Colombia played a leading role in establishing norms to manage violence and to protect subjects exposed to violence. In the later 1990s, the Inter-American Commission, traditionally less circumspect than the Inter-American Court, filed cases against the Colombian state for historic acts of violence perpetrated in violation of humanitarian law. In such cases, the commission claimed authority to apply humanitarian law in its elaboration of Convention rights. It justified this on the grounds that rights pertaining to humanitarian law reinforced Convention rights in some settings, and they could be used to inform the 'interpretation of the Convention provisions' in cases where human rights were violated in military environments.[50] This position implied that human rights law and humanitarian law could be applied together, as both bodies of law were mutually reinforcing.[51] As discussed, this indicated that protections for certain human rights could not be weakened by claims to military necessity.[52] Moreover, this implied that internal military environments were open to the penetration of international norms.

Following this, the Inter-American Court began, in specified areas, to invoke humanitarian law in proceedings against Colombia.[53] This was seen in the *Mapiripán Masacres* case regarding murders perpetrated by paramilitaries in Colombia, who were assumed to be acting with

[50] *Arturo Ribón Avila v. Colombia* (1997), para. 132.
[51] *Arturo Ribón Avila v. Colombia* (1997), para. 174.
[52] In cases against Peru, analogously, the Commission argued that common Article 3 of the Geneva Convention was applicable within the American system. See *Hugo Bustios Saavedra v. Perú* (1997), para. 58.
[53] *Las Palmeras v. Colombia* (2001).

support amongst state agents.[54] In this case, the court repeated its established jurisdictional caution, and it avoided describing conditions in Colombia unreservedly as war. However, it decided that such conditions constituted an internal conflict subject to humanitarian law. It presented this situation as a 'humanitarian crisis' in which the effects of violence had reached such intensity that they extended beyond actors immediately engaged in conflict and affected numerous persons, especially persons displaced by military conflict.[55] In such cases, the court again expressed the presumption that human rights law and humanitarian law formed convergent normative orders.[56] Indeed, the court declared that humanitarian principles had *erga omnes* status radiating into all spheres of society, such that failure to enforce humanitarian law provided grounds for human rights actions against public agents.[57] Owing to its internal conflicts, the Colombian state was placed under duty both to heighten its own observance of basic rights and to impose a system of rights across all parts of society, especially those exposed to military violence. The court supported this jurisprudence by claiming that both bodies of law were joined by their commitment to averting crimes that degrade humanity itself – to preventing *lesa humanidad*. Later, the court extended its reasoning in this regard, declaring the situation in Colombia a 'non-international armed conflict' to which the Geneva Conventions could be immediately applied.[58] This brought an essential transformation in the relation between the Colombian state and war, as it implied that war was not a condition factually defined by sovereign acts of the state.

In Colombia, the extended use of humanitarian law by the Inter-American Court was linked to domestic jurisprudence. After 1991, the Colombian Constitutional Court developed a body of case law that gave direct effect to humanitarian law, often using such law to promote the programmatic objectives of the constitution. Despite prevailing presidential declarations, the court decided to accept that its duty to enforce human rights law included an obligation to apply humanitarian law within Colombian territory, so that it construed Colombian society as a terrain directly subject to international military law. This gave great support to later jurisprudence of the Inter-American Court, which

[54] *'Mapiripán Masacre' v. Colombia* (2005).
[55] *'Mapiripán Masacre' v. Colombia* (2005), para. 96.58.
[56] *'Mapiripán Masacre' v. Colombia* (2005), para. 115.
[57] *'Mapiripán Masacre' v. Colombia* (2005), p. 110.
[58] *Comunidades afrodescendientes desplazadas de la cuenca del río Cacarica (Operación Génesis) v. Colombia* (2004), para. 221.

claimed that humanitarian law was enforceable in Colombia because it had been applied by a domestic tribunal.[59]

Constructive engagement with international humanitarian law was a feature of the Colombian Constitutional Court from an early stage. In 1992, the court declared that the 1991 constitution conferred binding domestic status on international human rights law and international humanitarian law.[60] Moreover, it claimed that the Geneva Conventions should be treated domestically as *jus cogens*, so that all laws and public acts violating them should be deemed invalid. This line of reasoning was reinforced three years later. By 1995, the court developed the doctrine, rooted in a constructive appropriation of French public law, that a body of norms existed forming the hard nucleus of the constitution – the *block of constitutionality* – which automatically assumed a superior position in the hierarchy of national constitutional norms. This doctrine implied that treaties and agreements signed and ratified by Colombia possessed the same status as constitutional laws, such that, using international treaties, the court was permitted to integrate new elements of international human rights law into the constitution. This doctrine was applied, for instance, to strengthen protection for certain human rights set out in the American Convention, and it incorporated rulings of the Inter-American Court in domestic law.[61] Through this doctrine, the court argued that international humanitarian law should be assimilated to the block of constitutionality, so that domestic law was required to reflect 'the content of international humanitarian law'.[62] In this, the court was careful to indicate that this incorporation of humanitarian law did not *of itself* signal the admission of a state of belligerency, and it did not subject the sovereignty of the state to external legal constraints. Yet it argued that the *jus cogens* quality of humanitarian law was such that all public authority was bound by a moral regime that controlled violence. Eventually, the court concluded that international humanitarian law should predetermine all acts of law, and it could be applied in conditions which governments refused to define as armed conflict: this meant that the application of international humanitarian law was in principle separate from any sovereign act of state.[63] In each respect, this analysis

[59] *Mapiripán Masacre' v. Colombia* (2005), para. 114.
[60] C-574/92.
[61] T-1391/01.
[62] C-225/95.
[63] C-291/07.

involved recognition of actors in the Colombian conflict as combatants in a war outside sovereign control, and it deeply altered the inherited construction of warfare as a sovereign act.

These assumptions were flanked by the construction of a normative order for Colombian society in which all modes of violence were subject to vigilant regulation. From an early stage, the Constitutional Court insisted that all military agents were bound by international humanitarian law. In particular, the court established the principle that 'military obedience' could not be cited as a reason for disregard of human rights law.[64] This principle then gave rise to additional expectations. For example, the court stipulated that all members of military forces should be seen as active protectors of a constitutional order which included the nucleus of humanitarian law. In this capacity, the court claimed, all military personnel were positively obliged to confront and prevent acts of aggression 'against the constitutional rights of persons' and 'in general manner, against human rights'.[65] One central function accorded to the military was to provide security against human rights abuses. At the same time, the court decided that all military personnel were bound by the 'absolute obligation to prevent non-recognition of international humanitarian law'.[66] This norm covered crimes of omission in which military agents had failed to prevent such violations. In these respects, members of the armed forces, even when acting within Colombian territory, were positioned as immediate subjects of international humanitarian law.

Through such reasoning, the Colombian Constitutional Court established a situation in which a constitution of military violence was created that, through its interpretation, penetrated further and further into Colombian society, so that actions and subjects bound by it grew rapidly. In this process, constitutional formation became detached from actual agreements in society, and it was shaped by interaction between national and international norm setters. First, this constitution provided a framework for the social environments in which violence occurred. From 1992, the Constitutional Court set out several rulings to define the duties of public agents in states of emergency, traditionally marked by the weakening of legal constraints on public bodies and acts of public violence. Second, by consequence, this constitution augmented legal protection for the subjects exposed to

[64] C-225/95.
[65] T-327/04.
[66] SU 1184–01.

violence and its effects. Through this conjoined process, warfare was interpreted as a generic social domain with a separate constitutional character, which transmitted norms across different spheres of society.

On the first point, in its early rulings, the court declared that the norms of humanitarian law must be upheld in states of emergency, which it placed under judicial control as a matter of designated responsibility.[67] It applied the same logic to human rights law, declaring that the suspension of core aspects of human rights law was prohibited in states of emergency.[68] Over a longer period, it established a body of rules regarding the declaration of the state of emergency and the conditions that should be applied within such conditions. These rules were modelled on decisions of the Inter-American Court and included provisions regarding the proportionality, the temporal limits and the public announcement of any declaration of exceptional conditions. These rules also included the insistence that, in any state of exception, certain basic rights should remain untouched. This insistence was linked to the increasingly strong conviction in favour of the block of constitutionality, which could be applied to all social terrains. To define such rights, the court enumerated rights contained in international conventions, such as rights of children and clear *jus cogens* rights. It added to these rights established under humanitarian law. It also declared that judicial rights 'inherent to the democratic form of government' must remain inviolable in militarized settings, such that all government actions in the state of exception could be subject to appeal or review. These judicial rights covered rights of individual legal petition – that is, they covered the submission of *tutelas* against public actions. This meant that, even in exceptional conditions, the strict line of accountability between state and citizens was not abrogated. These arguments were then condensed in the formula that the 'sole valid justification' for the imposition of a state of exception could be the utility of this condition for 'the defence of democracy', such that any act in a state of emergency that did not proportionately contribute to the ultimate strengthening of democracy could be declared illegal.[69] In these respects, the Constitutional Court effectively reserved to itself the power to control conditions of militarization in society and established a set of rules to ensure that public agents could not react to military conditions by transforming their constituted powers into

[67] C-574/92.
[68] C-295/93.
[69] C-802/02.

military powers. These provisions strongly echoed classical provisions in humanitarian law, implying that, in states of war, the fundamental form of government could not be altered, so that the quality of sovereignty remained independent of military potency. On this basis, the Colombian state was subject to laws of war in its own territory.

A vital innovation in this line of reasoning was that, under certain conditions, the Constitutional Court claimed for itself the authority to declare an effective state of emergency, against the will of government agents. Progressively, the court promoted the idea that, in certain localized situations, it possessed the entitlement to declare that a condition of constitutional crisis existed. Moreover, where it declared such a crisis, it was authorized to devise remedies to end the crisis, which included the power to instruct government bodies to implement specific exceptional measures. Through this, the court assumed the supreme monopoly of power in crisis situations, and it often exercised this power on the basis of international norms. The court classified crises warranting such intervention as *unconstitutional states of affairs*, which it construed as broad systemic conditions marked by the endemic failure of the government to meet the standards of protection for human rights set out in the constitution. Such unconstitutional conditions were defined as emergencies that affected large numbers of people, in common conditions of distress, which could not easily be addressed through single government actions, and which, for this reason, required the imposition of broad-ranging judicial remedies. Initially, this category of crisis was applied to specific problems in the public sector such as weak social security provisions for some groups or lack of timely payment of salaries.[70] Over time, this legal construct was expanded to cover less localized problems, and it acquired extensive application in circumstances created by the ongoing military conflicts.

On the second point, the court used this line of jurisprudence to widen the protections that it provided for victims of violence. For example, it developed such reasoning to designate the living conditions of persons displaced by war, which it attributed to a mass of systemic causes, which could not be rectified or removed by one simple set of actions. These causes, the court ruled, resulted in the violation of numerous rights which could not be addressed through regular legal proceedings. The rights whose violation demanded judicial intervention included the right to live in dignity, the rights of children, the right

[70] T-559/98.

to the free development of personality, the right to health, the right to free movement, the right to education, the right to work, the right to a minimum of food and the right to legal personality. Accordingly, the court reserved to itself the power to set out legislative directives where such rights were abused. Vitally, the rights subject to such protection included *the right to peace*, which, following international humanitarian law, was construed as the right of civilians not to be treated as targets of military violence.[71] By stating that neglect of the right to peace could be viewed as an indicator of an unconstitutional state of affairs, the court determined that it possessed jurisdiction over the military environment as a whole. In addressing such violations, the court decided that it possessed the authority to prescribe general systemic solutions, addressing different causes of constitutional crisis, and these solutions were justified by their potential efficacy in reinstating persons in the rights that had been systematically violated. The court then prescribed a series of measures to alleviate the mass violations of human rights, and it put into effect a monitoring system to ensure that these measures were enforced.[72]

In key respects, the jurisprudence regarding unconstitutional states of affairs formed an inverted construction of classical reasoning relating to states of exception.[73] In establishing this concept, the Constitutional Court decided that it could impose a state of emergency on the government, in circumstances where the government had tangibly failed in its constitutional duties. Accordingly, the government itself could be placed in an exceptional regime in which normal procedures regarding state action were suspended, and public agents were to receive directives from the high judiciary, often legitimated by international law. This contained the implication, further, that states of exception could not only be employed as instruments to combat challenges to state security or national security. Expressly, in such jurisprudence, states of emergency were conceived as legal frameworks to regulate and remedy conditions in which the security of individual persons was exposed to systemic risk. This inversion of traditional state-of-exception principles reflected in effect an inversion of the logic of securitization that commonly supports such reasoning. The leading ruling of the Constitutional Court on these

[71] T-025/04.

[72] T-025/04.

[73] In a recent ruling, C-383/2023, the court declared unconstitutional a state of emergency imposed in the La Guajira region on the grounds that the court had previously (T-302/2017) declared an unconstitutional state of affairs in this region and the measures ordered had not been fulfilled.

matters contained the statement that an unconstitutional state of affairs was to be imposed in an emergency until such a time as the government was again able to guarantee 'the right to personal security' of persons affected by the emergency. This was taken to mean that a state of emergency should be enforced until all persons suffering under the emergency obtained adequate protection for their basic rights; this involved the guarantee that the 'minimal conditions of security would be satisfied' for such persons, such that they could exercise their rights to live a 'life with dignity'.[74]

These demands framed the Colombian state within a substantially revised security constitution. In this jurisprudence, emergency laws were primarily deemed necessary, not to address security pressures of a military nature, but to cover security crises created by systemic individual vulnerability, induced by military conflict. Effectively, in such rulings, the state's traditional relation to warfare was constitutionally transformed: its legitimacy was defined by its ability, not to sustain military security, but to avert multiple personal insecurity in face of violence. This meant in effect that the provision of security was conceived as a process in which states were obliged to promote rights to avert personal insecurity, and the constitution of security was legitimated by the extent to which this was realized. Personal security was attached to governmental protection of individual rights, and – indicatively – actors responsible for collective military security were perceived as a potential cause of individual insecurity. This naturally meant that one military function of government was to protect citizens from the violence that it itself engendered, especially in its executive functions. These developments were flanked, after 2011, by a broad interpretation of the nature of an internal armed conflict, establishing the principle that all subjects affected by such conflicts should be treated as victims, with due rights of redress. To support this principle, the court followed the Inter-American Court in establishing a wide construction of the victim of military violence, indicating that a victim of violence is any person suffering harms that are tangibly caused by armed conflict. This meant that, inter alia, persons affected by displacement, by actions of private security providers and by actions of non-identified armed groups should be treated as subjects of a war zone, with claims elevated security and protection.[75] This also implied in effect

[74] T-025/04.
[75] C-781/12.

that military actions conducted for the sake of national security could be legal only if they demonstrated proportionate regard for the rights of vulnerable subjects. The court spelled out this logic, stating that measures taken in the defence of 'internal security' needed to be weighed against the interests of vulnerable subjects.[76]

Viewed from a long-term historical-sociological perspective, the Constitutional Court in Bogotá established legal constructs that touched on underlying principles of modern constitutionalism. As discussed, the original concept of the citizen that sustained modern constitutional law was distilled as a response to national security pressures, providing the centrepiece for a security constitution. The Colombian Constitutional Court declared that the citizen had to be defined as the source of legitimacy for government in new terms. In this revised construction, the citizen was presented as a figure who provided legitimacy for government to the extent that the government recognized the vulnerability of the citizen and organized its actions to diminish such vulnerability. Moreover, this construction implied that, either by design or omission, the government itself was a primary cause of subjective vulnerability amongst citizens, and the court was allowed to place the government in a security constitution to securitize citizens against the effects of its actions. In such reasoning, the original historical thread between the mobilization and the vertical integration of citizens and the construction of legitimacy was fundamentally altered, and the provision of individual security became the basis of citizenship in distinct form. On this account, the government was seen as acquiring legitimacy by recognizing multiple forms of security and insecurity, and by administering security for citizens through a complex web of duties, within an international normative system. In this system, the essential obligations of government were constructed, not through manifest bargaining with citizens, but through the recognition of citizens as vulnerable subjects.

In devising this construction of security and citizenship, the Colombian Constitutional Court also adopted a distinctive approach to the main institutional outcome of national citizenship: the sovereign state. Most tangibly, first, the court suggested that the state did not have the categorical authority to define conditions of war. Alongside this, the court stated that the powers of the sovereign state could be legitimately exercised only if they were deployed as part of a transnational

[76] See the discussion of the balance to be struck between national security policies and rights of indigenous communities in SU-383/03.

constitutional order assuming force in conditions of internal military conflict. At a different level, however, the court expressly proposed its jurisprudence as a technique for raising the obligations of state institutions, for bringing state organs into closer proximity to citizens in society and so – effectively – for augmenting the factual sovereignty exercised by the state. This was especially vital in the historical context of Colombia, because violence often occurred in remote regions where subjects affected by war had little access to governmental protection. In one judgment, the court declared that its insistence on the enforcement of human rights law and humanitarian law in conditions of military conflict was intended to force the state to demonstrate that it possessed, 'in Weberian terms', the monopoly of power in society – that it was a factually sovereign actor. In this ruling, the condition of sovereignty presupposed that the state could display its ability to guarantee human rights, to maintain social welfare and to discharge basic obligations to its citizens. Only by such means, the court opined, could the state be perceived as distinct 'from other centres of warlike power that have been erected in the country'.[77] Perhaps unintentionally, such reasoning was centred around a reformulation of the deep historical attachments between citizenship, sovereignty, welfare and warfare. In this account, the sovereign power of the state was defined, not by its ability to aggregate military force in society, but by its ability to impose a grammar of rights on society, ensuring the security of individual subjects in a condition of domestic pacification. Sovereign statehood, in other words, could be anchored only in a security constitution that was oriented, not towards the vertical extraction of military capacity, but to the lateral management of the effects of violence. As in other contexts, this process reflected a transformation of the position of military law in the state. Military law entered the state here as an instrument used to pacify national society and to predetermine the intervention between citizens and government, such that the state itself was bound domestically by international laws of war. As in South Africa, in fact, the attempt to create a constitution of violence fed into a wider ethic of transformative constitutionalism. Over time, the Constitutional Court cemented a complex body of social rights with heightened guarantees for education, pensions and cultural specificity, implying that the constitution of violence presupposes extensive social protection.

[77] SU-1150/00.

CONCLUSION

Post-1980s democracies were generally built on a substratum of international law, which created an international environment for domestic democracy and helped governments to organize their security functions. However, the post-military transitions in South America crystallized in clearest form the legal processes that broadly characterized this period of modern democratic formation. In this region, constitutional democracy developed through the emergence of a legal system in which violence inside and outside national society was not fully differentiated and basic democratic rights were defined and insulated by international military law. In Latin America, regime changes were structurally built on the principle that democracy required the construction of political subjects who could claim protection in a transnational constitution of violence. In this constitution, national governments appeared potentially as entities engaged in acts of occupation toward their own citizens. This process greatly intensified one aspect of the system of world law created after 1945. From the 1980s, states acquired constitutional form in an international security constitution, and international military law was used to manage many societies where strictly there was no war. This was linked to the fact that some military regimes that came to an end in the 1980s were originally conceived as parts of a global civil war, and their leaders projected themselves as actors in a transnational occupation system. Examples of the domestic use of humanitarian law appeared in other contexts, especially during decolonization in Africa. Yet in South America, the transitions reflected a paradigmatic process in which state legitimacy was partly detached from the vertical integration of citizens and directed towards the management of the violent lateral effects that such integration induced. The principle was established that democracy presupposed a constitutional order in which national governments are subjects of laws of war in their own societies.

CHAPTER NINE

CONSTITUTIONS AFTER WAR

It was claimed in previous chapters that post-1945 democracies were stabilized through a process in which constitutional norms originally created by war were transposed into a political order in which the military origins of constitutionalism lost some force. This was partly brought about by the fact that governments subjected themselves to military constitutions which shaped their deep legitimational interactions with society. This was also evident in the fact that welfare states became stronger; this meant that social individualization was reinforced, the socio-integrational relevance of military attachments decreased and military spending lost some constitutional significance. Importantly, welfare state formation often occurred as different political factions, traditionally separated by bitter social partitions, found common ground in supporting limited material redistribution, so that the effects of constitutional democracy in inducing lateral militarization in society were diminished. In these respects, constitutional democracy developed – in essential form – as the dialectical consequence of imperialism and related interstate conflict. On one hand, imperialism was the original force that propelled the evolution of constitutional law, and it led to the formation of governments that integrated citizens through political and social bargains, at least for persons originally located on the inside of imperial systems. However, such integration was always inherently precarious as, in parallel, interstate warfare promoted sequences of factional militarization at the domestic level that adversely affected constitutional systems. Eventually, most constitutions brought stability to democracy as they helped governments to manage the pacified integration of citizens through social and political rights, originally generated by military conflict. As discussed, after 1945, a growing number of states settled around a constitutional equipoise in which they balanced the impetus to social inclusion generated by warfare with an institutional system able to integrate social actors without immediate military purposes. This was often closely supported by the penetration of international law into domestic society, so that international law and domestic welfare provisions framed national polities in a system of *world law*. Overall, militarism, usually resulting from imperialism, formed the dialectical motor of constitutional democracy: constitutional democracy resulted from war, yet it was consolidated as constitutions transposed legal institutions arising from war onto peaceful premises. This stabilization of democracy meant that states were able to integrate their citizens in a vertical manner through electoral rights, yet they could also mitigate the lateral effects of such integration. This typically meant that intra-societal violence became weaker, but this was also reflected in reduced military conflicts between democratizing states.

This conjuncture meant that, after 1945, the constitutions of most democratic polities were partly severed from the force that had historically brought them into being – military violence. As discussed, the nexus between violence and constitutional law did not disappear. Yet immediately after 1945, a mode of constitutional government evolved that did not depend structurally on war and promoted social integration in a form separate from war. Then, from the 1980s, most constitutional systems were created without war. From the 1980s, for the first time in history, many states began to develop constitutions without warfare, and, with obvious exceptions, few constitutions resulted directly from war. One defining factor in the constitutional transitions of the 1980s was that frequently the deepening of constitutional rights was detached from domestic imperatives resulting from war, and constitutional rights were not instilled in national societies as governments were forced to bargain with their citizens to mobilize populations for collective security. This fact presents a paradox at the centre of constitutional history. From the 1980s, constitutional law became a global organizational form for government, and states in Latin America, Eastern Europe, parts of Africa and parts of Asia adopted enduring democratic constitutions. However, the globalization of constitutional law occurred at a moment in which constitutions were fundamentally transformed and removed from their social foundations.

The frequent absence of war in the constitutional transitions of the 1980s and 1990s left several defining legacies for constitutional practice. First, the impact of low background militarization in the transitions starting in the 1980s became evident in the fact that, as discussed, many constitutions were formed through the immediate alignment of national law to international law. This was already typical of transitions after 1945. However, the construction of national constitutions on international templates was greatly simplified from the 1980s as the frameworks for transition were already in place. In many cases, international law had provided directives for regime change before transition started.

This can be seen in many factors. As mentioned, this is illustrated by cases in Eastern Europe in which national courts assimilated international norms in constitutional law, at times without domestic constitutional approval.[1] One core determinant of constitution making in Eastern Europe was the Helsinki Accords (1975), which projected norms of governmental legitimacy for all Europe. By 1990, the Venice Commission had been established, which advised transitioning national governments about ways in which their constitutional systems could be adapted to transnationally accepted models, in essence establishing preconditions for constitutional legitimacy. The subsequent transition in the 1990s coincided with the UN's endorsement of the Paris Principles (1993), which encouraged states to establish institutions for protecting human rights. In Latin America, some national constitutions were created or reformed through the wholesale incorporation of international law. As mentioned, one example of this can be found in the constitutional reforms in Argentina in 1994, in which President Menem gave immediate effect to Argentina's international treaties, forming in essence a new constitution. More generally, most transitions in Latin America were created through gradual normative adjustment in which international norms played a guiding role. This is illustrated by the Chilean case. In Chile, constitutional reforms of 1989 revised Art. 5 of the 1980 constitution, giving higher status to international law, and this partly framed the regime change. In each case, the transition to democracy was effected through constitutional changes closely articulated with international law. In Africa, many transitions were initiated by sitting leaders, frequently because of

[1] This was especially marked in Hungary, where the existing constitution was not comprehensively rewritten after 1989 and judges interpreted international law to assimilate new norms in the constitutional text.

international pressure. For example, in Ghana in 1992, Jerry Rawlings was encouraged to submit to elections by international actors. Similar pressures were felt in Nigeria in 1999. In such cases, the impulses that underpinned post-1945 democracy building, in which democratic norms were largely detached from mobilized citizens, were often intensified.

Second, the impact of low background militarization in these transitions became tangible in the fact that, in the democratic polities created in and after the 1980s, many constitutions were established that were not embedded in robust welfare systems. Under earlier constitutions, the allocation of political rights had normally led to the allocation of welfare rights. From the 1980s, however, this convergence was reduced. This point is often overstated. It is sometimes claimed that the wave of constitution making that began in the 1980s was solely driven by global fiscal policies, which led to a universal decrease in welfare investment. Such outlooks often suggest that the use of international law to support new constitutions was part of an ideological shift in which global economic norms were enforced as a democratic design to reduce national fiscal deficits, to undercut national welfare systems and to increase capital mobility.[2] However, nuance is required in addressing such assertions.

In Eastern Europe, the democratic transitions after 1989 normally coincided with a perceived reduction in welfare spending as the full-employment policies that characterized states in the Soviet sphere of influence were abandoned. These policies had provided effective social security for most citizens, and their termination caused great personal precariousness. However, patterns of welfare investment after the late 1980s varied greatly in different European countries. Social expenditure in new democracies was often administered by organizations with deep historical roots, so that welfare provisions were reformed in distinct ways. Moreover, some European countries acquired constitutions that declared provision for social rights a primary indicator of legitimacy. Examples are found in Arts 67–70 of the Polish Constitution (1997). Despite these caveats, however, relatively depleted protection for social rights was an important feature of post-1989 European constitutional politics. In some contexts in Eastern Europe, the basic social infrastructure that created welfare states in Western Europe was lacking, as trade unions were defined by historical

[2] See for a summary of this construction (Doyle 2010: 294–295).

hostility to communism and had limited commitment to welfare state formation. This meant that one central actor that had traditionally negotiated social rights in constitution-making periods was weakly represented.

By contrast, in most states in South America that underwent democratization from the 1980s, constitutions were created to reorganize political systems where, prior to reform, the military had formed a primary vector of social integration and social investment had been limited. Peru formed an outlier in this regard, as the military regime under Velasco Alvarado (1968–75) had a powerful welfarist bias. The post-1964 military regime in Brazil also promoted some social security measures to reduce the appeal of organized labour. Yet some Latin American states had internalized global economic dictates before transition, reflecting their loyalties in the Cold War. On one hand, early transitions in Latin America appeared to reflect wider economic imperatives. As mentioned, the transition that ended the military regime in Argentina in 1983 was a defining example of democratic transformation motivated by international norm setters, and it was flanked by measures to deregulate the public economy and to reduce the power of trade unions.[3] By the 1990s, Argentina had adopted an increasingly anti-collectivist model of political economy, which was supported by the constitutional incorporation of international human rights law. Such liberalizing policies were facilitated by the fact that trade unions in Argentina had been implicated in the military regime, and the end of the dictatorship formed a policy opening both for the rejection of military rule and for the abandonment of economic collectivism. Such emphases were also pronounced in other states. For example, democratic transitions in Chile and Bolivia were first cemented by governments with limited commitment to social spending. Constitutional reform in Bolivia was promoted in 1994 by the government of Sánchez de Lozada, which was often resented for its external economic alignment. On the other hand, in a relatively short time, some states in Latin America – notably Chile, Argentina and Brazil – developed increasingly expansive welfare systems which involved large-scale economic transfers for healthcare, income security and public education. From roughly 2000, various Latin American states accomplished something with only limited precedent in modern global history – that is, they created welfare states whose origins could

[3] Gaudio and Domeniconi (1986: 427).

not be traced to the integration of populations mobilized for or affected by war. Brazil exemplified this. Increases in social spending were already visible in Brazil in the 1990s, in the longer wake of the transition, including education subsidies for poorer families introduced by President Cardoso (*Bolsa Escola*). However, during Lula's presidency starting in 2003, far-reaching welfare packages were introduced. These included family support packages (*Bolsa Familia*) and new healthcare reforms.

Striking in these processes is that increases in social spending in Latin America performed integrational functions analogous to those seen in Europe after 1945. The building of welfare states in Latin America from circa 2000 involved the direct transfer of integrational functions from the army to institutions with distributional responsibilities. In Brazil, illustratively, Lula's promotion of social investment after 2003 created a situation in which the role of military actors in civil administration decreased. Social investment specifically targeted remote regions such as the Amazon, where military organizations had traditionally assumed civil governance functions.[4] As social investment increased in such regions, resources were channelled into new organizational structures, which meant that the army lost some administrative importance. In Argentina, the beginning of Kirchner's policy of increasing social spending coincided with reforms to civil–military relations and the termination of earlier amnesty laws for perpetrators of military crimes (2003). In Colombia, social spending remained relatively low after 1991, and the government did not establish a full welfare state. After 2002, President Uribe increased defence budgets. Subsequently, however, integration functions were partly transferred from military actors to welfare organizations. Social budgets were expanded and social spending was used, as discussed, to promote expansive models of citizenship and to construct solid political infrastructure in regions where governmental penetration had been low. Such spending policies were specifically designed to create a new integrational apparatus in distant parts of society, partly because weak state infrastructure had been a key cause of military conflict.[5]

In African transitions, the switch from militarism to welfarism was less pronounced. In many societies, the instruments for welfare provision

[4] In the Amazon region, the central focus of state power is the military. The Centro de Instrução de Guerra na Selva, a centre for military training for war in tropical environments, has operated in Manaus since March 1964.

[5] See background discussion in Chapter 4.

that existed before transitions were part of the developmentalist structure of the state, often supported by military units. Further, informal sources of social protection retained a primary role in insulating social agents after transition. However, over a longer period, some reformed African states began to redirect resources into social provision, including educational investment. This was pioneered in South Africa, where provisions in Art. 27 of the 1996 constitution created extensive welfare rights and Art. 29 established far-reaching education rights. Other African countries, typically those with relatively robust democracies, developed constitutionally defined welfare systems. For example, the revised constitution of Cape Verde (1999) used illuminating vocabulary to determine the government's security obligations. This constitution curtailed the powers of government to suspend constitutional clauses for the sake of national security, but Arts 61–3 protected very broad-ranging rights to material and professional security. The 2010 constitution of Kenya protected core social rights, creating an obligation for the state to administer welfare to citizens unable to work (Art. 43(3)). This gave rise to the Social Assistance Act in 2013.

Despite these variations, the constitutional context of the 1980s had the immediate distinguishing feature that, in many transitions, institutions expanded electoral democracy without promoting policies to augment provisions for social rights. As discussed, the weakening of the historical nexus between political rights and social rights was partly due to the international constellation of the time. The move to democracy was partly realized as states engaged in realignment in the security domain. However, this was also connected to the global economic policy shift in the late 1970s and early 1980s, whose core tenets acquired influence in global institutions through the 1980s. In some countries in Africa and South America, constitution making was clearly linked to initiatives in international public policy, and the growth in the number of democracies coincided with the implementation of policies promoting debt reduction and lower public-sector employment in low-income economies. In many settings, constitution making was reflected in a hostility to trade unions, which had frequently been co-opted into dictatorial regimes.[6] This tended to bring a reduction in public spending, as it reduced the bargaining power of organized labour. This tendency was reinforced by the fact that most

[6] This was especially prominent in Argentina after 1983. But the role of trade unions was weakened through reforms in other states – for example, Bolivia and Ghana.

constitutions were created after the weakening of Soviet influence in Eastern Europe, which reduced the ideological competition that produced incentives for governments to create constitutions with a strong social component. Indicatively, the Brazilian constitution of 1988 was the main transitional constitution written before the end of Soviet influence, and it contained extensive labour-rights provisions (Arts 6–11), whose force was later curtailed. Moreover, this retreat from social rights was not exclusively a feature of states in a process of democratization. The reduction of public spending, or at least diminished commitment to welfare investment, was a prominent aspect of public policy in established democracies in the 1980s. By this time, key democratic states such as the USA, the UK and the FRG had embarked on structural experiments in which democracy was – variably – detached from post-1945 ideals of selective economic redistribution. In this period, crucially, many parties of the centre right partly renounced the commitment to welfare spending that had formed the cornerstone of most post-1945 democracies. In the USA and the UK, this process was linked to intensified ideological hostility to the Soviet Union in the 1980s and, after 1989–91, to anti-Communist triumphalism. These ideological patterns dissolved the traditional consensus between left and right that had supported the solidification of constitutional democracy after 1945.

At the same time, the weakening of the social component of constitutional law that began in the 1980s can be more immediately attributed to the fact that many constitutions came into being in contexts not immediately defined by actual warfare. Discernibly, the absence of warfare meant that, in many transitions, democratic institutions were created in contexts in which previous determinants of public spending and social rights formation did not exist. In the 1980s, many pre-transitional states had partial military features, and national governments secured some legitimacy by claiming exposure to pressing military threats. As mentioned, in Latin America, such threats were defined in the context of global civil war. In Eastern Europe, these threats resulted from Cold War polarities. However, in virtually all settings, the actual social force of military violence had been limited, and few societies moved towards democratic constitutionalism because of affiliations created in war. Consequently, military roles were not as strongly constitutive of political entitlement as in earlier periods of constitutional formation, and governments did not allocate rights to citizens because of shared sacrifice or obligations linked to recent military service. In particular, in the 1980s and 1990s, most democratic states were not required to establish benefit systems for demobilized soldiers or dependants of dead soldiers, so that the immediate military pressure on public spending was weaker than in earlier constitutional environments.[7] From the 1980s, further, democratizing governments were not confronted with populations that had been collectively armed for engagement in military actions. As a result, governments were not exposed to the risk that their populations could utilize military instruments to secure their rights. As discussed, in different historical contexts, the prospect that recently militarized populations may seek to enforce their political and social rights autonomously, through anti-systemic associations, had decisively shaped constitution-making actions. In most previous periods of democratization, the management of demobilized populations affected wider policies for social distribution. From the 1980s, however, the impetus for political and social inclusion that emanated from pre-transition militarization was weakened. The value of social rights as instruments to bargain for the pacified integration of citizens was reduced, and this in turn meant that the willingness of governments to commit to social spending was curtailed. This was closely connected to the collapse of the Soviet Union, whose ideological presence had driven up social spending in Western Europe and even encouraged right-leaning parties to offer material benefits to electorates.

On each count, the incentives for the maintenance of high levels of public spending were not pronounced in the constitutional transitions of the 1980s. In virtually all previous constitution-making environments, levels of public spending increased through warfare had been partly carried over into peacetime as resources invested in the army were directed into post-war pacification programmes. Before the 1980s, most importantly, constitutional guarantees for extended political rights usually brought expanded social rights, and, almost invariably, each wave of political enfranchisement brought increased welfare investment. In the 1980s, this conjoined trajectory was dissolved. At this time, public-spending policies established under pre-transitional regimes could be suspended by governments with relative impunity. In other words, from the 1980s, political rights were no longer constructed as a clear military-constitutional bargain between governments and

7 On the vital role of this factor in forming national welfare systems, see Obinger, Grawe and Dörr (2020).

citizens, and this tended to soften pressures on governments to increase allocation of social rights.

This constellation placed constitutional law in an altered position towards the residues of imperialism. As discussed, military conflict, usually related to imperialism, had provided the historical mainspring for the creation of constitutional rights. This was always a dialectical process as the military forces that entered national societies through imperialism both consolidated constitutional law and generated modes of violence that constitutions could not administer. However, after 1945, constitutional structures that had originated in military pressures were stabilized in a form that redirected social integration processes away from military organization. As examined, this was partly caused by the reinforcement of social rights in which core welfare rights (healthcare, income security, pensions and education) were differentiated from the military sphere of influence. In contexts defined by strong social rights, the exercise of political rights proved less likely to cause acute social conflict and to unbalance the political apparatus. In the 1980s, however, many constitutions were established in societies where the social institutions required to support constitutional functions were not strongly consolidated. This was the first time that constitutions were *fully post-imperial*. At this point, many states obtained constitutions in order to change their position in the global security landscape, but, traditional inter-imperial military rivalries were not strong intra-societal determinants of constitutional organization. In essence, this meant that the dialectical tendency of warfare to promote bargains that sustained democracy disappeared, and citizens were integrated in a set of political rights without the presence of social rights to sustain political integration. As a result, the patterns of constitution making that occurred in and after the 1980s formed a new model of post-imperial constitutionalism. Constitutions created after the 1980s were marked by the tendency, fundamental to democratic constitution making after 1945, to construct their citizens on a template defined by human rights law. As examined, international military law played an important role in this process. In this respect, they perpetuated the legacy of constitutions created after 1945. Yet at the same time, they did not construct their citizens on a template defined by welfare commitments. As a result, they were marked by a global alignment in the political dimension of basic rights, but they did not establish strong measures to absorb the conflicts released by vertical integration. This meant that they weakened some aspects of the global polity model (world law) that originally supported this system.

Against this background, the following sections analyse ways in which, in different polities created after the 1980s, constitutions reacted to the fact that part of the dialectic substructure of constitutional law was weakened. In most cases, the absence of warfare produced a new trajectory along which national polities developed, and this was often expressed in the fact that the force of constitutional law in supporting democratic integration became attenuated. In some instances, constitutions lost their capacity to steer national societies away from militarized subject formation. The weak presence of war as a determinant of constitutional organization frequently had the outcome, paradoxically, that some constitutions lost their pacificatory force, so that *the absence of war* was often manifested in *renewed constitutional militarism*. Indeed, the first wave of conclusively post-imperial constitution making eventually gave rise to modes of constitutional formation more typical of societies defined by inter-imperial pressures. The construction of the system of world law, which initially grew out of war, was palpably destabilized through this process.

CONSTITUTIONS WITH NO WAR 1: NEW DEMOCRACIES

Over a longer period, some constitutions that took shape in the 1980s and 1990s began to demonstrate weak integrational force, such that, in some societies, constitutional norms lost some ability to sustain democratic legitimacy for government. This can be associated with the disputed status of social rights in constitutions created and transformed after the 1980s. Across a range of cases, constitutional orders founded after the 1980s were afflicted by crisis because of their limited provisions for social welfare, so that controversies about welfare repeatedly eroded the legitimating effects of constitutional law. In many cases, this meant that governments struggled reliably to manage vertical integration, to generate predictable support for policies, and to avert deep intra-societal hostilities. Eventually, some constitutions reverted to models of legitimation in which military patterns of conflict and coercion came to the fore. This tendency became visible in different variations, and renewed military emphases became evident in different social dimensions. Generally, however, many constitutional systems began to display or rely on patterns of legitimation with strong military aspects. Some systems veered towards *vertical militarization*, in which states applied military violence to effect social control, often linking this to international policies and exploiting global dichotomies as sources of loyalty. By contrast, some systems veered towards *lateral militarization*, as states induced harsh polarization to obtain legitimacy, dividing societies into potentially military conflicts between rival associations. Over a longer period, a complex remilitarization of democracy began to occur in which democratic integration became a source of violent conflict.

These phenomena can be observed in different constitutional trajectories in Eastern Europe. In most Eastern European countries, as mentioned, the path to democratization was originally based in a partly externalized model of legitimacy, defined by powerful protections for individual rights, deep incorporation in international normative systems and strong provisions for judicial authority. Within a decade, however, this model had begun to show signs of weakness. This relatively uniform constitutional model mutated into distinctive patterns of semi-constitutional government in which military integration and legitimation acquired new influence.

One prominent and distinctive example of such developments is Russia. Russia's experiment in democratization beginning in the 1980s was based in a constitutional trajectory that saw the establishment of individual political rights without a strong commitment to social investment. On one hand, the restructuring in Russia in the 1990s recalled patterns of political transformation in Eastern Europe after 1918. At this time, Russia emerged from within the Soviet Union from 1991 as a polity with a limited tradition of pure nationhood, evolving as a nation state by separating itself from the geographical structures originally created by a continental empire. Before 1989–91, the Soviet Union was not an empire in any typical sense of the word; unlike other empires, it did not impose an unequal citizenship regime on citizens living in different regions or with different ethnicity, it was not strongly based in transfers of capital and resources from the colonies to metropolitan centre, and it employed some policies that clearly privileged members of non-central regions. However, the territorial form of the Soviet Union resulted from an imperial past, and some regions were incorporated in the Soviet Union by unilateral acts. Russia was also discredited by military failures in Afghanistan through the 1980s. Moreover, up to the late 1980s, military service played an important role in linking different territories, and memories of military sacrifice in World War II played an important symbolic role in unifying different parts of the Union.[8] In the 1990s,

[8] For example, Uzbek workers in Moscow often protested against racism by saying that shared sacrifice in World War II should have made all Soviet citizens equal.

therefore, Russia acquired shape as a post-imperial nation. The 1993 constitution of Russia was rather atypical in that it established a strong presidency whose incumbent exercised designated functions separate from the executive. The constitution also had a semi-military background, as it was rapidly introduced to cement the political command of Boris Yeltsin after he had dissolved the parliament in a setting marked by civil violence. Yet, from 1993, the Russian polity was based in a constitution that mirrored international templates. For example, it provided for full enfranchisement and gave strong protection to individual rights, including private monetary, personal civil and political rights. It also established a constitutional court to protect individual rights and to limit the regulatory powers of government. This construction of legitimacy was declared in Art. 18 of the 1993 constitution, which gave human rights general status in constitutional law.

These institutional changes were initially supported by the integration of Russia in international normative communities, prompted by pro-Western policies adopted by the Russian leadership after 1991 and later reinforced by Russian accession to the ECHR. Indeed, the 1993 constitution gave direct effect to international law (Art. 15(4)). Through this process, the integrational role of military determinants in Russian policy was diminished as Russia moved out of the Cold War environment into a redefined global arena and the government signalled a more favourable relation to Germany and the USA. This entailed a symbolically vital realignment in Russian national security policies in which it was expected that international military pressures (current and recollected) would lose force as determinants of legitimacy. The initial reframing of the legitimacy of the Russian polity in accordance with international standards coincided with strategic moves by the Russian government to acquire membership in Western security systems. These moves included Russian collaboration in NATO-related organizations such as Partnership for Peace (1994). As a result, the transformation in Russia involved a twofold reformulation of governmental legitimacy in which the authority of government was separated from its traditional geopolitical imagery and concentrated on internationally defined rights. This formed a relatively typical attempt to separate social integration from military violence and to move governmental legitimacy onto individualistic premises.

One distinctive feature of this process was that the shift away from military integration in Russia was not supported by provisions for social welfare. Importantly, the reorientation towards individual rights occurred in an extremely precarious social environment as the economic reforms enforced with the constitution led to acute social vulnerability and insecurity. In fact, conditions of economic implosion meant that public institutions often had limited societal control and, in the face of acute economic collapse, they were subject to mass colonization by private actors.[9] Because of this, the ability of public bodies to articulate with citizens through stable sets of rights was restricted in both the political and social dimensions. At one level, this led to large-scale alienation from formal institutions, as basic services were provided by informal actors, including gangs and criminal bosses. However, this also meant formal individualization promoted by law had limited effect in society, as constitutional guarantees for rights weakened political institutions and had generally deleterious outcomes. Both in the dimension of individual rights and in the dimension of welfare protection, the constitutional transition in Russia had a deeply unpropitious social basis.

In the decade after 2000, the Russian constitutional system embarked on a distinctive line of redefinition. In this process, constitutional guarantees for some individual rights retained relatively high status, yet, at the same time, the political rights projected as preconditions of constitutional democracy were weakened. In its first dimension, this process was reflected in the fact that, after 2000, new laws were introduced that facilitated access to judicial institutions for citizens. In 2001–2, all major procedural codes in Russia were renewed in accordance with Russia's international obligations.[10] These laws meant that judicial bodies were reinforced, legal formalization was promoted and local manipulation of judicial outcomes was limited. This was flanked by the intensified integration of Russia into international legal structures, as judicial reforms meant that the assimilation of rights set out in the ECHR took greater effect in domestic law. Of course, many cases heard in the European Court of Human Rights were filed against Russia. Yet the ECHR acquired deep reach in Russian society, and it discernibly affected patterns of legal reasoning and political decision-making.[11] As the legal reforms took effect, however, the presidency became less constitutionally constrained and restrictions on political competition likely to challenge

[9] See Taylor (2011: 25).
[10] This applied to the Criminal Procedure Code (2001), the Code on Administrative Offenses (2001), the Arbitration Procedure Code (2002) and the Civil Procedure Code (2002).
[11] See the discussion in Thornhill and Smirmova (2018).

the presidency were increased. By the early 2010s, the Russian constitution was constructed in part as an administrative constitution in which individual interactions between citizens and government were subject to increasing normative control. This tendency increased after 2015, with the introduction of a new code for administration litigation, which increased opportunities for litigation against public bodies. This meant that individual citizens could seek redress against public bodies, so that central government could impose heightened control on local institutions across the vast domains within the Russian frontiers. However, at the same time, the extent to which citizens could exercise the political rights to shape acts of legislation was reduced, and the presidency increasingly detached itself from effective political control. In some respects, the emphasis that Putin placed on individual rights in administrative law was always conceived as part of a process of domestic securitization in which international norms were harnessed to serve internal security imperatives. From 2000, the government encouraged individual citizens to litigate against public bodies partly as a mechanism to reinforce state capacity and to exercise greater control over individual interactions.[12]

As this new constitutional order took shape, the Russian government increasingly manufactured new, more symbolic forms of legitimacy. In the first instance, this constitutional system relied increasingly on the projection of strong leadership as an instrument to link society to the political system, constructed around President Putin. Initially, the growing personalization of political leadership in the presidency was one stream in the Russian constitutional system. Over time, however, the construction of legitimacy moved away from constitutional channels, and military techniques for projecting legitimacy acquired new importance. On one hand, this became evident – externally – in the renewed militarization of the larger post-Soviet space. This had actually been initiated by the USA, who used post-Soviet regions in Central Asia as a land route to Afghanistan from 2001. However, the fact that some former constituent units of the Soviet Union were incorporated in pro-Western military alliances after 2000 provided a basis for the reemphasis of national security in the Russian polity, meaning that the Russian government began to explain its legitimacy

[12] Putin announced this policy in an open letter to the Russian voters of 25 February 2000. Putin explained this policy as designed to *unify legal space* in Russia. One of Putin's most important early orders was Decree No. 1486 of 10 August 2000, 'On Additional Measures to Ensure the Unity of the Legal Space in the Russian Federation'.

within traditional military polarities. This legitimational shift gained momentum through Russian incursion in the Crimea, internationally defined as part of Ukraine. In the first instance, this renewed turn to militarism brought constitutional practice into conflict with the original international orientation of the constitutional system. By 2015, recognition of the authority of international norms as part of Russian law was clearly curtailed, and the growing importance of national security imprinted an anti-globalist bias in the constitutional order. This was reflected in measures to reduce the liberty of national judicial bodies in their use of international norms, in surveillance of international organizations in Russia and in growing reliance on military policies to stabilize popular support for the government.[13] After circa 2015, Putin's government began to treat oppositional actors as combatants, partitioning domestic society into rival groups in a semi-military conflict. This eventually gave rise to constitutional changes that further reduced governmental competition by limiting scope for the rotation of the presidency.

In each step, Russian constitutional law since circa 2000 was shaped slow, often contradictory legitimational redirection, in which the premise of constitutional order moved away from individual rights and towards national security. This followed a trajectory, well established through twentieth-century history, in which a state exiting an imperial environment was unable to institutionalize an integrational structure for its citizens. Through a complex intersection of national and international forces, the logic of legitimation based in the protection of individual rights ceded ground to more classical militaristic motivational designs. As a result, citizens were attached to the state through constructions of citizenship, not as a quality of individual rights holding, but as members in an externally threatened security community.

This realignment in the legitimational base of the state was partly determined by Russia's distinctive position in the global community of states. The deep cause of this can be found in the fact that, after 1991, post-Communist Russia was incorporated in a transnational normative system, reflected in the domestic internalization of human rights law. Yet, at the same time, Russia was excluded from a transnational security system – in fact, it was placed outside a security system (NATO), many of whose members remained overtly hostile to Russia. Unlike in many

[13] See Russian Constitutional Court, Ruling on Merits No. 21-P of 14 July 2015.

other post-Communist states, the security-related motives for Russia to comply with human rights were weak, and human rights had little force as part of a security constitution. After circa 2010, the incremental turn away from rights as institutions of governmental legitimacy at the domestic level occurred alongside the isolation of Russia in the domain of international security. Despite such prominent causes, however, the legitimational force of constitutional rights in Russia was weak from the outset, and the preconditions for the integration of citizens in a democratic constitutional order were always unstable. First, after 1991, political rights were implemented in Russia in a context of acute economic hardship, such that, as mentioned, few citizens were able to exercise political rights in a fully reflexive fashion. The construction of welfare structures to support constitutional order and to stabilize the exercise of individual rights was almost entirely absent at this time, and most Russian citizens suffered a catastrophic decline in living standards. Second, after 2000, the incorporation of internationally defined rights became stronger in the domestic legal order, but the protection of such rights was designed partly to serve technical prerogatives of internal security and institutional consolidation. Such rights were separated from both political rights, which became weaker after circa 2008, and social rights, which were never fully established.

On each count, the remilitarization of citizenship in Russia was – at least partly – the product of a constitutional conjuncture in national society. Importantly, the intensification of military patterns of citizenship occurred as the force of human rights law weakened, and the government projected alternative patterns of integration to support its authority. By circa 2014, Russia entered a constitutional trajectory on which militarism replaced individual rights as an essential source of integration and legitimation. This was strongly flanked by the promulgation of traditional identities as the premise for constitutional duties. For example, constitutional reforms introduced in July 2020 established a guarantee for Russian cultural identity. This was also linked to positive invocations of Russia's imperial past. By 2022, Russia had approached the full militarization of citizenship, in which the internal interactions between state and citizens of the state were directly correlated with the mobilization of external military capacity. Illuminatingly, many Russian soldiers killed in the war with Ukraine came from poor families, and their dependents received large sums of money in compensation for their deaths, so that military sacrifice served as a source of social security. Overall, amongst patterns of remilitarization, Russian formed a case of strong vertical militarization. This can be traced to the fact that individual rights had limited force in the post-1991 polity, which was in turn closely connected to the absence of social rights. Both factors combined to cause a systemic failure of constitutional integration.

In less unsettling fashion, similar tendencies can be observed in other parts of Eastern Europe that converted to constitutional rule in the late 1980s and early 1990s.[14] As discussed, for example, the Polish state was historically sustained by highly militarized constitutional constructs in which military loyalties, shaped by global ideological hostilities, had an intense impact on the definition of citizenship. Through the drafting of the constitutions that followed 1989, security concerns remained prominent. For example, leaders in the transitional period, such as Lech Wałęsa, advocated obligatory military duties for all male citizens. In the longer aftermath of 1989, traditional ideals of popular mobilization and territorial defence, reflecting the Polish military tradition, retained influence.[15] Yet at a practical integrational level, external compliance with international human rights law played an at least equal role in cementing constitutional government through the 1990s. As mentioned, transitional actors supported the use of international human rights law partly because of experiences with military rule in the 1980s. The interim constitution passed in 1992 did not contain a separate catalogue of rights, so that protection of rights was entrusted to the courts and the *Sejm*. The 1997 constitution established more formal protections for basic rights, strongly reflecting international expectations regarding the protection of human dignity as the source of personal rights (Art. 30). In this realignment, however, the shift towards the protection of single rights was not strongly supported by provisions for social rights. As mentioned, the 1997 constitution set out some social rights (Arts 67–70), but these were weakly justiciable, and their realization was subject to commensurate legislative decisions.[16] Before 1997, Poland experienced a shock process of privatization during and after transition, partly dictated by international bodies such as the World Bank, which created long-term poverty. Later, successive governments promoted moderately high levels of social spending, but integration of labour remained low and unemployment high.[17] This was partly exacerbated by the fact that political parties with strong

[14] I am grateful to Atina Krajewska for reading and commenting on the following sections.
[15] Maj (2017: 301–4).
[16] Morawska (2006: 244).
[17] I am following analysis in Mikołajewicz (2003: 363–365).

welfare commitments were discredited because of their association with socialist governments.

Over a longer period, the constitutional system created in Poland in the 1990s began to fracture, and the models of individual integration that supported the constitution lost some purchase in society. By the second decade of the twenty-first century, politicians were able to acquire constitutional authority by mobilizing new constructs of legitimacy, often seen as displaying a populist approach to legitimation. First, from circa 2005, it became more common for parties seeking election to motivate voters by appealing to deep-lying historical identities, often connected to Catholicism.[18] In many instances, second, such techniques for constructing support were attached to anti-globalist attitudes as the enforcement of international human rights norms was presented as an external dictate that had undermined organic constructs of solidarity. Eventually, this was expressed in policies that weakened Poland's commitment to the protection of minority rights, especially rights for sexual minorities and rights regarding reproductive freedoms, not easily aligned to ideas of moral community promoted by the Roman Catholic Church.[19] For this reason, third, attempts to stimulate collective solidarity to legitimate government often included hostility towards judicial actors. Judicial institutions became objects of criticism as they were seen as organs that established norms with constitutional effects without reasonable claim to express genuine solidarities in society, imposing heteronomous principles at the core of the polity. This resulted in far-reaching changes to judicial institutions designed to tie them to pro-government attitudes. This history was linked to the perception that courts often formed vectors for internationally established minority rights, so that, allegedly, such rights were established in constitutional law without connection to intra-societal agreements.[20]

In complex parallel to these constructions, fourth, the Polish constitutional system began to construct legitimacy around military identities. In the first instance, this occurred in paradoxical fashion, in the later 1990s. At this time, Poland positioned itself squarely within the Western security community; Poland joined NATO in 1999, which

[18] This began with the first government including Prawo i Sprawiedliwość (PiS) in 2005.

[19] The most important example is the anti-abortion ruling (2020) of the Constitutional Court, whose judges had been largely appointed by the government.

[20] At the beginning of the PiS government starting in 2015, the courts found support for gay rights in Polish law. See the 2016 Supreme Court case, Akt I KZP 20/15. However, PiS supported local governments that sought to ban open shows of homosexuality.

had been the long-term goal of Polish governments since the transitional reforms in 1989–90.[21] In the longer aftermath of this step, military imagery became more central to the legitimational system as dichotomies inherited from the Cold War were exploited to support the increasingly anti-globalist policies that framed government. Progressively, after 2010, governmental legitimacy was built, simultaneously, around anti-Russian sentiment and increasing hostility towards international norms. Initially, this placed the Polish government in the contradictory position that it extracted legitimacy from its membership in a Western security community while at the same time projecting legitimacy in anti-globalist terms, which partly negated the principles endorsed by the security community on which it relied. Ultimately, however, the militarization of constitutional discourse in the Russian Federation created an environment in Poland in which the fusion of anti-globalist nationalism and security policies sanctioned by the Western security community became more globally palatable. This was not lastly the case because Poland was a reliable participant in international security coalitions, and Polish militarism contained a strong anti-Russian core. Following Russian encroachment in Ukraine, security commitments assumed a central role in the projection of governmental authority, and the military emphasis of citizenship historically characteristic of Polish society acquired new visibility. For example, 2016–17 saw the formation of a new reservist army, the Army for Territorial Defence, which reflected interwar military models.[22] As in the 1930s, parties to the right of the political spectrum began to demand the 'militarization of the people'.[23]

Two points have salience in this legitimational redirection. First, increasing militarism in the Russian Federation created a security constellation in Poland that favoured classical military constructions of citizenship. Second, this setting was utilized by political elites to inflame intra-societal antagonisms, and differing governments constructed legitimacy by linking partitions in society to international conflicts. By 2015, this security environment saw the construction of a governmental system that promoted the sharp polarization of Polish society as the increased attachment of legitimacy to security commitments was strongly flanked by strategies of internal exclusion. For example, governments supported by strong military rhetoric introduced

[21] Kupiecki (2015: 26).
[22] Dz.U. 2016 poz. 2138. For analysis see Michalak (2017: 27).
[23] Maj (2017: 312).

policies that reduced protection for minorities and accentuated already existing antagonisms between social groups separated by value orientations or regional position. In some parts of Poland, the changing security environment witnessed the informal mobilization of militias, recruited for loosely defined anti-Russian movements. This was at times flanked by favourable attitudes towards the military past of Poland entailing a positive evaluation of Piłsudski and interwar militarism.[24] At the same time, governments promoting military identities began to support their claims to authority by implementing strategically targeted welfare policies. Unlike other polities in Eastern Europe, Poland did not experience deep recession after the financial crisis of 2008.[25] However, the years after 2008 brought a conservative economic shift leading to welfare retrenchment and increased inequality. Subsequently, from 2015, governments that supported nationalist solidarities prioritized welfare provision for social groups likely to share strong attachments to Catholicism and to subscribe to anti-Russian views. Overall, the Polish context provides a congruent model of lateral and vertical militarization in which constitutional legitimacy was primarily generated by intra-societal antagonism, but this tendency converged with strategic vertical militarization. Indicatively the conservative government was voted out of office in the elections of 2023 partly because of anxieties that it could marginalize Poland in international security communities, making it more vulnerable to Russia. The maintenance of liberal constitutional order was partly a security-related choice.

Although ostensibly opposed, strong symmetries can be observed in the constitutional trajectories of Russia and Poland from the 1990s. In the early 1990s, both polities moved – to some degree – away from models of legitimacy attached to security, and both promoted social integration through the assimilation of international human rights law. For distinct but overlapping reasons, however, the force of human rights law was weak in both polities, and the ability of the constitutional order to bring society into convergence through human rights law was limited. Incrementally, then, the weakness in the societal effects of human rights law was displayed through the re-emergence of legitimational discourses attached to security. As mentioned, in the case of Russia, international memberships and expectations of international compliance were always selectively promoted – that is, Russia

[24] Recent commentaries on territorial defence policies have expressed strong connections to earlier military traditions. See for one example Jakubczak (2020: 27, 91).

[25] See Golinowska (2008: 134).

was invited to join international human rights communities at a time when international security communities were being consolidated that were openly hostile to Russia.[26] This created a conjuncture that was always likely to induce backlash against constitutional government. In both Russia and Poland, the reorientation towards individualistic constructs of citizenship occurred in conditions where limited provisions were made for personal security, so that the social premises for governmental legitimacy were weak. In both societies, the experience of constitutional erosion occurred in a context that was shaped in part by the fact that constitution making in the 1980 and 1990s did not reflect the outcome of deep-rooted solidarities and they did not establish deep social commitments to support constitutional law. Paradoxically, the re-emergence of military solidarities after circa 2008 reflected – in part – the absence of a constitutional order formed by war, as the second tier of democratic law, preserving social rights to integrate society, did not develop in conjunction with the system of individual human rights.

In the relation between Russia and Poland, the link between legitimation through security and the weakening of rights-based constitutional norms acquired emblematic expression. However, in other parts of Eastern Europe, the connection between constitutional weakening and classical patterns of external animosity was also pronounced. For example, in key respects, Hungary pioneered the path towards democratic crisis in Eastern Europe. In the years after 2010, Hungarian governments under Viktor Orbán systematically asserted strong national identities as the basis for social organization. From this time, Hungary saw far-reaching constitutional changes that reflected deep opposition to global norms and normative communities, expressing a tendency to organize governmental institutions around a relatively unchecked executive. These changes were also marked by hostility to judicial bodies responsible for applying international norms.[27] At the same time, these policies were supported rhetorically by a reimagining of the Hungarian past. Through this, renewed emphasis was placed on Hungary's earlier imperial structure and a sympathetic attitude to the

[26] During the crisis years under Yeltsin, NATO expanded its influence into the 'security vacuum' left by the end of Soviet influence, creating a security community whose members frequently showed implacably anti-Russian attitudes. The idea of NATO enlargement was sparked by renowned friends of global democracy such as Dick Cheney. Polish membership in NATO was advocated by Zbigniew Brzezinski (Hill 2018: 110).

[27] In Hungary, legislation starting in 2011 reduced the power of the courts, flanked by selective judicial appointments.

soft Fascist governments connected to Horthy in the 1920s was promoted. As in Poland, this process can be directly traced to the weakly rooted constitutional system adopted after 1989. In its first steps, the Hungarian transition was largely led by judicial activists, and it was not supported by strong protections for social rights. This can also be connected to the fact that international integration policies were discredited by the financial crisis of 2008. This crisis brought substantial retrenchment to the welfare system in Hungary, and it was utilized by the government to authorize welfare cuts, partly to the specific detriment of minorities.[28] Unlike Poland, the pattern of legitimational reorientation in Hungary was not strongly attached to anti-Russian attitudes, and increasing authoritarianism at the domestic level was only marginally connected to external hostilities. In fact, Orban promoted cordial relations with Putin's government. Nonetheless, the constitutional landscape in Hungary exemplified the tendency towards internal disintegration and lateral antagonism in societies with weak welfare systems. These constitutional conditions were also marked by the strategic reassertion of military identities.

Analogous developments became visible in Latin America, where global ideological polarities acquired slightly different resonance. As outlined, in some Latin American polities that underwent constitutional transition in the 1980s, welfare states were constructed in the longer aftermath of regime change. This process of welfare state formation was distinctive in that several governments initiated relatively large increases in social spending, covering all key areas of the welfare state (including education), without linking these policies to social solidarities created through warfare. Also characteristic in this process was the fact that, unlike welfare state formation Europe after 1945, most welfare states in Latin America were based in the policy preferences of one political party, and at times in those of one single politician. As discussed, the dominant feature of most post-1945 European welfare states was that, over time, they were put in place by overarching cross-party coalitions: many welfare states were built, at least in part, by parties of the right. In the Latin American context, the close linkage of welfare policies to single groups of individuals meant that social support for welfare reforms remained relatively fragile, and it was often tied to popular enthusiasm

[28] One expert analysis claims that this period saw 'massive welfare state retrenchment', with social spending decreasing by about 14 per cent. This same article explains how the authoritarian shift after 2010 brought deep welfare cuts, including the imposition of public works programmes (Szikra 2014: 488–493).

for particular personalities.[29] Moreover, far-reaching welfare reforms were introduced in the relatively favourable economic conjuncture before 2008, when politicians of the left could generate revenue for social spending without deep taxation measures, likely to alienate wealthier voters. However, in the longer wake of 2008, the economic constellation that had propitiated such welfare reforms evaporated, albeit with a longer delay than in Europe and the USA. In the years after 2010, underlying social support for welfare policies and social rights regimes became more precarious in much of Latin America. Political parties began successfully to mobilize substantial sectors of the population against pro-welfare fiscal regimes, often creating support by promoting the polarization of society around attitudes to welfare. In such contexts, the erosion of social rights systems began to release new, highly conflictual modes of governmental legitimation in society. In some cases, politicians acquired influence by promoting patterns of legitimacy which supplanted both preconditions of constitutional democracy – human rights and social welfare – and directed legitimation once more towards militarism.

In some polities in Latin America, backlash against constitutional rule, based in individual rights, assumed relatively moderate form, notably in Chile. In other parts of the continent, this backlash became enmeshed with military policies. In Colombia, as mentioned, social welfare policies traditionally had limited reach. However, the period beginning in circa 2010 saw the expansion of welfare policies.[30] Such policies were partly instigated by judicial bodies, which promoted the enforcement of human rights law to increase public spending and to create a stronger infrastructure for national government. As discussed, such policies were closely linked to peacebuilding initiatives, so that the consolidation of the state around social rights, rooted in international frameworks, went hand in hand with designs for the pacification of society. In Colombia, by consequence, opposition to welfare policies always had a military component. Factions that rejected welfare investment were usually hostile to actors on the political left that sought to terminate the military conflict as hostility to welfarism entailed hostility to the material infrastructure that supported peace. The main backlash against infrastructural reinforcement occurred in the elections of 2018 as Iván Duque became the president of Colombia. This led to the creation of a government that openly declared the non-existence of armed conflict in Colombia. At the beginning of Duque's

[29] Examples are Lula in Brazil and Kirchner in Argentina.

[30] After 2010, Santos's presidency saw substantial reduction in extreme poverty, reflected in enhanced unemployment protection legislation in 2013.

presidency, Ernesto Macías, the president of the Colombian Senate, stated that, in Colombian territory: 'Neither a civil war nor an armed conflict has existed.' Instead, he defined the Colombian civil conflict as violence caused by 'a terrorist threat against the state'.[31] Reflecting such beliefs, Duque's government showed reduced commitment to recognition of the peace agreements established to end civil conflict. Moreover, Duque was hostile to bodies that had created a constitution for violence in society, and he resolved both to place limits on the authority of the judiciary and to reduce the force of the American Convention in Colombian jurisprudence.[32] Alongside this, Duque's government ushered in a period of committed anti-welfarism. This was even reflected in some decisions of the Colombian Constitutional Court, which, contrary to its earlier policies, placed limits on social spending.[33] This change of direction gave rise to a clear, albeit limited remilitarization of Colombian society. Although 2018 did not lead to the recommencement of encompassing civil war, some regions saw intensified conflict between the regular army and insurgents. Moreover, military engagement in economic conflicts become more frequent and intense. The years after 2018 saw increased violence against minorities such as Afro-Colombians and indigenous communities as protective regimes put in place before 2018 were weakened.

The most striking militarized backlash against the social premises of constitutional rule occurred in Brazil.[34] The election of Bolsonaro in 2018 marked the central moment in a process of rapid retrenchment of welfare spending, which had already been in decline since 2015.[35] One reason for Bolsonaro's electoral success was that he gained the support of military figures who had become hostile to democracy owing to the creation of a truth commission (2012), which investigated military crimes perpetrated before 1985.[36] Once in power, Bolsonaro's government was marked by the frequent assumption of office by military actors, so that some aspects of civilian government were partly eroded, and the military captured important ministerial positions, acting as part of a vertical anti-welfare bloc. Moreover, basic functions performed by

[31] Parts of the speech are printed in the newspaper *Semana* (7 August 2018).
[32] With other leaders in South America, in 2019, Duque issued a joint communication to the Inter-American Commission on Human Rights demanding an increase in the autonomy of national courts within the Inter-American Human Rights System.
[33] This argument is developed in C-110/19.
[34] Lucas Delgado kindly helped me with this section and provided some additional data.
[35] Healthcare spending amounted to 1.24 per cent of the Brazilian GDP in 2016, falling to 1.15 per cent of GDP in 2019. In 2016, education spending amounted to 1.64 per cent of GDP, falling to 1.27 per cent of GDP in 2020.
[36] See an analysis in Victor (2022: 125).

the army expanded. Bolsonaro's reduction of social investment led to the erosion of the institutional networks that had attached different regions, especially those in remote areas, to the polity, as the policies used to create a geographical infrastructure for national society were depleted.[37] This meant that the military became the primary centre of social coordination in regions affected by depleted infrastructure, especially the Amazon, so that the management of the loosely colonized regions that form Brazil was partly coordinated by the army. Indicatively, as governmental control of the Amazonian regions weakened, government policies towards the region became more strongly focused on assertions of sovereignty and rejections of international conventions.[38] This military reorientation in government was underscored by the promotion of strong national identities, combining anti-globalism, expressed through hostility to international human rights regimes, with anti-minority outlooks, expressed in hostility to indigenous rights and protections for sexual minorities. This reorientation was also underpinned by a rhetoric of global civil war as Bolsonaro's authoritarian policies were presented as part of a global front against communism. In this respect, Bolsonaro's government established a direct rhetorical connection with the Brazilian military regime of the 1960s.[39] Bolsonaro's government also involved attacks on the constitution. It created an apparatus that reduced constitutional guarantees for individual rights, especially in the social domain. It was sustained by attempts to weaken the force of international judicial institutions in Brazil, involving harsh attacks on judicial bodies and to reinforce executive powers, linking the executive more fully to the military. After his removal from office, Bolsonaro's supporters presented themselves as protagonists in military conflict both with political opponents and with their primary institutions. In January 2023, they launched an attempt to destabilize the constitutional structure of society by informal military means. In each point, this regime formed a paradigmatic example of a constitutional system that redirected its integrational processes from human rights and welfare to militarism.

Importantly, the militarization of Brazilian society under Bolsonaro became manifest in the fact that the national government devolved some governance duties to military organizations. On one hand, the

[37] Presidential Decree 9.759 (11 April 2019) abolished the National Councils and repealed the National Social Participation Policy.

[38] Bolsonaro's rejection of concerted environmental policies regarding the Amazon was often supported by the claim that such policies weakened Brazil's sovereignty over border regions.

[39] See p. 368.

policy was adopted to deploy militias to combat criminality. Militias were typically deployed notionally in actions to combat drug trafficking and in other policing functions. However, militias were also used to supress minority and dissident groups, and they clearly formed part of the substructure of the regime.[40] In addition, in legislation of 2008/9, the Lula government had assigned some policing duties to more formal military bodies. Through this process, pacification units with special military training (Unidades de Policia Pacificadora) were established, and they were utilized to maintain security in parts of Rio de Janeiro, viewed as beyond the reach of law. The deployment of military resources for civil-political ends is a grey area in Brazil as the *policia militar* can be utilized at the state level for political security. In February 2018, the regular army was authorized by the Senate to accompany pacification units in Rio de Janeiro. As the government became more authoritarian under Bolsonaro, however, the militarization of policing became more systematic. At one level, this process simply formalized the use of military methods to regulate violent crime.[41] At a different level, this process invoked strong memories of internal colonization in which historically the army had played a leading role. Rhetorically, criminalized urban environments were depicted as lawless spaces requiring military pacification in which military units were deployed as 'expeditionary forces'.[42]

Overall, the course of Brazilian constitutionalism after 2015–16 entailed the partial demolition of the model of state-building and social integration based in social investment and rights-based constitutional norms. This was replaced by a nationalist counter-model under Bolsonaro in which social order was imposed vertically by military organizations, with clear similarities to units operating in an occupation system. At a more lateral level, Bolsonaro's policies also included the deployment of military actors, and he promoted the use of local militias and remnants of the military dictatorship for purposes of social regimentation. Indicatively, he presented several social movements as terrorist organizations, including the movement of landless peasants, which he implicitly placed outside the system of legitimate competition, justifying informal violence against them. Accordingly, developments in Brazil embodied a process of constitutional legitimation combining vertical

40 From 2017 to 2020, gun ownership in Brazil increased by more than 100 per cent.

41 See Sampó, Quirós and Petrino (2019: 159).

42 Souza (2015: 207). On the imperial legacies conjured by this process, see Rodrigues, Mendonça and Morato (2021: 102).

and lateral militarization, in which vertical elements became very prominent. Through this reorientation, the structural-integrational force of the polity was discernibly weakened, especially in areas at its geographical and social perimeters.

In these developments, a core paradox of constitutionalism became manifest. As discussed, constitutional democracy acquired shape, generally, as a political system that was the dialectical result of military pressures. These dialectical outcomes were realized, above all, in the configuration of democracy after 1945. At this time, democracy assumed a form defined by universal electoral inclusion. But, at the same time, the strong legitimational emphasis on political rights contained in early or classical constitutionalism was made sustainable by the fact that constitutions promoted general, reinforced protections for social rights. Most importantly, this corpus of social rights softened the impact of political rights in the state, allowing national governments to displace some of their integrational functions away from simple political representation and political conflict management. At the same time, democracy was supported by individual rights, linked to international law, which predetermined interactions between government and citizens and prevented the use of military in national societies. In key respects, the convergence of these sets of rights established constitutional orders as complex and multifocal systems of integration able to avert the intense politicization of social conflicts. This construction of government usually intersected with wider patterns of individualization in society, which were reinforced by the different constitutional rights stabilized at the governmental level, strongly supported by international law. The longer-term implication of this was that, after 1945, moderately stable constitutional systems were established, and they secured an organizational complex for managing interactions between government and society without acute internal antagonism. Through this process, constitutional structures forged by warfare diminished the military propensities of society and weakened the military emphasis of national citizenship roles.

By circa 1980, the link between military organization and constitution making was largely severed. Armies retained roles in creating constitutions in the 1980s and 1990s, but most constitutions were drafted outside wartime contexts. As mentioned, in many cases, an external system of international norms formed the basis for constitution making, so that constituent agency was partly transferred to the international arena. However, as the role of military conflicts lost force in defining the constitutional obligations of government, the basic functions of many constitutions changed. At a primarily legal level, this was mainly reflected in the relative weakness of social rights. More sociologically, this was reflected in the fact that the social substructures that had supported encompassing social welfare provisions (military solidarities, rescaling of public spending from war to peace, persistent presence of demobilized soldiers) were absent. As a result, constitutional systems created from the 1980s onwards showed relatively low capacity to integrate society through social welfare policies. In many polities, the weak integrational force of constitutional law meant that alternative models of constitutionalism acquired appeal, in which strong national identities and intense political conflicts were again utilized to underpin national governments. In most cases, such constitutional reorientation involved an express commitment to positioning national citizenship in a global military context. In the examples considered in this chapter, constructs of national citizenship were reattached to international conflicts, such that, in each case, the integrational role of citizenship became associated with military loyalty. In each case, further, this entailed the intensification of domestic conflicts in which national populations were partitioned into antagonistic groups strongly linked to global military oppositions. In some cases, military units began to operate against oppositional groups at the national level. On this basis, it became possible to observe a deep correlation between deficient integration at the national level, caused remotely by the weak entrenchment of social rights, and the emergence of militarized patterns of citizenship. In such cases, typically, polities were eventually directed onto military trajectories, in part, because their constitutions were not originally shaped by war.

CONSTITUTIONS WITH NO WAR 2: OLDER DEMOCRACIES

Such tendencies towards remilitarization became most widely visible in constitutional systems established in and after the 1980s. However, semi-military patterns of constitutional redirection were not exclusive to relatively new democracies. On the contrary, it became a general characteristic of constitutional systems that they tended to produce compensatory, militaristic patterns of legitimacy in circumstances where their basic integrational functions lost force. As mentioned, the wave of constitution making that commenced in the 1980s coincided with a global turn against social spending. The resultant fact that many constitutions were created that lacked strong integration mechanisms promoted the military reconstruction of legitimacy in many new democracies. However, similar phenomena could be observed in older democracies shaped by this period. In and after the 1980s, constitutions of older democracies were also placed, albeit less tangibly, on new normative foundations. This was caused, primarily, by the fact that the fifth wave of constitutional democratization was defined by a background that favoured liberal policy making, which meant that many existing democratic states that provided global support for democratization cut or limited domestic social spending. At the same time, constitutional reordering after the 1980s coincided with broad ideological reconfiguration caused by the collapse of the Soviet Union. This meant that constitutional governments had less incentive to promote social investment to weaken Communist sympathies amongst their constituents. Owing to this, the deep consensual form of many polities, held together by cross-party commitments to welfare state formation and to the rejection of Communism, was weakened. In broad terms, the fifth wave of constitutional formation reflected a constellation in which the social rights that supported constitutions in older democracies were eroded, and the distant legacies of military conflict, expressed in the post-1945 social agreements, had limited impact. The fifth wave of constitution making, in its entirety, was shaped by the reduced effect of obligations resulting from warfare. This fact enduringly shaped the techniques for generating legitimacy promoted by constitutions in older democracies, and it tended to direct democracy towards more violent preconditions.

In the USA, for example, constitutional democracy was effectively achieved in the 1960s. This was strongly linked to the influence of global military pressures. After 1945, the USA contributed to promoting constitutional rule in Europe, although its impact in South America deviated greatly from this role. Such external prerogatives were strongly reflected in domestic policies in the USA, as, in the Cold War environment, public spending increased exponentially, and minority groups acquired stronger representation. By the 1980s, however, the welfarist emphases of American government had been reduced. Moreover, the collapse of the Soviet Union limited the pressure on the American government to project legitimacy through plans to guarantee material security, which had been central to democratization in Western Europe after 1945.

These factors meant that, by the 1980s, the government of the USA had undermined the welfarist preconditions for democracy, at home and abroad, and the USA encouraged democracy internationally without promoting social spending. In the longer aftermath of the 1980s, however, two key constitutional processes developed in the USA.

First, from the 1980s, patterns of inter-party consensus regarding social spending that partly originated in World War II were eroded. As in other countries, this collapse of consensus was partly displayed in the fact that different political parties advocated reduced social spending, so that the agreements about state responsibilities that had supported democracy were undermined. This was not an entirely linear process as some presidencies brought selective increases in social spending. For example, the first Obama administration implemented new, expanded policies in healthcare, although this was not matched in other areas of social investment such as education.[43] Yet, the longer period from the 1980s was marked both by reduced commitment to social spending, and, equally importantly, by the fact that social spending became an increasing focus of social and political division. Second, this collapse of the post-war consensus gave rise to several subsidiary phenomena, each of which reinforced its own cause. For example, this process led to the intensification of conflict between different social groups. In central respects, such conflicts ran along traditional ethnic and socioeconomic fissures, as political parties increased their appeal by expressing hostility to minority groups marked by high dependence on public resources. In fact, the reduction of welfare investment was specifically driven by the fact that factions whose own welfare position was fragile could be motivated to support the exclusion of minorities and marginal social groups.[44] By 2016, it had become possible for politicians to win the support of some social groups who were natural beneficiaries of welfare policies by turning them against other potential welfare beneficiaries on racial grounds, leading to a reduction of material well-being for all. This resulted from the fact that political parties were able to promote strong collective identities amongst their adherents, linking subjects in society to populist constructions of national

[43] On one calculation, educational investment per pupil decreased after Obama became president (See www.statista.com/statistics/203118/expenditures-per-pupil-in-public-schools-in-the-us-since-1990, last accessed 4 February 2024).

[44] The white male with no college education was the typical voter profile amongst Trump supporters in 2016.

interest. This in turn was backed by an increasingly strategic rejection of international norms and obligations.[45]

Ultimately, the selective promotion of lateral hostility between social groups acquired prominence through the Trump presidency. This was displayed at a day-to-day level in the management of resentment against regime opponents, and in the promotion of anti-minority actions, amongst the government's electoral base. This was clearly displayed as Trump was elected out of office, as he advocated the mobilization of informal military units to overturn the federal constitution in 2021. In this process, the outgoing president was able to direct his support against core national institutions, effectively defining these institutions as enemies in civil conflict. As in Brazil, the Trump regime contained clear para-constitutional dimensions in which the legitimacy of the government (the presidency) was defined in opposition to the constitutional order of the state. At the same time, the Republican Party began to present itself in part as an anti-constitutional organization existing in a state of partial mobilization against established institutions. Elements in the established Republican Party clearly supported political militarism. Eventually, actors inciting horizontal militarization failed to dislodge constitutional democracy because the regular army did not support such policies, and regular military units could not (at that point) be co-opted for a full *coup d'état*. In these points constitutional crisis in the USA embodies strong *lateral militarization* with some clear potential for vertical militarization.

Analogous processes became observable in the UK. In the UK, from the 1980s, a series of governments rejected the original pro-welfare consensus that had taken form in the aftermath of 1945, so that the political rights embedded in constitutional law lost their correlation with welfare rights. In the first instance, this retrenchment was conducted in an environment of deepened class division in the 1980s, marked by heightened trade union activism. As in the USA, this was eventually expressed in a post-1989 consensus, in which both main political parties limited their policy commitments to social investment. Of central importance in this process was that the Conservative Party abandoned its traditional role as an investor in social welfare. After the financial crisis of 2008, then, the UK saw very far-reaching cuts in social spending, affecting core areas such as income security, healthcare and education.

[45] Examples are Trump's attitudes to migration from Mexico and rejection of the International Criminal Court.

Against this background, governments were able to capitalize on the loss of integrational structure in society by constructing subjects around binary definitions of national belonging and membership. As in other polities, this tendency became manifest in political campaigning with an anti-immigration bias, and in strong hostility to institutions with responsibility for implementing international norms in the domestic polity. This mode of subject construction ran through the debates around Brexit, before and after the referendum of 2016. As in the USA and Brazil, this resulted in a situation in which potential beneficiaries of welfare investment – working-class citizens – became partly allied to a political partly that was clearly (if not always consistently) hostile to welfare state formation. As in the USA and Brazil, moreover, this tendency gave rise to a governmental system with a para-constitutional edge in which some sectors of society were mobilized against the system of political representation. Through the longer aftermath of the Brexit referendum, governments presented their legitimacy, linked to the immediate manifestation of the will of the people, as a quality with higher authority than the constitutional form of the state. This became clear as Boris Johnson openly rejected primary constitutional provisions regarding parliamentary sovereignty. As a result, the UK appears as a model of moderate *lateral militarization*. Unlike in the USA, the reimagining of constitutional legitimacy in the UK was strongly tied to international security policies. The assertion of strongly nationalized subjectivities as the root of government was linked, first, to discomfort with the German role in European security policies, and, more strongly, to anti-Russian sentiment.

In key respects, populism developed as a weak form of militarism, and many governments straddled the division between these regime types. In contemporary society, populist constructions of legitimacy have often formed a prelude to militarism. This can be seen – for example – in the case of Russia under Putin and in Israel under Netanyahu, both of which have their origins in populist techniques for consensus management. As mentioned, this can also be seen in the actions of the Bharatiya Janata Party, which has frequently combined populist appeals and policies to stimulate lateral militarization. Moreover, as stated, governments defined as examples of populism usually revolve around patterns of legitimation that are common in governments seen as examples of militarism. Both types of government have the tendency to extract legitimacy from uncertain welfare systems and diminished individual security, and even to attach welfare benefits to pro-regime actions and attitudes. Likewise, in both populist and military governments, the discrediting of judicial bodies is prevalent, and judicial actors are often accused of undermining both national solidarity and national security. This is also clearly visible in Israel, where populist militarism is supported by attacks on the judiciary, including allegations that the courts are in sympathy with external military actors. Inherent in both systems, vitally, is the fact that governments promote conflict in both the lateral and the vertical dimensions of society, as intensified lateral conflict is used as a pretext for stronger use of prerogative force at the vertical level. Also inherent in both models is a tendency to link internal factions to external threats and to partition domestic society around external antagonisms, so that the border between internal and external politics becomes unsettled. Accordingly, populism and militarism fall at different points on the same legitimational spectrum, and the relation between them is fluid.

CONCLUSION

Overall, experiences of constitutional construction since the 1980s display different patterns of crisis, from complete democratic collapse, to increased authoritarianism, to recurrent threats of sabotage. In different ways, these cases can be grouped together as examples of an emergent paradigm in which democratic subject formation has been detached from the integration system (world law) created after 1945. This paradigm has strong variations, but it tends to coalesce around some degree of social militarization in the vertical or the lateral dimension of society, or frequently in both. In particular, the erosion of constitutional democracy is typically marked by the fact that welfare institutions lose the power to support the exercise of individual political rights, so that governments obtain legitimacy by forcing political subjects into violent collectives directed towards external or internal adversaries, or both. This in turn tends to create a hostility to international normative principles. On both counts, government usually acquires an executive bias and the sets of rights that traditionally framed executive authority lose force. As mentioned, one process at the core of modern society is that welfare states replaced military bodies as organs of social integration. In cases of constitutional crisis, this process is often partly reversed. In its effects, these tendencies often recreate, albeit in weakened form, characteristics of constitutions formed in societies shaped by military or inter-imperial rivalry. For example, in extreme cases, such constitutions mobilize citizens for external violence and reproduce classical military contracts. In some cases, government resumes some characteristics of a system of internal colonization, as military bodies acquire increased authority in managing links between government and citizens. More generally, such constitutions draw legitimacy from global dichotomies, so that international divisions are reproduced in internal antagonisms, and the primary partition between the inside and the outside of society is weakened.

CHAPTER TEN

NEW SECURITY CONSTITUTIONS

The weakening of democratic integration in constitutional law is not solely caused by occurrences inside nation states. On the contrary, constitutional law has also been redirected towards new patterns of military integration by organizations in the international domain, and recent developments in the global security environment have undermined some constitutional balances that support modern democracy. As explained, constitutional democracies were consolidated after 1945 as they simultaneously stabilized constitutional rights that originated in militarism *and* detached political interactions from military propensities in society. Through this, democracy came to repose on a dialectic of military violence as war drove mass inclusion through rights, but, partly as a result of legal norms created by war, these rights were separated from militarism. This was visible in the organic construction of many constitutions. By the early twenty-first century, however, this formative logic of democratic constitutional law had been eroded in many settings. As analysed in this chapter, the preconditions that supported both classical constitutionalism, rooted in military bargains and post-1945 constitutionalism, and sustained by an international form to stabilize such bargains, became unsettled. This is not to say that constitutional democracy approached global disintegration at this point. Yet core legitimational logics underpinning democracy were discernibly weakened and constitutional models more typical of militarized societies reappeared. By this time, as discussed, the domestic preconditions for democracy were depleted, and, in parallel, the internal role of international norms in securing democracy was revised.

However, these factors were partly caused by changes in global security landscapes, which began to challenge the deep web of national and international norms around which constitutional democracies had been designed. In consequence, constitutions began to rearticulate more traditional imperial functions. That is, they again focused on societal control and territorial occupancy, they re-emphasized executive functions and they established legal orders in which the partition between conflicts inside and conflicts outside society lost some force.

NEW SECURITY LANDSCAPES

The reconfiguration of constitutional law by changes in international security settings can be partly traced to the political importance ascribed to terrorism, which was increasingly perceived as a global threat after the suicide attacks in New York and Washington in 2001. Of course, terrorism had long existed as a tangible security risk before this time, and most constitutions contained provisions to address potential cases of terrorism.[1] In fact, many constitutions had been shaped by responses to actors defined as terrorists.[2] Further, terrorism had become an object for international policy making before 2001. Yet, from this point, governments began to accentuate national security prerogatives related to terrorism as distinct sources of legitimacy. Owing to the increasingly transnational nature of terrorism, national security prerogatives were partly reconceived and governments began to concentrate their security resources on averting sui generis threats associated with terrorism.

Initially, the increased anxiety about terrorism meant that governments and politicians simply placed heightened emphasis on conventional security policies, presenting terrorist violence as a critical threat to their basic legitimacy. In such instances, many governments projected classical exceptionalist arguments to define their responses to terrorist violence. On one hand, governments often presented terrorism as an external existential threat, standing in some analogy to acts of war. This was clearly the case in the USA, where, from 2001, terrorists were declared *unlawful enemy combatants* and actions against terrorism were

[1] A paradigmatic formulation is found in an earlier ruling of the Constitutional Court of the FRG, stating that the guarantee of security provides the 'essential and final justification' of the state itself: BVerfG 49,24 – Kontaktsperre-Gesetz.

[2] See discussion of South Africa at p. 360.

described as a war on terror.[3] Later, in 2015, President Hollande stated that France was in a state of war, following terrorist attacks in Paris. Such constructions of terrorism as a military threat are not entirely without justification. As discussed, in the longer wake of 1945, military conflict increasingly took place in uncertain social and legal contexts in which distinctions between formal warfare, conducted by official military organizations, and informal violence were not always evident. Further, terrorism can be interpreted as one extreme manifestation of a wider process in which, after 1945, military conflict was separated from high-intensity warfare and it was more frequently conducted as asymmetrical violence, especially in postcolonial settings.[4] In its motivations, moreover, terrorism occupies a space with proximity to war. Of course, its perpetrators mainly attack civilians. Yet they usually aim to harm individual persons to the extent that these individuals are subjects of a given government, so that harm done to civilian subjects is calculated as harm done to their government or to their society in its totality. More generally, a definition of terrorism became widespread before and after 2001 that construed terrorism in constitutional terms, indicating that terrorism was a mode of violence that attacked the deepest values that democratic societies contain. The minimal threshold for the categorization of a violent criminal as a terrorist is now typically that she or he is a person whose actions constitute a collective threat to the most substantial principles on which a society and its citizens rely. Different accounts have presented governmental reactions to terrorism as one instance in a persistent confrontation between constitutional ideals and military violence in which violence intruded on the consensual, rights-based structure of constitutional rule.[5] Accordingly, one observer explains that terrorism is 'an act of public violence' which is performed by a citizen to undermine 'public government by intimidation or coercion'.[6] In such definitions, public reactions to terrorism were often proposed as vital indicators of political legitimacy – terrorism was projected as a phenomenon close to a moral war, implying that, in responding to terrorism, governments could use special measures to protect the most precious obligations that tie them to their citizens.[7] Importantly,

[3] This designation was upheld by the US Supreme Court in *Hamdi v. Rumsfeld*, 542 U.S. 507 (2004).
[4] Münkler (2006: 222).
[5] See analysis in Brooks (2004: 714).
[6] Lavi (2011: 802).
[7] Writing in *The Guardian* (14 December 1999), Jack Straw, UK Home Secretary, declared that antiterror legislation was intended to defend 'democratic values'.

a definition of the terrorist was implied in UN resolutions and EU Council Framework Decisions that construed terrorism as violence containing an attack on democratic society as a whole.[8]

At a more fundamental level, however, the increasing importance of terrorism as a security threat meant that governmental duties were proportioned to new forms of violence, and the position of such violence in relation to national security systems became ambiguous. Inevitably, as constitutional law was historically interwoven with the management of national security threats, the rise of terrorism challenged deeply rooted premises of constitutional law. In particular, it challenged both core parts of the military-dialectical balance in which constitutional rights had historically been constructed and states had integrated their citizens.

First, the rise of terrorism changed the physical and legal locus of violence in relation to which governments defined their security obligations. Terrorism is often perpetrated by transnational agents and organizations, and some perpetrators of terrorism operate within international support networks. To this extent, terrorism mirrors more classical security threats. However, acts of terrorist violence are typically committed inside the physical borders of national societies in terrains not classified as war zones. Consequently, the distinction between the inside and the outside of national societies becomes unstable as governments are exposed to terrorism. Owing to this uncertain geographical position, further, terrorists are not easily separable from other criminal actors and many atrocities defined as terrorism resemble other acts of violence which are subject to regular criminal jurisdiction. Despite the symbolic importance of terrorism as a threat to the structure of democratic society, it is frequently uncertain how such acts can be differentiated from other acts of violence that affect many victims. Often, acts of terrorism are perpetrated by nationals of the government against whom violence is directed, and the specific motivation for violence is unclear.[9] This means that the definition of a violent act as an example of terrorism often depends on the ethnic or regional provenance of its perpetrator, as the term 'terrorism' is most

[8] In the UN, see the Preamble to the Resolution of the UN Human Rights Commission 1998/47. In the EU, see the decision that 'terrorism constitutes a threat to democracy, to the free exercise of human rights and to economic and social development', set out in Council Framework Decision of 13 June 2002 on combating terrorism (2002/475/JHA).

[9] Examples include the attacks on the London underground in 2005 and in Manchester in 2017, which were at least partly perpetrated by members of local populations with limited claim to political motivation. In the USA, the concept of the American-citizen enemy combatant was used to address this ambiguity in *Padilla v. Hanft*, 423 F.3d 386 (4th Cir. 2005).

easily used to label acts committed by members of minority populations in affected societies. For such reasons, terrorism poses a security threat in face of which the security obligations of states are not fully manifest. In fact, although states usually claim that the provisions of collective security against terrorism is a higher-order constitutional duty, most crimes of 'terrorists' are processed under criminal law.[10]

Second, the rise of terrorism placed the violence in relation to which governments explain their security duties in a new temporal domain. That is, as terrorism emerged as a security challenge, governments attached their legitimacy to the management of violence of a semi-military nature, which did not depend on legal declarations of conflict and whose outbreak was not subject to any conventions of war. This meant that governments were required to take action against violence that they at least presented as a potentially permanent threat, which could not be limited by formal-legal understandings of the beginnings and ends of combat situations. This had the consequence, on one hand, that governments expressed their legitimacy through the provision of security in abstract form, not related to distinct and identifiable circumstances. On the other hand, this meant that governments connected their legitimacy to the provision of security without an obvious temporal focus or object. There is much evidence to illustrate this. For one prominent instance, Donald Rumsfeld stated after 9/11 that government actions against terror would not address terrorism as 'a single event', but they would involve 'a very broadly based campaign to go after the terrorist problem where it exists' without geographical specificity – 'in countries across the globe'.[11]

Third, the rise of terrorism placed the violence to which governments are exposed in a domain whose social effects differed from those of more conventional conflict. This was the case for the simple reason that, unlike the classical deployment of military force, governmental provision of security against terrorism does not depend on the extensive mobilization of national populations. Terrorist violence is a latent threat affecting limited numbers of persons in society, and it is perpetrated by small organizations. Consequently, governments typically react to such violence through measures that do not require the large-scale integration of citizens in military actions. In some cases, governments have mobilized substantial military forces in pursuit of putative terrorists.[12] Yet generally

[10] The Manchester attack of 2017 was classified as a case of terrorism, but relevant legal cases were heard under normal criminal law.
[11] Pentagon briefing, published in the *Washington Post* (18 September 2001).
[12] The obvious examples are military deployments in Afghanistan and Iraq.

the organization of governmental security in face of terrorism requires only the participation of a narrow group of actors. In this regard, the transformation of security threats caused by the rise of terrorism profoundly altered the foundations of constitutional law. This transformation meant, to some degree, that governments attached their legitimacy to the provision of security in matters in which their reliance on citizens was limited. As a result, governments were not compelled to integrate their citizens as actors vital to the administration of national security policies, and the interdependence between governments and citizens that characterized the long history of constitutional law was weakened. The original basis of constitutional interaction between governments and citizens was modified by this simple fact.

As discussed in the following, the effects of these processes can be observed in several constitutional tendencies. In brief, however, the rise of terrorism altered constitutional law, first, because it changed the deep-lying historical bargaining structures that grew from the governmental provision of security. However, it also modified the dialectical effects of violence that configured constitutional rights after World War II. As terrorism increasingly became a matter for international regulation, it unsettled the specific dynamics that had shaped constitutional formation after 1945. As mentioned, after 1945, many states began to organize their powers domestically by reflecting on their proximity to military regimes, often using international norms to modify the terms of their interaction with citizens and to secure the basic architecture of democracy. Through this, international law softened governmental actions towards individual citizens, as it often placed limits on executive actions. The rise of terrorism substantially weakened this constitutional dynamic. Through the rise of terrorism, international norms acquired, in certain cases, a new function and many states used international principles to justify the erosion of basic rights and to reinforce executive powers. In both respects, the causal forces that had imposed basic rights on constitutionally ordered institutions lost intensity.

TERRORISM, EMERGENCIES AND EXECUTIVES

At the most specific level, transnational terrorism challenged constitutional law because it confronted governments with a form of violence that was not easily captured by conventional emergency laws. As mentioned, governments defined terrorism as a threat to their fundamental normative structure, and many governments relied on exceptionalist arguments to explain their responses to terrorism, internally and externally. In so doing, governments framed their responses to this threat in a classical exceptionalist perspective. However, terrorism gave rise to a new mode of exceptionalism which affected the constitutional order of states in new ways.

Traditionally, provisions for states of emergency in the constitutions of democratic states usually declared that certain constitutional rights could be suspended in specified situations to protect higher-order principles of democracy. This approach became rooted in the idea of strategic constitutional defence, and, at least ideal-typically, it implied that, where limitations on basic constitutional provisions were enforced, the reasons for the emergency should be manifest for all citizens. Of course, such provisions normally stipulated that emergency powers could be used both against external and internal actors, and they frequently allowed the imposition of emergency rule on selective grounds, against anti-systemic organizations in national society. However, in the classical democratic construction, the state of emergency was a constitutional reality that was palpably different from conditions covered by normal law. A state of emergency was imposed as a government provided an account, implicitly, of the primary principles that it wished to defend, and it suspended some constitutional norms in achieving this goal. A state of emergency, in this sense, was defined as a legal interlude in which the constitution itself remained unchanged; in fact, emergencies served to solidify the essential core of the constitution as the constitution reappeared with full authority after the emergency had passed.[13] This classical approach is echoed in important recent analyses which indicate that emergency laws may be justified if open public debate is conducted to explain their necessity, such that people affected by circumscribed deprivation of rights must know why this is the case.[14] In classical democratic doctrine, states of emergency had particular implications for executive power. In emergencies, executives were authorized to discharge core legislative functions, and agents in the executive acquired circumscribed responsibilities for social protection and pacification.[15]

The historical observations presented in previous chapters indicate ways in which states of emergency were entangled in complex manner with the societal bargains that determined the allocation of constitutional

[13] See, for example, Art. 48 of the German constitution (1919), Art. 91 of the German constitution (1949), Arts 16 and 36 of the French constitution (1958) and Art. 228 of the Polish constitution (1997).

[14] Gross (2003: 1118).

[15] See the classical claim that exceptional executive authorization may be required for constitutional protection in Schmitt (1928: 112).

rights. As discussed, in the gradual evolution of most democracies, periods of emergency tended to reduce constitutional rights for specified periods, as governments were faced with intense actual violence. However, the longer structural effect of emergency laws usually differed from their immediate implications. Over time, democratic governments exposed to military emergencies were compelled to engage in negotiations with their citizens, and they tended to elevate protections for rights. Indeed, the expansion of executive force during emergencies was usually correlated with the longer-term thickening of procedural rights, political rights and social rights made available to citizens, at least in broadly democratic polities. This was observable at crucial stages in the history of modern democracy. For example, World War I saw both intense executive expansion and dramatically increased use of emergency legislation in all belligerent societies, partly extending after 1918. Yet, as examined, World War I led, typically, to the exponential increase of each set of constitutional rights, if only for a short period. Similarly, the aftermath of 1945, notably, was a period marked by greatly augmented executive power, but it also led to the unprecedented expansion of public-law rights – in administrative law, electoral law and social welfare law.[16] This complex fusion of executive expansion and the reinforcement of constitutional rights was usually caused by the fact that war brought an experience of emergency, which was focused around a defined external threat, which affected all members of society. That is, military emergencies placed governments and their populations under extreme collective strain, and, in response, governments entered new obligations and discharged new duties towards citizens, which, specifically, executive agencies were required to accomplish. Visibly, emergency situations became central stages in the formation of democracy, such that constitutional rule evolved in a dialectic of exceptionalism in which military experiences had constituent force. As discussed, this dialectic was less strongly realized in societies under external imperial control, where periods of military conflict did not reliably solidify new rights.[17] In many societies under colonial rule, military conflict led to the heightened use of internal violence, often via emergency courts.[18] However in societies on the metropolitan side of imperial systems, war typically placed downward pressure on rights for a short time and then, after conflict, it intensified the rights connecting citizens to the

[16] See pp. 176, 378–9.
[17] See pp. 149–51.
[18] See pp. 149–51, 358.

state. After 1945, as discussed, most constitutions utilized international law to stabilize these rights in a form detached from war.

By contrast, terrorism created a distinct mode of political exceptionalism, and it had an unusual impact on constitutional structure in many polities.[19] Most governments reacted to threats resulting from terrorism by claiming – symbolically – that terrorism constitutes an exceptional global environment, requiring states to fulfil heightened protective duties. However, in strict constitutional terms, governments usually addressed terrorist violence in improvised ways. In fact, few governments declared in determinate legal categories that they were operating in states of emergency as they addressed terrorist risks, and few governments clarified how such risks actually affected their constitutional form. In some polities, such as the UK and the USA, that introduced new security laws related to terrorism, constitutional powers for declaring a state of emergency are limited.[20] In most constitutional settings, the impact of terrorism became tangible, not in measures to protect higher constitutional principles, but in ad hoc legislation, which led to the (partly acknowledged) weakening of the legal norms that usually constrain executive powers.[21] However, the exceptionalist premises for such measures were deeply ambiguous. Indeed, in many cases, perpetrators of terrorist violence did not occupy an exceptional legal space, and they did not pose any obvious threat to the system of government as a whole. As mentioned, in many cases, governments struggled to differentiate terrorists from ultra-violent criminals, and the precise constitutional principles that demand protection in face of terrorism, apart from a general injunction to avert mass violence, are not easy to declare.[22]

In addition, the form of exceptionalism inherent in terrorism altered constitutional law because, in the face of terrorism, many governments were able to proclaim the provision of security as a free-standing duty detached from other obligations. As examined, the bargains at the core of constitutional law hinged, historically, on the fact that states were

[19] My view is close to the claim that, in policies addressing designated terrorist risks, 'the application of the emergency paradigm has broadened considerably', such that 'normalcy can no longer be distinguished from emergency' (Greene 2018: 34, 48).

[20] Illustratively, the US constitutional system provides for suspension of habeas corpus (Art. I/9), but it does not allow an explicit grant of power to address emergencies. See the analysis in Issacharoff and Pildes (2004).

[21] See, for example, the UK Civil Contingencies Act (2004).

[22] As mentioned, victims of the Manchester Arena bombing were killed by a fellow Mancunian. Of the four perpetrators of the London 7/7 bombings, only one was born outside the UK, and he had lived in Britain from early childhood (Walker 2007: 225).

required to mobilize large sectors of their population for war, and this occurred in relation to a manifest external threat, for a legally circumscribed period of time. In most contexts, persons involved in the organization of security (soldiers) received a set of political and social rights to motivate them to participate in the organization of security. Constitutions thus developed as an internal apparatus to secure national sovereignty. Through the rise of terrorism, however, the rights-producing effects of national security strategies were necessarily curtailed and the pressures that forced governments to bargain over rights were diminished. In particular, it proved specific to the nature of terrorism that governments were able to promise security as a right separated from the complex of rights that formed national citizenship as a political condition, and governments frequently pledged commitment to provide security in a form that placed other rights in a weakened position. On this basis, the dialectic of violence at the core of constitutional law was modified. The commitment to the provision of security in isolation from other rights has featured strongly in governmental policy statements since circa 2000. For example, this tendency was displayed in governmental reasoning regarding relevant policy obligations.[23] This tendency became evident in priority statements of politicians.[24] This tendency also appeared in judicial decision-making in national and supranational courts.[25] In such declarations, obligations attached to security became dissociated from other rights. Of course, none of this is unusual in times of warfare, as most periods of warfare saw the privileging of security over other state duties. But, in reaction to terrorism, such privileging occurred on a protracted basis in the face of threats of a legally unspecified nature.

In many polities, by consequence, exposure to terrorism created a pattern of exceptionalism that separated governments from the historical dialectics of collective violence, weakening the pressures that engendered rights as elements of constitutional rule. This is primarily manifest in the fact that, in cases of perceived threats arising from terrorism, governments typically limit protections for primary *procedural rights*. In the USA, for example, the most controversial reaction to

[23] This is evidenced in legal rulings in the UK. In some cases, the Home Secretary specifically weighed rights of individuals against the public interest in security, privileging the latter. See the justification in *Pham (Appellant) v Secretary of State for the Home Department (Respondent)* [2015] UKSC 19, at para. 108.

[24] After 9/11, ministers of the interior in Germany and Austria declared that security should be placed above basic rights in the hierarchy of governmental obligations (Michaelson 2006: 11).

[25] European Court of Human Rights, *Ghoumid and others v France* (52273/16) (25 June 2020).

terrorism is expressed in policies of executive detention, in which real or potential terrorists are incarcerated under executive orders, entailing a limitation of habeas corpus rights. Such orders often involve a hybridization of laws of war and laws of peace.[26] Many persons detained in such circumstances are American citizens who are treated as combatants. Such persons are denied both protections for combatants under international law and habeas corpus rights under constitutional law. In fact, these provisions created a special court system for persons suspected of terrorist activities, and this court system assumed extraterritorial reach.[27] However, some widening of executive authority is a broad feature of governmental responses to terrorism. As a general norm, for example, governments have used national security risks to authorize otherwise legally questionable surveillance policies, including invasive access to private data and communications.[28] This is especially frequent in social domains possessing potential relevance for terrorism such as transnational communication, banking and finance. In some instances, governments have weakened otherwise solid constitutional protections for rights of habeas corpus and access to court for persons suspected of terrorist crimes.[29] In some examples, this tendency has found support at the international level, as UN directives regarding asset freezing for persons suspected of terrorism have clearly breached guarantees for access to law in national constitutional systems.[30] This reduction in protections for procedural rights is at times manifested in the most essential dimension of legal subjectivity – in rights to citizenship itself. In some settings, it has become frequent for governments to exercise powers of citizenship deprivation over suspected terrorists. In many cases of citizenship deprivation, procedural rights for persons affected by such decisions have been weakly protected, and broad discretionary powers have been reserved for executive bodies.[31] In virtually all cases, such acts of legal exclusion have been conducted in a manner that is selectively detrimental to minority communities, as

[26] Detention, Treatment, and Trial of Certain Non-citizens in the War against Terrorism, 66 Fed. Reg. 57, 833 (13 November 2001).

[27] Gross (2003: 1017–9).

[28] See provisions for 'enhanced surveillance procedures' in the US Patriot Act (2001).

[29] See *Rumsfeld v. Padilla*, 542 U.S. 426 (2004).

[30] See the ECHR rulings regarding the Swiss government's failure to provide a remedy in imposing UN-mandated anti-terror orders: *Nada v Switzerland* [2012] ECHR 1691 (12 September 2012); *Al-Dulimi and Montana Management Inc. v Switzerland* (Application no. 5809/08) ECHR (21 June 2016). This judicial trend is considered in illuminating manner in Tzanakopoulos (2011: 134–136).

[31] *Begum v Home Secretary* [2021] UKSC 7.

citizenship deprivation is most easily imposed on persons who have more than one nationality.

Analogous developments are also manifest in the sphere of *political rights*. As mentioned, terrorism has often been defined as an assault on the fundamental political fabric of democracy.[32] In some countries, governments have justified the imposition of heightened security measures regarding terrorism by claiming that strict guarantees are required to support political rights.[33] In such accounts, acts combating terrorism are presented as acts of constitutional defence. Yet reactions to terrorism have frequently lowered constitutional protections for rights of political participation.

These outcomes are seen in a range of examples. At a most manifest level, some governments utilized the threat of terrorism to control access to the political system, limiting the basic exercise of political rights. For example, some authoritarian governments treated terrorism as a pretext to prohibit political parties, diminishing competition for public office. Important examples of this can be seen in the Central Asian region. Until his death in 2016, Karimov's government in Uzbekistan used the threat of terrorism, associated with the post-independence civil war in Tajikistan, the alleged regional proliferation of Islamist movements and the proximity of conflict in Afghanistan, to suppress political opposition and to secure the unaccountability of government. This was strongly linked to the fact that Uzbekistan became an ally of the USA after 2001, as it provided military access to Afghanistan in return for American finance. In this case, the Uzbek government utilized US anti-terror strategies to confer transnational legitimacy on its policies of political repression, which involved rigid control of freedom of movement and the imposition of harsh internal security controls. The aftermath of 9/11 saw the broad legitimation of extreme authoritarianism in Uzbekistan, and it was only after the deployment of indiscriminate violence by the government in the Fergana valley in 2005 that the international community withdrew support from the regime. In this case, the USA used the spectre of Islamic terrorism to advance militarily into regions which, only a decade earlier, had been inner components of the Soviet Union. In other polities, the provision of security against terrorism has been

[32] See examples at pp. 475–6, where antiterror actions are legitimated because they are deemed vital for the defence of democracy.

[33] In France, President Hollande constructed a militarized antiterror regime around the defence of positive values such as human rights and freedoms attached to citizenship. In analysing France, one account describes President Hollande's 'discursive construction of security as the bedrock of human rights' (Bogain 2017: 482).

specifically deployed as a pretext to manage the political arena and to reduce competition for access to political office. In some polities in Africa, for example, UN directives regarding security have been implemented as justifications for the exclusion of certain movements from the political arena.[34] In such instances, the construction of terrorism as a security threat stood in the path of longer trajectories of democratization, and it was utilized to narrow channels of communication with the political system, to curtail the political rights of many organizations.

In more consolidated democracies, many governments used terrorism to manage and constrain the exercise of political rights. For example, in France, several associations that represent Muslims have either been dissolved or subject to heightened state control; some have been required to sign a 'republican contract' to obtain public funding.[35] In more extreme instances, governments have utilized security threats to marginalize regime opponents, and simple critics of the government have been labelled terrorists in terms that legitimated the use of violence against them. This is evident in some primarily democratic polities such as Colombia and Brazil. In Colombia, as analysed, different presidents have argued that the civil conflict demands blanket securitization against terrorists. In Brazil, as discussed, President Bolsonaro classified different protest groups as terrorists, which provided justification for increased use of violence by the government. In India, similar tactics have been deployed by Modi, who amended existing antiterror laws in 2019, using enhanced powers to incarcerate regime opponents. Elements of this closely replicated the constitutional emergency of 1975–7, which itself mirrored aspects of colonial-era security strategies.

At a less deliberate level, governments that sponsored strong antiterrorist initiatives tended almost inevitably to depreciate the standing of political rights. The weakening of political rights appears in the simple fact that, in face of security threats connected with terrorism, powers of legislation are transferred to political actors, usually in executive bodies, who are not strongly bound by specific acts of legislation, so that rights of collective participation in lawmaking are retrenched. In addition, the implementation of national security policies to prevent terrorism spills over into policies that restrict political liberties more widely. This can often be seen in legislation introduced after terrorist

[34] See discussion in Whitaker (2007: 1025).

[35] Loi no 2021–1109 (24 August 2021), Loi confortant le respect des principes de la République. Associations dissolved since 2020 include: Baraka City, Le Collectif contre l'islamophobie en France (CCIF) and Cheikh Yassine. Rachel Pougnet informed me of this.

violence, in which the range of political activities covered by national security legislation is expanded. This tendency became immediately obvious after 9/11, as the Patriot Act in the USA gave the federal government extended powers of political surveillance. Parts of this legislation were then emulated globally, and national security laws allowing intensified monitoring of political activities became commonplace. In such cases, the diminution of protections for political rights necessarily means that, in responses to terrorism, intra-organic counterweights to executive power are reduced and executive agents can operate at a heightened degree of autonomy.

In each point, the impact of terrorism partly counteracts the complex military dialectic at the core of constitutional law. Following the terrorist attacks of 2001, it became habitual for governments to associate terrorism with war and to claim military authorization in combating it both internally and extraterritorially. This alignment of terrorism to war reduced constraints on executive power in foreign policy, as governments exploited anxiety about terrorism to mobilize military force against other countries.[36] This alignment also weakened rights-based constraints in internal policies. Yet, the longer-term outcome of these processes differed greatly from more typical historical reactions of constitutional systems to warfare. These processes provided only limited expression for the rights-constituting dimensions of political exceptionalism. In fact, they partly replicated constitutional trajectories in earlier imperial societies. On one hand, they mirrored constitutional conditions on the inside of earlier imperial polities, where governments were able to use executive force to limit the push for constitutional inclusion.[37] But they also mirrored conditions on the colonial side of imperial systems, where subjects lacked military leverage on government and violence instilled a tiered citizenship regime in society. Recent history has seen a transformation of the post-1945 pattern of the occupation constitution, and an international order has emerged that, in some respects, facilitates governmental control of society.

NEW OCCUPATION CONSTITUTIONS 1

Changes in the form of constitutional law are not only determined by the policies of national governments concerning transnational terrorist violence. As mentioned, security policies in the international domain

[36] See pp. 495–6.
[37] See pp. 143–7.

have also had important consequences for constitutional law. The rise of terrorism occurred as part of a global security landscape in which international organizations were already acquiring new powers to influence decisions in national societies. Above all, terrorism acquired salience as a security challenge at a point when the UN Security Council was becoming more assertive in discharging its responsibilities regarding international security. Incrementally, these processes shaped constitutional systems at the national level, and changes in the emphasis of international law affected the deep preconditions of democratic constitutionalism.

The changing role of the Security Council can be partly attributed to the fact that, in the longer aftermath of the Cold War, the UN was released from some geopolitical constraints that had previously restricted its actions. The Security Council was originally conceived as an organ close to an executive body for the UN, possessing a small membership, authorized to react to pressing security threats, but without effective legislative functions for individual states. Chapter VII of the UN Charter, in its initial wording, conferred on the Security Council the power to intervene in disputes between sovereign states and, in some cases, to help to 'restore international peace and security' (Art. 42). In the early 1990s, however, the Council issued an increasing number of resolutions that declared military situations a threat to peace. In many such cases, these resolutions referred to events inside national societies, which would not have normally been subject to the authority of the Security Council. Through the 1990s, the Security Council modified its traditional definition of the threat to peace to cover problems such as state fragmentation, actions of mercenaries and other national emergencies.[38] In this process, organs of the UN moved away from their conventional deference to sovereign national governments in domestic military contexts. A transnational security domain was tentatively consolidated that altered central axes of the conventional security system, such that the principle of sovereign authority was qualified and the range of security challenges subject to international directives was widened.

The increase in the importance of security threats relating to terrorism was closely connected to this expansionary process, and, as the Security Council enlarged its general remit, terrorism was increasingly

[38] See for one example the reasoning in Resolution 733 (1992) concerning civil violence in Somalia which engaged the UN in its responsibility for 'maintenance of international peace and security'. See the analysis in De Wet (2004: 157) and Talmon (2005: 180–181).

identified as a mode of violence subject to international regulation. In the early 1990s, the Security Council had already begun to use its broadened construction of the threat to peace to address terrorism, notably in Resolutions 748 (1992) and 883 (1993) regarding the responsibility of Libya for the attack on an aeroplane in British airspace (Lockerbie bombing) and its duty to extradite suspects for trial.[39] In Resolution 748 (1992), the Council declared that 'the suppression of acts of international terrorism ... is essential for the maintenance of international peace and security'. It also stated that demands contained in this resolution relating to the extradition of Libyan nationals, and conditions regarding military, commercial and diplomatic relations with Libya, should prevail over other international agreements. It also established a committee to monitor compliance with such demands. On this basis, the Security Council indicated that terrorism could be construed in partial analogy to war, and it assumed the power to decide both when terrorism constituted a threat to international peace and when national governments were involved in supporting it. This process was by no means simple as it presupposed that the Council could precisely identify the point at which terrorism reached such intensity that it should be classified as war, assuming international dimensions.[40] One result of these developments was that the Security Council asserted legislative authority that significantly exceeded competences that it had previously claimed. Through the 1990s, the Council assumed powers to legislate in questions relating to terrorism that altered its constitutional definition. For example, in Resolution 1267 (1999), the Council imposed a sanctions regime on member states to combat terrorism linked to Al Qaeda. In doing this, it deviated from established precedent, as it had not previously claimed the authority to resolve matters reaching beyond a particular dispute or delineated conflict.[41] It expanded such competences in unforeseen ways, proposing resolutions in matters not strictly related to or emanating from interstate disputes, and penetrating deep into social domains subject to national constitutional norms.[42] In such steps, the Security Council in

39 See the analyses in De Wet (2004: 167) and Fox (2008: 2003).

40 Tzanakopoulos (2011: 60).

41 It had only created 'legal obligations' in relation to a 'specific controversy with clear geographic boundaries' (Helfer 2008: 81).

42 On this process, see Szasz (2002: 903). On the unprecedented nature of these provisions, see Helfer (2008: 82) and Ní Aoláin (2021: 34–36), and on their lack of authorization see Fremuth and Griebel (2007: 341, 360).

effect widened the definition of interstate war to incorporate terrorism, and, by this means, it enlarged its own authority and legislative force.

This trend culminated in the aftermath of 2001. At this point, the Security Council passed a series of rulings intended to have direct effect and to induce substantial legal reforms in all states in the UN, with far-reaching implications for the global legal order. In late September 2001, the Security Council passed Resolution 1373, accorded general obligatory force, which has emblematic significance in this process. This Resolution stipulated that international terrorism formed a threat to international peace and security, and it could justify military self-defence. It introduced a series of provisions under Chapter VII of the UN Charter that prescribed legislative measures to combat terrorism to UN member states, to the effect that, amongst other requirements, all states were obliged to freeze the assets of terrorist suspects, and all states were expected to criminalize financing of terrorist organizations.[43] This Resolution stipulated that all states should provide information to other states about the locality of possible terrorists. Most strikingly, it set out potential norms of criminal law for national legislators, and it established presumptions regarding penalties to be imposed by national governments on persons found guilty of terrorist violence.[44] It also created a new international body, a Committee of the Security Council, whose function was 'to monitor implementation of this resolution, with the assistance of appropriate expertise'. This Committee received reports from states on their introduction and implementation of relevant legislation. Accordingly, the legislative acts of the Security Council acquired an designated executive enforcement mechanism.[45]

Through such provisions, the Security Council established its authority to shape domestic constitutional acts in many contexts as it acquired the capacity to reach into domestic polities and legal systems to establish norms capable of overriding national constitutional protections. Alongside this, the Security Council established its authority to predetermine the international acts of national states. For example, Resolution 1373 contained provisions regarding the management of refugees in cases where a suspicion existed that applicants for asylum

[43] This was anticipated in asset-freezing provisions in Resolution 883 (1993) regarding the Lockerbie bombing.

[44] On the multiple bodies that now issue 'model laws', whose purpose is to harmonize counter-terrorism provisions across domestic regimes, see de Londras (2022: 121–153).

[45] This was flanked by provisions to help states draft legislation to meet their obligations under the resolution, so that relevant laws were instilled from outside in national polities (Ward 2003: 300).

may have engaged in terrorist activity. This created at least the possibility that UN resolutions could contravene norms of international law (i.e. the Refugee Convention) acknowledged as having *erga omnes* standing. Subsequent decisions, notably Resolution 1540, reinforced directives regarding asset freezing and the immediate incorporation of international norms, expressing the same presumption that its content would be put into effect as national law. Some resolutions recognized that certain affected states would struggle to meet the demands placed on them by such exigencies and they contained provisions for other states to assist them in their implementation.[46]

Here, exaggeration needs to be avoided. Such provisions did not form a universal security constitution, and they took effect, variably, within and alongside a broad range of national legal orders. Nonetheless, many states introduced new security laws because of these resolutions. Across different polities, these resolutions promoted a normative system in which constitutional rights not related to security were subject to adverse pressure. Some institutional counterweights were created to avert this process, and extreme examples of governmental use of security rights to curtail other rights have been denounced at the international level.[47] Yet, in Security Council resolutions, the right to security was projected in a form that could override other rights, and the fact that it was enshrined in international law meant that it could displace rights protected in national constitutional orders with little obstruction. Moreover, the standing of the Security Council meant that these provisions could be enforced with limited constitutional debate, and related controversy was largely displaced into judicial bodies. Indicatively, in some polities, some parts of Security Council resolutions, which were put into effect by national legislatures or executives, were contested by national or transnational courts on grounds of legality. One reason for this was that provisions for persons designated as terrorists frequently failed to provide legal avenues for such persons to challenge this designation. As a result, some national courts declared invalid laws or orders prompted by the UN resolutions by ruling that they breached international norms

[46] Of Resolution 1373, one account explains how: 'States were required to legislate domestically against terrorism, essentially presenting mandatory legislative accommodation by international fiat' (Gross and Ní Aoláin 2006: 403).

[47] Note the claim that measures taken by the Security Council are bound by 'basic human rights' (De Wet 2004: 217, 370). See the report submitted by Martin Scheinin (2010), as 'Special Rapporteur on the Promotion and Protection of Human Rights and Fundamental Freedoms while Countering Terrorism'.

regarding access to court (habeas corpus).[48] Similar rulings were reached by international human rights courts.[49]

The development of these new security landscapes contained deep implications for constitutional law and altered the formative premises of constitutional law, both in its classical pre-1945 and in its post-1945 construction. At a primarily level, one result of this constellation was that the classical military mainspring of constitutional democracy was weakened. The transnational security architecture defined security obligations for nation states that did not require bargaining between governments and citizens, so that governments assumed increased military authority without granting correlated rights. Simultaneously, however, antiterrorism law created legal constructions that altered the relation between war, law and legal protection that had conferred distinct features on constitutional law after 1945.

As discussed, key elements of national constitutional law after 1945 were defined by the fact that human vulnerability was treated as a transnational object of law. Through this, legal protections for vulnerable subjects reached from the international domain into national law, and constitutional guarantees for single subjects, usually expressed in human rights law, connected the national legal system to the international legal system. This reflected the perception that the experiences of violence on the inside and on the outside of national societies were deeply connected. This was flanked by transformative processes inside national societies in which political subjects were separated from military affiliations, and historical intergroup conflicts were softened. Through the rise of terrorism, however, the relation between international law and national law in the construction of subjective vulnerability was modified, and the figure of the terrorist – as a transnational violent actor – placed this relation on new foundations. Through the rise of terrorism, the construction of members of national societies as transnational subjects persisted. That is, terrorism produced a legal architecture in which national citizens were defined as potential victims of violence of a transnational nature, as persons exposed to threats of a transnational character and as subjects directly implicated in international law.[50] At the international level, human vulnerability

[48] See the UK case *HM Treasury v Ahmed* [2010] UKSC 2.

[49] See cases in international courts against the implementation of UN directives at note 30, p. 483.

[50] One sympathetic commentary on Security Council resolutions declares that they are necessary because of the 'proven mobility of terrorists', the 'permeability of borders' and the fact that terrorists may exploit some states with weak antiterror infrastructures (Rosand 2005: 548).

is widely used to justify the imposition of protective norms (resolutions) by the Security Council. For example, resolutions of the Security Council have been framed by declarations of solidarity with victims of terrorism.[51] At the national level, human vulnerability is taken as a principle to justify the obligations of governments towards their citizens.[52] In this regard, the deep convergence between national and international violence that defined the post-1945 legal order for managing violence after 1945 was recreated. However, in this process, increased emphasis was placed on the protection of subjects from violence perpetrated, not by their own governments, but by transnational terrorists, and the vulnerability of individual subjects was emphasized to justify new powers assumed by national governments.

In this respect, the redefinition of the source of violence in relation to which governments owe obligations to their citizens has partly revised the relation between international law and constitutional law. In the longer aftermath of 1945, international law tended to imprint the form of a protective constitution in national societies. In broad terms, international law combined with constitutional law to form a thick system of norms, framing state actions in a structure of individual rights and obviating state violence towards citizens. However, this constitution has acquired an altered form, and it has been affected by a change in the emphasis of international law. In some respects, modern constitutional law developed after 1945 by constructing national society in some analogy to civil war in which international norms moderated the behaviour of state agents towards citizens. More recently, the axis of protection moved from the relation between citizens and their own states to the relation between citizens and terrorists, and, through this, state organizations were able to reconsolidate some powers, and the limits on their actions were reduced. As mentioned, one feature of contemporary counterterrorist legislation is that it is based, at the international level, in a revised definition of war. Through the rise of terrorism, constitutional law again drew some

[51] As a framing position, the Security Council declared 'its profound solidarity with the victims of terrorism' in Resolution 2617 (2021).

[52] After 2001, the US Department of Defense established the principle that official antiterror policies comprised the sum of 'defensive measures used to reduce the vulnerability of individuals and property to terrorists acts'. Most tellingly, in declaring a state of emergency on 16 November 2015, President Hollande stated that his 'will was to use the entire force of the state to serve the protection of our co-citizens'. This plan was to include internal use of the police forces and the army, connected to simultaneous intensification of military actions abroad. He also declared that it was vital to develop the French constitution to 'allow public authorities' to act more effectively against *terrorisme de guerre*.

legitimacy from the protection of subjects in a world of transnational violence, such that society was observed in some analogy to civil war. However, this new construction of violence created protective duties that reduced the normative constraints on the executive power of states in their own societies.

This broad tendency towards the reconstruction of the relation between citizen and government can be observed in specific legal phenomena. As discussed, this is evident in the fact that, in responding to terrorism, some governments give security imperatives primacy over other constitutional laws. For example, some states locate their citizens in legal categories close to those reserved for external combatants. Further, some governments define terrorists as foreign fighters, and some place their own nationals suspected of terrorism in detention centres with military features. National citizens placed in detention centres by their own governments are usually deprived both of constitutional rights that they could claim as citizens and of the internationally defined rights that they might claim as soldiers. Protections given to citizens in antiterrorist detention units in their polities are in some cases far below those dictated by common norms of international humanitarian law. Indicatively, the suspension of the Geneva Conventions has been authorized for persons suspected of terrorism and detained in their own societies; this suspension was expressly demanded in military orders issued by US President Bush in 2007.[53] In each respect, the rise of terrorism led to the depletion of rights both at the constitutional and the international level. In extreme cases, as mentioned, governments have used the transformation of violence inherent in terrorism as a framework to expand military control over society, declaring different categories of regime opponent terrorists and utilizing expanded executive powers to remove rival factions from the system of political competition.

In these respects, a constitutional order has taken shape in which governments have acquired augmented pacification functions towards some agents in their own societies. In some aspects, this process meant that governments assumed roles as actors in a global conflict in which their own domestic domains are potential battlegrounds. This reflected certain similarities with late-imperialist environments in which states acted as organs in wars uncertainly positioned between the national and the international sphere. Indeed, in some settings, this reflected

[53] Executive Order 13440, 20 July 2007 (rescinded 2009).

important similarities with administrative practices in societies on the colonial (external) side of imperial systems. In such contexts, states applied executive measures in which the distinction between military law and constitutional law was unclear, and citizenship rights could easily be reduced when states were exposed to military threats.

NEW OCCUPATION CONSTITUTIONS 2

This transformation of the historical roots of constitutional law is reflected in other tendencies in the international security landscape. In recent history, the widening of the powers of international organizations in regulating terrorism has been mirrored in the fact that some organizations assumed augmented enforcement roles vis-à-vis sovereign national states. Through the increasing regulation of transnational violence, global security policy began to construct a new legal structure that cut deep into national constitutional systems. This brought far-reaching changes to the societal sources of constitutional law, involving adjustments to inherited understandings of international law. This process also induced the partial reproduction of some constitutional elements more typical of imperial environments, and it re-patterned constitutional law as a legal order used to sustain external acts of annexation. In some respects, these developments meant that constitutional law was partly realigned to its function as an instrument for managing territorial control. In fact, the legal instruments that, after 1945, had directed constitutional law away from territorial control, became responsible for the reconsolidation of such functions.

This transformation can be seen in the fact that, after the end of the Cold War in 1989–91, the number of international missions supported by the UN increased, and their focus and purposes changed. Before this time, the UN had only conducted a small number of military operations. These had mainly been organized as peacekeeping initiatives, or as missions in regions affected by decolonization conflicts. From the early 1990s, the engagement of the UN in military operations became more frequent and the UN increasingly initiated actions in conflicts that did not have an interstate dimension.[54] This change in policy direction reflected an expanded definition of 'collective security' and the widening of the mandate of the Security Council.[55] Such

[54] See Ottaway and Lacina (2003: 74).
[55] This was set out in the *Report of the UN Secretary-General: Agenda for Peace* (1992).

interventions intersected with the increasingly widespread conviction that the international community, represented through the UN, was under obligation to intervene in some civil conflicts or potential civil conflicts, especially where societal circumstances threatened to give rise to mass humanitarian catastrophes. Like the rise of humanitarian law after 1945, this transformation was strongly connected to experiences of extreme ethnic violence. United Nations interventionism found increased support after the genocide in Rwanda, to which lack of UN intervention was widely perceived as a contributory factor. Eventually, the principle that the international community has a responsibility towards persons in circumstances of extreme vulnerability in their own societies was addressed in *The Responsibility to Protect* report drafted by an independent International Commission on Intervention and State Sovereignty, convened in 2000. This principle was formally endorsed by the UN in 2005, and it was repeatedly affirmed as a directive norm in Resolution 1674 (2006) of the Security Council.

Manifestly, these developments need to be treated as distinct from changing patterns of security law relating to transnational terrorism, as such measures were meant to prevent atrocities in contexts marked by existing civil war or extreme intergroup antagonism. In certain respects, however, these changes were constitutionally linked to the outcomes of security threats related to terrorism. This link was manifest in the fact that the international community accepted a mandate to protect persons in conditions of extreme vulnerability at the same time that global antiterror programmes were implemented by Western powers, especially the USA and the UK. Frequently, in fact, the mandate to protect vulnerable subjects was invoked to support military actions against states that, rightly or wrongly, became associated with international terrorism.

From the outset, the concept of a duty to intervene in matters subject to the authority of sovereign states possessed precarious legitimacy and it was susceptible to misuse. Before the responsibility to protect was formally endorsed by the UN as a transnational obligation, this concept had been selectively utilized by Western governments – especially that of the UK – in the mobilization of military resources against Iraq in 2003.[56]

[56] The notion that there may be sufficient humanitarian grounds for removal of a foreign government came to be known as the Blair doctrine. The major report on the Responsibility to Protect was largely finalized before 9/11. For comment see Wheeler (2005: 98). In 2005, President Bush's second inaugural address contained the pledge to support the 'great objective of ending tyranny' – 'by force of arms when necessary'.

This war, and subsequent military occupation, was justified by its advocates through a fusion of diverse international law principles, ranging from the right to pre-emptive self-defence to vague moral claims that it reflected humanitarian imperatives.[57] In addition, the duty to intervene has been unevenly interpreted. In some cases, the reasons for declaring a given situation a potential humanitarian disaster or human rights crisis have been questionable. This also became clear during Western intervention in Iraq and in subsequent acts of belligerent occupation. Although the initial military acts against Iraq were not formally approved by the UN, territorial occupation and, more clearly, governmental transformation in Iraq were partly authorized by the UN in Resolution 1483 of the Security Council. In subsequent instances of international intervention, such as NATO-led military intervention in Libya (2011), the UN proved a little more forthcoming in providing support for military intervention on humanitarian grounds. First, the UN stated that Muammar Gaddafi was threatening to inflict harm on peaceful protestors, which could, if realized, have constituted crimes against humanity.[58] Then, although it shied away from sanctioning a 'foreign occupation force' in Libya, the UN authorized external control of Libyan airspace through imposition of a no-fly zone and stated that 'all necessary measures' could be used to protect civilians. This was justified by the assumption that Gaddafi had acted in breach of 'international law, including international humanitarian law, human rights and refugee law'.[59] The ensuing intervention led to the toppling of a regime and the extrajudicial killing of a leader whose worst period of repressiveness had long passed.[60] Further, this intervention did little to avert humanitarian crisis. Instead, it directly contributed to two civil wars, in Libya and in Mali, and it caused a death toll that probably surpassed any human suffering it may have prevented. Alongside this, in this setting, the mandate derived from the duty to protect was patchily interpreted, and foreign organizations did not always invoke this duty uniformly. In Libya, NATO forces were less rigorous in protecting citizens from actors that helped to overthrow the government than they were in using force against the outgoing regime.[61]

[57] For analysis of the doctrine of pre-emptive self-defence in this context, see Moir (2010: 77).
[58] Security Council Resolution 1970 (2011).
[59] Security Council Resolution 1973 (2011). The US representative at the Security Council said: 'The United States stood with the people of Libya in their struggle to exercise their fundamental rights.'
[60] Kuperman (2013: 126).
[61] Genser (2018: 444).

An important general outcome of these processes is that they promoted a new ethic of interstate behaviour in the face of military conflict. These developments allowed states effectively to designate a situation a zone of military conflict without any actual presence of war, enabling governments to deploy military resources in such zones. After 1989, as mentioned, it became increasingly common for the Security Council to classify human rights violations or internal conflicts with human-rights dimensions as threats to international peace. This meant that states with influence in the UN could decide that some conditions in other states could be classified as examples of warfare, which meant that powers granted under Chapter VII of the UN Charter could be used in relation to internal conflicts. Moreover, in principle, these developments meant that the constitutional order of the UN was redefined as tolerance for violations of state sovereignty increased and the categorical prohibition of aggressive war central to the UN Charter lost force.[62] Through this, the defence of human rights served as part of a system of proportionality, which could be strong enough, in some settings, to outweigh more established norms of international law. Notably, international interventions motivated by human rights contravened older norms of interstate conflict. Many such interventions led to violent regime change, entailing the transformation of the sovereign form of government of the invaded society. Such processes manifestly conflicted with existing international norms, notably Art. 43 of the regulations attached to the Hague Convention (1907), intended to prevent the transformation of sovereign institutions by occupying powers.[63] In such conditions, then, new constitutions were often implanted in national societies, entailing the complete transfer of power and the fundamental redefinition of sovereignty.

In these respects, the redirection of international security policy after 1989 showed tendencies similar to those that occurred in antiterror law. Together, both bodies of law formed a transnational executive structure whose provisions could be used to abrogate both national constitutional law and established principles of international law. Both legal domains were shaped by a conceptual extension of war, which observed war as a diffuse societal condition and provided a warrant for executive authorization in circumstances designated as warfare. As a result, the social spheres, internal and external, in which governments were able to claim

[62] On this possibility, see Fox (2008: 303).
[63] See discussion in Wheatley (2006: 549) and Carcano (2015: 340).

authority to protect people from military violence increased dramatically. At one level, this mirrored the constitutional order formed after 1945, which was rooted in an extended concept of war. In recent developments, however, the constitution of violence that had shaped post-1945 democracies was inverted. After 1945, international norms were imposed to frame and limit the powers of national executives, to stabilize constitutions in social contexts already defined by war and to bring an end to war. Under the new constitutional system, basic rights themselves formed justifications for military incursion.

As mentioned, through the transformation of security risks at the end of the twentieth century, the role of basic rights in framing the social position of legal subjects changed. At this time, the right to security, or the governmental duty to guarantee security, was partly differentiated from other sets of rights. In some settings, it became the building block for an altered constitutional order in which governments were able to impose restrictive norms on their populations. This process was largely caused by a revision of the inherited concept of war in which governments designated members of their societies as military adversaries. At the same time, governments began to re-embark on trajectories of territorial annexation in which they acted, not as single belligerent states, bound by laws of war, but as members of military consortia which claimed justification through a revised understanding of warfare and of state obligations in the face of war. In such contexts, the provision of security for vulnerable subjects was used to justify the occupation of foreign countries and the replacement of existing regimes with externally ordained forms, often rooted in putative provisions for basic rights. Frequently, as discussed, this resulted in the greatly increased violation of human rights. A fact of fundamental importance in these processes is that, through such expansion of war, governments began to reproduce aspects of imperial politics. In particular, the distinction between the inside and the outside of national societies, and the related distinction between war and peace, was reconfigured. On this basis, some governments construed their own domestic societies in analogy to war zones, as parts of an international war in which violence against domestic adversaries could be transferred to other domains. Moreover, some governments eroded the difference between domestic domains and the domains subject to sovereign control of other states, claiming authority to define constitutional norms beyond their borders. This reproduced the classical imperial constellation in which spaces inside and spaces outside imperial states were unified by violence.

NEW OCCUPATION CONSTITUTIONS 3

One obvious factor in these processes is that, through the redefinition of war, armies frequently became actual agents of constituent power, so that the constitutional impulse of the 1980s, where military agents were removed from constitutional roles, was weakened. In some settings, recent years have seen the re-emergence of the patterns of occupation constitutionalism that took shape after 1945, where international bodies played an active role in democratic constitution making in former authoritarian states. Constitutions have been implemented in Iraq and Afghanistan, and a constitution has been drafted for Libya, which were partly designed to bring these polities into line with international assumptions regarding human rights law. The constitution-making situation in Iraq was partly constructed through a resolution of the UN Security Council, which established an order of occupation for Iraqi territory.[64] The creation of the Iraqi constitution was then formally endorsed by the Security Council, which deemed this a process in which 'the aspirations of the Iraqi people' could be realized.[65] Of course these polities were frequently seen as states that hosted terrorists, so that new constitutions were observed as a means to limit threats to international peace supposedly emanating from their territories. Such contexts reflected a process of externalized democratization in which some national governments strongly attached to international organizations enacted an international constituent power to shape government in other polities.

However, the difference between such contemporary constitution-making environments and the lines of occupation constitutionalism established after 1945 is self-evident. Most recent constitutions created following external intervention have been established because foreign military actors acquired roles in affected societies, not for reasons of self-defence nor to defend other countries exposed to belligerent acts, but rather in order, strategically, to promote regime change and to create a new constitutional system. Often, democracy was promoted (not established) through the meditated liquidation of existing institutions. Through this process, human rights law was frequently redesigned as a justification for military intervention, and constitutional law, giving strong expression to human rights, became

[64] Security Council Resolution 1483 (2003).
[65] Security Council Resolution 1511 (2003).

an instrument to secure external influence in a particular territory. In key respects, as discussed, human rights law was employed to vindicate international acts that otherwise were in clear breach of international law. The imposition of new regimes in post-authoritarian states after 1945 was frequently seen as illegal in international law.[66] However, such states had been invaded in due exercise of prerogatives granted under international law. In more recent cases, occupation constitutions have been imposed as part of a retroactive justification of military intervention, even in cases where invasion induced far greater human rights violations than would, in probability, have been the case had invasion not take place. In central respects, the claim that territorial occupancy may be required to ensure that human rights are protected is close to the assumption of a custodial duty, in which states justify their presence in other sovereign territories by claiming the moral duty to educate the populations of such territories towards democracy. Such events recall international acts of constitutional supervision in the Ottoman Empire in the nineteenth century and, more exactly, the tutelary mandates imposed in the same area in the aftermath of 1918.[67] Indicatively, constitutions in Libya, Iraq and Kosovo have all been initiated or created because of international involvement, in each case in former Ottoman regions.

In such contexts, as in other security domains in contemporary society, international law entered a trajectory on which it dialectically undermined its original constitutional effects. The patterns of international law that became prevalent after 1945 served in essence to transpose military norms into national society and to protect citizens from governments acting as analogues to military organizations in their interactions with their own citizens. This was based in a thick system of *world law*, reflecting the sense that military conflict traversed the divide between national and international society. In recent history, a new expansive construction of warfare has evolved, which also indicates that violence must be subject to global control. However, this construction at times diminishes individual protections against unmandated authority. In some cases, it has been utilized to sustain the external promotion of military violence inside sovereign territories.

66 See p. 341.

67 One observer has argued that this marks a return to trusteeship arrangements, in which human rights are applied to justify wardship (Wilde 2009: 134).

CONCLUSION

A set of linked socio-constitutional preconditions can be identified for modern democracy. First, after 1945, basic rights produced through military bargains were located on relatively secure premises by international law and domestic welfare systems. Owing to this, national societies with democratic features were subject to legal regimes in which citizens appeared as subjects of transnational violence. These features of democracy were strongly shaped by military conflicts that defined World War II and by the ideological antagonisms that characterized the Cold War. These features have been unsettled by several factors that typify contemporary security environments. In key respects, in fact, contemporary security policies weaken formative elements of democratic constitutionalism. This is seen in the fact that the basic military bargaining mechanisms that underpin democracy are diminished. Perhaps more fundamentally, this is also evident in the fact that the protective regimes resulting from international law have been qualified, and the post-1945 construction of global war has been restated in a form that can easily acquire repressive or interventionist implications. In central points, these developments have had the result that some aspects of imperialist constitutionalism have again become prevalent. At the core of this process is a potential weakening of international law as a source of democracy as democratization is associated with acts of military violence.

CONCLUSION

This book has sought to illustrate how, through its history, constitutional law has developed in complex conjunction with imperialism. From the beginning, constitutional law took shape as an internal organizational structure that allowed states to adapt their functions to the pressures of an international society increasingly defined by imperialism, and it formed a mechanism for creating governmental legitimacy that was strongly connected to military necessities. This character of constitutional law originated in the intensification of imperialism after circa 1750, when national governments were forced to increase domestic military support for their actions. To achieve this, governments established immediate individual linkages with their subjects and conducted processes of *vertical integration* in their societies, which reduced the social importance of local and religious bodies. These processes were usually consolidated by constitutional order: constitutions served both to organize the vertical integration of society and to soften or at least control the lateral conflicts that such integration engendered. Naturally, such processes occurred at different locations in imperial systems; some took place in the metropolitan parts of empires, and some took place in colonized societies, separating themselves from imperial rule. Generally, however, constitutions marked a dialectical reaction of national governments to imperialism. On one hand, virtually all constitutions contained a particular *post-imperial* emphasis. That is, they located states on foundations distinct from those of pure imperial rule and they created polities held together by voluntary, often increasingly democratic affiliations between citizens. However, the democratic fabric of constitutional law had a strategic valence in the context of imperialism and most states used constitutional law to position themselves in the world of empires. The societal bargains expressed in constitutional law often reconfigured elements of imperialism. Most constitutions were, simultaneously, post-imperial and part of a cycle of imperial restructuring.

On these grounds, this book challenges some influential outlooks in constitutional law, sociology and international relations. This book argues, first, that constitutional law was typically produced in situations where states were forced to stabilize the deepening interactions between their internal and external environments, and this was typically caused by imperialism. In this context, constitutional law projected popular sovereignty as the primary legitimating norm for government because this form proved militarily expedient, and the principle that government derived authority from the sovereign people allowed governments to extract increased military capacity from society. This basic constitutional norm enabled states to design their internal sovereignty in a form that supported their external sovereignty as they were challenged by other states. This meant that constitutionalism became a common, often semi-isomorphic model for arranging government functions in the age of high imperialism. In most settings, constitutions legitimated by popular sovereignty were formed as societies underwent structural transformation because of external imperial pressures.

Second, this book argues that states that embarked on a trajectory of constitutional organization almost invariably showed propensities for militarism, and they defined their legitimacy in terms that conflicted with international order. The societal process of vertical integration connected with constitutional law was part of an inherently expansionist dynamic in national societies, and it usually resulted in increased internal and external militarization. For this reason, warfare was a common event in societies whose states were assuming constitutional form, and, in many such cases, warfare and democratization were causally interlinked. Many wars resulted, specifically, from democratization processes instilled in society by constitutional texts, and the pressures released by constitutional constructions of legitimacy were frequent causes of war – civil war, interstate war and wars with internal and external aspects.

Third, accordingly, this book argues that, in key respects, most national societies developed on a design that was not entirely distinct from that of empires, and most national polities organized their societies through constitutional norms and procedures first used to consolidate empires. Even where constitutions were conceived as texts to order nations in distinction from empires, they frequently mirrored the convergence between nations and empires, and they enacted provisions to organize society in imperial form. On one hand, of course, constitutional systems that developed in empires had markedly different effects for subjects at different positions in imperial environments. It is self-evident that, in the imperial polities of nineteenth-century Europe, institutions in regions that evolved on the metropolitan side of empires provided far higher levels of constitutional protection for citizens than those in regions located at the colonial side. However, even in such empires, the metropolitan side and the colonized side of society were typically shaped, at least in part, by related forces and imperatives. In many settings, further, the formation of national society was not always clearly distinct from the formation of an empire, and national integration and imperial construction were two parts of the same process. In different settings, constitutions usually discharged functions in which imperial and national imperatives overlapped. Most importantly, both nations and empires were typically formed by military directives, containing elements of military occupation, and constitutions served to organize societies in a form proportioned to the requirements of the army. This military emphasis normally remained palpable in postcolonial constitutional systems.

On these grounds, the book adopts a stance against the commonplace perception that the modern sovereign state is defined by a clear distinction between its internal and its external functions, deploying less violence in the internal dimension. Most states developed in a form in which the inside and the outside of national society were not fully differentiated, and many states translated external violence into internal violence, and vice versa. Constitutions were usually established to allow states to manage the interface between the internal and the external functions. However, few constitutions achieved this, and the deep links between these functions stimulated military conflicts that traversed both domains. The major crises of constitutionalism in modern history occurred in periods when, often for reasons arising inside national societies, the partition between internal and external violence lost solidity. To rectify common misconceptions, it is essential to observe how, until after 1945, the empire, not the nation state, was the dominant political and constitutional form in world society.

Against this background, this book argues that constitutional law only provided a widespread foundation for democracy after 1945, which coincided with a profound transformation of global imperialism. This democratic stabilization was linked to the construction of a normative order (*world law*) that altered the deep relations between constitutional law and military violence. On one hand, such stabilization depended on the emergence of a corpus of international norms, through which states partly separated their legitimacy from modes of social integration connected to warfare. At the same time, such stabilization presupposed the emergence of organizational systems inside democratic societies that were able to absorb the lateral conflicts that vertical integration generated. This was achieved – diversely – through the establishment of welfare states, including institutions providing mass education. In both respects, dialectically, democratic constitutional systems were founded after 1945 through a process in which rights resulting from bargains that were originally of a military nature were stabilized in a normative system detached from war. This conjuncture marked a decisive shift towards a post-imperial constitutional order.

On this basis, in turn, the book argues that constitutional democracy is a fragile and uncertain artefact about whose origins our knowledge is limited and often ill-constructed. It argues that the pathway towards constitutional democracy usually resulted from societal pressures which were not essentially democratic, or at least that the bargaining structures around which democracy developed were framed and put into effect by non-democratic military events, so that democracy is of essentially contingent nature. For this reason, it concludes that constitutional rule acquired solid democratic form as constitutional law was detached, in part, from the motivations that brought it into being, and this occurred in the unusual environments that were shaped by the legacy of the great inter-imperial wars, starting in the 1930s. Prior to that point, with a few exceptions, democracies had either only been incompletely formed or they had produced modes of violence that fractured their institutional structure. Seen in this light, constitutional democracy appears as a rather precarious product of World War II, galvanized by a distinct combination of internal solidarities and external norm formation, at once resulting from yet also solidified against the societal experiences global warfare caused. In addition, constitutional democracy appears as a characteristic product of the Cold War, as Cold War polarities forced different factions in national governments in many societies to adopt welfare policies which they were frequently willing to abandon after the reduction of the social risks resulting from the Cold War.

Underlying this analysis is a deeper sociological claim about the impact of vertical integration on national societies. As mentioned, it is implied throughout the book that constitutions took shape as societies were formed on an increasingly vertical model in which norms of individual political integration and lines of individual interaction between states and citizens were partly defined by military imperatives. Observed schematically, this was a process in which integration functions originally ordered by local and religious bodies were transferred, incrementally, to military organizations. However, this integration pattern had effects that undermined the sovereign form of the state that constitutions were expected to sustain, as it generated lateral conflicts that legally ordered states were unable to absorb. It was only as patterns of vertical integration were both subject to a higher-order constitution and directed from military bodies towards welfare states that constitutional democracy became a robust form of government. The growing diffusion of international law and the formation of welfare states with broad coverage usually created an apparatus in which constitutional states were able to reduce the tensions caused by vertical integration and to obviate extreme conflicts at the horizontal level of society. Normally, this proved decisive for the consolidation of democracy.

The future of constitutional democracy appears strongly linked to knowledge of these facts. Much evidence indicates that still today, if constitutions are not supported by the protective dimensions of international law and they lack a substructure that promotes societal individualization via welfare provisions, democracy will be unstable. Indeed, where constitutional systems do not have these preconditions, it is to be expected that some pattern of militarization, with either a vertical or a lateral emphasis, will unsettle democratic structures. The realities that took form after 1945 may have provided a contingent framework for constitutional democracy. But the structural processes that underpinned this framework were deeply embedded in the societies whose governments assumed constitutional and democratic form at this time, and these processes are usually destabilized when the above preconditions are absent.

BIBLIOGRAPHY

Abad, Iván Orozco (1989), 'La guerra del presidente'. *Análisis Político* 8: 73–78.

Abad, Iván Orozco (1992), *Combatientes, rebeldes y terroristas: Guerra y derecho en Colombia*. Bogota: Editorial Temis.

Abrahamian, Ervand (1982), *Iran between Two Revolutions*. Princeton, NJ: Princeton University Press.

Adelman, Jeremy (2010), 'The Rites of Statehood: Violence and Sovereignty in Spanish America, 1789–1821'. *Hispanic American Historical Review* 90(3): 391–422.

Ágoston, Gábor (2005), *Guns for the Sultan: Military Power and the Weapons Industry in the Ottoman Empire*. Cambridge: Cambridge University Press.

Ahmad, Feroz (1969), *The Young Turks: The Committee of Union and Progress in Turkish Politics*. London: Hurst.

Ahmad, Feroz (2014), *The Young Turks and the Ottoman Nationality: Armenians, Greeks, Albanians and Arabs 1908–1918*. Salt Lake City: University of Utah Press.

Ajnenkiel, Andrzej (1972), *Spór o model parlamentaryzmu polskiego*. Warsaw: Książka i Wiedza.

Ajnenkiel, Andrzej (1980), *Polska po przewrocie majowym: Zarys dziejów politycznych Polski 1926–1939*. Warsaw: Państwowe Wydawnictwo Wiedza Powszechna.

Akami, Tomoko (2012), 'The Nation-State/Empire as a Unit of Analysis in the History of International Relations: A Case Study in Northeast Asia, 1868–1933', in Isabella Löhr and Roland Wenzlhuemer (eds.), *The Nation State and Beyond: Governing Globalization Processes in the Nineteenth and Early Twentieth Centuries*. Berlin: Springer, pp. 177–208.

Akçam, Taner (2004), *Armenien und der Völkermord: Die Istanbuler Prozesse und die türkische Nationalbewegung*. Hamburg: Hamburger Edition.

Aksan, Virginia H. (2007), *Ottoman Wars 1700–1870: An Empire Besieged*. Harlow: Pearson.

Albi, Julio (1987), *La defensa de las Indias (1764–1799)*. Madrid: Ediciones Cultural Hispánica.

Algar, Hamid. (1969) *Religion and State in Iran 1785–1906: The Role of the Ulama in the Qajar Period*. Berkeley: University of California Press.

Ali, Imran (1988), *The Punjab under Imperialism, 1885–1947*. Princeton, NJ: Princeton University Press.

Allon, Yigal (1970), *The Making of Israel's Army*. London: Vallentine, Mitchell.

Almario García, Óscar (2013), *Castas y razas en la independencia neogranadina, 1810–1830: Identidad y alteridad en los orígenes de la Nación colombiana*. Bogota: Universidad Nacional de Colombia.

Almarza Villalobos, Ángel Rafael (2019), 'Ciudadanía, votos y armas. Elección de diputados en los llanos venezolanos y neogranadinos para el Congreso General de Colombia: 1820–1821'. *Estudios de historia moderna y contemporánea de México* 55: 3–40.

Alpert, Michael (1982), *La Reforma Militar de Azaña (1931–1933)*. Madrid: España Ediciones.

Altrichter, Helmut (1977), *Konstitutionalismus und Imperialismus: Der Reichstag und die Deutsch-russischen Beziehungen 1890–1914*. Frankfurt: Peter Lang.

Alves, João Luiz (1917), *O Estado de guerra e o estado de sítio*. Rio de Janeiro: Imprensa Nacional.

Anderson, Fred (1984), *A People's Army: Massachusetts Soldiers and Society in the Seven Years' War*. Chapel Hill: University of North Carolina Press.

Anderson, Fred (2000), *Crucible of War: The Seven Years' War and the Fate of Empire in British North America, 1754–1766*. London: Faber.

Andújar Castillo, Francisco (1991), *Los militares en la España del siglo XVIII: Un estudio social*. Granada: Universidad de Granada.

Andújar Castillo, Francisco (2004), *El sonido del dinero. Monarquía, ejército y venalidad en la España del siglo XVIII*. Madrid: Marcial Pons.

Anghie, Antony (2005), *Imperialism, Sovereignty and the Making of International Law*. Cambridge: Cambridge University Press.

Antaramian, Richard E. (2020), *Brokers of Faith, Brokers of Empire: Armenians and the Politics of Reform in the Ottoman Empire*. Stanford, CA: Stanford University Press.

Anyanwu, Ogechi E. (2011), *The Politics of Access: University Education and Nation-Building in Nigeria, 1948–2000*. Calgary: University of Calgary Press.

Araujo, Ricardo Nambuco (2012), 'L'art français de la guerre: Transferts de la doctrine de la guerre révolutionnaire au Brésil (1958–1974)'. *Cahiers des Amériques latines* 70: 39–58.

Archer, Christon I. (1977), *The Army in Bourbon Mexico, 1760–1810*. Albuquerque: University of New Mexico Press.

Atassi, Karim (2014), *Syrie, la force d'une idée: Architectures constitutionnelles des régimes politiques*. Paris: L'Harmattan.

Augustyniak, Urszula (2004), *W służbie Hetmana I Rzeczypospolitej: Klientela wojskowa Krzysztofa Radziwiłła (1585–1640)*. Warsaw: Semper.

Aydinli, Ersel (2004), 'The Turkish Pendulum between Globalization and Security: From the Late Ottoman Era to the 1930s'. *Middle Eastern Studies* 40(3): 102–133.

Azaña, Manuel (1918), *Estudios de política francesa contemporánea: La política militar*. Madrid: Biblioteca Calleja.

Azcárate, Gumersindo (1892), *El régimen parlamentario en la práctica*, second edition. Madrid: Librería de Fernando Fe.

Baba, Gürol and Jay Winter (2022), 'The Wilsonian Moment at Lausanne, 1922–1923'. *Journal of Modern European History* 20(4): 536–553.

Bachof, Otto (1951), *Die verwaltungsgerichtliche Klage auf Vornahme einer Amtshandlung*. Tubingen: Mohr Siebeck.

Baczkowski, Michał (2017), *Galicja a wojsko austriackie 1772–1867*. Krakow: Towarzystwo Wydawnicze 'Historia Iagellonica'.

Badem, Candan (2010), *The Ottoman Crimean War (1853–1856)*. Leiden: Brill.

Balfour, Sabastian (1997), *The End of the Spanish Empire 1898–1923*. Oxford: Clarendon.

Ballbé, Manuel (1983), *Orden público y militarismo en la España constitucional*. Madrid: Alianza Editorial.

Bandeira, Esmerelda O. T. (1919), *Direito, justiça e processo militar*, second edition. São Paulo: Francisco Alves.

Bandeira, Moniz (1995), *O expansionismo brasileiro e a formação dos estados na Bacia do Prata: Da colonização à Guerra de Tríplice Aliança*. Brasilia: Editora UnB.

Barajas, Justo Alberto Huerta (2016), *Gobierno y administración militar en la II República española*. Madrid: Boletín Oficial del Estado.

Barbosa, Ruy (1892), *O estado de sitio: Sua natureza, seus effeitos, seus limites*. Rio de Janeiro: Companhia Impressora.

Barkawi, Tarak (2017), *Soldiers of Empire: Indian and British Armies in World War II*. Cambridge: Cambridge University Press.

Barkey, Karen (2008), *Empire of Difference: The Ottomans in Comparative Perspective*. Cambridge: Cambridge University Press.

Barnett, Michael N. (1992), *Confronting the Costs of War: Military Power, State, and Society in Egypt and Israel*. Princeton, NJ: Princeton University Press.

Bartolini, Stefano (2000), *The Political Mobilization of the European Left, 1860–1980: The Class Cleavage*. Cambridge: Cambridge University Press.

Basu, Subho (2023), *Intimation of Revolution: Global Sixties and the Making of Bangladesh*. Cambridge: Cambridge University Press.

Baumgart, Peter (1984), 'Die Annexation und Eingliederung Schlesiens in den friderizianischen Staat', in Peter Baumgart (ed.), *Expansion und Integration: Zur Eingliederung neugewonnener Gebiete in den preußischen Staat*. Cologne: Böhlau, pp. 81–118.

Bayat, Mangol (2020), *Iran's Experiment with Parliamentary Governance: The Second Majles, 1909–1911*. Syracuse, NY: Syracuse University Press.

Beaufre, André (1972), *La guerre révolutionnaire: Les formes nouvelles de la guerre*. Paris: Fayard.

Bedjaoui, Mohammed (1961), *Law and the Algerian Revolution*. Brussels: Publications of the International Association of Democratic Lawyers.

Bein, Werner (1994), *Schlesien in der habsburgischen Politik: Ein Beitrag zur Entstehung des Dualismus im Alten Reich*. Sigmaringen: Thorbecke.

Béland, Daniel and André Lecours (2008), *Nationalism and Social Policy: The Politics of Territorial Solidarity*. Oxford: Oxford University Press.

Ben-Eliezer, Uri (1995), 'A Nation-in-Arms: State, Nation, and Militarism in Israel's First Years'. *Comparative Studies in Society and History* 37(2): 264–285.

Ben-Eliezer, Uri (2019), *War over Peace: One Hundred Years of Israel's Militaristic Nationalism*. Berkeley: University of California Press.

Benvenisti, Eyal (1993), *The International Law of Occupation*. Princeton, NJ: Princeton University Press.

Berbel, Márcia Regina (1999), *A nação como artefato: Deputados do Brasil nas cortes portuguesas 1821–1822*. São Paulo: Fundação de Amparo à Pesquisa do Estado de São Paulo.

Berber, Friedrich (1964), *Lehrbuch des Völkerrechts*, vol. III. Munich: Beck.

Berenhorst, Georg Heinrich von (1872), *Betrachtungen über die Kriegskunst*, third edition. Leipzig: Fleischer.

Berezwoski, Cezary (1934), *Powstanie państwa polskiego w świetle prawa narodów*. Warsaw: Wydawnictwo 'Themis Polska'.

Berger, Stefan and Alexei Miller (2015), 'Introduction', in Stefan Berger and Alexei Miller (eds.), *Nationalizing Empires*. Budapest: Central Eastern European Press, pp. 1–30.

Berkes, Niyazi (1964), *The Development of Secularism in Turkey*. Montreal: McGill University Press.

Berkowitz, Edward and Kim McQuaid (1988), *Creating the Welfare State: The Political Economy of Twentieth-Century Reform*. New York: Praeger.

Berlepsch, Hans-Jörg von (1984), *'Neuer Kurs' im Kaiserreich? Die Arbeiterpolitik des Freiherrn von Berlepsch 1890 bis 1896*. Bonn: Neue Gesellschaft.

Beşikçi, Mehmet (2012), *The Ottoman Mobilization of Manpower in the First World War: Between Voluntarism and Resistance*. Leiden: Brill.

Beşikçi, Mehmet (2013), 'Mobilizing Military Labor in the Age of Total War: Ottoman Conscription before and during the Great War', in Erik-Jan Zürcher (ed.), *Fighting for a Living: A Comparative Study of Military Labour 1500–2000*. Amsterdam: Amsterdam University Press, pp. 547–580.

Best, Werner (1940), *Die Verwaltung in Polen vor und nach dem Zusammenbruch der polnischen Republik*. Berlin: R.v. Decker's Verlag.

Bilder, Mary Sarah (2004), *The Transatlantic Constitution: Colonial Legal Culture and the Empire*. Cambridge, MA: Harvard University Press.

Billaud-Varenne, Jacques Nicolas (1794), *Rapport fait a la convention sur la théorie du gouvernmement démocratique*. Paris: Imprimerie du tribunal révolutionnaire.

Bílý, Matěj (2022), *The Warsaw Pact, 1985–1991: Disintegration and Dissolution*. Abingdon: Routledge.

Bitis, Alexander (2006), *Russia and the Eastern Question: Army, Government and Society 1815–1833*. Oxford: Oxford University Press.

Blainey, Geoffrey (1988), *The Causes of War*, third edition. New York: Free Press.

Blanco Valdés, Roberto L. (1988), *Rey, Cortes y fuerzas armadas en los origenes de la España liberal, 1808–1823*. Valencia: Edicions Alfons el Magnanim.

Blaufarb, Rafe (2001), 'Noble Privilege and Absolutist State Building: French Military Administration after the Seven Years' War'. *French Historical Studies* 24(2): 223–246.

Blaufarb, Rafe (2002), *The French Army 1750–1820: Careers, Talent, Merit*. Manchester: Manchester University Press.

Blauvelt, Timothy K. (2003), 'Military Mobilisation and National Identity in the Soviet Union'. *War & Society* 21(1): 41–62.

Bley, Helmut (1968), *Kolonialherrschaft und Sozialstruktur in Deutsch-Südafrika 1894–1914*. Hamburg: Leibniz.

Bloxham, Donald (2005), *The Great Game of Genocide: Imperialism, Nationalism and the Destruction of the Ottoman Armenians*. Oxford: Oxford University Press.

Blythe-Stason, Edwin (1946), 'Administrative Law. Developments: 1940–1945 (A Service for Returning Veterans)'. *Michigan Law Review* 44(5): 797–810.

Böckenförde, Ernst-Wolfgang (1969), 'Der Westfälische Frieden und das Bündnisrecht der Reichsstände'. *Der Staat* 8(4): 449–478.

Bockhoff, Ernst Hermann (1937), *Völker-Recht gegen Bolschewismus*. Berlin: Nibelungen.

Bogain, Ariane (2017), 'Security in the Name of Human Rights: The Discursive Legitimation Strategies of the War on Terror in France'. *Critical Studies on Terrorism* 10(3): 476–500.

Boister, Neil (1991), 'The ius in bello in South Africa: A Postscript?' *Comparative and International Law Journal of Southern Africa* 24(1): 72–87.

Bolivar, Simon (1961), *Decretos del Libertador*, 3 vols. Caracas: Imprenta Nacional, vol. I.

Bonald, Louis Gabriel Ambroise, Vicomte de (1818), *Opinion sur le projet de loi relatif au recrutement de l'armée*. Paris: Le Normant.

Borges, Vavy Pacheco (1992), *Tenentismo e Revolução Brasileira*. São Paulo: Brasiliense.

Borja, Miguel (2010), *Espacio y guerra: Colombia Federal 1858–1885*. Bogota: Editorial Universidad Nacional de Colombia.

Bougrab, Jeannette (2002), *Aux origines de la constitution de la IVe République*. Paris: Dalloz.

Boysen, Jens (2008), *Preußische Armee und polnische Minderheit: Royalistische Streitkräfte im Kontext der Nationalitätenfrage des 19. Jahrhunderts (1815–1914)*. Marburg: Herder-Institut.

Branche, Raphaëlle (2016), *La torture pendant la guerre d'Algérie 1954–1962*, new edition. Paris: Gallimard.

Brass, Paul R. (2011), *The Production of Hindu–Muslim Violence in Contemporary India*. Seattle: University of Washington Press.

Briquet, Pierre (1728), *Code militaire ou compilation des ordonnances des roys de la France*, 3 vols. Paris: Imprimerie royale, vol. I.

Brissot, Jacques-Pierre (1792), *Troisième discours, sur la necessité de la guerre*. Paris: Imprimerie du patriote français.

Brocheux, Pierre and Daniel Hémery (2001), *Indochine: La colonisation ambiguë*, new edition. Paris: La Découverte.

Brodowska-Kubicz, Helena (1986), 'Kształtowanie się świadomości społecznej i narodowej chłopów w XIX stuleciu'. *Acta Universatatis Lodziensis* 24: 3–19.

Broers, Michael G. (2001), 'Noble Romans and Regenerated Citizens: The Morality of Conscription in Napoleonic Italy, 1800–1814'. *War in History* 8(3): 249–270.

Brooks, Rosa Ehrenreich (2004), 'War Everywhere: Rights, National Security Law, and the Law of Armed Conflict in the Age of Terror'. *University of Pennsylvania Law Review* 153 (2004): 675–761.

Brower, Daniel (2003), *Turkestan and the Fate of the Russian Empire*. London: Routledge.

Brunkhorst, Hauke (2002), *Solidarität: Von der Bürgerfreundschaft zur globalen Rechtsgenossenschaft*. Frankfurt: Suhrkamp.

Bucholc-Srogosz, Katarzyna (2007), *Departament Wojskowy Rady Nieustającej w latach 1775–1789 i 1793–1794*. Poznan: Wydawnictwo Poznańskie.

Burbank, Jane and Frederick Cooper (2011), *Empires in World History: Power and the Politics of Difference*. Princeton, NJ: Princeton University Press.

Burbano, Pablo Casado (1982), *Las fuerzas armadas en el inicio del constitucionalismo español*. Madrid: EDERSA.

Burgorgue-Larsen, Laurence and Amaya Úbeda de Torres (2011), '"War" in the Jurisprudence of the Inter-American Court of Human Rights'. *Human Rights Quarterly* 33(1): 148–174.

Burkholder, Mark A. and D. S. Chandler (1977), *From Impotence to Authority: The Spanish Crown and the American Audiencias, 1687–1808*. Columbia: University of Missouri Press.

Bushnell, David (1954), *The Santander Regime in Gran Colombia*. Newark: University of Delaware Press.

Buzan, Barry (1991), *People, States and Fear: An Agenda for International Security Studies in the Post–Cold War Era*, second edition. New York: Harvester.

Buzan, Barry and Ole Waever (2003), *Regions and Powers: The Structure of International Security*. Cambridge: Cambridge University Press.

Caban, Wiesław (2001), *Służba rekrutów z Królestwa Polskiego w armii carskiej w latach 1831–1873*. Warsaw: Wydawnictwo DIG.

Cagaptay, Soner (2006), *Islam, Secularism and Nationalism in Modern Turkey: Who Is a Turk?* Abingdon: Routledge.

Calbet, María Teresa González (1987), *La Dictadura de Primo de Rivera: El Directorio Militar*. Madrid: El Arquero.

Callahan, Raymond A. and Daniel Marston (2010), *The 1945 Burma Campaign and the Transformation of the British Indian Army*. Lawrence: Kansas University Press.

Calleja, Eduardo González (1998), *La razón de la fuerza: Orden público, subversión y violencia política en la España de la Restauración (1875–1917)*. Madrid: Consejo Superior de Investigaciones científicas.

Calleja, Eduardo González (2005), *La España de Primo de Rivera: La modernización autoritaria 1923–1930*. Madrid: Alianza.

Callwell, C. E. (1896), *Small Wars: Their Principles and Practice*. London: Harrison & Sons.

Cambon, Pierre-Joseph (1793a), *Rapport et projet de décret sur la conduite des généraux français dans les pays occupés par les armées de la République*. Paris: Imprimerie Nationale.

Cambon, Pierre-Joseph (1793b), *Rapport et projet de décret, sur la conduite à tenir et les pouvoirs à donner aux Généraux françois chargés de l'expédition de la Hollande*. Paris: Imprimerie Nationale.

Cameron, Meribeth E. (1931), *The Reform Movement in China 1898–1912*. Stanford, CA: Stanford University Press.

Campbell, Randolph B. (1989), *An Empire for Slavery: The Peculiar Institution in Texas, 1821–1865*. Baton Rouge: Louisiana State University Press.

Campos, Francisco (1942), *Direito constitucional*. Rio de Janeiro: Edição Revista Forense.

Campos, Francisco (2001), *O Estado nacional: Sua estrutura, seu conteúdo ideológico*. Brasilia: Senado Federal, Conselho Editorial.

Canal, Jordi (2000), *El Carlismo: Dos siglos contrarrevolución en España*. Madrid: Alianza Editoria, S.A.

Capefigue, Jean-Baptiste (1864), *Le Congrès de Vienne et les traités de 1815. Vol. IV*. Paris: Amyot.

Carcano, Andrea (2015), *The Transformation of Occupied Territory in International Law*. Leiden: Brill.

Cardozo, Juan Alberto Rueda (2006), 'Reformas liberales al fuero militar en Colombia y Nueva Granada, 1820–1857'. *Anuario de Historia Regional y de las Fronteras* 11(1): 217–287.

Carl, Horst (1993), *Okkupation und Regionalismus: Die preussischen Westprovinzen im siebenjährigen Krieg*. Mainz: Zabern.

Carpenter, Stephen Cullen (1815), *Select American Speeches: Forensic and Parliamentary. Vol. 1*. Philadelphia, PA: Campbell.

Carvalho, José Murilo de (2011), 'República, democracia e federalismo Brasil, 1870–1891'. *Varia historica* 27(45): 141–157.

Castro, Celso (1995), *Os Militares e a República: Um estudo sobre culture a ação política*. Rio de Janeiro: Zahar.

Castro, Celso (2012), *Exército e nação: Estudos sobre a história do exército brasileiro*. Rio de Janeiro: Editora FGV.

Castro, Tatiana de Souza and Gabriel Faustino dos Santos (2022), 'Regime de exceção e tutela dos direitos individuais: A discussão da Revisão Constitucional de 1926 e a limitação do habeas corpus na prática jurisprudencial'. *História do Direito* 2(3): 118–142.

Cénat, Jean-Philippe (2010), *Le roi stratège: Louis XIV et la direction de la guerre (1661–1775)*. Rennes: Presses Universitaires de Rennes.

Chanet, Jean-François (2006), *Vers l'armée nouvelle: République conservatrice et réforme militaire, 1871–1879*. Rennes: Presses Universitaires de Rennes.

Chaparro, Juan Carlos Rodríguez (2010), *Las relaciones politico-militares el marco de la transición política en Colombia 1810–1838*. Bogota: Academia Colombiana de Historia.

Chojnowski, Andrzej (1979), *Koncepje polityki narodowościowej rządów polskich w latach 1921–1939*. Wroclaw: Wydawnictwo Zakładu Narodowego im. Ossolińskich.

Christiansen, E. (1967), *The Origins of Military Power in Spain 1800–1854*. Oxford: Oxford University Press.

Çiçek, M. Talha (2014), *War and State Formation in Syria: Cemal Pasha's Governorate during World War I, 1914–1917*. London: Routledge.

Ciesieski, Tomasz (2009), *Armia koronna w czasach Augusta III*. Warsaw: Wydawnictwo DIG.

Clarke, Ben (2005), 'The Juridical Status of Civilian Resistance to Foreign Occupation under the Law of Nations and Contemporary International Law'. *University of Notre Dame Australia Law Review* 7: 1–22.

Cock, Jacklyn (1989), 'Conscription in South Africa: A Study in the Politics of Coercion'. *South African Sociological Review*: 1–22.

Código militar (1881). Bogotá: Zapata.

Coelho, Edmundo Campos (2000), *Em busca de Identidade: O Exército e a política na sociedade brasileira*. Rio de Janeiro: Editora Record.

Cohen, Julia Phillips (2014), *Becoming Ottomans: Sephardi Jews and Imperial Citizenship in the Modern Era*. Oxford: Oxford University Press.

Coleccion de los Decretos y órdenes que han expedido las Cortes Generales y extraordinarias desde su instalacion de 24 de Setiembre de 1810 hasta 19 de Febrero de 1823. Vol. VII. Madrid: Imprenta Nacional.

Colley, Linda (2021), *The Gun, the Ship and the Pen: Warfare, Constitutions and the Making of the Modern World*. London: Profile.

Collins, Bruce (2010), *War and Empire: The Expansion of Britain 1790–1830*. Abingdon: Routledge.

Conde Calderon, Jorge (2014), 'La conversión de milicianos y guerrilleros en ciudadanos armados de la República de Colombia'. *Historia Caribe* 9(25): 17–37.

Conde Calderón, Jorge (2019), 'De esclavos a soldados de la patria: El Ejército Libertador como garante de la libertad y la ciudadanía'. *Co-Herencia* 16(31): 79–100.

Conge, Patrick J. (2000), *From Revolution to War: State Relations in a World of Change*. Ann Arbor: University of Michigan Press.

Coppolani, Jean-Yves (1980), *Les élections en France à l'époque napolienne*. Paris: Albatros.

Cornell, Sarah E. (2013), 'Citizens of Nowhere: Fugitive Slaves and Free African Americans in Mexico, 1833–1857'. *Journal of American History*, 100(2): 351–374.

Cornette, Joël (1993), *Le roi de guerre: Essai sur la souveraineté dans la France du Grand Siècle*. Paris: Payot et Rivages.

Corvisier, André (1964), *L'armée française de la fin du XVII siècle au ministère de Choiseul: Le soldat. Vol. I*. Paris: PUF.

Corwin, Arthur F. (1967), *Spain and the Abolition of Slavery in Cuba, 1817–1886*. Austin: University of Texas Press.

Costa, Ana Paula Pereira (2006), 'Organização militar, poder de mando e mobilização de escravos armados nas conquistas: A atuação dos Corpos de Ordenanças em Minas colonia'. *Revista de História Regional* 11(2): 109–162.

Costa, Wilma Peres (1998), 'A questão fiscal na transformação republicana – continuidade e descontinuidade'. *Economia e Sociedade* 7(1): 141–173.

Costeloe, Michael P. (1986), *Response to Revolution: Imperial State and the Spanish American Revolutions, 1810–1840*. Cambridge: Cambridge University Press.

Craig, Albert M. (1961), *Chōshū in the Meiji Revolution*. Cambridge, MA: Harvard University Press.

Cronin, Stephanie (1997), *The Army and the Creation of the Pahlavi State in Iran, 1910–1926*. London: Tauris.

Cronin, Stephanie (2014), *Armies and State Building in the Modern Middle East: Politics, Nationalism and Military Reform*. London: Tauris.

Crook, Malcolm and John Dunne (2014), 'The First European Elections? Voting and Imperial State-Building under Napoleon, 1802–1813'. *Historical Journal* 57(3): 661–697.

Cruz, Adolfo León Atehortúa (2001). 'Las fuerzas militares en Colombia: De sus orígenes al Frente Nacional'. *Historia y espacio* 17: 133–166.

Dąbrowski, Stefan (1922), *Walka o rekruta polskiego pod okupacją*. Warsaw: Perzyński, Niklewicz i S-ka.

Dahl, Adam (2018), *Empire of the People: Settler Colonialism and the Foundations of Modern Democratic Thought*. Lawrence: University of Kansas Press.

Dal Lago, Enrico (2018), *Civil War and Agrarian Unrest: The Confederate South and Southern Italy*. Cambridge: Cambridge University Press.

Damas, Carrera Germán (2010), *Colombia 1821–1827: Apprender a edificar una Republica moderna liberal*. Caracas: Fondo Editorial de Humanidadores y Educación.

Daranowski, Piotr (1989), 'Pozycja traktatów w porządku prawnym PRL'. *Acta Universitatis Lodziensis: Folia Iuridica* 41: 5–43.

Da Silva, Paulo Sérgio (2006), *A Constituição brasileira de 10 de Novembro de 1937. Um retrato com luz e sombra*. São Paolo: UNESP.

Dassel, Kurt (1998), 'Civilians, Soldiers, and Strife: Domestic Sources of International Aggression'. *International Security* 23(1): 107–140.

Davies, Brian L. (2016), *The Russo-Turkish War, 1768–1774: Catherine II and the Ottoman Empire*. London: Bloomsbury.

Davison, Roderic H. (1963), *Reform in the Ottoman Empire, 1856–1876*. Princeton, NJ: Princeton University Press.

Delbanco, Andrew (2018), *The War before the War: Fugitive Slaves and the Struggle for America's Soul for America's Soul from the Revolution to the Civil War*. New York: Penguin.

De Londras, Fiona (2022), *The Practice and Problems of Transnational Counter-Terrorism*. Cambridge: Cambridge University Press.

Depalo, William A. (1997), *The Mexican National Army 1822–1852*. College Station: Texas A&M University Press.

De Montaud, Inés Roldán (2000), *La Restauración en Cuba: El fracaso de un proceso reformista*. Madrid: CSIC.

Devereux, Robert (1963), *The First Ottoman Constitutional Period: A Study of the Midhat Constitution and Parliament*. Baltimore, MD: Johns Hopkins University Press.

De Wet, Erika (2004), *The Chapter VII Powers of the United Nations Security Council*. Oxford: Hart.

Dickerson, Oliver Morton (1970), *Boston under Military Rule 1768–1769*. New York: Da Capo Press.

Dickinson, Frederick R. (2013), *World War I and the Triumph of a New Japan, 1919–1930*. Cambridge: Cambridge University Press.

Dickinson, John (1774), *A New Essay on the Constitutional Power of Great-Britain over the Colonies in North America*. Philadelphia, PA: Almon.

Dmowski, Roman (2020), *Wobec rodzących się totalitaryzmów: Wybór pism*. Krakow: Wydział Studiów Międzynarodowych i Politycznych Uniwersytetu Jagiellońskiego.

Dmowski, Roman (2021), *Niemcy, Rosja i Kwestia Polska*. Wroclaw: NORTOM.

Doise, Jean (1994), *Un secret bien gardé: Histoire militaire de l'affaire Dreyfus*. Paris: Seuil.

Dolhnikoff, Miriam (2007), *O pacto imperial: Origens de federalism no Brasil*, second edition. São Paulo: Globo.

Domínguez, Ercilio (1905), *Colección de leyes y decretos militares concernientes al ejército y armada de la República Argentina. Vol. I*. Buenos Aires: Compañía Sud-americana de Billetes de Banco.

Doratioto, Francisco (2002), *Maldita guerra: Nova historia da Guerra do Paraguai*, third edition. São Paulo: Companhia das Letras.

Dörr, Nikolas, Lukas Grawe and Herbert Obinger (2020), 'The Military Origins of Labor Protection Legislation in Imperial Germany'. *Historical Social Research* 45(2): 27–67.

Doyle, David (2010), 'Politics and Privatization: Exogenous Pressures, Domestic Incentives and State Divestiture in Latin America'. *Journal of Public Policy* 30.3 (2010): 291–320.

Drea, Edward J. (2009), *Japan's Imperial Army: Its Rise and Fall, 1853–1945*. Lawrence: Kansas University Press.

Drozdowski, Marian (2017), *Podstawy finansowe działalnośći państwowej w Polsce 1764–1793: Działalnośc budżetowa Sejmu Rzezczypospolitej w czasach panowania Stanisława Augusta Poniatowskiego*. Poznan: PTH.

Drummond, José Augusto (1986), *O Movimento Tenentista: A intervenção política dos oficiais jovens (1922–1935)*. Rio de Janiero: Graal.

Dryzek, John and Robert E. Goodin (1986), 'Risk-Sharing and Social Justice: The Motivational Foundations of the Post-War Welfare State'. *British Journal of Political Science* 16(1): 1–34.

Dubois, Laurent (2004), *Avengers of the New World: The Story of the Haitian Revolution*. Cambridge, MA: Harvard University Press.

Dubois-Crancé, Edmond Louis Alexis (1790), *Lettre de M. Dubois de Crancé, député du département des Ardennes, a ses commettans; ou Compte rendu des travaux, des dangers et des obstacles de l'Assemblée nationale, depuis l'ouverture des États-généraux, au 27 avril 1789, jusqu'au premier août 1790*. Paris: Imprimerie Nationale.

Dukwicz, Dorota (2015), *Rosja wobec sejmu rozbiorowego warszawskiego (1772–1775)*. Warsaw: Instytut Historii Pan.

Dulany, Daniel (1766), *Considerations on the Propriety of Imposing Taxes in the British Colonies*, second edition. London: Almon.

Durkheim, Émile (1950), *Leçons de sociologie*. Paris: PUF.

Duus, Peter (1995), *The Abacus and the Sword: The Japanese Penetration of Korea, 1895–1910*. Berkeley: University of California Press.

Eckhardt, Krzysztof (2012), *Stan nadzwyczajny jako instytucja polskiego prawa konstytucyjnego*. Rzeszów: Wyższa Szkoła Prawa i Administracji Przemyśl–Rzeszów.

Edling, Max (2014), *A Hercules in the Cradle: War, Money, and the American State, 1783–1867*. Chicago, IL: Chicago University Press.

Egnal, Marc (1988), *A Mighty Empire: The Origins of the American Revolution*. Ithaca, NY: Cornell University Press.

Eisenstadt, S. N. (1993), *The Political Systems of Empires*, second edition. New Brunswick, NJ: Transaction.

Eissa-Barroso, Francisco (2016), *The Spanish Monarchy and the Creation of the Viceroyalty of New Granada (1717–1739): The Politics of Early Bourbon Reform in Spain and Spanish America*. Leiden: Brill.

Ejiogu, E. C. (2007), 'Colonial Army Recruitment Patterns and Post-Colonial Military Coups d'état in Africa: The Case of Nigeria, 1966–1993'. *Scientia Militaria: South African Journal of Military Studies* 35(1): 99–132.

Elias, Norbert (1976), *Über den Prozeß der Zivilisation. Vol. II.* Frankfurt: Suhrkamp.

Erickson, Edward (2001), *Ordered to Die: A History of the Ottoman Army in the First World War.* Westport, CT: Greenwood.

Erickson, Edward (2003), *Defeat in Detail: The Ottoman Army in the Balkans, 1912–1913.* Westport, CT: Praeger.

Esherick, Joseph W. (1976), *Reform and Revolution in China: The 1911 Revolution in Hunan and Hubei.* Berkeley: University of California Press.

Esherick, Joseph W., Hasan Kayali and Eric Van Young (2006), 'Introduction', in Joseph W. Esherick, Hasan Kayali and Eric Van Young (eds.), *Empire to Nation: Historical Perspectives on the Making of the Modern World.* Lanham, MD: Rowman & Littlefield, pp. 1–34.

Esquivel Triana, Ricardo (2009), *Neutralidad y orden: Político exterior y military en Colombia, 1886–1918.* Bogota: Editorial Pontificia Universidad Javeriana.

Evered, Emine Ö. (2012), *Empire and Education under the Ottomans: Politics, Reform, and Resistance from the Tanzimat to the Young Turks.* London: Tauris.

Fahmy, Khaled (1998), 'The Nation and Its Deserters: Conscription in Mehmed Ali's Egypt'. *International Review of Social History* 43(3): 421–436.

Fatton Jr., Robert (2007), *The Roots of Haitian Despotism.* Boulder, CO: Rienner.

Fawaz, Leila Tarazi (2014), *A Land of Aching Hearts: The Middle East in the Great War.* Cambridge, MA: Harvard University Press.

Fehrenbacher, Don E. (2002), *The Slaveholding Republic: An Account of the United States Government's Relations to Slavery.* Oxford: Oxford University Press.

Fernandez Marchena, Juan (1982), *La Institución militar en Cartagena de Indias en el siglo XVIII 1700–1810.* Seville: E.E.H.A.

Fernandez Marchena, Juan (1983), *Oficiales y soldados en el ejercito de America.* Seville: E.E.H.A.

Ferreira, Oliverios S. (2000), *Vida e morte do partido fardado.* São Paulo: SENAC.

Ferry, Jules (1892), *Le gouvernement de l'Algérie.* Paris: Colin.

Fertig, André Aila (2010), *Clientelismo politico em tempos belicosos: A Guarda Nacional do Rio Grande do Sul na defesa do Império do Brasil (1850–1873).* Santa Maria: Editoraufsm.

Fick, Carolyn E. (2007), 'The Haitian Revolution and the Limits of Freedom: Defining Citizenship in the Revolutionary Era'. *Social History*, 32(4): 394–414.

Figueroa, Federico Bito (1985), *El problema tierra y esclavos en la historia de Venezuela.* Caracas: Universidad Central to Venezuela.

Findley, C. V. (2012). *Bureaucratic Reform in the Ottoman Empire: The Sublime Porte, 1789–1922*. Princeton, NJ: Princeton University Press.

Finkelman, Paul (1986), 'Slavery and the Northwest Ordinance: A Study in Ambiguity'. *Journal of the Early Republic* 6(4) 343–370.

Fisher, J. R. (1970), *Government and Society in Colonial Peru: The Intendant System 1784–1814*. London: Athlone.

Flacks, Richard (1967), 'The Liberated Generation: An Exploration of the Roots of Student Protest'. *Journal of Social Issues* 23(3): 52–75.

Flórez Bolívar, Roicer Alberto and Sergio Paolo Solano (2014), 'Educando al buen ciudadano: Las guardias nacionales en la Provincia de Cartagena, Colombia, 1832–1857'. *Anuario de Estudios Americanos* 67(2): 605–633.

Fonseca, Annibal Freire da (1916), *Do poder executivo no Republica Brazileira*. Rio de Janeiro: Imprensa Nacional.

Forrest, Alan (2006), *Napoleon's Men: The Soldiers of the Revolution and Empire*. London: Hambledon.

Förster, Jürgen (2007), *Die Wehrmacht im NS-Staat: Eine strukturgeschichtliche Analyse*. Munich: Oldenbourg.

Forsthoff, Ernst (1968), 'Verfassungsprobleme des Sozialstaats', in Ernst Forsthoff (ed.), *Rechtsstaatlichkeit und Sozialstaatlichkeit: Aufsätze und Essays*. Darmstadt: Wissenschaftliche Buchgesellschaft, pp. 145–164.

Fortin, Katharine (2012), 'Complementarity between the ICRC and the United Nations and International Humanitarian Law and International Human Rights Law, 1948–1968'. *International Review of the Red Cross* 94(888): 1433–1454.

Fox, Gregory H. (2008), *Humanitarian Occupation*. Cambridge: Cambridge University Press.

Fraleigh, Arnold (1971), 'The Algerian Revolution as a Case Study in International Law', in Richard A. Falk (ed.), *The International Law of Civil War*. Baltimore, MD: Johns Hopkins University Press, pp. 179–243.

Fremuth, Michael and Jörn Griebel (2007), 'On the Security Council as Legislator: A Blessing or a Curse for the International Community'. *Nordic Journal of International Law* 76(4): 339–362.

Frey, Sylvia R. (1991), *Water from the Rock: Black Resistance in a Revolutionary Age*. Princeton, NJ: Princeton University Press.

Frisch, Hillel (2011), *Israel's Security and Its Arab Citizens*. Cambridge: Cambridge University Press.

Fung, Edmund (1980), *The Military Dimension of the Chinese Revolution: The New Army and Its Role in the Revolution of 1911*. Canberra: Australian National University Press.

Gałędek, Michał (2017), *Koncepcje i projekty nowego ustroju administracji dla przyszłego Królestwa Polskiego: Studium z dziejów myśli administracyjnej*. Gdansk: Arche.

Ganiage, Jean (1968), *L'expansion de la France sous la Troisième République (1871–1914)*. Paris: Payot.

Gárate, Elizabeth Salmón (2016), 'Aproximación institucional del DIH y el DIDH: Tendencias actuales en la jurisprudencia de la Corte Interamericana de Derechos Humanos'. *Ius et veritas* 52: 330–354.

García Leon, José M. (1983), *La milicia nacional en Cadiz durante el trienio liberal 1820–1833*. Cadiz: Ediciones de la Caja de Ahorros de Cádiz.

Garon, Sheldon (1987), *The State and Labor in Modern Japan*. Berkeley: University of California Press.

Garrido, Margarita (1993), *Reclamas y representaciones: Variaciones sobre la política en el Nuevo Reino de Granada, 1770–1815*. Bogota: Banco de la República.

Gaudio, Ricardo and Hector Domeniconi (1986), 'Las primeras elecciones sindicales en la transicion democratica'. *Desarrollo Economico* 26(103): 423–454.

Gawron, Przemysław (2010), *Hetman koronny w systemie ustrojowym Rzeczypospolitej w latach 1581–1646*. Warsaw: Neriton.

Gawrych, George W. (1988), 'Kemal Atatürk's Politico-military Strategy in the Turkish War of Independence, 1919–1922: From Guerrilla Warfare to the Decisive Battle'. *Journal of Strategic Studies* 11(3): 318–341.

Gay, José Contreras (1993), *Las milicias provinciales en el Siglo XVIII: Estudio sobre los regimientos de Andalucía*. Granada: Instituto de Estudios Armerienses.

Gelpi, Christopher (1997), 'Democratic Diversions: Governmental Structure and the Externalization of Domestic Conflict'. *Journal of Conflict Resolution* 41(2): 255–282.

Genser, Janet (2018), 'The United Nations Security Council's Implementation of the Responsibility to Protect: Review of Past Interventions and Recommendations for Improvement'. *Chicago Journal of International Law*, 18(2): 420–501.

Giddings, Franklin Henry (1901), *Democracy and Empire: With Studies of Their Psychological, Economic and Moral Foundations*. New York: Macmillan.

Gierowski, Józef (1953), *Między saskim absolutyzmem a złotą wolnością: Z dziejów wewnętrznych Rzeczypospolitej w latach 1712–1715*. Wroclaw: Wydawnictwo Zakładu Narodowego im. Ossolińskich.

Gingeras, Ryan (2016), *Fall of the Sultanate: The Great War and the End of the Ottoman Empire 1908–1922*. Oxford: Oxford University Press.

Girard, Georges (1921), *Racolage et milice (1701–1715): Le service militaire en France à la fin du règne de Louis XIV*. Paris: Plon.

Gleditsch, Nils Petter (1992), 'Democracy and Peace'. *Journal of Peace Research* 29(4): 369–376.

Gneist, Rudolf (1966), *Der Rechtsstaat und die Verwaltungsgerichte in Deutschland*. Darmstadt: Wissenschaftliche Buchgesellschaft.

Go, Julian (2011), *Patterns of Empire: The British and American Empires 1688 to the Present*. Cambridge: Cambridge University Press.

Goclon, Jacek (2013), 'Gabinety Królestwa Polskiego 1917–1918: Skład, funkcjonowanie i działalność'. *Krakowskie Studia z Historii Państwa i Prawa* 6(2): 149–178.

Godechot, Jacques (1992), *La Grande Nation: L'expansion révolutionnaire de la France dans le monde de 1789 à 1799*. Paris: Aubier.

Gohier, Urbain (1899), *L'Armée contre la nation*. Paris: Éditions de la Revue Blanche.

Golinowska, Stanisława (2008), *Modele polityki społecznej w Polsce i Europie na początku XXI wieku*. Warsaw: Fundacja im. Stefana Batorego.

Gómez, José Cepeda (1990), *El ejército español en la política española (1787–1843): Conspiraciones y pronunciamientos en los comienzos de la España liberal*. Madrid: Fundación universitaria español.

González Calleja, Eduardo (2015), 'Construcción y defensa del Estado en la Segunda República Española (1931–1936)'. *Crónica Jurídica Hispalense: Revista de la Facultad de Derecho (Universidad de Sevilla)* 13: 121–140.

Gordon, Joel (1992), *Nasser's Blessed Movement: Egypt's Free Officers and the July Revolution*. Oxford: Oxford University Press.

Gould, Elija H. (2012), *Among the Powers of the Earth: The American Revolution and the Making of a New World Empire*. Cambridge, MA: Harvard University Press.

Graber, Doris Appel (1949), *The Development of the Law of Belligerent Occupation 1863–1914: A Historical Survey*. New York: Columbia University Press.

Graebner, Norman A. (1955), *Empire of the Pacific: A Study in American Continental Expansion*. New York: Ronald Press.

Grawe, Lukas (2020), 'The Influence of Military Considerations on the 1869 *Reichsvolksschulgesetz* in Imperial Austria'. *Historical Social Research* 45(2): 143–163.

Greene, Alan (2018), *Permanent States of Emergency and the Rule of Law: Constitutions in an Age of Crisis*. Oxford: Hart.

Greene, Jack P. (1963), *The Quest for Power: The Lower Houses of Assembly in the Southern Royal Colonies 1689–1776*. Chapel Hill: University of North Carolina Press.

Greene, Jack P. (1994), *Negotiated Authorities: Essays in Colonial Political and Constitutional History*. Charlottesville: University Press of Virginia.

Griffin, Patrick (2007), *American Leviathan: Empire, Nation, and Revolutionary Frontier*. New York: Hill and Wang.

Groniowski, Krzysztof (1963), *Realizacja reformy uwłaszczeniowej 1864 roku*. Warsaw: Państwowe Wydawnictwo Naukowe.

Gross, Oren (2003), 'Chaos and Rules: Should Responses to Violent Crises Always Be Constitutional?' *Yale Law Journal* 112(5): 1011–1134.

Gross, Oren and Fionnuala Ní Aoláin (2006), *Law in Times of Crisis: Emergency Powers in Theory and Practice*. Cambridge: Cambridge University Press.

Grünhagen, Colmar (1890), *Schlesien unter Friedrich dem Großen, I (1740–1756)*. Breslau: Wilhelm Koebner.

Grynwaser, Hipolit (1951), *Pisma I: Kodeks Napoleona w Polsce. Demokracja szclachecka 1795–1831*. Wroclaw: Wydawnictwo Zakładu Narodowego im. Ossolińskich.

Guibert, Jacques-Antoine-Hippolyte (1803), *Defense de système de guerre*, volume 2, in *Oeuvres militaires de Guibert*. Paris: Magimel, IV.

Gumz, Jonathan (2018), 'International Law and the Transformation of War, 1899–1949: The Case of Military Occupation'. *Journal of Modern History* 90(3): 621–660.

Gunasti, Susan (2016), 'The Late Ottoman Ulema's Constitutionalism'. *Islamic Law and Society* 23(1–2): 89–119.

Gürke, Norbert (1937/8), 'Der Begriff des totalen Krieges'. *Völkerbund und Völkerrecht* 4: 207–212.

Gürsoy, Yaprak (2017), *Between Military Rule and Democracy: Regime Consolidation in Greece, Turkey, and Beyond*. Ann Arbor: University of Michigan Press.

Habermas, Jürgen (1973), *Legitimationsprobleme im Spätkapitalismus*. Frankfurt: Suhrkamp.

Habermas, Jürgen (1990), *Strukturwandel der Öffentlichkeit: Untersuchungen zu einer Kategorie der bürgerlichen Gesellschaft*, new edition. Frankfurt: Suhrkamp.

Habermas, Jürgen (2008), 'Konstitutionalisierung des Völkerrechts und die Legitimationsprobleme einer verfassten Weltgesellschaft', in Winfried Brugger, Ulfrid Neumann and Stephan Kirste (eds.), *Rechtsphilosophie im 21. Jahrhundert*. Frankfurt: Suhrkamp, pp. 360–379.

Hacısalihoğlu, Mehmet (2007), 'Inclusion and Exclusion: Conscription in the Ottoman Empire'. *Journal of Modern European History* 5(2): 264–286.

Hadden, Sally E. (2001), *Slave Patrols: Law and Violence in Virginia and the Carolinas*. Cambridge, MA: Harvard University Press.

Hanioğlu, M. Şükrü (2001), *Preparation for a Revolution: The Young Turks, 1902–1908*. Oxford: Oxford University Press.

Halicz, Emanuel (1986), *Dokumenty Komitetu Centralnego Narodowegu i rządu narodowegu 1862–1864*. Wroclaw: Wydawnictwo Zakładu Narodowego im. Ossolińskich.

Haller, Stanisław (1926), *Naród a armja*. Krakow: Księgarnia Krakowska.

Hämmerle, Christa (2022), *Ganze Männer? Gesellschaft, Geschlecht und Allgemeine Wehrpflicht in Österreich-Ungarn (1868–1914)*. Frankfurt: Campus.

Hammond, John Craig (2014), 'Slavery, Sovereignty, and Empires: North American Borderlands and the American Civil War, 1660–1860'. *Journal of the Civil War Era* 4(2): 264–298.

Hampel, Józef (2008), *Chłopów polskich drogi do demokracji. Studia i szkice.* Krakow: Wydawnictwo Naukowe Akademii Pedagogicznej.

Hancock, David (1995), *Citizens of the World: London Merchants and the Integration of the British Atlantic Community, 1735–1785.* Cambridge: Cambridge University Press.

Hartmann, Christian (2010), *Wehrmacht im Ostkrieg: Front und militärisches Hinterland 1941/42*, second edition. Munich: Oldenbourg.

Heffter, August Wilhelm (1855), *Das europäische Völkerrecht der Gegenwart.* Berlin: Schroeder.

Helfer, Lawrence R. (2008), 'Nonconsensual International Lawmaking'. *University of Illinois Law Review* 1: 71–126.

Helg, Aline (2004), *Liberty and Equality in Caribbean Colombia 1770–1835.* Chapel Hill: University of North Carolina Press.

Hellegers, Dale M. (2001), *We the Japanese People: World War II and the Origins of the Japanese Constitution. Vol. II.* Stanford, CA: Stanford University Press.

Henderson, Errol A. (2002), *Democracy and War: The End of an Illusion?* Boulder, CO: Lynne Rienner.

Herbst, Stanisław (1983), *Z dziejów wojskowych powstania kościuszkowskiego 1794 roku.* Warsaw: Książka i Wiedza.

Herrera, Fernando Botero (2003), *Estado, Nación y provincial de Antioquia: Guerras civiles e invención de la region 1829–1863.* Medellin: Hombre Nuevo.

Hietala, Thomas R. (1985), *Manifest Design: Anxious Aggrandizement in Late Jacksonian America.* Ithaca, NY: Cornell University Press.

Higginbotham, Don (1988), *War and Society in Revolutionary America: The Wider Dimensions of Conflict.* Columbia: University of South Carolina Press.

Higginbotham, Don (2005), 'War and State Formation in Revolutionary America', in Eliga H. Gould and Peter S. Onuf (eds.), *Empire and Nation: The American Revolution in the Atlantic World.* Baltimore, MD: Johns Hopkins University Press, pp. 54–71.

Hill, William (2018), *No Place for Russia: European Security Institutions since 1989.* New York: Columbia University Press.

Hinderaker, Eric (1997), *Elusive Empires: Constructing Colonialism in the Ohio Valley, 1673–1800.* Cambridge: Cambridge University Press.

Hinnebusch, Raymond A. (1990), *Authoritarian Power and State Formation in Ba'thist Syria: Army, Party, and Peasant.* Boulder, CO: Westview.

Hintze, Otto (1962), *Staat und Verfassung: Gesammelte Abhandlungen zur allgemeinen Verfassungsgeschichte*, edited by Gerhard Oestreich, second edition. Gottingen: Vandenhoeck & Ruprecht.

Hoensch, Jörg K. (1970), 'Der Streit um den polnischen Generalzoll 1764–1766: Zur Rolle Preußens und Rußlands beim Scheitern der Finanzreform Stanisław Augusts'. *Jahrbücher für Geschichte Osteuropas, Neue Folge*, 18(3): 355–388.

Holton, Woody (1999), *Forced Founders: Indians, Debtors, Slaves, and the Making of the American Revolution in Virginia*. Chapel Hill: University of North Carolina Press.

Hopkins, Stephen (1765), *The Rights of Colonies Examined*. Providence, RI: William Goddard.

Horne, Gerald (2014), *The Counter-Revolution of 1776: Slave Resistance and the Origins of the United States of America*. New York: New York University Press.

Humphreys, Leonard A. (1995), *The Way of the Heavenly Sword: The Japanese Army in the 1920s*. Stanford, CA: Stanford University Press.

Ibáñez Rivas, Juana María (2016), 'El derecho internacional humanitario en la jurisprudencia de la Corte Interamericana de Derechos Humanos'. *Revista Derecho del Estado* 36: 167–198.

Ilski, Zdzisław (2022), *System wyborczy do Izby Poselskiej parlamentu Polski przedrozbiorowej, Księstwa Warszawskiego i Królestwa Polskiego*. Wroclaw: Oficyna Wydawnicza ATUT.

Inglot, Stefan (ed.) (1952), *Próby reform włosciańskich w Polsce XVIII wieku: Wybór źródeł*. Wroclaw: Wydawnictwo zakładu narodowego im. Ossolińskich.

Issacharoff, Samuel and Richard H. Pildes (2004), 'Emergency Contexts without Emergency Powers: The United States' Constitutional Approach to Rights during Wartime'. *International Journal of Constitutional Law* 2(2): 296–333.

Jakubczak, Ryszard (2020), *Powszechna Obrona Terytorialna w bezpieczeństwie narodowym RP*. Warsaw: Fundacja Historia i Kultura.

Janas, Eugeniusz (1998), *Konfederacja wojska koronnego w latach 1661–1663: Dzieje i ideologia*. Lublin: Wydawnictwo Uniwersyetu Marii Curie-Skłodowskiej.

Janke, Peter (1974), *Mendizabal y la instauración de la monarquía constitucional en España (1790–1853)*. Madrid: Siglo XXI de España.

Jaundrill, D. Colin (2016), *Remaking Military Service in Nineteenth-Century Japan*. Ithaca, NY: Cornell University Press.

Jędrysiak, Jacek (2014), 'Granica wschodnia w pruskim planowaniu obronnym w latach 1815–1830'. *Przegląd Historyczno-Wojskowy* 15: 7–32.

Jewuła, Łukasz, Tomasz Kargol and Krzysztof Ślusarek (2015), *Dwór, wieś i plebania: W przestrzeni społecznej zachodniej Małopolski w latach 1772–1815*. Krakow: Towarzystwo Wydawnicze 'Historia Iagellonica'.

Joint Committee on Indian Constitutional Reform. Vol. I. (1934). London: His Majesty's Stationery Office.

Jones, P. M. (1995), *Reform and Revolution in France: The Politics of Transition, 1774–1791*. Cambridge: Cambridge University Press.

Jureit, Ulrike (2019), 'Europa als postsouveräner Raum: Über Imperialität, Großraumkonzepte und postsouveräne Herrschaft', in Eva Marlene

Hausteiner and Sebastian Huhnholz (eds.), *Imperien Verstehen: Theorien, Typen, Transformationen*. Baden-Baden: Nomos, pp. 101–127.

Jurkowski, Roman (2001), *Ziemiaństwo polskie kresów północo-wschodnich 1864–1904: Działalność społeczno-gospodarcza*. Warsaw: DiG.

Kacprzak, Michał (2009), *Ziemia dla żołnierzy: Problem pozyskania i rozdysponowania gruntów na cele osadnictwa wojskowego na kresach wschodnich 1920–1939*. Lodz: Ibidem.

Kaczmarczyk-Klak, Katarzyna (2018), 'System rzadów w Polsce w latach 1918–1922'. *Studia Prawnicze KUL* 1(73): 57–80.

Kamissek, Christoph (2018), *Kriegslust und Fernweh: Deutsche Soldaten zwischen militärischem Internationalismus und imperialer Nation (1770–1870)*. Frankfurt: Campus.

Kania, Leszek (2019), *Wyroki bez apelacji: Sądy polowe w wojsku polskim w czasie wojny z Rosją Sowiecką 1919–1921*. Zielona Góra: Uniwerstytet Zielonogórski.

Kansu, Ajkuf (2000), *Politics in Post-Revolutionary Turkey, 1908–1913*. Leiden: Brill.

Kant, Immanuel (1976), *Zum Ewigen Frieden*, in Werkausgabe, edited by Wilhelm Weischedel. Frankfurt: Suhrkamp, vol. IX: pp. 195–251.

Kapila, Shruti (2021), *Violent Fraternity: Indian Political Thought in the Global Age*. Princeton, NJ: Princeton University Press.

Karmi, Ilan (2010), *The Jewish Community of Istanbul in the Nineteenth Century: Social, Legal and Administrative Transformations*. Istanbul: Gorgias Press.

Karp, Matthew (2016), *The Vast Southern Empire: Slaveholders at the Helm of American Foreign Polity*. Cambridge, MA: Harvard University Press.

Karpat, Kemal H. (1982), '*Millets* and Nationality: The Roots of the Incongruity of Nation and State in the Post-Ottoman Era', in Benjamin Braude and Bernard Lewis (eds.), *Christians and Jews in the Ottoman Empire: The Functioning of a Plural Society*. New York: Holmes & Meier, pp. 141–170.

Karpat, Kemal H. (2001), *The Politicization of Islam: Reconstructing Identity, State, Faith and Community in the Late Ottoman State*. Oxford: Oxford University Press.

Karwacki, W. L. (1975), *Łódz w latach rewolucji 1905–1907*. Lodz: Wydawnictwo Łódzkie.

Kasprzycki, Remigiusz (2016), 'Dezercje i unikanie służby w Wojsku Polskim w latach 1918–1939'. *Dzieje Najnowsze* 3: 87–106.

Kaufmann, Franz-Xaver (1973), *Sicherheit als soziologisches und sozialpolitisches Problem*, second edition. Stuttgart: Enke.

Kayali, Hasan (1997), *Arabs and Young Turks: Ottomanism, Arabism and Islamism in the Ottoman Empire, 1908–1918*. Berkeley: University of California Press.

Kayali, Hasan (2021), *Imperial Resistance: The Great War's End, Ottoman Longevity, and Incidental Nations*. Berkeley: University of California Press.

Kelsen, Hans (1945), 'The Legal Status of Germany according to the Declaration of Berlin'. *American Journal of International Law* 39(3): 518–526.

Kemal, Ghazi Mustapha (1929), *A Speech Delivered by Ghazi Mustapha Kemal, President of the Turkish Republic*. Leipzig: Koehler.

Kęsik, Jan (1998), *Naród pod bronią: Społeczeństwo w programie polskiej polityki wojskowej 1918–1939*. Wroclaw: Wydawnictwo Uniwersitetu Wrocławskiego.

Khalid, Adeeb (2006), 'Backwardness and the Quest for Civilization: Early Soviet Central Asia in Comparative Perspective'. *Slavic Review* 65(2): 231–251.

Khoury, Philip S. (1987), *Syria and the French Mandate: The Politics of Arab Nationalism 1920–1945*. Princeton, NJ: Princeton University Press.

Kienemann, Christoph (2018), *Der koloniale Blick gen Osten: Osteuropa im Diskurs des Deutschen Kaiserreichs von 1871*. Paderborn: Schöningh.

Kieniewicz, Stefan (1953), *Sprawa włościańska w powstaniu styczniowym*. Wroclaw: Wydawnictwo Zakładu Narodowego im. Ossolińskich.

Kienitz, Sabine (2008), *Beschädigte Helden: Kriegsinvalidität und Körperbilder 1914–1923*. Paderborn: Schöningh.

Kiepurska, Haline (1974), *Warszawa w Rewolucji 1905–1907*. Warsaw: Wiedza Powszechna.

Kier, Elizabeth and Ronald Krebs (eds.) (2012), *In War's Wake: International Conflict and the Fate of Liberal Democracy*. Cambridge: Cambridge University Press.

Kivelson, Valerie A. and Ronald Grigor Suny (2017), *Russia's Empires*. New York: Oxford University Press.

Kłaczewski, Witold (1993), *Abdykacja Jana Kazimierza: Społeczeństwo szlacheckie wobec kryzysu politycznegu lat 1667–1668*. Lublin: Wydawnictwo Uniwersyetu Marii Curie-Skłodowskiej.

Klafkowski, Alfons (1946), *Okupacja niemiecka w Polsce w świetle prawa narodów*. Poznan: Wydawnictwo Instytutu Zachodniego.

Klose, Fabian (2009), *Menschenrechte im Schatten kolonialer Gewalt: Die Dekolonisierungskriege in Kenia und Algerien 1945–1962*. Munich: Oldenbourg.

Klüber, Jean Louis (1819), *Droit des gens moderne de l'Europe*. Stuttgart: Cotta.

Knoblauch, Edward (1997), 'Mobilizing Provincials for War: The Social Composition of New York Forces in 1760'. *New York History* 78(2): 147–172.

Knouff, Gregory T. (2004), *The Soldiers' Rebellion: Pennsylvania in Arms and the Forging of Early American Identity*. University Park: Pennsylvania State University Press.

Koçunyan, Aylin (2018), *Negotiating the Ottoman Constitution 1839–1876*. Paris: Peeters.

Koehler-Derrick, Gabriel and Melissa M. Lee (2023), 'War and Welfare in Colonial Algeria'. *International Organization* 77(2): 263–293.

Kolb, Robert (1998), 'The Relationship between International Humanitarian Law and Human Rights Law: A Brief History of the 1948 Universal Declaration of Human Rights and the 1949 Geneva Conventions'. *International Review of the Red Cross* 324: 409–419.

Kolb, Robert and Sylvain Vité (2009), *Le droit de l'occupation militaire: Perspectives historiques et enjeux juridiques actuels*. Brussels: Brulant.

Kolla, Edward James (2017), *Sovereignty, International law, and the French Revolution*. Cambridge: Cambridge University Press.

Kołłątai, Hugo (1790), *Prawo polityczne narodu polskiego*. Warsaw: Grölla.

Kołłątai, Hugo (1954), *Listy Anonima i prawo polityczne narodu polskiego*. Warsaw: Państwowe wydawnictwo naukowe.

Komarnicki, Wacław (1922), *Polskie prawo polityczne (Geneza i system)*. Warsaw: Nakładem Księgarnia F. Hoesicka.

Kowecki, Jerzy (1963), *Pospolite ruszenie w insurekcji 1794*. Warsaw: Wydawnictwo Ministerstwa Obrony Narodowej.

Kozelsky, Mara (2019), *Crimea in War and Transformation*. Oxford: Oxford University Press.

Kozłowski, Jerzy (2004), *Wielkopolska pod zaborem pruskim w latach 1815–1918*. Poznan: Wydawnictwo Poznańskie.

Kraay, Hendrik (2002), 'Em outra coisa não falavam os pardos, cabras, e crioulos: O "recrutamento" de escravos na guerra da Independência na Bahia'. *Revista Brasileira de História* 22: 109–126.

Krebs, Ronald R. (2006), *Fighting for Rights: Military Service and the Politics of Citizenship*. Ithaca, NY: Cornell University Press.

Krebs, Ronald R. (2009), 'In the Shadow of War: The Effects of Conflict on Liberal Democracy'. *International Organization* 63(1): 177–220.

Krepinevich, Andrew F. (1986), *The Army and Vietnam*. Baltimore, MD: Johns Hopkins University Press.

Kreuder-Sonnen, Christian and Bernhard Zangl (2015), 'Which Post-Westphalia? International Organizations between Constitutionalism and Authoritarianism'. *European Journal of International Relations* 21(3): 568–594.

Kriegseisen, Wojiech (1989), *Samorząd szlachecki w Małopolsce w latach 1669–1717*. Warsaw: Państwowe Wydawnictwo Naukowe.

Krotofil, Maciej (2002), *Ukraińska Armia Halicka 1918–1920*. Torun: Wydawnictwo Adam Marszałek.

Kruse, Volker (2015), *Kriegsgesellschaftliche Moderne: Zur strukturbildenden Dynamik großer Kriege*. Konstanz: UVK.

Kuenne, Robert E. (1993), *Economic Justice in American Society*. Princeton, NJ: Princeton University Press.

Kuethe, Allan J. (1978), *Military Reform and Society in New Granada, 1773–1808*. Gainesville: University Press of Florida.

Kuethe, Allan J. and Kenneth J. Andrien (2014), *The Spanish Atlantic World and the Bourbon Reforms*. Cambridge: Cambridge University Press.

Kukulski, Jerzy (1995), *Sądy gminne w Królestwie polskim: Studium społeczno-historyczne*. Kielce: Wyżsa Szkola pedagogiczna im. Jana Kochanowskiego.

Kulecka, Alicja (2016), *Ku społeczeństwu obywatelskiemu: Czas walk i polemik 1863*. Warsaw: Wydawnictwo Uniwersystetu Warszawskiego.

Kulesza, Władysław T. (1985), *Koncepcje ideowo-polityczne obozu rządzącego w Polsce w latach 1926–1935*. Wroclaw: Wydawnictwo Zakładu Narodowego im. Ossolińskich.

Kulikoff, Allan (1992), *The Agrarian Origins of American Capitalism*. Charlottesville: University Press of Virginia.

Kundu, Apurba (1998), *Militarism in India: The Army and Civil Society in Consensus*. London: Tauris.

Kuperman, Alan J. (2013), 'A Model Humanitarian Intervention? Reassessing NATO's Libya Campaign'. *International Security* 38(1): 105–136.

Kupiecki, Robert (2015), 'Strategia Bezpieczeństwa Narodowego RP 2014 jako instrument polityki państwa: Uwarunkowania zewnętrzne i aspekty procesowe'. *Bezpieczeństwo Narodowe* 1: 11–36.

Kupisz, Dariusz (2008), *Wojska powiatowe samorządów Małopolski i Rusi Czerwonej w latach 1572–1717*. Lublin: Wydawnictwo Uniwersyetu Marii Curie-Skłodowskiej.

Lafontaine, Fannie (2005), 'No Amnesty or Statute of Limitation for Enforced Disappearances: The *Sandoval* Case before the Supreme Court of Chile'. *Journal of International Criminal Justice* 3(2): 469–485.

Landau, Zbigniew and Jerzy Tomaszewski (1967), *W dobie inflacji 1918–1923*. Warsaw: Książka i Wiedza.

Lang, Andrew F. (2017), *In the Wake of War: Military Occupations, Emancipation and Civil War America*. Baton Rouge: Louisiana State University Press.

Lange, Richard (1948), 'Das Kontrollratsgesetz Nr. 10 in Theorie und Praxis'. *Deutsche Rechts-Zeitschrift* 3(5): 155–161.

Lanz, Laureno Vallenilla (1961), *Cesarismo Democratico: Estudios sobre las bases sociologicas de la Constitución de Venezuela*, fourth edition. Caracas: Tipografia Garrido.

Lasso, Marixa (2006), 'Race War and Nation in Caribbean Gran Colombia, Cartagena, 1810–1832'. *American Historical Review* 111(2): 336–361.

Lasso, Marixa (2007), *Myths of Harmony: Race and Revolution during the Age of Revolution, Colombia 1795–1831*. Pittsburgh, PA: University of Pittsburgh Press.

Lauterpacht, Hersch (1952), 'The Problem of the Revision of the Law of War'. *British Yearbook of International Law* 9: 360–382.

Lavi, Shai (2011), 'Citizenship Revocation as Punishment: On the Modern Duties of Citizens and Their Criminal Breach'. *University of Toronto Law Journal* 61(4): 783–810.

Lawrence, Mark (2017), *The Spanish Civil Wars: A Comparative History of the First Carlist War and the Conflict of the 1930s*. London: Bloomsbury.

Leffler, Melvyn P. (1984), 'The American Conception of National Security and the Beginnings of the Cold War, 1945–48'. *American Historical Review* 89(2): 346–381.

Legieć, Jacek (2013), *Służba rekrutów z Królestwa polskiego w armii rosyjskiej w latach 1874–1913*. Kielce: Wydawnictwo Uniwersytetu Jana Kochanowskiego.

Lehnstaedt, Stephan (2012), 'Das Militärgeneralgouvernement Lublin: Die "Nutzbarmachung" Polens durch Österreich-Ungarn im Ersten Weltkrieg'. *Zeitschrift für Ostmitteleuropa-Forschung* 61: 1–26.

Lengnich, Gottfried (1746), *Ius Publicum Regni Poloni. Vol. II*. Gdansk: Rüdiger.

Léonard, Émile G. (1958), *L'Armée et ses problèmes au XVIIIe siècle*. Paris: Plon.

Leroux, Denis (2014), 'La "doctrine de la guerre révolutionnaire": Théories et pratiques', in Abderrahmane Bouchène, Jean-Pierre Peyroulou, Ouanassa Siari Tengour and Sylvie Thénault (eds.), *Histoire de l'Algérie à la période coloniale*. Paris: La Découverte, pp. 526–532.

Lerp, Dörte (2016), *Imperiale Grenzräume: Bevölkerungspolitiken in Deutsch-Südwestafrika und den östlichen Provinzen Preußens 1884–1914*. Frankfurt: Campus.

Levi, Margaret (1996), 'The Institution of Conscription'. *Social Science History* 20(1): 133–167.

Levy, Jack S. (1988), 'Domestic Politics and War'. *Journal of Interdisciplinary History* 18(4): 653–673.

Lewis, Michael (2000), *Becoming Apart: National Power and Local Politics in Toyama, 1868–1945*. Cambridge, MA: Harvard University Press.

Lewandowski, Enrique Ricardo (1985), 'Notas sobre o conceito de guerra revolucionária e sua expressão legal'. *Revista da Faculdade de Direito, Universidade de São Paulo* 80: 210–217.

Lignereux, Aurélien (2023), *L'Empire de la paix. De la Révolution à Napoléon: Quand la France réunissait l'Europe*. Paris: Passés composes.

Lindner, Ulrike (2011), *Koloniale Begegnungen: Deutschland und Großbritannien als Imperialmächte in Afrika 1880–1914*. Frankfurt: Campus.

Linklater, Andrew (2017), *Violence and Civilization in the Western States-Systems*. Cambridge: Cambridge University Press.

Llano, Alonso Valencia (1988). *Estado soberano del Cauca: Federalismo y regeneración*. Bogota: Banco de la República.

Lleixa, Joaquim (1986), *Cien años de militarismo en España: Funciones estatales confiadas al Ejército en la Restauración y el Franquismo*. Barcelona: Editorial Anagrama.

Logevall, Fredrik (2012), *Embers of War: The Fall of an Empire and the Making of America's Vietnam*. New York: Random House.

Łojek, Jerzy (1986), *Geneza i obalenie Konstytucji 3 Maja: Polityka zagranicza Rzeczypospolitej 1787–1792*. Lublin: Wydawnictwo Lubelskie.

Łopatecki, Karol (2013), *Organizacja, prawo i dyscyplina w polskim i litewskim pospolitym ruszeniu (do połowy XVII wieku)*. Bialystok: Instytut Badań nad Dziedzictwem Kulturowym Europy.

López, José Hilario (1833), *Exposición que hace al congreso de la Nueva Granada en 1831 sobre los negocios a su cargo*. Bogota: Espinosa.

López Garrido, Diego (1982), *La Guardia Civil y los orígenes del Estado centralista*. Barcelona: Editorial Critica.

Łotys, Zbigniew (2005), *Problem niepodległości w świadomości Polaków epoki stanisławowskiej*. Olsztyn: Olsztyńska Szkoła Wyższa im J. Rusieckiego.

Luard, Evard (1986), *War in International Society: A Study in International Sociology*. London: Tauris.

Lynch, Christian Edward Cyril (2011), 'O momento oligárquico: A construçao institucional da república brasileira (1870–1891)'. *Historia Constitucional* (12): 297–325.

Lynch, John (1986), *The Spanish American Revolutions 1808–1826*. New York: Norton.

Lynn, John (1984), *The Bayonets of the Republic: Motivation and Tactics in the Army of Revolutionary France, 1791–1794*. Urbana: University of Illinois Press.

Lynn, John (1989), 'Toward an Army of Honor: The Moral Evolution of the French Army, 1789–1815'. *French Historical Studies* 16(1): 152–173.

Maciejak, Maciej (2014), *Bitwa pod Szczekocinami 6 Czerwca 1794*. Zabrze: Wydawnictwo inforteditions.

Madariaga, María Rosa de (2002), *Los Moros que trajo Franco: La intervención de tropas coloniales en la Guerra Civil Española*. Barcelona: Ediciones Martínez.

Madison, James, Alexander Hamilton, and John Jay (1987 [1787–8]), *The Federalist Papers*. London: Penguin.

Maj, Ewa (2017), 'Obrona terytorialna i wojska obrony terytorialnej w myśli politycznej Polski współczesnej'. *Bezpieczeństwo. Teoria i Praktyka* 3: 297–316.

Majer, Diemut (2002), *Nationalsozialismus im Lichte der juristischen Zeitgeschichte. Ideologie – Staat – Besatzungsregime in Europa 1939–1945*. Baden-Baden: Nomos.

Makris, Alexandros (2023), 'Domestic Dimensions of a Transnational Problem: Social Welfare for Veterans in Greece (1912–1940)'. *War & Society* 42(3): 251–266.

Malec, Dorota (2015), 'Obywatelstwo państwa polskiego w świetle orzecznictwa Najwyższego Trybunału Administracyjnego 1922–1939'. *Miscellanea Historico-Iuridica* 14(2): 73–96.

Malešević, Siniša (2019), *Grounded Nationalisms: A Sociological Analysis*. Cambridge: Cambridge University Press.

Mallinder, Louise (2016), 'The End of Amnesty or Regional Overreach? Interpreting the Erosion of South America's Amnesty Laws'. *International and Comparative Law Quarterly* 65(3): 645–680.

Mancke, Elizabeth (2005), *The Fault Lines of Empire: Political Differentiation in Massachusetts and Nova Scotia, ca. 1760–1830*. New York: Routledge.

Mann, Michael (1987), 'Ruling Class Strategies and Citizenship'. *Sociology* 21(3): 339–354.

Mann, Michael (2012), *The Sources of Social Power: Volume 2, The Rise of Classes and Nation-States, 1760–1914*. Cambridge: Cambridge University Press.

Mansfield, Edward D. and Jack Snyder (1995), 'Democratization and the Danger of War'. *International Security* 20(1): 5–38.

Mansfield, Edward D., and Jack Snyder (2002), 'Democratic Transitions, Institutional Strength, and War'. *International Organization* 56(2): 297–337.

Ma'oz, Moshe (1968), *Ottoman Reform in Syria and Palestine 1840–1861: The Impact of the Tanzimat on Politics and Society*. Oxford: Clarendon.

Maoz, Zeev and Bruce Russett (1993), 'Normative and Structural Causes of Democratic Peace, 1946–1986'. *American Political Science Review* 87(3): 624–638.

Marchet, Gustav (1915), *Versorgung der Kriegs-invaliden und ihrer Hinterbliebenen*. Warnsdorf: Strache.

Marichal, Carlos (1980), *La revolución y los primeros partidos políticos en España: 1834–1844*. Madrid: Ediciones Cátedra.

Marichal, Carlos (1999), *La bancarrota del Virreinato: Nueva España y las finanzas del Imperio Español, 1780–1810*. Mexico City: El colegio de México.

Markiewicz, Grzegorz (2013), 'Stanowisko głównych polskich ugrupowań socjalistycznych w Łodzi w latach 1905–1907 wobec kwestii autonomii Królestwa Polskiego'. *Studia z historii społeczno-gospodarczej* 12: 57–72.

Marr, David G. (2015), *Vietnam: State, War, and Revolution (1945–1946)*. Berkeley: University of California Press.

Marston, Daniel (2014), *The Indian Army and the End of the Raj*. Cambridge: Cambridge University Press.

Marston, Jerrilyn Greene (1987), *King and Congress: The Transfer of Political Legitimacy, 1774–1776*. Princeton, NJ: Princeton University Press.

Marszałek, Piotr Krzysztof (1995), *Rada Obrony Państwa z 1920 roku: Studium prawnohistoryczne*. Wroclaw: Wydawnictwo Uniwersytetu Wrocławskiego.

Marszałek, Piotr Krzysztof (2011), *Najwyższe władze wojskowe w systemie ustrojowym II Rzeczypospolitej*. Wroclaw: Prawnicza i Ekonomiczna Biblioteka Cyfrowa.

Martin, Vanessa (2013), *Iran between Islamic Nationalism and Secularism: The Constitutional Revolution of 1906*. London: Tauris.

Martínez, Juan José Benavides (2014), *De milicianos del rey a soldados mexicanos: Milicias y sociedad en San Luis Potosí (1767–1824)*. Madrid: Editorial CSIC.

Martins Filho, João Roberto (2008), 'A influência doutrinária francesa sobre os militares brasileiros nos anos de 1960'. *Revista Brasileira de Ciências Sociais* 23: 39–50.

Marzec, Wiktor (2016), *Rebelia i reakcja: Rewolucja 1905 Roku i plebejskie doświadczenie polityczne*. Lodz: Wydawnictwo Uniwersyetu Łódzkiego.

Mason, Matthew (2006), *Slavery and Politics in the Early American Republic*. Chapel Hill: University of North Carolina Press.

Mattos, Carlos de Meira (1975), *Brasil: Geopolítica e destino*. Rio de Janeiro: Sindicato Nacional dos Editores de Livros.

Mavrogordatos, George Th. (1983), *Stillborn Republic: Social Coalitions and Party Strategies in Greece, 1922–1936*. Berkeley: University of California Press.

May, Robert E. (1973), *The Southern Dream of a Caribbean Empire, 1854–1861*. Baton Rouge: Louisiana State University Press.

Mażewski, Lech (2010), *Bezpieczeństwo publiczne: Stany nadzwyczajne w Rzeczypospolitej Polskie oraz Polskiej Rzeczpospolitej Ludowej 1918–2009*. Torun: Adam Marszałek.

Mazur, Karol (2006), *W stronę integracji Koroną: Sejmiki Wołynia i Ukrainy w latach 1569–1648*. Warsaw: Neriton.

McAlister, Lyle N. (1957), *The 'Fuero Militar' in New Spain*. Gainesville: University of Florida Press.

McCann, Frank D. (1984), 'The Formative Period of Brazilian Army Thought, 1900–1922'. *Hispanic American Historical Review* 64(4): 737–765.

McCord, Edward A. (1993), *The Power of the Gun: The Emergence of Modern Chinese Warlordism*. Berkeley: University of California Press.

MccGwire, Michael (1998), 'NATO Expansion: "A Policy Error of Historic Importance"'. *Review of International Studies* 24(1): 23–42.

McDonnell, Michael A. (2007), *The Politics of War: Race, Class, and Conflict in Revolutionary Virginia*. Chapel Hill: University of North Carolina Press.

McEnroe, Sean F. (2012), *From Colony to Nationhood in Mexico: Laying the Foundations, 1560–1840*. Cambridge: Cambridge University Press.

McFarlane, Anthony (1993), *Colombia before Independence: Economy, Society and Politics under Bourbon Rule*. Cambridge: Cambridge University Press.

Mędrzecki, Włodzimierz (2002), *Młodzież wiejska na ziemiach Polski centralnej 1864–1939: Procesy socjalizacji*. Warsaw: Wydawnictwo DIG.

Meeker, Michael E. (2002), *A Nation of Empire: The Ottoman Legacy of Turkish Modernity*. Berkeley: University of California Press.

Menou, Jacques (1791), *Premier rapport sur Avignon et le Comtat Venaissin*. Paris: Imprimerie Nationale.

Metinsoy, Murat (2021), *Power of the People: Everyday Resistance and Dissent in the Making of Modern Turkey, 1923–38*. Cambridge: Cambridge University Press.

Meyer, Jean (1983), *Le poids de l'état*. Paris: PUF.

Meyer, John W., Francisco O. Ramirez, Richard Rubinson and John Boli-Bennett (1977), 'The World Educational Revolution'. *Sociology of Education* 50(4): 242–258.

Michaelsen, Christopher (2006), 'Balancing Civil Liberties against National Security? A Critique of Counterterrorism Rhetoric'. *University of New South Wales Law Journal* 29(2): 1–21.

Michalak, Artur (2017), 'Cele, zadania, struktura i funkcje wojsk obrony terytorialnej w XXI wieku'. *Bezpieczeństwo. Teoria i praktyka* 28(3): 27–36.

Michalski, Jerzy (1964), *Polska wobec wojny o sukcesje bawarską*. Wroclaw: Wydawnictwo Zakładu Narodowego im. Ossolińskich.

Michalski, Jerzy (ed.) (1954), *Historia Polski 1764–1795: Wybór tekstów*. Warsaw: Państwowe Wydawnictwo Naukowe.

Mielnik, Hubert (2020), *Sądownictwo polskie (nieniemieckie) w dystrykcie Lubelskim Generalnego Gubernatorstwa w latach 1939–1944*. Lublin: Wydawnictwo Uniwersyetu Marii Curie-Skłodowskiej.

Mikołajewicz, Zbigniew (2003), 'Ekonomiczne i społeczne skutki procesu transformacji w Polsce'. *Annales Universitatis Mariae Curie-Skłodowska. Sectio H, Oeconomia* 37 (2003): 361–373.

Misra, Kashi P. (1980), 'Paramilitary Forces in India'. *Armed Forces & Society* 6(3): 371–388.

Moir, Lindsay (2010), *Reappraising the Resort to Force: International Law, Jus Ad Bellum and the War on Terror*. Oxford: Hart.

Molenda, Jan (1999), *Chłopi, Naród, Niepodległość: Kształtowanie sie postaw narodowych i obywatelskich chłopów w Galicji i Królestwie Polskim w przededniu odrodzenia Polski*. Warsaw: Neriton.

Moliner, Antonio (1997), *Revolución burguesa y movimiento juntero en España: La acción de las juntas a través de la correspondencia diplomática y consular francesa, 1808–1868*. Lleida: Milenio.

Monerri Molina, Beatriz (2019), *Las Cortes del Estatuto Real (1834–1836)*. Madrid: Dykinson.

Monsalvo Mendoza, Edwin (2013), 'Ciudadanía, vecindad y sufragio en Cartagena 1810–1834'. *Revista Historia y Memoria* 6: 171–204.

Monteiro, Góes (1934), *A Revolução de 30 e a finalidade política do Exército*. Rio de Janeiro: Adersen.

Montoyam, Luis Horacio Botero (2014), *La opinión en la formación de la ideología de la independencia en la Nueva Granada*. Medellin: Sello Editorial.

Morawska, Elżbieta (2006), 'Prawa i wolności socjalne w Konstytucji RP: Zagadnienia systemowe'. *Kwartalnik Prawa Publicznego* 6(2): 229–252.

Moreau, Odile (2007), *L'Empire ottoman à l'âge des réformes: Les hommes et les idées du 'Nouvel Ordre' militaire, 1826–1914*. Paris: Institut Français d'Études Anatoliennes, Maisonneuve & Larose.

Morgan, Edmund S. (2003), *American Slavery, American Freedom*. New York: Norton.

Morrison, Alexander (2021), *The Russian Conquest of Central Asia: A Study in Imperial Expansion, 1814–1914*. Cambridge: Cambridge University Press.

Morrison, Michael A. (1997), *Slavery and the American West: The Eclipse of Manifest Destiny and the Coming of the Civil War*. Chapel Hill: University of North Carolina Press.

Morvan, Jean (1904). *Le soldat imperial (1800–1814). Vol. II*. Paris: Plon.

Motta, Paulo Roberto (1971), *Movimentos Partidários no Brasil*. Rio de Janeiro: Editora FGV.

Müller, George Friedrich (1760), *Königlich-Preußisches Krieges-Recht*. Berlin: Verlag der Haude und Spenerschen Buchhandlung.

Munévar, Oscar Fabián (2008), 'El irrespeto a la real justicia: El estamieno military in Cartagena de Indias', in César del Río and Saúl Rodríguez Hernández (eds.), *De milicias reales a militares contrainsurgentes: La institución militar en Colombia del siglo XVIII al XXI*. Bogota: Editorial Universidad Javeriana, pp. 203–219.

Münkler, Herfried (2006), *Der Wandel des Krieges: Von der Symmetrie zur Asymmetrie*. Göttingen: Velbrück.

Murray, Christina (1987), 'The ANC in Court: Towards International Guidelines in Sentencing'. *Journal of Southern African Studies* 14(1): 140–146.

Myrdal, Gunnar (1960), *Beyond the Welfare State: Economic Planning and Its International Implications*. New Haven, CT: Yale University Press.

Nabuco, Joaquim (2003), *O abolicionismo*. Brasilia: Senado Federal, Conselho Editorial.

Nadelhaft, Jerome J. (1981), *The Disorders of War: The Revolution in South Carolina*. Orono: University of Maine at Orono Press.

Nascimento, Carla Silva (2009), 'A "Questão Militar": Indisciplina e crise política em meio à crise hegemônica imperial (1868–1889)'. *Militares e Política* 4: 7–22.

Nascimento, Fernanda (2014), 'Un nuevo espíritu: La modernización del Ejército brasileño en las páginas de la revista A Defesa Nacional, durante el primer gobierno de Vargas (1931–1937)'. *Locus* 20(1): 281–303.

Naumann, Friedrich (1900), *Demokratie und Kaisertum*. Berlin: Buchverlag der Hilfe.

Nehru, Jawaharlal (1951), *The Discovery of India*, third edition. London: Meridian Books.

Neimeyer, Charles Patrick (1996), *America Goes to War: A Social History of the Continental Army*. New York: New York University Press.

Nemo, Jean (1956), 'La guerre dans le milieu social'. *Revue Défense Nationale* 12: 605–623.

Neocleous, Mark (2006), 'From Social to National Security: On the Fabrication of Economic Order'. *Security Dialogue* 37(3): 363–384.

Neto, Franchini Helio (2019), *Independência e Morte: Política e Guerra na Emancipação do Brasil 1821–1823*. Rio de Janeiro: TOPBOOKS.

Newman, John Paul (2015), *Yugoslavia in the Shadow of War: Veterans and the Limits of State Building, 1903–1945*. Cambridge: Cambridge University Press.

Ní Aoláin, Fionnuala (2021), 'The Ever-Expanding Legislative Supremacy of the Security Council in Counterterrorism', in Arianna Vedaschi and Kim Lane Scheppele (eds.), *9/11 and the Rise of Global Anti-Terrorism Law: How the UN Security Council Rules the World*. Cambridge: Cambridge University Press, pp. 34–55.

Nielsen, Christian Axboe (2014), *Making Yugoslavs: Identity in King Aleksandar's Yugoslavia*. Toronto: University of Toronto Press.

Niewęgłowska, Aneta (2011), *Federacja Polskich Związków Obrońców Ojczyzny*. Warsaw: Neriton.

Nkrumah, Kwame (1968), *Handbook of Revolutionary Warfare*. London: Panaf.

Nogueira, Octaciano (2005), *A Constituinte de 1946: Getúlio, o Sujeito Oculto*. São Paulo: Martins Fontes.

Nord, Philip (2012), *France's New Deal: From the Thirties to the Postwar Era*. Princeton, NJ: Princeton University Press.

Nowak, Magdalena (2007), *Narodowy i Ukraińcy: Narodowa Demokracja wobec mniejszości ukraińskiej w Polsce 1922–1939*. Gdansk: Wydawnictwo Uniwersytetu Gdańskiego.

Nunes, Castro (1956), *Do mandado de segurança e de otros meios de defesa contra atos de poder público*, fifth edition. Rio de Janeiro: Revista Forense.

Nuñez Florencio, Rafael (1990), *Militarismo y Antimilitarismo en España (1888–1906)*. Madrid: Consejo Superior de Investigaciones Científicas.

Nycz, Michał (2016), *Geneza reform skarbowych sejmu niemego: Studium z dziejów skarbowo-wojskowych z lat 1697–1717*. Oshpitzin: Napoleon V.

Obinger, Herbert (2020), 'Conscription, the Military, and Welfare State Development'. *Historical Social Research* 45(2): 7–26.

Obinger, Herbert, Lukas Grawe and Nikolas Dörr (2020), 'Veteranen-und Kriegsopferversorgung und Sozialstaatsentwicklung in Australien, Deutschland, Österreich und den USA'. *Politische Vierteljahresschrift* 61(3): 473–501.

Obinger, Herbert and Carina Schmitt (2020), 'World War and Welfare Legislation in Western Countries'. *Journal of European Social Policy* 30(3): 261–274.

Ochimowski, Feliks (1919), *Prawo administracyjne*. Warsaw: Księgarnia F. Hoesicka.

Olson, Alison Gilbert (1992), *Making the Empire Work: London and American Interest Groups 1690–1790*. Cambridge, MA: Harvard University Press.

Olszewski, Henryk (2002), *Sejm w dawnej Rzeczypospolitej: Ustrój i idee. Vol. I.* Poznan: Wydawnictwo Naukowe UAM.

Olwell, Robert (1998), *Masters, Slaves, and Subjects: The Culture of Power in the South Carolina Low Country 1740–1790*. Ithaca, NY: Cornell University Press.

Omissi, David (1994), *The Sepoy and the Raj: The Indian Army 1860–1940*. Basingstoke: Palgrave.

Oneal, John R. and Bruce M. Russet (1997), 'The Classical Liberals Were Right: Democracy, Interdependence, and Conflict, 1950–1985'. *International Studies Quarterly* 41(2): 267–293.

Onuf, Peter S. (1987), *Statehood and Union: A History of the Northwest Ordinance*. Notre Dame, IN: University of Notre Dame Press.

Organiściak, Wojciech (2002), 'Polskie "Artykuły wojskowe" z 1775 roku'. *Kwartalnik Historyczny* 109(1): 41–59.

Ortega, José Varela (1977), *Los amigos políticos: Partidos, elecciones y caciquismo en la Restauracíon (1875–1900)*. Madrid: Alianza Editorial.

Ortiz Mesa, Luis Javier (2004), *Fusiles y plegarias: Guerra de guerrillas en Cundinamarca, Boyacá y Santander, 1876–1877*. Medellin: Universidad Nacional de Colombia.

Ortiz-Ospina, Esteban and Max Roser (2016), 'Government Spending'. OurWorldInData.org. https://ourworldindata.org/government-spending.

Ostanek, Adam Adrian (2019), *W służbie ojczyźnie: Wojsko Polskie w systemie bezpieczeństwa województw południowo-wschodnich II Rzeczypospolitej (1921–1939)*. Warsaw: Wojskowa Akademia Techniczna.

Osterhammel, Jürgen (2009), *Die Verwandlung der Welt: Eine Geschichte des 19. Jahrhunderts*. Munich: Beck.

Ottaway, Marina and Bethany Lacina (2003), 'International Interventions and Imperialism'. *SAIS Review (1989–2003)* 23(2): 71–92.

Pahlavi, Pierre and Éric Ouellet (2009), 'Guerre irrégulière et analyse institutionnelle: le cas de la guerre révolutionnaire de l'armée française en Algérie'. *Guerres mondiales et conflits contemporains* 235(3): 131–144.

Park, James William (1985), *Rafael Nuñez and the Politics of Colombian Regionalism, 1863–1886*. Baton Rouge: Louisiana State University Press.

Parla, Taha and Andrew Davison (2004), *Corporatist Ideology in Kemalist Turkey: Progress or Order?* Syracuse, NY: Syracuse University Press.

Parrott, David (2001), *Richelieu's Army: War, Government and Society in France, 1624–1642*. Cambridge: Cambridge University Press.

Parsons, Talcott (1965), 'Full Citizenship for the Negro American? A Sociological Problem'. *Daedalus* 94(4): 1009–1054.

Paruch, Waldemar (1997), *Od konsolidacji państwowej do konsolidacji narodowej: Mniejszości narodowe w myśli politycznej obozu piłsudskiego (1926–1939)*. Lublin: Wydawnictwo Uniwersitetu Marii Curie-Skłodowskiej.

Paula Marques, Raphael Peixoto de (2013), 'Estado de exceção e mudança (in) constitucional no Brasil (1935–1937)'. *Historia Constitucional* 14: 353–386.

Pearce, Adrian J. (2014), *The Origins of Bourbon Reform in Spanish South America, 1700–1763*. Basingstoke: Macmillan.

Pearl, Christopher R. (2020), *Conceived in Crisis: The Revolutionary Creation of an American State*. Charlottesville: University of Virginia Press.

Pedersen, Susan (2015), *The Guardians: The League of Nations and the Crisis of Empire*. Charlottesville: Oxford University Press.

Perez Garzon, Juan Sisinio (1978), *Milicia nacional y revolución burguesa: El prototipo madrileño 1808–1874*. Madrid: Consejo superior de Investigaciones científicas Institut 'Jeronimo Zurita'.

Peri, Yoram (1983), *Between Battles and Ballots: Israeli Military in Politics*. Cambridge: Cambridge University Press.

Perlmutter, Amos (1969), 'The Praetorian State and the Praetorian Army: Toward a Taxonomy of Civil–Military Relations in Developing Polities'. *Comparative Politics* 1(3): 382–404.

Pesek, Michael (2005), *Koloniale Herrschaft in Deutsch-Ostafrika: Expeditionen, Militär und Verwaltung seit 1880*. Frankfurt: Campus.

Pessoa, Mário (1971), *O direito da segurança nacional*. São Paulo: Revista dos Tribunais.

Phelan, John Leddy (1978), *The People and the King: The Comunero Revolution in Colombia, 1781*. Madison: University of Wisconsin Press.

Pictet, Jean S. (1960), *The Geneva Conventions of 12 August 1949, Commentary Geneva Convention Relative to the Treatment of Prisoners of War*. Geneva: International Committee of the Red Cross.

Piegzik, Michał A. (2016), *Problem reformy armii Rzeczpospolitej w dobie Sejmu Czteroletniego*. Zabrze: Wydawnictwo infortedition.

Pigeard, Alain (2003), *La conscription au temps de Napoléon: 1798–1814*. Paris: Bernard Giovanangeli.

Pijaj, Stanisław (2003), *Między polskim patriotyzmem a habsburskim lojalizmem: Polacy wobec przemian ustrojowych monarchii habsburskie (1866–1871)*. Krakow: Towarzystwo Wydawnicze 'Historia Iagellonica'.

Pimenta, João Paulo G. (2006), *Estado e nação no fim dos Impérios Ibéricos no Prata 1808–1828*, second edition. São Paulo: HUCITEC.

Pinto, Bilac (1964), *Guerra revolucionaria*. Rio de Janeiro: Forense.

Pinzón de Lewin, Patricia (1994), *El ejercito y las elecciones: Ensajo histórico*. Bogota: CEREC.

Podolska-Meducka, Aldon (2011), *Od wojny do wojny: System świadczeń wojennych w Polsce w latach 1918–1923*. Warsaw: Oficyna wydawnicza szkoła głóna handlowa w Warszawie.

Pohl, Dieter (2008), *Die Herrschaft der Wehrmacht: Deutsche Militärbesatzung und einheimische Bevölkerung in der Sowjetunion 1941–1944*. Frankfurt: Fischer.

Pönitz, Carl Eduard (1842), *Die Eisenbahnen als militärische Operationslinien*. Adorf: Verlags-Bureau.

Pontoriero, Esteban Damián (2012), 'Pensamiento militar y legislación de defensa en la Argentina'. *Historia y problemas del siglo XX* 3(3): 149–165.

Ponzani, Michela (2011), 'Trials of Partisans in the Italian Republic: The Consequences of the Elections of 18 April 1948'. *Modern Italy* 16(2) (2011): 121–138.

Popławski, Antoni (1774), *Zbiór niektórych materii politycznych*. Warsaw: Drukarnia Pijarów.

Popović-Obradović, Olga (2013), *The Parliamentary System in Serbia 1903–1914*. Belgrade: Helsinški odbor za ljudska prava u Srbiji.

Posner, Eric A. and Adrian Vermeule (2003), 'Accommodating Emergencies'. *Stanford Law Review* 56: 605–644.

Powell, Ralph L. (2015), *Rise of the Chinese Military Power*. Princeton, NJ: Princeton University Press.

Pownall, Thomas (1781), *The Right, Interest and Duty of Government as Concerned in the Affairs of the East Indies*. London: Almon.

Prado Arellano, Luis Ervin (2019), 'Desplegando el Estado: Los ejércitos republicanos en las provincias del Cauca, 1832–1855'. *Historia Caribe* 14(35): 149–178.

Prakash, Gyan (2019), *Emergency Chronicles: Indira Gandhi and Democracy's Turning Point*. Princeton, NJ: Princeton University Press.

Preuß, Hugo (1915), *Das deutsche Volk und die Politik*. Jena: Eugen Diederichs.

Preuß, Hugo (2008), *Gesammelte Schriften. Vol. IV*, edited by Detlef Lehnert. Tubingen: Mohr Siebeck.

Preuss, Ori (2012), 'Brazil into Latin America: The Demise of Slavery and Monarchy as Transnational Events'. *Luso-Brazilian Review* 49(1): 96–126.

Price, Don C. (1974), *Russia and the Roots of the Chinese Revolution, 1896–1911*. Cambridge, MA: Harvard University Press.

Pro Ruiz, Juan (1998), 'La política en tiempos del Desastre', in Juan Pan-Montojo (ed.), *Más se perdío en Cuba: España, 1898 y la crisis de fin de siglo*. Madrid: Alianza Editorial, pp. 151–260.

Provence, Michael (2017), *The Last Ottoman Generation and the Making of the Modern Middle East*. Cambridge: Cambridge University Press.

Provost, René (2002), *International Human Rights and Humanitarian Law*. Cambridge: Cambridge University Press.

Przeniosło, Marek (2003), *Chłopi Królestwa Polskiego w latach 1914–1918*. Kielce: Wydawnictwo Akademii Świętokrzyskiej.

Przeniosło, Marek (2014), 'Placówki werbunkowe Departamentu Wojskowego Naczelnego Komitetu Narodowego na terenie okupacji austro-wegierskiej 1915–1916'. *Res Historica* 37: 65–80.

Qichao, Liang (1916), 'Xinmin Shuo' [新民说] in Liang Qichao, *Yinbingshi Wenji* [饮冰室文集]. Beijing: Commercial Press.

Quarles, Benjamin (1961), *The Negro in the American Revolution*. Chapel Hill: University of North Carolina Press.

Quesnay, François (1768), *Physiocratie, ou constitution naturelle du gouvernement le plus avantageux au genre humain. Vol. I*, edited by P. S. Dupont. Leiden.

Rabinovich, Alejandro (2012), 'La militarización del Río de la Plata, 1810–1820: Elementos cuantitativos y conceptuales para un análisis'. *Boletín del Instituto de historia argentina y americana 'Dr. Emilio Ravignani'* 3(37): 11–42.

Raim, Edith (2013), *Justiz zwischen Diktatur und Demokratie: Wiederaufbau und Ahndung von NS-Verbrechen in Westdeutschland 1945–1949*. Munich: Oldenbourg Wissenschaftsverlag.

Ramelli Arteaga, Alejandro (2009), 'El derecho internacional humanitario ante la Corte Interamericana de Derechos Humanos'. *Anuario Mexicano de Derecho Internacional* 9: 35–68.

Ramirez, Francisco O. and Marc J. Ventresca (1992), 'Building the Institution of Mass Education: Isomorphism in the Modern World', in Bruce Fuller and Richard Rubinson (eds.), *The Political Construction of Education: The State, School Expansion and Economic Change*. New York: Praeger, pp. 47–59.

Ranalletti, Mario (2010), 'Aux origines du terrorisme d'État en Argentine: Les influences françaises dans la formation des militaires argentins (1955–1976)'. *Vingtième Siècle: Revue d'histoire* 105(1): 45–56.

Ratajczyk, Leonard (1975), *Wojsko i obronność Rzeczypospolitej 1788–1792*. Warsaw: Wydawnictwo Ministerstwa Obrony Narodowej.

Ravina, Mark (2017), *To Stand with the Nations of the World: Japan's Meiji Restoration in World History*. Warsaw: Oxford University Press.

Re, Rohit, and Ornit Shani (2023), 'Assembling India's Constitution: Towards a New History.' *Past & Present* 263(1): 204–248.

Real Declaracion sobre puntos esenciales de la ordenanza de milicias provinciales de España (1767). Madrid: Oficina de Antonio Marin.

Reglamento para las milicias de infanteria y caballeria de la Isla de Cuba (1769), Madrid: Por Juan de San Martin.

Reid, James J. (2000), *Crisis of the Ottoman Empire: Prelude to Collapse 1839–1878*. Stuttgart: Steiner.

Reynolds, Douglas B. (1993), *China, 1898–1912: The Xinzheng Revolution and Japan*. Cambridge, MA: Harvard University Press.

Ribeiro, Marly Martinez (1967), 'Revisão constitucional de 1926'. *Revista de Ciência Política* 1(4): 65–114.

Rieu-Millan, Marie Laure (1990), *Los diputados americanos en las Cortes de Cadiz (Igualdad y Independencia)*. Madrid: Consejo Superior de investigaciones científicas.

Rigouste, Mathieu (2009), *L'Ennemi intérieur: La généalogie coloniale et militaire de l'ordre sécuritaire dans la France contemporaine*. Paris: Décuverte.

Rink, Martin (1999), *Vom 'Partheygänger' zum Partisanen: Die Konzeption des kleinen Krieges in Preußen 1740–1813*. Frankfurt: Lang.

Ritter, Gerhard A. (1991), *Der Sozialstaat: Entstehung und Entwicklung im internationalen Vergleich*, second edition. Munich: Oldenbourg.

Robeiro, Gladys Sabina (2002), *A liberdade em construção: Identidade nacional a conflitos antilusitanos no Primeiro Reinado*. Rio de Janeiro: Relume Dumará.

Robespierre, Maximilien (1950), *Œuvres complètes. Vol. VI*. Paris: Presses Universitaires de France.

Robespierre, Maximilien (1954), *Œuvres complètes. Vol. VIII*. Paris: Presses Universitaires de France.

Robespierre, Maximilien (1958), *Œuvres complètes. Vol. IX*. Paris: Presses Universitaires de France.

Robinson, Shira (2013), *Citizen Strangers: Palestinians and the Birth of Israel's Liberal Settler State*. Stanford, CA: Stanford University Press.

Rodríguez, Jaime E. (2012), *'We Are Now the True Spaniards': Sovereignty, Revolution, Independence and he Emergence of the Federal Republic of Mexico, 1808–1824*. Stanford, CA: Stanford University Press.

Rodrigues, Thiago, Thaiane Mendonça and Tadeu Morato (2021), 'A Guerra para Dentro: Pacificação como doutrina e prática das Forças Armadas do Brasil'. *Revista Brasileira de Estudos de Defesa* 8(2): 99–104.

Rogers, Alan (1974), *Empire and Liberty: American Resistance to British Authority 1755–1763*. Berkeley: University of California Press.

Rohloff de Mattos, Ilmar (2017), *O tempo saquaremo*, seventh edition. São Paulo: HUCITEC.

Romanones, Conde de (1920), *El ejército y la política*. Madrid: Renacimiento.

Rosand, Eric (2005). 'The Security Council as Global Legislator: Ultra Vires or Ultra Innovative'? *Fordham International Law Journal* 28(3): 542–590.

Rosenfield, Luis (2020), 'A crise do pensamento constitucional da Primeira República: O debate da década de 1920'. *Estudos Ibero-Americanos* 46(3): 1–17.

Rosswurm, Steven (1987), *Arms, Country, and Class: The Philadelphia Militia and 'Lower Sort' during the American Revolution, 1775–1783*. New Brunswick, NJ: Rutgers University Press.

Rostworowski, Emanuel (1957), *Sprawa aukcji wojska na tle sytuacji politycznej przed sejmem czteroletnim*. Warsaw: Panstwowe Wydawnictwo Naukowe.

Roth, Markus (2009), *Herrenmenschen. Die deutschen Kreishauptleute im besetzten Polen – Karrierewege, Herrschaftspraxis und Nachgeschchte*. Gottingen: Wallstein.

Rotteck, Carl von (1816), *Ueber stehende Heere und Nationalmiliz*. Freyburg: Herdersche Universitäts-Buchhandlung.

Rougier, Antoine (1903), *Les Guerres civiles et le droit des gens*. Paris: Larose.

Roure, Agenos de (1920), *A Constituinte Republicana. Vol. I*. Rio de Janeiro: Imprensa Nacional.

Rousseau, David L. (2021), *War and Rights: The Impact of War on Political and Civil Rights*. Ann Arbor: University of Michigan Press.

Rovinello, Marco (2020), *Fra servitù e servizio: Storia della leva in Italia dall'Unità alla grande guerra*. Rome: Viella.

Roy, Srirupa (2007), *Beyond Belief: India and the Politics of Postcolonial Nationalism*. Durham, NC: Duke University Press.

Roynette-Gland, Odile (2000), *'Bons pour le service': L'expérience de la caserne en France àla fin du XIXe siècle*. Paris: Belin.

Roynette-Gland, Odile (1997), 'L'armée dans la bataille sociale: maintien de l'ordre et grèves ouvrières dans le Nord de la France (1871–1906)'. *Le Mouvement social* 179: 33–58.

Rubenstein, Jérémy (2022), *Terreur et séduction: Une histoire de la doctrine de la 'guerre révolutionnaire'*. Paris: La Découverte.

Ruddiman, John A. (2014), *Becoming Men of Some Consequence. Youth and Military Service in the Revolutionary War*. Charlottesville: University of Virginia Press.

Rummel, Rudolph J. (1995), 'Democracies Are Less Warlike Than Other Regimes'. *European Journal of International Relations* 1(4): 457–479.

Sabato, Hilda (2018), *Republics of the New World: The Revolutionary Political Experiment in Nineteenth-Century Latin America*. Princeton, NJ: Princeton University Press.

Saes, Guillaume Azevedo Marques de (2013), 'Uma interpretação das causas da rebelião militar contra a ordem imperial no Brasil na década de 1880'. *Lutas Sociais* 17(30): 18–29.

Saler, Bethel (2015), *The Settlers' Empire: Colonialism and State Formation in America's Old Northwest*. Philadelphia: University of Pennsylvania Press.

Samper, José and María Samper (1886), *Derecho publico interno de Colombia. Vol. I*. Bogota: Impr. de 'La Luz'.

Sampó, Carolina, Ludmila Quirós and Jessica Petrino (2019), 'La Guerra urbana en Río de Janeiro: De las Unidades de Policía Pacificadora a la militarización (2008–2018)'. *Revista de Relaciones Internacionales, Estrategia y Seguridad* 14(1): 151–166.

Samuś, Pawel (2013), *Wasza kartka wyborcza jest silniejsza niż karabin, niż armata: Z dziejów kultury politycznej na ziemiach polskich pod zaborami*. Lodz: Wydawcnictwo Uniwersytetu Łódzkiego.

Sánchez Torres, Rafael (2013), *El precio de la guerra: El estado fiscal-militar des Carlos III (1779–1783)*. Madrid: Marcial Pons.

Sancho, Vicente (1814), *Proyecto de una constitución de las milicias nacionales*. Madrid: Empfrenta Espinosa.

San Miguel, Evaristo (1836), *De la Guerra civil de España*. Madrid: Miguel de Burgos.

Santa Rosa, Virginio (1976), *O sentido do tenentismo*, third edition. São Paulo: Alfa-Ômega.

Santos, Luís Cláudio Villafañe (2003), 'O Império Brasileiro: Guerras e Nacionalismo'. *Prohistoria: Historia, políticas de la historia* 7: 87–106.

Sardenberg, Idálio (1987), 'Princípios fundamentais da Escola Superior de Guerra'. *Revista da Escola Superior de Guerra* 8 (1987): 9–15.

Saull, Richard (2001), *Rethinking Theory and History in the Cold War. The State, Military Power and Social Revolution*. London: Cass.

Savary, Jean-Julien (1825), *Guerres des Vendéens et des Chouans contre la République française. Vol. III*. Paris: Baudoin.

Scheinen, Martin (2010), 'Report of the Special Rapporteur on the Promotion and Protection of Human Rights and Fundamental Freedoms while Countering Terrorism'. https://digitallibrary.un.org/record/697664?ln=en.

Schindling, Anton (1991), *Die Anfänge des immerwährenden Reichstags zu Regensburg: Ständevertretung und Staatskunst nach dem Westfälischen Frieden*. Mainz: Von Zabern.

Schlochauer, Hans-Jürgen (1948), 'Zur Frage eines Besatzungsrechts für Deutschland'. *Archiv des Völkerrechts* 1(2): 188–218.

Schmid, Carlo (1949), *Speech of 18.11.1948 in Parlamentarischer Rat, Verhandlungen des Hauptausschusses*. Bonn: Bonner Universitäts-Buchdruckerei Scheur.

Schmid, Jürg H. (1956), *Die völkerrechtliche Stellung der Partisanen im Kriege unter besonderer Berücksichtigung der Genfer Konvention zum Schutze der Kriegsopfer vom 12. August 1949*. Zurich: Polygraphischer.

Schmidt, Karl (1948), 'Die Neuregelung des Besatzungsrechts'. *German Yearbook of International Law* 1: 123–128.

Schmidt, Richard (1927), 'Der preußische Einheitsstaat und der deutsche Bundesstaat: Gedanken zur Revision des Artikels 18 der Reichsverfassung und des Gesetzes zur Ausführung der Neugliederungsbestimmungen'. *Zeitschrift für Politik* 16: 201–241.

Schmitt, Carl (1928), *Verfassungslehre*. Berlin: Duncker und Humblot.

Schulz, Matthias (2009), *Normen und Praxis: Das Europäische Konzert der Großmächte als Sicherheitsrat, 1815–1860*. Munich: Oldenbourg.

Scott, Rebecca J. (1985), *Slave Emancipation in Cuba: The Transition to Free Labor, 1860–1899*. Princeton, NJ: Princeton University Press.

Sehgal, Manu (2021), *Creating an Early Colonial Order: Conquest and Contestation in South East Asia, c. 1775–1807*. Oxford: Oxford University Press.

Seidel, Robert (2006), *Deutsche Besatzungspolitik in Polen. Der Distrikt Radom 1935–1945*. Paderborn: Ferdinand Schöningh.
Seidenfus, Ricardo Antônio Silva (1985), *O Brasil de Getúlio Vargas e a formação dos Blocos: 1930–1942. O proceso do envolvimento brasileiro na II Guerra Mundial*. São Paulo: Editora Nacional.
Shafir, Gershon (2017), *A Half Century of Occupation: Israel, Palestine, and the World's Most Intractable Conflict*. Berkeley: University of California Press.
Shah, Aqil (2014), *The Army and Democracy: Military Politics in Pakistan*. Cambridge, MA: Harvard University Press.
Shannon, Timothy J. (2000), *Indians and Colonists at the Crossroads of Empire: The Albany Congress of 1754*. Ithaca, NY: Cornell University Press.
Shulman, Mark R. (1999), 'The Progressive Era Origins of the National Security Act'. *Dickinson Law Review* 104: 289–330.
Shy, John (1965), *Toward Lexington: The Rise of the British Army in the Coming of the American Revolution*. Princeton, NJ: Princeton University Press.
Shy, John (1976), *A People Numerous and Armed: Reflections on the Military Struggle för American Independence*. New York: Oxford University Press.
Silva, Hélio (1969), *1934: A constituinte*. Rio de Janeiro: Civilização brasileira.
Silva, Luiz Geraldo (2013), 'Gênese das milícias de pardos e pretos na América portuguesa: Pernambuco e Minas Gerais, séculos XVII e XVIII'. *Revista de História (São Paulo)*: 111–144.
Silva Jardim, Antônio da (1978), *Propaganda republicana (1888–1889)*. Rio de Janeiro: Ministério da Educação a cultura.
Sinha, Manisha (2000), *The Counter-Revolution of Slavery: Politics and Ideology in Antebellum South Carolina*. Chapel Hill: University of North Carolina Press.
Siollun, Max (2009), *Oil, Politics and Violence: Nigeria's Military Coup Culture (1966–1976)*. New York: Algora.
Sisson, Richard and Leo E. Rose (2000), *War and Secession: Pakistan, India, and the Creation of Bangladesh*. Berkeley: University of California Press.
Skocpol, Theda (1992), *Protecting Soldiers and Mothers: The Political Origins of Social Policy in the United States*. Cambridge, MA: Harvard University Press.
Slemian, Andréa (2009), *Sob o Império das leis: Constitução e unidade nacional na formação de Brasil (1822–1834)*. São Paulo: HUCITEC.
Śleszyński, Wojciech (2007), *Bezpieczeństwo wewnętrzne w polityce państwa polskiego na ziemach połnocno-wschodnich II Rezczypospolitej*. Warsaw: Oficyna Wydawnicza RYTM.
Śliva, Michał (2005), 'Wpływ rewolucji 1905 roku na Galicję'. *Przegląd Nauk Historycznych* 42(8): 163–172.
Small, Melvin and J. David Singer (1982), *Resort to Arms: International and Civil War, 1816–1980*. Beverly Hills, CA: Sage.
Smethurst, Richard J. (1974), *A Social Basis for Prewar Japanese Militarism: The Army and the Rural Community*. Berkeley: University of California Press.

Smith-Rosenberg, Carroll (1992), 'Dis-covering the Subject of the "Great Constitutional Discussion", 1786–1789'. *Journal of American History* 79(3): 841–873.

Snyder, Jack (2000), *From Voting to Violence: Democratization and Nationalist Conflict*. New York: Norton.

Soares, Rodrigo Goyena (2020). 'Os militares e os usos políticos do abolicionismo'. *Anos* 90(27): 1–15.

Sohrabi, Nader (2011), *Revolution and Constitutionalism in the Ottoman Empire and Iran*. Cambridge: Cambridge University Press.

Sohrabi, Nader (2018), 'Reluctant Nationalists, Imperial Nation-State, and Neo-Ottomanism: Turks, Albanians, and the Antinomies of the End of Empire'. *Social Science History* 42(4): 835–870.

Sosin, Jack M. (1967), *The Revolutionary Frontier 1763–1783*. New York: Holt, Rinehart and Winston.

Souza, Luís Antônio Francisco de (2015), 'Dispositivo militarizado da segurança pública: Tendências recentes e problemas no Brasil'. *Sociedade e Estado* 30: 207–223.

Stanek, Wojciech (1991), *Konfederacje generalne koronne w XVIII wieku*. Torun: Adam Marszałek.

Stankiewicz, Witold (1963), *Konflikty społeczne na wsi Polskiej 1918–1920*. Warsaw: Państwowe Wydawnictwo Naukowe.

Stawecki, Piotr (1981), *Polityka wojskowa Polski 1921–1926*. Warsaw: Wydawnictwo Ministerstwa Obrony Narodowej.

Steele, Ian K. (1986), *The English Atlantic 1675–1740: An Exploration of Communication and Community*. Oxford: Oxford University Press.

Stokes, Anthony (1783), *A View of the Constitution of the British Colonies in North-America and the West Indies at the Time the Civil War Broke Out on the Continent of America*. London: White.

Stone, John Lawrence (2006), *War and Genocide in Cuba, 1825–1898*. Chapel Hill: University of North Carolina Press.

Strachan, Hew (2004), *Financing the First World War*. Oxford: Oxford University Press.

Strang, David and Patricia Mei Yin Chang (1993), 'The International Labor Organization and the Welfare State: Institutional Effects on National Welfare Spending, 1960–80'. *International Organization* 47(2): 235–262.

Stroynowski, Andrzej (2005), *Opozycja sejmowa w dobie rządów rady nieustającej: Studium z dziejów kultury politycznej*. Lodz: Wydawca wyższa szkoła studiów międzynarodowych.

Stuke, Markus (2017), *Der Rechtsstatus des Kriegsgefangenen im bewaffneten Konflikt: Historische Entwicklung und geltendes Recht*. Tubingen: Mohr.

Suarez, Santiago-Gerardo (1984), *Las Milicias: Instituciones militares hispanoamericanas*. Caracas: Fuentes para da historia de Venezuela.

Sugita, Yoneyuki (2019), *Japan's Shifting Status in the World and the Development of Japan's Medical Insurance Systems*. Singapore: Springer.

Szasz, Paul C. (2002), 'The Security Council Starts Legislating'. *American Journal of International Law* 96(4): 901–904.

Szczepański, Janusz (2000), *Społeczeństwo Polski w walce z najazdem bolszewickim 1920 roku*. Warsaw: Pułtusk.

Szczygielski, Wacław (1970), *Konfederacja barska w Wielkopolsce 1768–1770*. Warsaw: Instytut Wydawniczy Pax.

Szczygielski, Wocjiech (1994), *Referendum trzeciomajowe: Sejmiki lutowe 1792 roku*. Lodz: Wydawnictwo Uniwersitetu Łódzkiego.

Szczygielski, Wojciech (2009), 'Z dyskusji parlamentarnej nad powołaniem Komisji Wojskowej w początkach obrad Sejmu Wielkiego'. *Przegląd Nauk Humanistycznych* 8(2): 63–98.

Szikra, Dorottya (2014), 'Democracy and Welfare in Hard Times: The Social Policy of the Orbán Government in Hungary between 2010 and 2014'. *Journal of European Social Policy* 24(5): 486–500.

Szumski, Jerzy (2002), *Uwłaszczenie chłopów w północno-wschodniej części Królestwa Polskiego 1848–1871*. Bialystok: Wydawnictwo PRYMAT.

Szymborski, Grzegorz (2020), *Działania zbrojne w Rzeczypospolitej podczas interwencji rosyjskiej 1764 roku*. Zabrze: Infort.

Talmon, Stefan (2005), 'The Security Council as World Legislature'. *American Journal of International Law* 99(1): 175–193.

Taylor, Brian (2011), *State Building in Putin's Russia: Policing and Coercion after Communism*. Cambridge: Cambridge University Press.

Thalhofer, Elisabeth (2010), *Entgrenzung der Gewalt: Gestapo-Lager in der Endphase des Dritten Reiches*. Paderborn: Schöningh.

Thénault, Sylvie (2011), *Une drôle de justice: Les magistrats dans la guerre d'Algérie*. Paris: La Découverte.

Thibaut, Clément (2005), *Repúblicas en armas: Los ejércitos bolivarianos en la Guerra de Independencia en Colombia y Venezuela*. Bogota: Instituto Francés d'études andines.

Thomas, Martin (2005), *The French Empire between the Wars: Imperialism, Politics and Society*. Manchester: Manchester University Press.

Thomas, Martin (2012), *Violence and Colonial Order: Police, Workers and Protest in the European Colonial Empires, 1918–1940*. Cambridge: Cambridge University Press.

Thornhill, Chris (2021), *Democratic Crisis and Global Constitutional Law*. Cambridge: Cambridge University Press.

Thornhill, Chris and Maria Smirnova (2018), 'Litigation and Political Transformation: The Case of Russia'. *Theory and Society* 47: 559–593.

Tickner, Arlene B. and Rodrigo Pardo (2003), 'En busca de aliados para la "seguridad democrática": La política exterior del primer año de la administración Uribe'. *Colombia internacional* 56–57: 64–81.

Tilly, Charles (2004), *Contention and Democracy in Europe, 1650–2000*. Cambridge University Press.

Tise, Larry E. (1987), *Proslavery: A History of the Defense of Slavery in America, 1701–1840*. Athens: University of Georgia Press.

Tomaszewski, Janusz (2019), 'Odrodzenie Wojska Polskiego 1918–1921'. *Wrocławskie Studia Politologiczne* 27 199–212.

Toppe, Andreas (2008), *Militär und Kriegsvölkerrecht: Rechtsnorm, Fachdiskurs und Kriegspraxis in Deutschland 1899–1940*. Munich: Oldenbourg.

Totman, Conrad (1980), *The Collapse of the Tokugawa Bakufu 1862–1868*. Honolulu: University of Hawaii Press.

Touscoz, Jean (1963), 'Etude de la jurisprudence interne française sur les aspects internationaux de l'affaire d'Algérie'. *Annuaire français de droit international* 9(1): 953–969.

Tovar Mora, Jorge Andrés and Hermes Tovar Pinzón (2009), *El oscuro camino de la libertad: Los esclavos en Colombia, 1821–1851*. Bogota: Universidad de lo Andes.

Trinquier, Roger (1961), *La Guerre moderne*. Paris: La Table Ronde.

Troch, Pieter (2015), *Nationalism and Yugoslavia: Education, Yugoslavism and the Balkans before World War II*. Oxford: Bloomsbury.

Trzeciakowski, Lech (1973), *Pod pruskim zaborem 1850–1918*. Rzeszow: Wiedza Powszechna.

Tucker, Robert W. and David C. Hendrickson (1982), *The Fall of the First British Empire: Origins of the War of American Independence*. Baltimore, MD: Johns Hopkins University Press.

Turfan, M. Naim (2000), *Rise of the Young Turks: Politics, the Military and Ottoman Collapse*. London: Tauris.

Tusell, Javier (1977), *La Crisis del caciquismo andaluz (1923–1931)*. Madrid: Cupsa.

Tutino, John (2018), *Power, Sovereignty and Silver: Mexico City, 1808 in an Age of War and Revolution*. Albuquerque: University of New Mexico Press.

Tzanakopoulos, Antonios (2011), *Disobeying the Security Council*. Oxford: Oxford University Press.

Umegaki, Michio (1988), *After the Restoration: The Beginning of Japan's Modern State*. New York: New York University Press.

Üngör, Uğur Ümit (2011), *The Making of Modern Turkey: Nation and State in Eastern Anatolia, 1913–1950*. Oxford: Oxford University Press.

Üngör, Ugur Ümit and Mehmet Polatel (2011), *Confiscation and Destruction: The Young Turk Seizure of Armenian Property*. London: Bloomsbury.

Uribe de Hincapié, María Teresa (1996), 'Proceso histórico de la configuración de la ciudadanía en Colombia'. *Estudios políticos* 9: 67–76.

Uribe de Hincapié, María Teresa and Liliana María López Lopera (2008), *La Guerra por las soberanías: Memorias y relatos en la Guerra civil de 1859–1862*. Medellin: La Careta.

Uricoechea, Fernando (1978), *O minotauro imperial: A burocratização de estado patrimonial brasileiro no século XIX*. Rio de Janeiro: DIFEL.

Vagts, Alfred (1981), *A History of Militarism*. Westport, CT: Greenwood.

Vallée, Gustave (1937), *La Conscription dans le département de la Charente (1798–1807)*. Paris: Sirey.

Velazquez, Maria del Carmen (1950), *El estado de guerra en Nueva España 1760–1808*. Mexico City: El Colegio de México.

Verhandlungen der verfassunggebenden Nationalversammlung. Vol. 329 (1920), Berlin: Druck und Verlag der Norddeutschen Burchdruckerei und Verlags-Anstalt.

Vianna, Oliveira (1939), *O Idealismo do Constitução*. São Paulo: Companha Editora Nacional.

Victor, Fabio (2022), *Poder camuflado: Os militares e a política, do fim da ditadura à aliança com Bolsonaro*. São Paulo: Companhia das Letras.

Villa, Alejandro Valencia (1991), *La humanización de la guerra: Derecho internacional humanitario y conflicto armado an Colombia*. Bogota: Ediciones uniandes.

Villa Patiño, Carlos Alberto (2010), *Guerra y construcción del Estado en Colombia 1810–2010*. Bogota: Universidad Militar Nueva Granada.

Vinkovetsky, Ilya (2018), 'Strategists and Ideologues: Russians and the Making of Bulgaria's Tarnovo Constitution, 1878–1879'. *Journal of Modern History* 90(4): 751–791.

Vinson III, Ben (2001), *Bearing Arms for His Majesty: The Free-Colored Militia in Colonial Mexico*. Stanford, CA: Stanford University Press.

Volkmann, Hans-Erich (2016), *Die Polenpolitik des Kaiserreichs: Prolog zum Zeitalter der Weltkriege*. Paderborn: Ferdinand Schöningh.

Voßkuhle, Andreas (2011), 'Hugo Preuß als Vordenker einer Verfassungstheorie des Pluralismus'. *Der Staat* 50(2): 251–267.

Vovchenko, Denis (2016), *Containing Balkan Nationalism: Imperial Russia and Ottoman Christians*. Oxford: Oxford University Press.

Waibel, Dieter (1996), *Von der wohlwollenden Despotie zur Herrschaft des Rechts: Entwicklungsstufen der amerikanischen Besatzung Deutschlands*. Tubingen: Mohr.

Walkenhorst, Peter (2007), *Nation-Volk-Rasse: Radikaler Nationalismus im Deutschen Kaiserreich 1890–1914*. Gottingen: Vandenhoeck und Ruprecht.

Walker, Clive (2007), 'The Treatment of Foreign Terror Suspects'. *Modern Law Review* 70(3): 427–457.

Ward, Curtis A. (2003), 'Building Capacity to Combat International Terrorism: The Role of the United Nations Security Council'. *Journal of Conflict and Security Law* 8(2): 289–305.

Ward, Harry M. (2006), *George Washington's Enforcers: Policing the Continental Army*. Carbondale: Southern Illinois University Press.

Ward, Matthew C. (2003), *Breaking the Backcountry: The Seven Years' War in Virginia and Pennsylvania, 1754–1765*. Philadelphia: University of Pennsylvania Press.

Wąsicki, Jan (1980), *Ziemie polskie pod zaborem pruskim: Wielkie Księstwo Poznańskie 1815–1848*. Warsaw: Państwowe Wydawnictwo Naukowe.

Waswo, Ann (1977), *Japanese Landlords: The Decline of a Rural Elite*. Berkeley: University of California Press.

Watt, Lori (2009), *When Empire Comes Home: Repatriation and Reintegration in Postwar Japan*. Cambridge, MA: Harvard University Press.

Weart, Spencer R. (1998), *Never at War: Why Democracies Will Not Fight One Another*. New Haven, CT: Yale University Press.

Webb, Stephen Saunders (1979), *The Governors-General: The English Army and the Definition of the Empire, 1569–1681*. Chapel Hill: University of North Carolina Press.

Webb, Stephen Saunders (1995), *Lord Churchill's Coup*. New York: Norton.

Webb, Stephen Saunders (1997), 'Army and Empire: English Garrison Government in Britain and America, 1569 to 1763'. *William and Mary Quarterly* 34(1): 1–31.

Weber, Max (1921), *Gesammelte Politische Schriften*. Tubingen: Mohr.

Weber, Max (1921/2), *Wirtschaft und Gesellschaft: Grundriß der verstehenden Soziologie*. Tubingen: Mohr.

Weber, Petra (2010), *Gescheiterte Sozialpartnerschaft – Gefährdete Republik? Industrielle Beziehungen, Arbeitskämpfe und der Sozialstaat. Deutschland und Frankreich im Vergleich (1918–1933/39)*. Munich: Oldenbourg.

Wehler, Hans-Ulrich (1972), *Bismarck und der Imperialismus*, third edition. Cologne: Kiepenheuer & Witsch.

Weill, Sharon (2014), *The Role of National Courts in Applying International Humanitarian Law*. Oxford: Oxford University Press.

Weiner, Myron (1991), *The Child and the State in India: Child Labor and Education Policy in Comparative Perspective*. Princeton, NJ: Princeton University Press.

Weiss, Thomas G. (2004), 'The Sunset of Humanitarian Intervention? The Responsibility to Protect in a Unipolar Era'. *Security Dialogue* 35(2): 135–153.

Wempe, Sean Andrew (2019), *Revenants of the German Empire: Colonial Germans, Imperialism, and the League of Nations*. Oxford: Oxford University Press.

Werneck Sodré, Nelson (2010), *História Militar do Brasil*. São Paulo: Editora Expressão Popular.

Westlake, John (1894), *Chapters on the Principles of International Law*. Cambridge: Cambridge University Press.

Wettengel, Michael (2022), *Revolution von 1848/49 in Hessen: Die hessischen Staaten, Nassau, Waldeck und Frankfurt*. Frankfurt: Kramer.

Wheatley, Steven (2006), 'The Security Council, Democratic Legitimacy and Regime Change in Iraq'. *European Journal of International Law* 17(3): 531–551.

Wheeler, Nicholas J. (2005), 'Victory for Common Humanity: The Responsibility to Protect after the 2005 World Summit'. *Journal of International Law and International Relations* 2(1): 95–106.

Whitaker, Beth Elise (2007), 'Exporting the Patriot Act? Democracy and the "War on Terror" in the Third World'. *Third World Quarterly* 28(5): 1017–1032.

White, Richard (1991), *The Middle Ground: Indians, Empires and Republics in the Great Lakes Region, 1650–1815*. Cambridge: Cambridge University Press.

White Paper on the Application of the Geneva Conventions of 1949 to the French-Algerian Conflict (1960). New York: Algerian Office.

Wieck, William M. (1977), *The Sources of Antislavery Constitutionalism in America, 1760–1848*. Ithaca, NY: Cornell University Press.

Wierzbicki, Leszek Andrzej (2011), *Pospolite ruszenie w Polsce: W drugiej połowie XVII wieku. Ostatnie wyprawy z lat 1670–1672*. Lublin: Wydawnictwo Uniwersytetu Marii Curie-Skłodowskiej.

Wilde, Ralph (2009), 'From Trusteeship to Self-Determination and Back Again: The Role of the Hague Regulations in the Evolution of International Trusteeship, and the Framework of Rights and Duties of Occupying Powers'. *Loyola of Los Angeles International and Comparative Law Review* 31 (2009): 85–142.

Wilkinson, Steven I. (2004), *Votes and Violence: Electoral Competition and Ethnic Riots in India*. Cambridge: Cambridge University Press.

Wilkinson, Steven I. (2015), *Army and Nation: The Military and Indian Democracy since Independence*. Cambridge, MA: Harvard University Press.

Williams, Chad L. (2010), *Torchbearers of Democracy: African American Soldiers in the World War I Era*. Chapel Hill: University of North Carolina Press.

Wimmer, Andreas (2013), *Waves of War: Nationalism, State Formation, and Ethnic Exclusion in the Modern World*. Cambridge: Cambridge University Press.

Wimmer, Andreas and Brian Min (2006), 'From Empire to Nation-State: Explaining Wars in the Modern World, 1816–2001'. *American Sociological Review* 71(6): 867–897.

Wimmer, Jan (2019), *Wojsko polskie w drugiej połowie XVII wieku*. Oshpitzin: Napoleon V.

Winnicki, Zdzisław Julian (2017), *Rada Regencyjna Królestwa Polskiego i jej organy (1917–1918)*. Wroclaw: Wektory.

Winter, Jay (2022), *The Day the Great War Ended, 24 July 1923: The Civilianization of War*. Oxford: Oxford University Press.

Woloch, Isser (1986), 'Napoleonic Conscription: State Power and Civil Society'. *Past & Present* 11: 101–129.

Woźnicki, Marek (2014), 'Reformy ceł i podatków w Rzeczypospolitej w latach 1764–1766'. *Annales Universitatus Mariae Curie-Skłodowska* 69: 151–166.

Wrzosek, Mieczysław (1988), *Wojsko Polskie i operacje wojenne lat 1918–1920*. Bialystok: Dział Wydawnictw Filii UW.

Wyszczelski, Lech (2006), *Wojsko Polskie w latach 1918–1921*. Warsaw: Neriton.

Wyszczelski, Lech (2015), *Konflikty narodowe i wewnętrzne II Rzeczypospolitej: Konflikty z sąsiadami opór mniejszczószi narodowych, strajki chłopskie i robotnicze*. Warsaw: Bellona.

Yaycioglu, Ali (2016), *Partners of the Empire: The Crisis of the Ottoman Order in the Age of Revolutions*. Princeton, NJ: Princeton University Press.

Yilmaz, Hale (2013), *Becoming Turkish: Nationalist Reforms and Cultural Negotiations in Early Republican Turkey 1923–1945*. Syracuse, NY: Syracuse University Press.

Yong, Tan Tai (2005), *The Garrison State: The Military, Government and Society in Colonial Punjab, 1849–1947*. New Delhi: Sage.

Young, Louise (1998), *Japan's Total Empire: Manchuria and the Culture of Wartime Imperialism*. Berkeley: University of California Press.

Zaghi, Carlo (1986), *L'Italia di Napoleone dalla Cisalpina al Regno*. Turin: UTET.

Zaporowski, Zbigniew (1992), *Sejm Rzeczypospolitej Polskiej 1919–1939: Działalność posłów, parlamentarne koncepcje Józefa Piłsudskiego, mniejszości narodowe*. Lublin: Wydawnictwo Uniwersytetu Marie Curie-Skłodowsiej.

Zeleza, Paul Tiyambe (2016), *The Transformation of Global Higher Education, 1945–2015*. Basingstoke: Palgrave.

Zhao, Suisheng (1995), *Power by Design: Constitution-Making in Nationalist China*. Honolulu: University of Hawaii Press.

Zielińska, Zofia (2012), *Polska w okowach 'systemu północnego' 1763–1766*. Krakow: Wydział Historyczny Uniwersytetu Warszawskiego.

Zilversmit, Arthur (1967), *The First Abolition of Slavery in the North*. Chicago, IL: Chicago University Press.

Ziring, Lawrence (1971), *The Ayub Khan Era: Politics in Pakistan 1958–1969*. Syracuse, NY: Syracuse University Press.

Zollmann, Jakob (2010), *Koloniale Herrschaft und ihre Grenzen: Die Kolonialpolizei in Deutsch-Südwestafrika*. Gottingen: Vandenhoeck und Ruprecht.

Zürcher, Erik J. (2010), *The Young Turk Legacy and Nation Building: From the Ottoman Empire to Atatürk's Turkey*. London: Tauris.

Życiński, Stanisław (1992), *Reforma wojskowa na Sejmie Czertoletnim (1788–1792) i jej unwarunkowanie polityczne*. Szczecin: Wydawnictwo naukowe Uniwersytetu szczecińskiego.

INDEX

CAMBRIDGE STUDIES IN LAW AND SOCIETY

Books in the Series

Diseases of the Will: Alcohol and the Dilemmas of Freedom
Mariana Valverde

The Politics of Truth and Reconciliation in South Africa: Legitimizing the Post-Apartheid State
Richard A. Wilson

Modernism and the Grounds of Law
Peter Fitzpatrick

Unemployment and Government: Genealogies of the Social
William Walters

Autonomy and Ethnicity: Negotiating Competing Claims in Multi-Ethnic States
Yash Ghai

Constituting Democracy: Law, Globalism and South Africa's Political Reconstruction
Heinz Klug

The Ritual of Rights in Japan: Law, Society, and Health Policy
Eric A. Feldman

Governing Morals: A Social History of Moral Regulation
Alan Hunt

The Colonies of Law: Colonialism, Zionism and Law in Early Mandate Palestine
Ronen Shamir

Law and Nature
David Delaney

Social Citizenship and Workfare in the United States and Western Europe: The Paradox of Inclusion
Joel F. Handler

Law, Anthropology, and the Constitution of the Social: Making Persons and Things
Edited by Alain Pottage and Martha Mundy

Judicial Review and Bureaucratic Impact: International and Interdisciplinary Perspectives
Edited by Marc Hertogh and Simon Halliday

Immigrants at the Margins: Law, Race, and Exclusion in Southern Europe
Kitty Calavita

Lawyers and Regulation: The Politics of the Administrative Process
Patrick Schmidt

Law and Globalization from Below: Towards a Cosmopolitan Legality
Edited by Boaventura de Sousa Santos and César A. Rodríguez-Garavito

Public Accountability: Designs, Dilemmas and Experiences
Edited by Michael W. Dowdle

Law, Violence and Sovereignty among West Bank Palestinians
Tobias Kelly

Legal Reform and Administrative Detention Powers in China
Sarah Biddulph

The Practice of Human Rights: Tracking Law between the Global and the Local
Edited by Mark Goodale and Sally Engle Merry

Judges beyond Politics in Democracy and Dictatorship: Lessons from Chile
Lisa Hilbink

Paths to International Justice: Social and Legal Perspectives
Edited by Marie-Bénédicte Dembour and Tobias Kelly

Law and Society in Vietnam: The Transition from Socialism in Comparative Perspective
Mark Sidel

Constitutionalizing Economic Globalization: Investment Rules and Democracy's Promise
David Schneiderman

The New World Trade Organization Knowledge Agreements: Second Edition
Christopher Arup

Justice and Reconciliation in Post-Apartheid South Africa
Edited by François du Bois and Antje du Bois-Pedain

Militarization and Violence against Women in Conflict Zones in the Middle East: A Palestinian Case-Study
Nadera Shalhoub-Kevorkian

Child Pornography and Sexual Grooming: Legal and Societal Responses
Suzanne Ost
Darfur and the Crime of Genocide
John Hagan and Wenona Rymond-Richmond

Fictions of Justice: The International Criminal Court and the Challenge of Legal Pluralism in Sub-Saharan Africa
Kamari Maxine Clarke

Conducting Law and Society Research: Reflections on Methods and Practices
Simon Halliday and Patrick Schmidt

Planted Flags: Trees, Land, and Law in Israel/Palestine
Irus Braverman

Culture under Cross-Examination: International Justice and the Special Court for Sierra Leone
Tim Kelsall

Cultures of Legality: Judicialization and Political Activism in Latin America
Javier Couso, Alexandra Huneeus, and Rachel Sieder

Courting Democracy in Bosnia and Herzegovina: The Hague Tribunal's Impact in a Postwar State
Lara J. Nettelfield

The Gacaca Courts, Post-Genocide Justice and Reconciliation in Rwanda: Justice without Lawyers
Phil Clark

Law, Society, and History: Themes in the Legal Sociology and Legal History of Lawrence M. Friedman
Edited by Robert W. Gordon and Morton J. Horwitz

After Abu Ghraib: Exploring Human Rights in America and the Middle East
Shadi Mokhtari

Adjudication in Religious Family Laws: Cultural Accommodation, Legal Pluralism, and Gender Equality in India
Gopika Solanki

Water on Tap: Rights and Regulation in the Transnational Governance of Urban Water Services
Bronwen Morgan

Elements of Moral Cognition: Rawls' Linguistic Analogy and the Cognitive Science of Moral and Legal Judgment
John Mikhail

Mitigation and Aggravation at Sentencing
Edited by Julian V. Roberts

Institutional Inequality and the Mobilization of the Family and Medical Leave Act: Rights on Leave
Catherine R. Albiston

Authoritarian Rule of Law: Legislation, Discourse and Legitimacy in Singapore
Jothie Rajah

Law and Development and the Global Discourses of Legal Transfers
Edited by John Gillespie and Pip Nicholson

Law against the State: Ethnographic Forays into Law's Transformations
Edited by Julia Eckert, Brian Donahoe, Christian Strümpell and Zerrin Özlem Biner

Transnational Legal Ordering and State Change
Edited by Gregory C. Shaffer

Legal Mobilization under Authoritarianism: The Case of Post-Colonial Hong Kong
Waikeung Tam

Complementarity in the Line of Fire: The Catalysing Effect of the International Criminal Court in Uganda and Sudan
Sarah M. H. Nouwen

Political and Legal Transformations of an Indonesian Polity: The Nagari from Colonisation to Decentralisation
Franz von Benda-Beckmann and Keebet von Benda-Beckmann

Pakistan's Experience with Formal Law: An Alien Justice
Osama Siddique

Human Rights under State-Enforced Religious Family Laws in Israel, Egypt, and India
Yüksel Sezgin

Why Prison?
Edited by David Scott

Law's Fragile State: Colonial, Authoritarian, and Humanitarian Legacies in Sudan
Mark Fathi Massoud
Rights for Others: The Slow Home-Coming of Human Rights in the Netherlands
Barbara Oomen

European States and Their Muslim Citizens: The Impact of Institutions on Perceptions and Boundaries
Edited by John R. Bowen, Christophe Bertossi, Jan Willem Duyvendak, and Mona Lena Krook

Environmental Litigation in China: A Study in Political Ambivalence
Rachel E. Stern

Indigeneity and Legal Pluralism in India: Claims, Histories, Meanings
Pooja Parmar

Paper Tiger: Law, Bureaucracy and the Developmental State in Himalayan India
Nayanika Mathur

Religion, Law and Society
Russell Sandberg

The Experiences of Face Veil Wearers in Europe and the Law
Edited by Eva Brems

The Contentious History of the International Bill of Human Rights
Christopher N. J. Roberts

Transnational Legal Orders
Edited by Terence C. Halliday and Gregory Shaffer

Lost in China? Law, Culture and Society in Post-1997 Hong Kong
Carol A. G. Jones

Security Theology, Surveillance and the Politics of Fear
Nadera Shalhoub-Kevorkian

Opposing the Rule of Law: How Myanmar's Courts Make Law and Order
Nick Cheesman

Ironies of Colonial Governance: Law, Custom and Justice in Colonial India
James Jaffe

The Clinic and the Court: Law, Medicine and Anthropology
Edited by Ian Harper, Tobias Kelly, and Akshay Khanna

The World of Indicators: The Making of Government Knowledge through Quantification
Edited by Richard Rottenburg, Sally E. Merry, Sung-Joon Park, and Johanna Mugler

Contesting Immigration Policy in Court: Legal Activism and Its Radiating Effects in the United States and France
Leila Kawar

The Quiet Power of Indicators: Measuring Governance, Corruption, and Rule of Law
Edited by Sally Engle Merry, Kevin E. Davis, and Benedict Kingsbury

Investing in Authoritarian Rule: Punishment and Patronage in Rwanda's Gacaca Courts for Genocide Crimes
Anuradha Chakravarty

Contractual Knowledge: One Hundred Years of Legal Experimentation in Global Markets
Edited by Grégoire Mallard and Jérôme Sgard

Iraq and the Crimes of Aggressive War: The Legal Cynicism of Criminal Militarism
John Hagan, Joshua Kaiser, and Anna Hanson

Culture in the Domains of Law
Edited by René Provost

China and Islam: The Prophet, the Party, and Law
Matthew S. Erie

Diversity in Practice: Race, Gender, and Class in Legal and Professional Careers
Edited by Spencer Headworth, Robert L. Nelson, Ronit Dinovitzer, and David B. Wilkins

A Sociology of Constitutions: Constitutions and State Legitimacy in Historical-Sociological Perspective
Chris Thornhill

A Sociology of Transnational Constitutions: Social Foundations of the Post-National Legal Structure
Chris Thornhill

Genocide Never Sleeps: Living Law at the International Criminal Tribunal for Rwanda
Nigel Eltringham

Shifting Legal Visions: Judicial Change and Human Rights Trials in Latin America
Ezequiel A. González-Ocantos

The Demographic Transformations of Citizenship
Heli Askola

Criminal Defense in China: The Politics of Lawyers at Work
Sida Liu and Terence C. Halliday

Contesting Economic and Social Rights in Ireland: Constitution, State and Society, 1848–2016
Thomas Murray

Buried in the Heart: Women, Complex Victimhood and the War in Northern Uganda
Erin Baines

Palaces of Hope: The Anthropology of Global Organizations
Edited by Ronald Niezen and Maria Sapignoli

The Politics of Bureaucratic Corruption in Post-Transitional Eastern Europe
Marina Zaloznaya

Revisiting the Law and Governance of Trafficking, Forced Labor and Modern Slavery
Edited by Prabha Kotiswaran

Incitement on Trial: Prosecuting International Speech Crimes
Richard Ashby Wilson

Criminalizing Children: Welfare and the State in Australia
David McCallum

Global Lawmakers: International Organizations in the Crafting of World Markets
Susan Block-Lieb and Terence C. Halliday

Duties to Care: Dementia, Relationality and Law
Rosie Harding

Insiders, Outsiders, Injuries, and Law: Revisiting 'The Oven Bird's Song'
Edited by Mary Nell Trautner

Hunting Justice: Displacement, Law, and Activism in the Kalahari
Maria Sapignoli

Injury and Injustice: The Cultural Politics of Harm and Redress
Edited by Anne Bloom, David M. Engel, and Michael McCann

Ruling Before the Law: The Politics of Legal Regimes in China and Indonesia
William Hurst

The Powers of Law: A Comparative Analysis of Sociopolitical Legal Studies
Mauricio García-Villegas

A Sociology of Justice in Russia
Edited by Marina Kurkchiyan and Agnieszka Kubal

Constituting Religion: Islam, Liberal Rights, and the Malaysian State
Tamir Moustafa

The Invention of the Passport: Surveillance, Citizenship and the State, Second Edition
John C. Torpey

Law's Trials: The Performance of Legal Institutions in the US 'War on Terror'
Richard L. Abel

Law's Wars: The Fate of the Rule of Law in the US 'War on Terror'
Richard L. Abel

Transforming Gender Citizenship: The Irresistible Rise of Gender Quotas in Europe
Edited by Eléonore Lépinard and Ruth Rubio-Marín

Muslim Women's Quest for Justice: Gender, Law and Activism in India
Mengia Hong Tschalaer

Children as 'Risk': Sexual Exploitation and Abuse by Children and Young People
Anne-Marie McAlinden

The Legal Process and the Promise of Justice: Studies Inspired by the Work of Malcolm Feeley
Jonathan Simon, Rosann Greenspan, Hadar Aviram

Gift Exchanges: The Transnational History of a Political Idea
Grégoire Mallard

Measuring Justice: Quantitative Accountability and the National Prosecuting Authority in South Africa
Johanna Mugler

Negotiating the Power of NGOs: Women's Legal Rights in South Africa
Reem Wael

Indigenous Water Rights in Law and Regulation: Lessons from Comparative Experience
Elizabeth Jane Macpherson

The Edge of Law: Legal Geographies of a War Crimes Court
Alex Jeffrey

Everyday Justice: Law, Ethnography, and Injustice
Sandra Brunnegger

The Uncounted: Politics of Data in Global Health
Sara L. M. Davis

Transnational Legal Ordering of Criminal Justice
Gregory Shaffer and Ely Aaronson

Five Republics and One Tradition
Pablo Ruiz-Tagle

The Law Multiple: Judgment and Knowledge in Practice
Irene van Oorschot

Health as a Human Right: The Politics and Judicialisation of Health in Brazil
Octávio Luiz Motta Ferraz

Shari'a, Inshallah: Finding God in Somali Legal Politics
Mark Fathi Massoud

Policing for Peace: Institutions, Expectations, and Security in Divided Societies
Matthew Nanes

Rule of Law Intermediaries: Brokering Influence in Myanmar
Kristina Simion

Lactation at Work: Expressed Milk, Expressing Beliefs, and the Expressive Value of Law
Elizabeth A. Hoffmann

The Archival Politics of International Courts
Henry Redwood

Global Pro Bono: Causes, Context, and Contestation
Edited by Scott L. Cummings, Fabio de Sa e Silva and Louise G. Trubek

The Practice and Problems of Transnational Counter-Terrorism
Fiona de Londras

Decoupling: Gender Injustice in China's Divorce Courts
Ethan Michelson

Anti-Constitutional Populism
Martin Krygier, Adam Czarnota and Wojciech Sadurski

Lawyers in Conflict and Transition
Kieran McEvoy, Louse Mallinder and Anna Bryson

The Ghostwriters: Lawyers and the Politics behind the Judicial Construction of Europe
Tommaso Pavone

The Sentimental Court: The Affective Life of International Criminal Justice
Jonas Bens

Practices of Reparations in International Criminal Justice
Christoph Sperfeldt

Seeking Supremacy: The Pursuit of Judicial Power in Pakistan
Yasser Kureshi

The Power of the Jury: Transforming Citizens into Jurors
Nancy S. Marder

Undue Process: Persecution and Punishment in Autocratic Courts
Fiona Feiang Shen-Bayh

Discounting Life: Necropolitical Law, Culture, and the Long War on Terror
Jothie Rajah

Clean Air at What Cost? The Rise of Blunt Force Regulation in China
Denise Sienli van der Kamp

Law and Precarity: Legal Consciousness and Daily Survival in Vietnam
Tu Phuong Nguyen

Prosecutors, Voters and The Criminalization of Corruption in Latin America: The Case of Lava Jato
Ezequiel A. Gonzalez-Ocantos and Paula Muñoz Chirinos

Entangled Domains: Empire, Law and Religion in Northern Nigeria
Rabiat Akande

The Social Constitution: Embedding Social Rights Through Legal Mobilization
Whitney K. Taylor

Out of Place: Fieldwork and Positionality in Law and Society
Edited by Lynette J. Chua and Mark Fathi Massoud

Negotiating Legality: Chinese Companies in the U.S. Legal System
Ji Li

Law and Jewish Difference: Ambivalent Encounters
Mareike Riedel

www.ingramcontent.com/pod-product-compliance
Lightning Source LLC
LaVergne TN
LVHW010339220926
848484LV00004BB/935

* 9 7 8 1 3 1 6 5 1 3 9 4 1 *